1,000,000 Books

are available to read at

www.ForgottenBooks.com

Read online
Download PDF
Purchase in print

ISBN 978-0-282-39408-0
PIBN 10850140

This book is a reproduction of an important historical work. Forgotten Books uses
state-of-the-art technology to digitally reconstruct the work, preserving the original format
whilst repairing imperfections present in the aged copy. In rare cases, an imperfection in
the original, such as a blemish or missing page, may be replicated in our edition. We do,
however, repair the vast majority of imperfections successfully; any imperfections that
remain are intentionally left to preserve the state of such historical works.

Forgotten Books is a registered trademark of FB &c Ltd.
Copyright © 2018 FB &c Ltd.
FB &c Ltd, Dalton House, 60 Windsor Avenue, London, SW19 2RR.
Company number 08720141. Registered in England and Wales.

For support please visit www.forgottenbooks.com

1 MONTH OF
FREE
READING

at

www.ForgottenBooks.com

By purchasing this book you are
eligible for one month membership to
ForgottenBooks.com, giving you
unlimited access to our entire
collection of over 1,000,000 titles via
our web site and mobile apps.

To claim your free month visit:

www.forgottenbooks.com/free850140

* Offer is valid for 45 days from date of purchase. Terms and conditions apply.

English
Français
Deutsche
Italiano
Español
Português

www.forgottenbooks.com

Mythology Photography **Fiction**
Fishing Christianity **Art** Cooking
Essays Buddhism Freemasonry
Medicine **Biology** Music **Ancient
Egypt** Evolution Carpentry Physics
Dance Geology **Mathematics** Fitness
Shakespeare **Folklore** Yoga Marketing
Confidence Immortality Biographies
Poetry **Psychology** Witchcraft
Electronics Chemistry History **Law**
Accounting **Philosophy** Anthropology
Alchemy Drama Quantum Mechanics
Atheism Sexual Health **Ancient History**
Entrepreneurship Languages Sport
Paleontology Needlework Islam
Metaphysics Investment Archaeology
Parenting Statistics Criminology
Motivational

HISTORY OF CHRISTIAN THEOLOGY IN THE APOSTOLIC AGE.

History of Christian Theology
in the Apostolic Age.

BY

Wilhelm Eugen

EDWARD REUSS,

PROFESSOR IN THE THEOLOGICAL FACULTY, AND IN THE PROTESTANT SEMINARY
OF STRASBOURG.

TRANSLATED BY ANNIE HARWOOD,
FROM THE THIRD EDITION.

WITH A PREFACE AND NOTES BY
R. W. DALE, M.A.

VOLUME II.

LONDON:
HODDER AND STOUGHTON,
PATERNOSTER ROW.
—
MDCCCLXXIV.

Watson and Hazell, Printers, London and Ayles

TABLE OF CONTENTS.

VOLUME II.

BOOK SIXTH.

BOOK SEVENTH.

THE THEOLOGY OF JOHN.

APOSTOLIC AGE.

CHAPTER I.

THE EPISTLES OF PAUL.

IT is not necessary to show, by any lengthened demonstration, that our acquaintance with the theology of Paul must be derived from his epistles, in comparison with which every other source of information would be not only inadequate, but superfluous, and apt even to lead us into error. We shall take occasion here, however, to make a few observations in detail on this point, which will more clearly define our views with regard to it, and which will have at least the merit of novelty for many of our readers.

As a general principle, we regard all the epistles of Paul as equally adapted to bear witness to his theology. It is true that doubts have repeatedly arisen as to the authenticity of one or other of those epistles, and latterly these doubts have been asserted with singular emphasis in a celebrated school which has almost succeeded in baffling criticism itself. But they appear to us, in the majority of cases, strangely exaggerated, and built upon a very fragile foundation; as, for example, when they assail documents which bear so plainly the impress of their Pauline origin as the epistles to the Philippians, to Philemon, the First Epistle to the Thessalonians, and the Second to Timothy. And even where these doubts are held in common by scholars perfectly independent of each other, and whose critical judgment is entitled to all respect,—as, for instance, in relation to the pastoral epistles and the Epistle to the Ephesians,—we must withhold our assent to their opinions, till they have been established by more conclusive arguments and evidences more clear and irrefragable than any yet adduced in the discussions. We believe that the authenticity of all these epistles, as they have been received by ecclesiastical tradition, may still be defended successfully, and we have on various occasions endeavoured to do our part towards such a result. But should we be ultimately compelled to abandon this ground, and to abstain from quoting some of these epistles as of such doubtful authorship that we might be confounding the thoughts of different minds, we should not even then feel that the exposition we are about to give of the Pauline system would be altered in any of its essential characters. For, whatever may be said by the critics to whom we have referred, we have not been able to discover in any of the epistles called in question or rejected by them, any doctrinal statement of importance which is either in direct contradiction with the teaching of the epistles they accept as genuine, or which contains anything not found in them. A change in the formula, a variation in the mode of expression, does not constitute a divergence of thought. We shall carefully note these variations as we proceed, and weigh their importance; but we shall not pause now before little obstacles which the interested imagination of the *savans* is too ready to magnify into mountains. From our point of view, indeed, the apostle is released from all the fetters of a rigid and narrow formalism.

There are, however, some of the epistles demanding more than others the attention of the historian, whether as containing more directly doctrinal matter, or as treating the subject in a manner more systematic and complete. The Epistle to the Romans stands foremost in this category, because it possesses these qualities in a pre-eminent degree, and should therefore be made, as far as possible, the basis of any exposition of the views of its author. The first eight chapters of that epistle present a full and explicit summary of the anthropology and soteriology of the Gospel; that is to say, of its teaching in relation to man and to salvation; only it treats rather of the question of the work of redemption in itself than of the person and dignity of Christ as the Redeemer. The same aspect of the doctrine is treated in some chapters of the Epistle to the Galatians, but more succinctly, and consequently less clearly, so that the exegete is constantly in need of the commentary which the other epistle furnishes. The first four chapters of the Epistle to the Ephesians contain also a sort of general statement of Christian theology, but from a new point of view,—one supplied by speculation rather than by experience. It is needless to point out the other passages which may serve best to define or to explain the various parts of the system. Each epistle, in truth, furnishes its own contingent of that which the old theologians called the *dicta probantia*; but we shall find no passages so isolated that the doctrinal views they contain are peculiar to themselves, and receive no confirmation or explanation from other parallel passages.

It may be interesting, again, to know the chronological order of the documents which we shall consult. We have already had occasion to refer to this point, the practical importance of which is beginning to be recognized, and which deserves yet more careful attention for the sake even of the conservative school of criticism. We shall here merely indicate the results to which we have been led by a careful examination of the texts, and which we have fully stated and sustained in another work.*

The oldest epistles of Paul that have come down to us (for we take it as a fact that many of them have been lost) are those to the Thessalonians, written from Corinth between the years A.D. 53 and 54. Next to these comes the Epistle to the Galatians, written at Ephesus immediately after Paul's arrival in that city, in the year 57 A.D. Then, after a journey through the island of Crete, Greece (where he made a short stay), Illyria, and Macedonia, the apostle wrote at Corinth the Epistle to Titus, and about the same time, or shortly after, the First Epistle to Timothy. On his return to Ephesus, about Easter,

* "Geschichte der Heiligen Schriften des Neuen Testaments."

A.D. 59, he wrote that which we call the First Epistle to the Corinthians, and during the following winter he sent from Macedonia the Second Epistle to the same Church. In the spring of the following year, during his third sojourn at Corinth, he composed the Epistle to the Romans. During his captivity in Cæsarea, from the year A.D. 60 to 62, he wrote the epistles to the Ephesians and Colossians, and to Philemon. Carried to Rome in 62, he, almost immediately on his arrival, despatched the Second Epistle to Timothy; and lastly, towards the end of his captivity, and shortly before his death, the Epistle to the Philippians, which is the latest we possess. This chronology, it will be observed, differs considerably from that commonly received. We candidly admit that there are several points for the determination of which we are not in a position to adduce irrefragable arguments,—as, for example, with reference to the First Epistle to Timothy, which has hitherto seemed to baffle all the sagacity of the critics. But we maintain positively that the commonly accepted chronology (which consists essentially in placing the three pastoral epistles after the rest, while accepting them as genuine, and in dating from Rome all the epistles written in captivity) is ill-founded and arbitrary, especially as it can only be sustained by recourse to the old fable of the second captivity. This latter hypothesis is not only quite superfluous for the reconstruction of the biography of the apostle, but is supported by arguments which will not bear investigation.

It will be seen from the category we have given, that we reject altogether the Epistle to the Hebrews, as belonging to the Pauline series. In truth, there is nothing left in our day but a baseless preconception in favour of such a supposition, while against it is the unanimous voice of the ancient Church, the opinion of our great reformers and their confessions of faith. We shall have to allude again to this fact, and shall then more fully vindicate our conclusions. It would be out of place to do so here.

It will be remarked, again, that we do not include among our sources of information a book which our readers may perhaps have expected us to name—we mean the Acts of the Apostles. This contains, it is true, many of Paul's discourses, but they are discourses which do not go beyond the circle of the ideas common to the preaching of all the apostles; there is nothing in them distinctively characteristic of the theology of Paul. We may even say that they convey very imperfectly the true spirit of that apostle. The historian who gave them to the world probably had in his possession materials supplied by his memory or by tradition, but he was not mainly desirous to bring into full relief the Pauline theology, properly so called. We shall have occasion elsewhere to give a doctrinal synopsis of the book of the Acts, and we shall see, by the special end which the author proposed to himself in writing it, that he may be of great assistance to us in ascertaining the religious position of the Churches of primitive times, but that we cannot look to him as a guide in the study of our present subject.

From the writings of Paul alone, then, must we seek to derive his theology. These writings are not only cast into an epistolary form, but are genuine letters addressed to particular readers. They might all very aptly be described as pastoral letters, if usage had not appropriated that name exclusively to a few of them in distinction from the rest. The apostle deals with the religious and ecclesiastical condition of the communities to which he writes, and in which he had previously filled the office of pastor or spiritual director. The letters have therefore an essentially practical end in view, and are prompted by the need he feels of maintaining his influence as pastor during his enforced absence from the Churches. This peculiar relation is the occasion of the very marked difference between the epistles of Paul and the so-called catholic epistles, a difference of manner which strikes the reader at once, and independently of the yet greater diversity soon discovered in the subject-matter. It is important to recognize the first of these characteristics, because of the influence it exerts on the form and method of the teaching of the epistles.

On this subject a question arises which it is important to determine before entering on the system itself to which our

attention is now directed. Will these epistles, written under
the influence of casual and temporary necessities, and taking in
their teaching probably the form demanded by these accidents
of circumstance, suffice to meet our present purpose ?

This question seems to us a very fair one. In truth, the
epistles are addressed, without exception, to persons already
familiar with evangelical ideas; they are not designed in any
case to give elementary or complete instruction to their readers.
Doctrines are introduced fragmentarily and incidentally, or are
simply alluded to as matters already well understood. The
actual teaching of Christianity had been given orally, and
doubtless in a complete and connected form; while in his
epistles the apostle had always in view the necessities of those
to whom they were immediately addressed, the disciples whom
he knew, whom he had himself taught, whom he visited from
time to time, and not the possible requirements of a future
generation, to whom these same epistles have become the sole
medium of communication with the mind of their author.
Under these conditions, is it likely that the epistles will give
us all that we desire to know? May we not expect in a system
derived from them to find gaps here and there ?

We cannot accept the reply to this question given by our
old theologians, namely, that the Holy Spirit has provided that
all should be written which was necessary to salvation. This
is not the question. Our salvation is not the point at issue,
nor does that depend on the existence of a page more or less ;
the point to be determined is whether, with the documents we
possess, we can trace the logical and systematic connection in
which the apostle Paul presented the truths of the Gospel, both
in the sphere of subjective reflection and of public instruction.
And we have a right to propose this question, because the
epistles of Paul form but a very small part of the great sum
of his apostolic labours.

We submit a few considerations calculated to reassure us in
reference to the doubts which this question may raise. We
observe, first, that after all the Pauline system is not so com-
plicated a matter as might be imagined from the ponderous

bulk of dogmatism accumulated in the arsenals of the schools. It starts from a few very simple principles which we can trace through all the subsequent detailed applications. These principles once recognized and rightly understood, the reconstruction of the system is not a matter of much difficulty, the more so as everything in it tends to a practical application, and to the edification of the Church. On this principle, every part of the system is connected with questions accessible to the least skilled intellect, and thus always presents one aspect in which it may be apprehended by the religious feeling, by the Christian conscience, and by common sense, even while in another aspect it may include speculative and transcendental elements which practised theologians alone can appreciate.

We may observe, again, in reference to the views peculiar to the apostle Paul,—those which encountered the strongest opposition in the prejudices of traditional religion,—that he is careful to reiterate them on every occasion, and to set them forth with ever new demonstration. We may be very sure that matters on which he only touches once, obscurely * or in passing, though they may form a part of his creed, and cohere in some way with his system, have not formed the basis of his teaching, and will not help us much in tracing the peculiar current of his thought. It would be scarcely too much to say that a misconception of his meaning on these points need not compromise our views on the essential parts of his theology.

A purely literary estimate of the epistles of Paul would lead us away from the field of our present investigation. The subject, however, is so attractive, and French literature possesses so few studies of this kind, that we may perhaps be pardoned if, in concluding these preliminary remarks, we

---

* We may cite, as an instance, the passage relating to the glorification of nature (Rom. viii. 19, and foll.), or that other passage, also without any direct parallel, treating of Antichrist (2 Thess. ii.), and more particularly the famous passage (Rom. v. 12, and foll.) which establishes the typical relation between Adam and Christ. This latter passage, nevertheless, has been made the starting-point of the ecclesiastical system of Pauline theology.

yield to the desire to say a few words on this aspect of his writings.

Just as the inner life of Paul was under the ruling power of one idea, which exercised an influence as profound as it was various on all the relations of the apostle and on all the spheres of his marvellous activity, so his epistles all bear the impress of a grand uniformity of method, allied to a rare affluence in the modes of expression. They all commence with salutations more or less solemn, addressed to the readers, and with thanksgivings to God for that which has already been accomplished, whether in the particular community addressed, or elsewhere for the establishment of His kingdom. They are divided almost always, unless extraordinary circumstances call for a different method, into a doctrinal or theoretical, and a moral or practical part. They conclude with private matters,—news, commissions, personal references, and desires dictated by love and piety.

But in a plan so uniform,—so little adapted, as it would seem, to promote freshness and vivacity,—how faithfully does the style mirror the individuality of the writer! Doubtless, it is not classical or correct: the rhetoric fulness, the sonorous cadence, the finished diction, all are wanting. The concision of the syntactic forms requires study rather than simple reading. But what a wealth of language! what fertility of expression! Unfinished sentences, ellipses more or less difficult to fill up, parentheses which divert at once the pen of the writer and the mind of the reader, daring omissions in the argument defying logic, pictures drawn as true to life as to art, rhetorical figures of every sort,—all these express in turn and with inimitable force the characteristics of a quick and culti-vated mind, the affections of an ardent and deeply sensitive soul, and show how the pen, ready and daring as it was, was too slow a medium for the thoughts of the writer. The multi-tude of comparisons, of graceful metaphors taken from animate and inanimate nature, from public and private life, from civil relations and sacred rites, and expanding easily into spiritual allegories, all these do honour to a brilliant imagination worthy of a son of the East. Antitheses sometimes paradoxical, telling climaxes, pressing and irresistible questions not to be parried by the reader, exclamations full of startling force, irony over-turning opposition,—a vivacity, in short, which allows the reader no rest, alternates with tender and touching effusions of feeling which carry captive the heart.

It must ever be borne in mind, further, that it was Paul who imprinted on the Hellenic idiom its peculiar Christian character, and that he was thus in a manner the creator of the theological language of the Church. It is impossible to estimate the difficulties he had to encounter here. The religious vocabulary he found ready for his use was of the very poorest, and often he could only triumph over this obstacle (one which genius alone can appreciate and genius alone could subdue) by concentrating a whole world of ideas in a single word. Unfortunately, in endeavouring to reverse the process, and derive the many ideas from their one symbol, the schoolmen have often failed, and torn and mangled fragments of the original thought have been all that have come out of the process.

The form of Paul's teaching, especially when he speaks calmly, is essentially dialectic. The speculative and mystical elements of his convictions and of his preaching, were so closely allied in his mind by a severe and rigorous method, that he was never in danger of being carried away by his imagination or by mere fanciful enthusiasm. It was one of his great aims always so to give a reason of the faith that was in him, that he might awaken the same faith in others. His theology, however, is widely removed from the cold scholasticism of the rationalist, which would sacrifice all feeling and life to definition and analysis. But we must pause here a moment to note a fact which has never till now been fully appreciated. There is one portion of the Pauline theology in which dialectic reasoning seems to predominate; there is another portion which is chiefly characterized by the language of religious feeling. The union of these two elements in one mind, as it is here met with, is a thing so exceptional, so peculiar to Paul, that science in all ages has found the utmost difficulty in rightly balancing the two. The traditional theology of the orthodox schools has more and more slighted the second element, giving attention exclusively to the first; and the Gospel so treated has become, we venture to say, a system of jurisprudence rather than a religion, and its ethical essence has been sacrificed to the absolute dominion of a syllogism. It is for us not to fall into the opposite error, but to re-establish the equilibrium of the two elements as it really existed in the mind of the apostle.

Paul was wont to have recourse for his demonstrations to Holy Scripture, and inasmuch as his method in this respect was the same as that of the Jews and Judæo-Christians, we need not dwell on it more fully here after what we have already said on that point. In so far as he struck out new paths for himself, we shall study his exegesis, when we come to it in the natural order of our subject.

CHAPTER II.

GENERAL OUTLINE OF THE PAULINE THEOLOGY.

WE have now to inquire what is the fundamental and formative idea, the basis of the system of Paul, the principle which gives to it a logical unity, and which may help us in its reconstruction. This preliminary investigation cannot be a very difficult task, and unless we wilfully close our eyes to that which is most clear and positive in Christian theology, we can without hesitation lay our finger upon the essential principle with which the apostle starts. There seems to us, however, a necessity to go still further back, and not to be satisfied with any axiomatic summary of the system whatever, but to trace such axiom itself to the source whence it must have been derived. This fact anterior to the theory we find in the life of the apostle, which will serve better than any speculative reasoning to throw light on his system The doctrine of Paul is the natural corollary of his history. To study his history from the psychological point of view is the best and only way to comprehend his teaching. This study the apostle himself was the first to engage in; his inner life was to him a sort of mirror, in which the Gospel revelation took form and colour; it was at the same time the touchstone by means of which he tested its true worth. This is also the reason why so many Christians have a peculiarly intimate knowledge of this system; they have passed through similar experiences, which have become to them at once the clearest explanation and the highest commendation of a theology which remained a sealed and dead letter to those who had no other key to its interpretation than that furnished by books or by a religious routine. We are justified therefore in saying that just as the life of Paul is the key to his theology, so the life of the Christian will be its demonstration.

We shall not need to write a long biographical article in order to illustrate what we have just said. A few general observations will suffice to bring out the justness of the principle. The details of the history are too familiar to all to need repetition here, and indeed it is rather in the inner life of the apostle than in his outward history that we shall discover the light we seek.

The life of Paul divides itself into two periods very distinct from each other. There is, first, his life under the law, the life of a rigid Pharisee, seeking to make himself acceptable to God—seeking, that is, a legal righteousness by a fanatic zeal in the performance of every supposed duty. There is, again, his life under the Gospel, the life of the devoted apostle, happy in his mission, making it the great business of his existence, but without boasting in any strength of his own for its accomplishment, or in any title earned by his success to a recompense of reward; on the contrary, recognizing in all humility his own insufficiency, and the grace which constantly came to his aid. The two periods of this life, so utterly dissimilar, are separated the one from the other by the simple, abrupt fact of his conversion on the road to Damascus—a conversion which however psychologists have sought to explain it, always appeared to Paul himself as the direct and immediate effect of a Divine intervention, in which neither his memory or reflection could ever discern the operation of any natural cause. As he looked back from the second period of his life, its earlier stage seemed to him sometimes as an aberration, pardonable perhaps because he was sincere in his errors, but more often as a sin for which he could never atone, and which in any case deserved to forfeit just that which he had most ardently sought to secure, the blessedness, the reward of righteousness. As he looked into his own heart, and questioned his own consciousness, he was fully convinced that he owed his conversion in

no way to himself, that his feet had not been turned out of
the path of error he had been pursuing by any power or will
of his own, but that it was God Himself who, by a special
revelation of Christ, had come to save him. He thus learned
gratefully to ascribe this salutary change to the grace of God,
from whose hands he thankfully and adoringly received it.
He felt that henceforth he was bound to walk worthy of that
grace, that it might never be withdrawn from him; that it
could never again be with him a question of reckoning with
God as if he had any merit of his own, any virtue that he
might cast into the balance. If obedience to his new duties
became easy to him, if his efforts were sustained and accomplished the desired end, he regarded it as a gift of the same
grace, and not as any matter of personal glorying for himself.
But that which formed the crown of his happiness was that
consciousness of peace and reconciliation, which filled him with
a joy as intense as it was pure. It was the certainty that the
great debt he had contracted by the falseness of his former life
no longer rested upon him, that it was remitted in view of the
new life given, in view of the solemn surrender he had made
of any claim to personal merit; in view, finally, of the boundless
confidence he had placed in the inexhaustible love of God his
Saviour. All this gave him the strength he needed to do
battle with the world, and sustained his hopes of the glorious
triumph of the kingdom of Christ.

We shall find in the Pauline system, as we come to unfold
it, all the features we have thus broadly traced, and which we
have gathered from the numerous passages in which Paul
speaks of his own history and experience.*

But we are not satisfied with thus grasping the fundamental
idea of his theology, and bringing out its essentially psychological character. As we have spoken of a system, it is incumbent
on us to show that it is not we only, but Paul himself, who
cast his teaching into a systematic shape and form. A mind
so argumentative as that of Paul could not fail to arrange his

---

* Gal. i. 11, and foll.; 1 Cor. xv. 8, and foll.; Phil. iii. 6, and foll.;
2 Cor. iv. 7, and foll.; 1 Tim. i. 12, and foll.

ideas on a definite plan, and to group them according to their
natural relations. We therefore expect to find him enunciating
in some part of his writings the division which he adopts, the
method he follows. Nor are we disappointed. In the Epistle
to the Romans, at the very point where he commences his
exposition of the religion of the Gospel, he brings together all
the doctrinal theses on which it rests, and enumerates them
categorically, so that they contain the programme of his
ulterior demonstration, and indicate to us the track we must
follow in order to apprehend it aright :—

" But now the righteousness of God *without the law is manifested*, being witnessed by the law and the prophets ; even the
righteousness of God which is by faith of Jesus Christ *unto all
and upon all them that believe*: for there is no difference : for
all have sinned, and come short of the glory of God; being
justified freely *by His grace through the redemption that is in
Christ Jesus.*" *

The subject of this passage, and consequently the fundamental idea around which all the others are grouped, is
righteousness. It is immediately and twice over characterized
from the Gospel point of view by the addition of the genitive
of God, which distinguishes it from every other quality to which
this name is commonly applied.

This righteousness of God is presented under a double aspect,
and the system accordingly divides itself into two parts, the
one negative or polemic, the other affirmative or dogmatic.
The second is, without doubt, the more important, and of the
wider significance ; but the first is not the less indispensable.
The latter, having reference to the past, is represented as to its
substance by the words *the law*, as to its position in the system
by the negative particle *without*. The former, having regard

---

* Νυνὶ ΧΩΡΙΣ ΝΟΜΟΤ ΔΙΚΑΙΟΣΤΝΗ Θεοῦ ΠΕΦΑΝΕΡΩΤΑΙ, μαρτυρουμένη
ὑπὸ τοῦ νόμου καὶ τῶν προφητῶν, δικαιοσύνη δὲ Θεοῦ διὰ πίστεως Ἰησοῦ Χριστοῦ,
ΕΙΣ ΠΑΝΤΑΣ καὶ ἐπὶ πάντας ΤΟΤΣ ΠΙΣΤΕΤΟΝΤΑΣ· οὐ γάρ ἐστι διαστολή.
πάντες γὰρ ἥμαρτον, καὶ ὑστεροῦνται τῆς δόξης τοῦ Θεοῦ, δικαιούμενοι δωρεὰν ΤΗΙ
ΑΤΤΑΤ ΧΑΡΙΤΙ ΔΙΑ ΤΗΣ ΑΠΟΑΤΤΡΩΣΕΩΣ ΤΗΣ ΕΝ ΧΡΙΣΤΩΙ ΙΗΣΟΤ.
Rom. iii. 21, and foll.

to the future, is represented by the word which refers to the *Gospel revelation.*

In the first part the apostle distinguishes and draws attention to three facts which correspond to three aspects of his negative thesis. There is, first, the historic side, or the fact of the *universality of sin.* Here we shall find him investigating the causes and describing the effects of sin, both being regarded by him as lying at the basis of the decrees of God, and as forming the premises of the system which is to deal with them. In the second place, there is the *polemical side,* properly so called, or the fact of the *insufficiency of the law.* Here we shall find him analyzing the nature, the moral effects, and providential design of the *anterior* revelations, more particularly of the Old Testament, and demonstrating their temporary character. Lastly, there is the *religious side,* or the fact of man's secret desire for deliverance from his state of misery. Here we shall find the description of the threefold bondage of man—under sin, under guilt, under the law—and of the gloomy prospect (the coming short of *the glory of God*) connected with it. This last fact brings us at once to the second part, which treats of the consolation given to the man who is conscious of his desperate state.

In this second part we have then the setting forth of the *Gospel*—that is to say, of the good news to be proclaimed to the sinner. It consists in teaching him that his salvation is possible, that henceforth there is access for him to God by the way long predicted, but not hitherto opened. *God wills the salvation of man by Christ.* This is the simplest expression of the Gospel. This statement of it names three persons placed in a particular relation, the knowledge of which relation forms the basis of this theology. It is God who wills the salvation of His creatures; it is Christ who procures that salvation for them; it is man by whom it is to be obtained. The motive power with God is *grace;* the act of Christ is *redemption;* the medium for man is *faith.*

Such is the outline of the Pauline system as it may be deduced directly from the text we have analyzed. We shall not for the present pursue it further. The second part is very slightly sketched here: of the various details which it comprehends, and the numerous subdivisions which it suggests, we shall speak at length presently. We shall endeavour to show by other passages of his writings that these subdivisions are indicated generally by the apostle himself. It is with a view to render the comprehension of the system more simple to our readers that we confine ourselves for the present to what has been said. The system will unfold itself in its fulness before their eyes as they advance, and they will not fail to note its dialectic completeness, when they have grasped the scope of its religious import.

CHAPTER III.

OF RIGHTEOUSNESS.

WE shall not be surprised to find at the basis of Paul's theological system a proposition purely and simply borrowed from Mosaism. When he enlisted under the banner of the Gospel, he would not commence by repudiating the sum and substance of his former faith as an error and a lie. Such an act of absolute repudiation of the past might beseem a pagan, an idolator; but for a converted Jew, Judaism still rested upon the basis of a Divine revelation; the Gospel did not open with a divorce from the law. Paul, as a Christian, might undoubtedly regard and apprehend the relations of the two dispensations in a manner different from that to which as a disciple of Gamaliel he had been accustomed; but he did not cease to recognize that there were bonds of union and relationship between Judaism and Christianity, truths and axioms common to both, and above all in both the same God.

We have said, then, that the starting-point of evangelical theology, as formulated by Paul, is a proposition borrowed from Judaism. We may add that it was one of capital importance in the Judaic system. *The condition of blessedness is righteousness:* this was the fundamental axiom of the doctrines of the Old Testament; this is also the basis upon which, from a dialectic point of view, the religious theory is founded which the great apostle developes and applies in his epistles.

We shall not dwell here on the fact, otherwise well ascertained, that the written law and the prophets did not hold out to the people of Israel any hope of a recompense beyond the grave. They ever stimulated and sustained the moral energy of the nation by promises made in the name of God for the future. These promises, merely earthly and political in the beginning, were raised gradually into a higher sphere; and in the apostolic age, without being completely spiritualized, they had become generally associated, both in the teaching of the schools and in the popular mind, with the future life and the inauguration of a more perfect and happier world. The religious faith of Judaism, especially in the latter times, had found in these hopes its highest and dearest expression.

The same hopes the Gospel adopted and confirmed, raising them into its own sphere, and gradually spiritualizing them. It accepted also the condition which Mosaism had attached to the realization of the promises,—the necessity, namely, of righteousness. But it is in the appreciation and definition of this one means of attaining to blessedness, in the exposition of the particular relation between it and the facts of the Gospel, that Paul struck out a new path for himself, along which we must follow him.

Let us once more call to mind briefly what in Judaism was understood by *righteousness.** We must not attach to the word the meaning it bears in our civil language. The idea of the theocracy will lead us to its true signification. Men, who stand to God in the relation of subjects to a King, must endeavour to perform all that is demanded of them. Their acts must be in exact accordance with the sovereign will to which they bow. The question is not one of motive in the acts performed, of the feelings which prompt or accompany those acts, but of the actual thing done. If these are in perfect harmony with the command given, it constitutes righteousness—that is, legal perfection. It was to this legal, external, material perfection, so to speak, that Judaism aspired; the law is called, in view of the end thus proposed, a law of righteousness;† it was considered possible for and

---

* צְדָקָה, δικαιοσύνη.

† Rom. ix. 31, νόμος δικαιοσύνης.—Phil. iii. 4, and foll.

incumbent on the individual to attain to this end, to make himself thus righteous, in short, by his own efforts and merit.*

This was what Paul had learnt in the school of Judaism.† The ideal aim of his life had been the punctual performance of the law; his zeal and courage were sustained by the hope of appearing before God as righteous, and thus gaining his title to blessedness. Now it must be observed that this principle of a close relation between present righteousness and future felicity, has in it nothing which repels the reason or which is contrary to the conception of God. If there was any error in the use made of it, the theory at least was not in fault. Paul therefore does not repudiate it. He still proclaims that it is the fulfilment of the law—the positive or the natural law—which will secure for man the declaration of the favour of God, and the prospect of a glorious reward. He still repeats that without being righteous no man can claim a part in the heavenly inheritance.‡

* 'Ιδίαν, Rom. x. 3 ;
† Phil. iii. 4, and foll.
‡ Rom. ii. 13, and foll. ; 1 Cor. vi. 9, 10.

CHAPTER IV.

OF SIN.

SIDE by side with this principle, Paul places another which is
no less fundamental, and which in combination with the foregoing will give us his whole system. The one, which is purely
theoretical, had been derived from the conception of God; the
other, which is simply historical, is based upon experience and
conscience. Both are alike true, and yet they seem to be contradictory and incompatible with each other. They constitute
a kind of antinomy, as it is called in logic, but an antinomy of
far graver moment than any which merely baffles speculative
reason, since this touches man in his highest interests, and
opens before him a gloomier vista than one of doubt and error
simply. It is this very antinomy which the Gospel, in default
of all other philosophy, is destined to resolve. .

The theoretic principle affirms that no man can attain to
happiness without righteousness. Historical experience declares directly that no man possesses this righteousness; that,
on the contrary, all without exception are in the sight of God
sinners.

We have just said that, with Paul, this second fundamental
principle of the evangelical theology was sustained by experience. In fact, he does not anywhere give a speculative
demonstration of it—one based, that is, on some theological
premise. In order to establish it, he appeals simply to the
observations which any man can make on those about him,
and more particularly to the inner consciousness of every
individual. In order to help all in this study of themselves,

which, painful as its results are, is full of instruction for those who seriously pursue it, the apostle divides men into two classes —those who have and those who have not received a positive law from God;* in other words, the Jews and the Gentiles; and he then applies his principle to both categories.†

It is true, he says, that the Gentiles have not received any positive law—that is, a revelation of the will of God at any particular portion of their history; but they do not thus escape responsibility towards God because of their sins; for, in default of such positive commandment, they have received two other laws equally divine, which may stand them in its stead —that, namely, which is manifested in nature, and that which speaks in their conscience. By the former they may learn to know God, the almighty and all-wise Creator, who perpetually reveals Himself in His creatures;‡ by the latter they ought to recognize the obligation to worship, and the way to please Him.§ This constituted a *law* ‖ for them perfectly analogous to that of the Jews, both in its source and in its end. They had not profited, however, by these revelations; they had worshipped the creature rather than the Creator, and had fallen in consequence of this error into the most terrible moral corruption. In losing God they had lost themselves, and contracted an immeasurable debt of moral guilt.¶ Thus, though they were without law in the historical sense of the word, as we have explained above, they were yet chargeable with transgression of the Divine law,** of sin in the moral and positive sense, no less than the possessors of the written law.

The culpability of the Jews is still more evident. The knowledge of the will of God was made so easy to them, that their transgressions were without excuse. The very explicitness of their law, its minuteness in all details of duty, left

* Οἱ ἄνομοι, οἱ ὑπὸ νόμον, 1 Cor. ix. 20, and foll.; Gal. iv. 5.
† Rom. i., ii.
‡ Acts xiv. 15—17; xvii. 24—28; Rom. i. 20:
§ Rom. ii. 15; i. 32.
‖ Rom. ii. 27.
¶ Rom. i. 23—32; Eph. iv. 17—19.
** Ἀνομία, 2 Cor. vi. 14; Rom. vi. 19; Titus ii. 14.

them without any cloak of ignorance to cover their sins. And yet experience proves that the Jews also failed to fulfil the law. For, on the one hand, they misconceived its spirit, they perverted it by making it a matter of purely outward observance, by reducing it to an *opus operatum*, as scholastic theology would have termed it; on the other hand, they found it impossible never to neglect any minute item of those innumerable commandments contained in the law, and· yet the obedience demanded was to be absolute and entire.*

It is, then, an established fact that all men, to whatever ⌐nation or religion they belong, are sinners.†

It follows naturally that none has any valid title to the possession of happiness. The condition not being fulfilled, ⸱the Divine promise becomes null and void; all mankind has forfeited its highest good, its sublimest hope.‡

To what has just been said we add a single remark. Paul, from his historical point of view, is speaking only of the Jews and the Gentiles, but it is easy to see that all that he says is ·equally applicable to men who might not come directly under either of these categories. This is evident from the psychological considerations which he goes on to present; and, indeed, the terms Jews and Gentiles, though borrowed from the positive facts of his own day, have also an abstract and general signification, which will render them always applicable to a theology perfectly independent of circumstances.

This fact of sin § once admitted as the general and habitual condition of man, the question of its cause and its origin naturally presents itself. The apostle was bound to enter ·upon it; he has solved it, and made it a very essential element in the economy of his system. He devotes himself to a psychological study of human nature, and these are the discoveries he makes.

* Rom. ii. 1—3, 21—24.
† Πάντες ὑφ' ἁμαρτίαν εἰσί, Rom. iii. 9 ; comp. 19.
‡ 'Υστεροῦνται τῆς δόξης τοῦ θεοῦ, Rom. iii. 23.
§ We do not enumerate here the passages in which we find the terms ἁμάρτημα, ἁμαρτία, παράπτωμα, etc. We shall meet with these again as we go on to analyze the theological ideas connected with them.

In the nature of man, from the moral point of view, two hostile principles are in active operation,—the one good, the other evil. The former is called the spirit, and is the depositary of the ideas of natural religion, of the knowledge of God, of His will, of the moral law; it is to this that every Divine manifestation is addressed, and to which every impulse to act according to the will of God, or, which amounts to the same thing, according to the moral law, appeals.* This principle is the motive power, the condition of a life agreeable to God; of a life of righteousness, as Paul speaks; of a virtuous life, as we should call it in our speech of to-day. The second principle is the flesh. This is in all things the reverse of the former; it represents in general the sum of all that is opposed to the mind and will of God; from it comes every impulse to violate the moral law; it is the spring and source of unrighteousness and vice; that which we call sensuality is but a partial expression of the idea conveyed by the *flesh*.†

These two principles are in perpetual warfare. If for a moment one of them seems overcome or enchained, neither is ever destroyed; both preserve always some power of resistance, some hope of victory.‡ Unhappily, the good principle, in this incessant conflict sustained with the evil, habitually succumbs, or at least never achieves over it a lasting mastery.

---

* This is a misconception of the apostle's account of human nature—if by human nature is meant the condition of man previous to regeneration. The "spirit" is not what Reuss describes in the text, "the depositary of the idea of natural religion," etc. The "spirit" is that new element of life which man receives in response to his faith in the Lord Jesus Christ. Before regeneration there is a knowledge, more or less imperfect, of the moral law, and there may be a conflict between the higher affections of the moral nature and those inferior impulses which betray a man into sin, but the "spirit" is present only in the regenerate soul.—ED.

† A series of expressions which we shall note in passing are derived from this twofold psychological thesis. Κατὰ σάρκα (κατὰ πνεῦμα) ζῆν, περιπατεῖν, εἶναι; τὰ τῆς σαρκὸς (τοῦ πνεύματος) φρονεῖν, ἐν σαρκὶ (ἐν πν.) εἶναι, Rom. viii. 4—13.

‡ Ἡ σὰρξ ἐπιθυμεῖ κατὰ τοῦ πνεύματος, τὸ δὲ πνεῦμα κατὰ τῆς σαρκὸς, ταῦτα δὲ ἀλλήλοις ἀντίκειται, Gal. v. 17.

The term which Paul uses to describe this antagonism may apply to both opposing tendencies, but it serves more particularly to designate the evil principle, wherever it is employed in an ethical sense. Every motion of the flesh, every impulse of desire on its part, is a lust, an appetite, in the evil sense of the word.* The epithets which usually accompany this word sufficiently mark its import. The lust of the flesh is evil, blind, delusive, since it is in contradiction with the true interests of man; unhappily, it is also natural to our heart and to the world at large to which we by birth belong.†

Every victory of the flesh over the spirit is a sin; or, to speak more exactly, we recognize as sin every act in order to the consummation of which the flesh has to gain such a preliminary victory. These victories as they are repeated become more and more easy; the flesh finally gains the ascendant over the spirit, and exercises a sway no longer contested; sin, from being an isolated fact, becomes a habit, a tendency, a general disposition. This disposition is unhappily the ordinary condition of man. In his natural development, and while he is left to himself, he is under the empire of the flesh, he is the slave of sin. The combat is generally an unequal one, and the spirit never achieves the full and definite supremacy it ought to exert; it is at most at intervals that its efforts are crowned with a momentary success, which, because so short-lived, is of no value.‡

Paul never loses sight of this fundamental idea of his religious psychology, but the terms which he uses in its application and in his theological discussions vary in many respects, and seem to be based on differing conceptions. In truth, since he is describing an internal conflict, a kind of schism between the faculties of the same individual, we can well conceive of a sort of double consciousness in the writer himself. The *I* may comprehend his whole personality, and thus include

---

* Ἐπιθυμία, Rom. vi. 12; xiii. 14; 1 Thess. iv. 5; Titus iii. 3, etc.

† Ἐκ, σαρκός, Gal. v. 16, 24; Eph. ii. 3; κακή, Col. iii. 5; ἀνόητος, 1 Tim. vi. 9; ἀπάτης, Eph. iv. 22; καρδίας, Rom. i. 24; κοσμική, Titus ii. 12.

‡ Ἐγώ σαρκικός εἰμί, πεπραμένος ὑπὸ τὴν ἁμαρτίαν, Rom. vii. 14.

the two conflicting powers;* or, again, the I may represent only the higher and spiritual element, thus distinguished from the lower and carnal, as from something foreign to its true self;† or, lastly, the I may mean the personality already under the power of sin, and thus having lost, so to speak, the better part of itself.‡ This last is the expression of the common experience; the first is based upon man's psychological study of himself, while the second is the utterance of the religious or Christian idea. With this mode of expression is connected that other in which Paul speaks of an inner man,§—that is to say, of a personal being truly deserving the name of man, but concealed or kept in bondage by something foreign and external to itself.

Here is a series of terms which all represent the same psychological fact, but in a different manner. The spirit and the flesh may both be considered as not self-governing, but as placed under the dominion of an external law. The spirit is under the law of God, the flesh under the law of sin. The former is also called "the law of the mind," the second the "law in the members,"‖ the members being the organs of the flesh in the consummation of the acts to which it prompts, as the mind is the organ of the spirit to which God addresses

---

* Rom. vii. 25.

† Rom. vii. 17, 20, 24.

‡ Rom. vii. 18.

§ Ὁ ἔσω ἄνθρωπος, Rom. vii. 22 ; 2 Cor. iv. 16 ; Eph. iii. 16.

‖ Νομὸς θεοῦ, ἁμαρτίας, τ. νοὸς, τ. μελέων. The word νοῦς has different meanings : it signifies at first simply what we call reason, apart from any moral functions—the mode of thought, the direction of the mind (Rom. i. 28 ; xiv. 5 ; Eph. iv. 17 ; Phil. iv. 7 ; 1 Tim. vi. 5 ; 2 Tim. iii. 8 ; Titus i. 15). In a particular case it designates the free and spontaneous action of the human mind, in opposition to the state of ecstasy (1 Cor. xiv. 14, and foll.) In a series of other passages it relates to the moral dispositions, the manner of life, the ethical principles (Rom. xii. 2 ; Eph. iv. 23 ; 1 Cor. i. 10). We have just seen it placed in contrast to σάρξ (Rom. vii. 23, 25), as representing the spiritual element in man ; elsewhere it is combined with this word, νοῦς τῆς σαρκὸς (Col. ii. 18), to designate the carnal element or tendency. Νοῦς Χριστοῦ (1 Cor. ii. 16) is, without doubt, the deeper apprehension of the Gospel.

Himself in order to enforce His will. These expressions, the law of sin, the law in the members, are evidently suggested by the requirements of the parallelism. The fundamental relation, as shown above, is not changed by these various formulas, which only differ from those before used by pointing out the more immediate causes of the inner antagonism. But it would be wrong to conclude from these terms, the *members* or the *body*,* that Paul regards sin as inherent in the very substance of the flesh, a theory which would lead at once to Manicheeism,—that is, to the system which proclaims the radical antagonism, the absolute dualism between matter and spirit, as between two elements of different origin. Paul does not go beyond the simple psychological observation to which we have alluded, and in this part of his system, even more than elsewhere, he is careful not to enter the region of more or less perilous metaphysics. He goes no further than the fact of the opposition between the natural man and God.†

If we grasp the idea of a law of God by which the spirit is governed, the fact that the spirit triumphs over the flesh appears naturally as an act of obedience to that law, and a life regulated by it is a life for God or according to His will.‡ In this case, which we put here hypothetically, the *ego* is consciously made one with God, and there is no more opposition to the practice of the Divine law. On the contrary, when the flesh gains the dominion, when the senses and the passions form the rule and end of life, it is a life for self, the life of an egoist.§

There is yet one other variation to be noted in the language employed. Sometimes the flesh is described as powerful and victorious.‖ Again it is represented as too weak to follow the

---

* Σῶμα τῆς σαρκὸς, τῆς ἁμαρτίας, Col. ii. 11 ; Rom. vi. 6.

† Κατὰ ἄνθρωπον is the equivalent of κατὰ σάρκα, and is opposed to κατὰ θεόν.

‡ Ζῆν τῷ θεῷ, Gal. ii. 19.

§ Ζῆν ἑαυτῷ, 2 Cor. v. 15 ; Rom. xiv. 7.

‖ Rom. vii. 23.

motion of the spirit.* We see at once that these are but two
phases of the same fact.

We shall conclude with a remark which may seem superfluous after all that has gone before, but which we cannot
pass over because Paul himself gives emphasis to it. This
universality of sin, deplored by the apostle, is not only the
character of the generation then living. He does not imitate
the moralists, preachers, or writers of satires, who have often
represented their own contemporaries as more corrupt than
their fathers. He declares positively that all men who have
ever lived from the very first, have been in the same moral
condition.†

We have now to verify the effects and consequences resulting to man from this state of sin. In part these are manifest
now and here; in part they hang over him as a menace for the
future.

In the present time, the sinful man may find himself in two
very different positions, corresponding to two distinct stages of
the knowledge he has of himself, and consequently of his own
moral misery.

One man is alive to his sins, and seeks to avoid their repetition; he makes efforts to resist the principle of sin, but the
victory ever eludes him; in moments of weakness and supine-
ness he yields afresh, and falls when he least expects it;
he knows the good, and wills and desires it, but finds no
strength in himself to cleave to and realize it, or rather he is
constantly brought into collision with a stronger force which
breaks and paralyzes his will. This is the conflict, ever renewed and ever issuing in failure, which the apostle describes
so eloquently in a famous passage of his writings.‡ Hence arises
a feeling of bitter disappointment, a sort of despair which will
plunge man into an abyss of misery,§ or will issue in a stolid
indifference.

* Rom. vi. 19.
† Πάντες ἥμαρτον, Rom. v. 12.
‡ Rom. vii. 15—23.
§ Ταλαίπωρος ἐγὼ ἄνθρωπος, Rom. vii. 24.

And this constitutes that second stage of the moral consciousness, of which we spoke just now. He who is unhappy enough to sink thus low, has no more courage even to attempt to resist evil. He is insensible * to the shame of sin, deaf to the voice of conscience, inaccessible to the counsels of peace; he is, in a word, in a state of stupefaction, of moral lethargy, which well deserves the name of death.†

The future is fraught with consequences yet more fearful; it presents itself to the man under the darkest colours. He who has gone afar off from God, and who has no power and no will to bridge over the great gulf between them, how shall he stand before his Judge? If a man fails to fulfil all the duties prescribed by the law of God, is he not condemned already, already under a curse from which there is no escape? ‡ How much heavier must that curse be upon one who has provoked it by his own indifference? But in both cases alike, the blessedness annexed to the fulfilment in all points of the Divine commands is necessarily withheld, hopelessly lost, and its dark reverse is all to which the sinner can look forward.

God, in His justice, can but punish. This necessity is designated by an anthropomorphic term, borrowed from the Old Testament (where such repeatedly occur), the word *anger*, § from which, however, we must carefully dissociate all idea of passion or human affection. It might be better called the reprobative justice of God. Now, since we are all sinners, and since the moral consciousness, from its very first awakening, brings with it the sense of guilt already contracted; or, in other words, since by the natural play of our powers, the flesh has already gained the mastery over the spirit, even before conscience has taught us to recognize the antagonism of the two elements, it follows that in our natural state, and at the very commencement of our conscious existence, we find our-

---

* Ἀπηλγηκὼς ἑαυτόν, Eph. iv. 19.

† Νεκρὸς ἐν τοῖς παραπτώμασι, Col. ii. 13; comp. Eph. ii. 1, 5; ἀπηλλοτριωμένος τῆς ζωῆς τοῦθεοῦ, Eph. iv. 18.

‡ Κατάρα, Gal. iii. 10.

§ Ὀργή, Rom. i. 18; ii. 5, 8; iii. 5; Eph. v. 6; Col. iii. 6, etc.

selves already under the stroke of this Divine reprobation, or, as the apostle says, "we are children of wrath." *

The punishment reserved for the sinner is necessarily deprivation of the blessedness promised to the righteous. This purely negative aspect of it is conveyed by different terms all equally expressive of the idea of death to *die*, to *perish; death is the wages of sin*; sin is the goad of death,† and many similar expressions. In the passage last quoted, the figure of the goad is borrowed from the practice of the husbandman of urging on the beasts at plough by means of a pointed instrument. It conveys therefore the idea that sin urges on death, death being regarded as a power acting under the pressure of another force. Lastly, man in his natural state, finds himself in a condition which leads him to his ruin; and that which Paul calls the *body of death* ‡ is not the physically mortal frame, but the disposition which by sin leads to damnation.

It is at once obvious that the question here is not that of physical death, or rather that the idea of the unhappy state, both present and future of the sinner, is not exhausted by the fact of the cessation of the present life. The terms, however, which we have just enumerated, are really borrowed in the first instance from the phenomenon of natural death. At the time when the Hebrew people began to form their religious

---

* Εσμεν τέκνα φύσει ὀγῆς, Eph. ii. 3. In view of what is said in Rom. v. 13, on the necessity of the intervention of a law because of transgression, we find it impossible to translate this expression by such a phrase as this: we are by our very *birth* children of the curse. The meaning of the word φύσις is determined by a very explicit parallel passage in Rom. ii. 14, where it signifies also, and in view again of the moral condition, the natural development of the faculties, apart from the positive law. ["By nature," as Reuss says, does not mean "by our birth;" the expression is the precise antithesis of "by grace." Of Adam, after he sinned, it might be said that "by nature" he was a child of wrath; it was owing to God's supernatural grace that he became a child of God.—ED.]

† Τὰ ὀψώνια τῆς ἁμαρτίας θάνατος, Rom. vi. 23; comp. v. 16; vii. 5, and foll.; 2 Cor. vii. 10, etc.; ἀποθνήσκειν, Rom. viii. 13; ἀπόλλυσθαι, Rom. ii. 12; ἀπώλεια, Phil. iii. 19; τὸ κέντρον τοῦ θανάτου ἡ ἁμαρτία, 1 Cor. xv. 56.

‡ Σῶμα τοῦ θανάτου, Rom. vii. 24.

language, death appeared to them as the end of all existence, the gloomy dwelling in the shades of the dead not deserving to be called life. To the ancient Israelites, therefore, this separation from earth was a thing fraught with terror; to them nothing seemed so desirable as a prolonged old age, the utmost possible postponement of those bitter farewells. To them the idea of life was the natural synonym for happiness; death was the image of every kind of evil. When at length the power of the Messianic hope, with all its far-reaching consequences, had suggested and fostered the belief in a resurrection and a recompense beyond the grave, the old phraseology, slightly modified in meaning, might still serve to mark the two conditions, so essentially in contrast, of the life to come. The names of life and death applied to them with singular aptness, the former representing far more than the mere continuity of physical existence, the latter not intending at all to set forth the cessation of that continuity. All the horror which the vision of the grave had been wont to inspire in the ancients, now centred in the idea of being shut out from the kingdom of Messiah; and what comparison could better describe the joy of having a part in that kingdom, than the supreme satisfaction men had once felt in being saved from a danger which threatened existence itself, and in enjoying a happy old age whose peaceful days were to be lengthened out indefinitely? Thus life meant blessedness; and the absence of blessedness was called death.

This last expression is further justified from another point of view. After the change that had passed upon the eschatological ideas of the Jews, physical death, which had been at first so terrible to all, because beyond it all was blank, retained the same aspect, or became even more terrible to those to whom it was now the prelude to a condition of positive woe; while to others, the hope which filled their souls outweighed the anguish of the bitter moment. To the one, death was the path to joy; to the others, the future appeared as a deathless death.*

* This is a very unsatisfactory account of the terminology of St. Paul and of the New Testament writers generally, concerning the future of

Death had been appointed by God in the beginning * to be the chastisement of the transgression of His will. It is true that this penalty had only been made a distinct threat in view of one particular sin. But the same punishment was subsequently applied, *imputed*, without any fresh decree, to those who had committed any sin whatever. Transgressions were infinitely diversified in their object and their form; but the punishment remained the same for all; all were alike disobedient and blameworthy, and the difference of the conditions in which the individuals were placed in relation to the positive laws of God (not all having received them by formal promulgation), made no difference at all in their doom; those who have sinned without law shall perish independently of law; and those who sin having the law, shall be judged by the law.†

the wicked. Both our Lord and His apostles insist so constantly on the final destruction of the impenitent, that it is difficult to understand how the doctrine of everlasting suffering could have obtained a footing in the Church. "Eternal death" is not an eternal dying. The death of the body is the death of that by which we are related to the region of the phenomenal and the temporal; eternal death is the death of that by which we are related to the real and the eternal.—ED.

* We shall allude again presently to the passage in Rom. v. 12, and foll., which many of our readers may, no doubt, expect that we should discuss here. For the moment, we direct attention only to ver. 14, which belongs to our present subject. Paul has in view these two facts : that sin existed prior to the Mosaic law (ver. 13), and that in the Scripture a penalty is nowhere expressly announced, after the threat uttered to Adam (Gen. ii. 17), till the lawgiving from Sinai. Men, from Adam to Moses, sinned not, ἐπὶ τῷ ὁμοιώματι τῆς παραβάσεως Ἀδάμ, after the manner of Adam—that is to say, not against an express command.

† Ὅσοι ἀνόμως ἥμαρτον ἀνόμως καὶ ἀπολοῦνται, καὶ ὅσοι ἐν νόμῳ ἥμαρτον, διὰ νόμου κριθήσονται, Rom. ii. 12.

CHAPTER V.

OF THE LAW.

IN view of a corruption so universal, and to which such fearful consequences are attached, it is natural to inquire what means are there to remedy the one and to remove the other. This is the sum and substance of theology. Paul, in the investigation of this great question, proceeds by way of exclusion. Convinced that the root of the evil was found in the men themselves, he arrived directly at the conviction that they would seek in vain in their own nature, in their own powers and faculties, for the means of ameliorating their state, and gaining any assurance of future good. So long as they looked in this direction, they could not but fail of their end. While going about to establish their own righteousness, they were not submitting themselves under the righteousness of God.* Here the term *their own righteousness* is relative, and stands for that to which man may attain by his own efforts; the righteousness of God is the absolute righteousness which God requires, and which alone can be of worth. Between these two there is a broad gulf, and there can be no surer way to fail of the second than by clinging persistently to the first.

The means of attaining salvation are, then, not to be found in man, but without him. Where then are we to look for them? Paul, as a Jew, turns first to the law of Moses. That law appeared to him as a positive Divine revelation; as such

---

* Τὴν ἰδίαν δικαιοσύνην ζητοῦντες στῆσαι, τῇ δικαιοσύνῃ τοῦ θεοῦ οὐχ ὑπετάγησαν, Rom. x. 3. Paul is speaking here of the Jews, but what he says is to him an absolute truth.

it demanded absolute obedience, and promised happiness in return. But before coming to the question, How can man be saved? Paul had already demonstrated the universality of sin. He had found that the Jews, though they had the law, did not escape the power of sin; he himself, while fully convinced of the claims and privileges of the law, while devoted to the commandments of God, was conscious of sin within. This experience must in itself show him the insufficiency of the law, its powerlessness to do what was required of it, its weakness because of the presence of sin in the flesh. This fact, translated into a doctrinal form, would be the assertion that the law could neither secure to man, nor enable him to achieve, the victory of the spirit over the flesh; consequently that it could not help him in the attainment of righteousness—that is, of a disposition absolutely conformed to the will of God, and to eternal salvation as the result of such a disposition.*

This, then, is the first doctrinal statement, properly so called, which we find in the writings of Paul, according to the plan we are following in our exposition. It is obviously purely negative; it does not yet unfold the evangelical idea itself; but it prepares the way. It is so important, not only as a basis of doctrine, but as a fact of history, that we may be allowed to pause over it a moment, in order to estimate rightly the significance of the terms composing it.

And first let us endeavour to arrive at an exact definition of the word *law*.

Primarily, this word signifies, purely and simply, the law of Moses as contained in the Pentateuch,† or even a particular article of that law.‡

The Jews, however, had already in their common speech extended the circle of this notion, and designated by the term *law* the entire Old Testament, less in the literary sense,

---

* Ἐν νόμῳ οὐδεὶς δικαιοῦται παρὰ τῷ θεοῦ, Gal. iii. 11; comp. ii. 16; Rom. iii. 20, and foll., to the end of chap. iv.; Acts xiii. 39.

† Νόμος Μωσέως, Rom. v. 13, 20; 1 Cor. ix. 8, and foll.; xiv. 34; Gal. iii. 17, 19, etc.

‡ Rom. vii. 2.

according to which the *prophets* * were added, to complete the idea of the volume, than in the theological sense, all the other books being thus regarded as corollaries of the Mosaic legislation.† It may be boldly affirmed that in most of the passages in which Paul makes use of the word *law*, it is in the historical or literary sense; the allusion is to the Old Testament as a whole, not to the Pentateuch in particular; on this account the term has most frequently that which was called in the old theology the *economic* signification—that is, it stands for the entire Old Testament economy.

This more or less general application of the term does not therefore exert any influence upon the doctrinal statements we are about to consider. For our subject, it is more important to show that Paul, when he speaks of the law, makes no difference between its various precepts, whatever their nature or import, but treats them all as forming a compact and homogeneous body, all the parts and elements of which present the same characteristics. From our Christian standpoint we are accustomed to distinguish between the moral and the ritual portion of the Old Testament, and to declare the one to be explicitly confirmed by the Gospel, and of permanent obligation on the Church; the other to be as explicitly abrogated by Christ. We have not here to inquire to what extent and in what sense such a distinction is legitimate and sustained; we merely assert that Paul does not make it, and that it has no place in his system. Any one maintaining the contrary, proves by the very attempt that he has not understood the apostle. He will find great difficulty, moreover, in producing a single passage in support of his theory; while if our assertion needs such demonstration, we can fully support it by quotation. Thus all that is written in the book of the law is declared to be equally necessary, and placed under the same punitive sanction, and the relation of the law to righteousness and salvation, pointed out by the apostle, extends to the whole

* Rom. iii. 21.

† Rom. ii. 13; iii. 19; x. 4; 1 Cor. xiv. 21, etc.; comp. Rom. ii. 17, and foll.; Phil. iii. 5, and foll.

law.* Lastly, the law is contrasted broadly with the spirit, as
two principles which cannot co-operate.† But it is superfluous
to continue quotations; the system as a whole is an emphatic
denial of the statement we are opposing.

We maintain, then, that the disciple of Christ was not led
at all to modify his convictions as a disciple of the Pharisees,
in relation to the indissolubility and entire homogeneity of all
the parts of the law. He might, indeed, proclaim the decadence
of the entire code, without excepting a single line, but he never
could make a provisional selection among its precepts, retaining
some and rejecting others. The works of the law ‡ are all actions
done at the behest of the law,—all legal actions, without distinction as to what we call moral or spiritual. They comprise,
therefore, not only fasts and tithes, circumcision, and other like
institutions, but also a man's duties towards his neighbour ;.
and the law is called *a law of works*,§ inasmuch as it leads to
a course of action in harmony with its injunctions, inasmuch
as it wills that a man should act according to certain precepts
which it lays down for him, without distinction as to the object
or motive of his acts. The "*men who are of the works of the
law*"‖ are then all those who are placed in such a position that
their moral character can or ought to be judged solely by the
conformity of their acts to the letter of the law.

For the true character of the law (and this is the essential
point of the system) is that of an authority external to man, a
power foreign to his nature, which comes to present and to
prescribe to him a code of commandments,.and which exacts a
passive, strict, absolute obedience,—an obedience to be tested
by its actual results, not by the spirit which may have led to
it. Provided the act of obedience is rendered, the law is satisfied; it is not its province to inquire whether the man obeyed
from a happy moral impulse, or from fear of punishment.

* Gal. iii. 10, 21.
† Gal. v. 18.
‡ Ἔργα νόμου, Rom. iii. 20, and foll. ; ix. 32 ; Gal. ii. 16 ; iii. 2, and.
foll., etc.
§ Νόμος ἔργων, Rom. iii. 27.
‖ Οἱ ἐξ ἔργων νόμου ὄντες, Gal. iii. 10.

3. *

"*The law is not of faith*," * it is said; in other words, the test
of the status of the individual, in the eye of the law, is not a
disposition of soul, but an outward act; the *opus operatum*
is the one essential.† The law, then, is called a *law of commandments*,‡ because it consists in a series of such commandments, the reason of which man may not perceive, which may
be even repugnant to him, but which are all invested with
that character of irrefragable authority which we have just
indicated. These commandments man will not find in his own
heart, at least not in the first instance, but in a book, in the
letter of Scripture,§—that is to say, in a sphere external to
himself. From this point of view there is no difference whatever between what we call moral precepts and ordinances presumed to be purely ritual.

But we go a step further. The arguments which Paul uses
with reference to the Mosaic law, will apply for the most part
with equal justice to every kind of law, not only to the positive,
but to that which we call *natural law*, that which is manifested by the voice of conscience.‖ For the latter stands in
exactly the same psychological relation to man as the positive
law. This point we shall find more fully established as we
follow the course of the apostle's argument.

We shall first verify the natural effect of the law as he traces
it, and its relation to sin. Here experience teaches us at the
outset two psychological facts, which become at once axioms of
the highest importance in theology : the law incites to sin; the
law awakens the consciousness of sin.

The carnal tendency, the propensity to sin, exists in man
before the moral consciousness.¶ The latter only comes to us
with the law,—that is to say, when any law whatever seeks to

---

* Ὁ νόμος οὐκ ἔστιν ἐκ πίστεως, Gal. iii. 12.

† Ὁ ποιήσας ζήσεται, Gal. iii. 12 ; comp. v. 3.

‡ Νόμος τῶν ἐντολῶν, Eph. ii. 15 ; comp. Rom. vii. 8—13.

§ Ἐγγράμμασι, 2 Cor. iii. 7 ; Rom. ii. 27, 29.

‖ Rom. ii. 14, 15 ; vii. 7—25, especially ver. 22, 23.

¶ There is no need to remark that the point under notice here is the
conscientia legis, the *moral consciousness*, not the inner law itself, commonly
called *conscience*.

direct the course of our actions. It is essential to remember here that the function of the law is simply to dictate, to command, nothing more. By it we learn to know our duty ; but for its fulfilment we are left to the natural play of our instincts. The conflict between the flesh and the spirit begins as soon as the law has spoken ; and as has been said already, the flesh generally gains the day.*

It is obvious at once that the significance of this fact goes far beyond a mere act of the reason ; it exerts an almost direct influence upon the will, and becomes the cause of a result diametrically opposed to the design of the law. The law doubtless addresses itself to the spirit ;† it places itself in relation with the spiritual element in man ; but as it does not impart to him any new powers in addition to those which he has by nature, not only it does not render the victory over the flesh any more easy, but it becomes itself the accidental cause of sin. In fact, as every command arouses within a man a conflict between the two principles, and as it is possible for every such conflict to issue in a defeat of the good, the law multiplies indefinitely the occasions to sin. Without the law, sin would be, so to speak, slumbering, dead,‡ existing hypothetically or virtually,—that is to say, as a possibility, but not as an actual fact. This condition continues so long as man remains without the consciousness of law.§ By the commandment, especially if it is given in the negative form, or as a prohibition, sin is stimulated, excited ; it has placed before it an object of desire ;‖ it is developed and strengthened by the unlawful desire, which repeats itself more and more readily ; and. nothing helps so much to render the tendency to sin irresistible, as the prodigious number of commandments with which the law returns again and again to the charge, prolonging indefinitely the melancholy experience of stern provocation, rebellious lusts

---

* τὴν ἁμαρτίαν οὐκ ἔγνων εἰ μὴ διὰ νόμου, Rom. vii. 7.

† Ὁ νόμος πνευματικός, Rom. vii. 14.

‡ Χωρὶς νόμου ἡ ἁμαρτία νεκρά, Rom. vii. 8.

§ Ἐγὼ ζῶν χωρὶς νόμου ποτέ, Rom. vii. 9.

‖ Τὴν ἐπιθυμίαν οὐκ ᾔδειν, εἰ μὴ ὁ νόμος ἔλεγεν· οὐκ ἐπιθυμήσεις, Rom. vii. 7.

unequal struggles, desperate defeats.* The picture is, not
overdrawn, the colours are not too strong, and the results,
unhappily, but too familiar. The heathen poet had described
this study of oneself, with mournful truth, before the apostle :
"*Nitimur in vetitum semper petimusque negata.*"

It must be observed, nevertheless, that the law gives man a
criterion of the morality of his actions. Without it, he would
not know what he was doing ; he would have no standard by
which to estimate the relation subsisting between his acts
and the will of God. Such involuntary ignorance would
absolve the man from every sort of responsibility.† This
axiom of civil law has certainly only a very limited application in morals ; but in theory, and speaking absolutely,
it cannot be contested. With the law, ignorance ceases, and
responsibility begins. Sin, as an actual or objective fact, being
invariably present in a man who has reached this stage of
development, the law makes him conscious of it.‡ This was
the second psychological fact we mentioned, and which Paul
proceeds to translate into an axiom of theology.

But before passing on to it, let us sum up once more what
has just been said, to show that the law which should have
led man to salvation by the fulfilment of its commands,§
actually produces precisely the opposite result. Good, just,
holy in itself,‖ it is the cause or at least the occasion of
transgression, and consequently of death,¶ by the whole series
of psychological and moral phenomena which we have just
analyzed. Yes, it is the law, in a word, which makes it
incumbent upon God to show His wrath.**

All will now grant that we are right in saying that Paul
speaks of the law in such a manner that his assertions apply
no less to the natural law which we find in our conscience,

* Ἡ δύναμις τῆς ἁμαρτίας ὁ νόμος, 1 Cor. xv. 56.
† Ἁμαρτία οὐκ ἐλλογεῖται μὴ ὄντος νόμου, Rom. v. 13 ; comp. iv. 15.
‡ Διὰ νόμου ἐπίγνωσις ἁμαρτίας, Rom. iii. 20.
§ Ὁ ποιήσας αὐτὰ ζήσεται, Rom. x. 5.
‖ Rom. vii. 7, 12, 16.
¶ Εὑρέθη μοι ἡ ἐντολὴ ἡ εἰς ζωὴν αὕτη εἰς θάνατον, Rom. vii. 10 ; 2 Cor. iii. 6.
** Ὁ νόμος ὀργὴν κατεργάζεται, Rom. iv. 15.

than to the positive law contained in the books of Moses. The same phenomena appear in both cases, because in both there is the same Divine origin, and the same human nature; consequently the same relations of authority and power, and, finally, the same effects. Moses is not more eloquent than our own heart; conscience can speak as loud as any prophet; but it can no more hinder us from sinning than Moses and the prophets can force us to be saints. The fine passage in the Epistle to the Romans already repeatedly referred to in this chapter,* will strike us with fresh point and power if we explain it from this general and essentially psychological point of view.

Having once established and explained this psychological phenomenon, we are prepared to follow the apostle through a series of theological statements which are of the highest importance in his whole system, and which constitute in part its peculiar and special character among the beliefs of the time.

If every positive law proceeding from God, whether in‧scribed upon the individual conscience of men in general, or once solemnly proclaimed from Mount Sinai to the chosen people, has the effect we have just described; if such is its natural and necessary connection with sin, theology is without doubt bound to ask what can have been the purpose of God in giving His law.

To this question Paul replies, first, that the design of the law cannot have been to render man just; for this end it has never at all fulfilled. God would then have chosen means insufficient to attain His ends; or, to speak more exactly, the means devised by Him have produced a result the very reverse of what He intended. 'Now such a supposition is, on the very face of it, inadmissible. All that comes from the hand of God is good;† the law, then, must be good; it must be fit for the work to which it is designed; that work, therefore, must be something other than man's justification.

* Rom. vii. 7, and foll.
† Rom. vii. 12.

Let us bear in mind, in order to understand the full scope
of this assertion, that the man who seeks to be recognized and
declared as *just* before God, his sovereign Judge, is bound to
fulfil all that God enjoins in His law. But in this work, his
moral strength constantly breaks down; his efforts slacken at
times, or even cease altogether for a season. But it is established by a clear declaration of God,* that the first transgression
of a Divine command, even were it an isolated transgression,
would be a violation of the indispensable condition of blessedness, and would not only forfeit any claim to its enjoyment,
but render man liable to condemnation and the curse. It may
be said generally, that if righteousness is to result from a complete sum of isolated acts, it will never be realized, since the
weakness of man will never allow him to maintain unbroken
the entire series of these acts, and no after-efforts of his can
avail to supply the omissions.

It is then evident that the design of the law cannot have
been to render man righteous, or to establish that righteousness. If the law had been able to give life to man, that effect
would have been seen, and there would have been no necessity
to seek any other means of salvation;† but for such an end
the law was feeble and futile.‡ The natural and necessary
result produced by the law will show us what was the end
for which God gave it. When we look more closely into the
question, we shall see by the very multiplicity of its effects
upon the moral condition of man, that it was designed to
serve many ends, and that it has been in the hands of God a
powerful instrument in preparing the way for that dispensation which was finally to lead men to the desired goal.

The first result we shall notice, which is at once the most
striking and the most to be deplored, is that the law augments
the number of sins, that it provokes them, so to speak, that it

* Gal. iii. 10.
† Εἰ γὰρ ἐδόθη νόμος ὁ δυνάμενος ζωοποιῆσαι, ὄντως ἂν ἐκ νόμου ἦν ἡ δικαιοσύνη,
Gal. iii. 21.
‡ Ἀδύνατος ἀσθενής, Rom. viii. 3; comp. iii. 20, and foll.; iv. 15; ix. 31;
Gal. ii. 16, and foll.; iii. 11, etc.

incites man to fill up more and more the measure of his guilt. This, then, is the first purpose it is meant to serve.[*] The law brings death; and the priesthood which it instituted, so far from being a tutelary power over Israel, was a ministry of death and condemnation.[†] This statement seems strangely paradoxical; it even approaches blasphemy; and yet it unquestionably has its place in the system as a whole. We shall discover presently its relations to evangelical ideas, properly so called. For the present it is sufficiently explained and justified by the close connection in which it stands with the statement following.

The second result, which we have already verified as a fact, and which consequently we regard as the second purpose of the law, is that it makes man conscious of his moral wretchedness, and shows him sin in its natural ugliness. By it, man is perpetually reminded of his shortcomings; he is overwhelmed by the sense of his weakness and sin; lastly, there is aroused in him an earnest desire to be delivered, by whatsoever means, from this unhappy state. This desire becomes the more keen as he comes to perceive how sin works like a poisonous serpent, infecting with its corrupt and deleterious influences even the law, which is in itself divine and good, and thus making its own deformity the more conspicuous by its antagonism to the most sacred things.[‡] Man thus learns to know sin as it is, and realizes that he is in himself too weak to resist it. It is obvious that this second result is closely associated with the first, and forms, so to speak, its corollary. And as the consciousness of this state is the preliminary and indispensable condition of the change to be wrought, the necessity of this operation of the law becomes clear.

Paul adverts to a third design, which does not belong to quite the same category of facts. The naturally carnal mind of man threatened him, and with him the entire race, with

* Ὁ νόμος παρεισῆλθεν ἵνα πλεονάσῃ τὸ παράπτωμα, Rom. v. 20.

† Διακονία θανάτου, κατακρίσεως, 2 Cor. iii. 6—9.

‡ Ἵνα φανῇ ἁμαρτία, διὰ τοῦ ἀγαθοῦ μοι κατεργαζομένη θάνατον, ἵνα γένηται καθ' ὑπερβολὴν ἁμαρτωλός, Rom. vii. 13.

utter ruin, if the unbridled play of the passions met with no effectual check. The law was therefore given as a salutary curb upon their violence; it was to be a sort of schoolmaster to prevent man, by external discipline, from doing the evil from which his own reason and heart were not strong enough to restrain him.* In the interpretation which we give to this passage, and in the consequences we derive from it in relation to the Pauline system, we are not following the commonly received opinion, which regards the term *schoolmaster* as conveying a different idea, that of a progressive education. We do not deny, as will presently be shown, that such an idea lies at the basis of the theory, but we do not think the term in question is designed to express it. In fact, that term is contrasted in the context with others which express the idea of liberty, of emancipation, and not of perfection considered as the fruit of an education given. It is itself explained by other terms which convey the idea of a heavy yoke, a hard and repressive rule.† It is employed in the same way elsewhere,‡ in opposition to the word *father*, in illustration of the different feelings which influence the father and the master in the control of those committed to them.

We may gain yet another view of the purpose God designed to fulfil by the promulgation of the law, if we take into consideration the twofold relation in which it stands to the Gospel revelation.

In the first place, the law appears as a factor in the education of men, as labouring to lead them on to something beyond its own sphere. It is a means used, not to secure the effect resulting directly from its own action, but to lead through that direct result to another more remote.

In the second place, and for this same reason, the law appears as a preparatory thing, as having for itself only a temporary value. As it did not always exist, so it has not the privilege

---

* Τῶν παραβάσεων χάριν . . . ὁ νόμος παιδαγωγὸς ἡμῶν γέγονεν, Gal. iii. 19, 24.

† Συγκλείειν, φρουρεῖν, Gal. iii. 25, and foll.

‡ 1 Cor. iv. 15.

of an endless life, while there are purposes of God which, existing before the law, are intended also to survive it.

These two ideas seem to us to be expressed and summed up in that phrase,' so rich in condensed meaning, " *Christ is the end of the law.*" * This word *end* may very well convey at once the idea of a goal or term towards which the law tends, and that of a cessation or abrogation of the law when that end was attained.

The same idea is discoverable also, but expressed in a less striking manner, in several other analogous passages. Thus it is said, the law *intervened,*† placed itself, that is, between two points,—namely, between the sin of Adam, whence date the miseries of our kind, and the redemption effected by Christ, whence dates our restoration. Evidently, the law here forms a sort of link or transition between the two capital facts placed at either extremity. The transitory character of the law is also expressed in these words; it has been given to exercise its power and govern man until the day when the promised Seed should come to fulfil His mission; ‡ its pedagogic, that is to say, its corrective and repressive office, was to cease from the moment that a new order of things, having as its vital element faith in Christ, should come to take its place.

In making this statement that Christ is the end of the law, the apostle has already passed beyond the sphere of mere psychological experience, and of a simple theological estimate of the facts attested by it. He has entered the special domain of Christian theology; he has broken with Judaism; he assigns to the latter a place different to that hitherto appropriated to [it by faith; he cancels its authority, and asserts for the Gospel a higher dignity, a character which places it above the vicissitudes of time, and claims for it the power of an endless life. The Gospel is henceforth regarded as the antithesis of the law, and we shall find this

* Τέλος νόμος Χριστός, Rom. x. 4.

† Παρεισῆλθεν, Rom. v. 20.

‡ Ἄχρις οὗ ἐλθῃ τὸ σπέρμα, etc., Gal. iii. 19, 25.

opposition constantly brought before us in the further course
of this study.

While establishing this antithesis, however, the apostle is
still careful to declare that his theology does not contradict
the law, that it is not hostile to it, nor tends to overthrow *
it; on the contrary, that it maintains, as no other system
can, its spirit and intention, since the law itself, rightly understood, wills and predicts the new economy of grace.   The
prophets had proclaimed it afar off, and the promises made
to Abraham were not connected with the letter of the law,
but with faith, that they might be of universal application.†

This latter fact especially is brought out on every page
of the epistles, by numerous quotations taken from the Old
Testament, for the purpose of theological demonstration.   It
would be a grave mistake to regard these citations as
argumenta ad hominum as a compliance with the dialectic
method of the Jews, or, again, as purely homilectic comparisons.   On the contrary, Scripture is regarded as a great
whole, one body of revelations, having its aim beyond itself,
in the future, and organized in view of a new dispensation. ‡
Its deepest meaning cannot therefore be recognized till after
the fulfilment of that new dispensation;§ but it remains no
less true that the Gospel revelation rests upon the predictions
of the prophets, and that the preaching of the apostles will
naturally have the same basis.‖

* Νόμον οὖν καταργοῦμεν, Rom. iii. 31.
† Rom. i. 2 ; iv. 13, 16.
‡ Gal. iii. 8, 22.
§ 2 Cor. iii. 11, 13, and foll.
‖ Rom. xvi. 26.

CHAPTER VI.

OF THE GOSPEL.

HITHERTO we have confined our attention to Paul's epitome of theological reflection upon the antecedents of the Gospel. We now proceed to inquire what are his views and teachings in relation to the Gospel itself. Before entering on this new series of facts and ideas, however, let us take one more comprehensive glance at the former series, so as to have a clear and definite impression upon our minds of the views set forth in the epistles on the subject of the law.

It follows from what has been said, that man, so long as he is under the dominion of law (whether the law of Moses or any other), is unhappy and in a state of bondage, unless indeed he have lost all feeling, which is a more unhappy condition still. His position appears to him one of *servitude*,* and that in a threefold aspect.

First, he feels himself crushed under the enormous burden of his guilt, under the weight of his many sins, a burden of which he is not only utterly unable to free himself, but to which he adds daily by fresh transgressions. He is like an insolvent debtor constantly in terror of his creditors, ever liable to be apprehended by the arm of the law, without any means of freeing himself, and still increasing day by day the sum of his liabilities.†

In the second place, he is overwhelmed with the sense of his weakness, which is such that, in spite of all his efforts

---

* Δουλεία.

† 'Υπόδικος τῷ θεῷ, Rom. iii. 19.

and all his struggles, the flesh gains perpetually new victories over the spirit, and thus acquires an ever-growing ascendancy. The chances of success for the spirit and the good principle diminish in the same proportion, and the absolute dominion of sin becomes more manifest after every fresh fall.*

Lastly, he is tormented by the terror of the law, which is ever before him, reiterating its precepts and prohibitions without giving him the strength necessary to obey, threatening him with the wrath of God in case of transgression, and not helping him in any way in the fulfilment of duty; filling him thus with anguish and terror, and refusing to lend him any aid when his soul cries out for that joyful strength which would enable him to walk in the good way.†

Like all slavery, this triple servitude cannot but seem very heavy and burdensome to man, and render him supremely unhappy. He is thus naturally led to sigh after deliverance, and the idea of slavery consistently leads to that of redemption,‡ that is of a ransom.

The necessity of a redemption arises out of the weakness of man, who has no power to redeem himself. The notion of a ransom implies a third person, who, placing himself as mediator between the master and the slave, procures freedom for the latter by means of a ransom paid.

The desire for redemption arises from a consciousness of the misery of bondage. This desire must be awakened before redemption can be realized. The slave must have first the desire to be redeemed. As we have just seen, the design of the law is to awaken this desire.

* Δοῦλοι τῆς ἁμαρτίας, Rom. vi. 6, 20; vii. 14; Titus iii. 3.

† Πνεῦμα δουλείας εἰς φόβον, Rom. viii. 15; comp. ζυγὸς δουλείας, Gal. v. 1. It is well known that in Biblical language (Hebraic) the terms which we translate by *fear* have not always a bad signification: φόβος θεοῦ may be a very legitimate feeling, and commendable (2 Cor. vii. 1; Eph. v. 21), or at least natural to the man who knows his own weakness (1 Cor. ii. 3; 2 Cor. vii. 15; Eph. vi. 5; Phil. ii. 12). Here, in combination with the idea of slavery, it is of course contrasted with the relation of a father to his children.

‡ Ἀπολύτρωσις.

Lastly, the possibility of redemption is based upon the existence of the good principle in man. When we speak of redemption, we imply that there is something to be redeemed, delivered from bondage. It is the spirit which is thus enslaved, not annihilated, by the flesh. If the spirit were utterly defiled and debased,—changed, so to speak, into the very substance of the flesh, or killed like a plant which has been deprived at once of its sap and of its organs of nutrition—redemption would no longer be a possibility. Men do not redeem a corpse, to which liberty could be of no avail.

The announcement of this threefold redemption is called the *Gospel*, the good news.

As good news, the Gospel declares and brings to man all that hitherto he has been wanting; in a word, it releases him from his burden; it satisfies his wants; it changes his fear into joy; or, at least, it tells him that all this may be and in a manner is already accomplished. Here in a few words is the glad message: *a way is opened for man to become righteous before God, by grace and faith, no longer by merit and works,*—namely, by the redemption in Christ Jesus.* It will be remembered that we have already had occasion to quote this same passage to supply the basis of our exposition.

The Gospel is described by different terms taken from the different relations included in the statement we have just cited. It is called the Gospel of God,† because God is the Author of the salvation it proclaims. It is the Gospel of salvation,‡ in reference to its object. It is the Gospel of grace,§ in allusion to the source whence it flows. It is the Gospel of Christ,∥ as He

---

* Rom. iii. 21—24. It is this fundamental thesis which the apostle has in view whenever he speaks simply of the *Gospel* (Rom. i. 16; Gal. ii. 2, etc.), with the exception of a few passages in which the word signifies rather the act or ministry of preaching (1 Cor. ix. 14, the second time; v. 18, the second time; 2 Cor. viii. 18; Gal. ii. 7; Phil. ii. 22; iv. 3, etc.)

† Θεοῦ, Rom. i. 1; xv. 16; 2 Cor. xi. 7, etc.

‡ Τῆς σωτηρίας, Eph. i. 13.

§ Τῆς χάριτος, Acts xx. 24.

∥ Χριστοῦ, Rom. xv. 19; comp. i. 9; 1 Cor. ix. 12, 18; Gal. i. 7, etc.

is the Mediator of salvation. It is the Gospel of peace,* since the enjoyment of peace is one of its blessed results.

And as the Gospel is always presented to men under the form of a discourse, a word, it is similarly spoken of as the word of God, of Christ, of life.† To other names by which it is described we shall allude presently.

This Gospel is emphatically *the truth*, for it contains all the elements of a knowledge of God and of His will, or, as we should say in our day, of religion and morality, which are necessary for the salvation of man.‡ Let it be observed that the term *truth*, as used by Paul and other writers of the New Testament, does not represent only what is called theoretic truth, the assurance and adequate knowledge of certain facts, but also practical truth, or the principles and practice of duty. The Gospel, as the subject of preaching, is called the word of truth.§

The passage to which we have just referred as epitomizing the whole theology of Paul, and more especially the positive portion which we have yet to examine, ontains a series of antitheses, very essential to his system, not only as regards its substance, but also its form, and the constant recurrence of which in the following chapters will convince us increasingly, that the apostle was conscious of the opposition in which his theology stood to the old doctrines. This circumstance alone may help us to appreciate the vast advance made by evangelical teaching under Paul, since that teaching was in its commencement comprised in a circle within which such antitheses were absolutely unknown or impossible.

It is not needful for us to enumerate them, so clearly do they

---

* Τῆς εἰρίνης, Eph. vi. 15.

† Λόγος θεοῦ, 1 Cor. xiv. 36; 2 Cor. ii. 17; Titus ii. 5, etc.; λόγος Χριστοῦ, Col. iii. 16; 1 Thess. i. 8, etc.; λόγος ζωῆς, Phil. ii. 16.

‡ 2 Cor. iv. 2; vi. 7; 2 Thess. ii. 13; 1 Tim. ii. 4; iii. 15; iv. 3; 2 Tim. ii. 25; iii. 7; Titus i. 1.

§ Eph. i. 13; Col. i. 5; 2 Tim. ii. 15; Ἀλήθεια τοῦ εὐαγγελίου, Gal. ii. 5, 14; v. 7; Eph. iv. 21, is the *true* Gospel as opposed to a falsified Gospel. Ἀλήθεια τοῦ θεοῦ, Rom. ii. 2; iii. 7; xv. 8, is simply the veracity of God.

come out from the text we have just transcribed. All our readers must have noted them for themselves. Bondage and freedom, law and Gospel, merit and grace, works and faith, wrath and love, death and life; such are the principal anti-nomies, an examination of which will furnish the apostle with the materials of his theological deductions. We shall be careful as we proceed to note the finer shades which analysis may trace in these main and fundamental ideas. We con-fine ourselves for the moment to tracing the outline of the division suggested to us by the fundamental formula of the whole Pauline theology. This outline we have already com-menced; we shall carry it now into further detail, so as to unfold before our readers more and more of this system, which is as rich in thought as it is ingenious in its logical form.

The first part of the system treats of God as the author of salvation, and regards Him under three aspects: 1st, from the ethical point of view—that is to say, in His love or *grace,* which is the primary source of all that is done for the welfare of man; 2nd, from the metaphysical point of view—that is, in *His decrees,* the exercise of His will as the immediate result of His love; 3rd, from the religious point of view—that is, in the *plan of salvation,* the mode by which He puts into operation His saving purpose.

The second part treats of Christ as the Mediator of salvation; and He also is regarded from three points of view: 1st, doctrinally, that is in His own person and nature—*the Son;* 2nd, mystically, that is in His work or office—*the Saviour;* 3rd, historically, that is in the place He occupies in the chain of human destinies—*the Second Adam.*

The third and last part treats of man, the heir of salvation, and considers him also in a threefold light: 1st, in His indi-vidual relation, that is in the acceptance of the salvation offered to him by God in Christ; this is *faith.* 2nd, in his social relation, that is in the exercise of his Christian duty to further the designs of God among his fellow-men; this is *love.* 3rd, in a theological aspect, that is in the living anticipation of the final and full realization of these designs; this is *hope.*

CHAPTER VII.

OF GOD AS THE AUTHOR OF SALVATION.

THE evangelical theology of Paul, as we have shown above, is based upon the fact that under the dominion of the law man is the object of the reprobation of God: he has nothing to expect but the infliction of a righteous anger. For the law, so far from helping him to act in conformity with the will of God, excites his evil passions, impels him to transgress, is at the same time his accuser and the witness to establish his guilt; so that, in short, it may be said that the law itself calls forth the wrath of God,—that is, it leaves the justice of God no alternative but to punish.

Justice, however, is not the sole attribute of God which natural as well as positive revelation has taught man to know. There is another element no less great and powerful in the Divine essence, the manifestation of which is to be seen everywhere, not only in external nature and in the government of the world, but still more in the numberless benefits so bountifully bestowed upon men, both individually and collectively. This attribute is love. God has no pleasure in the death of creatures whom He formed for life and happiness; on the contrary, He wills that they shall all be saved from such a doom.* He is the God of love; love is the very essence of His being.† This love is the principle to which man's hope clings, on which it fastens.‡ It is because God loves that He offers to man the

* Πάντας ἀνθρώπους θέλει σωθῆναι, 1 Tim. ii. 4.
† 2 Cor. xiii. 11.
‡ Rom. viii. 39.

means and the prospect of a happy future.* It is the conviction that he has been thus loved first which gives man power
to love in return.† Lastly, the name " beloved of God"‡ belongs
peculiarly to those in whom the feeling of the love bestowed
upon them has become a principle of life and happiness.

This love of God, in the circumstances of its most special
manifestation, is called *mercy*. For men in their natural state
are unhappy and hopeless, seeing no escape from their misery;
it is then, humanly speaking, a sentiment of pity which leads
God to offer them a helping hand;§ it is especially in all that
relates to the forgiveness of sins that God reveals His love;
and where disobedience has been manifested on the part of
man, there the Divine mercy is manifested in its turn; it becomes, so to speak, the heritage of sinful man.‖ So persistent
is that mercy, that it might be said to wrestle with the per-
versity of man, as though it would not be put aside. It deals
with the misery of the whole race, while it reveals itself in the
providential direction of the individual.¶

But there cannot be any self-contradiction in God, any
opposition between His attributes. It is impossible that His
love and His justice should come into collision, that the one of
these manifestations of the Divine Being should be, so to speak,
neutralized or absorbed by the other, or sacrificed to it. Both
must remain in their freeness and entirety, and the wisdom of
God will find means fully to satisfy both. If justice were
simply to give way to love, the sacred and immutable law
which God has laid down for the moral world, would be thenceforth powerless and void; transgression would find a yet wider
and freer field, and the old guilt, effaced by Divine mercy,
would soon be succeeded by a longer and blacker catalogue of
sins. If love were to be silent in the presence of justice, not

* Rom. viii. 37; 2 Thess. ii. 16.
† Eph. v. 1.
‡ Ἀγαπητοῖς θεοῦ, Rom. i. 7; xi. 28; 2 Cor. xiii. 13; Rom. v. 5.
§ Ὁ θεὸς, πλούσιος ὢν ἐν ἐλέει, διὰ τὴν πολλὴν ἀγάπην αὐτοῦ . . . ἐνέδειξε
τὸν πλοῦτον τῆς χάριτος αὐτοῦ, κ.τ.λ., Eph. ii. 4; Rom. v. 8; xi. 30.
‖ Τὸ ὑμέτερον ἔλεος, Rom. xi. 31, and foll.; v. 20.
¶ 2 Cor. iv. 1; 1 Tim. i. 13, 16.

4 *

only would humanity become the prey of the most terrible despair, but God would see His work perish without being able to deliver it from going down into the pit.

What means, then, has Divine wisdom found (we speak after the manner of men) to secure the claims of justice without doing violence to the promptings of love? Paul expresses it in a phrase as sententious in form as it appears paradoxical in substance, that God might *be just*, he says, and at the same time be *the Justifier*.* The whole theology of the apostle is comprised in these words; and our exposition will be, in fact, an analysis of them. But we shall proceed to it systematically, and without deviating from the course we have marked out.

We said that the wisdom of God had discovered a way whereby to satisfy at once His justice and His love. Let us not, however, for a moment imagine that this way had to be sought and found at some period in the history of man when God had learned or discovered that there was no other means to save him. Such a mode of representing the subject cannot be that of the apostle; it would be unworthy of God, contrary to all rational conception of His divinity; it would be making God's plan a mere expedient, a sort of palliative employed as a last resource; and instead of exalting the wisdom of God, it would be a proof that in the beginning that wisdom had been at fault. God must have determined from all eternity the design of creation, namely, the blessedness of rational beings. He must have known from all eternity the measure of power to be given to His creatures; it is impossible to suppose that He should have discovered in course of time an error in His calculation concerning the relation of the means to the end.

No; Paul declared plainly and positively that the means which God intended to employ to bring men to a state of happiness, were chosen and determined by Him from the beginning; the whole scheme, the combination of those means, that which forms the subject of evangelical preaching, is a plan formed in

* Εἰς τὸ εἶναι αὐτὸν δίκαιον καὶ δικαιοῦντα, Rom. iii. 26.

the counsels of God from all eternity.* This plan is so emphatically a thing immutable, anterior, and superior to any accidental necessity that might arise, that it is itself called the
wisdom of God,† and is thus identified with a co-eternal
attribute of the Divine Being. This wisdom is contrasted
with that of men as being essentially different in its nature, so
that in order to comprehend the wisdom of God, the first step
is to forget the wisdom of men, though in the judgment of the
wise of this world the wisdom of God is but folly.‡ God is
in the view of Paul the alone truly wise.§ The purpose of God
is further represented as independent of all contingent circumstances, by the employment of the word *goodwill* or *pleasure,*‖
which implies necessarily the idea of the most entire subjective
liberty.

Even the prophets of the old covenant had some conception,
more or less definite, of such a plan. It was their special mission to speak of it to the people of God, to preach the Gospel
as by anticipation, even to declare its basis and conditions, and
to give utterance to the promises which belonged to it in the
peculiarly evangelical sense.¶ Nevertheless, speaking generally
and comparatively, this revelation was still far from complete.
The plan of God could not as yet be understood, because the
manifestation of Him who was to carry out that plan had not
yet taken place. There remained a mystery, a hidden thing,
which only the ultimate revelation of God in Christ could
make plain.** We lay stress upon the difference in the idea of a
mystery as the term is used in the writings of Paul, and the
scholastic sense, according to which it signifies an incomprehen-
sible dogma. In all the passages in which the apostle uses this

---

* Πολυποίκιλος σοφία τοῦ θεοῦ ἣν ἐποίησεν ἐκ Χριστῷ Ἰησοῦ κατὰ πρόθεσιν
τῶν αἰώνων, Eph. iii. 10, 11 ; comp. i. 4, and foll.; 2 Tim. i. 9.

† 1 Cor. ii. 7 ; comp. i. 21, 24; Col. ii. 3.

‡ 1 Cor. i. 20, and foll. ; ii. 5, and foll.; iii. 18, and foll.

§ Rom. xvi. 27.

‖ Εὐδοκεῖν, εὐδοκία, 1 Cor. i. 21; Eph. i. 5, 9.

¶ Rom. i. 2 ; Titus i. 2; Rom. iii. 21; ix. 4; Gal. iii. 16.

** Μυστήριον, ἀποκάλυψις, Rom. xvi. 26 ; 1 Cor. ii. 7—10; Gal. iii. 23;
Col. i. 16, and foll. ; Eph. iii. 3, and foll.; 2 Tim. i. 10 ; Titus i. 3.

word, he contrasts the mystery with the revelation which dispels it; while with the schoolmen of the Church, the mystery begins with the revelation.

Paul describes God's plan of salvation sometimes as the mystery of God, or more fully as the mystery of the will of God, in relation to Him as its Author; sometimes as the mystery of Christ, because He is its Mediator and Executor; sometimes as the mystery of faith or godliness, in reference to its practical conditions; lastly, as the mystery of the Gospel, inasmuch as it is the subject of the apostolic preaching.* As this plan comprises a number of various elements, he uses sometimes the plural number, and speaks of all mysteries.†

The plan of God is then eternal—anterior to time; but in forming it, God had also determined the moment and the era when it should be revealed to the world. This era was doubtless that most appropriate and favourable to its realization; it might be justly called "due time," "the fulness of time,"‡ and in comparison with the previous period, the time of ignorance of God's will,§ this final era of revelation and fulfilment is spoken of as the "dispensation of the fulness of times."‖

Until this epoch, the men who were to be heirs of salvation, to whatever religious category they might belong,¶ were like minors** placed under the power of tutors and governors, until the time appointed by the will of the Father. These tutors represent the elementary means of instruction which the pagan and Jewish world already possessed.†† These rudiments are poor indeed compared with the Gospel, and of little avail, since they can never enable man to fulfil the end of his existence;

* M. τοῦ θεοῦ, Col. ii. 2; 1 Cor. iv. 1; μ. τοῦ θελήματος, τ. θ., Eph. i. 9; μ. τοῖ Χριστοῦ, Eph. iii. 4; Col. iv. 3; μ. τῆς πίστεως, 1 Tim. iii. 9; μ. τῆς εὐσεβείας, 1 Tim. v. 16; μ. τοῦ εὐαγγελίου, Eph. vi. 19.
† 1 Cor. xiii. 2.
‡ Καιροὶ ἴδιοι, Titus i. 3; 1 Tim. ii. 6.
§ Χρόνα ἀγνοίας, Acts xvii. 30; comp. Eph. iv. 18.
‖ Πλήρωμα τῶν καιρῶν, τοῦ χρόνου, Eph. i. 10; Gal. iv. 4.
¶ Gal. iii. 27, and foll.
** Νήπιοι, Gal. iv. 1, 3.
†† Στοιχεῖα τοῦ κόσμου, Gal. iv. 3, 9; Col. ii. 8, 20.

nevertheless they are a proof that God was not willing to leave His children without some salutary and protective tutelage,* even when all the relations between Him and them seemed to be broken. Truth was not apprehended by the world before the appearing of Christ. The Gentiles might indeed have arrived at it both in a theoretical and practical sense,† that is to say as to their religious beliefs and moral principles, but they attained not to it. The Jews had yet more help. They had a positive law, and in this law a relative form of the absolute truth,‡ and yet they missed the way of salvation. A new and last revelation, fuller and more unexceptionable than the foregoing, was then to crown this work of human education.

To this all the purposes of God were tending. They were directed especially to two points, corresponding to the two necessities of humanity of which we have before spoken, and really comprehending a third. In the first place, the debt already contracted by men had to be cancelled; next, a means must be devised to save them from contracting a fresh liability. This means consisted in proposing to them new terms of salvation, terms less difficult, or rather less impossible to be met, and in imparting to them at the same time new strength to avail themselves of them. It is evident that, in this way, not only guilt and sin might be done away, but the law also, which gave constant occasion to sin, would become superfluous, and mankind would be released from the threefold bondage under which it had so long groaned.

We shall see presently how all these results were to be attained, and what methods the Divine wisdom proposed for their happy realization. For the present, we have yet to establish the general point of view from which the apostle judges of the nature and scope of these designs. He has shown us man confronted with a law by the fulfilment of which he would secure happiness for himself, but ever repelled by the *justice* of God, which could not be satisfied with the very imperfect obedience

---

* Παιδαγωγὸς, Gal. iii. 24.

† Rom. i. 18, 25; ii. 8.

‡ Μόρφωσιν τῆς ἀληθείας, Rom. ii. 20.

he had to offer, so that he could look for nothing but reprobation. Now this same man, having been brought at length to
acknowledge with humility that he has no merit of his own
to plead, turns from God's justice to His grace, and receives
gratefully, as a free gift, that happiness which he had hitherto
vainly sought, and which, while it was refused to him as the
meed of his worthless works, is now freely granted to the
trustful surrender he makes of himself to the arms of everlasting love.*

The term grace means essentially the same as mercy, love;
etymologically, however, it has a less general sense than the
latter, and expresses more directly than the former the intervention of God's sovereign will, an act not determined by anything
on the part of man.† Grace is then naturally opposed to works
considered as meritorious: the two ideas or facts are incompatible.‡ It forms the antithesis to justice, and all that can
be regarded as the legitimate effect of justice.§ It is always
freely offered‖ to any who will accept it, but none can claim or
deserve it. The more man recognizes it as a free gift, the

---

* Τῇ χάριτι ἐσμεν σεσωσμένοι διὰ τῆς πίστεως, Eph. ii. 5, 8; Titus iii. 5.

† The word χάρις is one of those most frequently employed by Paul,
yet we only quote now a small number of passages for this reason. We
cannot include here any of the passages where it stands for such benefits
as result from right speech (as, for example, Eph. iv. 29; Col. iv. 6), nor
other more numerous passages where it expresses gratitude (τῷ θεῷ), etc.,
or a benefit conferred by man on man (2 Cor. viii., passim). Elsewhere it
alludes to a particular effect of the grace of God, an individual experience
(Eph. iv. 7; Phil. i. 7; Rom. xii. 6; 1 Tim. i. 14; 2 Cor. iv. 15; πᾶσα χάρις,
ix. 8). More especially does the apostle delight to trace his calling to
grace (2 Cor. xii. 9; 1 Cor. xv. 10; Gal. i. 15; Eph. iii. 7); he thus describes the mission which he has received, and in which he glories (Rom.
i. 5; 1 Cor. iii. 10; Gal. ii. 9; Eph. iii. 2, 8), or the authority resulting
from that mission (Rom. xii. 3; xv. 15), or the mode of action becoming
a dignity due to Divine grace (2 Cor. i. 12). In desiring this grace to his
readers at the commencement and close of all his epistles, he has in view
the spiritual necessities of men, and the assurance that these can only be
satisfied by the full and free gifts of their common Father.

‡ Rom. xi. 6; 2 Tim. i. 9.

§ Rom. v. 15, 19, 20, 21; vi. 1.

‖ Δωρεά, δῶρον, δώρημα, δωρεάν, Rom. iii. 24; v. 16; Eph. ii. 8; χάρισμα,
Rom. v. 15; vi. 23, contrasted with ὀψώνιον, wages, xi. 29.

more will he magnify its greatness and preciousness.* Grace is so emphatically the dominant thought in the theoretic portion of the Gospel, that the word is often used by the apostle to designate the Gospel plan as a whole, in opposition to the old covenant.†

Grace is then the primary source (and as contrasted with works the sole source) of the salvation of man. Properly and primarily, then, it is God Himself who should be called our Saviour.‡ Now we have already shown that the decrees of God concerning the salvation of men are eternal; there can be no question of a revolution in the providential government of the world, as there can be no change in the essence of God Himself. The eternity of the decree is one more security for its final fulfilment. These eternal decrees, however, are only revealed and brought to man's knowledge in time and successively; from the human point of view, therefore, there appears to be a change in the relations between God and the world; and Paul, placing himself at this stand-point, uses the expressions suggested by such an idea.

Thus regarded, two orders of things present themselves to our notice, two successive economies or plans. A very simple and natural figure occurs to the mind of the apostle to render his thought more popular. God is regarded as the head of a household, who gives his orders and makes his arrangements so that his subordinates may work together for the good of all, and carry out his will. These arrangements, as a whole, form what might be called the order (or organization) of the house of God,§ and systematic phraseology speaks of the two

* Eph. i. 6, 7; ii. 7.

† Gal. ii. 21; v. 4; Col. i. 6; Rom. v. 2; Titus ii. 11, etc. As Christ is the Mediator of the grace of God, it is repeatedly called χάρις Χριστοῦ (Gal. i. 6; 2 Cor. viii. 9; 2 Thess. i. 12). It is properly a grace granted: ἐν Χριστῷ (1 Cor. i. 4; 2 Tim. ii. 1).

‡ Σωτήρ, 1 Tim. i. 1; ii. 3; iv. 10; Titus i. 3; ii. 10; iii. 4; comp. 1 Cor. i. 21; 1 Tim. ii. 4, etc.

§ Οἰκονομία τοῦ θεοῦ. This word has also another meaning in the language of Paul. The apostle regards himself in his capacity of apostle as steward of the household of God, οἰκόνομος; his office is an οἰκονομία, a stewardship (1 Cor. iv. 1; ix. 17; Eph. iii. 2; Col. i. 25; Titus i. 7).

economies, that of the old and that of the new covenant, each
having what might be called its own peculiar constitution, its
surety or mediator, its legal basis and prospective promises.*

The new economy is called the economy of mystery, inasmuch as it had been but recently revealed, after being long
veiled from the eyes of the majority, and only dimly and
occasionally perceived by the prophets themselves.   It is also
spoken of as the economy of faith, because faith is, as it were,
its organic law.   It is further described as the economy or
" dispensation of the fulness of times,"† which may refer to the
fact that the new revelation, or, which amounts to the same
thing, the advent of the new order of things, took place at the
period before appointed of God,—that is, in the fulness of the
times ; the context, however, seems to favour another explanation, according to which this is the economy which is to last
to the end of time, and then to receive its full glory and final
perfection.   This last economy, though founded upon an idea or
a fact very simple in itself, is described as the most incompre-
hensible thing, as an inexhaustible treasure, an unfathomable
depth of wisdom,‡ which not only the prophets but the angels
themselves desired, but failed to look into,§ till it pleased God
to reveal it to the world.

The fulfilment of the purposes of God, in so far as they relate
to the salvation of men, comprehends two elements, the means
offered by God to man for the attainment of salvation, and
the obligations imposed on man in order to a right use of those
means.   This corresponds to the two other aspects of the
Gospel of which we have yet to speak.   The first to which
we now come, is comprised in the idea or in the fact of the
mission of the Saviour Jesus Christ.‖

* Οἰκ. τοῦ μυστηρίου, Eph. iii. 9.
† Οἰκ. τοῦ πληρώματος τῶν καιρῶν, Eph. i. 10.
‡ Rom. xi. 33.
§ Eph. iii. 9, and foll.
‖ Let us observe, in passing, one expression peculiarly Pauline, which
appears to us designed to set forth that it is by His Son Jesus Christ that
God has been brought into relations with man : θεὸς καὶ πατήρ 'I. Χρ.
(Rom. xv. 6; 2 Cor. i. 3; xi. 31; Eph. i. 3; Col. i. 3.)

CHAPTER VIII.

OF THE PERSON OF CHRIST.

THE only point of importance which the theology of Paul had to teach in relation to Christ, was the nature and manner of the saving work undertaken by Him in behalf of humanity. But that work could not be understood without a knowledge of the person by whom it was wrought; the theory relating to it would have no sufficient basis apart from a true conception of Christ Himself. We have then, in the first place, to speak of the Saviour, and of His peculiar nature.

We shall observe first that the specially doctrinal epistles, those to the Romans, to the Galatians, and to the Ephesians, do not touch at all on this part of the system. We conclude, therefore, that the apostle had nothing really new to advance on the subject. In fact, the few passages which may guide us contain almost the very same indications which we have already noted, and which we shall find in other of the apostolic writings,—indications so simple and concise, that ecclesiastical theology soon pronounced them insufficient for the purposes of science.

The conception of the person of Christ, as it is set forth in the writings of Paul, comprises two constituent elements already partially familiar to us. The first is the metaphysical idea of a primitive revelation of God, conceived as a hypostasis, or distinct personal manifestation, in the divine essence, this hypostasis becoming subsequently the source and the cause of all later revelations, and notably therefore of creation also. This idea we have already traced in Jewish philosophy, with which apostolic Christianity held it in common.

The second element is the idea, which is at once historical and theological, that this hypostasis became man in the person of Jesus. This second idea, while foreign to Judaism, was not at all peculiar to the apostle Paul.

We subjoin the details of his teaching on this point.

Jesus Christ unites in His own person a twofold essence, human and divine. "*He is made of the seed of David according to the flesh, and declared to be the Son of God according to the spirit.*"*

Paul says nothing, or at least very little, on the relation of these two essences or elements. The nature of their union, the precise time when it took place, the mode in which it was accomplished,—things which occupied the speculative science of the ancient Church during long ages, and in reference to which Protestantism has fixed on still more exact formularies,—all these questions are not even touched here, and theology is under an illusion in thinking that mere exegesis has been the basis of the solutions given at various times, or that it can ever be capable of deciding among them.

The existence of the human element is proved by the birth of Christ; the existence of the divine, by His resurrection.†️ But it is expressly said the divine element is the essential;

---

* Γενόμενος ἐκ σπέρματος Δαβὶδ κατὰ σάρκα, ὁρισθεὶς υἱὸς θεοῦ κατὰ πνεῦμα, Rom. i. 3, 4; comp. 1 Tim. iii. 16; 2 Tim. ii. 8. In the first of these passages it is said that Jesus Christ was of the race of David *according to the flesh*, while *according to the spirit* He belongs to a higher sphere, and was the Son of God. As this is the only passage in Paul's epistles which contains such an expression, we must explain it by the aid of philology alone; and this will not easily discover in the words κατὰ σάρκα and ἐκ σπέρματος Δαβὶδ the idea of a supernatural generation, especially when it is remembered that the apostle goes on to prove the presence of the divine nature by the resurrection, and by a narrative analogous to that of the gospels. The phraseology used by Paul being thus insufficient to support the ecclesiastical theory, we must suppose that the apostle did not yet feel the necessity of any speculative theology in reference to it. [Rom. i. 3, 4, has nothing to do with the "supernatural generation" of our Lord. The resurrection, Paul says, was that by which our Lord was *shown* or "declared" to be the Son of God; what *constituted* Him the Son of God is another question altogether.—ED.]

† Gal. iv. 4; Rom. i. 4.

the human, but the adopted, added, external element.* This
implies the idea of a humiliation, a sort of emptying, a laying
aside, and leads us directly to represent to ourselves the union
of the two natures as the alliance of a divine spirit with a
human body, an explanation recommended by its very simplicity, but which has never found favour with theologians.
It is true that it is not thus distinctly stated in the texts, but
they contain not a word to the contrary.†

As to the human element, there can be no doubt of its
objective reality, though in the passage last quoted there occur
expressions which may be translated by the terms form,
resemblance, *habitus*,‡ and which might be supposed to refer
to a mere appearance, a simple analogy, as docetism has, in
fact, taught. § In view, however, of the many passages where
the *corporeal materiality* (if we may be permitted such an
expression) is asserted as a fact, the terms in question cannot
be thus construed; and the author made use of them, doubtless, in order to give prominence to the presence of the divine
element contained, concealed, as it were, in an outward form,
which so far from revealing it, suggests rather an existence of
a different and inferior order.

The human nature of Christ comprehends certain particular
facts, which are of importance in their relation to His work,
and which we here enumerate before proceeding. These are:
First, The *body* itself, expressly called a *body of flesh*,‖ to
mark the absolute identity of His nature with ours, an identity

* Ἐν μορφῇ θεοῦ ὑπαρχων, μορφὴν δούλου ἔλαβεν, Phil. ii. 6, 7.

† By such a union as Reuss describes in the text between "a divine
spirit" and "a human body," God would not have become "man;"
Christ would have been a manifestation of God, but not God manifested
in human nature and in a human history. In 1 Tim. ii. 5, Paul expressly
declares that Jesus Christ is "man;" but this implies a human soul as
well as a human body. It is true that it is St. Paul's manner to speak of
Christ as a manifestation of God "in the *flesh*," but it is a grave misconception to suppose that when he speaks of the "flesh" he refers only to
the physical nature of man.—ED.

‡ Μορφή, ὁμοίωμα, σχῆμα.

§ Comp. Μόρφωσις as opposed to δύναμις, 2 Tim. iii. 5; Rom. ii. 20.

‖ Σῶμα τῆς σαρκός, Col. i. 22; comp. Rom. i. 3; viii. 3; 1 Tim. iii. 16.

of substance, and of the faculties and conditions of existence.
Second, The infirmities allied with such a body;* that is to
say, not only the capacity of suffering, but, in general, all the
physical necessities which keep mortals in a continual state of
subservience.   Third, The yoke of the law, to which the Son
of God submitted by the very fact that He was born a Jew,
setting aside any other end which that submission might be
designed to subserve.† Fourth, The sufferings, ‡ not only those
of His passion, but all the rebuffs, insults, and persecutions
which throughout His whole career He had to endure from
the world. Fifth, Death itself.§ There is but one characteristic
of man's estate in which He had no share, namely, sin.||

As to the divine element, the first remark which suggests
itself is one akin to that we have just made upon the human
nature of Christ. Here, again, we find such expressions as the
form, the *image*¶ of God, suggestive of a mere resemblance or
analogy,—of an image which should come to the help of intelligences unable to rise to the perfections of God, by reflecting
these in a less transcendent manner; but such is not the real
meaning or scope of the writer's words. To him the divine
nature has also an objective reality; it exists *really*** in the
person of Christ, and he employs other terms only to make it
possible for the reader to distinguish between the Son and the
Father.

Paul speaks in several places of the divine nature of Christ,
but nowhere with greater fulness than in the Epistle to the
Colossians.†† We there find the dogma of the hypostasis of the
Word, which we have already noted elsewhere. We shall
observe, however, that he does not elaborate any theory on the
point, or treat it scientifically; that he does not even use the

* 'Ασθενεία, 2 Cor. xiii. 4.
† Gal. iv. 5.
‡ Παθήματα, θλίψεις, 2 Cor. i. 5 ; Phil. iii. 11 ; Col. i. 24.
§ Phil. ii. 8.
|| 2 Cor. v. 21 ; comp. Gal. ii. 17 ; Rom. viii. 3.
¶ Μορφή, Phil. ii. 6 ; εἰκών, 2 Cor. iv. 4 ; Col. i. 15.
** Σωματικῶς, Col. ii. 9.
†† Col. i. 15, and foll.

terms which custom has appropriated to it, and which we find elsewhere in the theology of the apostles; and for this reason, that whenever Paul begins to touch on these transcendental questions, the need of a practical and popular teaching at once asserts itself, and he turns aside from the metaphysical aspect of the doctrine to deal with the ethical.

Let us now take a glance at the passage quoted from the Epistle to the Colossians. We shall find in it, first of all, and very readily, the elements of the theological doctrine to which we lately alluded. When the apostle calls Christ the image of the invisible God, he expresses the idea of a primitive revelation of the Deity, emerging from the sphere of pure abstraction, where it is inaccessible to the reason, and becoming concrete and personal. He then speaks of the creation as the ulterior revelation made through the organ of this divine personality, and claims for this revelation the character of indefinite and permanent duration, which is called in popular speech the upholding of all things. The language of the schools is to be traced still more plainly when he speaks of the fulness of the Godhead* as dwelling in Christ; for this word *fulness* is the term appropriated in metaphysics to designate the totality of the attributes of Deity, considered a sa series of forces or powers, and the word *dwell* indicates the simultaneous presence of all these attributes in the person of the Word.

But it is just this leading term, the Word, which is conspicuously absent in this passage, and in the Pauline epistles generally, though it cannot have been unknown to their author. This proves that his design was not to set forth the theory itself, but to make a practical use of it; he therefore only took up that which appeared to him at the time necessary.

We must not fail also to observe, further, that the argument of the apostle did not go on to develop all the natural and necessary consequences of the great principle of the divine hypostasis, as we find them afterwards established by the doctors of the Church. In giving, so to speak, a slight sketch of them here, he makes use of an expression which must have

---

* Πλήρωμα τῆς θεότητος κατοικεῖ ἐν αὐτῷ.

seemed to the theology of the Church, from its point of view, to accord ill with the system strictly understood. He calls Christ " the first-born of every creature,"* and thus likens Him, in a manner, to created beings. This expression did not at all . harmonize with Jewish philosophy, from which Paul borrows the term first-born, nor has it ever been accepted by the philosophy of the Catholic Church.

We shall not draw any conclusion from the fact h ere established by a natural exegesis, unfettered by the bonds of any system. We shall simply repeat that this system did not receive its completion from apostolic hands; that the theologians who came after the apostles went beyond the letter of their teaching; and that they themselves had quite a different end in view from that of gratifying the demands of speculative inquiry.

For the rest, Christ is at once man and God; both names

§ Πρωτότοκος πάσης κτίσεως. The word πρωτότοκος always implies the idea of resemblance or homogeneity of one individual with a succession of others following. He is the first-born of many children (Matt. i. 25 ; Luke ii. 7; Rom. viii. 29; Heb. xi. 28); the first to rise from the dead, followed by many others (Col. i. 18 ; Rev. i. 5); the first generation of Christians, inasmuch as it was not to be the last (Heb. xii. 23); or, according to another explanation, the faithful of the Old Testament, thus named in relation to those of the New. Everywhere the genitive added to the word designates the category to which the πρωτότοκος belongs. Now κτίσις signifies always creatures (Rom. i. 25 ; viii. 19—22, 39 ; 2 Cor. v. 17 ; Gal. vi. 15 ; Col. i. 23). By the addition of πᾶσα, any possible doubt that might remain as to the significance of the word is removed. Rom. i. 20 is the only place where κτίσις signifies the act of creation, but this in no way alters the case, for the first-born of the act of creation would certainly be the first creature. (Comp. Rev. iii. 14.) [Mr. Llewellyn Davies has the following note on the phrase in Col. i. 16 : " The only exact *translation* of these words is ' first-born of all creation ; ' (not ' first-born of *every* creature,' as in E. V.,) and from this title it might, without doubt, be logically inferred that the Son was a part of creation. But this phrase belongs to a class of expressions in which the strictest grammatical sense is by no means always what is meant. We do not infer from the phrase, ' fairest of all her daughters, Eve,' that Eve was one of her own daughters. And πρωτότοκος πάσης κτίσεως *might* be written by one who meant to convey that the Son was begotten *before* any

are therefore distinctly applied to Him.* But Paul uses still
more frequently another designation, indicative of the peculiar
nature of the Saviour's person; he calls Him the Son of God,†
a name which throws much light upon the twofold relation of
which we are here speaking.

The condition or character of a son implies two things:
first, as to the essence, the relative equality and homogeneity
proved by the expressions and passages cited above; secondly,
as to the relation of the persons, a certain inequality. The
latter is sufficiently indicated by the following facts: it is said,
first, that the totality of the divine attributes was communicated to the Son by the freewill of the Father; ‡ it might be

part of creation. It would scarcely be maintained that St. Paul would
have applied the term κτισθείς to the Son. It is a fair and natural way of
explaining the words, to say that the Son, with reference to 'all creation,'
occupied the place of 'first-born.' He is prior to and at the head of all
existence. The next sentence is sufficient to correct any false impression
that St. Paul was speaking of the Son as a created being." Sufficient
emphasis, however, does not seem to be laid by Mr. Davies, in this excellent note, on the position of the πρωτότοκος among ancient nations generally,
and especially among the Jews. The word came to denote supremacy of
position quite as much as priority of birth. The "first-born" was, under
the father, the head of the household. That the idea of mere priority was
subordinate in St. Paul's mind to supremacy seems to be shown by the
words which follow: Christ's relation to "the whole creation" is that of
the Heir to the inheritance, "for in Him all things were made." In relation to the Father, He is "the image of the invisible God;" in relation
to the universe, He is Proprietor and Prince.—ED.]

* Ἄνθρωπος, 1 Cor. xv. 21; 1 Tim. ii. 5; Rom. v. 15; θεός, Rom. ix. 5;
Titus ii. 13. At least, this is the simplest and most natural explanation
of the two passages. I may remark, however, in passing, that among the
most orthodox Fathers, and in the height of the controversy with Arian-
ism, many would not accept such an interpretation.

† Υἱὸς τοῦ θεοῦ. We do not speak here of the name of Christ, which
belongs properly to Jewish eschatology, and designates the office, not the
nature, of the Saviour. As to the name Son of God, it is needless to
quote the seventeen passages where it occurs.

‡ Εὐδόκησε, Col. i. 19. [St. Paul does not say "it pleased the Father
that in Him should all fulness dwell," but τᾶν τὸ πλήρωμα, "all the
fulness was pleased to dwell in Him." This gives a different colour to the
passage.—ED.]

said, in abstract terms, that the fact of the revelation depends
upon that will; but such an expression is not found in the
text.   In the second place, we read of the obedience or subjection of the Son.*   Lastly, His present glory is represented
as reward conferred because of His sacrifice.†

But the passages we have just quoted are not the only ones
which lead us to say that the relation of the Son to the Father
is, according to Paul, one of subordination.   He recurs to it repeatedly and very explicitly.‡   We might be disposed to regard
such subordination as something temporary and transitory,
characteristic only of the earthly life of Jesus, and this is the
ordinary expedient employed to remove the difficulty which
the official theology of the Church finds in the expressions of
the apostle; but it is insufficient; for one of the passages
quoted in the last note leads us beyond the sphere of earth,
and declares plainly the definitive subordination of the Son.§
The separation of the two persons by different and very remarkable designations,‖ is, in general, too strongly marked to
allow us to suppose a subtle dogmatic distinction in the language of the apostle, between the different conditions through
which Jesus Christ had to pass.   We may further appeal to
the phrase " *the God and Father of our Lord Jesus Christ,*" explained above, without any necessity for making the genitive

* 'Υπήκοος, Phil. ii. 8.   [But the " obedience " is predicated in relation
to that period of voluntary humiliation with which the whole passage is
dealing.—ED.]

† Διὸ, Phil. ii. 9; Eph. i. 20.   [Here St. Paul is speaking of the glory
conferred on the Incarnate Son, after His voluntary humiliation.—ED.]

‡ 1 Cor. iii. 23; xi. 3; xv. 28.

§ The Incarnate Son, inasmuch as He unites in Himself the divine and
the human, must be in a very true sense " subordinate " to the Father.
The subordination must continue as long as human nature, though
glorified, remains in union with the personality of the Eternal Word,
and as the dissolution of that union is inconceivable, the subordination
will never cease.   But this does not affect, as Reuss appears to suggest,
the essential and eternal relation of the divine personality of our Lord to
the Father.   Nor is there anything in it to disturb what he calls the
" official theology of the Church."—ED.

‖ Θεος—κύριος: θεος—μεσίτης, 1 Cor. viii. 6; 1 Tim. ii. 1; Eph. iv. 4—6.

dependent on the two subjects, as several interpreters have done.

Undoubtedly, the idea of subordination does not harmonize with the Athanasian Creed; and from that standpoint it is a logical fallacy like that contained in the phrase, "the *first-born* of every creature;" but we think that the expedient of a temporary subordination, adopted as a desperate resource in view of an inexorable text, is quite as much opposed to the speculative theorem of the *homousia*, or equality and absolute consubstantiality of the two divine persons. It is mere playing with words to deny it. We shall see that John in his theology carefully avoids these rocks on either hand.

CHAPTER IX.

THE WORK OF CHRIST.

THE Son of God appeared in the person of the man Jesus, at the time determined by the wisdom of God, and was sent by God to work out the salvation of men in the manner chosen and appointed by Him: 1. *Jesus Christ came into the world to save sinners.* 2. *That which the law could not do, God sending His own Son condemned sin in the flesh.* 3. *In the fulness of time God sent forth His Son to redeem them that were under the law.**

These three passages all alike describe the work of Christ, but each of them presents the purpose of His mission under a different aspect; and it is only by putting them all together that we can meet all the requirements of the system. We need merely to call to mind the threefold bondage under which we have already described man as groaning; and we shall then see how these three passages, taken together, indicate as the aim of the mission of Christ, the threefold deliverance which is needed and sought. The first passage promises to sinners freedom from the guilt already contracted by sins committed. The second promises to those who are weak through the flesh, effectual aid in the battle with sin, and ultimate victory. The third promises to those who are kept in terror by the perpetual threatenings of the law, redemption from a yoke

---

* 1°. Χριστὸς Ἰησοῦς ἦλθεν εἰς τὸν κόσμον ἁμαρτωλοὺς σῶσαι, 1 Tim. i. 15. 2°. Τὸ ἀδύνατον τοῦ νόμου . . . ὁ θεὸς τὸν ἑαυτοῦ υἱὸν πέμψας . . . κατέκρινε τὴν ἁμαρτίαν Rom. viii. 3. 3°. Ὅτε δὲ ἦλθε τὸ πλήρωμα τοῦ χρόνου ἐξαπέστειλεν ὁ θεὸς τὸν υἱὸν αὐτοῦ ἵνα τοὺς ὑπὸ νόμον ἐξαγοράσῃ, Gal. iv. 4.

which presses heavily on them, without securing to them any righteousness.

Under these three relations, Christ appears to us as a Saviour; His mission is to save,* or if we adhere to the idea of our bondage, He is a Deliverer. As however this bondage is deserved, and enfranchisement may not be given to the detriment of any third party, we arrive at the idea of a redeemer and a redemption; that is to say, of a ransom paid for the liberation of a slave.†

This then is the design of the mission of Christ. We have now to inquire what was required of Him in its fulfilment.

His work could not consist simply in giving instruction, in inculcating new principles of morality, better than any before possessed by men, or in preaching to them with more urgency the necessity of amending their lives, or in setting before them a holy example. All this, no doubt, He did, and Paul himself several times presents Jesus to his readers as a model to be followed,‡ or reminds them of His teaching, and of particular words spoken by Him.§ But nowhere does this point of view appear as essential, and we may even venture to ask whether Paul did himself believe that which has since been made the main characteristic of more than one apologetic system; namely, that the morality of the Gospel, that is, the body of teaching given by Christ in relation to the special duties of men, is superior to that of Mosaism.‖

---

* Σωζειν comes from σόος, safe and sound, and signifies properly to heal, to preserve life from an imminent danger. The word is frequently used by Paul, though he only once applies it in relation to Christ (1 Tim. i. 15); the substantive σωτήρ rarely occurs (Eph. v. 23; Phil. iii. 20) except in the pastoral epistles, where it is employed sometimes of God, sometimes of Christ (2 Tim. i. 10; Titus i. 4; ii. 13; iii. 6). Add to it the phrase ἡ σωτηρία ἡ ἐν Χριστῷ (2 Tim. ii. 10).

† Ἀγοράζειν, 1 Cor. vi. 20; vii. 23; ἐξαγοράζειν, Gal. iii. 13; iv. 5; λυτροῦσθαι, Titus ii. 14; λυτρωτής, Acts vii. 35; ἀντίλυτρον, 1 Tim. ii. 6; ἀπολύτρωσις, passim.

‡ 1 Cor. xi. 1; Eph. v. 2; 1 Thess. i. 6; Phil. ii. 5.

§ Acts xv. 35; 1 Cor. vii. 10.

‖ It is quite true that St. Paul was far enough from contending that

Similiar instructions, moreover, are within the province of any other teacher, of the apostles or their successors, and cannot therefore constitute the essential or main element in the altogether exceptional and extraordinary mission of the Son of God, especially as that preaching and teaching, however eloquent, solid, and admirable they may be, do not by themselves produce the desired redemption. The purpose of Christ not being comprehended in that which is commonly called moral reformation, the preaching of morality could not be the principal means employed by Him.

The work of Christ, to speak first in a general manner, is His *life*. In that life, the essential point was the entire absence of sin.[*] Jesus Christ was the first who possessed this character of holiness or righteousness; the first over whose spirit[†] the flesh never gained the victory; the first, finally, in whom sin found itself wholly baffled.[‡] It is true, that in this victory of the spirit over the flesh He had not to pass through the same kind of struggle which in ordinary men leads to the opposite result; to Him this victory was natural and necessary

the characteristic element of the new faith is its superior morality ; but it is evident from the kind of exhortations which he addresses to his converts, that to him the revelation of God in Christ transfigured the old moral precepts and created new obligations. Truthfulness is not only enforced with a new motive, but is exalted to a new sphere, when he says, " Putting away lying, speak every man truth with his neighbour, for *we are members one of another*." Not only is theft forbidden,—Christian men are to "labour" that they "may have to *give* to him that needeth." They are to be "kind one to another, tender-hearted, forgiving one another, even as God for Christ's sake hath forgiven them." Moral duties arise out of moral relations, and as the revealed and actual moral relations of men have both undergone a wonderful change as the result of the coming of Christ, moral duties have undergone a similar transformation. It is a shame to the Christian philosophy of this country that Aristotle's Ethics should still be our text-book in morals; long before this we ought to have had a science of Christian Ethics.—ED.

[*] 2 Cor. v. 21; Gal. ii. 17. The technical term of the schools, ἀναμαρτησία, is not found in the epistles. Instead of it we meet with ὑπακοή and δικαίωμα (Rom. v. 18, 19).

[†] Πνεῦμα ἀγιωσύνης, Rom. i. 4.

[‡] Rom. viii. 3.

by the very fact of His divine nature.* But this in no way alters its character. Sin had found its master and conqueror, and that conqueror had incorporated Himself with humanity, which He could therefore make a sharer in the benefits of His triumph.

Since righteousness is defined as the perfect fulfilment of the law, the absence of sin in the person of Jesus Christ may also be expressed or represented by these same terms, and according to the fundamental idea of his theological system, Paul is naturally led to present the fact in this particular form. Christ, in coming into the world, and in being born as a man, had not placed Himself under any rule of life less severe than that of the Jews, which was the most rigorous imposed upon men at all; He was under their law.† His righteousness therefore was precisely the same as that demanded of other Jews.

Now, in this life of Christ (we are speaking of course of His earthly life) there are two acts of paramount importance, which theology is bound to consider specially when treating of the life of the Saviour: we refer to His death and His resurrection. For the moment we confine ourselves to pointing out the peculiar characteristics of these two facts, a more complete investigation of their relation to other parts of the system being reserved for the succeeding chapters.

In reference to His death,‡ which should not be dissociated from the sufferings preceding it,§ we may observe first, that it

---

* This is expressly said in the passage recently quoted from Rom. i. 4, where πνεῦμα stands for the divine nature. [It is not the New Testament view that the victory of Christ over sin was "natural and necessary." All the New Testament writers who refer to His temptations and conflicts imply that both were real. But this raises the old question whether we are to ascribe to our Lord the *posse non peccare* or the *non posse peccare.*—ED.]

† Γενόμενος ὑπὸ νόμον, Gal. iv. 4.

‡ Θάνατος, αἷμα, σταυρὸς, etc.

§ Reuss has failed to notice that, in relation to the atonement, St. Paul, like all the other New Testament writers, never associates the sufferings which preceded our Lord's death with the death itself. These sufferings,

was not deserved, as is the death of men generally;* that it was therefore an act of Christ's free will, who gave up His own life.† If side by side with such an expression as this, we find another, according to which God gave His Son,‡ and Christ suffered in obedience to His Father's will,§ there is no necessary contradiction between the two statements. The will of two persons meets in the pursuit of a common end; the liberty of the one is not impaired by any coercive authority on the part of the other; on the contrary, it is the same impulse of love which dictates to both the part they take in the work of salvation.||

With regard to the resurrection, it is said to be the work, not of Christ Himself, but of God;¶ nevertheless it is connected in the closest possible manner with the fact of the death, both in relation to the time and to the very nature of things, and still more in reference to its value and meaning. The two facts are perfectly inseparable, not only in the personal history of Christ Himself, but of the believer also.** It may even be said that the resurrection is, in one sense, of greater relative importance than the death:†† for beside the material or theological value, which is the same for both events, the resurrection has a further formal or argumentative value, since without it the death of Jesus would remain one of a series of ordinary and, so to speak, accidental events of the same kind. The resurrection alone proves that here was

in their view, gave emphasis to Christ's example and to the revelation of His love, but it does not appear that they thought of them as contributing to the value of His atoning sacrifice. In this the old idea of sacrifice was preserved. It was necessary that the sacrificed victim should *die*, but not necessary that it should be tortured.—ED.

* Rom. v. 12.
† Παρέδωκεν ἑαυτὸν, Eph. v. 2; Gal. ii. 20.
‡ Rom. viii. 32.
§ Phil. ii. 8.
|| Rom. viii. 35, 37; 2 Cor. v. 14; Gal. ii. 20; Eph. iii. 19; v. 2, 35.
¶ Rom. iv. 24; viii. 11, etc.
** Rom. iv. 25; vi. 4, and foll.
†† Χριστὸς ὁ ἀποθανὼν μᾶλλον δὲ καὶ εγερθείς, Rom. viii. 34.

something divine;* it will ever remain therefore the pivot of all evangelical teaching. †

We assert once again, that all which has just been briefly said in reference to the life, death, and resurrection of Christ can only be understood in its clearness and full significance, when we have learned how these facts are associated with the saving purposes of God, and how each of them contributes to the realization of His benevolent design. We have not yet noticed all the elements in this combination, and must therefore confine ourselves for the present to generalities.

The principal point established by what we have just said, and which will form ultimately the subject of our doctrinal studies, is that the death and resurrection of Christ stand in the closest connection with the salvation of men; ‡ He was delivered to death for our sins; He was raised again for our justification.

It will be readily observed that in this statement there are two pairs of correlative facts—death and resurrection, sin and justification. [It is evident that the two former, taken together, and not isolated, took place in view of the two others, equally regarded here as inseparable. Just as it would be absurd to say that the death of Christ has nothing to do with man's justification, so would it be to assert that His resurrection must be, in theological analysis, completely dissociated from the fact of sin.

The same thesis is often partially reproduced in other expressions which convey only one of its elements at once.

For instance, Paul delights to repeat that Christ suffered death for our sins, since He Himself had no sin.§ As a general rule the preposition here employed signifies *for the benefit of, in commodum,* etc., and this would give a plausible sense in

---

* Rom. i. 4.

† 1 Cor. xv. 14.

‡ Παρεδόθη διὰ τὰ παραπτώματα ἡμῶν καὶ ἠγέρθη διὰ τὴν δικαίωσιν ἡμῶν, Rom. iv. 25.

§ ʽΟ Χριστὸς ἀπέθανεν ὑπὲρ τῶν ἁμαρτιῶν ἡμῶν, 1 Cor. xv. 3; comp. Rom. v. 6, and foll.; vi. 10; 1 Cor. viii. 11; 2 Cor. v. 14, 21.

relation to men, who certainly are advantaged by the death of Christ. In this view, however, not only would there be no explanation of the relation of causality between the death of Christ and the salvation of men, but the meaning suggested does not accord with the object, *sins;* for it cannot be said that Christ died for the benefit of our sins. We shall have occasion presently to examine more closely the theological idea which gave rise to this elliptical formula.

We find the apostle, however, adverting quite as frequently to the essential connexion existing between the resurrection of Christ and the future felicity of saved man. If in this aspect he dwells chiefly on our own resurrection, we shall call to mind that the two ideas of life and blessedness are correlatives, as we have already shown.*

We come now to a sort of antithetic parallelism between the destiny of Christ and that of men. Their life in sin caused His death; His death without sin shall be to them the cause of life.

In order that this may be possible, it is necessary that this parallelism become something more than a form of logic, it must correspond to a physical fact; between Christ and man there must be a close community of life; man himself must die with Christ, to rise again with Him. This is the main point of the whole system, and will furnish the explanation and demonstration of the dogmatic theses which we have given above in the form of simple assertions. But before passing on to these we must glance at yet another aspect of the relation of Christ to humanity. We have gained some conception already of the vast importance which the theology of Paul attaches to the death of Christ,† but we must observe also that the apostle felt that this very fact, apart from all theological reflection on it, was the stone of stumbling, ‡ which would come into collision with the ideas of a people whose hopes of the future were resting upon a totally different basis.

* Ὁ ἐγείρας Ἰησοῦν καὶ ἡμᾶς διὰ Ἰησοῦ ἐγερεῖ, 2 Cor. iv. 14; comp. Rom. viii. 11; 1 Cor. xv. 12, and foll., 20.

† 1 Cor. ii. 2.

‡ Σκάνδαλον, 1 Cor. i. 23; Rom. ix. 33; Gal. v. 11.

CHAPTER X.

OF THE TYPICAL RELATION BETWEEN THE OLD AND THE NEW COVENANT.

THE death and resurrection of Christ bring us to a point at which the entire human race enters upon a new period of its existence and development,—a development which will differ in most important respects, altogether different from anything before realized. This fact fills the mind of the apostle; he pauses to contemplate it from this new point of view; he soon discovers a constant and often antithetic parallelism between the two periods. He at once recognizes that this parallelism does not belong only to the domain of history and experience, that it is not confined to certain moral characteristics more or less decided, but that it is the effect of a providential arrangement, and deserves therefore to be the subject of theological study. The two dispensations or *economies* of which we have already spoken are brought face to face, or rather succeed each other in such a manner that the former is the more or less material, but always typical, image of the latter; the latter, the more or less spiritualized reflection, the ideal reproduction of the former.

This is what is meant by the typical relation between the old and new covenant.*

A relation of this kind may exist between two moral or

---

* "An Old Testament type is the exhibition, in an inferior form, of a truth, a principle, a law, which is revealed in a higher form in the Christian dispensation."—*The Jewish Temple and the Christian Church*, by R. W. Dale, p. 162. For a discussion of this question, see *The Jewish Temple*, etc., pp. 153—162.—ED.

religious facts, as when Paul speaks of the blameworthy conduct of the Israelites in the desert* as typical, and makes the application to his readers. More generally, however, it is the historical facts of the Old Testament, and especially the sacred and legal institutions of the Jewish people, which are spoken of as types of the revelation of the Gospel. In this case the first term of the comparison is more especially regarded as having a prophetic character, a relative dignity; it appears as preparatory, transitory, as a mere shadow,—that is, as a thing having no inherent reality or value; while the other term of the comparison, that which belongs to the sphere of the Gospel, contains all that is definite, durable, essential, or, to continue the figure, is the substance which casts the shadow.

The Old Testament thus is or contains the *shadow of the future*, while in Christ alone, and by Him, is manifested all that was real in the old symbolic forms.†

The technical term used to designate the fact which contains the prophetic image is the type, the model;‡ and as it receives a new value, a special signification, from the relation in which it is placed with a corresponding evangelical fact, it may also be called an *allegory* ; § for that term properly indicates in rhetoric a sense different from that contained in the mere letter. But as this sense cannot be truly discerned till after the revelation of the new order of things, and generally escapes

---

* 1 Cor. x. 11.

† Σκιὰ τῶν μελλόντων, Col. ii. 17 ; τὸ δὲ σῶμα Χριστοῦ. Σῶμα, in a parallel antithesis, expresses the idea of *reality*, we might say of *materiality*, in opposition to what we call figure or symbol. Comp. Col. ii. 9, where σωματικῶς expresses the certainty of the real subjective existence of the divine attributes in the person of Christ.

‡ Τύπος, model, example, in the moral sense, Phil. iii. 17; 1 Thess. i. 7 ; 2 Thess. iii. 9; 1 Tim. iv. 12; Titus ii. 7; in the theoretical or didactic sense, Rom. vi. 17; in the prophetic sense, Rom. v. 14. We see from 1 Cor. x. 6, 11, how closely connected the moral is with the theological sense. The conduct of the Israelites in the desert is called τύπος ἡμῶν, in view of the practical teaching which the reader is to derive from it for his own benefit; and τύπος ἐκείνοις συμβαίνων, in view of the providential direction of the events designed to subserve this prophetic purpose.

§ Ἀλληγορία, Gal. iv. 24.

those who occupy any other standpoint, it is called a *mystery*,*
that is to say, a thing hidden until made plain by the new
revelations given in the fulness of time. Lastly, as the typical
meaning is, for the most part, disengaged from a material
fact, an object belonging to the sphere of the senses, it may
be regarded as the soul or spirit of that fact,† which is thus
spiritualized. Its interpretation is therefore a spiritual process,
and the objects in question are themselves said to be spiritual,
inasmuch as they contain such a sense.‡

Paul, the oldest Christian writer, was also, as far as we can
prove, the first to open the rich mine of typological comparison between the Old and New Testaments. We may
safely take it for granted that the few examples which we
find in his epistles, are not the only essays and discoveries
of this kind suggested to him by his biblical studies. The
other apostles were also in the habit of using the same kind
of interpretation, and often found in it such striking parallels
of truth, that several of these were subsequently converted
into dogmatic formularies by the theologians of the Church.
This is the case especially, though not exclusively, with those
that occur in the Epistle to the Hebrews, of which we shall
speak again presently. As to the typological comparisons
contained in the various books of the New Testament, it is
not necessary to go over them separately in the case of each
writer. The method and the principle are the same with all
who use them. We may observe, however, that this typological
method could only become prevalent as Christian theology cast
off the yoke of Mosaic legalism ; no need of it could be felt so
long as the law was still held to be materially binding, and the
application of this spiritual and suggestive principle was at
once the effect of the anti-Judaic tendency, and the surest
means of justifying it.

* Μυστήριον, Eph. v. 32.

† Πνευματικῶς, πνευματικά, 1 Cor. x. 3, 4 ; comp. ii. 14.

‡ Another technical expression, to which we may here advert in passing,
is παραβολή (Heb. ix. 9), a word which etymologically means any parallelism, but in common use a parallelism designed to teach.

The most characteristic institutions of Mosaism were thus
shown to possess a moral meaning, which gave them a permanent value at the very time when, in a literal and historical
sense, their decadence was declared. And this moral sense so
commended itself by its simplicity and naturalness, that its
figurative origin was forgotten, and it passed readily into
the popular religious language of the day. Thus the circumcision of the flesh, made by hands, was changed into a circum-
cison of the heart, received not materially, but spiritually, by
union with Christ, and hence came to be called simply the circumcision of Christ, as that which alone henceforward deserved
the name.* Again, the rites of a yearly feast, by which the
people of God were bound to observe certain external duties
during the days appointed, became the basis of a moral allegory
of wide import, and designed to teach the disciples of Christ
the permanent necessity of purification in a higher sense.†
The sacricfies to be presented to God were to be spiritual; ‡
faith was the offering God required; the persons of the believers themselves were to take the place of the victims of
olden times, and they were to find life instead of death in the
surrender. Here then is worship in the spiritual sense; all the
members of the Church were henceforth invested with a priestly
character, and the apostle more especially performed the litur-
gical functions by order and in the name of Jesus Christ, carrying the Gospel as a sacred instrument, and leading to the altar
converted pagans, as the most acceptable sacrifice to God, one
on which He Himself set the sanctifying seal of His Holy
Spirit.§
     Thus, by an ingenious exegesis, which disposed of the letter,
while it magnified the spirit, the Pauline theology succeeded
in filling the flaccid forms of a worship perishing for lack of
nourishment, with a new life, all the more durable that it was

* Eph. ii. 11; Rom. ii. 29; comp. Acts vii. 51; περιτομὴ καρδίας, Col.
ii. 11; Phil. iii. 3.
† Ἄζυμα ἀληθείας, 1 Cor. v. 6, and foll.; comp. Matt. xvi. 6; Luke xii. 1.
‡ 1 Peter ii. 5; Phil. ii. 17; θυσία ζῶσα, Rom. xii. 1; λογικὴ λατρεία, ibid.
§ Rom. xv. 16.

independent of anything material. The same method was applicable to other departments of the religious life of the Israelites. We shall find it applied to their conceptions of the end of all things, and we shall trace it in several doctrinal propositions relating to the person and work of Christ, of which we shall speak as we proceed.

The most familiar and important of these typical parallels in the writings of Paul, is that which compares Adam and Christ, assigning to each a position at once analogous and different, in relation to humanity. It is of the more moment rightly to understand this, since it has given rise in the Church to interpretations as dubious as they are widely adopted.

In two passages* Paul contrasts Christ with Adam, as type and antitype, and calls Christ the future Adam, the second man, the last Adam. †   The parallelism contains various points of comparison, in regard to each of which the protoplast on the one hand, and the Saviour on the other, is placed at the head of a class or series of men, differing from each other by corresponding characteristics.

There is, first, the physical relation: the first Adam was of the earth, earthy; he had a material, earthly body, a body therefore mortal and corruptible; such is our present body, a body of flesh and blood, formed in the image of that of our first father, and unfit to inherit the kingdom of God; the second Adam is the Lord who came down from heaven, and is there again in glory. He is clothed in a heavenly, spiritual body, which has nothing in common with our mortal, corruptible flesh. Those, then, who belong to Him, who are in fellowship with Him by the new birth of the spirit, as we are connected with the first Adam by our natural birth,—these shall, in their turn, put on the heavenly incorruptible body, the pledge of an endless life.

In the second place, there is the physical relation. The first Adam became, by the breath which God breathed into him,

---

* Rom. v. 12, and foll.; 1 Cor. xv. 45, and foll.

† Δεύτερος, ἔσχατος, μέλλων.

a living soul; his life was of an animal nature,* that is, it consisted in the natural play of the organs designed for the preservation of the body, and in the action of the appetites which stimulated their exercise. It is not a question here of the higher faculties, because in reality these are not the mainspring of an unregenerate man's life. The second Adam possesses and communicates a nature altogether different. The principle of his life is the spirit, the divine breath of an essence and a power far more elevated, not needing gross material organs for its development, not exhausting itself with time, but assuring to him who receives it a true and lasting life.

There is, thirdly, the moral relation; the first Adam sinned, and by him sin entered into the world. The men who succeeded him all sinned without exception, and in this respect there was no difference between the period which preceded the giving of the law from Mount Sinai, and that which followed it. A communion, a solidarity, is established in this respect between all men and their first father. The second Adam sinned not; and His life, regarded as one single grand act, was an act of righteousness,† a life perfectly agreeable to the will of God. The men who follow Christ (and the apostle soon shows how profound a meaning he attaches to that word), the men of the second race, who enter into communion with Christ by faith, attain to the same exemption from sin, to the same righteousness as His.

There is, lastly, the teleological or ultimate relation, the most important of all. The consequence or effect of the sin of the first Adam was death. God had forewarned him of this. Death was, then, the direct and due reward of his deed. His descendants sinned like him, and death came upon them also, but without their having received any declaration from God of the penalty contingent on their transgression. They sinned, then, in this respect, not as Adam sinned,‡ that is, not in view of a positive penalty, since this

---

* Ψυχικός.   † Δικαίωμα.

‡ Μὴ ἐπὶ τῷ ὁμοιώματι τῆς παραβάσεως Ἀδάμ.

was not definitively proclaimed till the giving of the law. The fact that they all thus died is the proof that they were all sinners; for otherwise, and in the absence of any positive law,* it could not be clearly proved that they had sinned. The death which the first man had merited by the transgression of a positive command, he transmits to all his descendants, since † all are in a community of sin with him. The second Adam was exempt from death, by His own nature, doubtless, but also by the absolute absence of sin. This exemption from death, or, in other words, the life which He possesses in Himself, is transmitted by Him to the second race of men—to those who are by faith brought into a community of righteousness with Him.

It is mainly in view of this last relation that the apostle insists on the fact, that between the two terms of the typological parallel there is a very marked inequality in favour of the second Adam, or rather of those who belong to Him. This inequality is uppermost in his mind, and he reverts to it three times in succession,‡ without even then succeeding in making his thought quite clear, because of the many ellipses he introduces into his syllogistic statements. The inequality, however, seems to consist in the following points: first, in the fact that, in the natural race, one single instance, the sin of Adam, was the basis of the condemnation of many;§ while in the spiritual race, grace and life were manifested in spite of the numerous sins of many sinners. Secondly, it is to be observed that death appeared as wages due and deserved, while life is a grace, a free gift.|| Lastly, to the race of the second Adam the prospect of a happy futurity acquires a higher degree of certainty, because a pledge of it is even now given in the justifying fellowship of believers with Christ.¶

Some have added a fourth point of comparison which leads to the same result. The reasoning of the apostle in these

---

* Rom. v. 13.   § Κατάκριμα, v. 16.
† Ἐφ' ᾧ; comp. 1 Cor. xv. 22. || Rom. v. 15.
‡ Rom. v. 15—17.   ¶ Rom. v. 17.

verses might appear to be based upon the fact that the word *death* is used in its proper and physical sense, while *life* represents, not simply its opposite, but contains the further idea of happiness.

We do not share this opinion. In each—and this is a very essential point—the first member of the parallel which relates to Adam, is not presented by Paul as any new and unknown thing which he was charged to reveal to the world. It is the second member which possesses the character of novelty, and which is of capital importance to his entire system. The other, Paul only cites as a fact already familiar, since it belonged to Bible history, which was the subject of popular instruction in the synagogue, and the schools had already made it a part of their theological system. There appears to be here, however, an original thought peculiar to our author, namely, the spiritualization of the idea of death, inasmuch as the Jews attached to it a physical sense only, while in Paul's idea the two senses are generally inseparable. We lean the more to this view of the subject, because Paul * does not regard mortality as in itself a thing contrary to the nature of man; it, is only abnormal in its penal and condemnatory character.

These are all the elements of theology we are able to discover in these celebrated passages. The speculation of the schools has doubtless felt the need of something more; it has elicited from the texts other theorems, the value and truth of which we have not now to discuss. Historical exegesis must be careful not to amalgamate the postulates of philosophy with the positive results of literal interpretation. On a point of doctrine so important we must be on our guard, as writers of history, against making use of expressions not found in the texts or documents we are handling. We may reasonably suppose that the expressions used by the apostle appeared to him sufficiently clear and complete to convey his thought. It must be in his own writings, and not in those of authors of a distant age, that we must seek any further aid we may

* According to 1 Cor. xv. 47.

need, while still reserving to every age, to every school, to every individual, the right to cast fresh aid upon the subject, light derived from private reflection, with a view either to modify the theory itself or the method taken to establish it.

Thus, to cite a few examples, Paul does not say a word of any change passing upon human nature in consequence of the sin of Adam. On the one hand, this doctrine would be in contradiction with what he teaches about creation;[*] on the other, it would not coalesce with what he says of the eternity of the divine decrees concerning salvation in Christ. It is, indeed, beyond doubt, that if Adam had been created impeccable, if by nature he had been perfect and averse to sin, he would not have fallen under temptation. The fact of sin proves it to be a natural possibility. The passage in Romans vii., analyzed at so much length by us in a previous chapter, applies to Adam as much as to any other man. We readily grant to the moralists that the repetition and habit of sin lowers the moral condition of man, but that has nothing to do with the theological theories as to human nature, and Paul nowhere speaks of this particular fact.

Neither can we find a word in his writings about the imputation of the sin of Adam, in the absolute sense of that scholastic term; for in that case it would be necessary to speak in the same way of an imputation of the merit of Christ apart from any condition. On both sides we are bound first to take account of an accessory fact of great importance, and which is, to Paul, the cardinal point of the doctrine; and next, not to make any mistake as to what it is which he speaks of as imputed. That which is imputed is not sin, but the penalty of sin—death; it is not the merit, but that which, to preserve the parallel, we might call the effect of the merit—namely, life. The former passes upon those who enter into community of life with Adam,—that is, who sin like him; the latter is given to those who enter into community of life with Christ,— that is, who are righteous by faith. It is evident that the

* 1 Cor. xv. 45—47.

Augustinian formula does not take into account this parallelism of the respective conditions, and that it substitutes, at the same time, cause for effect, when it uses the term imputation. Paul[*] does not intend to say that by the simple fact of the holy life of Jesus Christ *all* men are justified; he means to say that they are so virtually or conditionally,—that is to say, *if they have faith;* just as the other member of the sentence cannot signify simply that *all* men are condemned for the sin of one man, but rather that sin brings upon them all a like punishment, *inasmuch as all* have actually become sinners; so the men of the second race[†] are not certainly declared righteous except as they enter by faith into fellowship with the obedience of their Head. This is a condition so natural and so familiar that Paul did not feel it necessary to state it. It follows that the corresponding ellipsis must exist in the preceding phrase, which then signifies that all men of the first race are declared sinners, inasmuch as by their own acts they have become sharers in the disobedience of their Head. The *declaration* is in both cases a judicial act of God, as the word exactly expresses;[‡] it is made in the first case by the infliction of the punishment, in the second by the bestowment of life.[§]

* Rom. v. 18.

† Πολλοί, v. 19.

‡ Καθιστάναι.

§ What St. Paul says of the relation of all men to Adam, is his way of stating the obvious fact of the *solidarité* of the human race in sin and suffering. There is a similar *solidarité* in Redemption between all who are redeemed.—ED.

CHAPTER XI.

OF FAITH.

GOD sent His Son into the world to save men; for this end Christ was born and died. It only remains for us to ask how that end is realized, how that salvation is wrought and obtained. The reply is very simple so long as we look only at the fact itself; but as we wish to proceed methodically in our exposition, we have to choose between several different points of view which may furnish us with the elements of a logical division. As to the time, for instance, we may speak of the beginning, the progress, the consummation of the work of salvation. As to the persons engaged, we must mention successively the part taken by God, by Christ, and by man, as all concurring in the same work. As to the objective extension of that work, we shall have to consider the individual, the Church, the kingdom of God. As to the faculties of the soul which are specially called into play, or the inner dispositions more particularly manifested, we shall have to trace the exercise of reason and feeling, will and activity, patience and joy.

Paul himself does not take up exclusively any one of these standpoints. We also shall endeavour, as far as possible, to combine them, so as to secure, on the one hand, the means of embracing in one view the system in all its fulness, without exposing ourselves, on the other hand, to the danger of making Paul merely the exponent of our own views. On the following plan we hope to be able to arrange easily all the various parts of this suggestive system.

Our fundamental idea, one which certainly expresses the true thought of the apostle, is to refer all to God, whose purpose appears to us the cardinal point, the motive principle, the centre of the whole work of salvation. From this point of view, we shall first inquire how man recognizes this purpose, how this exercise of his reason reacts at once upon his heart, touches it, and brings it into a new and indispensable condition. This essentially receptive disposition is faith. In the next place, we shall find man endeavouring, to the extent of his powers, to co-operate in God's design, to become a fellow-labourer in His work. This essentially active disposition is *love*. Lastly, we shall find him concentrating his thoughts upon the ultimate and perfect fulfilment of God's purpose, which he has not only truly discerned, but which he has, so to speak, appropriated; he willingly suffers now, that he may have a share in that future joy, the prospect of which comforts him in all his sorrows, and forms a perpetual stimulus to his zeal and activity. This essentially expectant disposition is *hope*.

It will be seen that this division comprises almost all the different points of view which we have enumerated. For in speaking of faith we shall be led to look at the individual, and to study the beginning of the work of salvation in its most limited sphere; love will naturally lead us to speak of the community at large, the condition and progress of which correspond to a second stage of the same work, its outward extension; lastly, what we shall have to say of hope will relate to the establishment, in the widest sphere, of the kingdom of God. Lastly, in each of these three sections we shall have to speak successively of the part of God, of Christ, and of man in these different phases of the work of salvation,— a mode of division which may commend itself as the most natural of all.

We commence with the definition of faith. It is of the highest importance to form a correct idea of the meaning of this term. A just appreciation of it is the key to the entire Pauline system; and any error, however partial, on this point, any misconception, even accidental, as to the import of this expression, must necessarily mislead any one seeking to arrive at the true meaning of the apostle. Yet it is not easy to give the exact definition required; Paul himself does not supply it anywhere; the Greek word corresponding to it has really very various significations, and that which is most important for the theological theory, and to which we shall more particularly refer, is so rich and so emphatic, that it cannot be exhausted in a few words. Our readers will then excuse us if, on account of the importance of the subject, we enter fully into it here, even after having already treated the philological part of the question.

Etymologically, there is in this word and its derivatives the twofold notion of trust and fidelity. A comparison with the same word in other languages,—the German, *trauen* and *Treue*; Latin, *fides*, *confido*, etc.,—shows that these two ideas are very closely connected. This primal meaning is found repeatedly in the writings of Paul.*

With this idea of trust, that of *belief* is nearly allied, that is, the simple persuasion that a fact is true,† and in this sense *belief* may be contrasted with *knowledge*.‡ Most frequently, this persuasion or conviction is placed in connection with religious facts or ideas. Thus, there is one series of passages in which no mention is made of the special object of religious conviction, or in which the Christian element implied is ex-. pressed by accessory terms only.§

* Thus πίστις θεοῦ (Rom. iii. 3) is the faithfulness with which God fulfils His promises. (Comp. ἀπιστία, Rom. iii. 3; πιστὸς ὁ θεός, 1 Cor. i. 9; 1 Thess. v. 24, etc.; and the numerous passages—for example, Gal. v. 22, 1 Cor. xiii. 7—where πίστις is enumerated among the social virtues.) Hence again the passive, πεπίστευμαι, *was committed to me* (Gal. ii. 7; 1 Tim. i. 11); πίστις, trust in God (contrasted with ἀπιστία), Rom. iv. 19, 20.

† *Fürwahrhalten*, 1 Cor. xi. 18; Rom. vi. 8.

‡ 2 Cor. v. 7.

§ The Οἰκεῖοι τῆς πίστεως, for example (Gal. vi. 10), are those who belong to the same family (οἰκία) by faith. In Rom. xiv. 2, 22, 23, the reference is simply to the presence or absence of any religious conviction whatever in an ordinary act of life, in itself indifferent. In πίστις τοῦ εὐαγγελίου

Thus far the word *faith* is used only as expressing a general idea; but it is far more frequently employed to designate the Christian faith in its special acceptation. In order to get a complete comprehension of it, we shall be careful to follow what we may call the genetic development of the idea, commencing with its origin and tracing it through all its successive phases.

Christian faith begins with or is born out of the hearing of Gospel preaching. It is, then, in its origin, the simple belief that that preaching proclaims a truth, that it speaks true.* The preaching itself is called "*the word of hearing*,"† because the first condition of its efficacy is that it be heard.

As we are already acquainted with the subject of the preaching, we may conclude that the subject of faith is also the death of Christ for man, and the fact that, on account of that death, God is willing to grant him His favour. "*The faith of the Gospel*" ‡ is then the conviction of the truth of this twofold historic and dogmatic assertion, or of any particular portion of that Gospel made the subject of preaching, as the case may be.§ In a great number of passages an intellectual apprehension ‖ of the will of God, and of the revelations given of it, is pointed out as a thing indispensable for the believer.¶

But the notion of faith is far from being exhausted by this act of the understanding. Conviction, at first theoretic only, and confined within the sphere of the reason, produces at once an impression upon the soul, which receives the fact of the death of Christ as irrefragable proof of the love of God to men. This impression awakens a corresponding feeling in man, an inclination towards God, a desire to love Him in return, and, above all, a sense of reliance, based upon the

(Phil. i. 27) it is the genitive which determines the nature of the preceding word (comp. 1 Cor. ii. 5; xiii. 2; xv. 14, 17; Eph. i. 13).

* Ἡ πίστις ἐξ ἀκοῆς, Rom. x. 14—17.

† Λόγος ἀκοῆς, 1 Thess. ii. 13.

‡ Πίστι- τοῦ εὐαγγελίου, Phil. i. 27.

§ For instance, 1 Thess. iv. 14; Rom. vi. 8; 2 Thess. ii. 11, and foll.

‖ Γνῶσις, ἐπίγνωσις.

¶ 1 Tim. ii. 4; iv. 3; 2 Tim. ii. 25; iii. 7; Titus i. 1; Col. i. 6, 9, and foll.; ii. 2; iii. 10; Eph. i. 17; iv. 13; Rom. x. 2; 2 Cor. ii. 14; iv. 6.

grace thus manifested. At first, it was the understanding which was thus enlightened, now it is the heart which glows with a new and living fire.* This second element is also contained etymologically in the word faith (*fides*). With it the practical life of faith begins. The conviction of which we spoke at first was based upon the consciousness of sin; the trust of which we are speaking now, implies the renunciation of every sort of personal merit, and the grateful acceptance of the favour freely offered in God's name.

There is, however, yet a third element indispensable to a full realization of the idea of faith. The understanding and the heart are not the only faculties of the soul which are interested. The will also must be enlisted. But here there is more required than what we call man's own good resolutions of amendment; these will not carry him far; for they are often made under transitory influences, and forgotten as soon as formed. The result of faith is, we might almost say, the opposite of all this; it is the abnegation of the man's own will, the abdication of self, the surrender of personal independence and of the uncontrolled exercise of the powers of the soul; it is, in short, an absolute subordination of the whole human personality to the personality of the Saviour, an identification with His ideal existence, complete communion with Him. We arrive here at a capital dogma of the Pauline theology, that indeed which may be said to govern all the rest. Faith, according to this apostle, is essentially mystical in its nature,—that is, it lies beyond the limits of analysis, and can be apprehended only in the secret of the soul. For it may be laid down as a fundamental principle, that in this faith the life of the individual is merged in a life not its own, which is at once ideal and real, and its infallible model and exemplar. The consciousness of the individual must be modified by such a union, and that change Paul expresses when he says, "it is no more I that live, but Christ who liveth in me."† Instead of a life regulated by worldly and carnal

* Ἡ ἀγάπη θεοῦ ἐκκέχυται ἐν ταῖς καρδίαις ἡμῶν, Rom. v. 5; comp. x. 9, 10.
† Ζῶ δὲ, οὐκέτι ἐγὼ, ζῇ δὲ ἐν ἐμοὶ Χριστός, Gal. ii. 20.

principles, a new life is born, the principle of which is faith. He who lives by this life is, so to speak, born of faith.*

Faith, then, according to Paul, is at once an act of the reason or conviction, an act of the heart or trust, an act of the will or self-surrender. The last element is the most important of the three, the only one which makes faith the centre of the whole system, since by it alone does faith become the means of justification. In fact, if the personality of the sinner charged with guilt, and exposed to punishment, is lost, merged in that of another, then the object of the divine anger disappears also. If the man becomes one with Christ, living by His Spirit, and according to His will, instead of following the impulses of his own carnal affections, he possesses henceforth a power which will make him victorious over sin. In a word, if Christ is the principle of his life, and lives in him, the man will no more need the precepts of a law external to himself, and therefore inferior. The three-fold redemption is accomplished; the threefold bondage of guilt, of sin, and of the law is broken; man has returned to his normal relation to God, and "*his faith is counted to him for righteousness.*"†

Faith thus defined forms an antithesis to the law in more than one respect.

The law sought to bring righteousness by the merit of works; it is therefore called the law of works.‡ Faith implies the avowal that no such merit is possible, that all depends on the grace of God,§ and the new order of things is even called "*the law of faith,*"‖ as though more strongly to emphasize this contrast.

The law had reference to outward and legal acts, externally regulated by its prescriptions; it did not deal with the motives concurring to prompt to obedience. Faith, on the contrary, is

---

* 'Ο ἐκ πίστεως, Gal. iii. 7, and foll. ; Rom. iii. 26.

† 'Η πίστις λογίζεται εἰς δικαιοσύνην, Rom. iv. 5, and foll.

‡ Νόμος τῶν ἔργων, Rom. iii. 27.

§ Διὰ τοῦτο ἐκ πίστεως (ἡ ἐπαγγελία) ἵνα κατὰ χάριν, Rom. iv. 16.

‖ Νόμος πίστεως, Rom. iii. 27.

an inward spiritual thing, and tests and weighs the most secret springs of our actions.

Lastly, the law divided men into various hostile camps or categories. Faith, which alone is accessible to all, is also the only power which makes all one.*

We are anxious to take an exhaustive view of our subject, to place before the eyes of our readers all that is connected with it in the thought and in the phraseology of the apostle. The idea of faith is with him more comprehensive and more complex than with any other of the New Testament writers, for he includes in it religious or moral phenomena, which elsewhere are only connected with it externally and as among its consequences. Thus we may say that the word *faith*, in the writings of Paul, corresponds to what we are accustomed to call *Christianity* in the abstract sense of the word, the sum of the disposition and actions regulated by the principles of the Gospel,† or even more simply still, the Christian Church and doctrine.‡ We may add that all the terms just analyzed are

* Οὐκ ἐστὶ διαστολή, Rom. iii. 22; comp. Gal. iii. 28, etc.

† Rom. i. 8, 12; xii. 3, 6; xiv. 1; 2 Tim. i. 5; 2 Cor. x. 15; 1 Tim. v. 8, 12; 1 Thess. iii. 5, and foll.; Col. i. 4, etc.

‡ Gal. i. 23; Phil. ii. 17. Hence πιστεύειν, to become a Christian, to receive baptism (Rom. xiii. 11; 1 Cor. iii. 5; xv. 2, 11); ὑπακοὴν πίστεως (Rom. i. 5; xvi. 26) is conversion to Christianity; the apostle of Jesus Christ is a διδάσκαλος ἐν πίστει (1 Tim. ii. 7), and faith itself is the correlative of truth (comp. iv. 6); οἱ πιστεύοντες, οἱ πιστοί, Christians, members of the Church (Eph. i. 19; 1 Thess. i. 7; 1 Tim. iv. 10; v. 16; 1 Cor. xiv. 22; 2 Cor. vi. 15; Col. i. 2; Titus i. 6, etc.) The contrary, a holding aloof from the Christian community and its ways, is designated by ἀπιστία and ἄπιστοι (Rom. xi. 20, 23; 1 Tim. i. 13; 1 Cor. vi. 6; vii. 12, and foll.; xiv. 22, and foll.) In some cases this πιστεύειν may refer rather to a special aspect of the Christian dispensation. In Rom. xv. 13, it relates more particularly to its universality; in 1 Cor. iv. 13, Col. ii. 12, to its evidences, the principal of which is the resurrection of Christ; in Gal. iii. 22, and foll., Eph. ii. 8, etc., to the antithesis between redemption by the grace of Christ and by the merit of the obedience of the law; in 2 Thess. i. 10, to the hope of the Gospel. It is easy, however, to see that these various applications do not at all affect our fundamental definition. In Rom. i. 17 (ἐκ πίστεως εἰς πίστιν) the word on its first occurrence desig-

ås frequently employed as they are diversely construed. We find sentences where the preposition seems to represent a more general or less intimate relation, a simple reliance *on* Christ, not including the mystical conception ;* others where it seems to mark specially hope or confidence in something future secured *by* Christ ;† others where it expresses the idea of perfect communion *in* Christ.‡ This last form of expression is so peculiarly congenial and dear to Paul, that he uses it even when it is not necessary ; for instance, he speaks of faith *in* His blood,§ although the idea is not of communion with the blood of Christ, but of confidence in the efficacy of that blood. Again, we find the expressions *to believe on Christ* in a passage which treats of the entire New Testament dispensation, of which Christ is the centre,‖ and *to believe Christ* in another, which points rather to the pledge given by Christ of the realization of the object of faith ;¶ lastly, we have briefly *the faith of Christ*,** which, like the construct case in the Hebrew syntax, expresses the idea of intimate relation. We may advert to one passage†† in which three of these seven formulas are used in succession, which proves that if they are not synonymous etymologically, they are so in theology. It is needless to say that the word faith, used alone and without any addition, has repeatedly, in Paul's writings, this profound and complex meaning.‡‡ This faith is called a mystery,§§ inasmuch as its

nates faith as the principle which justifies in an abstract manner ; on the second, the faith which justifies the believer as *in concreto.*

* II. εἰς Χριστόν, Col. ii. 5 ; Phil. i. 29 ; Rom. x. 14 ; comp. πρὸς, Philem. 5, and 1 Thess. i. 8.

† II. ἐπὶ Χριστῷ, 1 Tim. i. 16 ; comp. Rom. iv. 5, 24.

‡ II. ἐν Χριστῷ, Gal. iii. 26 ; Eph. i. 15 ; 2 Tim. iii. 15.

§ Rom. iii. 25.

‖ 1 Tim. iii. 16.

¶ 2 Tim. i. 12 ; comp. Titus iii. 8.

** Rom. iii. 22 ; Eph. iii. 12.

†† Gal. ii. 16.

‡‡ Rom. ix. 30, 32 ; x. 6, 8 ; iv. 13, 14 ; v. 1, 2 ; Gal. iii. 2, 5, and foll., 23, 25 ; Phil. i. 25 ; 2 Tim. iv. 7, etc. See especially 2 Cor. xiii. 5, where πίστις corresponds to Χριστὸς ἐν ὑμῖν.

§§ 1 Tim. iii. 9.

nature and import were unknown before the revelation of Christ; it is unique and the same for all,* inasmuch as there is but one Saviour. Thus the expression to believe, used alone, may express the sum of all the elements which we have discovered in our analysis, and which are all indispensable to salvation;† and if we find more than one passage in which the term appears to be used without any special reference, we may safely attach to it, at least in a general manner, the idea of the normal relation with the Saviour.‡

Faith, again, which is to be the essential and fundamental disposition of all who will belong to Christ, and claim their share in the benefits He bestows, is a passive thing, especially as to its intellectual element. It is received, accepted, not of necessity scientifically examined. Many members of the Church stop at this point of their religious development, without rendering their relation to Christ, the relation on which their salvation depends, incomplete or sterile. Some, however, but a smaller number, go on to a theological and speculative study of this relation, make it the theme of their meditation, and thus add to faith knowledge;§ this, without being indispensable, is yet a precious gift of the Spirit.

Such is a general view of the faith on which the salvation of man depends, and which, in this respect, takes the place of works; but the mysterious life of this faith and its momentous effects demand a deeper analysis than any mere definition of the term or the subject. We now proceed to complete this study by a series of chapters, in which we shall follow the order of thought indicated by the apostle himself,|| speaking first of the operation of God, then of the subjective experience of man, and lastly of the part taken by Christ in this primary sphere of the Christian life.

* Eph. iv. 5.
† Rom. iv. 11; x. 4; 1 Cor. i. 21, etc.
‡ Philem. 6; 2 Cor. i. 24; Eph. vi. 16; Col. i. 23; 2 Thess. i. 11; 1 Tim. iii. 13, etc.
§ Γνωσις. 1 Cor. xii. 8, 9; comp. 2 Cor. viii. 7; see also Col. ii. 3; 1 Tim. vi. 20; 2 Cor. ii. 6; 1 Cor. xiii. 2, 8.
|| Rom. x. 13, 14.

CHAPTER XII.

OF ELECTION.

WE have already spoken of God as the Author of the salvation of men; we have seen that He has purposed that salvation, and are well assured that the means He has chosen are those most fit to accomplish His will; it remains for us to show here that in the application of those means to individuals, the 'initiative belongs no less to Him. His operation in this respect may be described under three heads, arranged in a certain chronological order.

Experience tells us that all men do not accept the Gospel, that all do not believe, that many remain indifferent to its preaching, or even show hostility to it. This fact* may be explained first, in a very simple and natural and at the same time practical manner, by saying that God wills the salvation of all,† but that many by their own perverseness and obstinacy reject the offered salvation,‡ and thus choose their own perdition. This explanation has in its favour what is called common sense, and moreover morality is directly interested in enforcing its practical consequences. We shall not be surprised, therefore, to find Paul frequently laying stress on those consequences.

Nevertheless, speculation in analyzing the idea of the Divine omniscience, in so far as it is able to comprehend it, that is to say, without rendering it independent of the notion of time, arrives at a totally different theory, and enunciates the thesi

---

* Ὁ τὰ πάντα ἐνεργῶν κατὰ τὴν βουλὴν τοῦ θελήματος αὐτοῦ, Eph. i. 5, 11.
† 1 Tim. ii. 4; comp. 1 Thess. v. 9.
‡ Rom. x. 16.

of *election*. It says: Just as God had, before all time, decreed absolutely· the salvation of men by Christ, so has He also chosen the individuals who are to be made heirs of salvation.* The formula used by the apostle to convey this thought contains several terms which it will be well for us to examine specially. These set forth, on the one hand, the *decree* of God in the absolute and abstract sense; on the other hand, a choice or predestination in the concrete and individual sense.† The

---

* Ἐξελέξατο ἡμᾶς πρὸ καταβολῆς κόσμου . . . καὶ ἐκληρώθημεν προορισθέντες κατὰ πρόθεσιν αὐτοῦ, Eph. i. 4, 11. [Reuss seems to me to read the early verses of Eph. i. in the light of controversies which have greatly agitated the Church since apostolic times, but of which the apostles knew nothing. St. Paul says that God chose us "in Christ," not that He chose some among those that were *out of Christ*, and determined to bring them into union with Him. The thought seems to be this : Before the foundation of the world, God determined that all who are in Christ should constitute a distinct race, separate from the rest of mankind, called to special privileges and prerogatives ; *they*—not the Jewish nation—are the true people of God; *they*—not the mere natural descendants of Abraham— constitute the "elect race ;" and they are destined to be holy and without blame before God. He goes on to say that, in God's great love, they were predestinated unto the adoption of children by Jesus Christ unto Himself. The passing away of the special prerogatives of the Jewish race indicated no change in God's purpose. From the very first, " before the foundation of the world," He meant to do what He is doing now. This was the " mystery," as St. Paul afterwards calls it, which " in other ages was not made known to the sons of men," but which it was Paul's glory to preach among the Gentiles. God's real purpose was revealed at last. From the very first He meant to have a very different kingdom from that visible and earthly state which had sprung from the Jewish patriarchs. The true " elect race " consists of all who are in Christ, and if God's will were done, all men would belong to it. Reuss puts the Calvinistic interpre- tation upon St. Paul's words, and interprets them as meaning that God has settled who shall believe in Christ. According to the Calvinistic theory, some men who are still " children of wrath," to use a phrase of St. Paul's, are among the " elect," and will, therefore, some day become children of God. This is a mode of thought utterly foreign to St. Paul. The only " elect " persons that he ever speaks of are those who are actually in Christ. They are " elect " *because* they are in Him. The ·blessedness and glory of the " elect " are to be seen only as we become one with Him. We are elected, not that we *may* be in Christ, but as being in Him.—ED.]

† Comp. 1 Cor. i. 27, 28.

absolute decree is evidenced by the individual election.* It is God, then, who works all things according to the good pleasure of His will,† a phrase in which one of the two closing words would be altogether needless except to give emphasis to the idea of the absolute.

These terms, it is true, do not occur very frequently in the writings of Paul, but there can be no doubt as to their signification. Christians are called the elect, ‡ not as a historical assertion, and to represent them as a class or company of remarkably virtuous people, but as an affirmation of the doctrine that they owe to Divine grace their privilege of belonging to the Church. They are spoken of as the *elect* simply, or as the elect of God, or as elect in Christ, thus designating at the same time the Divine Persons on whose operation the individual election depends. The election itself is an election of grace, an expression which excludes any notion of personal merit, and implies, further, the obtaining of certain benefits constituting a privilege.§ From the metaphysical point of view which commands this whole question, it is important to show that the apostle really connects his thesis, as philosophy‖ has always done, with the idea of the Divine omniscience, so that we cannot err as to the nature and basis of the doctrinal theory we are setting forth. All the rest is but an inevitable corollary from this fundamental idea, which is therefore the only point open to critical question.

* Ἡ κατ᾽ ἐκλογὴν πρόθεσις, Rom. ix. 11. We may here refer to the passage in 2 Thess. ii. 13, according to the reading, εἵλετο ὑμᾶς ἀπ᾽ ἀρχῆς. We prefer this in any case to the other (ἀπαρχὴν), because the latter contains an exaggeration contrary to the history itself, and even a slight error in syntax. It may be observed, also, that by the former reading we get united in one sentence the whole series of ideas essential to the Gospel.

† Ὁ τὰ πάντα ἐνεργῶν κατὰ τὴν βουλὴν τοῦ θελήματος αὐτοῦ, Eph. i. 5, 11.

‡ Ἐκλεκτοί, 2 Tim. ii. 10; θεοῦ, Rom. viii. 35; Col. iii. 12; Titus i. 1; ἐκ κυρίῳ, Rom. xvi. 13.

§ Ἐκλογὴ χάριτος, Rom. xi. 5 (comp. v. 7, where ἐκλογὴ is put for ἐκλεκτοί). The same thought is conveyed also in the ἐκληρώθημεν, referred to above (Eph. i. 11), since κλῆρος and its derivatives always convey the idea of possession, either actual or future.

‖ The προγινώσκειν (Rom. viii. 29) precedes the προορίζειν.

Election being an act of the will of God, and it being impossible for the will of God to fail of its purpose, it follows that the elect must necessarily and infallibly attain salvation. God Himself will provide the means, and guide His chosen to the right use of them; He will dispose and prepare them, not only for the final glory, but for all that precedes it.*

We are anxious to make a few more observations on this important subject, and to endeavour to enter yet more fully into the views of the apostle. Chapters nine to eleven of the Epistle to the Romans contain various statements which will help to throw light upon this point in his system.

Some have thought that all difficulties were removed (and especially those arising out of a just recognition of the claims of morality), by supposing the Pauline theory of predestination to be as follows: All men are sinners; none can make any claim to blessedness; all have deserved condemnation; if God were to be simply just, He might deliver all indiscriminately to eternal death; but He does not so; He chooses out some, to whom He grants salvation. The elect have no ground for boasting, for they do not owe their privilege to their own deserts; those who are not chosen have no ground for complaint, for God was under no obligation towards them; they receive only what they had merited.

Many theologians or exegetes, we say, have satisfied themselves with this explanation, and brought themselves to believe that this is a true representation of Paul's theory. We willingly admit that on many points it might be sufficient, and that in the ninth chapter of the Epistle to the Romans, the examples of Ishmael and of Pharaoh, and still more the quotations from the prophets, do not oppose and even seem to favour it.† The preference shown by God for Isaac over his brother offers the less difficulty, since according to the tradition of the Jewish schools there were sufficient grounds for such a choice. That God should harden the heart of Pharaoh does not imply that He forcibly changed an innocent man into a sinner; the

---

* Προετοιμάζει εἰς δόξαν (Rom. ix. 23), εἰς ἔργα ἀγαθά (Eph. ii. 10).

† Rom. ix. 7, 17, 25—29.

sense is simply that He did not touch him by His grace, but left him to his own naturally hostile and impious disposition. Lastly, when Hosea and Isaiah are appealed to, to prove that God rejects one rebellious people and gives grace to another, that He saves only a small number of those who have excited His just anger, that a complete and deserved destruction such as came upon Sodom is averted solely by the fact of the divine ´ mercy—all this, it seems to us, is quite in harmony with the view given above.

But there are in the same chapter two other passages which will in no way lend themselves to such an interpretation, and in which Paul pointedly guards against the slightest possibility of error or uncertainty.

Let us observe first what he says in regard to the election of Jacob and the rejection of Esau, who are presented here as types of the elect and the reprobate generally. These were twin children of one father and mother, as all men are the creatures of the same God; and before they were born, before they had done either good or evil, the one was chosen, the other rejected. Nay, more; not only does God thus act towards them, but He had before declared that He should so act, so that this unequal destiny was recognized as the effect of the sovereign will of God, and not as a consequence of any act of the individuals. The principle of absolute predestination was thus placed beyond the possibility of any false interpretation.*

* Οὐκ ἐξ ἔργων ἀλλ' ἐκ τοῦ καλοῦντος, ἵνα ἡ κατ' ἐκλογὴν πρόθεσις τοῦ θεοῦ μένῃ, Rom. ix. 11. [We shall miss the meaning of any author, inspired or uninspired, if we fix on isolated sentences and sever them from the process of thought with which they are vitally and organically connected. St. Paul is not contending in this passage that God has a *right*—whether as the effect of His arbitary choice or on other grounds—to confer on any man, or on any race, exceptional distinctions and privileges; he is contending that God's "election" of the Jewish race has not come to nothing. "The word of God "—His promise to Abraham—had been kept, notwithstanding that rejection of the great mass of the Jewish people on account of unbelief, which might make it appear to some that the divine word had "taken none effect;" this is the thesis which the apostle has to maintain. He maintains it by showing that from the beginning the promise to Abraham was not understood as including all his natural descendants.

Now it would be a false interpretation to say that God knows beforehand if a man will persist in evil or if he will repent; and that He regulates predestination according to this foreknowledge. The doctrinal thesis is thus deprived of its most essential element, and the elimination of works, which is the point on which the apostle is insisting, is lost sight of.

The other passage * is still more significant. The potter, it is said, may make at his own pleasure, out of the same lump of clay, various vessels: some designed for an honourable, some for a degrading use. Now we have not to do here with a historical fact, the terms of which were given, but with an image freely chosen for the sake of the argument, and consequently much more apt, if that be possible, to express the inner thought of the theologian. Now the clay is an inert mass, having in itself no positive quality which might determine its form or use. The clay does not make itself into a

" They are not all Israel which are of Israel." Ishmael was not the heir of the Abrahamic promise, although he was the child of the patriarch : " In Isaac shall thy seed be called." Jacob and Esau were twins, but before the children were born it was said " the elder shall serve the younger ; " and in the subsequent history of their descendants, so far were the children of Esau from inheriting the special favour of God, that Malachi said, " Jacob have I loved, but Esau have I hated." This, however, was *not* said of the children before they "had done any good or evil." The subordination of Esau to Jacob was the effect of the divine appointment, and was *confessedly not inconsistent with the divine promise to Abraham ;* this is what St. Paul is specially anxious about : the hating of Esau, or rather of Esau's descendants, was the result of their sin. There was no thought, however, in St. Paul's mind about Jacob and Esau being, as Reuss says, types of the elect and the reprobate. St. Paul is contending that God is under no obligation because of His promise to Abraham to make all Jews heirs of the kingdom. He shows this by reminding his Jewish readers that Ishmael and Esau were excluded from the special advantages which before our Lord's coming were the inheritance of the Jewish people ; had this exclusion been the result of the sin of Ishmael and Esau, it might have been answered that all God's promises were conditional, and that Ishmael and Esau had forfeited them ; but St. Paul says, *No—quite apart from the obedience or disobedience of particular descendants of Abraham,* God did not interpret His promise as obliging Him to make them all heirs of the promise.—ED.]

* Rom. ix. 20, and foll.

7 *

vessel; before being thus shaped by the hands of the potter, it is as fit for one form as another; it is the free will, we might almost say the arbitrary fancy, of the workman which decides the use to be made of it. The potter makes of the same dead mass, which is neither good nor bad, two sorts of vessels; thus without any regard to what we call man's individual worth, a worth altogether fictitious and imaginary, God, from all eternity, and before the first sin of the first man,* *creates* some for eternal glory simply to show His boundless mercy, and prepares others for condemnation † solely to display the power of His anger, so that in the moral world there are vessels of grace and vessels of wrath, just as in the potter's workshop there are vessels unto honour and dishonour. ‡

* Comp. Eph. i. 4.

† Προετοιμάζει εἰς δόξαν, ἵνα γνωρίσῃ τὸν πλοῦτον τ. δ. . . . καταρτίζει εἰς ἀπώ-λειαν, θέλων ἐνδείξασθαι τὴν ὀργὴν καὶ τὸ δύνατον αὐτοῦ.

‡ Σκεύη ἐλέους, ὀργῆς, etc. [The illustration of the potter and the clay must have been familiar to the Jewish readers of this epistle, and the ethical element introduced into the illustration by Jeremiah (chap. xviii.) would be present to those for whom St. Paul is writing. In Jeremiah, the potter is represented as *failing* in the first instance to give to the clay the form which he desired; the vessel is "marred in the hands of the potter." Failing to make the vessel which he desired, "he [makes] it again another vessel," gives it another form, fashions it for another and probably an inferior use. And this change is distinctly attributed by the prophet to the quality of the "clay." A nation which God has destined to an honourable use is "marred" in His hands through its own sin; God then assigns to it an inferior destiny,—may even destroy it altogether. The arbitrariness of the divine decrees, the disregard of all ethical considerations in distributing the destinies of the human race, which so many have found in the illustration of the potter and the clay, is the very position which, as Jeremiah used it, the illustration was intended to condemn. "Behold, as the clay is in the potter's hand, so are ye in mine hand, O house of Israel. At what instant I shall speak concerning a nation, and concerning a kingdom, to pluck up, and to pull down, and to destroy it; *if that nation, against whom I have pronounced, turn from their evil, I will repent of the evil that I thought to do unto them.*" (Jer. xviii. 6—8.)

It would be very singular if an illustration which had been used by Jeremiah to show that the decrees of God are, so to speak, *changed* by the character of men, were used by St. Paul to enforce the theory of fatalism. Nor is it used for any such purpose. Vessels may be formed by the

All this is singularly clear, and assuredly no exegetical arguments can henceforth avail to overturn the system which Augustine, Calvin, Gomar, and their followers, have built upon these premises. That Paul teaches, or does not teach, that grace is irresistible; that he does or does not assert in so many words that God creates sin in man; that he is or is not explicitly a ·

potter for manifold purposes, as nations are appointed by God to minister variously to the development of the resources of human nature and the beneficent designs of the divine government. Egypt, Rome, and Greece were to the Jews " vessels of dishonour " compared to the elect race, and yet Egypt, Rome, and Greece had each a service that was honourable in itself. " Of the same lump "—this is the point of St. Paul's argument— God made the descendants of Isaac and the descendants of Ishmael, the descendants of Jacob and the descendants of Esau,—constituting " the children of the promise" kings and priests to Himself, but not leaving the others unblessed. The curious thing is that interpreters, Reuss among them, imagine that St. Paul teaches that as a potter makes some vessels with the express intention of destroying them, so God determines, of His own free will, to fashion some men for eternal destruction. Who ever heard of a potter making a vessel in order to destroy it? The vessels of which St. Paul speaks as " vessels of wrath " are vessels which were put on to the potter's wheel in order to be formed for some useful and honourable purpose,—perhaps the most honourable of all,—but were " marred." The idea of the potter was not fulfilled : as it turned out, they were "fitted" for nothing but "destruction." But even *these*, though it was God's will to make His wrath and power known on the finally impenitent, God " endured with much long-suffering ; " He tried to make the best of them, but the material was so bad and unworkable that He could do nothing with it. After " much long-suffering," real and honest long-suffering, intended to bring men to repentance, He can do nothing but destroy those who continue to reject His authority and His grace.

I am sensible how impossible it is in a note to refute an interpretation which has been wrought into the very substance of the thought of the Church. I am sensible, too, that having his mind filled with the illustration as employed by Jeremiah, in which the human ethical element is absolutely dominant over the divine decree, and never dreaming that it was possible for any one to suppose that he intended to represent the divine decree as disregarding the moral character and actions of men, St. Paul uses expressions which are perilously bold ; but the general movement of his thought throughout the ninth chapter of the Romans, instead of being favourable to the Calvinistic theory, appears to me to be intentionally and even vehemently opposed to it.—ED.]

supralapsarian, is of little moment; the fact remains that no human logic, starting from the principles enunciated above, can escape these strictly necessary consequences. But what then becomes of morality, practical Christianity, Gospel preaching? If man can do nothing, absolutely nothing, cannot even listen when God calls, since God must first open his ears, and may refuse to do so; if the decree is eternal alike to salvation and to condemnation, then each may wait with stolid indifference till the event shall reveal the fate from which escape is in any case impossible; he may abandon himself to licentiousness or to despair, it makes no difference; for, we repeat it, his destiny depends in no way upon his efforts, or the direction he may give to his life.* The common expedient adopted by those who hold the theories of predestination, the attempt to prop up morality by saying that no one can know if he is elected or not, is an evasion fraught with illusion, since after all the determination of God was formed before the man's birth. How many men are there whose moral energy would not sink under the pressure of a conviction so overwhelming?

And can this be indeed the doctrine of Paul? Why then does he say to the Corinthians, "*Run*," if to the Romans he means to say your running shall avail nothing? † Why say to Timothy that "God will have all men to be saved"? ‡ Why give so many exhortations if they must be either ineffectual, even when they produce an impression upon the hearer, or superfluous if they have no power at all to touch him? Why are so many promises given by a man who is not in the secret counsels of God, and who has not turned over the leaves of the book of life, there to read the names of the elect? To what end are faith and charity? Of what good is the Gospel, or Christ Himself, since all is said, done, decreed beforehand?

Ah, indeed! if the final utterance of the Christian revelation be contained in that image of the potter and his clay, it is a bitter mockery of all the deep yearnings and legitimate

---

* Οὐ τοῦ θέλοντος οὐδὲ τοῦ τρέχοντος, Rom. ix. 16.

† Τρέχετε, 1 Cor. ix. 24; οὐ τοῦ τρέχοντος, Rom. ix. 16.

‡ 1 Tim. ii. 4.

desires of a soul aspiring after God. It would be at once the satire of reason against itself, and the suicide of revelation.

But we are not left here to merely critical or philosophical considerations. We are writing history. Let us keep to our proper sphere, and seek in our author himself the solution of this great enigma. A thinking man may almost always be understood by others who think for themselves, and if there is anywhere a flaw in his argument, there will be some way of discovering it, and of seeing at the same time how it stands related to the truth.

First of all, it is a fact worthy of remark, and not sufficiently noted, that the apostle, in the dissertation from which we have taken our principal quotations, has not properly in view individuals, but masses—the two great sections of humanity which he so often contrasts, the Jews and the Gentiles. It is in reference to the general relation between them and the providential government of our race, that he brings forth his arguments. Regarded closely, the whole of this ninth chapter, intimately connected as it is with the two following, is not speaking of predestination in the ordinary, scholastic, or Calvinistic sense of the word. This great section of the Epistle to the Romans is designed to explain theologically a material and historical fact—namely, the repugnance of the great majority of the Jews to the Gospel, a repugnance which seemed about to make them lose all the advantages promised of old, and thus, as it were, to belie God who had held out to them such a prospect. We have here, then, Paul's explanation of this fact, which struck his mind, and which had already been pointed out by the Saviour. "God," he says, "hath given them the spirit of slumber, eyes that they should not see and ears that they should not hear;"* only an insignificant minority does not share in this blindness, as if reserved to be the root and stock of a new growth.† But this blindness, this partial hardening of Israel, forms a part of the secret purposes of God, which are only revealed by the event itself; it is

* Rom. xi. 8.
† Rom. xi. 4, 5, 16.

designed to be the occasion and the cause of the conversion of
the Gentiles.* When these shall have been brought within the
pale of the Church, the turn of Israel will also come.† For the
present, and in their actual relation to the Gospel,‡ the Jews
are without; they are enemies for your sake, O Gentiles, as
though to open the door to you; but absolutely,§ and according
to the unchangeable decrees of God, they are still His beloved;
the benefits to the enjoyment of which they were formerly
called, shall never be lost to them; they also in the end shall
obtain mercy.‖ Glorious philosophy of history! worthy indeed
to call forth the enraptured adoration of the apostle.¶ The
individual is lost sight of in the great march of historic events,
and the judgment pronounced upon these will be all the more
true for being thus raised above the sphere of details and
accidental phenomena.

But it is just this very circumstance which proves to us the
insufficiency of the theory. In historical crises of this nature,
and especially in those of which Paul is here broadly tracing
the mysterious vicissitudes, the individual is sacrificed to the
interests of the masses. Yet the God of the Gospel is assuredly
the God of individuals also. Why must He cause to perish,
or allow to perish, so many of the Jews for the benefit of a
number (greater no doubt) of Gentiles? Was there no other
way for these to be saved? Or if, indeed, these perverse Jews
refused the Gospel, must Paul of necessity lay that opposition
to the charge of God? In short, does not the broad, elevated,
admirable theory of the eleventh chapter resolve itself thus,
under another aspect, into the sorrowful, narrow, disheartening
theory of the ninth? Does there not lie beneath this teaching,
also, the refusal to reply to a most natural and legitimate
question? Does not it also imply those hard words, "Who art
thou, O man, that repliest against God? Shall the thing formed
say unto him that formed it,Why hast thou made me thus?"**

* Rom. xi. 11, 15, 25 (μυστήριον).
† Rom. xi. 26 (πλήρωμα).
‡ Κατὰ τὸ εὐαγγέλιον, Rom. xi. 28.
‖ Κατὰ τὴν ἐκλογὴν Rom. xi. 28.
§ Rom. xi. 29, 31, 32.
¶ Rom. xi. 33, and foll.
** Rom. ix. 20.

This very question suggests a few closing reflections, not critical, but explanatory, upon this point in the apostle's theory. Although essentially all Bible writers take the same standpoint, we shall make these remarks here, because Paul is the only one who attempts to establish it by argument. His logic fails him, as it has failed all the philosophers, ancient and modern, and of every school, who have sought to solve the problem of the connection between omniscience, or divine prescience, and the freedom of man. In the concrete question which he is treating, and from which he starts, he insists upon the fact that Jacob was chosen without any merit of his own, in order to make the Jews feel that human merit is not the ground of salvation, that natural sonship does not constitute men heirs of the promises given to the fathers, that the Gentiles might as freely share in them by the grace of God, who was about to show the world that His kingdom was not enfeoffed to any one people. As he proceeds to carry out this perfectly just and legitimate idea to its farthest issues, even to the borders of a paradox, from which Paul is never wont to recoil, he proclaims with equal boldness the counterpart of this idea—namely, that rejection also is the effect of the sovereign will of God, and not the consequence of demerit. Esau is rejected as Jacob is chosen, because God wills it;* there is no other reason; and this second fact is established less on the ground of God's prescience than of His absolute sovereignty. But if our reason can and is bound to accept the first fact of election without merit, it is shocked, repelled by the second,— rejection without demerit. The common sense of the apostle at once suggests to him this natural objection, "Why then does he yet find fault?" And for all reply, he can only lower man to the level of inert matter, in order to save his logic.

The problem is plainly beyond the scope of human reason; and on this very ground, revelation itself has not been able to offer a solution of it, since revelation, while it is able to supply man with new ideas, is not able to change the laws of his nature and to give him faculties which creation has withheld.

* Rom. ix. 15.

Thus it can give him just conceptions of the moral relations between the world and God, but it cannot make him comprehend the very essence of God, or the nature and means of His operation upon the universe, since to do this, it would need to raise man to the level of God Himself. It does not even tell him on these matters (and herein is its wisdom) as much as philosophy claims to teach. Subject as we are in all our life, and thought, and action to the restrictions of time and space, it is impossible for us to comprehend how God exists, thinks, acts, independently of space or time, and no revelation can enlighten us in the matter. Consequently the apostle, like any other man entering on such a subject, strikes against a rock, which he would have done wisely not to approach.

As we examine more closely into the theology of Paul, we find him elsewhere steadily keeping at a distance from this dangerous coast, and content with meeting at once the requirements of religious faith and practical morality. The former demands the absolute sovereignty of God alike in wisdom and power; the latter asserts, with no less emphasis, the liberty of man. Consequently, where God is concerned, dogmatic theology insists upon the complete independence of His will and action, and uses expressions which approach the doctrine of predestination; where man is concerned, moral teaching insists upon his free will, and invites him by hopes and threats to labour for his own salvation. The theoretical and the practical view are both alike true, but because of the weakness of our understanding, which is not able to harmonize them in one metaphysical formula, they are true to us only on condition of being kept distinct from each other.

One word more. Judaism, in the time of the apostles, proclaimed simply and broadly the predestination of Israel and the repudiation of the Gentiles. National prejudice dominated religious thought, and the practical morality of the Pharisees was itself so lax that it dared not find a flaw in the theories of the schools. Hence, also, it is that the expressions which represent these theories are so familiar to the authors of the New Testament. They employ them generally without

feeling the difficulties they suggest, and they use them with
reference to an actual division of the human race, analogous to
that which formed the basis of the theology of the synagogue.
Judæo-Christianity ignored even the presence of the problem
concealed, as if designedly, by this point of view, apparently so
simple and legitimate; we shall see John raising a corner of
the veil, and then at once letting it fall again. Paul alone
frankly faces the question; and if he cannot answer it successfully, so far from reproaching him with his failure, we venture
to say that by so doing he shows himself to be the only true
theologian among his contemporaries. True knowledge alone*
is able to recognize clearly the limits imposed upon it.

* Γνῶσις καθὼς δεῖ γνῶναι, 1 Cor. viii. 2; comp. xiii. 9.

CHAPTER XIII.

OF CALLING AND THE HOLY SPIRIT.

GOD thus, before the creation of the world, chose those whom
He destined to eternal blessedness: this is, as we have said,
the act of His sovereign will lying at the basis of the work of
salvation. His second act consists in bringing the elect into
a state of salvation. Here, again, they are supposed to be perfectly passive. All the activity is on the part of God, and is
spoken of as His calling.* This calling takes place in time
and successively, in the order which God is pleased to follow
with the individuals called, while the election is made once for
all, and before all time.†

Calling, in the phraseology of Paul, is not a mere invitation
or exhortation addressed to an individual in the name of God,
by the medium of an apostle or other messenger, and to which
man may or may not respond, according to the disposition
of the moment. Doubtless, apostolic preaching is the most
ordinary outward medium, through which the knowledge of
the Gospel is brought to men,‡ or by which God is placed in
connection with the individual. The very term *calling* is

---

* Ἡ κλῆσις, τὸ καλεῖν.

† In all that St. Paul says of the "calling" of believers, he is under
the control of the characteristic ideas of the Old Testament. As those
who are in Christ are the true elect (see Note, p. 95), they have also
received that divine call which separated Abraham, and with him his
descendants, from the rest of mankind.—ED.

‡ This is clear from the frequent use of the word κηρύσσειν and of its
derivatives and synonyms (Rom. x. 14, and foll.; Gal. iii. 2, 5; 2 Tim.
ii. 1, 2, etc.)

borrowed from this mode of communication, and does not prejudice in any way the effect which it may naturally produce.
But the theological meaning of the term is far from being thus
exhausted.* To this outward invitation there is added, as an
invariable and essential element, a corresponding inward feeling
produced directly by the contact of the soul with God. *Calling*,
in the sense in which Paul uses it, cannot fail or remain
ineffectual. In truth, calling and election are, with him, one
and the same thing, with the one exception of the different
epochs, which man—always obliged to apply the measure of
time to the operations of God—necessarily assigns to the two
acts in question. If the calling could by possibility fail in the
case of one individual, the omniscience of God, on which the
theory of election is based, would be at fault, and the system
would be overthrown by its own inconsistency.†

All this the apostle says in express terms: "whom He did
destinate, them He also called; and whom He called, He justified."‡ Christians are first chosen, and then as a consequence
called.§ To call and to elect are thus two synonymous terms
even from the human point of view,|| and calling is of grace,¶
an effect of the sovereign will of God, like election itself,** first
because it is not a general and universal invitation, independent
of its eventual effect, but is in fact a privilege†† granted only to
some, and which can never be slighted or offered at a venture.

* So far is this from being the case, that even in 2 Thess. ii. 14, we should
not translate διὰ τοῦ εὐαγγελίου in the sense of *by means of the preaching
of the Gospel*, but rather by the entire dispensation of which it treats.

† We see, then, that Paul attaches to the word καλεῖν quite a different
sense from that which it has in the gospels, where it is placed in opposition
to ἐκλέγεσθαι (Matt. xx. 16, etc.), while the apostle practically identifies
these two terms. The term καλεῖν, with its derivatives, does not appear at
all in the theology of John.

‡ Οὓς προώρισε, τούτους καὶ ἐκάλεσε, καὶ οὓς ἐκάλεσε, τούτους καὶ ἐδικαίωσε,
Rom. viii. 30.

§ Κατὰ πρόθεσιν κλητοί, Rom. viii. 28.

|| Rom. ix. 24.

¶ Rom. xi. 29.

** Εὐδοκία, Gal. i. 15; Phil. ii. 13; comp. 2 Tim. i. 9.

†† Ἀξιοῦν, 2 Thess. i. 11.

Christians are thus spoken of as those who are called* more
especially to life, to the kingdom of God and to His glory;
to peace,† in relation to the end or definitive result of the
calling; or into liberty and hope,‡ both these being either
the conditions of the calling, or its direct effect upon the dispositions of the soul. §

That which is beyond a doubt is that the calling is always
and invariably ascribed to God, who is on this account spoken
of sometimes simply as *He who calleth*.|| The expression,
the called of Christ, which occurs once only, must therefore be
explained as containing two distinct ideas, closely connected
however,—called (by God) in Christ, or called (by God) to the
salvation which is in Christ.¶

With this idea of calling, we have already stepped out of the
sphere of metaphysics, to enter without further transition that
of evangelical mysticism; for the manner in which the calling
is effected or wrought in man, can be understood by the light
of the inner experience alone. Understanding, reason, have
nothing to do with it, and can give no explanation of it.

The non-elect and uncalled are spoken of as the lost,** but
this term is not so much the antithesis of the *called* as of the
saved, and will be explained presently.

---

* Κλητοί, 1 Cor. i. 24.   This designation is less frequent than that of
ἐκλεκτοί, and only occurs in the formulas of greeting (Rom., 1 Cor.)   It
must have been of common use in ordinary life, however, since it has
given rise to such expressions as κληθῆναι, in the sense of becoming a
Christian (1 Cor. vii. 18, and foll.; comp. Eph. iv. 1); κλῆσις is then
the epitome of the circumstances which characterized the formation of the
community (1 Cor. i. 26; comp. 1 Tim. vi. 12; 1 Thess. ii. 12; 2 Thess.
ii. 14).

† Col. iii. 15 (ἐν εἰρήνῃ); 1 Cor. vii. 15 is quite a different thing.   The
reference, there, is to concord and peace in the household.

‡ Gal. v. 13; Eph. i. 18; iv. 4; comp. 1 Thess. iv. 7.

§ As to the phrase ἡ ἄνω κλῆσις (Phil. iii. 14), it is difficult to say if it
is best rendered as the calling to heaven, or as the calling which comes
from heaven.

|| Ὁ καλῶν, Gal. v. 8; Rom. ix. 11; 1 Thess. v. 24; ὁ καλέσας, Gal. i. 6.

¶ Rom. i. 6.   This would be confirmed by Eph. i. 11, if the variation
ἐν ᾧ ἐκλήθημεν is preferred.   Comp. 1 Cor. i. 9; εἰς κοινωνίαν, τ. Χρ.

** Ἀπολλύμενοι, Cor. i. 18; 2 Cor. ii. 15; iv. 3; Thess. ii. 10.

The analysis of the idea of calling thus leads us to perceive that the work of man's salvation begins without participation on his side; and that it is God alone who both prepares and brings salvation. But the operation of God does not terminate here; it is manifested again in a third stage, and by a fact of more direct importance. We refer to the *communication of the Holy Spirit.*

Before examining this fact in the particular place it occupies in the general system, it will be well for us to call to mind a few preliminary thoughts, which will help us to connect it with other Biblical ideas. As a general rule, Paul when he speaks of the Spirit of God, keeps within the limits of the Old Testament language, and there are but faint indications, in a few isolated passages of his writings, of the first elements of a theological speculation which subsequently, as we know, was largely developed in the schools.• Thus logic, taking the place of what had been originally the expression of the poetic genius of the Hebrew tongue, eliminates from the conception of God in its totality, the particular conception of His Spirit, just as we can think of the human spirit apart from the man himself, as a particular element of his being.* But we must not fail to observe a capital difference between these two terms of comparison. Man is really a complex being; he *has* a spirit, and there is nothing to hinder us from separating in our thoughts the various elements of which it is composed; for this separation has a real foundation in fact. But it is quite otherwise with God, in relation to whom such a distinction must be always ideal and purely suppositious. God *is* a Spirit; He is indivisible. The Spirit of God is, then, nothing else than God Himself; it cannot be a question of separating His Spirit from something else which should be the *substratum,* so to speak, or incomplete residue of the Deity. The comparison indicated in the passage referred to is clearly made for quite another end, than to serve as the basis of a metaphysical theory. We affirm that here, as everywhere else, the expression

* 1 Cor. ii. 10, and foll.

employed by the apostle is the very same term, in such general
and ancient use, by which the language of Scripture seeks to
render more concrete and vivid an idea essentially abstract,
and beyond the range of human reason—the idea of God.
Thus every act whatsoever which our reason recognizes as
proceeding from God, will be naturally ascribed to His Spirit,
because where there is action there is the concrete notion of
One who acts: reason cannot rise into the region of pure abstraction; and this is the idea conveyed by the Hebrew
writers in using this expression. Every manifestation of the
thought or will of God, whether spoken of as creation, preservation, government, judgment, inspiration, or otherwise, is
then an act of the Spirit of God. If the Bible, in making use
of this expression, had designed to establish a metaphysical
principle, it could not have stopped short of the conclusion,
rigorously deducible from the premises, that God *in abstracto*
never acts. This axiom was in fact stated by the contemporaries of the apostles; and if the apostles did not directly make
use of it, it was because they had in view in their teaching
another purpose than that of the schools.

We may take it, then, as established, that the metaphysical
side of the question of the Holy Spirit is not touched in these
epistles, and that the apostle leaves this problem to the discussion of later philosophers. This fact is directly confirmed
by another still more important. In the theology we are at
present studying, the question is really of the Spirit of God,
only in so for as it is communicated to certain men—that is, in
the ethical point of view. Now this ethical design, on account
of which the attribute of *holiness* is so uniformly and exclusively prefixed to the name of the Spirit, as well as the general
fact of a communication of the Spirit and the ideas flowing
from it, seem unfavourable to the development of the idea of a
personality, if they do not altogether exclude it. We shall find,
indeed, from numerous other passages which will presently
come before us, that Paul speaks of it frequently as an object,
a force, which may be compared in its nature and its operation to material forces. Thus, the Spirit of God received by

man is a fire which must not be quenched,* which should, on
the contrary, be stirred when it grows low and dull,† which
communicates its heat to our whole being; ‡ it is a conquering
sword to be used against temptation;§ it is a leaven which
works with holy energy in the heart of man, raising it towards
God, and producing a result which is contrasted with the intoxi-
cation caused by physical intemperance; ‖ it is, lastly, a field
which will yield only good fruit, and pre-eminently eternal life,
in return for the seed sown in it.¶ Again, every manifestation
of this power from on high is called a *spirit*, so that there are
many spirits.** The manifestations of an opposite origin, of
contrary tendency, are spoken of by the same name,†† but are
not therefore necessarily to be personified.

All this brings us directly to the main theme of this
chapter. That Spirit of God, which is by its very nature
a holy Spirit, that is, antipathetic to sin, is communicated by
God to men whose own spirit craves indeed after the good,
but cannot attain to its realization because of the yoke of the
flesh.

On the part of God, this communication is designated by the
terms to *give*, to *procure* for, to *send*; on the part of man, by
the term to *receive*.‡‡ These expressions in themselves show
us that in this relation God alone is active, man passive. We
shall arrive at the same result, if we inquire at what time,
according to the system of Paul, this communication of the
spirit is made. We shall show by indisputable quotation that
it takes place simultaneously with the calling.

Men are said to have received the Spirit by hearing the

* 1 Thess. v. 19.
† 2 Tim. i. 6.
‡ Rom. xii. 11.
§ Eph. vi. 17.
‖ Eph. v. 18.
¶ Gal. v. 22; vi. 8.
** 1 Cor. xii. 10; xiv. 12, 32.
†† 2 Cor. xi. 4; 1 Tim. iv. 1.
‡‡ Διδόναι, 2 Cor. i. 22; 1 Thess. iv. 8; ἐπιχορηγεῖν, Gal. iii. 5; Phil. i. 19;
ἀποστέλλειν εἰς τὰς καρδίας, Gal. iv. 6; λαμβάνειν, Rom. viii. 15.

Gospel preaching, which calls forth or produces faith.* This must necessarily signify that the Spirit is given at the same time that the divine calling (which, as we have shown, is always effectual) reaches the individual, under the form of an apostolic invitation. Both divine facts are inseparable, or rather it is the same fact regarded under the two aspects of the end and the means, or of the form and the result. Otherwise this entire sentence would have this evidently inadmissible sense, that whoever hears with his outward ears the Gospel preached, no matter what his disposition of mind, receives at once the Spirit of God.

It follows, again, from another passage,† that the confession of Jesus, and consequently the manifestation of faith, is an effect of the communication of the Spirit. In the same manner,‡ that communication precedes the consciousness we have of the love of God to us, a consciousness which is again only an element of faith. We may say, then, that the communication of the Spirit does not take place when faith is perfected, but faith is wrought and fully realized when that communication has taken place. But the two spiritual phenomena are indivisible, so that it may also be truly said that the *promise* of the Spirit is linked with the *fact* of faith.§

The nature of this communication, or the relation in which the Spirit of God places Himself with our spirit in this mystical operation, may be regarded in two different ways.

We may, first, consider the Spirit of God as existing and acting in us, side by side with the human spirit, as essentially one with the latter in its operation and effects, but essentially distinct in the conception we must form of it. This point of view has been already indicated by the quotations made above, —the gift of the spirit and other parallel terms. It is explicitly stated in one passage,‖ where the analysis of a fact at

---

* Ἐξ ἀκοῆς πίστεως, Gal. iii. 2, 5.
† 1 Cor. xii. 3.
‡ Rom. v. 5.
§ Gal. iii. 14 ; comp. Eph. i. 13.
‖ Rom. viii. 16.

once religious and psychological, leads the writer to separate the two elements. The popular expression of this point of view is found in the idea that our spirit is assisted and strengthened by the Spirit of God, in its henceforward victorious conflict with the flesh,* and that the various faculties of the soul are thus brought into a state of sanctification and power till then unknown to them.† We shall be reminded here of the antithesis between the life after the flesh and the life after the Spirit,‡ an antithesis too closely connected with the anthropology of Paul's system. to allow us to attach to it any other meaning.

But we may also represent to ourselves the Spirit of God as having taken the place of our spirit, identifying itself with it; or, to put it in another form, we may think of the human spirit as absorbed, so to speak, by the Spirit of God. The writings of Paul furnish us with a series of expressions exactly conveying this idea. Thus the word *communion*,§ according to the general tenor of the system, can signify nothing short of this mystical union. The antithesis between the law of the spirit and the law of sin‖ ought also to be mentioned here, because it is most in harmony with the whole system to recognize in these two principles, two powers disputing together for the entire possession of the man. Again, when it is said that the Spirit of God dwells in us,¶ or even more definitely that our body is the temple of the Holy Ghost which dwelleth in us, ** the idea of the human spirit as having a distinct and separate existence is lost; the Spirit of God has actually taken the place of our own spirit, and is, so so speak, individualized in the persons of the faithful.†† Lastly, this forms the basis of

* Eph. iii. 16.
† Col. i. 8; 2 Tim. i. 14; Rom. ix. 1; xiv. 17; xv. 13, 16, 30; 1 Thess. i. 6.
‡ Rom. viii. 4, 6, 13; Gal. v. 16, and foll., 25.
§ Κοινωνία, 2 Cor. xiii. 13.
‖ Rom. viii. 2.
¶ Οἰκεῖ, Rom. viii. 9; 2 Tim. i. 14.
** 1 Cor. vi. 19; comp. iii. 16.
†† Rom. viii. 26, 27.

one of the favourite allegories of the apostle, in which he represents all believers as having but one and the same spirit, the
Spirit of God, and thus jointly forming one body.* All these
expressions, as well as the idea which underlies them all, are
essentially mystical, and consequently are in close relation
with the fundamental idea of the calling, as we have already
exhibited it. They are therefore more in harmony with the'
rest of the system, truer equivalents of its original idea than
those connected with the former point of view.

We shall conclude this part of our exposition by drawing
attention to the fact, that the most perfect expression of this
mystical idea, explicitly states the absolute unity of the Spirit
of God with the spirit of man : "He who is joined to the Lord
is *one* spirit."†

The communication of the Spirit once made, and the mystical union once accomplished, man possesses and carries
within himself a new principle, powerful enough to assure to
him the victory over the flesh, and the possibility of leading a
life holy and acceptable to God. Henceforward he is no more
under the dominion of the flesh, like a slave, but is guided by
the spirit, like a free man.‡ He is a spiritual man.§ In analyzing this idea of direction by the Holy Spirit, we shall find

* Ἐν ἑνὶ πνεύματι ἡμεῖς πάντες εἰς ἓν σῶμα ἐβαπτίσθημεν, 1 Cor. xii. 13.
The word βαπτίζειν in this passage must be understood of the spiritual
baptism, as in the parallel passage, 2 Cor. i. 21, the word χρίειν.

† Ὁ δὲ κολλώμενος τῷ κυρίῳ ἓν πνεῦμά ἐστι, 1 Cor. vi. 17.

‡ 2 Cor. iii. 17 ; Gal. iii. 3 ; Rom. viii. 5 ; πνεύματι θεοῦ ἄγεσθαι, Rom.
viii. 14.

§ Πνευματικός, Gal. vi. 1 ; 1 Cor. ii. 13, and foll. ; iii. 1. We notice
here that the last term has also other special meanings. He is called also
πνευματικός, who has attained to a higher degree of Gospel understanding,
which again stands in close connection with the other meaning (1 Cor.,
loc. cit.) ; again, one who is honoured with occasional special and extraordinary inspirations is so called (1 Cor. xii. 1 ; xiv. 1, 37). We find
again, further on, the σῶμα πνευματικόν (1 Cor. xv. 44). On the other
hand, to this chapter of our exposition belongs the expression χαρίσματα
πνευματικά, or simply τὰ πνευματικά, the advantages or spiritual gifts of
those who are in communion with God by Christ, and who have consequently the Holy Spirit (Rom. i. 11 ; xv. 27 ; 1 Cor. ix. 11 ; Eph. i. 3).

the two elements of a constant direction of the will, and a per-severing direction of the life and actions.*

This communication of the Spirit, the third and last act which Paul ascribes to God in connection with faith, is also the principal thing, the culminating point of His operation upon man. Forgiveness of sins, sanctification, justification, all that is most important in the work of salvation, is referred to the influence of the Spirit of God, an influence naturally in-separable from the person of the Saviour.† With the Spirit man receives all that he needs to enable him victoriously to resist sin; he no longer requires an outward commandment, a legal prescription to teach him what he ought to do, to instruct and guide him in the path of duty. Hence that familiar and important antithesis of the Law and the Gospel, the letter and the spirit, which is so prominent in the Pauline system. The old legal economy provoked transgression, and led to death, be-cause of the natural weakness of man; the new economy of the Gospel and of the Spirit, by giving man the strength which was lacking to him before, successfully subdues sin, and leads to life.‡ The life of the believer, an entirely new life, separated from all that went before it by a change so radical that it may be compared to a death followed by a resurrection, this life has henceforward as its soul and principle, the spirit, not the letter.§ The letter enjoined the circumcision of the flesh, and secured to him who observed it, to the Jew according to the law, the approval of his countrymen; the spirit effects another circumcision, which removes the impurity from the heart; and he who submits to it—an Israelite indeed—is alone sure of the approval of God.‖ We shall observe in the next chapter the practical consequence of this fact.

It is needless to add explicitly that the communication of the Spirit is always annexed to the calling. But the calling

---

* Τὸ θέλειν, τὸ ἐνεργεῖν, Phil. ii. 13.

† 1 Cor. vi. 11.

‡ Τὸ γράμμα ἀποκτείνει, τὸ δὲ πνεῦμα ζωοποιεῖ, 2 Cor. iii. 6, 8.

§ Καινότης πνεύματος, παλαιότης γράμματος, Rom. vii. 6.

‖ Rom. ii. 27, 29.

itself, being an integral element of the redemptive economy, or, in other words, inseparable from the fact of the mission of Christ, it follows that the gift of the Spirit and communion with Christ are two correlative facts. The requirements of analysis may sometimes have led science to fix differently the chronological order of the facts of regeneration ; but it will be more exact, and at the same time more safe, not to press this logical analysis too far on ground which is not properly its own. It follows, again, that the terms *" to have the Spirit of God," " the Spirit of Christ," " to be in Christ," "for Christ to be in a man,"* * are all perfectly synonymous, as is further proved by a passage in which all these are employed indiscriminately.† In fact, we cannot conceive of two sources of the Spirit which is to be communicated to man, still less of two natures in that Spirit ; the substitution of one expression for another is explained quite simply by the fact that the phases of the inner metamorphosis of the man, while they are distinguishable by theological analysis, are in their essence perfectly inseparable. We shall not be surprised, then, to find three expressions, apparently different, and even opposed to each other, united in the same passage.‡ The Spirit is the Spirit of the Lord, because it is the principle of the new life of the man in communion with Christ ; Christ Himself is the Lord of the Spirit, as the head of the community of which the Spirit is the principle ; nay, more, the Lord Himself is the Spirit, inasmuch as it is by the mystical union of the believer with the Saviour, that the new spirit enters into the man. This last expression is unquestionably the most complete and adequate of the three, but it also clearly shows, by the absolute identification of the Redeemer and the Holy Spirit, that there is in all this no approach as yet to metaphysical speculation concerning a trinity of persons in the Deity.§

* Πνεῦμα θεοῦ ἔχειν, πνεῦμα Χριστοῦ ἔχειν, Χριστοῦ εἶναι, Χριστὸν ἔν τινι εἶναι.
† Rom. viii. 9, 10.
‡ 2 Cor. iii. 17, 18, Πνεῦμα κυρίου, κυρίου πνεύματος, ὁ κύριος τὸ πνεῦμα.
§ We may observe in passing, what is indeed a consequence of the remarks just made, namely, that the communication of the Holy Spirit,

This communication of the Holy Spirit completes the operation of God in regard to the work of faith. Henceforward, the man in whom all that we have just described has been accomplished, stands in an entirely new relation to his Creator. This relationship is that of a *child of God.** It is by the possession of the Spirit that we recognize ourselves as God's children.†

We ought, perhaps, to have reserved our remarks on this relation till we have noticed the other parts of the system yet to be treated, in order to complete the picture of regeneration. Paul himself seems to make it the crown of evangelical doctrine, which he reaches only at the close of his exposition of free salvation and justification by faith—that is to say, in the eighth chapter of the Epistle to the Romans, and immediately before writing its sublime and eloquent peroration. As we have adopted, however, on mature reflection, a plan according to which we shall treat in succession of the part taken by God, by Christ, and by man in the work of redemption, this particular point—the sonship of Christians—naturally belongs here. The institution of this relation is, in truth, an act of God. The word which Paul employs to designate it‡ properly signifies adoption, and this signification harmonizes perfectly

---

otherwise called inspiration, has essentially a moral end. In this respect there is no difference between Paul and his colleagues. Much more rarely is it a question of intellectual *illumination* (1 Cor. ii. 12, and foll. ; iii. 40 ; Eph. i. 17 ; iii. 5 ; Col. i. 9). Divine teaching is then compared to a light. Paganism was in darkness (Eph. v. 8). Judaism had yet a veil upon its eyes (2 Cor. iii. 13, and foll.) With the Gospel light comes, φωτισμός, φῶς (2 Cor. vi. 14 ; Col. i. 12 ; 2 Cor. iv. 4, and foll. ; Eph. i. 18 ; iii. 9), so that the believers live in full daylight, in the clear noon. But the apostle still urges that this light does not exclude ignorance merely, but also vice, the child of night (1 Thess. v. 5 ; Eph. v. 9 ; Rom. xiii. 12). Can it be needful to add that inspiration and illumination, in all the possible meanings of those words, are the heritage of all true believers, and not the prerogative of a few ? .

* Ὅσοι πνεύματι θεοῦ ἄγονται, οὗτοί εἰσι τέκνα (υἱοὶ) θεοῦ, Rom. viii. 14, and foll. ; ix. 8 ; Eph. v. 1 ; Phil. ii. 15 ; comp. Gal. iii. 26.

† Gal. iv. 6.

‡ υἱοθεσία.

with the idea we are now analyzing. For God adopts us; He declares His willingness to recognize us as His children,* inasmuch as by our fellowship with His only Son, who is perfection itself, we are made sharers in that perfection, and consequently in the love of God.† Paul, however, intends by this term less the act of adoption than the filial relation which follows on it, with the accessory idea of the boundless confidence with which a child throws himself into the arms of his father.‡ The designation of God as our Father is of such frequent occurrence that it seems needless to cite passages in proof of it.

This idea, or the fact of the filial relation of the believer to God, has a practical importance in the system as a whole. We may observe, first, the contrast between this relation and that which preceded it. Under the law, man was a slave; now he is free, § a child of the house. The¯fear which once tormented him gives place to love.‖ But as a child, he is also an heir ¶ of his father, a co-heir with the Son of God, and has claims which could never belong to the slave. We shall have occasion to allude again to this idea.

In concluding this chapter upon the operation of God in the work of faith, we would direct the reader's attention, by the analysis of one more passage,** to the fact that in the mind of Paul all these ideas are found associated together in the manner in which we have set them forth. "*Knowing*," he writes

* Eph. i. 5.

† It is as a simple consequence of the use of the figure that the children of God are called the brethren of Christ (Rom. viii. 29); but this expression takes away from the mystical character of the other.

‡ Rom. ix. 4; viii. 15; Gal. iv. 5. The use of the Syro-Chaldaic 'Αββᾶ is explained by the simplicity of the feeling which dictates the prayer. The latter was habitually offered in the sacred language, even by persons who, like Paul, used only Greek in common conversation. Compare Mark xiv. 36.

§ 'Ελεύθερος, Gal. v. 13.

‖ Rom. viii. 14, and foll.

¶ Κληρονόμος, Gal. iv. 7.

** 1 Thess. i. 4, 5. We must not forget that these are the earliest lines we possess of the apostle's writings.

to the Thessalonians, "brethren beloved, your election of God," (he knew it by the very success he had had among them,) "for our Gospel" (the outward and occasional cause of conversion) "came not unto you in word only," (which might have been the case if the calling had been a mere invitation,) "but also in power" (calling being always an efficacious act,) "and in the Holy Ghost," (communicated with the calling,) "and in much assurance" (on your part, the effect being your filial trust in God your Saviour).

CHAPTER XIV.

OF REGENERATION.

HAVING traced out the line of Paul's remarks on the direct action of God in the work of salvation, we proceed to look at man himself, and to take into consideration that which passes within him,—the result of the calling and communication of the Holy Spirit. It follows, from all that has gone before, that it is only in a very limited sense we can speak here of an act of the man himself. We have already sufficiently shown that, in truth, it is God alone who acts in all that is most essential to salvation.

Thus it is needless to say that, in regard to divine election, man has absolutely nothing to do; for this first act of the supreme will is accomplished before the very birth of the individual.

We pass, then, at once to the second act—the calling. What is the position of man in relation to this? Let us bear in mind that calling, in the language of Paul, is never a simple invitation, which might be of itself without direct or necessary influence upon the individual will. On the contrary, the effect is sure and infallible. Submission to the call, or, as it may be put, the act of surrender to the invitation of God, being an implied necessity, it is evident that this act also is produced by the divine will. Now, as the calling reaches the man through the outward form of preaching, the corresponding result will be an eager hearing, an obedience,* which may be

---

* ὑπακοή, Rom. vi. 16; comp. x. 17, and foll.; ὑπακούειν τῷ εὐαγγελίῳ, x. 16; ὑπακοὴ Χριστοῦ, 2 Cor. x. 5; ὑπακοὴ πίστεως, Rom. i. 5.

characterized either by the subject of the preaching (obedience to the Gospel and to Christ), or by the feeling with which it is received (the obedience of faith).

So far the theory. But we here find ourselves confronted with a new illustration of the fact we have already had occasion to point out, namely, that Paul does not adhere rigorously to his principle, and that in practice he asserts the claims of human'freedom quite as unhesitatingly as in theory he had vindicated the absolute and independent will of God. More than once he speaks of this obedience as a free and spontaneous act of the man.* The apostles are commissioned to invite all nations, but the appeal is not always crowned with success.† In truth, it cannot be said that this mode of expression is in contradiction with the other; for those who do not obey may always be regarded as not having been called. Nevertheless, this last use of the word belongs evidently to a different train of thought from the former, and one in which the theological idea of the calling is completely lost.

The calling is followed immediately by the communication of the Holy Spirit, and by this faith is wrought. We have, then, here to consider more particularly the change which takes place in a man in connection with this twofold divine dispensation. Here, again, we shall first place ourselves at the theoretical standpoint.

We have shown already that faith is essentially a mystical union with Christ, an abdication, therefore, of the man's own individuality, and that the communication of the Holy Spirit causes a complete metamorphosis of the human being, as to the conditions of his spiritual existence. From these two elements results the notion of regeneration—that is to say, of

---

* Rom. i. 5 ; xv. 18 ; xvi. 26.

† Rom. x. 16 ; 2 Thess. i. 8. Compare also the expressions ἀπείθεια, ἀπειθεῖν, Rom. xi. 30, and foll.; xv. 31 ; υἱοὶ τῆς ἀπειθείας, Eph. ii. 2 ; v. 6 ; Col. iii. 6, which are synonymous, etymologically and theologically, of ἄπιστος, ἀπιστία, Rom. xi. 20, and foll. ; Titus i. 15, etc. These last terms are also used simply to designate the Gentiles, without implying the idea of a rejection of the Gospel (1 Cor. vi. 6 ; vii. 12, and foll. ; x. 27 ; xiv. 22, and foll. ; 1 Tim. v. 8, etc.)

a change so complete that the new state is in all points the opposite of the old, and that, from the spiritual point of view, nothing is transmitted from the latter to the former. " Old things are passed away," says the apostle ; " behold, all things are become new." *

The idea of regeneration, like that of faith, is one of the most fundamental in the system of Paul. It expresses the great act of the life, as faith expresses the relation, the influence on which all the rest depends. It is clear that these two ideas are correlatives.

It is to be observed that the very term regeneration, now so familiar to us, is found only once in the writings of the apostle Paul.† The reason is that the religious feeling was not as yet governed by scientific requirements, as has been increasingly the case with the theologians of the Church. The idea itself, however, occurs repeatedly and under the most various forms. We shall attempt to collect and classify these expressions.

We have first those which convey the idea of a spiritual creation, forming a parallel with the physical creation or the natural birth of man. In this aspect the regenerate is spoken of as *a new creature. God's handiwork;* he is said to be created *in Christ, by Christ, after God.* We need not dwell on the fact that creation is here ascribed sometimes to God, sometimes to Christ; this is only a confirmation of that which we have already remarked more than once on the relation of the two persons. ‡

We have, again, the numerous passages in which the idea of renovation is made prominent, the image of a new man

---

* Εἴ τις ἐν Χριστῷ, καινὴ κτίσις, 2 Cor. v. 17.

† Παλιγγενεσία, Titus iii. 5. None of the other writers of the New Testament use it. In Matt. xix. 28, it has quite another sense, and refers to Jewish eschatology.

‡ Καινὴ κτίσις, Gal. vi. 15 ; ποίημα θεοῦ, Eph. ii. 9 ; κτισθέντες ἐν Χριστῷ, v. 10, or κατὰ θεόν, iv. 24; Χριστὸς ὁ κτίσας, Col. iii. 10 ; 1 Cor. viii. 6. Let us here note, in passing, the figurative expression νέον φύραμα, new leaven (1 Cor. v. 7), borrowed from the sacred rites of the Passover Feast. This figure occurs again in Rom. xi. 16, and without the adjective, which shows how familiar it was in the homiletic style of the apostle.

in contrast with the old.* As this renewing consists in the substitution of a set of good qualities for a corresponding set of bad, Paul delights in using a frequent figure of the Old Testament, and speaks of a change of garments. The popular rhetoric of Hebrew literature was wont to say of a moral quality, such as courage, justice, or any other, that it became the girdle of the reins. Thus, the apostle also says, Put off the old and put on the new man;† and he even indulges in longer or ·shorter allegories developing the same comparison, and adding to it that of military armour. ‡

A third descriptive and figurative expression, analogous to those we have just named, is that of a metamorphosis, a change of form.§ The new form to be appropiated is naturally that of Christ, to whom we are henceforth to be *conformed.*|| This is indeed a mere figure, and in itself a very inadequate one, for regeneration consists in something altogether different from a change of outward form. It is the spiritual nature of the man which is to undergo a complete change, and the word *form* is far from exhausting this idea. We may make the same remark in reference to the expression *putting on Christ,*¶ which also fails adequately to convey the idea of regeneration, if we adhere to the etymological meaning of the word. To this we shall advert again.

The term which we might expect to meet with here rather than any other, and which is so frequent in other books of the New Testament, that which we have translated by amendment, conversion, or repentance, occurs but very rarely in Paul's epistles. In three passages ** it has no meaning beyond a moral reformation, in the common acceptation of the word.

* Καινός, νέος, παλαιὸς ἄνθρωπος, Eph. ii. 15; iv. 22, and foll.; Rom. vi. 6; Col. iii. 9; ἀνακαινοῦσθαι, ἀνανεοῦσθαι, Col. iii. 10; Eph. iv. 23; 2 Cor. iv. 16; ἀνακαίνωσις, Rom. xii. 2; Titus iii. 5.

† Ἐκ-ἐνδύσασθαι, Eph. iv. 22, 24; Col. iii. 9, 10.

‡ Eph. vi. 11—17; Rom. xiii. 12; 1 Thess. v. 8; Col. iii. 12.

§ Μεταμορφοῦσθαι, Rom. xii. 2.

|| Σύμμορφοι εἶναι, Rom. viii. 29; comp. κατ᾽ εἰκόνα, Col. iii. 10.

¶ Χριστὸν ἐνδύσασθαι, Rom. xiii. 14; Gal. iii. 27.

** Μετάνοια, Rom. ii. 4; 2 Cor. vii. 9; xii. 21.

Only once* is it employed of the conversion of the Gentiles to Christianity. It is obvious that the term did not seem to the apostle adapted to convey in all its fulness his conception of regeneration.†

If we pass on to a more detailed analysis of that conception, we shall at once discover in it two elements easily to be distinguished, though inseparable in fact—the cessation of an old and the commencement of a new condition. If we adopt the image of a birth for the latter, that of a death naturally suggests itself for the former. We have already found the same figure of death representing vice and its punishment; we meet with it here in a third application, different from the two former, namely, as the destruction of the evil elements—that is, of sin, or of the flesh—in man.

This destruction is, then, the result of the act of regeneration, or, to speak more exactly, is one of its constituent elements. It is in this sense Paul says to the Romans, "Reckon ye yourselves to be dead indeed unto sin, but alive unto God through Jesus Christ our Lord."‡

Regeneration, as comprising these two elements of a death and a resurrection, is naturally placed in direct relation with the death and resurrection of Jesus Christ. This relation has been understood by some as if the historical fact were a symbol of the psychological, and had furnished the figurative phraseology used concerning it. But the idea of the apostle goes unquestionably far beyond a mere ideal analogy, and sets before us the fact of an objective and real relation.

We are thus brought once again into the region of evangelical mysticism; what we have set before us is nothing less than identification with the death and the life of the Saviour, and

---

* 2 Tim. ii. 25.

† Nor does it; and the common use of this term, as though it were equivalent to regeneration, is a sign of theological decadence.—ED.

‡ Λογίζεσθε ἑαυτοὺς νεκροὺς μὲν εἶναι τῇ ἁμαρτίᾳ, ζῶντας δὲ τῷ θεῷ ἐν Χριστῷ Ἰησοῦ, Rom. vi. 11. This passage must not be confounded with another (ch. viii. 10) which belongs to a different train of thought, and which treats of the physical mortality resulting from sin, and of the spiritual life in Christ, which is the pledge of the future resurrection.

all that is figurative is the expression, since the reference is
not to the physical existence of the Christian. The believer,
says Paul, dies with Christ to rise again with Him; and this
phrase is not to be explained away as a mere play upon words
or an ingenious analogy; it is the application of the great
principle of personal union, according to which the personal
existence of the man is really lost ·in that of Christ, who
repeats, so to speak, His own life, with its two main facts,
in every individual who surrenders himself to Him. A whole
set of terms derived from this parallelism might be quoted
in support of the view which we have just advanced as the
only one admissible. We have, for example, the expressions
*to be crucified, to die, to be buried, to be raised again, to live
with Christ.** The whole is summed up in this saying, " If we
are planted together" (united by spiritual coalescence) "in the
likeness of His death, we shall be also in the likeness of His
resurrection."† In this phrase, the word *coalescence*, or *plant-
ing together*, borrowed from vegetation, describes the mystical
union; the term *likeness* shows the inadequacy of the figure
to the reality of the fact; the *resurrection*, according to the
context, must be understood not of the future resurrection of
the body, but of the spiritual resurrection now realized; the
future tense only expresses the certainty of the result when
once the causes are admitted as really existing.

With this idea of regeneration Paul associates the Christian
rite of baptism. This rite, it need scarcely be said, has for
him, as for the Church in general, the ordinary signification,
namely, that of a consecration of those who are entering the
community. We shall have to speak of it again presently in

---

* Συσταυροῦσθαι, συναποθνήσκειν, συνθάπτεσθαι, συνεγείρεσθαι, συζωοποιεῖσθαι,
συζῆν, Rom. vi. 4—8; Col. ii. 11—13; iii. 1; 2 Tim. ii. 11; Gal. ii. 19;
v. 24; vi. 14. In Eph. ii. 5, 6, a passage the terms of which seem to
demand a similar explanation, some distinguished exegetes, basing their
opinions upon the close of the sentence, prefer to refer the whole to the
future resurrection. It would be safer to say that here the two ideas are
blended.

† Εἰ σύμφυτοι γεγόναμεν τῷ ὁμοιώματι τοῦ θανάτου τοῦ Χριστου, καὶ τῆς ἀναστάσεως
ἐσόμεθα, Rom. vi. 5.

this aspect. But Paul explains it also in a special manner,
which may be noticed here. The form in which baptism was
originally administered, that of a total immersion of the person
in water, suggests to him the idea of a double parallelism of
baptism with the two phases of regeneration, and with the
death and resurrection of Christ. The death of the old man,
the burial of the Saviour, and immersion in baptism, are
parallel and correlative facts; * and, unquestionably, the new
moral birth, the resurrection of Christ, and the coming up
out of the water, are so likewise, though not in any passage
explicitly so stated.† But Paul is speaking also of the baptism
of regeneration in a more popular manner, and without allusion
to the mystical ideas associated with that fact, when he
regards it as the symbol of a moral purification, a symbolic
washing. ‡

It only remains for us to speak of the effects of regeneration.
These have been already touched upon in the chapter devoted
to the definition of faith, and in that which treated of the
communication of the Holy Spirit; we have only now to add
those elements and new theological terms which our present
special point of view supplies.

Regeneration is followed by a new life, a life necessarily
opposed in all things to that which went before, opposite in
its principle, tendency, and acts. §

Here, again, we cannot but admire the variety and fulness
of the theological language of our author. Sometimes he is
content to characterize the second period of the life of the

* Συνετάφημεν τῷ Χριστῷ διὰ τοῦ βαπτίσματος εἰς τὸν θάνατον, Rom. vi. 4;
comp. Col. ii. 11.

† The phrase βαπτίζεσθαι εἰς τὸν θάνατον Χριστοῦ is thus explained. It is
difficult to say if this same parallelism is present to the mind of the
apostle when he says simply βαπτίζεσθαι εἰς Χριστὸν (Gal. iii. 27), or if he
has then in view only spiritual communion generally. Rom. vi. 3
might be brought forward in support of the first explanation ; 1 Cor.
x. 2 of the latter.

‡ Καθαρίζειν, λοῦτρον, ἀπολούειν, Eph. v. 26; 1 Cor. vi. 11; λοῦτρον
παλιγγενεσίας, Titus iii. 5 ; comp. ii. 14.

§ Ἐν καινότητι ζωῆς περιπατήσωμεν, Rom. vi. 4.

converted man by the psychological fact which we have
found lying at the basis of his system; he speaks of *living
in the Spirit, walking after the Spirit, and not after the
flesh;* * and the idea suggested is not of the natural man
obeying by preference his own right principle, but of the
regenerate man, obedient to the Spirit of God, which is given
him to be his constant guide.   In other passages, the union of
the believer with God and Christ is but vaguely intimated,
and we are led to think rather of an outward submission:
he is said to *live unto God, unto the Lord.*†   This idea is
more fully defined by a series of expressions which mark a
consecration to God, and consequently a corresponding forsaking
of the service of the flesh.‡

Believers are *consecrated in Christ Jesus, by the Holy Ghost,*§
the new vital principle excluding the old.   The corresponding
Greek word is commonly translated by our word *sanctified,*
and we do not deny that practically the idea is the same.
But the etymological signification should not be slighted; it
is richer and more in harmony with the general tone of the
theology we are studying.   That which is called the *sanctification of the Spirit* ‖ is then properly this same consecration, inasmuch as it is wrought by the Spirit of God; and as it
cannot take place without faith, Christ is *our sanctification;*¶
that is to say, this consecration is the result of our relation to the Saviour.   Sanctification is, then, the normal state
of the believer.**   Hence, again, the frequent designation of
the members of the Church by a term which properly signifies the devoted or consecrated †† ones, and which we very

* Ζῆν πνεύματι, Gal. v. 25 ; κατὰ πνεῦμα περιπατεῖν οὐ κατὰ σάρκα, Rom. viii.
4—13 ; com. Gal. iii. 3.

† Ζῆν τῷ θεῷ, Rom. vi. 11; Gal. ii. 19 ; τῷ κυρίῳ, Rom. xiv. 8; 2 Cor.
v. 15.

‡ Ἡγιάσθαι, 1 Cor. vi. 11.

§ Ἡγιασμένοι ἐν χριστῷ, 1 Cor. i, 2 ; ἐν πν. ἁγίῳ, Rom. xv. 16.

‖ Ἁγιασμὸς πνεύματος, 2 Thess. ii. 13.

¶ 1 Cor. i. 30.

** Rom. vi. 22 ; 1 Thess. iv. 3, and foll. ; 1 Tim. ii. 15, etc.

†† Ἅγιοι.—Ἡγιάσθαι, 1 Cor. vii. 14, to belong to the community.

inaptly translate *saints*, a term which would imply a proud and Pharisaic assumption of peculiar virtue.

But the apostle delights also to present in a yet more complete manner the idea, that the life of believers is to be henceforward the adequate expression of a perfect union with Christ, a life in Christ, a life of Christ in them.* We have already spoken of the figurative term, *to put on Christ*. It cannot be a sufficient explanation to suppose that this represents only in a general manner the moral qualities of the Christian. It is more natural to explain it as embodying the fact, that the regenerate man only begins to live as he becomes identified with the life of Christ.

We shall not need to carry further the analysis of this idea of a new life, so as to derive from it its practical consequences, or (to use the language of our day) to write a chapter on Christian ethics, enumerating the special duties of the believer. The Spirit of God is henceforward the leader of regenerate souls which are dead to sin; it follows, then, that they will do only that which is holy, good, and agreeable to God, and that everything which can be thus characterized will commend itself to them. If we sometimes find the word *law†* used by Paul to describe the motive of the acts of Christians, he uses it simply by the force of habit, and the inconsistency is further modified by the addition of the name of Christ. It is only by way of example that the apostle enumerates, in various places, what we may call the Christian virtues; ‡ we find, therefore, that the category is not always the same, nor is it given in any systematic order. If we attempt to draw up a catalogue of the terms by which Paul describes these Christian duties, we shall at once perceive that

* Ζῶ δὲ οὐκέτι ἐγώ, ᾖ δὲ ἐν ἐμοὶ Χριστός, Gal. ii. 20 ; λογίζεσθε ἑαυτοὺς ζῶντας τῷ θεῷ ἐν Χριστῷ, Rom. vi. 11.

† Gal. vi. 2, νόμος.

‡ 'Αρεταί, Gal. v. 22 ; Phil. iv. 8. · We may also compare here the still fuller and more frequent catalogues of vices ; these may serve as the complement to the others (Rom. i. 29, and foll. ; 1 Cor. vi. 9, and foll.; 2 Tim. iii. 2, and foll. ; comp. also 1 Cor. xiii. 4, and foll. ; 1 Tim. iii. 1, and foll.)

the majority of them have been already explained as having also a theological import. Sometimes they are expressions which, before being used to designate human qualities, have served to set forth the perfections of God; sometimes, before their application to the reciprocal duties between man and man, they have determined the fundamental relations of man with his Creator and Saviour. This supplies us with a fresh proof of the close connection which unites in evangelical Christianity, that which the science of the schools has too often abruptly separated—the doctrinal and the moral. We subjoin a few of these terms which are of more frequent occurrence than the rest; and to which we may call attention in passing, without attempting anything like a systematic and complete exposition of them.

Truth * is not simply the opposite of falsehood, but represents, generally, conduct in accordance with the will of God, or we might say is the true expression of the moral ideal set before us in the divine revelation. It is in this sense that it is contrasted with malice and unrighteousness.†

Righteousness ‡ does not mean simply the particular duty of rendering to every one that which is his due, or giving of alms to the poor;§ the idea is much more comprehensive. Like truth, it is the realization of the whole will of God, and we several times find the word joined to truth as its synonym.‖ It is virtue *in abstracto* as opposed to vice;¶ obedience to the divine law in contrast to rebellion against that law; ** in other words, the sum and substance of all that is contrary to the influence of Satan,†† and the intended result of the whole teaching of revelation.‡‡ Elsewhere, this term, standing *in*

* Ἀλήθεια, 2 Cor. xi. 10; Phil. i. 18, etc.
† 1 Cor. v. 8; xiii. 6; Eph. v. 9; vi. 14; 2 Thess. ii. 10, 12.
‡ Δικαιοσύνη.
§ Col. iv. 1; 2 Cor. ix. 10.
‖ Eph. iv. 24; v. 9; vi. 14; 2 Cor. vi. 7.
¶ Rom. vi. 13, and foll.
** Rom. v. 19; 2 Cor. vi. 14.
†† 2 Cor. xi. 15.
‡‡ 2 Tim. iii. 16.

concreto for a special manifestation of the will of God, is placed at the head of a series of similar qualities.*

Peace, a pacific disposition, (as well as all the other characteristics, longsuffering, gentleness, meekness, lowliness of mind,† which serve to secure a happy harmony among the faithful,) is naturally associated with love,‡ and must be of an essentially religious character, since it is based upon the consciousness of peace with God,§ unity of spirit,‖ and community of end.¶ The faults of others will not be harshly judged by men who know that their first duty is to watch over themselves, and not to trust in their own strength, and who can never forget how they themselves have been forgiven by Christ.**

Chastity †† is connected by the very etymology of the Greek word with the general idea of holiness—that is, of an exclusive consecration to God. This point of view, among others, will help to explain the peculiar esteem in which celibacy ‡‡ was held by Paul, a sentiment not in contradiction with the respect clearly expressed by him for the marriage state.§§ It is interesting to see the apostle making use alternately of two images apparently incompatible, to represent the close and ideal union between Christ and His Church: on the one hand, the conjugal union‖‖ is made the type of this relation; on the other, the Church is a chaste virgin affianced to Christ her Saviour.¶¶ Chastity is, then, strenuously insisted upon, and carnal lusts reprobated in view of a principle which regards the body as a

* 1 Tim. vi. 11; 2 Tim. ii. 22.
† Εἰρήνη, μακροθυμία, ἐπιείκειά, πραότης, χρηστότης, ταπεινοφροσύνη.
‡ 1 Cor. iv. 21.
§ Χαρά, Gal. v. 22.
‖ Rom. xiv. 17; Eph. iv. 3; 1 Cor. xiv. 33.
¶ Rom. xiv. 19; 1 Cor. vii. 15.
** Gal. vi. 1; Eph. iv. 2; 1 Cor. x. 12; Col. iii. 12, and foll.; Titus iii. 2, and foll.
†† Ἁγνότης, ἁγνεία.
‡‡ 1 Cor. vii. 1, 8, 32, and foll.
§§ Eph. v. 28, and foll.; 1 Tim. ii. 14, etc.
‖‖ Eph. v. 32.
¶¶ 2 Cor. xi. 2.

sanctuary, the abode of the Holy Spirit. Fornication, then,* is sacrilege, a greater sin than any a man could commit against an object in itself indifferent. The Christian, remembering that he is a member of a community which is bound in all circumstances to guard its sacred character, will not only himself abstain from every transgression of this nature,† but will regard as unworthy of him any connivance or tolerance towards those who have become guilty of such sin. ‡

We might multiply these examples, and show how uniformly Paul seeks the motives to his practical teachings, in the mystical ideas which form the essence of his theology, and not in those considerations of a different order from which the morality of the schools derives them. But we will not enlarge upon this subject here, referring our readers to the remarks we shall have to make presently on faith, grace, love, and other terms susceptible of a similar ethical analysis.

All the characteristics or virtues of the Christian are called " the fruits of the Spirit," § or from a slightly different point of view, the fruits of the light,‖ of that new light with which the Spirit illuminates the path of the believer; they are also called the fruits of the Gospel or of righteousness, or, what is the same thing, the fruits of freedom from sin, and submission to God; ¶ and all these variations in the terms employed, so far from assigning different origins to the practice of the same duties, only show afresh how close is the relation between all the various parts of the system. Lastly, it is said that the believer himself bears or produces fruit unto God;** fruits, that is, agreeable to God and

* 1 Cor. vi. 13—20 ; 1 Thess. iv. 3.
† 2 Cor. vi. 6 ; 1 Tim. v. 22 ; Titus ii. 5.
‡ 2 Cor. vii. 11 ; 1 Cor. v. 9.
§ Κάρπος τοῦ πνεύματος, Gal. v. 22.
‖ Eph. v. 9, according to the corrected editions. In the received text we have πνεῦμα.
¶ Col. i. 6 ; Phil. i. 11 ; Rom. vi. 22.
** Rom. vii. 4.

accepted by Him. These fruits* are undoubtedly works;†
since, however, they are not done in obedience to an outward and legal prescription, but from an inward impulse of
the Spirit, they are characterized as *good works.*‡ They are
the result or the consequence of the faith which saves, and
thus are mediately the works of God in us; they are not
the cause of our salvation, nor do they constitute any claim
to it. We admit, however, that these expressions are akin to
those of a less mystical morality. Thus *to do good* is an Old
Testament phrase, scarcely in accordance with the premises
we have seen laid down by Paul. §

Before concluding this first part of our present chapter, we
may pause a moment to consider the condition following on
the new spiritual birth, considered as a state of liberty in
exchange for one of servitude. It will be borne in mind that
that servitude was threefold—a bondage under guilt, under
the law, under sin. We have to speak here only of the last
two points.

We are freed from the power of sin, inasmuch as the Spirit
of God, who is strong and mighty in us, helps us to overcome
the flesh, or, to speak more correctly, inasmuch as we are made
one with Christ, and that with and in Him we have overcome
sin; for to be in Christ and to sin are things mutually incompatible.‖ Freed from the bondage of sin, and henceforward
yielding obedience to God only, who guides us by His Spirit,
we attain to eternal life, as the fruit of this happy change.¶

---

* The image grows into an allegory when it is carried out into sowing
and reaping, Gal. vi. 8.

† Ἔργα, Col. i. 10.

‡ Καλὰ, 1 Tim. vi. 18, etc.; ἀγαθά, 2 Cor. ix. 8 ; 2 Thess. ii. 17 ; 1 Tim.
v. 10 ; 2 Tim. ii. 21 ; iii. 17 ; Eph. ii. 10, etc.

§ Ἐργάζεσθαι, πράσσειν, ποιεῖν τὸ ἀγαθόν, 2 Cor. v. 10; Rom. ii. 10; xiii. 3;
Gal. vi. 10 ; Eph. vi. 8 ; ὑπομονὴ ἔργου ἀγαθοῦ, Rom. ii. 7 ; perseverance in
that which is good (Phil. i. 6), ἔργον ἀγαθόν, is the work of regeneration
itself.

‖ Gal. ii. 17.

¶ Ἐλευθερωθέντες ἀπὸ τῆς ἁμαρτίας, δουλωθέντες δὲ τῷ θεῷ, ἔχετε τὸν καρπὸν ὑμῶν
. . . . εἰς ζωὴν αἰώνιον, Rom. vi. 22 ; comp. v. 18.

This fact implies another as its natural consequence, namely, deliverance from the thraldom of the law. The law, in fact, so far from preventing the transgression of the commandments of God, or aiding in the fulfilment of duty, placed an obstacle in the way of obedience, and stimulated to sin. So long as it remains, it produces the same results, and freedom from sin cannot be real and final while the law continues in force. But we have no more need of the law. Instead of it, we have the Spirit of God to direct us, to prompt our actions; and this motive power, which has far more affinity with our new nature than the law had with the old, exerts also a far more powerful influence over us. The liberty which is in Christ is then at the same time opposed to the slavery of the law.* The law is done away,† not in the sense of denying its divine origin or the authority of its oracles,‡ but as a code in force to govern our lives;§ living by the new life which we have in Christ, we are dead to the law, || it has no more dominion over us. For the justified man, there is in theory no law.¶ To say that Paul means only that the ritual portion of the law is done away in Christ, while the moral retains its old position, is to show a misapprehension of the very rudiments of his system.

The delight in parallels which suggested so many of the technical terms used by the apostle, leads him to give the name of *law* here to the new order of things as to the old, though, in reality, the difference between the two is just this, that in the new there is no law. It is, so to speak, a new constitution in place of an old and abrogated constitution; the constitution of the spirit or of faith,**—one, that is, of which the spirit and faith are the fundamental principles, instead of

---

* Ἐλευθερία ἐν Χρ.—δουλεία τοῦ νόμου, Gal. v. 1, 13, 18 ; 2 Cor. iii. 17.
† Κατήργηται.
‡ Rom. iii. 31.
§ 2 Cor. iii. 11, and foll. ; Eph. ii. 15.
|| Κατηργήθημεν ἀπὸ τοῦ νόμου ἀποθανόντες, Rom. vii. 6.
¶ 1 Tim. i. 9 ; Gal. v. 23.
** Rom. viii. 2 ; iii. 27 ; contrast with Eph. ii. 15.

a constitution based upon a law expressed by letter and precept. Entering into this new constitution, I become an alien to the former—dead to it,* as it were; and the idea of the new birth is prominent in the whole of this series of images. In a word, *an order of things* based upon the operation of the Divine Spirit who sustains my *life* in Christ, *has made me free from an order of things* in which the operation of legal prescription † constantly ministered to the power of *sin* and led me to *death*. ‡ The slight ellipsis in this passage, notable in our translation, is easily filled up by a number of passages already quoted.

As we have observed, however, the term *law* is not properly applicable to the new order of things. The antithesis is more truly expressed by the terms law and grace.§ The latter marks much more clearly the radical change wrought in the relation between man and God, and by dispensing with that terrible name *law*, it brings us, if we may so say, into more full and free enjoyment of our liberty.

As to that liberty itself, it is surely not necessary that we should be reminded of Paul's warning against mistaking it for the absence of all rule, restraint, or duty—immoral license and lawlessness,‖ in the bad sense commonly attached to that word. On the contrary, a new obedience or subjection takes the place of the old; but while the latter was compulsory, hard, and hateful, the former is free, natural, and makes us happy.¶ In many passages this word *slavery*, which might seem at first repulsive, is used by the apostle as if expressly to remind us that man's true happiness, whether present or future, is to be found only in submission to God and to Christ. The term *servant*, or slave, when it occurs in the inscriptions

---

* Διὰ νόμου νόμῳ ἀπέθανον, Gal. ii. 19.

† Rom. vii. 16.

‡ Ὁ νόμος τοῦ πνεύματος τῆς ζωῆς ἐν Χριστῷ Ἰησοῦ ἠλευθέρωσέ με ἀπὸ τοῦ νόμου τῆς ἁμαρτίας καὶ τοῦ θανάτου, Rom. viii. 2.

§ Rom. vi. 14, 15.

‖ Ἀνομία, vice, crime, wickedness, impiety, Heb. v. 13; 1 Cor. ix. 21.

¶ Ὥστε δουλεύειν ἡμᾶς ἐν καινότητι πνεύματος καὶ οὐ παλαιότητι γράμματος, Rom. vii. 6.

of the epistles simply relates to the apostolic mission;[*] but elsewhere it has a wider meaning. The Christian is the slave or servant of God,[†] of righteousness,[‡] of the law of God,[§] as he once was the slave of sin and evil passions, and free from righteousness,[||]—rebellious, that is, against the law of righteousness.

The view we have just taken of the fact of regeneration brings it before us in the light of an instantaneous act, circumscribed within a space of time comparatively very brief; as an act consisting in the evolution of two phases, really distinct but closely connected, and most of all as an act complete and absolute in itself, not liable to any restriction or subsequent change. This essential character is not only asserted by very positive texts, but is a corollary of the theory previously demonstrated.

This theory, however, is not supported by experience. We do not find anywhere a regenerate man in whom no sin remains; nor were there any such men in the times of the apostle. In the very communities which he had founded, and in which he gathered his most faithful adherents, he perpetually discovered defects, errors, transgressions of every kind; and even in his own heart[¶] he could trace that which would have forbidden him, had he been so disposed, to believe in the realization of Christian perfection, or of a faith which should leave nothing to be desired.

We shall not, then, wonder to find in his epistles another set of expressions, and another train of thought, in which regeneration is represented rather as a matter of slow and gradual accomplishment, as a tendency, as a struggle. From this point of view we can understand the many exhortations,

---

[*] Rom. i. 1; Phil. i. 1; Titus i. 1; comp. Phil. ii. 22; Col. iv. 12.

[†] Rom. vi. 22; 1 Thess. i. 9; 1 Cor. vii. 22; Gal. i. 10; Eph. vi. 6; Rom. xiv. 18; Col. iii. 24; 2 Tim. ii. 24.

[‡] Rom. vi. 18, and foll.

[§] Rom. vii. 25.

[||] Ἐλεύθερος τῇ δικαιοσύνῃ, Rom. vi. 20.

[¶] Phil. iii. 11, and foll.

encouragements, warnings, reproaches, even threats, addressed
by him to the readers of his epistles, and which upon the
former theory are inexplicable.

An attempt has often been made to get rid of the contradiction between these two aspects of the same truth, by regarding
regeneration as the starting-point of a new life, an important
and decisive crisis, marking, so to speak, the date of a revolution in the man, after which a progressive amelioration will
become manifest in him, a greater facility of the spirit in
overcoming the flesh, new power to rise again from every fall,
and a happier assurance of pardon.

Our texts, however, do not favour this explanation. The
passages cited above are categorical. The theory makes no
exceptions. The idea of death applied to the renunciation of
sin implies absolute separation from the old infirmities; nay,
more, the preterite tense is used as referring to something
finally accomplished.* Nowhere do we find the apostle
speaking of a victory over the flesh henceforward rendered
more easy; such an expression would seem like an excuse,
a feeble compromise. The death and the resurrection are in
close and inseparable connection; were it otherwise, the relation with Christ, in view of which these mystical terms are
chosen, would have no existence; for Christ could not, being
once dead, remain in the tomb, nor could His resurrection be
an incomplete or gradual thing. Lastly, nothing is further
from the thought of the apostle, than any endeavour to accom-
modate to the weakness and indolence of man, a spiritual
transformation which ought to gain the full mastery of every
power of his being. Nor must we forget that all the expressions here used to designate a gradual moral amelioration, have
already had their meaning very clearly defined in the opposite
theory.

We cannot, then, in this way reconcile this theory with
practical life,—that is, with the language dictated by experience and by the necessities arising out of positive facts. The
reconciliation must be sought in some other way, and from a

* Rom. vi., *passim.*

point of view to which we shall have occasion to resort more than once.

The theory brings before us an ideal to which the reality does not correspond, but we need not on this account tamper with the theory, or lower the ideal, impoverishing it and detracting from its grandeur and beauty. On the contrary, this ideal should remain before the eyes of all, as a mirror in which they may easily and truthfully discern their own blemishes and shortcomings. The more they behold themselves in this mirror, the more should they be stimulated and encouraged to rise to the ideal set before them; and its grandeur and elevation will be the motive and measure of their progress. In all the spheres of his activity, man pursues an ideal end; the more exalted and difficult that end is of attainment, the nobler and grander will the effort be; and Christianity would never have helped on the progress of humanity, or would soon have ceased to do so, if the ideal it set before the community and the individual had been too low, too easily within the reach of our wonted indolence. Nothing is more opposed to the spirit of the Gospel, or more fatal to the morality which it would inspire, than any deception practised upon ourselves or others, as to the distance which ever separates us from the ideal, whether by representing it as less elevated than it really is, or by estimating too highly our own attainments. Vulgar rationalism has fallen into the first of these errors; pietism and Methodism have not always avoided the second. It would be hard to say which of the two is the more really contrary to the Gospel, or which has done most to falsify its precepts.

Theory and practice are two distinct things, and must not be confounded; each speaks its own language; we must guard against amalgamating the assertions relating to the two, or endeavouring to explain or modify the one by the other. Our duty is to show the radical difference between them.

According to the theory, wherever there is faith there is a new creature;* whoever has become a new creature sins no

* 2 Cor. v. 17.

more;* he who sins, then, is not a new creature,† and has not faith.‡ In actual fact we nowhere find this entire absence of sin; it cannot, therefore, be said that faith and regeneration, according to the theoretical view of them, have any real existence at all.

The theoretical deals with us as Christians; the practical exhorts us to become such. It is doubtless strange to see the apostle in his epistles perpetually blending these two points of view, and addressing his readers sometimes as if they were perfect Christians, at other times as if they needed to be gravely warned that they are yet far from such perfection. This difficulty disappears, however, when we take into account the individuality of the writer, who is ever ready at once enthusiastically to embrace the ideal which he sets before him, and at the same time to pay as much regard as the most impassive observer, to actual needs and natural capabilities. Rarely do we find united in the same person qualities so dissimilar and yet so really harmonious; and the incapacity of most men to place themselves in the same mental attitude, has furnished the official theology of the Church with some paragraphs equally singular and unfortunate.

According to the theory, the old man and sin are by the fact of regeneration *dead*. In the language of fact, all men, even those who belong to the Church, are exhorted to crucify both the one and the other.§

According to the theory, the fact of regeneration calls into existence a new man; it is spoken of as a *complete* renewal. In the language of experience, this renewing is a psychical phenomenon repeated day by day.‖

According to the theory, the fact of regeneration implies the idea of a change fully accomplished, by which the believer adopts or receives *immediately* the likeness of Christ. In

* Rom. vi. 6.
† Rom. viii. 7.
‡ Rom. vi. 16.
§ Νεκροῦν, θανατοῦν, Col. iii. 5 ; Rom. viii. 13.
‖ 2 Cor. iv. 16.

the language of experience, the apostle feels all the throes of childbirth for his yet imperfect disciples *till Christ be formed in them.*[*]

According to the theory, the calling and communication of the Holy Spirit imply the fulness of conviction, which, as it is itself only the beginning of faith, cannot be imperfect where faith itself is deemed to be perfect. In the language of practical life, the apostle labours to bring his converts into this full assurance, to make known to them the mystery of God and of Christ.[†]

According to the theory, Christians are consecrated to God, are pure, sanctified, holy, as surely as they are baptized and justified. In the language of experience, the sanctification which is ever the will of God,[‡] is the subject of exhortations addressed to men in whom it is not yet realized,[§] and prayer is ever offered to God that He would fulfil it in the believers.[||] When theology speaks of sanctification as of a fresh stage in the life of the Christian, subsequent to the moment of regeneration, it is not expressing the idea of Paul. Regeneration, in his theory, implies sanctification as it implies faith. Sanctification might be called a state succeeding regeneration, if the Greek word and the texts allowed us to take it as the synonym of *continuous holiness.* But this is not so. On the other hand, a continuous sanctification, that is to say the act of becoming sanctified by degrees, supposes an incomplete regeneration—an idea altogether alien to the theory which recognizes only that which is perfect.

According to the theory, the believer is always guided by the Holy Spirit, and Christ already lives in him. In the language of practical life, we find the necessity constantly reiterated, that the believer should be strengthened and sustained by means of apostolic exhortations, so that even the

---

[*] Gal. iv. 19, ἄχρις οὗ μορφωθῇ Χριστὸς.
[†] Col. ii. 2; comp. i. 9, 10.
[‡] 1 Thess. iv. 3, 7.
[§] 2 Cor. vii. 1; Rom. vi. 19.
[||] 1 Thess. v. 23.

apostle himself needs such help.* Christians are charged to watch and to stand fast.† It is always possible that they may fail to do so sufficiently,‡ and the apostle prays God to grant them§ (as if they did not yet possess) one good gift after another, without which, according to the theory, they could not be Christians at all.

Lastly, theoretically God is the Saviour of men; in practical language man is exhorted to work out his own salvation. ‖

We shall not wonder then to find the same practical exhortations speaking of a growth and progress in faith;¶ while in theory, faith is produced by divine power, and as a correlative of regeneration must be a thing positive and complete in itself, an imperfect faith not deserving the name.

In a word, the life of the Christian will be, in reality, a progressive movement, receiving its impulse from faith, and tending towards an end which theory sets before it as an ideal already realized, but which is actually so only in the person of Christ, from whom this theory has consequently borrowed the outlines of its portrait. Let us grow up into Christ, it is said, in all things, until we come to the fulness of the measure of the stature of a man in Christ.** In this allegory, the figure is taken from the growth of the human body. Imperfect Christians are compared to children.†† They are weak ‡‡ as children, especially in that their religious and moral consciousness has not as yet been able to free itself, whether from the superstitions of paganism, or from the asceticism of the synagogue. When they have arrived at perfection, they are called

---

* Rom. i. 11, 12 ; xvi. 25 ; 1 Thess. iii. 2, 13 ; 2 Thess. iii. 3.

† 1 Cor. xvi. 13 ; Phil. i. 27 ; 2 Thess. ii. 15, etc.

‡ 1 Thess. iii. 8 ; 1 Tim. ii. 15.

§ Eph. iii. 16, 17.

‖ Κατεργάζεσθε, Phil. ii. 12.

¶ 2 Cor. x.15.

** Αὐξήσωμεν εἰς Χριστὸν τὰ πάντα, μέχρι καταντήσωμεν εἰς ἄνδρα τέλειον, εἰς μέτρον ἡλικίας τοῦ πληρώματος τοῦ Χριστοῦ, Eph. iv. 13—15.

†† Νήπιοι, 1 Cor. iii. 1 ; Eph. iv. 14.

‡‡ Ἀσθενεῖς, ἀδύνατοι, 1 Cor. viii., passim ; ix. 22 ; Rom. xiv. 1, and foll. ; xv. 1 ; 1 Thess. v. 14.

adults,* as regards their understanding, their feelings, and in short all the qualities which constitute a Christian. Perfection itself, the sum of all the dispositions befitting the believer,† is called the full stature of Christ. The progress towards this end is analogous to physical development,‡ from which, however, it is carefully distinguished by a qualification which raises it into a higher sphere.§

* Τέλειοι, δύνατοι, 1 Cor. ii. 6; xiv. 20; Phil. iii. 15; Col. iv. 12.

† Τελειότης ἐν Χριστῷ, Col. i. 28; iii. 14.

‡ Τελειοῦσθαι, Phil. iii. 12.

§ Αὔξησις τοῦ θεοῦ, Col. ii. 19. [St. Paul's teaching cannot be rightly apprehended unless the principle which Reuss has illustrated at such length in the last few pages is constantly remembered. The oscillation of his thoughts between the "idea" of the Christian life and the actual life of Christian men is incessant. It is necessary, however, to remember that there was a moment in the history of every man who has received Christ, when the divine force which is ultimately to realize itself in the "idea" entered into the very centre of his personal life. That moment is critical and supreme. All that comes after it is but the development and revelation of an energy which then became the law of the man's life. —ED.]

CHAPTER XV.

OF REDEMPTION.

WE have now to consider, from a third and last point of view, the fact of the spiritual metamorphosis which the apostle includes under the general term of *faith*. Having already spoken of the operation of God and the experience of man, we have yet to regard this change in its relation to the work of Christ. It need scarcely be said that in all this the main fact remains ever the same. But this third point of view of which we are now speaking is of essential importance, since the Gospel teaches that it is through the mediation of Christ the salvation of man is effected. We shall then here find, side by side with the fact, as we have already recognized it, a new series of theological terms, for which the science of the Church has from the earliest days shown a peculiar preference. This phraseology corresponds with the three ideas of redemption, justification, and reconciliation; ideas directly based upon the doctrine of substitution, which we have already had occasion to vindicate, in determining the design and the import of the death of Jesus.

Let us speak first of redemption. It has been already made sufficiently clear that man, groaning under a yoke of threefold bondage, stands in need of a threefold enfranchisement. He needs to be delivered from the power of sin, and we have seen how this deliverance is effected by his mystical union with Christ in His death and resurrection. He needs to be delivered from the yoke of the law, and he has been so delivered, inasmuch as with the communication of the Holy Spirit, which he has received, a new principle of spiritual life is substituted for the old bondage of external authority. Lastly, he needs to be freed from the heavy burden of his former sins, the consciousness of which makes him miserable. It is of this third deliverance that we have now to speak; for it is to be observed that the word *redemption*, which, according to its etymology, may be applied equally to the other two, is by Paul always used in reference to this third deliverance.* This, however, may doubtless be merely accidental. Neither the term itself nor the system demands such a restriction. So true is this, that the word *to redeem* is used alike in reference to the power of sin,† and to enfranchisement from legal bondage.‡

Redemption, in this limited sense, or enfranchisement from the guilt already contracted by man, and on account of which he has deserved death, is effected by the three following facts or factors :—

1. *Christ dies;* He sheds His blood upon the cross with the purpose and design that His death shall stand in the stead of that to which men are justly liable on account of their sins. It is mankind who had merited death; it is Christ who dies.

2. *Man believes* in this intention and efficacy of the death of Christ; he receives with gratefulness the gift of the divine grace, by uniting himself to Christ spiritually and essentially, and becoming in Him a new creature.

3. *God accepts* this substitution in consideration of the man's faith, and remits to the man who has really become a new creature, the guilt of his former sins. This He does the more since this whole dispensation (this *economy*) is the fruit of His own sovereign will and wisdom.

---

* See Col. i. 14; Eph. i. 7; Rom. iii. 24. We may just remark here that in several passages to which we shall have to refer again, ἀπολύτρωσις signifies simply physical death and its results, inasmuch as it delivers us from the pains and tribulations of this present life (Eph. iv. 30; i. 14; Rom. viii. 23). But this has nothing to do with theology; it is simply a popular expression. In 1 Cor. i. 30, the meaning is not determined.

† Λυτροῦσθαι, Titus ii. 14; ἀγοράζω, 1 Cor. vi. 20; vii. 23.

‡ Ἐξαγοράζω, Gal. iii. 13; iv. 5.

To this brief exposition of the theory of redemption, we add a few special observations.

Redemption, as the word implies, is a setting free; he who obtains the grace of redemption is then a freedman by Christ,* a term which must be explained by the civil usages of the ancients in regard to their slaves, though the relation may not be absolutely the same here. It may quite as justly be said that the believer, by the very fact of his redemption, becomes the slave † of Christ, into whose service he passes when he leaves the service of sin.

But here occurs a much more important remark. We have argued on the idea of substitution, and this idea is unquestionably expressed in the following passage : " If one died for all, then were all dead; and He died for all, that they which live should not henceforth live unto themselves, but unto Him which died for them." ‡ It is impossible not to see that in this passage the preposition *for* does not signify merely *on behalf of*, but in *the place of;* otherwise the reasoning of the apostle would be without force, and the conclusion would not follow from the premise.

In the greater number of passages where this preposition is used in a similar context, it is impossible to distinguish precisely the shades of meaning which it may have. We shall find the same difficulty in John's writings. In the epistles of Paul, there is a series of passages in which the idea of substitution, properly speaking, does not belong to it, as, for example, where the preposition marks the love of one who devotes himself for another; § where it is contrasted with a hostile disposition; ‖ where it brings out the idea of a benefit conferred; ¶ where it refers to the purification of sin; ** where the

* Ἀπελεύθερος Χριστοῦ, 1 Cor. vii. 22.

† Δοῦλος, 1 Cor vii. 22.

‡ Εἰ εἷς ὑπὲρ πάντων ἀπέθανεν, ἄρα οἱ πάντες ἀπέθανον, ἵνα οἱ ζῶντες μηκέτι ἑαυτοῖς ζῶσιν, ἀλλὰ τῷ ὑπὲρ αὐτῶν ἀποθανόντι, 2 Cor. v. 14, 15.

§ Rom. v. 6, and foll.

‖ Rom. viii. 31, and foll.

¶ Rom. xiv. 15.

** Titus ii. 14; comp. Gal. i. 4; 1 Cor. xv. 3.

comparison of Christ with the paschal lamb seems, according to the symbolic sense of the Mosaic rite, to exclude such a meaning;* and elsewhere.† In a series of other passages the precise signification of the preposition cannot be determined. ‡ The number of texts is comparatively small in which the idea of substitution is indubitably conveyed, and these are principally those in which the figure of a ransom leads directly to it.§ In reference to purely human relations, the preposition has always another sense (*pro* in the sense of *propter* or *in commodum*), and it is only exceptionally we can discover the idea of substitution.‖ Rarely as it may be thus used, however, this sense appears to us explicitly established by some of the passages quoted, and it is further demanded by the whole spirit of the system.

At the same time, let it be well noted that there is a vast interval between this idea and the forensic or legal theory which gained wide acceptance among the schools of the middle ages, and which has become the formula or official explanation of our Churches—the theory, namely, of a *vicarious satisfaction*, material and objective. This theory, developed first by Anselm of Canterbury, passes by altogether the mystical aspect of the question, and transfers it entirely to the ground of what might be called divine jurisprudence. According to this teaching and to our symbolical books, the satisfaction is a priestly act, by which, conformably with the decrees of God, in obedience to which He acted, Christ satisfied divine justice, offended by the sins of men. As the offence had been infinite, none but an infinite, that is a divine Being, could offer this satisfaction. But that Being must be also man, so that the satisfaction should be given by humanity itself. Thus, the second Person in the Trinity became man, and laid upon Himself not only the guilt of man, for which He suffered, so as to

* 1 Cor. v. 7.
† For example, Eph. v. 25 ; 1 Cor. i. 13.
‡ 1 Cor. xi. 24 ; Gal. ii. 20 ; 1 Thess. v. 10.
§ 2 Cor. v. 21 ; Gal. iii. 13 ; 1 Tim. ii. 6 (ἀντίλυτρον).
‖ Rom. ix. 3.

satisfy the justice and the wrath of God (passive obedience,
penal satisfaction), but previously fulfilled in our place, and by
a similar substitution (*vicario nomine*), all the commandments
of the law (active obedience, legal satisfaction). By the latter
(*agendo*) He expiated our guilt; by the former (*patiendo*)
He delivered us from the penalty. It is evident that the
design of this theory is to find the material equipoise between
sin and expiation; it is a sort of legal contract between the
Son and Father, and in this contract the essential point is to
guard what may be called the acquired rights of divine
justice. Man is the subject of the contract, not one of the
contracting parties. The great discussion which agitated the
middle ages was to decide if, as the Thomists asserted, the
value of the blood of Christ exceeds the greatness of the guilt
(*satisfactio superabundam*), or if, as said the Scotists, it was
grace which gave to it this value (*satisfactio gratuita*); but
even this great discussion leaves untouched man's position in
relation to redemption.

There is not a word of all this weighing and calculating
scheme to be found in the whole writings of Paul. On the
contrary, the idea of an objective satisfaction (of Jesus Christ
in the place of the sinner) is based entirely upon a substitution
of ideas, a logical substitution, such as we have already traced
elsewhere, and which excludes at the very outset the purely
material and juridical explanation of Anselm and of orthodox
Protestant theologians. In truth, the death which the sinner
had incurred was eternal death—that is to say, a spiritual or
ethical chastisement; the death suffered by Jesus Christ was
physical, temporary death; in themselves these two facts
present no analogy, are not equivalents, and the one cannot be
substituted for the other in strict legal justice. The main,
essential, indispensable thing in order to any real substitution
is faith, which, in a purely mystical manner and apart from
all the combinations of scholasticism, transforms the physical
death of Christ into an equivalent of the spiritual death of
the old man. Substitution, and with it redemption, are then
actually accomplished, because and inasmuch as the old man

is become dead by mystical communion with the death of the Saviour, and not because God, like a common creditor, is satisfied by receiving the payment due to Him, without troubling to inquire whether it is the real debtor or another who has paid it. Nothing could be more foreign, more radically opposed to the idea of Paul, than this theory, worthy of Pharisaism. We repeat it, the pivot of the whole apostolic system is faith—always faith. So little does it treat of an equivalent, a legal consideration, offered to God in a juridical point of view, that Paul, in speaking of God, ascribes to Him qualities or motives absolutely incompatible with the idea of a strict and severe legality,—namely, longsuffering, generosity, forgetfulness of offences.*

To this observation we may add another, which will mark again the distance which divides the true and simple theory of the apostle from that which the scholasticism of later theologians has put in its place. The explanation which we have been led to give of the fact of regeneration shows plainly that the guilt which is remitted or pardoned, is that previously contracted, before the commencement of faith and the Christian life. In the passage in which Paul gives a definition of the fact, he expressly uses the formula pardon of *sins that are past*.† It is not, it cannot be on this theory, a question of sins following the moment of regeneration. Beside this passage, we have found two only which speak of the remission of sins, and in both cases the expression is synonymous with redemption, and on that very account it must be explained as in the passage first given. Thus the context shows that the

---

* Ἀνοχή, πάρεσις, Rom. iii. 25, 26 ; comp. Rom. ii. 4; 1 Tim. i. 16.

† Πάρεσις τῶν προγεγονότων ἁμαρτημάτων, Rom. iii. 25. [There is a double misconception in Reuss's account of this passage. St. Paul is not speaking of sins before regeneration as distinguished from sins after regeneration, nor is he speaking of the divine forgiveness of sins. "The sins which had passed" are the sins of the generations before Christ came, sins which God had not pardoned, but in His forbearance had *passed by* or *overlooked*. His true thought concerning these sins had not been revealed, but the revelation was made in the death of Christ.— ED.]

one passage * relates to eternal election, and the remission of
sins is connected with the fulness of the times, with the era
and fact of the Messianic manifestation.   This places us
at once on the ground of the most abstract theory; there
is no mention even of the individual application.   The
other passage † is only an extract from the preceding.   It
has, furthermore, been already shown that there can be no
question of sin in the regenerate, that it would be a breach
of logic, a contradiction *in adjecto*, to speak of remission of
sins in relation to regenerate souls, and Paul solemnly protests
against such an inconsistency.‡

There is yet a third remark deserving of careful consideration.   God was free to accept or to reject this substitution.   In
His capacity as Judge, He was under no obligation to receive
it, He had perfect liberty to refuse; for in very truth there
was not, in the judicial point of view, a valid substitution.   If
He, nevertheless, accepts it, He shows that He intends to let
grace act, and to adhere only to the form of justice;§ for it is
not possible that justice should be satisfied otherwise than
by the punishment of the really guilty party.   Redemption,
according to Paul, is not, then, as with Anselm, an act of
divine justice, but an act of grace, as has been sufficiently
explained in a previous chapter.

It will be appropriate to say a word here on a figure
employed by Paul, when he sets forth the deliverance from all
sin under the image of a debt in writing, remitted by the
destruction of the claim.‖   This destruction is effected by
Christ's nailing to His cross the document which makes man a
debtor.   The apostle would not have chosen this allegory, if
he had had to express the idea of a debt paid to the creditor
by another than the true debtor.   Christ does not here
pay a debt; He destroys a claim.   What is this claim, then ?

* Eph. i. 7, ἄφεσις.
† Col. i. 14.
‡ Rom. vi. 1, and foll.
§ Rom. vi. 1, and foll.
‖ Χειρόγραφον, Col. ii. 14, 15.

Evidently it is a document really written; it is the law which pronounces the penalty of death upon transgressors. This law Christ abrogates by the fact of His death, because that death opens another way than the way of the law, to life with God; redemption from bondage under the law goes side by side with redemption from legal guilt, the two being naturally inseparable. The law is done away by Christ; and we ourselves being united to Christ by faith,"* and consequently freed from the yoke of the law, are no more liable to suffer for the past, but are bound for the future to bring forth fruit unto God.

We close this chapter with one more observation of no small importance. We have already seen that Paul delights to trace in the old covenant the prophetic images of the new, the types of Gospel facts. We shall not, then, be surprised that he finds one for the redemptive death of Christ. Natural analogy easily leads him to it. In one passage, already repeatedly quoted,† which speaks of deliverance from old guilt, Christ is described by a term capable of two explanations. It is generally associated with that employed in the Greek translation of the Old Testament, to designate the covering of the sacred ark, on which the high-priest sprinkled some drops of the blood of the victim on the day of atonement. As allusion is made in the Epistle to the Hebrews to this ceremony, the conclusion has been at once drawn that it is referred to here also, and the patronage of Luther has done much to accredit it. But then Christ would be at once not only priest and victim, as He is represented in that epistle, but also the sacred furniture, which was to the Jews the symbol of the divine presence: in other words, He would be at once the one who offers and the one who receives the expiatory sacrifice. Such a combination might commend itself to our old theology, so bent on finding everywhere proofs of every dogma whatsoever; but we do not believe it entered into the idea of Paul. We prefer to take the word in question as the qualificative

---

* Rom. vii. 4.
† Rom. iii. 25, ἱλαστήριον, propitiatory.

adjective of a word easily omitted in such a case, the signification being a propitiatory *victim*. Christ would be thus
compared to a victim whose death on the altar is designed
to obliterate the first displeasure of God against men, and to
incline Him to restore to them His favour. This explanation
will embrace also another passage, in which it is said* that
Christ presented Himself to God as a victim and a sacrifice for
men, and that this sacrifice was agreeable to God.

Let it be observed that this image occurs only twice in our
epistles, and then, as it were, accidentally. It would be strange
indeed to make it the basis of the whole theology, when far
more full and lucid explanations are frequently given elsewhere
without a figure. Scholasticism has hastened to seize this image,
and has attached to it a series of questions, which in their
turn have been converted into dogmas. It has been asked,
to whom was the sacrifice offered ? what was its intention ?
what its value ? and so on. In the name of Paul, we refuse
to reply to these questions, and still more emphatically refuse
to make them the very basis of the system. Such comparisons
crowd into the mind without giving any right to speculation
to press them, or to derive from them other doctrinal consequences than those which the author may have had in view at
the moment when the images passed before him. Paul uses
the liberty which belongs to every man of comprehensive
thought, and whose mind embraces a wide horizon, to establish
relations between parallel facts, or to search out the harmonies
existing between different orders of things. Thus he compares
Christ to the paschal lamb,† and all will admit that the paschal
lamb had nothing to do with sin and expiation.‡ Shall it

* Eph. v. 2 ; προσφορά, θυσία.
† 1 Cor. v. 7.
‡ There is not the unanimity on this point which Reuss takes for
granted. There are many who accept the theory of Hengstenberg, who
in his Essay on the Sacrifices of Holy Scripture contends strongly for
the expiatory and vicarious character of the Passover sacrifice. "The
true root of all presentations of sin-offerings was the Passover, to which
in the main the Good-Friday of the Church of the New Covenant corresponds. That the Passover was a sin-offering is evident, even from the

then be concluded that the death of Christ had nothing to do
with these? Shall we on this ground proceed to deny substitution in every sense? Let one figure be fairly set against
another, and before making any one the basis of a theological
theory, let us always be careful to find the true *tertium com-
parationis*, the character common to the two terms by which
the comparison was suggested. The figure of a sacrifice is
found even in the sphere of morals.* Does this imply that there
is an analogy or identity between our own relation to humanity
and that of Christ? We adhere then in our estimate of the
name. The word signifies strictly, ' deliverance,' and then 'sacrifice of
deliverance,' or ' sacrifice of atonement.' But we learn the character of
the Passover as a sin-offering still more clearly from the account of its
first institution. When it was appointed that all the first-born in the
land of Egypt should die, the destroying angel—that is, the angel of the
Lord, in his revenging and punishing character—spared all those houses
which he found sprinkled with the blood of the paschal lamb, in sign of
the expiation of sin effected by it. He who had this token might be sure
of being spared and delivered (Exod. xii. 23). His sins were laid, as
it were, on the lamb, the type of innocence. He who slaughtered
the lamb confessed, in a symbolical language, that he also, no less
than the Egyptians, the children of this world, had deserved to be
an object of divine wrath; he declared that he could not claim deliverance on the ground of his own worth, or of any other title, but that he
expected it from the grace of God alone. According to the divine
promise to accept the blood of the innocent lamb in place of the blood of
the sinner, who recognized and felt himself to be such, those who made this
confession received the remission of the punishment of their sins. The
principle was thus laid down for all ages of the Church, that that which
distinguishes the Church from the world is the blood of atonement. Nor
was the festival of Passover, as celebrated in later times, a mere commemorative festival, as is clear from the continual slaughter of lambs for
sacrifices. Wherever there is a sacrifice instituted by God, we may be
certain that, provided it is brought in faith, there is a repetition of the
first benefit, which is distinguished from the subsequent ones only by its
forming the commencement of a long series. The paschal lamb was the
basis and root of the entire system of sacrifices : only as connected with
it had the remaining sin-offerings value and significance; without it
they were but as disjointed members. It was the true and proper
covenant-sacrifice, the sacrifice which represented in its highest form the
distinction between the world without God, and the people of God reconciled unto God."—Ed.

* Rom. xii. 1 ; Phil. ii. 17 ; iv. 18.

significance of the two former passages, to the general idea of a voluntary death which benefits men by being acceptable to God. The image carries us no further.

It is, morever, a fact that in the theology of Paul it is not the death of Christ, but the faith of man, which is the main thing, the pivot of the whole system; and this faith does not relate exclusively to the fact of the death of Christ, but also to the fact of His life. The holiness of that life, which we are to make our own by faith, exerts as great an influence* upon our justification as the sacrifice of His death. We are led to the same conclusion when we find that, in the thought of our apostle, the resurrection of the Lord is inseparable from His death, and that it even takes the pre-eminence both as an element of theological demonstration and in practical application. For in relation to the latter, the new birth, which cannot be dissevered from the idea of faith, is positively the essential thing, without which the death of the old man would be barren and meaningless. We are then justified in saying that the system is not based exclusively upon the fact of the death of Christ.†

* Rom. v. 19.

† St. Paul's conception of the relation between the death of Christ and human redemption was determined to an extent which Reuss altogether fails to recognize, by the Jewish idea of sacrifices for sin. There is nothing to be added to the general summary of St. Paul's opinion given early in the chapter, and there is very much in the later pages that cannot be overlooked without forming a most imperfect estimate of the Pauline doctrine. But such expressions as "redemption through *the blood*" of Christ, "made sin for us," "made a curse for us," originated in an idea of which this chapter gives no satisfactory account.—ED.

CHAPTER XVI.

OF JUSTIFICATION AND RECONCILIATION.

JUSTIFICATION is the declaration of God, by which remission of sins is granted to the man who is a sinner, in consideration of his faith.

We dwell on it here because it is the consequence, the corollary, so to speak, of the death of Christ and the faith of man. It does not, then, present any new idea to us, and all we have to do is to set forth by analysis the full meaning of the term, which is one of those most frequently employed in Pauline theology. In the passive† it signifies *to be declared just* by the decree of the supreme Judge. The question whether the man thus becomes just in reality, or in what sense he becomes so, is not for us to decide. It is enough ·to establish, on the one hand, that the declaration of such a Judge is beyond reversal; on the other, that the justification thus pronounced is essentially to be ascribed to grace. None but God, the Judge of the world, could make such a declaration or issue such a decree; He is therefore called simply the *Justifier.*† The act of the declaration itself is called *justification.* ‡

This declaration of the Judge is considered as made when the old guilt, accumulated during the whole period of the life of man preceding his regeneration, is cancelled or blotted out by the fact that the sinner becomes associated by faith with the

* Διϰαιοῦσθαι (Rom. ii. 13), δίϰαιον ϰαθίστασθαι (v. 19).
† Rom. iii. 26; iv. 5; viii. 30, 33.
‡ Διϰαίωσις, Rom. iv. 25; v. 18.

redeeming and vicarious death of Christ; in other words, it
takes place when the old man dies with Christ to rise again
with Him as a new man. For the sinner must needs *die*, but
God in His grace is pleased to substitute this mystical death,
which leads to life, for the physical death, the end of which is
damnation. " He who is dead," it is said,[*] " is freed from sin,"
or is *justified*. This passage, with a series of others which will
present themselves, proves clearly that the principle of justification is based essentially upon the death of the sinner himself,
and not upon any opinion whatever which he may hold concerning the death of Christ.

It follows naturally, that justification takes place, as to time,
simultaneously with redemption. This fact is not affected
by certain rhetorical phrases which seem to assert the contrary,
as, for example, where justification is named after sanctification, while in another passage it precedes it,[†] and redemption is even placed last,—an order which, if we attached any
doctrinal importance to it, would overturn the whole system.
Lastly, when we find the hope of righteousness[‡] (or justification)
spoken of, the reference is necessarily to man as he really is,
and to the fact that judgment is only actually pronounced
upon him in another life, though according to the theological
theory, the sentence is already passed.

Justification rests then, as we have seen, upon three facts all
equally indispensable, the grace of God, the blood of Christ,
the faith of man. If any one of these three elements were
wanting, justification would not take place, and consequently
there would be no salvation. We lay stress upon this point,
because it does not always receive due attention, the many (and
among them not a few so-called theologians) being only too
ready to regard the work of Christ as an *opus operatum*, the
benefit of which accrues to every baptized person, or at any
rate to all who believe in the dogma. We would only remark
that Paul, when he speaks of justification, does not as a rule

* Ὁ ἀποθανὼν δεδικαίωται ἀπὸ τῆς ἁμαρτίας, Rom. vi. 7 ; comp. iii. 24.
† 1 Cor. vi. 11; comp. i. 30.
‡ Gal. v. 5.

mention, at the same time, these three constituent elements, but generally one only.   Thus he names sometimes the grace alone,* sometimes the blood alone,† sometimes faith alone.‡ The expression to be justified in or by Christ § appears to embrace all the three elements, the name and person of Christ recalling at once God and the sinner, between whom Christ has come to establish a happy relation.   In the same way, the antithesis, justification by works,‖ or by the law,¶ involves also the three elements in question, inasmuch as all three are equally superfluous if man can attain salvation of himself— that is, by his own legal obedience.

   We resume our analysis.   He who is thus freed from the guilt of past sin, is spoken of as righteous ** in the theological sense of the word.   We are not to understand by this term a man who will henceforward abstain from sin (the idea conveyed by the word *saint*), but one whose former sins are once for all blotted out.   The qualification thus freely ascribed to him is called *righteousness*, in opposition to the state of sin, and his description as a sinner. ††   This righteousness is distinguished from anything else to which men might give the same name, by the addition of certain epithets, as the righteousness which is of faith,‡‡ thus placed in contrast with a righteousness derived from outward and legal obedience,§§ and still more

* Titus iii. 7.   † Rom. v. 9.
‡ Rom. iii. 28, 30 ; v. 1 ; Gal. ii. 16 ; iii. 8, 24.   There is no difference between the expressions δικ. πίστει, ἐκ π., διὰ π., and πιστεύεται εἰς δικ., Rom. x. 10.
§ Gal. ii. 17.
‖ Rom. iii. 20 ; Gal. ii. 16.
¶ Gal. iii. 11 ; v. 4.
** Δίκαιος, 1 Tim. i. 9.
†† Once δικαίωμα, Rom. v. 16; comp. 18; more frequently δικαιοσύνη. See especially Rom. vi. 13—20.
‡‡ Δικαιοσύνη πίστεως, Rom. iv. 11, 13 ; διὰ πίστεως, iii. 22; ἐκ πίστεως, ix. 30 ; x. 6 ; ἐπὶ τῇ πίστει, Phil. iii. 9.
§§ Δικαιοσύνη διὰ νόμου, Gal. ii. 21 ; ἐν νόμῳ, Gal. iii. 11 ; v. 4 ; ἐκ νόμου, Rom. x. 5 ; Gal. iii. 21 ; Phil. iii. 9.   Δικαιοσύνη ἐν νόμῳ (Phil. iii. 6), is not quite the same thing ; the context shows clearly that the writer is referring rather to a complete outward obedience to the law than to the moral qualification resulting to him who thus obeys.

emphatically as the righteousness bestowed or recognized by
God, the only valid righteousness in the eyes of the supreme
Judge,* as opposed to that which man claims as his own, and
with which he is satisfied.†

That we may omit nothing which relates to this idea of
justification, let us observe again that it is, firstly, a gift of
divine grace, like the redemption from which it flows;‡ secondly,
an act of substitution, faith being *imputed* as righteousness ;§
thirdly, in a measure, the act of Christ, who is *our righteousness*,‖ the result being put for the premise ; lastly, it is an unquestionable fact that, according to the theory, this righteousness will be henceforth the abiding characteristic of the believer.
Redemption from sin implies righteousness ; if this were
matter of dispute, we should have to commence by denying
the truth of the redemption, for he who is *free* from sin can
henceforth be the servant only of righteousness.¶

With this conception of righteousness, we are brought at
least in a sense, and in one aspect of it, to the final utterance
of dogmatic theology, since the design of that theology was
to restore the legitimate relation between righteousness and
happiness. The doctrine of righteousness in Christ is therefore as indispensable to the Gospel as the doctrine of faith,
and for the simple reason that it is essentially the same thing.
Hence, also, the new economy is called simply the law of
righteousness, as it is elsewhere called the law of faith, and the
apostolic ministry a ministration of righteousness.**

---

* Δικαιοσύνη ἐκ θεοῦ, Phil. iii. 9 ; or simply θεοῦ, Rom. 1. 17 ; iii. 21, 22 ;
x. 3 ; 2 Cor. v. 21.   It is a grave mistake to translate δικαιοσύνη θεοῦ by
justification, for it is not the declaration of God, it is the characteristic of
the man which Paul describes by this phrase.   It is always easy to recognize the passages in which this phrase designates an attribute of God Himself, for example, Rom. iii. 5, 25, 26.

† Ἰδία δικ.

‡ Δωρεὰ τῆς δικαιοσύνης, Rom. v. 17.

§ Λογίζεται, Rom. iii. 4—11 ; iv. *passim*, Gal. iii. 6.

‖ 1 Cor. i. 30.

¶ Ἐλευθερωθέντες ἀπὸ τῆς ἁμαρτίας ἐδουλώθητε τῇ δικαιοσύνῃ, Rom. vi. 18 ;
comp. v. 21 ; viii. 10.

** Νόμος δικαιοσύνης, Rom. ix. 31 ; διακονία δικ., 2 Cor. iii. 9.

We come now to the third fact which we have mentioned as the result of the work of Christ—namely, reconciliation. This, again, is only distinguished from the rest by the requirements of theological analysis, and not in relation to time.

In his natural state, man as a sinner is afar off, estranged from God; he is at enmity with Him.* This is an inevitable consequence of the tendency of the flesh to cast off obedience towards God.† But in this position, man cannot by possibility be happy; fear and distress of mind are his necessary portion.

This relation is changed by the help of Christ; that is to say, as the result of the union into which we enter with Him. The change thus wrought is sometimes described simply as a drawing near on our part, as an impulse imparted by Christ to bring us back to God,‡ and which, accompanied by a confidence full of hope and joy,§ is a direct effect of the operation of the Holy Spirit and of faith. ||

These terms, however, give us but a very popular description of the fact, and are far from reaching the sublimity of the true theological idea. They give a glimpse of it, however, and form a prelude, so to speak, to the scientific definition which we have to give of that which Paul calls reconciliation.¶ "God," he says, "is in Christ reconciling the world unto Himself, not imputing unto men their trespasses."** From this proposition, we shall derive the following characteristics of reconciliation.

It is God who reconciles men, who draws them to Himself; it cannot truly be said that He is reconciled to them, for no

* Ἀπηλλοτριωμένος καὶ ἐχθρὸς τῇ διανοίᾳ ἐν τοῖς ἔργοις τοῖς πονηροῖς, Col. i. 21.

† Rom. viii. 7.

‡ Προσαγωγή.

§ Παῤῥησία, πεποίθησις, Eph. iii. 12.

|| Eph. ii. 18; Rom. v. 2.

¶ Καταλλαγή.

** Θεὸς ἦν ἐν Χριστῷ κόσμον καταλλάσσων ἑαυτῷ, μὴ λογιζόμενος αὐτοῖς τὰ παραπτώματα αὐτῶν, 2 Cor. v. 19.

change takes place in the disposition of His mind.* We shall, therefore, find Paul speaking of the world being reconciled to God,† but never of God being reconciled to it. Man is passive in the act of reconciliation; he receives it.‡

The condition, or we may say the essence of reconciliation, is on our part the cessation of enmity, or, in other words, the death of the old man who was the enemy of God, and the birth of the new man; on the part of God it is the obliteration or non-imputation of the guilt already contracted, or, in popular language, the victory of grace over justice. Now as this change takes place in consequence of the mediation of Christ, we find here the whole series of expressions of which we have already spoken in the preceding chapters, and on which it is needless to enlarge again. Reconciliation is effected *by* or *in* Christ.§

Reconciliation is, then, as essential an element in the work of salvation as redemption and justification, or we might rather say it is the same fact regarded from a different point of view. Gospel preaching may be called simply the doctrine of reconciliation; ‖ the apostolic ministry, the ministry of reconciliation,¶ and the meaning conveyed is true and complete.

It follows from what has been said that the word *reconciliation* is in itself inaptly chosen, inasmuch as it suggests that which takes place between men, under similar circumstances, when there is a change in the mutual disposition of both

* 2 Cor. v. 18; see especially Col. i. 20 : εὐδόκησεν ἀποκαταλλάξαι τὰ πάντα διὰ Χριστοῦ εἰς αὐτὸν (θεόν). [There is no change effected in God's disposition towards men as the result of Christ's death; but there is a change in His relation to them; and it is this change in His relation to mankind which St. Paul speaks of in Cor. v. 18; and which, indeed, Reuss recognizes, though not very clearly, in the next paragraph, in which he describes reconciliation as consisting, on the part of God, in the obliteration or non-imputation of guilt, etc.—ED.]

† Rom. xi. 15.

‡ Λαμβάνει, καταλλάσσεται, Rom. v. 10, 11.

§ Διὰ Χριστοῦ (2 Cor. v. 18), ἐν Χριστῷ (v. 19), διὰ τοῦ θανάτου τοῦ Χριστοῦ (Rom. v. 10; Col. i. 22).

‖ Λόγος τῆς καταλλαγῆς, 2 Cor. v. 19.

¶ Διακονία τῆς κατ., 2 Cor. v. 18.

parties. The reconciliation spoken of in the theology of Paul is not a mutual reconciliation, but simply a return of man to God.* This must not be lost sight of in estimating the significance of the term *Mediator*,† which is only once applied to the person of Christ, but which occurs very frequently in the language of ecclesiastical theology. It would be an entirely false notion to deduce from this term the necessity of the intervention of a third person to secure, as it were, concessions on both sides, as is the case in mediation between men; and yet such is the conception often entertained by theologians with regard to it.‡ The intervention of Christ was doubtless necessary,—not, however, to incline God to receive men, but solely to incline men to return to God whom they had forsaken, and place themselves in such an attitude that God, without Himself changing in any degree, might receive them again into His favour. Hence Christ is also spoken of as the Reconciler.§

* But this ignores what Ruess has already acknowledged—that Reconciliation "on the part of God" is the obliteration or non-imputation of guilt, etc.—ED.

† Μεσίτης, 1 Tim. ii. 5.

‡ Something of this idea attaches to the mediator of a covenant, an expression which occurs in the Epistle to the Hebrews. Paul only uses it in speaking of Moses, Gal. iii. 19. In the 20th verse (which may be considered the most obscure in the whole New Testament, since there are three hundred different explanations of it,) he even appears to say that a mediator always supposes two contracting parties, in other words a legal synallagmatic convention, as was the case with the old covenant, but not with the new, in which God alone (εἷς) interposes, since that covenant rests upon His grace, His free mercy, and not upon any legal obligations.

§ Eph. ii. 16. We must pause a moment over 2 Cor. v. 20. Paul speaks in the imperative, καταλλάγητε τῷ θεῷ! It might be inferred from this that reconciliation is purely and simply on the part of men, and that the writer, who is here speaking to persons who are Christians, and therefore supposed to be already reconciled, forgets for the moment the theory, and speaks the language of common experience, as we have found elsewhere. It may, however, be explained in another way; the whole epistle is an apology for the Gospel ministry. Now we have already seen that Gospel preaching is called *the word of reconciliation*; the imperative exclamation of v. 20 is then merely the concrete form of that preaching, and is addressed here, not to the members of the Church, but to the world at large.

The reconciliation being thus accomplished, man stands in a new relation to God. This state, in contrast to that which preceded it, is called *peace.** Peace is represented sometimes as the result of justification, sometimes as that of the impartation of the Spirit;† but we already know that there is no real distinction, all these facts being simultaneous, and closely related to each other.

To the word *peace* itself we are naturally led to attach the ordinary sense, by the fact that it stands opposed to enmity.‡ It is easy to see, however, that this expression, in our modern tongues, does not exhaust its significance, and that it is really adequate only in a very limited number of passages, where, for example, the Gospel is called a Gospel of peace,§ a synonym obviously for the word of reconciliation. In most cases it is otherwise. Thus the apostle wishes peace to his readers in all the salutations with which he commences his epistles, and here the word is unquestionably the equivalent of the Hebrew term employed in the same circumstances, and which comprises every sort of well-being. || It is needless to say that in the lips of a minister of Christ, the allusion will be to spiritual rather than to material well-being; and the constant addition of the words "from God the Father," etc., shows clearly that it is a heavenly benediction, not a subjective disposition of the man, which is the good desired. The same remark will apply to the greetings with which several of the epistles close.¶

There may be some uncertainty about the term the *God of peace,* which occurs towards the close of several of the epistles,

---

* Εἰρήνη.

† Rom. v. 1 ; viii. 6.

‡ Ἐχθρά (comp. 1 Thess. v. 3).

§ Eph. vi. 15.

|| This is evident also from the text of several quotations from the Old Testament, (Rom. iii. 17 ; x. 15,) and from certain phrases in which its language is reproduced, as 1 Cor. xvi. 11. See also Rom. i. 7 ; 1 Cor. i. 3, etc. ; and the salutations of the epistles of Peter, of Jude, of the Second Epistle of John, and of the Revelation.

¶ Gal. vi. 16 ; Eph. vi. 23 ; 2 Thess. iii. 16.

in the expression of the writer's good wishes.* It might be
translated : The God from whom comes all true happiness and
salvation ; or, again, The God who wills that all men should be
brethren ;† or, again, The God who puts a blessed satisfaction
into the heart of His people, the natural effect of a sense of
reconciliation with Him. If the last interpretation be accepted,
the phrase belongs essentially to our present chapter. This
seems to be supported especially by the passage in which the
peace of God is represented as an inestimable good, and as
keeping the heart through Christ.‡

We may here speak of another sentiment frequently dwelt
upon as the privilege of the believer joined to God through
Christ. This is joy,§ the serenity of soul which preserves it
from all discouragement in adversity, which strengthens it to
meet danger and temptation, raises it above the vexations
of every-day life, and abundantly compensates to it all the
pleasures of the world.

In closing this chapter, and before proceeding further, let us
cast one more retrospective glance over the various ideas we
have just been analyzing. We have said that they all refer
to one and the same fact, regarded under different aspects.
We may say further that this difference, whether arising out
of the conception itself, or connected rather with the form of
its exposition, is of a nature to recall to us what we remarked
at the outset with regard to the two elements of the Pauline
theology—the rational and dialectic, the ethical and mystical
element. It will be readily seen that the idea of justification,
and the development given to it, rest mainly on the first
element, while that of redemption stands in more direct and
close relation with the second. This will explain to us also

* Rom. xv. 33; xvi. 20; 2 Cor. xiii. 11 ; Phil. iv. 9; 1 Thess. v. 23 ;
2 Thess. iii. 16 ; comp. Heb. xiii. 20.

† Eph. ii. 14, and foll.

‡ Phil. iv. 7 ; comp. Rom. xv. 23.   In Col. iii. 15 ; there is an error in
the text. It should read as in the MSS., εἰρήνη Χριστοῦ, and not θεοῦ, and
should be understood simply of the brotherly bond between Christians, a
consequence of their common union with Christ.

§ Rom. xii. 12 ; xiv. 17 ; xv. 13; Gal. v. 22 ; Phil. i. 25 ; 1 Thess. i. 6.

why the theology of the Church, that of Protestants especially, in making this idea of justification the basis of its whole system, has been more and more captivated by the charms of logical and legal argument, of a juridical theory, and has been thus led to neglect the more peculiarly Gospel element, which makes its appeal to the human conscience and to individual religious feeling.

CHAPTER XVII.

OF THE CHURCH.

WE have passed in review the thoughts and utterances of Paul in relation to the primary sphere of the Christian life, that which is limited to the individual, or rather which embraces his direct relations with God and with Christ. The centre of this sphere was the idea of faith—that is, the knowledge of the purposes of God concerning the salvation of man, and the individual appropriation of that salvation, by means of a mystic union with the Saviour.

We enter now on the second sphere, in which the Christian no longer stands alone in his relation to God and His grace, but in community with those of his fellows, whom a like relation to revelation, its author and its organ, has brought near and placed on the same footing with himself. Here the believer finds himself raised at once to a loftier position, to a higher level than he occupied before. So far, all that has been required of him may be described as a sort of negative activity, that is, he has been called upon to submit, to surrender himself to the operation of God, to obey an impulse from above, to accept that which was offered to him, not to resist a beneficent but .foreign power. Now, he is to become himself a real actor; he is to essay his own powers, and to exercise, in his turn, an influence on those around him. God invites him to take his part in the great work to be accomplished, and to labour for the advancement of the purposes of God, as if they were his own.

All that Paul teaches, in relation to this second sphere, its duties and the means to be employed, may be summed up in the idea and in the name of *love*,* which is thus the correlative of the idea and of the name of *faith*.

We may observe, at the outset, that this chapter is far more simple, far less rich in thought, than the preceding, partly because it is less closely allied to the mysticism of the Pauline theory, partly also because it contains only the practical application of principles already enunciated and explained. It is obvious also to remark, that we shall here find far less that is peculiar to our apostle; the ideas here set forth owe their individual colouring less to their origin or source, than to their connection with those in which we have already traced such individuality. We may add, in order to make this more evident, that the theory of Christian love is not based by Paul, like that of faith, upon a peculiar and subjective inner experience, but that it is an attempt to establish scientifically, and upon the basis of the results of that experience, two facts, supplied the one by history, the other by the moral consciousness—namely, the *Church* and *duty*.

As introductory to our subject, we may lay down a few general principles. We nowhere find in the writings of this apostle a logical definition of love in the strict sense. We gather, however, from many passages, among which we need quote only the noble panegyric so familiar to all readers of his epistles,† that he regards it as the disposition which is the necessary source of all Christian activity, as faith is the foundation of all Christian thought. Where love is wanting, the Christian element must be absent also. Faith and knowledge without it are valueless; the word without love is a mean-

---

* Ἀγάπη. We prefer the expression *love* to that of *charity*, which usage has sanctioned, for the simple reason that it is more exact. From ἀγάπη (a word radically different from ἔρως) the verb ἀγαπᾷν is formed, while charity will not supply us with any verb, for to *cherish* is not adapted to religious language. If the word *love* has another meaning, which no one will confound with that here conveyed, the word *charity* has also another, which is only too frequently confounded with the true. The apostle has so little fear of the words being misunderstood, that he only once adds an epithet limiting its significance to the spiritual sphere (Rom. xv. 30).

† 1 Cor. xiii.

ingless and empty sound; loveless activity profits nothing, and if it should assume the name of a sacrifice, it would be no better than a lie.* Love alone edifies, so far at least as edification depends upon ourselves.† And just as it is the ground and root of all Christian activity, so is it also the key of the arch, the crown of every Christian grace.‡ Hence it is we find here, as in the teaching of Jesus Himself, the whole morality of the law summed up or comprised in the commandment of love; or, rather, the apostle declares that all the law is fulfilled in this one great commandment.§

One point of leading importance is the close relation which exists between love and faith, the two being frequently conjoined, as though to represent the Christian virtues in their totality.‖ On a closer examination, we perceive that love is derived from faith,¶ faith being necessarily the source of all true good. On the one hand, the faith which is alone availing is a faith that works by love.** Faith apart from love would not be faith; love disjoined from faith would be no less an illusion. Thus when the subject is the active operation of faith,†† the apostle speaks of love, of the love which is the fruitful result of faith, and which is manifested in what are called *good works.*‡‡

The love of the Christian is shown necessarily by his active devotion to the interests of his fellow-creatures, since God can never require such services, but men alone. Considered, however, as a disposition of soul, as a motive power, as one of the very elements of the Christian life, love has a far more extended sphere, and lends its support, we might almost say its colouring, to all the tendencies of the inner nature. To

* 1 Cor. xiii. 1—3.
† 1 Cor. viii. 1.
‡ 'Επὶ πᾶσιν ἡ ἀγάπη ἥτις ἐστι σύνδεσμος τῆς τελειότητος, Col. iii. 14.
§ Gal. v. 14; Rom. xiii. 8, and foll.; πλήρωμα νόμου ἡ ἀγάπη.
‖ Eph. vi. 23; 1 Thess. iii. 6; v. 8; 1 Tim. i. 14; 2 Tim. i. 13, etc.
¶ 1 Tim. i. 5.
** Πίστις δι ἀγάπης ἐνεργουμένη, Gal. v. 6.
†† Ἔργον πίστεως, 1 Thess. i. 3; 2 Thess. i. 11.
‡‡ Ἔργα ἀγαθά, κόπος τῆς ἀγάπης, 1 Thess. i. 3.

love God and Christ is to the Christian a thing as natural as to love his neighbour.* Nay, more, love to God may be regarded as the source of all other manifestations of love, since to love and to believe is in reality the same thing.†

In relation to men, the system does not, as a general rule, make any distinctions among them when it speaks of love. Christian charity is universal,‡ even to the point of rendering good for evil. The Christian's motive to love so large as this, is the thought that God Himself thus loves all His creatures.§ In this broad sense, love can always manifest itself by intercessory prayer.|| But as there are limits to human energy, it is needful to economize its expenditure by restricting its sphere of action; the greatness of the effect produced will be in proportion to the just balance between the motive power and the sphere of its operation, or in other words between the means and the end. It is on this account the apostle exhorts the faithful to address themselves in their loving service primarily to the members of the household of faith;¶ not that he would so circumscribe their benevolence, but because he knows the circle of activity will widen of itself, as the power grows by exercise.

We now pass from these general and preliminary thoughts** to a more thorough examination of this second sphere of the Christian life, in which we shall again distinguish the different parts assigned to the three persons who co-operate in the work of regenerating humanity. Here, however, we shall

* Rom. viii. 28; Eph. vi. 24; 1 Thess. iii. 12; iv. 9.
† 1 Cor. viii. 3.
‡ Rom. xii. 17, 18.
§ 1 Tim. ii. 4; iv. 10.
|| 1 Tim. ii. 1.
¶ Gal. vi. 10; comp. Eph. i. 15; Col. i. 4; 2 Thess. i. 3.
** There are passages in which the term ἀγάπη represents, not a disposition of general application, but one of the many special manifestations of the Christian life—one virtue among many others (Gal. v. 22, etc.) If we use in such cases only the word charity, all difficulty is removed. [But the apostle's meaning is impoverished by changing "love" into "charity" here. As Reuss implies, there is really no difficulty; the apostle is not giving a scientific classification of "the fruits of the Spirit."—Ed.]

follow a different order from that which guided us in our previous analysis. Since man's activity is to be exerted on ground prepared for it, or in a form appropriate to the designs of God, it is of this form or ground we shall first speak. By the word thus used we mean the Church founded by Christ. The act of Christ and its results will occupy us first. We shall next inquire what help God has given to man in this particular direction, and shall observe, in conclusion, the active part which belongs to man himself.

Collectively, those who are called, and who have found salvation in Christ, are spoken of as the Christian *community*, or the *Church*. The latter word had among the Greeks a political meaning, and described a deliberative assembly. The Christians, who gradually came to prefer it to the word synagogue, as their separation from the Jews became more marked, had to add to the original term a special qualifying word, to mark its new and religious meaning; they thus spoke of the Church of God or of Christ.*

This term, however, is not always employed in the same sense; and in the writings of Paul, in particular, we readily distinguish three different meanings. At first it represents, according to classic usage, the assembly itself as a historical reality,—that is, the totality of persons assembled in a certain place at a given time.† It next stands for all the believers dwelling in the same city, and who might be supposed to meet together habitually for mutual edification. This is what we call a local church, a flock, a society (German, *Gemeinde*), in a restricted sense. This second signification so frequently occurs in the writings of the apostle Paul, that it would be needless to enumerate the passages.‡ Lastly, there is the ideal sense attached to the word, according to which it represents the great body of believers, without regard to the place of their

---

* Ἐκκλησία τοῦ θεοῦ, 1 Cor. xv. 9 ; τοῦ Χριστοῦ, Acts xx. 28, etc.

† 1 Cor. xi. 18 ; xiv., *passim*.

‡ See the salutations in the epistles, the places where Churches are spoken of in the plural (1 Cor. vii. 17 ; xi. 16, etc.), and the many passages where the name of a place is added.

habitation, or to the possibility of their all meeting together in any one spot; this is what we call the Church (Germ., *Kirche*). Perhaps the etymology of the word may give some clue to this extension of the original idea.* If so, it would then represent all those whom a special call has separated from the world. We are under no necessity, however, to resort to such an expedient in explanation of so natural a metonomic transition.

Of all the attributes of the Church, that which Paul mentions most emphatically, and which should first claim our attention here, is its unity. It is one as to the source of all its vital powers, as to the end to which it tends, and the spirit which animates it : *One body, one spirit, one hope, one Lord, one faith, one baptism, one God and Father of all.*† In this well-known passage, it is at once obvious that the various ideas passed in review do not follow any logical order, the main thought of the apostle being to bring into prominence that *unity* of which we just now spoke. Nor would anything be gained by attempting to follow this order here; many of the points enumerated we have already touched upon, others will come before us in the course of this chapter.

The idea of the unity of the Church rests primarily upon that of the unity of its Founder. Christ stands in this relation to the Church, not simply, as we know, in the historical sense, which would not necessarily imply the exclusion of all co-workers; but also, and essentially, in the theological sense, and by acts which could be performed by Himself alone. It is by virtue of these acts and their effects, of which we have already spoken at sufficient length, that He bears the name of *Lord*,‡ a name applied to Him more frequently than any other, and which should never be dissociated from the idea of the Church.

---

* 1 Cor. vi. 4; x. 32; xii. 28; Eph. i. 22; iii. 20, 21; v. 23—32; Gal. i. 13, etc.

† Ἐν σῶμα ἐν πνεῦμα, μια ἐλπìς; εἷς κύριος, μία πίστις, ἐν βάπτισμα, εἷς θεòς καì πατὴρ πάντων, Eph. iv. 4—6.

‡ Κύριος. We do not quote any passages here; there are more than three hundred in Paul's epistles, and these have doubtless done most to popularize the use of the name.

He is the Son of God in Himself, and independently of any historical relation; to all believers He is the Lord. The unbelieving alone reject Him in this capacity, and refuse to Him this title.*

The idea of the unity of the Church brings to our mind, at the same time, the fact that before the appearing of Jesus Christ, mankind was divided into two hostile parties, separated, so to speak, by a middle wall of partition,† that is, by the law, which assigned to each a different place in relation to God, and consequently a different destiny in the future. The law, having lost its obligatory character, the death of Christ having opened to all men, without distinction, a common way of salvation and justification, the separation ceased, the wall fell; peace and reconciliation were brought about between the two sections of humanity, as between mankind and God. All distinctions, in general, among mortals,—distinctions of nationality, of social position, of sex,‡—are lost as soon as union with Christ is realized, the new absorbing all the old relations.§ The Jews and the Gentiles had been enemies; the Christians recognized them, without distinction of race, as brethren. This name *brethren* they delighted to use, in speaking of each other, as at once distinguishing them from all other men,‖ and witnessing to the new spiritual relationship which united them to God and to Christ. Christ thus becomes the first-born among many brethren, who by Him are sons of God. ¶

* Ἀρνοῦνται, 2 Tim. ii. 12.

† Μεσότοιχον, Eph. ii. 14. and foll.

‡ Paul's remarks on the subordinate position of the woman (1 Tim. ii. 9, and foll. ; 1 Cor. xi. 2, and foll. ; Eph. v. 22, foll., etc.) do not refer to the religious relation of which we are here speaking. We may take this occasion to remark how wisely the apostle—in an age very unenlightened in this respect—reconciles the indefeasible claims of the spiritual nature, with the no less sacred duties of the social relation of the two sexes. Philosophy may express doubts as to the validity of the sometimes singular arguments on this point, which Paul derives from his Jewish dialectics, but it cannot repudiate his conclusions.

§ Gal. iii. 28 ; Col. iii. 11 ; 1 Cor. vii. 19 ; xii. 13.

‖ Ἀδελφόν ὀνομάζεσθαι, to be a Christian, 1 Cor. v. 11.

¶ Rom. viii. 29.

If once there were two peoples, separate and mutually hostile, now they are but one, the people of Christ,* bought with the price of His own blood, or the people of God to whom this name belongs in a sense far more peculiar than to those who in old times derived it from the laws and relations of a carnal sonship.† This is indeed the Israel of God,‡ composed of children according to the promise.§

Even this mode, however, of describing or emphasizing the idea of the unity of the Church does not appear to the apostle sufficiently expressive. There is another in which he still more delights, and which represents the fact by a most vivid figure. He speaks of an organic body, all the members of which, while differing as to the beauty of their form, the nature of their functions, the place they occupy, are yet all essential to the preservation of the living organism, and all contribute, in their measure, to its full development.‖ The allegory was designed to point to Christ as the Head (in the old acceptation of the word) of this body, and to lay stress upon the fact that the whole body was moved and animated by but one spirit.

This antithesis of the people of Christ and the ancient people of God, Israel according to the flesh,¶ would easily suggest the

---

* Titus ii. 14.
† 1 Cor. x. 18.
‡ Ἰσραὴλ τοῦ θεοῦ, Gal. vi. 16 ; comp. Rom. ix. 6.
§ Τέκνα τῆς ἐπαγγελίας, Rom. ix. 8.
‖ 1 Cor. xii. 12—27 ; comp. Rom. vii. 4, and foll. ; Eph. iv. 12—16 ; v. 23—30 ; Col. i. 18, 24; ii. 19 ; iii. 15. See also Eph. i. 23, an obscure passage, of which we venture to offer the following explanation. As a body, the Church not only has Christ for its Head, but it is also, according to another figure, *filled* with Christ as its spiritual principle ; Christ is the soul of the Church, the Church is the fulness (πλήρωμα), that is, the vessel filled to the brim with Him who is to penetrate its whole nature. And as, after all, Christ gives to the world nothing which does not come of God, the Church so filled is, from the ideal point of view, itself the fulness of God (πλήρωμα τοῦ θεοῦ, Eph. iii. 19). [Rather, the Church when called the Pleroma of Christ is represented as the sphere in which *all* that is in Christ is fully revealed.—ED.]
¶ Ἰσραὴλ κατὰ σάρκα, 1 Cor. x. 18.

idea of an absolute separation between the two periods of the history of religion, of a great gulf between the two economies. We do not find, however, anything of the kind. Both are bound together by the promises of God,* promises partially expressed in direct and explicit terms, partially contained in the prophetic and typical character of the former period. Thus God had made a covenant with Israel, by which that nation was distinguished from all others upon earth.† It was a government based upon promises, and ensuring their fulfilment ;‡ it thus held forth the prospect of a new covenant,§ a prospect realized in the Christian dispensation, which, in distinction from the preceding, received a special seal, not in the letter, but in the spirit. Hence the apostle so often alludes to the fact that this was the spirit of promise.‖

This new covenant, the covenant of redemption and reconciliation, the covenant based upon the abrogation of the law—in a. word, the covenant of faith brings to our mind, by all these distinctive titles, the fact of the death of Christ, by which all these results have been effected. It is a covenant sealed with the blood of Christ, as the old covenant was ratified by the blood of the sacrificial victim.¶ Thus the relation between Christ and His Church is as close as that between husband and wife ; the Church is part of His flesh and of His bones; no earthly relation can be more near and intimate. The original institution of marriage itself is a prophetic figure by which it is set forth.**

The symbol of this covenant is the Lord's Supper.‡‡ It is a common meal, in which all the brethren take part, at the common expense, and at the close of which, according to the

* Ἐπαγγελίαι, 2 Cor. i. 20 ; Rom. iii. 1, and foll. ; xv. 8 ; Gal. iii. 8, 16, and foll.
† Rom. ix. 4.
‡ Eph. ii. 12.
§ Καινὴ διαθήκη, 2 Cor. iii. 6.
‖ Gal. iii. 14 ; Eph. i. 33, etc.
¶ 1 Cor. xi. 25.
** Μυστήριον, Eph. v. 29, and foll.
†† Κυριακὸν δεῖπνον, 1 Cor. xi. 20, and foll.

Lord's direction, bread is broken and distributed among them all, the cup is offered to all, and they repeat the same words which Jesus had addressed to His disciples at His last supper with them under similar circumstances. The bread and wine, and the words which accompany their distribution, have thus a double application, a twofold symbolic meaning, apart from the commemoration of the person of the Saviour, which is also one end of this institution. The participation of all in the same bread, signifies the brotherhood of all who belong to the same body, the Church.* The participation of all in the same cup, signifies the share of all alike in the blood of Christ,† that is, in all that has been obtained for believers by the shedding of that blood. We need not pause here to show that these explanations, which the texts abundantly support, in no way favour the material interpretation of the sacramental words which has found acceptance in so many systems both ancient and modern. Suffice it to observe, first, that the words of the institution, as they are given by Paul, are less favourable to a material interpretation than in the form in which they appear in the gospels; we might almost suppose this to be designedly the case;‡ second, that Paul adds expressly, (he and Luke only) the idea of a commemorative object in the rite; third, that he attaches a different symbolic meaning to the communion in each kind.

It is right to advert here again, also, to the rite of baptism. We have seen that Paul makes this essentially the symbol of regeneration; but as it was always administered to those entering on Church membership, it follows naturally that it was also regarded as an initiatory rite. Christians were bap-

---

* Εἰς ἄρτος, ἓν σῶμα, 1 Cor. x. 17.

† 1 Cor. v. 16. If the word ποτίζεσθαι, 1 Cor. xii. 13, could be referred with certainty to the cup of the Holy Communion, we should find in it a third symbolical signification of this rite. It would represent also the communication of the Holy Spirit as the one Spirit of the Church.

‡ This is at once apparent on a comparison of the two formulas : 1st, "Drink ye all of it," that is, my blood, etc., Matt. xxvi 28 ; 2nd, "This cup is the new testament in my blood : this do," etc., 1 Cor. xi. 25 ; Luke xxii. 20.

tized into and in the name of Christ.* This formula might
be understood generally of the profession of faith which was
to accompany baptism. But in the mouth of Paul (though
he does not explain himself directly on the point) it undoubtedly contains the mystical meaning which is at the
basis of his whole system, and to which we are here naturally
led by the idea of the body of Christ and of His members.
Thus it is said, "For by one Spirit we are all baptized into
one body," † a phrase which shows us how entirely the
material aspect of the rite is merged by him in the spiritual, which he disengages from it, and which is with him
always the main thing. In fact, it might appear that the
baptism of the Spirit has completely superseded the baptism
of water.

This Church or society is then to be the sphere of the Christian's labour; here his love is to translate itself into deeds.
But here, again, he is not left to his own strength. God is ever
near to sustain him, and as He has already given him those
general dispositions which prompt to such activity, so He now
bestows on him those special qualities and capacities which he
is to use for the furtherance of God's designs.

The Gospel had already spoken of these special qualifications under the figure of talents committed to the servants of
a king, to be used by them to increase the common capital.
This figure has been so thoroughly apprehended, that the
word *talents* has come to have in modern languages, generally,
the broad sense of particular gifts of the human mind, by
which individuals are distinguished from each other. The
apostle Paul does not use this expression, but in substance the
idea repeatedly occurs in his writings. He regards the faculties which enable the individual to serve the cause of God and
the Church, as so many gifts of divine grace, which, in spite
of the variety of their form and application in practical life,
are so many manifestations of the same one and universal gift

* Εἰς Χριστόν, Rom. vi. 3 ; Gal. iii. 27 ; εἰς ὄνομα Χριστοῦ, 1 Cor. i. 13,
15.

† 1 Cor. xii. 13 ; ἐν ἑνὶ πνεύματι ἡμεῖς πάντες εἰς ἓν σῶμα ἐβαπτίσθημεν.

of the Spirit of God, which forms the distinctive characteristic of the Christian.*

We may observe, first, that the terms which describe this dispensation vary in form, without changing the fundamental idea. Properly, it is God who bestows these special gifts;† they are said to be given *in* and *with* the Spirit, as special manifestations of His presence; or to be *by* the Spirit as produced by Him; or, lastly, ‡ to be in the measure of His influence and operation. It might quite as justly be said that the Spirit Himself imparts these gifts,§ or that Christ ‖ does so, since He is also inseparably connected with all that is done in and for the Church. If there appears to be in this matter a purely arbitrary distribution among the members of the community, this is to convey the idea that he who may possess one or other of these gifts, is not to glory in it as a peculiar desert of his own, for there is to be an intercommunication of gifts among the members,¶ a sort of exchange by which each may obtain the gift of the other without losing his own; while each possessor is bound carefully to improve and cherish his own special talent.** The essential thing is that in each community no necessary gift be found wanting.††

The two passages from the epistles to Timothy, which we have just cited, are remarkable, again, as seeming to connect the communication of the gifts of the Spirit with the consecration to the Gospel ministry and the laying on of hands. This idea might appear to belong to a subsequent generation,

* Διαιρέσεις χαρισμάτων εἰσί, τὸ δὲ αὐτὸ πνεῦμα, ἑκάστῳ δὲ δίδοται ἡ φανέωρσις, τοῦ ποεύματος πρὸδ τὸ συμφέρον, 1 Cor. xii. 4, 7.

† 1 Cor. vii. 7 ; xii. 6, 18, 24 ; Eph. iii. 7 ; 2 Tim. i. 6.

‡ Κατὰ τὸ πνεῦμα, 1 Cor. xii. 8, 9 ; comp. κατὰ τὴν χάριν, Rom. xii. 6.

§ 1 Cor. xii. 11.

‖ Eph. iv. 7.

¶ Rom. i. 11.

** 1 Tim. iv. 14 ; 2 Tim. i. 6.

†† 1 Cor. i. 7, etc. In Rom. xii. 6, comp. v. 3, κατ' ἀναλογίαν τῆς πίστεως means, in the measure of the individual development of Christians in relation to their faith,—that is to say, their education, conviction, and Christian life. This shows that the special gifts depend in part on the subjectivity of those who obtain and possess them.

and to a later stage of the development of Christian thought, the gifts of the Spirit seeming to be reserved to a particular class of the faithful.* We do not think, however, that an example of special and individual application ought to be regarded as a contradiction to the general rule, to which it may fairly be held subordinate.

Thus furnished and adorned with the gifts of the Spirit, the individual enters the service of the Church. As the measure of his powers is necessarily limited, God assigns him his place in a particular and local community, and it is in working for this that he contributes his share to the general progress.

He finds himself thus placed in a new relation to Christ, the Head of the Church, of which he himself is a member. Christ is the Lord and Master of the Church; the believer is His servant and minister.† The modes of service are very varied.‡ Paul enumerates them without pretending to exhaust the catalogue. He names, for example, apostleship, prophecy, evangelization, administration, the care of the poor and the afflicted, the gift of healing, that of working miracles, etc.§ This category does not comprehend merely what we might call official duties; all co-operation in the work of the Church, the moral qualities which may serve as an example to others, conduct in harmony with the spirit of the Gospel, the social virtues, faith and charity, are alike included in the number of these

* Contrary to Rom. xii., 1 Cor. xii. ; comp. Acts viii. 15—17 ; xix. 6.

† Διάκονος.

‡ Διαιρέσεις διακονιῶν εἰσίν, ὁ δὲ αὐτὸς κύριος, 1 Cor. xii. 5.

§ 1 Cor. xii. 8—10, v. 28—30 ; Eph. iv. 11 ; Rom. xii. 4—7. The detailed reflections which this list may suggest do not belong to this history of theology. We simply refer our readers to competent exegetes. There are questions of philology and history, including that of the famous gift of tongues, on which the reader, who would like to know our views, may consult vol. iii. of the "Revue." We may observe, again, that the word διάκονος and its derivatives designate sometimes certain special functions, specially attention to the material wants of the community (Rom. xvi. 1 ; Phil. i. 1 ; 1 Cor. xvi. 15 ; 1 Tim. iii. 8, and foll.), elsewhere a special service casually rendered (Rom. xv. 25, 31 ; 2 Cor. viii., ix., passim ; 2 Tim. i. 18 ; Philem. 13) ; more frequently, however, the Gospel ministry, regarded as a charge entrusted to a man by God or by Christ (Rom. xi. 13 ;

gifts.* We may here say, in passing, that according to the old exegesis, these gifts of the Spirit were supposed to be something altogether miraculous, and granted exclusively to the Corinthian Church in the time of St. Paul. Had this been the case, it would seem the Spirit had but ill chosen His sphere. It is, in truth, melancholy to see how far ecclesiastical theology has deviated from the true evangelical principle, refusing to the believer of modern times precisely that which, according to the apostle, constitutes his essential and indispensable characteristic. By carrying the principle of inspiration to the extreme on the side of the letter, it has completely sacrificed its application to the spirit of the believer, thus reversing the real meaning of the apostle.

Paul loves to represent this labour for the spiritual good of the community by an allegory to which he frequently returns, and which has readily passed into the religious language of the Church. He compares the Church to a building,† more particularly to a temple, reared, or rather being reared, on Christ as its foundation, and the progressive completion of which is to be the work of all the faithful.‡ According to this figure, the terms *edification*,§ *to edify the Church*, which occur so frequently in the writings of the apostle, signify properly to co-operate for the advancement of the Church, whether by gaining for it new members, or still more by confirming and sanctifying those who are already in it, causing them to grow in faith and charity.‖ The image in itself represents the community as a whole, and refers to work undertaken for the general good.¶ It thus blends with the image of the body, which can refer only to the totality of believers, and their

1 Cor. iii. 5; 2 Cor. iii. 6, and foll.; iv. 1; v. 18; vi. 3; xi. 23; Eph. iii. 7; vi. 21; Col. i. 7, 23, and foll.; iv. 17; 1 Thess. iii. 2; 1 Tim. i. 12; iv. 6; 2 Tim. iv. 5.)

* 1 Cor. xii. 9; Rom. xii. 8, and foll.

† 1 Tim. iii. 15.

‡ 1 Cor. iii. 9—15; Eph. ii. 20, and foll.

§ Οἰκοδομή, οἰκοδομεῖν.

‖ 1 Cor. viii. 1; x. 23; Rom. xv. 20; 2 Cor. x. 8; xii. 19; xiii. 10.

¶ 1 Cor. xiv. 4, 12, 26.

common union with Christ.* By a metonomy, however, the word *edification* comes to mean, also, the spiritual good that one may do to another,† and it is in this sense that it is chiefly used in our own day.‡

We have yet another figure setting forth the same relations. Humanity is the field of God,§ in which the good seed is to be sown for eternity. God is the Master of the field, who apportions and directs the work ; the faithful entrusted with any share of the toil are His workmen.|| The apostles in a special manner do the work of the Lord,¶ but all the members of the Church may and ought to devote themselves to it.** Paul does not carry out this idea into an allegory, though it would have well borne such a development, and would have notably yielded this important principle, that the amount of pains to be bestowed upon Christian work must not be measured out in anticipation, by the worker's own direct share in the result.

---

* Eph. iv. 12, 16.

† Rom. xv. 2 ; xiv. 19 ; 1 Cor. xiv. 3, 17 ; 1 Thess. v. 11.

‡ Paul goes so far as to use the term in the absolute sense of progress made towards any end, good or bad, 1 Cor. viii. 10.

§ Γεώργιον.

|| Συνεργοί, 1 Cor. iii. 9.

¶ Ἔργον κυρίου, 1 Cor. xvi. 10 ; Phil. ii. 30.

** 1 Cor. xv. 58.

CHAPTER XVIII.

OF HOPE AND TRIAL.

WE now reach the third and last phase of the Christian life —hope.* The first represented a subjective and essentially individual experience; the second, activity in a wider sphere and in fellowship with other men. This third phase opens the prospect of the fulfilment of that which the first accepted in humble trust, and the second sought to hasten by zealous toil.

We have had occasion already to note that the facts which this prospect embraces, and which are sufficiently numerous, belonged also, almost without exception, to the theological sphere of Judaism, and still more generally to the eschatological horizon of the early Christians. What lies before us now, therefore, is not so much to write a chapter of the particular theology of Paul, as to show the identity of his convictions and teachings with those which prevailed at the time both in the Synagogue and the Church. We might confine ourselves to a few brief quotations, if the apostle had not attached to certain eschatological facts, furnished by the schools, Christian ideas which were entirely new, and by means of which the Church has been enabled, in this as in other spheres, to rise above the narrow limits of Jewish thought, to the height of the Gospel of the Spirit. Our readers will bear in mind that apostolic Christianity was at the beginning a religion of hope, inasmuch as it was immediately occupied with the near and certain fulfilment of all that the theology and national feeling of the Jewish people expected

* 'Ελπίς.

from Messiah; and that the difference between the eschatology
of the Synagogue and that of the primitive Church consisted
in three points: 1st, The Christians, convinced that Jesus
of Nazareth was the promised Messiah, believed in a second
coming of the Saviour, instead of the one advent expected by
the Jews. 2nd. The exclusiveness of Judaism gradually gave
place in the minds of the Christians to Gospel universalism;
3rd. The political element, which predominated in the hopes
of the Israelites, was altogether subordinated by the religious
and moral element, which the apostolic preaching brought into
prominence.

Let us now show first, very briefly, the relation which, in
the doctrine of Paul, hope sustained towards the other two
phases of the Christian life. Faith has for its essential
object, or we may say for its starting-point, all that God,
in His wisdom and inexhaustible love, has done to prepare
and open for the sinner a way of salvation. It is then to facts
belonging to the past, that faith is to attach the spiritual life
of man. Love is more especially the expression of that same
life, in so far as it relates to present duty. The domain of
hope is the future. Christian hope (such is the definition of
the apostle himself) has for its object all those good things
which, although promised to the elect, are not yet within their
grasp.

These benefits* are many, as we know; at least the terms
by which they are described are many and various; and hope
itself is defined in several ways, in view of this variety in its
object. It is sometimes spoken of as the hope of His appearing,† because that appearing is the condition and the pledge
of all that is to follow; again, as the hope of the resurrection,‡
deliverance from the bonds of death being the commencement
of our future existence, and the pledge of the ulterior promises
made to the faithful; again, as the hope of salvation,§ inasmuch

---

* Ὃ οὐ βλέπομεν ἐλπίζομεν, Rom. viii. 24.
† Ἐπιφανείας, Titus ii. 13.
‡ Ἀναστάσεως, 1 Thess. iv. 13.
§ Σωτηρίας, 1 Thess. v. 8; comp. Rom. viii. 20, 24.

as that term, which designates properly the act of saving, implies the negation of all peril, and consequently the affirmation of all good, prospectively enjoyed; again, as the hope of eternal life,[*] representing the same benefits under the aspect of life, that is of happiness, or in relation to their endless duration; again as the hope of glory,[†] or of the glory of God, by which the same happiness is set forth under the figure of splendour and brightness, the perfection of the outward no less than the inward life; again as the hope of righteousness,[‡] inasmuch as we believe God will accept us as righteous in view of our faith, so that we may be entitled to a share in the benefits prepared for the righteous; and righteousness is therefore here put for justification, the declarative act of God; lastly, as the hope of the Lord's coming,[§] inasmuch as all the hopes just enumerated will be fulfilled by Him at His advent. It is in this sense, again, Christ is said to be our hope. In relation to all these objects, our hope may be said to be laid up in heaven,[‖] because only as we reach heaven shall we enter upon the actual enjoyment of the hoped-for blessings.

Hope is further variously characterized according to the foundation on which it rests, which, again, may be regarded from different points of view. Thus we find the terms, " the hope of the Gospel," that is, a hope based on the Gospel;[¶] for the Gospel, proclaimed by God and under His sanction, is equivalent to a divine promise; "the hope of His calling,"[**] that is to say, a hope which has its warrant in the certainty of the individual calling; "hope in Christ,"[††] a phrase to which may be attached perhaps the same ideas as we have just mentioned in connection with the hope of the Lord's coming;

---

[*] Ζωῆς, Titus i. 2; iii. 7.

[†] Δόξης, Col. i. 27; Rom. v. 2; comp. 2 Cor. iii. 12.

[‡] Δικαιοσύνης, Gal. v. 5.

[§] Κυρίου, 1 Thess. i. 3; comp. 1 Tim. i. 1; Col. i. 27.

[‖] Ἀποκειμένη ἐν τοῖς οὐρανοῖς, Col. i. 5.

[¶] Εὐαγγελίου, Col. i. 23.

[**] Κλήσεως, Eph. i. 18; iv. 4.

[††] 1 Cor. xv. 19; 2 Cor. i. 10.

it denotes the hope which we derive through our relation with the Saviour; "hope in God,"* by which we are reminded that it is the will of God that man should be saved; hence, also, "the God of hope," † the God who awakens within us such a hope; we have, again, "the hope of the Scriptures," resting upon the promises of the Old Testament; ‡ and, lastly, we have a hope derived from our own experience, inasmuch as we prove by our perseverance in the practice of good, and our patience in evil days, that we are the true disciples of the Lord. §

The hope of the Christian, resting upon a basis so broad and sure, cannot fail him; ‖ on the contrary, it is of a nature to fill his heart with present joy, and to give him the foretaste of his final bliss.¶ It is a precious gift of divine grace.** It thus marks in an especial manner all the inestimable advantages of his position, compared with that of the Gentile who has no hope, not even the hope of the Jew.††

Such are the general ideas attached to the term *hope*, which may serve to complete its definition. We proceed now to trace, as we have done in the other two phases of the believer's life, the relations which this hope establishes between the three persons treated of by evangelical theology generally, and that of Paul in particular—God, Christ, and the believer. The order in which these three personages naturally present themselves for our contemplation, will be once more changed by the very nature of the ground, so to speak, on which we shall find them engaged. We shall address ourselves first to man, to whom this hope is given, because he will need to be prepared by patience and experience for its full realization. We shall next look at Christ, presenting Himself to man as the Conqueror

---

* 1 Tim. iv. 10 ; v. 5.

† Rom. xv. 13.

‡ Παράκλησις τῶν γραφῶν, Rom. xv. 4.

§ Δοκιμὴ ἐλπίδα κατεργάζεται, Rom. v. 4; comp. 2 Cor. i. 7 ; 1 Thess. ii. 19.

‖ Rom. v. 5.

¶ Rom. xii. 12.

** 2 Thess. ii. 16.

†† Eph. ii. 12; comp. 1 Thess. iv. 13.

of evil, and removing all the obstacles to the progress of His
saving work; His glorious return will be the signal for the
setting up of His kingdom. Lastly, we shall see God exalted
high over all, having accomplished all His designs, and
secured to His people an inheritance of glory incorruptible.

Paul shared the conviction and the hope of his colleagues,
and of all the members of the primitive Church, that the
second coming of Christ, and with it the close of the existing
order of things, and the foundation of a real and visible
kingdom of God, was imminent. "The Lord is at hand,"* he
says, in a passage in which it is impossible to understand a
purely spiritual presence. "The time is short,"† we read in
another passage of still plainer import. The period in which
he lived is spoken of as the end of the world, the last times
immediately preceding the beginning of a new era for
mankind.‡ And, as though to leave no doubt as to the necessity of understanding these phrases, not in a limited and
relative sense, but absolutely—in the sense, in short, attached
to them in the Jewish schools, he declares plainly that the
generation to which he himself belonged§ would not pass
away till the final scene of the world's drama had been enacted
before its eyes. The only limitation which he adds to this
assertion, is that some delay is not impossible, that the day of
Christ may not come, therefore, quite so immediately as some
had thought.‖ The event is sure, but the precise moment
cannot be fixed;¶ the Christian must therefore always be in
readiness, that he may not be taken unawares.

Until that day come,—a day anticipated at once with awe
and with desire,—there will be times of trial and tribulation
for the Church.** It will be a period of distress, of anguish,

* Ὁ κύριος ἐγγύς, Phil. iv. 5.
† Ὁ καιρὸς συνεσταλμένος, 1 Cor. vii. 29.
‡ Τὰ τέλη τῶν αἰώνων, 1 Cor. x. 11; καιροὶ ὕστεροι, 1 Tim. iv. 1; ἐσχάται
ἡμέραι, 2 Tim. iii. 1.
§ Ἡμεῖς οἱ ζῶντες, 1 Thess. iv. 15, and foll.
‖ 2 Thess. ii. 2.
¶ 1 Thess. v. 1.
** Καιροὶ χαλεποί, 2 Tim. iii. 1.

of calamity, of suffering of every description.* The Christian will not, however, be cast down by all this; on the contrary, he will rejoice; first, because he will remember that Christ also suffered for him, and his own sufferings will seem to bring him into fellowship with those of his Saviour, † and to be therefore a pledge of his final participation in the glory of Christ;‡ and, again, because he will regard them as a means in the hand of God, for educating and exercising him in a higher and stronger faith. § It is in this sense that the ills which befall Christians are called trials. ‖

The immediate effect of affliction upon the believer is patience.¶ This idea, in Paul's own language, is, however, more comprehensive than that we derive from the translation. It comprises three elements: 1st. Passive resistance to evil, or rather simple acquiescence in suffering.** 2nd. Active resistance, persistence or perseverance in previous convictions or resolutions, unshaken by fear or pain. †† 3rd. A quiet waiting for the end, an attitude of assurance and serenity of soul which no evil can disturb.‡‡ When God is spoken of as the God of patience,§§ it must be in the sense that He will satisfy this expectation of the soul and recompense this persevering faith.

This idea of a waiting, expectant attitude, indicated by the very etymology of the word, is paramount throughout this

---

* Παθήματα τοῦ νῦν καιροῦ, Rom. viii. 18 ; ἐνεστῶσα ἀνάγκη, 1 Cor. vii. 26 ; θλίψεις, 2 Cor. iv. 17 ; 2 Cor. vi. 4, and foll. ; Gal. iv. 14.

† Col. i. 24 ; 2 Cor. i. 5.

‡ Phil. iii. 10, 11.

§ Παιδεία, 2 Cor. vi. 9 ; Titus ii. 12 ; 1 Cor. xi. 32.

‖ Πειρασμοί, 1 Cor. x. 13. Πειράζειν and its derivatives are not very frequently used in Paul's epistles. It may be well, however, to observe that they contain all the different meanings found elsewhere, (see the following pages), even that of a simple examination, 2 Cor. xiii. 5.

¶ 'Η θλίψις ὑπομονὴν κατεργάζεται, Rom v. 3.

** Rom. viii. 25 ; xv. 4 ; 2 Cor. i. 6 ; vi. 4.

†† 1 Thess. i. 3 ; 2 Thess. i. 4 ; 2 Tim. ii. 10, 12 ; Rom. ii. 7 ; xii. 12 ; 2 Cor. xii. 12 ; Col. i. 11.

‡‡ 'Υπομονὴ τοῦ Χριστοῦ, 2 Thess. iii. 5.

§§ Rom. xv. 5

part of our subject; and it is on this account we have spoken of it here.*

In another aspect, the word in question contains, as we said, also the idea of active resistance, or of a struggle with evil regarded as a *trial*. Now, passing from the sphere of theory to that of experience, where we shall find, not Christians who have already realized the ideal, but, at most, men striving more or less imperfectly to approach it, this same resistance will come before us as a real conflict, as a wrestling with evil, which now presents itself in the form of *temptation*.†

To fight is then the destiny and the duty of the Christian. This fight is called emphatically a *good* fight,‡ on account both of the principle that prompts to it and the promise which is attached to victory. The victorious weapon used is faith. The apostle delights to describe, in suggestive allegories, the means of attack and defence placed at the disposal of the Christian.§

This warfare is to be waged, first of all, against our own moral weaknesses, as we have already elsewhere observed. It often arises out of the relations and occurrences of private and social life, the obstacles placed in the way of the good cause, the persecutions to which its defenders are exposed.‖ But all this is epitomized in one word, when it is said that the Christian warfare is against the devil and his kingdom.¶ The devil (called also by his Hebrew name Satan, and again simply *the wicked one* **) is represented as the prince and lord of the world, which is hostile to God; as the god of this world,†† all whose efforts are directed against the progress of

---

* We add a few more expressions of like meaning which the apostle occasionally uses : ἀναμένειν τὸν υἱόν, 1 Thess. i. 10 ; ἀπεκδέχεσθαι, Rom. viii. 19, 23, 25, 1 Cor. i. 7, Phil. iii. 20; ἀποκαραδοκία, Rom. viii. 19.

† Πειρασμός, Gal. vi. 1 ; 1 Thess. iii. 5.

‡ Καλὸς ἀγών, 1 Tim. vi. 12; comp. 1 Cor. ix. 24, and foll. ; Col. i. 29, etc.

§ Eph. vi. 13, and foll.; 1 Thess. v. 8 ; Rom. xiii. 12.

‖ Phil. i. 30 ; Col. ii. 1 ; 1 Thess. ii. 2 ; 2 Tim. iv. 7.

¶ Ἐνδύσασθε τὴν πανοπλίαν τοῦ θεοῦ πρὸς τὸ δύνασθαι ὑμᾶς στῆναι πρὸς τὰς μεθοδείας τοῦ διαβόλου, Eph. vi. 10.

** Ὁ σατανᾶς, Rom. xvi. 20, etc. ; ὁ πονηρός, Eph. vi. 16 ; 2 Thess. iii. 3.

†† Ὁ θεὸς τοῦ αἰῶνος τούτου, 2 Cor. iv. 4.

the kingdom of God. He is supported in his enterprise by an army of inferior spirits, who derive their power from him (as do the good angels from God), and who on that account are .called powers,* or simply *angels, demons, evil spirits.*† They inhabit the regions of the air,‡ which are, however, represented as a place of gloom, unless we interpret the term darkness in a moral sense.§ The devil is their head.|| He lays ambush for men. Those who are not converted, who do not listen to the voice of the Gospel, are wholly his; *he works in them,* as Paul says.¶ For the rest he is always on the watch; he sets snares in their path,** deceives, tempts,††

* Ἀρχαί, ἐξουσίαι, δυνάμεις, Rom. viii. 38 ; 1 Cor. xv. 24 ; Eph. vi. 12 ; Col. ii. 15. The good angels are spoken of by precisely the same names, or other synonyms, as θρόνοι, κυριότητες, Eph. i. 21 ; iii. 10 ; Col. i. 16 ; ii. 10. Neither exegesis nor the history of Jewish dogmas justifies us in distinguishing them into different classes of heavenly beings. We may refer to the word δαιμόνια, so common in our gospels, and which Paul uses only in 1 Tim. iv. 1, and 1 Cor. x. 20. According to the latter passage, it would appear (and this was the opinion of the early Church) that Paul regarded the gods of paganism as devils—that is to say, as real beings. Modern exegetes, taking their stand on 1 Cor. viii. 4, have preferred to take δαιμόνια in the classical sense. But the use of the word δαιμόνιον in the Hellenist idiom is so constant that it is impossible to assign to it in this single passage the classical meaning, which would moreover break the thread of the argument. After all, the difficulty is not so great. Paganism, as opposed to the kingdom of God, is of the devil ; idolatrous worship, since it robs God of the honour which is His due, is in truth a worship of the devil and of his power. It is the reality of the devil and his angels which Paul affirms, not the reality of the Olympic gods ; comp. 2 Cor. vi. 15.

† Ἄγγελοι, 2 Cor. xii. 7 ; 1 Cor. vi. 3 ; πνευματικὰ τῆς πονηρίας, Eph. vi. 12 ; δαιμόνια, 1 Tim. iv. 1.

‡ Eph. ii. 2 ; ἐν τοῖς ἐπουρανίοις, vi. 12.

§ Κοσμοκράτορες τοῦ σκότους, see Eph. vi. 12 ; 2 Cor. iv. 4. Paul is frequently speaking in a moral sense, whether he refers to vice (Rom. xiii. 12, Eph. v. 11,) or to the ignorance of men without the light of revelation (Eph. iv. 18, 2 Cor. iv. 6). These two facts, however, are so closely connected that it would be difficult always to separate them. See 1 Thess. v. 4, and foll. ; Rom. i. 21 ; Eph. v. 8, etc.

|| Ἄρχων, Eph. ii. 2.

¶ Ἐνεργῶν, Eph. ii. 2.

** 1 Tim. iii. 7 ; vi. 9 ; 2 Tim. ii. 26.

†† Πειράζει, 1 Cor. vii. 5.

seduces, beguiles them* by false doctrine, or by assuming the guise of an angel of light,† drawing them to himself by means of their own lusts and passions,‡ or, if he can effect no more, perpetually putting obstacles in their path.§ In a word, in one way or another, he seeks to injure the kingdom of Christ and to gain the advantage over Him.‖

Hence the exhortation addressed to Christians not to allow themselves to be taken captive by the devil at his will.¶ Those who follow him, who allow themselves to be led away by him,** are regarded as lost, unless after being given up for the time to him, for their chastisement and correction, they return to their true selves and to better feelings.††

Such is, in substance, the character, such are the conditions of the period which is to pass before the coming of Christ.‡‡ It is a time when vice and fleshly lusts and carnal desires will reign; an evil time,§§ and in most cases this is the sense to be attached to the expression *this present time, the time that now is,* even when the qualifying adjective is not given.‖‖ For this same reason it is a time of affliction and tribulation for the faithful.¶¶

He who boldly persists in this conflict, and holds out to the end, is said to have been *tried;* this is the fruit of his per-

---

* 1 Tim. iv. 1.
† 2 Cor. xi. 14.
‡ 1 Cor. vii. 5.
§ 1 Thess. ii. 18.
‖ 2 Cor. ii. 11.
¶ Eph. iv. 27.
** 1 Tim. v. 15.
†† 1 Cor. v. 5 ; 1 Tim. i. 20, παιδεία.
‡‡ Ὁ νῦν καιρός, ὁ νῦν αἰών, Rom. viii. 18; 2 Tim. iv. 10; Titus ii. 12.
§§ Gal. i. 4.
‖‖ Rom. xii. 2 ; 1 Cor. i. 20 ; ii. 6, and foll.; iii. 18, and foll.; ὁ αἰὼν τοῦ κόσμου τούτου, Eph. ii. 2. The term κόσμος in Paul's language has almost the same meaning as with John, but he does not use it in so strictly theological a sense.   It applies to the physical world, to men generally; and this is its most frequent meaning ; lastly, but more rarely, the apostle gives it a bad sense by adding οὗτος.
¶¶ Rom. viii. 18.

severance.* This, then, must express the judgment of God,
the seal of His approval.† This sentence is supposed to be
formally pronounced at the close of the Christian's life, who
having then been both proved and approved, stands accepted
before God.‡

* Δόκιμος, δοκιμή, δοκιμάζειν, Rom. v. iv. ; comp. 2 Cor. viii. 2.
† 2 Cor. x. 18.
‡ 1 Cor. xi. 19 ; 1 Thess. ii. 4 ; 2 Tim. ii. 15. We may pass by those
passages in which the reference is rather to public approval (δόκιμος τοῖς
ἀνθρώποις, Rom. xiv. 18), obtained by a conscientious fulfilment of
Christian duties (ἐν Χριστῷ, Rom. xvi. 10); comp. Phil. ii. 22 ; 2 Cor. ix.
13, etc.

CHAPTER XIX.

OF THE LAST TIMES.

THE conflict we have just described, as well as the charge addressed to Christians to wage and sustain it manfully, will last to the very moment of Christ's coming again. That happy period, which is to terminate a state of things so dark and painful, is called the end.*

With this second appearing of Christ, Paul, like the other apostles, connects all the great eschatological events which the Jews were wont to look for on the first coming of Messiah, whom they expected to appear once for all. These events are the resurrection, the judgment, and the setting up of the kingdom of God;† and it will be easy to show that the theology of the apostle was here at first built upon the common basis of the schools of his nation, and went but a little way in spiritualizing the doctrine of the Pharisees.

The return of Christ, who from the time of His death had become invisible to the world, is naturally regarded as a second revelation of His person; and because it is attended with results yet more important and decisive than His first manifestation in our earthly, human life, it is called simply the revelation of the Lord.‡ Then for the first time He will appear in all His glory and power; hence His return is sometimes

---

* Τὸ τέλος, 1 Cor. i. 8.

† Or, rather, the glorious manifestation of that kingdom; for Paul always thinks of the kingdom of God as being already established in the world.—ED.

‡ Ἡ ἀποκάλυψις τοῦ κυρίου, 1 Cor. i. 7 ; 2 Thess. i. 7; comp. Rev. i. 1.

described simply as His *appearing*,* without any qualifying term. As, however, His first sojourn with humanity was also an appearing,† the future manifestation is often distinguished as His *glorious* appearing,‡ in contrast to the state of humiliation in which He first came to earth ; or its permanence § is emphasized in contrast with the shortness of His former visitation, for the word translated *coming* in the text just cited properly signifies *presence.* || The appearing of the Lord then, according to the etymology, represents the whole future period of His sensible presence among His people, the indissoluble union which will thenceforth visibly exist between Him and them, while now it exists in spirit only. By a very natural metonomy, this term came in the end to designate the initial moment of this new era—the moment, that is, of Christ's reappearing.¶

Our readers will remember how prolific was the Judæo-Christian theory in descriptions of the coming manifestation of Christ. The writings of Paul contain some traces of the influence which these descriptions had exerted upon his imagination. Thus we find him speaking of Christ as descending from heaven amid fiery clouds and throngs of angels, and heralded by the blast of trumpets.** We would observe, however, that these are but isolated passages, and occur, moreover, in his earlier epistles, while in his later writings we meet with no allusions to such representations. His practical piety and his high appreciation of the Gospel, could not fail to make him turn away from these fanciful decorations of a doctrine, which he might at one time have received the more readily as a legacy from his early religious teaching. We do not say that he repudiated them altogether, but he certainly ceased to attach to them an exaggerated importance.

* Ἐπιφάνεια, 1 Tim. vi. 14 ; 2 Tim. iv. 1, 8.

† 2 Tim. i. 10.

‡ Titus ii. 13.

§ Ἐπιφάνεια τῆς παρουσίας, 2 Thess. ii. 8.

|| 1 Cor. xvi. 17 ; 2 Cor. vii. 6, etc.

¶ 1 Cor. i. 8 ; xv. 23 ; 1 Thess. ii. 19 ; iii. 13 ; iv. 15; v. 23 ; 2 Thess. ii. 1, 8.

** 1 Thess. iv. 16 ; 2 Thess. i. 7 ; 1 Cor. xv. 32.

It will be remembered also that Judæo-Christianity, continuing the studies of the Synagogue, was wont to exercise itself to discover the precursive signs of the end, and to fix its precise date. Paul was not altogether free from the same tendency. Sharing the general conviction of the nearness of Christ's appearing, he could not wholly withstand the temptation to trace the indications of its approach. He says, however, comparatively little on this subject; and if we except the famous passage on Antichrist,* (in which he repeats word for word, though with some appearance of mystery,† the theory derived by the rabbis from the book of Daniel,) we find nothing to add to the general expressions already quoted. Usually he is content with setting forth the practical side of the question; he expresses his hope that the Gospel will be carried into the farthest regions of the Gentiles before the close of the century;‡ he insists upon the necessity of preparing for the end, and of using diligently the span of time that remains; § lastly, he affirms that it is impossible to know the exact moment at which the Lord will come.|| Obviously this is the path in which it is safest for the Church to follow him, instead of losing itself in those apocalyptic reveries which have been the favourite and fatal aliment of so many sects, ancient and modern.

The fact which is placed in most immediate connection with

---

* 2 Thess. ii. 1—12.

† It is very difficult to say what personage Paul can have had in view in writing to the Thessalonians on the subject of Antichrist in the year 54. It is still more difficult to divine what was, in his view, the power which retarded his manifestation, τὸ κατέχον, v. 6. All conjectures that can be made on this subject are uncertain and precarious. If, however, Paul could not at this period determine the Antichrist to be expected, by means of the statements of contemporary history, it is at least certain that the power which hindered, could only be, in his view, the Roman empire, which, according to the exegesis of the time, was the fourth of the empires of which Daniel speaks, and was consequently to give place in the end to the kingdom of Christ.

‡ Rom. xi. 25, and foll.

§ Rom. xiii. 10—13; Eph. v. 16.

|| 1 Thess. v. 2.

the manifestation of Christ, is the resurrection of the dead.*
The dead, it is said, shall rise, they shall awake.† All these
expressions are figurative, and are derived from the image of
sleep in the grave.‡

Paul does not dwell largely upon the Judæo-Christian
description of the resurrection. We find, however, in his
writings, several characteristic traits common to those representations of the end. Thus he speaks of a succession of
signals given with the sound of the trumpet; at the last trump
appears an angel who calls the dead to come forth; these rise
at once from their graves, and ascend to meet the Lord in the
air, etc.§ All this belongs to an order of ideas anterior and
foreign to the system of Paul himself, and can have little
weight with us here. We pass on to other considerations
peculiar to his own mode of thought, which are at the same
time very suggestive in their evangelical import.

There are especially two aspects under which Paul connects
the Jewish dogma of the resurrection with Christian theology,
and he does so in a manner entirely new. Both are, in our
opinion, of the highest importance.

First, the resurrection of the dead is ascribed to God.‖ It is
an act of His almightiness, just like the resurrection of Jesus,
which anticipated it, and which is the pledge of that which is
to follow. But there are other passages in which this same
resurrection seems to be attributed to Christ. This occasions
no difficulty if it is remembered that the re-appearing of the
Lord gives the signal for the resurrection. But this mode of
thought or of expression may have a double meaning. We
may go no further than the simple Jewish idea that Messiah
raises the dead by command of God and as the instrument of
His will.¶ Evidently, in that case, the reference is to the

* Ἀνάστασις νεκρῶν, 1 Cor. xv. 21, 42 ; ἐξανάστασις ἐκ νεκρῶν, Phil. iii. 11.
† Ἀνίστανται, 1 Thess. iv. 16 ; ἐγείρονται, 1 Cor. xv. 52, etc.
‡ Κοιμηθέντες, 1 Cor. xv. 18.
§ 1 Cor. xv. 52 ; 1 Thess. iv. 16.
‖ 1 Cor. vi. 14 ; 2 Cor. i. 9 ; Rom. viii. 11.
¶ Ἡμᾶς διὰ Ἰησοῦ Χριστοῦ ἐγερεῖ, 2 Cor. iv. 14.

general resurrection, to a fact purely external and material.
The formula is slightly changed, the doctrine not at all; we
are still in the domain of Judæo-Christianity.

But the apostle Paul more frequently places the resurrection
of the dead in close and direct relation with the mystical
ideas of faith and regeneration. In this aspect of it, men in
whom the germ of the new spiritual life is already present
and active, have alone the prospect of a part in the second
resurrection, which is finally to vanquish death and chase
away the terrors of the tomb. The physical resurrection of
the future is inseparably linked to the spiritual resurrection
of the present; such is the Pauline, the Christian form of the
doctrine. Those who have no part in the first resurrection
—that which alone is of essential importance—will remain
strangers to the second. It is evident that here, as elsewhere,
the apostle makes an arbitrary use of the terms life and death;
their physical import is merged in their figurative acceptation.
From the Gospel point of view, there is life only in God and
in Christ; without these, there is only death; believers, the
regenerate, alone shall live; all others pass from temporal to
eternal death; the idea of the resurrection has no application to their future. Hence, in the passages where Paul
treats most at length of these things and of these hopes,*
he speaks expressly of the resurrection of Christians only,
a fact out of which has arisen the erroneous notion that
in his view the rest of mankind will be raised at another
time.†

This idea of Paul's, one of the most beautiful and profound
in his whole system, is also one of the most simple : it flows
naturally from the idea of regeneration and union with Christ.
So soon as this union, as we have described it above, is
accomplished, it follows that the new man cannot, any more
than Christ Himself with whom he is one, be held by the
bands of death. The twofold sense of the word death in this

---

* 1 Cor. xv. 23, and foll. ; 1 Thess. iv. 16, and foll.

† Some have even gone so far as to translate τὸ τέλος (1 Cor. xv. 24) by
ceteir.

deduction, does not in the least invalidate its logical force in the mysticism of the apostle. The passage* in which this idea appears most clearly set forth, refers rather to another series of religious facts; but in it, as in other similar passages, we can discern also the eschatological thesis which we are now considering. Expressions such as *being raised again with Christ* † indicate that the awaking now to the new spiritual life in Christ, is the preliminary and essential condition to awaking at last unto eternal life. The hope of the resurrection rests then entirely upon this union—that is to say, upon fahit and · regeneration. Those who can discover in the leading passage of the Epistle to the Corinthians,‡ only the deduction from the material fact of the resurrection of Christ, of the material fact of the resurrection of men, attribute to the apostle a paralogism of which the incongruity is obvious; and even if it were admissible, Paul would only have established the mere physical resurrection, and would have proved nothing as to the happiness, which is the one essential ele-ment in the conception of the future. From the fact that Christ (the Son of God) is raised from the dead, there can be no logical deduction of the fact that *all* men shall also be raised. Once again we repeat it, Paul is speaking only of believers. United to Christ in the secret and mystical meaning of the word, they are to pass with Him through the two phases of His existence—His death and resurrection. §

But if this is the adequate expression of the thought of Paul, it would be no less true to say that the resurrection is already virtually accomplished in the regeneration; the future return to life, after the death which awaits us all, will be only the consequence of this first palingenesis. Paul here makes only one distinction to be observed by us. Christ is already raised; for this reason he is called the first-fruits of the

---

* Rom. vi. 5, 8.
† Eph. ii. 5, 6; Col. ii. 12, 13.
‡ 1 Cor. xv. 12, and foll.
§ Συναποθανόντες συζήσονται.

dead,* and the first-born from the dead.† The faithful will also
rise presently and together.

We can now judge what is the true significance of the
passage in which it is said that as *in* Adam all die, so *in*
Christ shall all be made alive."‡ The preposition underlined
represents not the idea of a person being himself in an absolute manner the cause of life or death, but of fellowship with
a certain person entailing one or other of these results. We
may thus appeciate the fulness contained in the simple expression, "Christ our life." § We thus see also what Paul
means when he speaks of the significance to the believer ‖
of the resurrection of Christ; it is the pledge of his own resurrection just because he is in fellowship with the Saviour.
Lastly, we are able to explain the text ¶ in which the victory
over death and the manifestation of life are represented as
effects of the Gospel,—that is, they are declared to be possible
for those who embrace the Gospel.

Thus understood, the doctrine of the resurrection of the
dead—a doctrine which borders on materialism in Jewish
theology and in the orthodox system—appears in an entirely
new aspect, and is closely connected with the fundamental
idea of the Pauline theology.**

We now come to the second point to which we desire to
call the attention of our readers, and here again we find Paul
striking out an entirely new path, in which scholastic theology
has shown no inclination to follow him. This relates to the
nature of the resurrection body. The usage of Hebrew literature had rendered familiar the expression the resurrection of
the *flesh;* but by flesh the Old Testament always means man,
the human being, and does not restrict the term to its proper
and primitive meaning. It was very natural, however, that the

---

* Ἀπαρχὴ τῶν κεκοιμημένων, 1 Cor. xv. 21.

† Πρωτότοκος ἐκ τῶν νεκρῶν, Col. i. 18.

‡ 1 Cor. xv. 21, 22.

§ Col. iii. 4.

‖ Phil. iii. 10, δύναμις.

¶ 2 Tim. i. 10.

** Rom. iii. 20 ; 1 Cor. i. 29 ; Gal. ii. 16.

literal should prevail over the figurative sense, and that the dogma should come to mean the resurrection of the very body which we bear in this present life.

Paul speaks repeatedly and explicitly on this point. The actual organism, he says, is fitted for the necessities of this earthly life, and will cease with it,* since the physical functions which constitute the life of the body, especially all those which relate to its sustentation, and to the purposes of generation, will no more be needed in another life. Flesh and blood—that is, matter itself—will not inherit the kingdom of God.† It by no means follows, however, that the resurrection will be purely spiritual,—such a resurrection, for example, as might be argued from the philosophical notion of the incorruptibility of the soul, in opposition to the materiality of the body. This idea is foreign to the writings of Paul and to the New Testament generally. God alone possesses inherent immortality;‡ the notion of the indestructibility of the soul, of a continuity of life essentially inherent in it,—all, in short, that is called, in philosophy, immortality and its ontological evidence, lies beyond the circle of thought in which apostolic theology moves. But what is implied in the words of Paul is a metamorphosis of the body, a change of its perishable elements into the imperishable,§ a transformation of the feeble sickly, imperfect organism into one perfect, strong, glorious. Our present body has its vital seat in the soul—that is, in the natural play of certain animal, sensuous ‖ powers; the future body will have the spirit ¶ as its vital principle, and will be in its substance heavenly. The mortal element will be, so to

---

* 1 Cor. vi. 13.

† 1 Cor. xv. 50. We must be very careful not to take σὰρξ καὶ αἷμα literally, and without giving it a comprehensive meaning. Otherwise there would result the absurdity of a resurrection body retaining only the skin and bones of the present body. Σὰρξ καὶ αἷμα is elsewhere a rabbinical formula used to represent humanity, Gal. i. 16 ; Eph. vi. 12.

‡ 1 Tim. vi. 16.

§ Ἀφθαρσία, 1 Cor. xv. 42, and foll.

‖ Σῶμα ψυχικόν.

¶ Σῶμα πνευματικόν.

speak, absorbed by a more powerful element, namely, life.*
This idea springs again out of that of fellowship with Christ,
which recurs constantly as the fundamental idea of the whole
system. In truth, if our resurrection is a consequence of this
fellowship, it follows that the conditions of the one will be
in harmony with those of the other. We shall bear the body
of the heavenly man, of Christ glorified, as we now bear (and
as He Himself bore) the body of the earthly man, the first
Adam ;† and we must be careful not to reduce the significance
of the word *likeness*, used in the text to which we have referred, to that of a mere outward seeming. In a word,‡ He will
change our poor miserable body so as to make it like to His
own glorious body. Incorruptibility—freedom, that is, from all
tendency to decay, from the very possibility of death—belongs,
properly speaking, to God alone.§ There was none but Christ,
the very image of God, who could impart to the world such a
gift. ||

At the moment of His appearing, when the resurrection of
the dead is to take place simultaneously and generally, all
men will not have died; there will yet be a generation living
to witness this great and glorious climax in the world's
history. These men will be changed without passing through
the grave, but they will have no preference over the dead.¶
This fact, inasmuch as it is here announced for the first time,
is called a mystery.

The metamorphosis of the body, under the image of a grain
of wheat sown in the ground and rising again as the blade of
corn,** is elsewhere presented to our imagination as a change of

---

* 2 Cor. v. 4.

† 1 Cor. xv. 48, and foll., εἰκών.

‡ Μετασχηματίσει τὸ σῶμα τῆς ταπεινώσεως ἡμῶν σύμμορφον τῷ σώματι τῆς δόξης
αὐτοῦ, Phil. iii. 21.

§ Ἄφθαρτος, Rom. i. 23; 1 Tim. i. 17.

|| 2 Tim. i. 10.

¶ 1 Cor. xv. 51; 1 Thess. iv. 15. It is worthy of remark that in the
profound discussion of this subject, into which the apostle more than once
enters, he never says anything of unbelievers. His theology, no doubt,
has no application for them.

** 1 Cor. xv. 36, and foll.

raiment. *To be unclothed* is then the figurative term for death, the laying down of the earthly body; * *to be reclothed* represents the new state;† and the words immortality, incorruptibility, added to it, denote the properties of the new garment; finally, there is another term which signifies literally the putting on of a new garment over the old,‡ and which is applied to those who, being still alive at the coming of Christ, are changed without dying.

There remains but one point which needs explanation. The resurrection, being stated as a universal fact, comprehending all men, or at least all Christians, in one and the same instant, though they die at different periods divided from the final hour by longer or shorter intervals, what will be the intermediate destiny of each, between death and the resurrection day? To this question there is no exact and explicit reply in the passages which speak of the universal resurrection. The word by which Paul most frequently describes the fact of death,§ leads us to think of a state of sleep, unconsciousness, such as the ancient Hebrews supposed to be the condition of the dwellers in their *School*. It cannot be proved that this word relates exclusively to the body, and that the soul, while waiting, is separated from it, as is the tenet of the current orthodoxy of our day. On the contrary, Paul clearly teaches‖ that believers will only be reunited to Christ by and after the resurrection. And when it is said that the dead shall be restored to life at His appearing,¶ it is impossible to restrict the meaning to the body only; for in that case we should be authorized to ask what end will be answered by the restoration of the body, if life is possible without it. Here, then, is a flaw in the theory.

But this theory of a universal and simultaneous resurrection

---

* Ἐκδύσασθαι, 2 Cor. v. 4.
† Ἐνδύσασθαι, 1 Cor. xv. 53, 54.
‡ Ἐπενδύσασθαι, 2 Cor. v. 2.
§ Κοιμᾶσθαι, κεκοιμημένοι, the dead, 1 Cor. xv. 21; 1 Thess. iv. 13, etc.
‖ 1 Thess. iv. 17.
¶ 1 Cor. xv. 23.

is, in fact, taken from Judæo-Christianity, and harmonizes but ill with the system of Paul, which rests upon entirely different foundations. We shall not be astonished to find the religious consciousness of the apostle shaking off, at times, the fetters imposed upon it by this doctrine, and seeking a solution more in accordance with the premises of his own system. Thus the present life, which is represented as a temporary sojourn in a body which binds us to earth, is called absence, a separa- tion from our true home, which is with Christ.* To be parted from this body is to be joined to Christ, it is to find the home for which our hearts sigh.† By these same terms, the idea of an intermediate state is set aside; there is no more room for it; but the idea of a universal and simultaneous resurrection is rendered untenable also. In one of the last lines he ever penned,‡ the apostle expresses in other words the same conviction, that to be absent from the body is to be present with the Lord, that there will not be after death two consecu- tive and different states for the believer. And even before this,§ he seems to say plainly that, to the children of God, the enjoy- ment of happiness begins as soon as the body is laid down.‖

With the resurrection stands connected the thought of judgment. This is, again, a purely Judæo-Christian idea, and has no natural relation to the evangelical doctrine of Paul. For if, according to that doctrine, the resurrection itself is only a natural consequence of union with Christ, it follows logically that judgment is actually passed on this side the grave, if that union be real. And as this mystical theology does not speak of a resurrection of the unbelievers, neither can it treat of a final judgment by which they shall be separated from the faithful. The texts amply confirm these

* 2 Cor. v. 6, 8, ἐκδημεῖν.
† Ἐνδημεῖν.
‡ Phil. i. 23.
§ Rom. viii. 23.
‖ St. Paul's teaching concerning the condition of believers after death includes two elements: (a) they will be with Christ immediately; (b) their perfect glory will be consummated at the resurrection. These two elements can hardly be pronounced inconsistent with each other.—ED.

conclusions, arrived at by us from a conviction that the great logician would not be untrue to his premises. In fact, the word judgment is only used by Paul when he is dealing with popular ideas in a popular form. The resurrection, then, appears as a solemn assembly of men before the tribunal of God, each to receive his individual sentence, based upon his own actions, the good and the wicked being thus finally separated from each other by their merited penalties or rewards.* We repeat, this is pure Judæo-Christianity, which alone could argue of merit and reward; in a word, of salvation gained by a course of good conduct, and, so to speak, by the sweat of the man's own brow. If we look, on the other hand, at those well-known passages in which the resurrection is spoken of as grafted on faith, we shall seek in vain for any trace of such a final judgment.†

A few observations in detail will complete what we have to say on this subject. The phraseology which Paul uses in reference to the judgment is, as might be expected, essentially Jewish. First, God is represented as the Judge.‡ The judgment itself is pre-eminently a manifestation of anger.§ It would be needless to adduce evidence that such expressions belong to the style of the Old Testament. But we find another element, directly derived from the rabbis of the synagogue, namely, that the believers shall sit with God as judges of the unbelieving, and even of angels.‖ There are other expressions

---

* 2 Cor. v. 10; Rom. ii. 5.

† The great place which the anticipation of the final judgment held in St. Paul's personal religious life ought to have been recognized more fully. Nor is it true that there is any scientific or spiritual inconsistency between the doctrine of Justification by Faith and the Final Judgment. The serious difficulty consists in the fact that St. Paul's teaching implies that *after* the believer's inchoate blessedness with Christ which immediately follows death, he is to appear before the judgment-seat to receive his sentence. The difficulty is a serious one.—ED.

‡ Κρίσις θεοῦ, 2 Thess. i. 5; κρίμα τοῦ θεοῦ, Rom. ii. 2; κρινεῖ ὁ θεὸς τὸν κόσμον, Rom. iii. 6; 1 Cor. v. 13.

§ Ἡμέρα ὀργῆς, Rom. ii. 5; v. 9; ἡ ὀργὴ ἡ ἐρχομένη, 1 Thess. i. 10; comp. ἐκδίκησις, 2 Thess. i. 8.

‖ 1 Cor. vi. 2, 3.

more in accordance with evangelical teaching. Thus, when it is said that God will judge the world by Jesus Christ,* we trace the idea that judgment will be pronounced according to the attitude taken by men in reference to the Gospel. It is in this sense, again, that we must understand the expression "the judgment-seat of Christ," † the Christian naturally looking for his reward from the Master whom he has served.‡ All this clearly shows that it was very difficult to the apostle always to speak and think in conformity with his theological system, and that expressions constantly escape him borrowed from the current notions of his day, just as we speak of certain astronomical facts according to the impression which they make upon us through our senses. The Church ought to have recognized the incompatibility of the two trains of thought, and not to have endeavoured to force both into one system.

It remains for us to show that all which we have just described is the act of one and the same moment, or, according to Jewish phraseology, of one day. The coming of Christ, the resurrection, and the judgment, are simultaneous; there is no separating interval; and the passages we are about to quote will demonstrate conclusively that any other idea—the idea, for example, of a millenarian period intervening between the commencement and the close of these manifestations—is distinctly excluded by the eschatological system of Paul.

The Lord, it is said,§ will judge the quick and the dead at His appearing; and it is with reference to this appearing that the apostle describes the terrible manifestation of the Judge. Again, the coming of Christ and the day of judgment are placed in parallel lines,|| and the judgment itself is spoken of as the coming of Christ.¶ We would observe, further, the phrase " to judge the quick and the dead." ** This implies that at the

---

* Rom. ii. 16.
† Rom. xiv. 10 ; 2 Cor. v. 10.
‡ 2 Tim. iv. 8.
§ 2 Tim. iv. 1 ; 2 Thess. i. 7.
|| 1 Cor. i. 7, 8 ; comp. Rom. ii. 5.
¶ 1 Thess. ii. 19.
** 2 Tim. iv. 1 ; Rom. iv. 9.

time of Christ's coming all men will not be dead, but that all will have to appear before the Judge.   Now, if the judgment was not to take place till a thousand years after the coming of Christ, such a distinction would be meaningless.   Lastly, we draw attention to the fact that the expressions " the day of the Lord," " that day,"* are used alike for the appearing of Christ,† the resurrection,‡ and the judgment.§ Such a use of the terms, if it were not based upon the synchronism of the facts, must produce an inextricable confusion of ideas.

* Ἡμέρα κυρίου, ἐκείνη.
† 1 Thess. v. 2, 4 ; 2 Thess. i. 10 ; ii. 2, etc.
‡ Eph. iv. 30.
§ 1 Cor. i. 8 ; v. 5 ; 2 Cor. i. 14 ; 2 Tim. i. 18; iv. 8, etc.

CHAPTER XX.

OF THE KINGDOM OF GOD.

IMMEDIATELY on the consummation of the resurrection and the judgment, will commence the reign or kingdom of God.

This expression, as is well known, belongs to Judaism, and in the New Testament it is used in a modified sense by other writers beside Paul. It represents essentially a state of the world in which God is the sole director of all that transpires in the sphere of religion and morals, so that no tendency hostile to His will can prevail or even assert itself. Such a state, which the prophets in their artless enthusiasm had hoped to see established upon this earth, the colder and more practical theology of after-ages relegated to the life to come—partly, perhaps, because this lower world seemed unworthy of its realization, partly to free itself from the laborious duty of aiding in its accomplishment.

We shall now see what are the statements of Paul in his writings, with regard to the kingdom of God.* He speaks of it repeatedly by that familiar term, and calls himself like one of the old prophets, a worker for the kingdom of God.† In this view of it, the kingdom of God is a new condition of society, based upon moral regeneration, upon more direct union with God by His Spirit; in a word, it is a true theocracy.‡ But more generally this kingdom is represented by him as a future order of things, foreign to the earth and to existing conditions,

---

* Βασιλεία τοῦ θεοῦ, 1 Cor. vi. 9 ; xv. 50.
† Col. iv. 11.
‡ Rom. xiv. 17 ; 1 Cor. iv. 20.

in which the life of God, preached and prepared here below by the Saviour, will become perfect and blessed. For this reason, it is called the kingdom of the Son,* or, more fully, the kingdom of Christ and of God.† Jesus Himself, by whom this kingdom was virtually founded, is also its King; and it is in this capacity that He bears the name of Christ, the Anointed One,‡ a name which in the Old Testament designates kings in general, and, in a more special sense, the greatest of all kings. This name He bears even now, both because He came into the world to establish His kingdom, and because His work in this respect is even now accomplished. Already He is exalted and His name made high above every name that is named;§ in actual fact, however, He will not take possession of His kingdom until He comes again.‖

Here the question presents itself, where is the place of this kingdom? The prophets, whose horizon was still limited, supposed it would be established on earth, and we have seen that many Christians in early times held the same views on the subject. This conception is not altogether strange to Paul; at least he appropriates the poetic form under which the theology of his people loved to represent it. According to a passage which is variously explained, but which would have presented no difficulties, if the idea itself had not become foreign to the theology of the Church, external nature, all that surrounds man on this earth, yearns after a change which is to free it from the law of decay and death under which it now groans, and to make it a partaker in the incorruptible glory which is the promised inheritance of the sons of God. The coming of Christ is to fulfil this twofold aspiration. It is evident that this glorification of the material world, which is from that time no more to be a prey to all the physical ills which now disturb

---

* Col. i. 13. [But the apostle is here speaking of a kingdom actually existing, and into which Christian men are already "translated."—ED.]

† Eph. v. 5. [It is not clear that this passage, any more than the preceding one, refers to a future kingdom.—ED.]

‡ Χριστός.

§ Ὑψωθείς, Phil. ii. 9, 10.

‖ 2 Tim. iv. i.

its peace and ours, is anticipated in the hope that this world may thus be rendered a fit abode for the elect.

In other passages, however, the apostle rises to a region of thought in which earth is lost sight of. The more spiritual the idea of the kingdom becomes, (and none will deny that this spiritualizing tendency is very marked in the writings of Paul,) the more must this designation of a palpable place appear inappropriate. We do not adduce here the passage in which it is said that those who are raised from the dead will ascend to meet the Lord in the air, for this does not necessitate their permanent abode in those higher regions.* Neither is the well-known phrase that Christ is seated at the right hand of God at all decisive; for it so happens that the three passages in which it occurs † all refer to a period before the second coming. Nevertheless we maintain our ground for several reasons which appear to us conclusive. First, it seems to us that it would be altogether incompatible with the Christology of the apostle, to suppose a time coming when Christ would cease to be seated at the right hand of God. Again, the term *to sit down*, appropriated in apostolic theology to designate the permanent glory of Christ, is employed also in a passage of which the entrance of believers into the kingdom of God is the subject; and the mention made at the same time of heavenly places leaves no doubt as to the locality intended.‡ Again,§ the kingdom itself is called a heavenly kingdom, and the body which is to be substituted for the body we now bear, is in the same manner represented as to be given us from heaven.‖

But nowhere is there the slightest indication that Paul recognized two stages in the kingdom of God,—first a transi-

---

* 1 Thess. iv. 17.
† Rom. viii. 34 : Eph. i. 20 ; Col. iii. 1.
‡ Καθίζειν, Eph. ii. 6 ; comp. Phil. iii. 20.
§ 2 Tim. iv. 18.
‖ 2 Cor. v. 1. There are other details which we here pass over in silence. Paradise, the plurality of heavens, the third heaven (2 Cor. xii. 2, 4; Eph. iv. 10) are images, or, if we like so to call them, ideas borrowed from the current opinions of Judaism, and cannot be subjected to a theological analysis.

tory reign of Christ upon earth, and then an endless reign in heaven; two stages which, in the opinion of many theologians, will be separated from the resurrection of the unbelievers and the last judgment. We have already refuted this opinion above. The passages just quoted are equally opposed to it.

The kingdom of God, according to Paul, will comprehend not only the men called to enter into it, but also the angels, the hitherto privileged inhabitants of heaven. All together will then form one great community of beings worshipping God and acknowledging Christ as their common Head.* The angels, who take an interest now in the destinies of the Church, and revere the Son of God as their Creator and Lord,† will naturally be eager to welcome the elect as fellow-heirs in their blessedness, and to extend to them a brotherly hand in the covenant of peace.

There remains now only one last point to be considered in order to our obtaining a full view of the doctrine of Paul. We have just seen how man is to prepare himself for the consummation of all things, and how Christ victoriously completes the work begun on earth for the salvation of men. We have still to see that which God does on His part towards its realization, and how the end of the Gospel economy is actually attained.

We conclude this section, then, as we commenced the preceding, with the contemplation of the divine operations. For just as all things derive their origin from the will of God, in the spiritual as in the material world, so all also converge and meet in Him as their final goal. From first to last, Christ is but the Mediator of that will.‡

We have already seen what God has done for man in order to prepare him for salvation; we shall now see what it is He ultimately bestows upon him. We treat here of the benefits constituting what is called salvation, in so far as those benefits

* Ἀνακεφαλαιοῦνται, Eph. i. 10; Col. i. 20.
† Eph. iii. 10; i. 21; Col. i. 16.
‡ Εἷς θεὸς ὁ πατήρ, ἐξ οὗ τὰ πάντα καὶ ἡμεῖς εἰς αὐτόν, καὶ εἷς κύριος, Ἰησοῦς Χριστός, δι' οὗ τὰ πάντα καὶ ἡμεῖς δι' αὐτοῦ, 1 Cor. viii. 6.

are reserved for the future. For it must be borne in mind that there are benefits also which the believer enjoys in this present life, peace with God, the filial relation and other privileges, but more than all the spirit which is bestowed upon him, the gift of grace, which is the most important and the basis of all the rest, which indeed, in a sense, comprehends them all.

Thus this spirit is called a pledge, an earnest of good things to come,*—a figure which is not perfectly just, because it conveys rather the idea of a commercial contract than of the free grace of God. Elsewhere it is called the first fruits † in relation to the things which are to follow. A third image is that of a seal, a mark, by means of which God distinguishes His own, as masters in olden time were wont to mark their slaves. He sets on them the sign of the covenant, which is to serve as a pledge and security of the fulfilment of all His promises.‡ The old covenant also had its seal in the sign of circumcision.§ This simple analogy of itself aptly marks the spiritual character of the new covenant.

Believers have then to wait for the complete realization of certain benefits, which constitute a full salvation. The filial relation between them and God, to which the apostle delights to recur, here furnishes him with a new figure, repeatedly used but which has the weakness of all figures—it is only applicable in part. The children of God are the heirs of their father's possessions.‖ In this image the prominent idea is that of a future entrance upon a lawful inheritance, and the idea of the death of the actual possessor as a necessary preliminary, is dropped. This image, again, and the peculiar expression of it belong to the Old Testament.¶ The people of Israel had received the promise of the possession of Canaan, and each individual was to have his own share, or inheritance.* The

* Ὁ ἀρραβὼν τῆς κληρονομίας, Eph. i. 14 ; comp. 2 Cor. i. 22 ; v. 5.
† Ἀπαρχή, Rom. viii. 23.
‡ Σφραγίς, 2 Cor. i. 22 ; Eph. i. 13 ; iv. 30.
§ Rom. iv. 11.
‖ Εἰ τέκνα, καὶ πληρονόμοι, Rom. viii. 17 ; Gal iv. 7.
¶ Rom. iv. 13 ; Gal. iv. 30.
** Κλῆρος, Col. i. 12.

same idea is here transferred to the heavenly land of promise. The idea of inheritance—that is, of expectancy—predominates over that of possession. The phrase *heir of the kingdom* * is suggestive of a patrimony in reversion. The word *inheritance*, however, is also employed objectively in speaking of that into possession of which the Christian is to enter.†But it is everywhere expressly said that the question is not one of legal right of inheritance, but of a promise of divine grace. ‡

The enjoyment or entrance upon the possession of this heritage will take place when Christ comes again in glory and sets up His kingdom. The same expression may serve, then, to designate both facts. They are both manifestations :§ on the one hand, the manifestation of the Lord as such—that is, as King ; on the other, the manifestation of the children of God as such—that is, as heirs of His kingdom.‖

The term which denotes in the most general manner the blessings which the believer is warranted to expect, is *salvation*.¶ We are familiar with it already. It relates also to the first entrance into communion with Christ, because upon this all the rest depends. It is in view of this fact that God is called the *Saviour ;* ** and Christians are described as the *saved ;*†† to convert any one, and to bring him into the fold of the Church, is to save a soul ;‡‡ the time when a man hears the Gospel preached, and attends to the exhortation of an apostle, is to him the day of salvation.§§ In a word, it may be said that by the grace of God salvation is already at-

---

* Κληρονομεῖν τὴν βασιλείαν, 1 Cor. vi. 9, 10 ; xv. 50 ; Gal. v. 21.

† Eph. i. 14, 18 ; Col. iii. 24 ; κληρονομίαν ἔχειν ἐν τῇ βασιλείᾳ, Eph. v. 5.

‡ Gal. iii. 18, 29 ; Titus iii. 7.

§ Ἀποκάλυψις.

‖ Rom. viii. 18, and foll. : Ὅταν ὁ Χριστὸς φανερωθῇ τότε καὶ ὑμεῖς σὺν αὐτῷ φανερωθήσεσθε ἐν δόξῃ, Col. iii. 4 ; comp. 2 Cor. iv. 10, 11.

¶ Σωτηρία, Rom. i. 16 ; 2 Thess. ii. 13, etc.

** 2 Tim. i. 9 ; comp. Titus iii. 5.

†† 1 Cor. i. 18 ; 2 Cor. ii. 15.

‡‡ 1 Cor. vii. 16 ; Rom. xi. 14, 26 ; 1 Cor. ix. 22.

§§ 2 Cor. vi. 2.

tained.* Nevertheless it will only be enjoyed in reality and in its perfection in the kingdom of God, when time is no more, and all earthly relations have ceased; in other words, the idea itself belongs to a sphere not of this world. We have salvation, indeed, but we are saved by hope.† As time passes on, and we come nearer to the end of all things, so does our salvation draw nigh.‡ The verb *to be saved* is, therefore, used not only in the preterite, but also in the present,§ and still more often in the future,‖ since it comprehends the idea of a deliverance from the trammels and sufferings of this present life,¶ and since the obtaining of salvation is represented as the end of our earthly course.**

The term salvation is not the only one thus employed to describe both a present and a future state. There are two other terms which are its equivalents—redemption and adoption. We have already noticed three senses in which the word redemption applies to the actual state of the true Christian. He is redeemed,—that is, freed from guilt, from sin, and from the law. But he awaits another deliverance. He sighs for the time when he shall be delivered from the body,†† this body of infirmity, which causes him so much trouble and distress, which separates him from Christ,‡‡ and by that fact alone renders death desirable.§§ The day which shall put an end to time and usher in eternity, will be then also, and in a new sense, a day of redemption.‖‖

We may make a similar remark in reference to adoption. As believers, we are already the children of God, and we enjoy even now the happiness resulting from this relation; but on

---

* Eph. ii. 5, 8.
† Rom. viii. 24; comp. 1 Thess. v. 8.
‡ Rom. xiii. 11.
§ 1 Cor. xv. 2.
‖ Rom. v. 9, 10; x. 9; 1 Cor. x. 33; 1 Tim. iv. 16, etc.
¶ 2 Tim. iv. 18.
** 1 Thess. v. 9; 2 Tim. iii. 15.
†† Rom. viii. 23.
‡‡ 2 Cor. v. 6.
§§ Phil. i. 21—23.
‖‖ Ἡμέρα ἀπολυτρώσεως, Eph. iv. 30; comp. i. 14.

the complete enjoyment of all the prerogatives attached to this title, we shall only enter after death.*

It follows from all this that the benefits which constitute salvation do not belong exclusively to the sphere of the future life, and that the Christian must not be regarded as devoted here on earth to an existence of privation and absolute negation. On the contrary, he is even now so richly dowered, that even the ineffable blessedness which awaits him will bring to him nothing entirely new. The same observation will apply to most of the terms we have yet to enumerate.

We have, first, *life*. This begins with the union of the believer to Christ, before which man is regarded as dead. This life with and in Christ is the pledge or the guarantee of the future life; physical death will have no power to touch it.†
The term *life* is, however, usually employed to designate specially the life to come. It then contains implicitly the notion of blessedness, exemption from the various ills to which our present life is liable. Hence the life to come is called the true, real life,‡ that which alone deserves the name of life, because no prospect of death casts its shadow over it. This life is assured to us by the fact of Christ's victory over death; § but it is still hidden with Christ in God, until He shall come forth for His final manifestation.‖ It is, nevertheless, secure to the faithful, since their names are written in the book of life.¶ The difference between the two phases or periods of the believer's life is then purely accidental. It is a difference of duration. The present life** will end with the death of the body, but only to give place to the future life which shall be eternal.††

* Rom. viii. 19, 23.
† 1 Cor. xv. 12, and foll.; 2 Cor. v. 10, 11; Rom. v. 16.
‡ 'Η ὄντως ζωή, 1 Tim. vi. 19.
§ 2 Tim. i. 10.
‖ Col. iii. 3.
¶ Βίβλος ζωῆς, Phil. iv. 3.
** 'Η ζωή ἡ νῦν, 1 Tim. iv. 8.
†† 'Η ζωή ἡ μέλλουσα, αἰώνιος, Titus i. 2; iii. 7; 1 Tim. i. 16; vi. 12; Gal. vi. 8; Rom. ii. 7; v. 21; vi. 22, etc.

14 *

Apart from this circumstance, the idea does not contain in itself any distinct attribute by which we might recognize the nature of eternal life. We shall readily discover in it, however, by analogy, the element of happiness, since the idea of death included the element of utmost misery. This happiness, as we may gather from the different premises already analyzed, will consist essentially in the consciousness of reconciliation with God, or in the absolute peace of the heart, and in perfect union with God in Christ. The apostle abstains from any other description, which, as we know from the abuse since made of it, could be only sensuous or figurative.

The word life, moreover, characterizes the future existence only in relation to its spiritual and inner nature. In this it differs from the term *glory*, which conveys the idea of its outward conditions, since this is properly used to designate the manner in which an object presents itself to the eye, its appearance (*species*), and more particularly a brilliant and dazzling exterior. Glory is, therefore, essentially connected with the visible aspect of an object—its mode of manifestation. That object is here the body which the Christian is to receive. Its splendour, its glorious appearance, is contrasted with the miserable condition of his present body.* This, then, is the one attribute, of all that we shall here notice, which does not apply to the new life of the believers in this world. The antithesis between the body that now is and the body that shall be, expressed by the epithets applied to each, brings into prominence the infirmities and imperfections of the former, without revealing, in relation to the latter, anything more than the absence of these same properties.†

Glory is of God. The glory of God ‡ is the attribute of His person which sets forth the absence of all imperfection, of all that might disturb happiness; it represents an existence without shadow or suffering. Such is the existence given to Christ also, as the conqueror of death and sin, and

---

* Δόξα, ἀτιμία, 1 Cor. xv. 43.
† Σῶ: a ταπεινώσεως, δόξης, Phil. iii. 21.
‡ Δόξα θεοῦ, Rom. iii. 23 ; v. 2.

from Him it is transmitted to believers.* It is thus contrasted with all the calamities, privations, imperfections of the earthly life;† it is the condition of all the members of the kingdom of God,‡ and of the kingdom itself:§ this will be made manifest when that kingdom shall open its doors to the elect.||

The last expression used to describe the condition of the future life of the elect, is the verb *to reign*. It cannot be doubted that this term had its origin in the political hopes of the Jewish nation, which supposed that in the time of Messiah all other nations would be brought into subjection to it. Paul nowhere betrays this ambitious notion; with him, to reign means to have a part in the kingdom of God, in the community and felicity of the elect.¶ This word, then, contains no distinct idea to be added to those already given.**

Such are the definitions of the future condition of the elect which presented themselves to the mind of Paul, and which we gather from his phraseology. We may just add, in order to omit nothing, that, faithful to his fundamental thesis, according to which all these benefits accrue to the man only as he is united to Christ, the apostle uses also other terms, which draw attention at once to this union and to the heavenly blessedness of Christians. Thus they are called joint heirs with Christ;†† they shall live, shall be glorified, shall reign with Him.‡‡

We cannot pass from this subject without calling the

---

* 2 Cor. iii. 18.
† 2 Cor. iv. 17; Rom. viii. 18.
‡ 2 Tim. ii. 10.
§ 1 Thess. ii. 12.
|| Μέλλει ἀποκαλυφθῆναι, Col. iii. 4.
¶ Βασιλεύειν, Rom. v. 17.
** In the passage 1 Cor. iv. 8, which moreover contains some irony expressed by means of various figures, βασιλεύειν may also be referred to the idea of possession and enjoyment, and does not necessarily imply dominion or rule.
†† Συγκληρονόμοι, Rom. viii. 17.
‡‡ Συζήσονται, σονδοξασθήσονται, συμβασιλεύσουσι, 2 Tim. ii. 11, and foll.

CHRISTIAN THEOLOGY.

attention of our readers to a series of expressions relating to the future life and the condition reserved for each individual, which appear to be in contradiction with the whole Pauline system. These are the passages in which the purely legal point of view is maintained, at the sacrifice of the evangelical, and where we find allusions not to election and grace, not even to a simple co-operation of man in the work of salvation, but to merit and claims which he may plead before the Judge. We may enumerate the terms *render, reward, repay, recompense, the prize, the crown,* all used in figurative connection with man's own works, fightings, efforts, athletic games.‡ We might further cite the passages in which Paul glories in his own labours,§ as something which will form a plea for him with the Judge. What shall we say to all this? Can Paul have so far forgotten the principles on which he elsewhere so eloquently insists? ‖ This is not possible. His theory remains intact, his doctrinal system is ever true to the principles of the Gospel, as he has understood and uttered them. The inconsistency (for such it is) is not in the thought, but in the expression. The writer has allowed himself to make use of terms sanctioned by custom, and which are on the lips of all. The thinker adopts for the moment, and in his popular teaching, the language of the people—language which we never find him using when he is presenting the same ideas as the basis of the Christian faith. The Church has acted uniformly in the same manner; and the theologians who are most orthodox on the subject of justification, have used, in the homiletic style, expressions which they would have repudiated in their doctrinal expositions.

The system of Paul, in so far as we have been able to study and to comprehend it, is now before us in its completeness. We have nothing to add to it. The will of God is accomplished.

‡ Ἀποδιδόναι, 2 Tim. iv. 8 ; Rom. ii. 6, etc.; ἀνταπόδοσις, Col. iii. 24 ; μισθός, 1 Cor. iii. 8 ; ix. 17 ; βραβεῖον, Phil. iii. 14 ; στέφανος, 1 Cor. ix. 25 ; 1 Thess. ii. 19 ; 2 Tim. iv. 8 ; comp. Gal. ii. 2 ; Phil. ii. 16.

§ 1 Thess. ii. 19 ; 1 Cor. ix. 15 ; Phil. ii. 16.

‖ 1 Cor. iv. 7 ; xv. 10, etc.

The elect are brought into a state of blessedness by Christ. It follows necessarily that that blessedness will be liable to no withdrawal or change. It is everywhere described as eternal.*

But it is not eternal only; it must be regarded at the same time as immutable. There is nowhere any suggestion of various degrees of blessedness, by which some will be distinguished from others, nor of a progression or advancement, by which the felicities of one and the same man shall be gradually augmented.†

The same analogy at once leads us to the conclusion that the reprobate, who are excluded from happiness, have no prospect of a final change in their sad destiny. In fact, it is said that those who refuse to believe, shall receive as their penalty eternal death, perpetual banishment from the presence of the Lord and from His grace. It is true that there is no other passage in the epistles of Paul which asserts the eternity of punishment. But as this idea is perfectly in harmony with his whole system, we can dispense with further evidence. We cannot, however, pass over ‡ without remark, the interesting fact that the Pauline theology never dwells on the images of death and condemnation, while it delights to present those of life and blessedness. So true is this that the passages which are most explicit in reference to the last times, and which are also most strongly characterized by Jewish elements, say absolutely nothing of the fate of the condemned.

This unquestionable fact, this tendency, namely, of the apostle to dwell with complacency on the consoling aspect of the future, and to pass by the other side of the picture, has perhaps contributed to foster in the minds of some

---

* Ζωὴ αἰώνιος, αἰώνιος δόξα, 2 Cor. iv. 17 ; αἰωνία παράκλησις, 2 Thess. ii. 16 ; αἰώνιος οἰκία, 2 Cor. v. 1.

† It is only by an exegetical error that the idea of such a progression can be derived from 2 Cor. iii. 18, where the expression ἀπὸ δόξης εἰς δόξαν refers not to a gradation (from glory to glory), but, on the one hand, to the source of the glorification of believers, which is the glory of Christ (ἀπὸ δόξης Χριστοῦ), and on the other to the effect of that glory in our glorification (εἰς δόξαν ἡμῶν).

‡ 'Ολεθρος αἰώνιος, 2 Thess. i. 9.

theologians the belief in an ultimate restoration even of the condemned, and in a finally happy end for all creatures endowed with reason. This doctrine, advocated by many of the great thinkers both of the early Church and of modern times, but espoused also by enthusiasts of different schools, whose patronage has cast doubt upon it, has been combated with more vehemence than it demanded, by the rigidly orthodox of all confessions, with whom the eternity of punishment has always been a favourite dogma.

. We can discover no trace of this doctrine in the writings of Paul. The only passage which might be construed to contain it elementarily, is that in which it is said that after the appearing of Jesus Christ and the resurrection of the dead, will come the end; that Christ having reigned till He has put all enemies, even the last enemy, death, under His feet, will then deliver up the kingdom to the Father who gave it Him, and thus God will at last be all in all.* To these last words, the idea of universal restoration has been attached. But, taking the wider passage, we do not see that it contains anything more than has been set forth in the previous pages. When the elect shall have entered, after the resurrection, upon their eternal blessedness, Christ will have accomplished His mission, and finished His work: there will be no more need of a mediator. The union between God and His people will be perfect and immediate. After the victory gained over all the other enemies who here opposed themselves to the decrees of God, death alone will remain to be subdued, and that in its turn is vanquished by the resurrection of the elect.

Exegesis can find no more in these words. Nevertheless we admit that they may have a wider significance, if they are logically carried out to consequences not intended by the apostle. We need not dwell on the fact, which is sufficiently

---

* 1 Cor. xv. 24—28. [This passage simply affirms that the subordination of the Mediator to the Father will continue after the consummate triumph of the Mediatorial Kingdom: *then*, also, as now, shall the Son be subject under Him that put all things under Him, that God may be all in all.—ED.]

established by sound interpretation of the texts, but which the theology of the Church has never been willing to accept, that there is here no place assigned to the reprobate, that they are not even mentioned, and that this silence might seem to justify the hope of their final salvation. Nor will we lay stress upon another passage,* in which it is said that the divine mercy will in the end embrace all men, and where this word *all* has a sort of special emphasis attached to it. It may always be rejoined that the reference is to grace offered, and not to a necessary effect. It will be observed, again, that the pronoun here is collective, in its relation to the two great categories of Jews and Gentiles, and not to the totality of individuals of the human race. But there is another point of greater import- ance. Is it not a contradiction to represent death as itself vanquished—nay, even destroyed, and yet to leave under its power the majority of men? Must we not choose between the two alternatives? either we may adhere to the system and hold the eternal perdition of many, in which case death still remains as a power side by side with the power of God, which is a power of life or blessing; or, on the other hand, we may accept the fact of the destruction of death, as asserted in the passage quoted, and conclude from it the ultimate and final restoration of the lost.† This conclusion may be sustained by another consideration. If the highest glory of God consists in being all in all, it is plain that it would be a flaw in the perfection of God were He anything less than this; it would be a detraction from His glory, if in some, and those the greater number of mankind, He should be nothing. The religious conscience, no less than the logical sense, protests against any such imperfection in God and in the system. But here com- mences the province of speculation; the duty of religious exegesis is simply to ascertain with scrupulous impartiality what are the statements really made by each writer.

In concluding this entire section of our subject, we shall

---

* Rom. xi. 32.

† It is St. Paul's habit to speak of the *destruction* of the unsaved.—ED.

show in a few words that the division we have adopted in our
exposition of the theology of Paul, following the three categories of faith, love, and hope, is really that which was constantly present to the mind of the apostle himself, and that
he perpetually recurs to it; this he does even more often by
almost involuntary allusions, and in the natural course of his
thought, than by formal and systematic assertions.

In the earliest writings of his which have come down to
us,* he sums up the words of eulogy contained in his salutation, according to this trilogy of the phases and manifestations
of the Christian life.   Elsewhere, the spiritual armour of the
believer is made to consist in these three cardinal virtues.†
In other places, these suggest to the writer, by a natural association of ideas, various forms for his exhortations and
teachings;‡ and as hope cannot be called a quality or a virtue
in the same way as faith and love, patience is often in such
cases substituted for it.§   As a general rule, a little attention
will discover the same trilogy in various other passages,
although expressed in a manner which does not make its
presence at once evident. ‖

Although, however, Paul always thinks and reasons in the
forms of this trilogy, the three terms which compose it are
not in his view simply co-ordinate.   On the one hand, there
are many passages in which he names only faith and love,
without adding hope, which is thus regarded as subordinate
to the other two elements.¶   On another occasion he declares
that love is the greatest of the three.**   The attempt has been
made to discover the reason of this assertion.   It has been
said that faith and hope belong, properly speaking, only to
the present life, since faith is to be one day exchanged for

---

* 1 Thess. i. 3 ; comp. Col. i. 4.

† 1 Thess. v. 8.

‡ Eph. i. 15, 18 ; iii. 17, 18, 20.

§ Ὑπομονή, 1 Tim. vi. 11 ; 2 Tim. iii. 10 ; Titus ii. 2 ; 2 Thess. i. 3, 4.

‖ 2 Thess. ii. 17 (λόγος, ἔργον, ἐλπίς); Gal. v. 5, 6 ; Titus i. 1, 2.

¶ 2 Tim. i. 13; Titus iii. 15 ; Philemon 5 ; 1 Cor. xvi. 13 ; 2 Cor.
viii. 7 ; Eph. vi. 23 ; 1 Thess. iii. 6 ; 1 Tim. i. 5, 14 ; ii. 15.

** 1 Cor. xiii. 13.

sight—that is, for direct knowledge and actual possession,* and hope will cease by the very fact of its fulfilment.† Love, on the contrary, will abide for ever. This explanation is absolutely true in reference to hope only, for faith in the Pauline theology means communion with Christ, and can never cease even in another life. It would be more just to say that the superiority assigned to love is derived from the fact that faith and hope are qualities proper to man only, and intended to raise him above the sphere of earth, and to bring him into relation with heaven, while love is an attribute of God, communicated to man, to set on him the seal of his divine destiny.

* 2 Cor. v. 7.
† Rom. viii. 24, 25.

CHAPTER XXI.

PAULINISM AND JUDÆO-CHRISTIANITY.

In the exposition just concluded of the doctrine of Paul, we have naturally been led to give prominence to that portion of the evangelical teaching of the apostle, in which his subjective and individual conception is most directly brought out. We have not strictly avoided speaking of those points on which he more nearly coincides with earlier methods and ideas; but those in the treatment of which he strikes out an original course have necessarily claimed our chief attention. It is possible that the reader may thus have formed an impression that the interval between the two modes of thought is greater than we would really represent it; and that there is no redeeming affinity worthy of notice. Such is not the idea we have meant to convey; on the contrary, we recognize fully the double bond which attaches Paul on the one hand to Judaism, and on the other to Jesus Christ, while still leaving him entire liberty in the treatment of his ideas, and in the elaboration of his system. In order to dispel all uncertainty on this point, we shall devote a few concluding pages to the comparison of the two phases of the apostolic theology which have as yet come before us.

We have already had occasion to say that the individuality of Paul is especially marked in the two departments of sacred science which we call in our day anthropology and soteriology, the doctrine concerning man and his salvation. This assertion, which is fully sustained by facts, may be supplemented by the observation, that the other parts of the system of Biblical religion have not received from the hands of the apostle of the Gentiles a form very different from that which they had assumed before his time, whether in the Synagogue or in the Church.

Thus, for example, theology properly so called—that is to say, the series of dogmas relating to the person of God, His attributes, creation, providence, and the different modes of revelation—is left intact as a whole and in detail. Paul is very rarely led to give in any of his epistles direct teaching on these points, which proves that he had nothing new to impart to his readers. · The metaphysical theories to which these dogmas were made to lend themselves, first in the Jewish schools, then in those of the Gnostics, and finally in the Church itself, were unknown to him, or at least he made no attempt either to initiate them or to refute them in anticipation. The popular forms of scriptural teaching amply satisfy him,* and he is not even offended by the anthropomorphic expressions of which in the law and the prophets such free use is made, and which the Jewish scholasticism of the period sought as far as possible to eschew.

The idea most intimately connected with this theology—that of the theocracy and special election of the people of Israel—also underwent no radical change in his teaching. It is true that the universalist principle which lies at the foundation of the Pauline doctrine, was of a nature to break down the limits of Mosaic and Pharisaic exclusiveness. But, on the one hand, we have seen that Judæo-Christianity was not, as is often imagined, wholly inaccessible to ideas of this nature, although it admits them with extreme reserve; and on the other hand, it must not be forgotten that in rising to a higher point of view, Paul does not attempt to overthrow at once the ancient forms, or we might almost have said the limitations previously fixed by Providence. His judgment on the nature and origin of paganism is the same as that of the Old Testament and of his co-religionists; † Israel is always, in his

* Rom. i. 20, and foll.; 1 Tim. i. 17 ; vi. 16, etc.
† Rom. i. 18, and foll.; 2 Cor. vi. 14; Gal. ii. 15; Eph. ii. 11, foll., etc.

view, a privileged people ;* the admission of Gentiles into the evangelical community is compared to the grafting in of a wild branch upon a tree of nobler stock ;† and that tree is not a new creation; it has its roots at Sinai, or even it may be said they are struck before the tent of Abraham.‡

This brings us directly to another fact which will yet further confirm the foregoing remarks. The combination of the theocratic and particularist view with the principle of evangelical universalism ought to have led to a conflict, and revealed the contradiction between the two elements thus associated. But the theology of the apostle does not split upon this rock, because the exegesis, which he uses as a logical weapon, leads him to avoid it. This mode of exegesis is not peculiar to himself; it is the common heritage of all the Christian schools, and differs from that of the synagogue only because the evangelical principle forecasts its results without changing its methods. It may be said that nowhere has the revolution effected by the Gospel been less felt than in this important department of science, although the end to be attained, and which was always readily and completely attained, was here entirely new.

There is yet another point in regard to which the theology analysed in the present book does not differ at all from the popular notion which had preceded it. This is demonology, the doctrine concerning good and bad angels. Good angels appear here, as in the Jewish theory, as ministers of God in, the work of revelation,§ and attend Christ in His solemn coming to judgment.‖ In the present dispensation their function is to watch over the Church.¶ The evil angels, with the devil at their head, have been ever since creation** the

---

* Rom. iii. 1, and foll.; ix. 4, and foll., etc.
† Rom. xi. 17, etc.
‡ Rom. iv. 11, and foll.
§ Gal. iii. 19.
‖ 1 Thess. iv. 16.
¶ 1 Cor. xi. 10.
** 2 Cor. xi. 3.

authors of physical* and moral evil † in the world, and more
particularly the promoters of paganism, and of every sort of
opposition to the kingdom of God.‡ Pauline theology makes
no more attempt than Judæo-Christianity to investigate these
notions scientifically; it accepts them just as they had come
down from the simple tradition of earlier generations, and connects them only accidentally with the Gospel system.

We have already remarked that in his teaching in relation
to the close of the world's history, Paul does not deviate from
the then generally received ideas. We have spoken of this
at length, and need simply add here that the only two points
on which his theology goes beyond the narrowest form of
Judæo-Christianity, give but faint and distant indications of
the change which the Gospel was destined to produce in the
old theory. At least, these two theses (on the close connection
between the resurrection and faith, and on the nature of the
future body) do not lead him explicitly to retract a single
article of the whole series of eschatological facts enunciated
by the doctors of the synagogue.

Lastly, we believe there is ground for affirming that in the
capital doctrine relating to the nature of the person of Christ, ·
the two forms of teaching which we are now comparing stand
on the same level. It is, in truth, an opinion, very imperfectly
justified by history, that Judæo-Christianity rejected the
idea of the divinity of the Saviour. We have established the
contrary. The very utmost that can be said is that this idea
did not form the basis of the religious convictions of that school
in regard to Christ, and that it was content without arriving
by reflection at any exact and final conception on the subject.
It must even be admitted that many'Christians of this class
remained complete strangers to any spiritual or speculative
development of faith in this direction. But it is equally true
of the language used by Paul, that it was adapted to meet the
requirements of religious feeling rather than those of speculative

* 1 Cor. v. 5 ; 2 Cor. xii. 7
† 1 Thess. iii. 5, etc.
‡ 2 Cor. iv. 4 ; Eph. vi. 10, foll., etc.

thought. For all speculative purposes, it is surpassed by the formulas of ecclesiastical theology, and even by the phraseology of John, and of the Epistle to the Hebrews. We cannot, then, contrast the teaching of Paul with the ideas dominant among the first Christians in Palestine, as though it embodied a perfectly distinct system of doctrine.

We might very possibly trace still closer points of resemblance, if we were to go over all the details of the apostlic teaching. But we confine ourselves to what has just been said, because it suffices to sustain our first assertion. We have now to explain—and we must do so categorically—the fact of the divergence between the two formulas or systems; or, to speak more exactly, the fact of such a divergence being proclaimed broadly and repeatedly by Paul himself, and by his contemporaries, it will be for us to define its precise nature, and the points on which it bears.

In retracing our exposition, chapter by chapter, we might find theses, explanations, and arguments in great number, by and in which Paul leaves the common track to mark out for himself a new path, and is thus led in a direction which removes him from the errors of his predecessors, and of his own early surroundings, and finally places a gulf between the Synagogue and the Church, which in the commencement were so closely connected. But in pursuing this method we should lead our readers to suppose that the difference consists in a longer or shorter series of isolated dogmas, of articles of faith variously expressed by one or the other school—as is the case, for example, in the comparison that might be made in our own day between the several Protestant confessions of faith. Such is not our true idea. Details are almost lost sight of, in our view, in presence of the principle from which they flow, and the importance of that principle is such that it ought to absorb, so to speak, our whole attention. We have already shown, in the course of our historical narrative, that the adversaries of Paul stopped short at certain isolated questions, at that which seemed to them most negative and heterodox in his teaching, because in its practical application it was at the same time that which

was most concrete and palpable, that which would most
readily move the masses. Here we are not relating history,
but estimating a doctrine. It is right, then, that we should
trace it to its source, to its originating principle.

From this point of view, it may be said that the difference
between Paulinism and Judæo-Christianity is reduced to one
single principle. Both sides recognize salvation by Christ;
on both we find faith, hope, and charity; both speak of duty
and reward. But in Judæo-Christianity all this is a matter
of knowledge, instruction, understanding, of memory even, of
imagination often, and, lastly, of conscience, which is permeated
with it, and adopts it on the faith of a teaching supported by
tradition, and established by the written word. To Paul, and
according to his view, all these facts, all these convictions, are
the direct results of the religious feeling. He finds them in
himself, not as the creations or inventions of a spontaneous act
of his reason, but placed within him by the Holy Spirit of God,
and by Him vitalized and rendered fruitful. In both schools
a knowledge of Christ and His Gospel might have been gained
through the preaching of a missionary, or by the study of a
book. In the one, however, Jesus would have remained
primarily a historical personage, having his place, indeed, not
only in the past, but also in the present and the future, and
standing always at the summit of the scale of beings, exalted
to the right hand of God, having given commandments to His
disciples to be observed, and promised blessings by them to be
obtained. In the second or Pauline school, Christ reveals
Himself pre-eminently in the individual himself; it is in his
own spiritual nature that the man feels and finds Christ; His
death and resurrection become phases in the life of every
Christian; and that life itself is derived purely from the
intimate union of the two personalities, the individual
existence being renewed, fashioned, sanctified by and according
to the ideal and normal existence of the Saviour. In Judæo-
Christianity, even in its most elevated and honourable form,
the essential would always be, on the one hand, the practice
of duty, on the other, the prospect of the happy and complete

accomplishment of all the divine promises; and religion would consist in the close alliance of these two elements. In Paul's view, while he sacrifices no duty, and surrenders no promise, the essential element is faith; that is to say, the directness of the relation of the man with God by Christ, the inward consciousness of a state which reason and reflection could neither explain nor comprehend, and which hope itself could not conceive if it were not already realized. This state is at the same time religion. In Judæo-Christianity theology is the enumeration of duties and hopes; it is an eschatological asceticism. With Paul, theology is in its very essence the confession and profession of a feeling, the demonstration of its validity and of its power; and, lastly, the negation of all that could detract from its influence; it is a logical mysticism.

In comparing these two views of the concrete life of the individual and of the Church, it will be readily perceived that Judæo-Christianity alone has any need of a code of doctrine or precepts. The Pauline system can dispense with both; not that it will reject the one or neglect the other, but because it holds that no outward and formal legitimation of them is needed when their authority is established more directly by the witness of the Spirit, and, what is of more importance, is recognized by the spontaneous application or execution given to them. Hence it is that the Judæo-Christianity of the primitive age, as a theological system, adheres to the law of Moses, which is the only code it can acknowledge, none other as yet existing. Hence, also, it is that the theology of Paul proclaims the decadence of the law, and was apt to be regarded by the men of its age as the foe of the old dispensation, though nothing was further from the apostle's thought than to erase all the sacred traditions of earlier times.

It would be easy to show that a belief originally Jewish, such as is still found in the epistles of Paul, is ill adapted to the system of which we have just traced the fundamental principle. This proves only that the apostle, as a reformer in theology, sought first of all to lay a solid foundation for the new edifice, and to build up all its essential parts. Our reformers of the sixteenth century, to whom his theology served as a model and starting-point, pursued the same course, and did not remove at once the entire scaffolding of the theology which they found dominant in their day. The presence of some ideas which derive all their value and significance from their connection with an obsolete form of thought, is not necessarily obstructive to progress in new directions, provided the centre of gravity or the pivot of the system be changed at the same time. We shall find a remarkable illustration of this in one of the last chapters of our exposition of the theology of John; and a philosophical study of history teaches us generally that the development of humanity represents a chain all the links of which remain in unbroken connection.

We shall close the parallel we have just drawn with one reflection. It has not been our intention to pronounce any judgment upon the two systems we have expounded, whether by the analysis first given, or the subsequent comparison between them. Still less has it entered into our thought to ascribe to either one exclusively, and on psychological grounds, the monopoly of the Christian character. As theology—that is to say, as a logical presentation of evangelical facts and ideas, —the one may predominate over the other in the opinion of those who make theology their study, and Protestantism in particular has marked its preference in this respect. The remark we intended to make refers to another point. Setting aside theories and their scientific form, we have here two essentially different points of view—so different, that the same beliefs, the same evangelical truths, will present themselves under new aspects, as they are regarded from the one or the other. These are the rational standpoint and the mystical. We have clearly and adequately defined them already; we repeat that both are legitimate. So certainly is this the case that we have several times found Paul himself, and we shall presently find John also, passing from one to the other, without compromising the authority or force of his teaching. The explanation is this: reason and feeling are two faculties equally concerned in the appropriation of religious truth, but

15 *

not equally developed in all individuals. So long as this imperfection lasts, so long as perfect harmony is not established between our different modes of apprehending the facts of Christianity, so long these two points of view will appear opposed to each other, or will seem mutually exclusive. It would be a lamentable error to think that one or other of them ought to be absolutely proscribed.

CHAPTER XXII.

PAUL AND JAMES.

WE have already had occasion to remind our readers that men have a greater aptitude and inclination to grasp the differences between two facts which are analogous, or are brought into comparison, than the characteristics which may be common to both. The judgment in such a case becomes still more decisive if the facts to be compared are of a concrete nature, and connected with the actualities of life. Now as nothing is more concrete than proper names, the use of these easily leads to exaggeration in the direction indicated, and has a tendency to disguise the truth in some of its aspects. This was so in the apostolic age; and we have seen how the names of the apostles, inscribed on party banners, served to perpetuate the dissensions which divided the early Church. At this period, the two tendencies or systems which we have characterized in the foregoing pages, were distinguished, in popular language, by the names of Paul and of James. These names represented, in the minds of many, irreconcilable ideas, and time and repeated revisions of opinion were needed to obliterate or efface an antagonism which had wellnigh torn with schism even the infant Church.

This old cause of division in the primitive Church has been no less a stumblingblock to the science of modern times. Paul and James are again brought face to face, not indeed as the respective leaders of hostile parties in a community ready to gather round their names as watchwords, but as the writers of their respective books, brought before the tribunal of dogmatic exegesis to answer for their teachings, over the true meaning of which, and the divergence or harmony to be established between them, the war of words is daily renewed.

We have already spoken of James and of his epistle in the theoretic exposition of Judæo-Christianity. We only revert to the subject here to pause a moment on one special point which has always engaged the attention of theologians, and by which this epistle seems to be connected with the conflict of ideas now before us. Every one is familiar with the exegetical problem of the agreement or disagreement of Paul and James on the question of works and faith. Ever since Luther, basing his theology on the fundamental ideas of Paul, and particularly on the application made of them by Augustine, peremptorily rejected 'the epistle of James, as all but incompatible with the essence of the Gospel, and as hostile to the first principles of his own system, this isolation of one book of the canon from the rest has been a perpetual subject of embarrassment to theological science. It has not ceased to be so even now, though the Protestant schools, repudiating the inexorable rigidity of the dogmatic reformer, have long reinstated the epistle of James in the honoured roll of canonical writings. We have now to vindicate this procedure, in other words to prove the absence of any contradiction between two authors equally inspired; and there is an urgent necessity for arriving at a tranquillizing result on this difficult but interesting question, which is still provocative of diverse opinions. Looking at the long roll of champions who enter the lists in a cause which has the sympathies of all, we might suppose the result would be certain and speedy. But it would be more true to say that the perpetual renewal of the conflict shows how doubtful the issue still remains.

We, in our turn, have to enter upon this old discussion, which has been rather obscured than elucidated by the controversies of the last quarter of a century. Adhering to our historical method, we shall not concern ourselves with the practical result of our inquiries, and we may therefore entertain the more hope, if not of convincing those who start from another standpoint, at least of throwing some light upon

the question, and stating it more exactly than some who have
gone before us.

Let us first read once more the words of James,* from which
we may derive the positive teachings of that apostle. "What
doth it profit, though a man say he hath faith, and have not
works? can faith save him?" It is the religion of practical
life, not of fine words, which avails for good; by itself, the profession of the mouth is dead and void. It is only by works
that I can see if faith exists; without works, I defy any one
to prove to me that he has faith. The devils may believe;
it does not save them. It was the sacrifice of his son offered
by Abraham that justified the patriarch; the faith which he
had in God, and which rendered the sacrifice possible and
easy to him, was made perfect by the act which it produced.
Thus justification is clearly by works, and not by faith only.

In reference to Paul, we need only remark that his arguments tend, as all know, to the contrary conclusion, namely,
that justification is by faith alone, and not by works. Apparently, then, there is this startling contradiction between the
two theologians—a contradiction, as it would appear, intentional
and premeditated on the part of the later writer; the form of
his discourse shows that he has an opponent in view, and the
choice of Abraham as an example seems to leave no doubt
whose teaching it is he would controvert. This is the form in
which the question presents itself to the exegete.

In order to dispel this seeming contradiction between the
two statements, an attempt has generally been made, in our
days, to prove that the two terms which form its elements are
used with a different meaning by the two authors. Evidence
in support of this thesis being easy to adduce, most of the
theologians who have treated the subject are at once satisfied
that all has been said, and that henceforth the most perfect
harmony is re-established between the two texts. We shall
show how far this opinion is well-founded or false.

It is certain that by faith James means the conviction of the
reality of a religious fact; for example, the existence of God,

* James ii. 14.

or of duty, and the outward profession of that conviction. Such a profession may be an act of hypocrisy. In the most favourable case, it is the manifestation of a disposition of the mind, of a judgment of the reason, which does not necessarily go beyond the sphere of the intellect. Such a faith, James says, cannot save, and assuredly Paul never asserts the contrary.

With Paul, faith is a new and special relation into which the man enters with Christ, and by Him with God; it is, at once the principle and the form of a condition essentially different from the man's normal state; it is an entire life of thought, will, action,—a life which God animates with His own Spirit, and which can produce only that which is in accordance with such a divine origin. James does not say that in this view Paul is in error.

The works of which James speaks represent the fulfilment of Christian duties,—those, for example, towards widows and orphans, and the poor in general; he says expressly that he assigns to these acts a religious motive. But Paul is far from repudiating such works as alien to evangelical religion.

The works which Paul does repudiate are acts done under the coercion of an external law—acts of legal obedience, not the spontaneous product of an inward disposition generally conformed to the will of God. Such works are necessarily incomplete, and can never constitute the evidence of a perfect righteousness. But James says precisely the same thing.†

We gather, then, that the two apostles, in these contradictory statements of theirs, are speaking of very different things. Consequently, unless we are prepared to maintain that James was not even capable of understanding the language of Paul, unless we assert that he strangely misapprehended the meaning of the most elementary statements of his colleague's teaching, we cannot hold that he intended directly to attack that teaching, or to lay down an axiom in opposition and contradiction to the doctrine of Paul.

* James ii. 22.
† James ii. 10, and foll.

The idea of a direct polemical attack made upon Paul by James being thus set aside, we are met by a modified form of the same supposition. James, it is said, sought to oppose those who, having themselves ill understood the teaching of Paul, had set up the theory that a mere lip profession was sufficient for salvation, and that the practice of duty was a matter of indifference. James, we are told, would show these false teachers that they were giving to the words of the apostle a meaning that did not really belong to them.

If this was the intention of James, he is certainly not happy in his method of carrying it out; for in such a case he should have shown first of all what was the real meaning of Paul, and how the system of his false interpreters had corrupted the truth of his teaching, by wresting his words. The supposition that James was making an apology for Paul, and vindicating his principles from the wrong done them by a false application, is then as little tenable as the theory of a polemical purpose in the epistle. If we examine well the ground occupied by the two writers, the method they employ, the ideas they discuss, the principles they enunciate, we are necessarily led to the conclusion that James, the later writer, had no reference, direct or indirect, to his predecessor. It may be boldly affirmed that James had not before him a single epistle of Paul's when he composed his own; it may even be said that he had never read one of those epistles.

And here lies the very gist of the question. It is but trifling with words to pretend to have exhausted it by the negative reply we have just quoted, and which is given by so many theologians, who, content to have found it, imagine that nothing more is required to satisfy criticism. It is a mistake to suppose that harmony is implicity established between two systems when it is proved that the later was not written with the express intention of confuting the earlier. The practical and theoretical points of view are thus arbitrarily and often unwittingly confounded.

Now, from the practical point of view, the apostles are in perfect harmony. What, in truth, is the question? Not whether

faith ought to produce works. Both apostles urgently demand
a living and acting faith; and we defy the subtlest analysis
of the texts to discover the slightest difference between them,
in relation to the duties enjoined on the disciples of Christ
who are to inherit the kingdom of God.* It is only in the
sickly brain of the scholasticism of the sixteenth century, that
the absurd doctrine could have originated that works are
noxious to salvation.

The difference is elsewhere, but it has a real existence; it
lies in the theory. You ask, How is a man justified before
God? The answer which you receive is not the same from
both apostles.

Paul says: We must believe. It is faith which brings justification, pardon of sin,—in a word, salvation. Works have
nothing to do with it. Justification is by faith, and comes
before we have done anything whatever to merit it. It is
grace which makes faith thus availing. Where Christian faith
is, there works will be also; it is even necessary that there
should be works, otherwise the faith cannot be true and real;
but justification is bestowed, not because of the works which
follow it, but because of the faith which precedes them.

James says: A man must work; works secure his justification; he is not justified by faith alone.† Justification takes
place only in connection with works. Faith must indeed
concur to produce the works,‡ but unless the works are there,
faith is nothing; it is dead—that is, it is of no effect; it

* We should be doing an injustice to our readers if, after all that has
been already said, we should endeavour to prove this here by quotations
which we might give in abundance. There are analogies, or let us
rather say there is the most perfect conformity in this respect, not
only between Paul and James, but among all the apostolic writers. Let
us take, without selection, a few of the most striking principles laid down
in the Epistle of James; we shall find them readily elsewhere also; for
example, see ch. i. 12, and 2 Tim. iv. 7, 8; Rev. ii. 10; James i. 22,
and ‖Rom. ii. 13; 1 John iii. 7; James i. 25, and John xiii. 17; James
iii. 2, and Rom. iii. 23; 1 John i. 8; James i. 18, and John i. 13; 1 Peter
i. 23, etc.

† James ii. 24.

‡ Συνεργεῖν, James ii. 22.

becomes something—that is, it becomes efficacious and perfect only by the works which it produces.*

In reducing these two explanations to the simplest, at the same time to the least startling terms, we may say : According to Paul, faith, because it justifies, is the source of good works. According to James, faith, because it is the source of good works, justifies.

In these two formulas we have perhaps reduced the difference to its minimum ; we have at least not in any way exaggerated it. We have now to weigh its actual significance. This would be immense, if, for example, the formula of James implied that man by works, regarded as his own, could merit salvation. But this is not what he says. The apostle affirms explicitly that the power to do good comes from God, of whom it must be sought.† The difference would again be very great, and would involve consequences fatal to morality itself, if James by his mode of expression meant to represent the attainment of salvation as an easy thing, so that the natural and unregenerate man might without difficulty ensure it. But he says the very opposite ; he affirms that a single trans-gression is enough to forfeit all claim to any merit before God ; he denounces the common fallacy of regarding some trans-gressions as slight and insignificant; he declares that the love of God is incompatible with the love of the world; he brands as sin, not only the finished act, not only the evil desire in its first conception, but also the omission of a good deed, though not required of us by any positive or written law. He rises to the elevation of the Sermon on the Mount, and thus dispels any illusive hope man might entertain of meriting salvation by his own virtue.

And yet he says that works justify. This proves two things: first, that James regards the question as one of experi-ence, of actual fact,—that he looks at it, in a word, from the human side; while Paul's is the ideal, the theoretical view,—in other words, that of God. James says, with great simplicity,

---

* Τελειοῦται, James ii. 22.

† James i. 5, 17, and foll.

that in order to know if a man has faith, he, James, has a right to ask if the man has works; the fruits must be seen in order to judge of the root. This test he takes from the Master Himself,* and we believe that, in practice, Paul also knew no other method of judging of Christians. A true Christian is, according to him, a man who endures temptation,† one who is approved by his life. But in abstract theory, when he is estimating theologically the relations between man and God, a different course must be pursued. We must then rise above the series of successive facts which in their totality may decide our judgment on our fellow-creatures, and consider that God, who reads all hearts, there discovers the presence or absence of the very principle which should be the soul of the man's inner life, and consequently the motive of his actions. His judgment, thus anticipating, so to speak, the facts on which it seems to lean, rests upon a deeper basis—upon something which, important as it is, *we* cannot discern. He has therefore no need of the tentative method by which we must always be guided.

Nor is this all. The remarks we have just made touch on a vital point of evangelical theology. If James, as we said above, adheres to human experience in his estimate of the relation between works and salvation, it is because his religious ideas as a whole rest upon a different basis from the theological system of Paul. Paul could not have used the formula we are now discussing without abandoning altogether the mystical fact of regeneration, and all the ideas flowing from it; it was necessary in his view, that the whole life of the Christian should be traced back to one starting-point, to one first spring sufficiently copious to supply all its vital needs; it was necessary that it should be considered as something homogeneous, constant, continuous, without variations or fluctuations. And this is precisely what we find in the Pauline theory, and what we fail to find in the Judæo-Christian theology. To the latter, the life of the Christian always remains a compound fact, or rather a series of facts, having a common resemblance probably,

---

* Matt. vii. 16.

† Δοκιμος.

and highly commendable, but still bearing the character of an accidental succession, not exempt from interruptions and gradual changes, and subject to the inconstant operation of another series of facts, external and variable.*

There is then, in short, between the language of Paul and that of James neither more nor less difference than between a mystical theology and a popular morality. The former is not the less to be respected because it can never become popular; the latter is not the less excellent because it does not satisfy the requirements of religious thought. On the contrary, both are necessary and mutually helpful. It would be easy to prove this; indeed we have already proved it by the example of Paul, who preaches the two doctrines side by side. That he was able to look at the subject from both aspects, while James could not rise above his own point of view, only proves the superiority of Paul's genius. Our great reformers have well recognized the difference, and our modern apologists ought not to pass so lightly over that which presented itself as an incontestable fact to men, certainly not prejudiced against Scripture. But the latter have fallen into the error of admitting exclusively one side or the other of the question, and of unhesitatingly denouncing the exponents of the opposite theory. The fact that the Protestant Church has reversed on this point the judgment of its illustrious fathers, and has reinstated the Epistle of James in the canon, while still maintaining its own Pauline principle,—this fact in itself proves, not that the two formulas are identical, but that the Church in its practical life cannot dispense with the teaching of James.

* For those who have eyes to see, it will suffice to point to the phrase with which James concludes his argument (ch. ii. 16). He there calls faith the body, and works the spirit, determining the relative value of the two elements. Only ignorance or obstinacy could fail to recognize that Paul, if he had chosen to use the same image for the same purpose, would unquestionably have reversed it. This trait alone suffices to mark the divergence of the two conceptions.

BOOK SIXTH.

CHAPTER I.

THE EPISTLE TO THE HEBREWS.

IN tracing the historical picture of the Church in the first century, we have already prepared our readers for the fact, which is also very easy to explain from a psychological point of view, that the divergent tendencies which had at first divided the Christians into two camps, came in the end to coalesce through tacit and mutual concessions. It is true that each party still kept some uncompromising adherents, who were all the more disposed to exaggerate their particular differences from the isolation in which they soon found themselves. Attachment to the law, and, still more, personal antipathy to those who questioned its permanent obligation, led the partisans of traditional ideas into the sectarian schism of Ebionitism; and the logical rigidity of their opponents, on the other side, grew insensibly into Gnostic Antinomianism—that is, to the absolute rejection of all that belonged to the Old Testament. But between these two extreme parties, the body of the Church, now sufficiently strong to resist the action of a dissolvent within, as well as attacks from without, found its peace and equilibrium in the modification of those very principles, which the fanatics pressed to their extreme issues. It is matter of fact that official doctrine as it began to find expression during the second century, especially if we consider the corresponding development of the social constitution, was no longer the correct and authentic expression either of the old Judæo-Christianity, or of that Paulinism which had courageously advanced to the conquest of the world. This fact we are about to verify by the study of some literary monuments of the second half of the apostolic age—writings too slight and unsystematic to allow us to derive from them a complete system of doctrine, such as we have been endeavouring to trace in the epistles of Paul, but also too important to be passed by without a separate study of their theology. We shall see as we examine these documents how Christian teaching, in passing to another generation, lost more and more of its original colouring, how the spirit increasingly gave place to the letter, and how, more particularly, the fundamental principle of the Gospel, as Paul had discerned it in the teaching of the Saviour, lost little by little its force and distinctness.

Unhappily, the Pauline school was not fruitful in writers. Ecclesiastical history shows that in the two generations which followed the age of the apostles, and up to the commencement of patristic literature, there arose no theologian who adhered rigorously to the principles of Paul, and embodied them in a book. The only exceptions at all deserving recognition are the epistles (much interpolated, and perhaps altogether unauthentic,) which bear the names of Bishop Ignatius of Antioch, and the anonymous epistle to Diognetus. These are, in any case, of far too advanced a date to claim our attention now. It has not been, then, through the medium of books that this school has continued to exercise a paramount influence in the Church ; and as the history of this period supplies us with few proper names, we are not prepared to say if the apostle of the Gentiles left any successors worthy of him, at least in the elevation of their views and the constancy of their efforts. It must be indeed acknowledged generally that practical duties of every sort so absorbed the energies of the young community, that theology and literature could of necessity occupy but a secondary place. As we go back, however, to the more intimate circle of the friends and colleagues of Paul and their immediate successors, we meet with several whose names stand in direct connection with that portion of apostolic literature, the analysis of which will form the subject of the present book. As the gospel and the epistles of John occupy a place by themselves in this literature, and we reserve them for an entirely separate study, we shall now devote our attention specially, first, to four epistles, all more or less associated by their tendency with the teaching of Paul, and then to four historical books less directly involved in the progress of ideas, but nevertheless sufficiently instructive to be consulted by us, in the absence of more copious sources of information in reference to our present subject. The design of this exposition necessitates our beginning with the epistles.

Among these, the Epistle to the Hebrews, by far the most important and probably also the oldest, was only received into the canon at the commencement of the fifth century, although it was known and esteemed at Rome in the first· The reason of this tardy admission was that ancient writers were doubtful about its origin, some attributing it to Barnabas, others to Paul, others again to Luke or Clement,—hypotheses which have been all taken up in turn by modern critics, and supplemented by others of the same sort. Calvin and Luther, with their immediate followers, declared that they could not recognize Paul as the author of this scripture, and the confessions of faith of Lutheran Germany and reformed France implicitly sanctioned this opinion, without, however, ceasing to quote the epistle as of apostolic authority. Modern criticism has sought to confirm the judgment of the reformers by a series of arguments which we shall not reproduce. The literary question, the necessity of determining the individuality of the author, is subordinate in our history to the necessity of rightly understanding the theology of his book. Moreover, this study will do more to throw light upon the disputed point of its authorship, than all the philological or historical arguments which have been urged on either side, and far more than all the mutually contradictory testimonies of the fathers. If the impossibility of regarding Paul as the writer of the Epistle to the Hebrews is demonstrated to us by these intrinsic reasons, which can be alone decisive, we have no means of substituting another proper name for his. We need not refrain, however, from saying that, in that case, no conjecture appears to us more plausible than that of Luther, who was the first to point to Apollos of Alexandria as the probable writer of the epistle. All that we know of this disciple, of his relations with Paul, of the nature of his eloquence, of the method of his teaching, which Paul hints was above the grasp of the Corinthians,* and especially that which is said of the power of his exegetical demonstration,† harmonizes so perfectly with the most striking characteristics of the Epistle to the Hebrews, that we cannot but consider Luther's suggestion a very happy one, though it can never be more than an ingenious hypothesis. We the more gladly recognize the merit of his idea in this case, because the critical judgments of the great man are not always equally acceptable. Next to this hypothesis, that which bears most semblance of probability is the opinion of Tertullian, who names Barnabas as the author,—an opinion which, independently of other arguments, may profit by the growing repugnance of criticism to acknowledge that apostle to be the author of the epistle which now bears his name.

The Epistle to the Hebrews is, in chronological order, the first systematic treatise of Christian theology; for no epistle of Paul's can be thus denominated; and the fourth gospel, which deserves this name on more than one ground, must have been written at a somewhat later date. The Epistle to the Hebrews is not a letter, properly so called, written in view of a local necessity; and the few personal or circumstantial details added on the last page were certainly not the reasons which prompted the author to write. This book may have been already penned and actually concluded when occasion offered to make it useful to a particular circle of Christians, and in reference to them he may have added the thirteenth chapter. The

* 1 Cor. ii. 3.
† Acts xviii. 24, and foll.

Hebrews, whose name is inserted in the title by the care of a
later reader (also truly inspired), are not, as has been imagined,
the members of some isolated community, as, for example, the
Church at Jerusalem ; they are Jewish Christians, in general,
considered from a theoretical point of view. The discourse
itself (chapters i.—xii.), so distinguished by the clearness of its
arrangement, the elevation of its ideas, and its classic correctness of style, treats of the prerogatives which the Gospel may
claim over the Jewish law, and is designed to show to the
Christians who adhere to the latter, the inferiority and error
of their point of view, and the dangers which may result to
them from it.   This design gives to the writer's exposition
an entirely practical and almost homiletic character.
Throughout urgent exhortations interrupt, without enfeebling,
his theological argument ; and towards the close (chapter xii.)
these two elements blend in a peroration which is one of the
most eloquent pages of the entire Christian literature of the
first age.   It is needless to say that we should not look in a
treatise of this kind for a complete summary of Christian
theology, nor have we any ground for assuming that points
of doctrine not here touched upon formed no part of the
evangelical teaching of the writer.   Our duty will be first to
reproduce succinctly the teaching of his work, and then to
show the gaps which it leaves, and the means of so filling them
as to bring out the individuality of the writer.

The comparison between evangelical Christianity and legal
Judaism relates specially to two main points : the relative
dignity of the personages who represent the two dispensations,
as mediators between God and the world, and the nature of
the results or advantages secured by each.

In the former part, Jesus Christ is successively regarded
as the Revealer and as the High-priest.   In His capacity of
Revealer, He might be compared with the prophets of the Old
Testament generally, and with Moses in particular.*   But
the writer does not stop at these parallels.   The very variety
of form in the old revelations, and their incessant repetition,

* Heb. i. 1, πολυμερῶς, πολυτρόπως ; iii. 2, and foll.

as opposed to the one and final revelation by the Son, proves
the superiority of the latter. Again, Moses, the greatest of all
the prophets, received as the highest eulogy God could bestow
on him, the testimony that he had been a faithful servant in
the household of God; while Jesus Christ, no less faithful to
Him from whom He received His mission, is at once the
Founder and the Master of the house in which He serves.
This term *house** further reminds us of the two economies of
the Pauline theology.

There was here, also, another parallel to be traced, which
would mark yet more emphatically the dignity of the later
Revealer. We know that Jewish theology assigned this part
in the Sinaitic delivery of the law, not to a direct and personal
intervention of the Most High, but to angels, His delegates,†
beings, without contradiction, higher than any human prophet.
It is then to the angels that Christ is compared,‡ and it is this
comparison which supplies the writer with the opportunity
of exalting the prerogatives of the Son. The angels are simply
the ministers of the divine will, sent on their mission in the
interests of the men for whom salvation is prepared, and they
themselves are constrained to bow before the Son. Christ, on
the contrary, unites in Himself attributes which raise Him far
above the sphere of the angels. In relation to the outward
dignity in which He now presents Himself to the world, He is
said to be seated at the right hand of the Majesty on high; He
is the possessor or heir of all things.§ In relation to His essence,
His divine nature is affirmed explicitly and implicitly. He is
called God by the mouth of God Himself; ‖ more frequently,
however, the Son of God, or simply the Son ;¶ and the metaphysical import of the latter term is marked by the care taken
by the writer, to analyze it by means of formulas previously

---

* Οἶκος θεοῦ; comp. x. 21, antithesis of ἐν and of ἐπί.
† Heb. ii. 2.
‡ Heb. i. 4, 5, 6, 7, 14 ; ii. 5.
§ Heb. i. 2, 3, 13 ; viii. 1, κληρονόμος πάντων.
‖ Heb. i. 8.
¶ Heb. i. 2 ; iv. 14 ; v. 8 ; vi. 6, etc.

familiar in the schools.* He is the reflection of the divine perfection, the express image of God;† and it is clear, from the figures chosen, that the intention of the theology is to establish at once the divinity and the plurality of the persons in the Godhead, side by side with the monotheistic principle. As we read further that by Him God created the worlds,‡ that it is He who by His mighty will upholds and preserves all things,§ we understand without difficulty that the writer is striving to define the notion of the Creative Word, though he does not use the term *logos*. We recognize also in all these expressions, as in that of the First-born,‖ the same Christological ideas developed with more or less exactness by Paul and John, and which were based upon a yet more ancient metaphysical system.

The human nature of Christ¶ is only dwelt upon in relation to His work, of which we shall speak presently. He is man no less than God, and the familiar expression, Son of man, is designed, no doubt, to recall the fact of the incarnation.** This is represented as a temporary humiliation,†† by which He became a little lower than the angels, and subject to the sufferings of death.‡‡ But this humiliation itself was to result in a yet greater glory. By His sufferings He was to be raised to the heavenly place which was His of right, but to which He gained a new title by accepting voluntarily both the glorious mission of Saviour and the hard apprenticeship of sorrow, tears, shame, and death, in place of the heavenly felicity which He already possessed, and which He might still have kept.§§ This supreme glory, this undivided reign, is not indeed yet manifested to the world in all its fulness;‖‖ but the assurance of His henceforth

* See Book of Wisdom vii. 25, and foll., and generally Book I., ch. viii.
† Ἀπαύγασμα τῆς δόξης, χαρακτὴρ τῆς ὑποστάσεως, i. 3.
‡ Αἰῶνες, i. 2; comp. xi. 3.
§ Φέρων.
‖ Πρωτότοκος, i. 6.
¶ Αἷμα καὶ σάρξ, ii. 14.
** Heb. ii. 6.
†† Ἠλάττωσας βραχύ τι, ii. 7.
‡‡ Heb. ii. 7.
§§ Heb. xii. 2; v. 8, and foll. (ὑπακοή, ἔμαθεν). His mission, iii. 2, ποιεῖν.
‖‖ Heb. ii. 9.

deathless life * is the guarantee of the promises attached to His person, and the direct proof that death was for Him only the transition to perfection †—that is, to a state in conformity with His dignity. This is in all points, and almost in so many words, the explanation already given by the Epistle to the Philippians of the relation between the two stages in the life of Christ, although the difficulty which must always be felt in regarding His exaltation as a recompense—a difficulty which is avoided by John's explanation—is here rather less apparent. It must be observed, however, that the author only insists upon the humanity of Christ, in so far as that was essential to the work of redemption. He speaks, indeed, of Christ's relations with the race of David,‡ but in another passage he mentions as one of the distinctive characteristics of the Son of God, that He was without father, without mother, without descent; § as though he would thus break all the affiliating links between Him and preceding generations of men. It is confessedly difficult for us to comprehend the second term of this statement; but it is evident that the writer,

* Heb. vii. 8, 25 ; πάντοτε ζῶν.

† Τελειοῦσθαι, ii. 10 ; v. 9 ; vii. 28.

‡ Heb. vii. 14.

§ Heb. vii. 3; ἀπάτωρ, ἀμήτωρ, ἀγενεαλόγητος. [The argument is that, as a priest, Melchisedec is "without a genealogy," that he belongs to no consecrated line; the commencement of his priestly functions is not connected with the death of any predecessor; the close of them is not marked by the appearance of another who succeeded him. A priest "without" a priestly "father," "without" a "mother" belonging to the sacerdotal line, without a definite consecration signalizing his entrance into his office, without successors indicating that his functions had ceased,—held a position altogether unlike that of the priesthood that ministered in the Jewish temple,—belonged to altogether a different "order." It was these circumstances that made the priesthood of Melchisedec unique. In Psalms lxvii. and cx. the peculiarities of the priesthood of Melchisedec, who was, moreover, king as well as priest, had suggested a prophetic description of the coming Messiah, and it was with these two Psalms in his mind that the writer of this epistle connected Christ with the ancient princes of Salem. See, for a fuller development of the argument, "The Jewish Temple, etc.," by the Editor.—ED.]

preoccupied with the solution of the metaphysical part of the problem concerning the person of Christ, here passes by its historical side. In any case, it must be observed that by the two other terms of the passage, the Epistle to the Hebrews vindicates its consistency with itself, and its fidelity to the theory now received as orthodox; for if Jesus had no human father, it is evident that the ascending genealogy of his reputed father in no way affects His true descent.

In the comparison, then, between the revealers of the old and the new economy, the advantage is altogether on the side of the latter. The result is the same in the second parallel which the author traces, and on which he dwells with still more complacency. Jesus is there presented to us as a high-priest. In the old covenant, the relations of the faithful Jews with their God were sustained through the medium of a sacerdotal caste, with a high-priest at its head; the mission of this priest, chosen by God from among men, was to offer sacrifices for the expiation of sins.* The new covenant treats, in like manner, of sin and its expiation; in it, therefore, we find also a sanctuary, a sacrifice, and a high-priest. This high-priest is Jesus Christ. Resembling in many respects the high-priest by law appointed, He is greatly superior in many more important respects. Thus, Jesus did not take to Himself the priestly dignity; He was the Sent of God;† He made Himself the equal of men, and their brother,‡ becoming subject to the infirmities of their nature, and enduring the same temptations to which they are exposed, so that in all things He might be able to sympathise and help them. In these respects He is like unto Aaron. But He is also far above him, because His priesthood is eternal,§ while the priesthood of the old covenant was transmitted from father to son by reason of the inevitable death of each successive titulary; again, He is superior by his

* Heb. v. 1—4.

† Heb. v. 5; ἀπόστολος, iii. 1.

‡ Heb. ii. 17, 18; iv. 15.

§ Μένει εἰς τὸ διηνεκές, Heb. vii. 3; εἰς τὸν 'αἰῶνα, v. 6; vi. 20; vii. 23.

freedom from sin, being Himself without spot or blemish,* having nothing in common, as to His moral nature, with sinners, and having no need, like men who are priests, to commence each day by offering expiatory sacrifices for His own offences.† We may mention, as a third characteristic of the supremacy of His priesthood, that His priestly dignity was proclaimed in a more august manner, and by the oath of God.‡ All this, however, is as nothing in comparison with the inestimable benefits obtained from His sacrifice—benefits of which we shall have to speak presently, and in view of which the functions of the priests under the law appear miserably poor in their results. The epithets given to the high-priest of the new economy§ are thus completely justified. The name of Aaron could not suffice to set forth His dignity;‖ the Old Testament supplied another and more adequate type—the essentially prophetic figure of Melchisedec,¶ whose name and history are but the anticipation of the glory of the Son of God, at once priest and king, inaugurating a kingdom of righteousness and peace;** superior to Levi, who pays tithes to Him in Abraham; and to Abraham, who receives His blessing; and soaring high above humanity, to which He belongs neither by the ties of family nor by the conditions of a purely temporary existence. As we see into what strange misapprehensions exegetes have been led in reference to this famous and ingenious study of typology, we shall feel that the author had ground for saying to his readers, that the subject was one hard to treat intelligibly for those who were slow to comprehend anything beyond the mere elements of revelation.†† No interpretation can ward off from the writer of the epistle, the reproach of having indulged in a capricious and childish play of the imagination, unless it

---

* Χωρὶς ἁμαρτίας, Heb. iv. 15 ; vii. 26 ; ix. 14.
† Heb. v. 3 ; ix. 7.
‡ Ὁρκωμοσία, Heb. vii. 20, and foll.
§ Heb. iv. 14; x. 21 ; vii. 26 ; viii. 1, etc.
‖ Heb. vii. 11.
¶ Heb. v. 6 ; vi. 20 ; vii. 1, and foll.
** Βασιλεὺς εἰρήνης, etc., Heb. vii. ii ; i. 8.
†† Heb. v. 11, and foll.

takes boldly the ground we assume here, and avows that to the
author whose words we are studying the record in Genesis was
not a narrative, but a doctrinal statement; in other words, that
in his view Melchisedec had no historic reality, but was a prophetic or typical being.   This is very forcibly brought out by
the phrase in which the author speaks of Melchisedec as "*made
like unto the Son of God*"* (not that the Son of God was made
like unto Melchisedec) ; that is to say : we have in Melchisedec
not a true historical personage, but the typical and ideal representation of a theological fact, to be studied in the light of a
later revelation.   We may add, in concluding this first section
of our subject, that the Epistle to the Hebrews is the only book
of the New Testament which establishes and developes this idea
of the priesthood of Christ; and if we may judge by the example of Luther, it is this idea, so beautiful and suggestive in
itself, which has finally won for it the suffrages of theologians,
who were at first slow to accord to it canonical authority.

The second part of the epistle draws a parallel between
the respective effects of the priestly mediation of Aaron and
of Christ.   This parallel is based upon the familiar idea of two
covenants made by God with men; and it is the promises,
relations, results, and methods of these two covenants, which
form in turn the subject of the theological study of our author.
Let us observe, however, that in making use of this term
covenant we adhere to the ordinary sense of the corresponding
Greek term,† a sense which it always bears elsewhere, and in
most of the passages in this epistle also.   There is only one ‡
in which the author adopts the signification of *testament*, and
to this we shall advert separately.

Christ is then the Mediator§ or the Surety of a new covenant
which is better than the old by the very fact of its existence; for if the first had been sufficient, if it had been able
to realize its intention and its promises,‖ it would have left

* Ἀφωμοιωμένος τῷ υἱῷ, Heb. vii. 3.
† Διαθήκη.
‡ Heb. ix. 15, and foll. ; comp. Gal. iii. 15.
§ Μεσίτης, Heb. viii. 6 ; ix. 15 ; xii. 24 ; ἔγγυος, vii. 22.
‖ Τελειοῦν, Heb. vii. 19.

nothing to be desired,* and God would not have passed sentence upon it by holding out to the world the prospect of a new covenant.

We said that the two covenants are here compared, first, in relation to that which they promise. In substance, the promise is the same in both; at least it is expressed in the same terms. On Sinai, Jehovah had promised rest to Israel;† that is, a peaceful happiness, derived on the one hand from the quiet possession of Canaan, and on the other from dutiful obedience to His commandments. But the conquest achieved by Joshua‡ did not fulfil this promise because of the disobedience of the people. Long after this period, however, God by the mouth of David § opened anew the prospect of rest, to be obtained by those who should believe and obey, instead of hardening their hearts against the voice of His commandments. This rest, which might be called the Sabbath‖ of the people of God, their great day of peace and contentment after all the tribulations of this life,—as God too had His day of rest after the work of creation,—is to be sought yet in the future; the promise concerning it is not yet fulfilled, but it cannot fail, God having assured it with an oath. Since it holds out the promise of more perfect blessedness, it is guaranteed in a more solemn manner, and is thus in all points better than the first covenant.¶ The only requisite is to know its conditions, and to fulfil them.

This first point of the comparison gives us a glimpse of the nature of the relation between the two covenants. The writer has preluded this second phase of his parallel, by introducing successively the typical personages of Melchisedec, Moses, Aaron, and Joshua; and lastly (chapters viii.—x.) he raises points of resemblance, apparently arbitrary and accidental, to the height of theological and necessary facts. The old covenant is, especially

* Ἄμεμπτος, Heb. viii. 7, and foll.
† Κατάπαυσις, Heb. iii. 7, to iv. 11.
‡ Heb. iv. 8.
§ Psalm xcv.
‖ Σαββατισμός, Heb. iv. 9.
¶ Heb. viii. 6.

in its institutions, the image, the shadow, the prophetic counterpart of the new,* which alone has the very substance of the
promised blessings.† Thus the tabernacle of Moses (for it is this
which is described, according to the account in Exodus, and
not the temple of Jerusalem, as it was standing before its final
destruction,) was only the copy of a heavenly sanctuary,‡ shown
to the prophet upon Mount Sinai. This heavenly sanctuary has
then its various parts, its rites, and its priest, like the earthly
sanctuary ; § and by the law which forbade Aaron to pass within
the veil into the Holiest of All, save once in the year to atone
for his own and the people's sins, the Holy Spirit would show
that the way into the heavenly sanctuary was not yet opened to
men so long as the first tabernacle was still standing legally.‖

But by the very fact that God appointed a high-priest
after the order of Melchisedec,—a stranger, that is, to the
family of Levi,—He declared that the law itself which
had constituted the Levitical priesthood was abolished, or
that it had given place to a new law.¶ The old priesthood
obeyed a carnal commandment,—that is to say, it followed the
natural succession of individuals in a family; it made men
priests who were subject to every sort of infirmity;** the new
priesthood is established after the power of an endless life,
and thus the old might well be abrogated in favour of it. The
institution of the old law, the priesthood with its various
and repeated sacrifices, could never really take away sin,†† or

* Ὑπόδειγμα, σκιά, ἀντίτυπος, παραβολή, Heb. viii. 5 ; ix. 9, 24 ; x. i.

† Τὰ ἀληθινά, αὐτὴ εἰκών, τὸ τέλειον, ὁ τύπος, ibid. We know that to this
last word ecclesiastical terminology has attached a contrary meaning.
The type is the prophetic figure of the Old Testament ; the antitype is
its evangelical accomplishment. This view is based on chronological
data ; while our author, taking the ideal standpoint, and starting from
the idea of the eternity of the divine decrees, naturally finds the copy in
the earthly institution.

‡ Σκηνὴ ἐπουράνιος.

§ Ἅγιον κοσμικόν, Heb. ix. 1.

‖ Heb. ix. 6—8.

¶ Μετάθεσις, ἀτέθησις, Heb. vii. 12, 18.

** Heb. vii. 16, 28.

†† Heb. x. 2, and foll., 11.

purify the conscience of the sinner. So far from doing so, they only added to the torment of his conscience by the ceaseless reminder of his sins. It was vain for the law to pronounce that he was pure, while his sin-offering was consumed upon the altar; the voice of his conscience told him to the contrary. The law could not then bring to perfection,* that is, to perfect righteousness, those who by its aid sought to come near to God; they ever felt in the depths of their heart the insufficiency of the legal offerings.† The fear of death—that most cruel of all bondage‡—held them captive through their whole life. It was this insufficiency, this weakness, this inefficacy, which condemned the law, and commended the new dispensation, which will avail to bring us to God.§

We come now to the last point of the comparison—the means employed to effect the salvation of men. As we have already become acquainted with the methods of the old economy by our study of its results, it only remains for us to show what are the means employed in the new. These may be summed up in one very simple statement: it is by the blood of Christ that sinful man is purified and brought into possession of the promised blessings. This thesis contains three propositions, of which two are only passingly mentioned. Just as, in the old economy, the provisional covenant of God with Israel was ratified by a bleeding sacrifice,‖ so the blood of Christ¶ seals the eternal covenant of sanctified men, (that is, of men consecrated to God,) with Him who henceforth allows them free access into His holy presence.** And just as in civil life, the death of the testator is necessary before the heirs can be put in possession of that which he has bequeathed to them, so Christ died in order that His heirs, men delivered from the guilt contracted under the old covenant, may enter upon the

* Τελειῶσαι, Heb. x. 1.
† Heb. ix. 9.
‡ Heb. ii. 15.
§ Heb. vii. 18.
‖ Heb. ix. 19, and foll.
¶ Αἷμα διαθήκης αἰωνίου, Heb. x. 29; xiii. 20.
** Heb. x. 10, 19.

enjoyment of their eternal inheritance.* But these two propositions are plainly subordinate to the first, that of the necessity of the death of Christ for the purification of sinners. It is
on this the writer dwells with most emphasis. In former
times, he says, the blood of the slain animals, sprinkled on
persons who had contracted some Levitical or external defilement,† was supposed to restore the purity of the body, how
much more shall the blood of Christ, who through the eternal
Spirit,‡ (that is, in His divine nature, not subject to death,)
offered Himself to God, purge from the soul the defilement of
sin. Pardon§ cannot be obtained under the new covenant any
more than under the old, without shedding of blood; but since
this pardon is now real and positive,‖ there can be no more
repetition of the sacrifice. This has been offered once for all;¶
its effect has been complete deliverance, eternal redemption.**
Jesus is the author of this salvation, literally the leader,††
antesignanus, He who takes the initiative. By His death, He
has broken the yoke of him who had the power of death, that
is the devil?‡‡ The sanctuary of eternal life was closed against
us, but by the sacrifice of the body of Jesus on the cross, the
veil which hung before it is rent, and the way into the Holiest
really and finally opened.§§ This purification‖‖ is the ultimate
purpose of Christ's work on earth. The one great end of His
appearing in the fulness of time was to take away the actual
sins of the world, and to destroy sin as a power; and both
purposes have been accomplished by His sacrifice.¶¶ His blood

---

* Heb. ix. 15, and foll.
† Heb. ix. 13, and foll.
‡ Διὰ πνεύματος αἰωνίου.
§ Ἄφεσις, Heb. ix. 22.
‖ Heb. x. 17, 18.
¶ Θυσία, προσφορά, Heb. x. 10—14, etc. ; ἐφάπαξ, vii. 27 ; ix. 12 ; x. 10.
** Αἰωνία λύτρωσις, Heb. ix. 12 ; σωτηρία αἰώνιος, v. 9 ; vii. 25.
†† Ἀρχηγός, Heb. ii. 10.
‡‡ Heb. ii. 14.
§§ Ὁδὸς ζῶσα, Heb. x. 19, 20.
‖‖ Καθαρισμός, Heb. i. 3.
¶¶ Ἀναφέρειν τὰς ἁμαρτίας, ἀθέτησις τῆς ἁμαρτίας, Heb. ix. 26, 28.

cries to heaven like the blood of Abel,* but it has something greater to tell and to demand; it asks for pardon, not vengeance. Lastly, Jesus suffered outside the city, just as the victims were formerly consumed without the camp, after their blood had been brought into the sanctuary. Thus throughout the epistle, striking analogies multiply under the pen of the author, and serve to define the fundamental idea of his theology.

Jesus is then at once priest and victim in this great act of expiation. It is His own blood that He presents to God before the holy ark of the new covenant,—that is, before the throne of grace,—in order to render the Judge propitious to us.† The acceptance of His sacrifice is absolutely sure, since it is divine mercy itself, the grace of the Eternal, fulfilling an immutable‡ purpose, which has permitted that the Son should taste death for every man. It is the more important that those who are called to benefit by this grace § should not reject the gift of heaven,‖ but should show themselves worthy of it by brotherly love one towards another, by provoking one another to mutual love and to good works according to the will of God. The baptism of blood is to be the purification of their hearts, as the baptism of water is the symbolical ablution of their bodies;¶ the law of God is to be, according to prophetic promise, written henceforth in their minds,** so that they may not even need that any man should teach them; and they shall then be the children of God, and thus the brethren of Him who is by preeminence the Son.††

As children of God, and especially as beloved children, the men thus consecrated by the blood of Christ, and virtually already brought to perfection‡‡ by the sacrifice of the conse-

---

* Heb. xii. 24.

† Heb. vii. 25; ix. 24; iv. 16; Ιλάσκεσθαι, ii. 17.

‡ Χάρις, Heb. ii. 9; βουλὴ ἀμετάθετος, vi. 17.

§ Οἱ κεκλημένοι, Heb. ix. 15; κλήσεως ἐπουρανίου μέτοχοι, iii. 1.

‖ Heb. vi. 4; x. 29; x. 24; vi. 10; xiii. 21.

¶ Heb. x. 22.

** Heb. viii. 10; x. 16.

†† Υἱοί, Heb. xii. 5, and foll.; ii. 10; ἀδελφοί, ii. 11, 17.

‡‡ Οἱ ἁγιαζόμενοι, τετελειωμένοι, Heb. x. 14.

crating high-priest,* have actually still to pass through an
educational process,† more or less severe, in order to attain to
the end towards which, by ardent and repeated exhortations, the
whole epistle urges them to strive. The writer speaks of it as
a race, a fight, a course of trial, effort, labour, as we have found
the Christian life elsewhere described. But it cannot last
long. The revelation of Christ has taken place in the end of
the world,‡—that is, at the end of the preparatory period; His
sacrifice inaugurates a new era, an age of reformation,§ which
will very shortly ‖ be followed by the last day.¶ The certainty of this hope fills with joy even now;** for it opens
the wide prospect of future blessedness, of an eternal inheritance promised to those who do the will of God; the prospect, in a word, of salvation and life.†† This prospect will
be realized when Christ, who, as our Forerunner,‡‡ has already
entered heaven, and passed within the veil which as yet con-
ceals the Holiest of All, shall appear for the second time to
those who look for Him. He will then come, however, no more
to deal with sin,§§ but to introduce the redeemed into their
celestial home, into the city of the living God, a city with
firm foundations, built by God Himself, on another Mount Zion,
the new Jerusalem ‖‖ towards which now they are tending,
knowing, like the patriarchs before them, that here they have no
continuing city.¶¶ In this kingdom, which cannot be moved,***

* Ἁγιάζων, ii. 11.
† Παιδείαν ὑπομένειν, Heb. x. 32, 36 ; xii. 1, 7, and foll.
‡ Συντέλεια τῶν αἰώνων, Heb. ix. 26.
§ Καιρὸς διορθώσεως, Heb. ix. 10.
‖ Heb. x. 25, 37.
¶ Ἡμέρα, τέλος.
** Heb. iii. 6 ; vi. 1, 18 ; x. 23.
†† Μέλλοντα ἀγαθά, Heb. ix. 11; ἐπαγγελία κληρονομίας αἰωνίου, ix. 15 ;
x. 36 ; comp. i. 14 ; vi. 12, 17 ; σωτηρία, ii. 3 ; ix. 28, etc. ; περιποίησις
ψυχῆς, x. 39 ; ζῆν, xii. 9.
‡‡ Πρόδρομος, Heb. vi. 19, 20.
§§ Heb. ix. 28.
‖‖ Heb. xi. 10, 16 ; xii. 22.
¶¶ Heb. xiii. 14.
*** Βασιλεία ἀσάλευτος, Heb. xii. 27, 28.

which is to take the place of the heavens and the earth which are now, Jesus the great Shepherd of His sheep* will gather around Him, in the presence of God, the great Judge of the world, both the myriads of the angels and the just of every age† whose names are written in heaven, and who through the same Mediator will all be brought to the same perfection.‡

Such is the substance of the Epistle to the Hebrews in its doctrinal portion. From the writer's point of view, we may call it a treatise on transcendental theology; for he himself says that he aimed to write for the perfect,§ that is, for those who could bear strong meat, and whose reason was sufficiently exercised by use to grasp higher and fuller teaching.‖ Elementary instruction,¶ needful as it is for the many, lies far below the sphere which he aims to occupy in this epistle. We have followed him so far step by step, without mingling any reflections of our own with his systematic exposition; but we cannot pass on without examining his theology by the light of the Pauline theory. The analogies which this epistle presents with the teaching of Paul, are so many and so striking, that we cannot for a moment wonder that Paul should have been supposed to be its author. These analogies are to be traced in a series of terms common to both writers, no less than in the substance of the doctrinal ideas. Our readers cannot fail to have remarked this for themselves, and we have no need to dwell upon it. We may not, however, close our eyes to certain very remarkable differences, which, though we have no desire to exaggerate their significance, seem to us no less worthy of note because they have escaped the attention of superficial or prejudiced exegetes.

We avow at the outset, that, in an ethical point of view, the theology of this writer leaves nothing to be desired. He

* Ποιμὴν μέγας, Heb. xiii. 20.
† Πρωτότοκοι.
‡ Heb. xii. 22, 23.
§ Τέλειοι, Heb. v. 11, and foll.; vi. 1, and foll.
‖ Τελειότης, λόγος δικαιοσύνης.
¶ Ὁ τῆς ἀρχῆς τοῦ Χριστοῦ λόγος, τὰ στοιχεῖα.

declares that the Levitical sacrifices cannot produce purity of heart or rest of conscience. The great end of Christ's mission was to supply this lack, to re-establish the soul's peace with God, by purifying the conscience.* He describes this act by a term of his own, *the fulfilment*,†—that is to say, the progress and attainment of every man to the end for which he was designed. Applied to men, this uniformly implies moral perfection;‡ it is not only the cancelling of former sins, but also final and complete sanctification.§ So true is this, and so strongly does the author insist on perseverance in well-doing, that he goes so far as to declare, explicitly and repeatedly,‖ that a relapse into sin is always fatal; that it is equivalent to a repetition of the suffering inflicted upon Christ; and, lastly, that a tardy repentance, after such a fall, can be of no avail. The Romish doctors of the third century, and Luther in the sixteenth, loudly protested against this stern and paradoxical theory: they concluded from it that the writer could not have been an inspired apostle. If they had been content to say that his statement was not that of the so-called orthodox Church, we should have had nothing to object to their opinion; but we see nothing at variance with the Gospel in the assertion, that every man who proves by his acts that the knowledge of the truth has not benefited him morally, has no other expiation in which to hope.¶ The severe and paradoxical form of the assertion is not more strange than many of the sayings of Jesus, and the theory of Paul we have already shown to be, in more than one aspect, no less inexorable.

Nevertheless, we think the doctrine of Paul is favourably

---

* Heb. ix. 14.

† Τελείωσις.

‡ Heb. vii. 11, 18; x. 1, 14.

§ Heb. xii. 14, etc.

‖ Heb. vi. 4, and foll.; x. 26, and foll.; xii. 17.

¶ This exegesis is false: what is affirmed in chap. x. 26, *seq.*, is that if a man apostatizes from Christ, there is no sacrifice for sins left to him; the old sacrifices have passed away, and a Christian Jew cannot say that he will return to the faith of his fathers, for the institutions of that faith are obsolete.—ED.

distinguished from that of the Epistle to the Hebrews, by the presence of an element which is absent in the latter. In the great question concerning the relation between the atonement objectively offered by Jesus, and the salvation of the individual, Paul found the solution of the problem by associating the two facts in the closest possible manner, and in a way that satisfied the religious feeling, namely, by the idea of faith, based upon that of a substitution or of the communion of the man with the death and resurrection of the Saviour. This evangelical mysticism, which is the vital element in the Pauline theology, is here entirely wanting, and our readers have doubtless observed, that in our exposition the term faith and its derivatives have not yet occurred. This calls for some explanation.

The Epistle to the Hebrews uses the word very frequently, and sometimes also the verb formed from it, but in a sense entirely different from that of Paul. This is placed beyond question by the definition which the writer himself gives of the word.* Faith, he says, is firm persuasion† in relation to things hoped for, a solidly grounded conviction concerning things not seen as yet. A few lines further on he adds,‡ without faith it is impossible to please God, for he that cometh to God must believe that He is, and that He is the rewarder of them that diligently seek Him. Faith, then, is with him simply the conviction of the reason, the belief that a fact is true,§ especially when the fact in question is one that does not come within the range of the senses, and still more particularly when it is a future fact, the subject of promise, and to which a certain religious interest is attached. Thus regarded, faith is the synonym for the patient waiting for the fulfilment of the promises of God, for the hope professed, for the courage of the Christian in all his tribulations; finally, for perseverance as opposed to wavering and laxity of life.‖ It is in view of

* Πίστις, Heb. xi. 1.
† Ὑπόστασις, Heb. iii. 14 ; xi. 1.
‡ Heb. xi. 6.
§ Comp. Heb. iv. 2, 3 ; xi. 3 ; vi. 1.
‖ Heb. vi. 12 ; x. 22, and foll. ; 36, and foll. ; xiii. 6, and foll. ; μακροθυμία, ἐλπίς, ὑπομονή.

this courageous steadfastness that Jesus Christ, who has set us the example of it, is elsewhere spoken of as our leader in whom we conquer.* If yet further proof were needed, we could find it in abundance in the eleventh chapter, in which the writer enumerates all the examples of this faith, brought into prominence in Scripture history. We there see, in succession, Noah, Abraham, Sarah, Moses, and many others, commended on account of their immovable confidence in God with regard to the future benefits promised to them, of which they obtained no immediate possession.

In all this, there is no trace of the mystical idea attached to the term faith in the writings of Paul. We may say, further, that the accessory ideas of calling, justification, regeneration, are equally lacking in this epistle. Repentance† is expressly designated as something which does not belong to that portion of theology which the writer regards as worthy of speculative consideration. Righteousness‡ is with him truly a moral condition in conformity with the will of God, but it is a righteousness wrought as the result of outward trials ; and when it is spoken of as the righteousness which is by faith,§ we know that the reference is to the delight God has in seeing men trust in His promises. It is by this trust that the just shall live, while the unbelieving perish.|| In the noble passage borrowed from Jeremiah, in which it is said that the new covenant shall be written in the heart, and its laws henceforth faithfully observed, we seek in vain for any hint of faith in the Pauline acceptation of it, and material miracles¶ appear to be at least as much accounted of as the Spirit of God in the progress of the Gospel. Redemption is an external, objective, priestly act, taking place altogether apart from the individual who is to benefit by it. It is indeed

* Heb. xii. 1, 2 ; ἀρχηγὸς καὶ τελειωτὴς τῆς πίστεως.
† Μετάνοια, Heb. vi. 1.
‡ Δικαιοσύνη, Heb. xii. 11.
§ Heb. xi. 7.
|| Ἐκ πίστεως ζήσεται, Heb. x. 38. This passage is especially remarkable. The context compels us to construe ὁ δίκαιος ζήσεται ἐκ πίστεως, while Paul construes (Rom. i. 17 ; Gal. iii. 11) ὁ ἐκ πίστεως δίκαιος ζήσεται.
¶ Heb. ii. 4.

wrought in his behalf;* but it is not said that he appropriates it by a direct or active participation in it, influencing his own nature. We might be almost tempted to say that the writer of this epistle transfers to heaven the act of individual redemption, while Paul supposes it wrought within the soul of each believer. The efficaciousness of the sacrifice of Christ seems at least to be made dependent on the circumstance, that in His capacity as high-priest He is entered into heaven itself, there ever to intercede with God for us,† presenting His own blood as Aaron used to present the blood of the sacrificial goat.‡

We shall not attach undue importance to the fact that the polemical side of the Pauline theology scarcely appears in this book, if it may not be more truly said to be altogether absent. The author, writing for Jewish Christians, sought to convince without irritating them, to raise them to his point of view by a demonstration which should captivate their reason without exciting their prejudices. We cannot but remark, however, that the entire silence of this epistle on the relation between faith and works, is not easy to explain on the supposition that Paul was the writer. Nor is it less noticeable that the calling of the Gentiles, the universalist principle so uniformly characterizing Paul's writings in relation to the work of Christ, should here be also passed by in silence. We are far from intending to say that the writer repudiated that principle;§ as a disciple and friend of Paul, he could not do so; but assuredly the

* 'Υπέρ, in commodum, Heb. ii. 9; v. 1; vi. 20; vii. 25; ix. 24; xiii. 17.

† Heb. vii. 25.

‡ Heb. ix. 24. May we be allowed to make one remark, in passing, on the subject of this goat. Almost the whole of chapter ix. is devoted to the parallel between the sacrifice of Christ and the solemn atonement described in Levit. xvi. Now it is important to remember that in that solemnity two goats were presented,—the one offered as an atonement, the blood of which forms so important an element in the rite itself, and in the parallel; the other, not slain, but driven into the wilderness, *bearing the sins* of the people. Jesus is not compared to the latter, and the epistle never uses the expression that He *bore* our sins; it always speaks of His *taking them away*.

§ In spite of Heb. ii. 16.

17 *

apostle would never have carried the spirit of compromise so far as to pass over such a main point. That he does not do so, is further evident from the Epistle to the Romans, which is addressed to readers occupying precisely the same position as the Hebrews. He there pursues the very contrary course. The writer of this epistle speaks as if there were no Gentiles in the world. The people,* is with him the Jewish people; and in the more specially evangelical passages, there is nothing to compel us to go beyond this inner circle.†

With one more observation we close. The Epistle to the Hebrews proclaims, indeed, the decadence of the Mosaic law, and it is on this ground we have spoken of it first. But it cannot be said that in it the new economy appears as anything essentially different from the old, as is incontestably the case with the theology of Paul taken as a whole, and especially if we consider its psychological basis. Just as in this epistle we fail to find the mystical idea of faith, so does it also fail to mark the antithesis between faith and the law. It appears rather to recognize between the two dispensations simply a difference of degree or of progression,‡ the second being a new phase of development, retaining the outward form, but not the substance, of the earlier economy.

Many exegetes have even thought they could discover in one passage § proof that the writer regarded the law, not as *already* abrogated, but as destined *to fall by degrees* into desuetude. This is altogether erroneous. In order to understand the meaning of that passage, we must place ourselves, not at the chronological standpoint of the author, writing after the death of Jesus Christ, but at that of the prophet Jeremiah, whose words, quoted in the preceding verses, predict by implication the approaching abolition of the law.

Be this as it may, and placing Paul, as we do, far above the

---

* 'Ο λαός (the word ἔθνη is not used); Heb. v. 3; vii. 5, 11, 27; viii. 10; ix. 7, 19; x. 30; xi. 25.

† Heb. ii. 17; iv. 9; xiii. 12.

‡ Κρεῖττόν τι, Heb. xi. 40; comp. vii. 19, 22; viii. 6; ix. 23.

§ Heb. viii. 13; ἐγγὺς ἀφανισμοῦ.

writer of this epistle as an evangelical theologian, we must not be unjust to the distinguishing features of this work. In correctness of form and in clearness of exposition, we might even give our present writer the preference over Paul; and his theology itself is the more deserving the attention of the historian of doctrine, because it has exerted a great influence (far greater than is commonly believed) on the development of the ecclesiastical theory, and because many theologians have never gone beyond the conceptions here presented.

CHAPTER II.

THE EPISTLE OF PETER.*

THE position of Peter in the Church is well known. A sincere and devout Judæo-Christian, he had need of a special revelation to convince him that it was lawful to sit at meat with men not circumcised, and to baptize them. Yet again, later, his name served as a rallying-point for the party of legalism. From the testimony rendered to him by Paul himself, we cannot imagine that he shared the rigid views of the Pharisees; in the conferences at Jerusalem, he made efforts to bring about a reconciliation, and the two apostles parted good friends and colleagues. There remained, however, still some indecision of character about him, a certain weakness on small occasions, joined to a heroic courage in great emergencies. Just as, at an earlier stage in his history, his conviction boldly proclaimed at a critical moment, and the fidelity which made him draw his sword against a superior force, failed before the raillery of a few servants, so the eloquent orator of Pentecost, the courageous defender of the Gospel before the

---

* We use this abridged designation in speaking of what is called the *First* Epistle of Peter, because the irrefragable arguments of a criticism fully sustained by the testimonies of antiquity, and supported by the feeling of a large proportion of modern theologians of the first rank, from Calvin to Neander, go to prove that the Second Epistle of Peter, so called, is a production of much more recent date than the apostolic age. It does not therefore come within the scope of our history. We have quoted it several times parenthetically, in our exposition of Judæo-Christianity; for it must in any case, from its tendency and purpose, belong to that school, but it can have no place in our present chapter, which treats of an almost Pauline epistle.

Sanhedrim, allowed himself to be intimidated at Antioch by some obscure fanatics, and repudiated the principles he had openly professed, and which had been sanctioned by a heavenly vision. The theology taught by this disciple is naturally somewhat tinged by this fluctuation between opposite opinions.

The Epistle of Peter is quite as little a letter or epistle, properly so called, as that to the Hebrews. It is impossible to discover in this discourse any circle of readers primarily intended, distinctly characterized, or personally known to the writer. The address, though containing several geographical names, is far too general to be brought forward in contradiction of this statement. All the allusions to particular circumstances are so vague that it might be affirmed, at one point, that the apostle is addressing himself specially or exclusively to ethnico-Christians, at another to Judæo-Christians. The fact is that he is addressing all; and the early Church was perfectly right in placing this epistle in the same category as the first of St. John, as a Catholic epistle,—one, that is, addressed to believers in general.

In its contents it is essentially hortatory, and presents a series of moral exhortations relating to different general or special duties. It insists principally upon the hostile dispositions entertained by the world towards the Church, from which the author derives a powerful motive for a pure life, one that may serve as a model to others. His preaching, which is entirely practical, is sustained, on the one hand, by the general hopes guaranteed to believers by the Gospel, and, on the other, by the design and effects of the death of Christ.

It is evident, therefore, that we shall not find in this document a complete system of Christian theology, since it was not the intention of the author to give theoretical teaching. It is easy, nevertheless, to collect from it a series of doctrinal theses, which though they are not systematically developed, nevertheless furnish us with the materials for a tolerably correct estimate in this respect. Before passing on to this, however, we must point out one very singular fact in relation to this epistle, which has greatly influenced us in the choice of the place

assigned to it. This same Peter, whom we have seen so easily
swayed by circumstances in his apostolic life, we here find
placing himself as a writer in relations of dependence on those
who had gone before him. In fact, his letter, short as it is,
contains a long series of passages, copied more or less literally
from other epistles, and what is most curious to note, borrowed
partly from Paul, partly from James.* The fact cannot be
called in question, nor can it be ascribed to chance. Neither
does it find a sufficient explanation in the supposition that the
author, from want of practice in Greek composition, may have
had recourse to the writings of his predecessors. At the point
to which we have been brought by our estimate of men and
things at this period, it is impossible for us not to perceive in
this attempt to make Paul and James speak, as it were, with
one mouth, a direct intention, a premeditated method, a design,
in short, which harmonizes perfectly with the view we have
taken above. It must be observed that the dependence to
which we advert is not absolute; on the contrary, a considerable
number of terms and ideas point to individual and original re-

* See Peter i., and foll. = Eph. i. 4—7 ; Peter i. 3 = Eph. i. 3 ;
Peter i. 6, 7 = James i. 2 ; Peter i. 14 = Eph. ii. 3 ; Rom. xii. 2 ;
Peter i. 21 = Rom. iv. 24 ; Peter i. 24 = James i. 10, and foll.
   Peter ii. 5 = Rom. xii. 1 ; Peter ii. 6—10 = Rom. ix. 25, 32, and
foll. ; Peter ii. 11 = Rom. vii. 23 ; Peter ii. 13 = Rom. xiii. 1—4 ;
Peter ii. 13—17 = Gal. v. 13 ; Peter ii. 18 = Eph. vi. 5.
   Peter iii. 1 = Eph. v. 22 ; Peter iii. 9 = Rom. xii. 17 ; Peter iii. 22
= Rom. viii. 34 ; Eph. i. 20.
   Peter iv. 1 = Rom. vi. 6 ; Peter iv. 8 = James v. 20 ; Peter iv. 10,
and foll. = Rom. xii. 6, and foll.
   Peter v. 1 = Rom. viii. 18 ; Peter v. 5 = Eph. v. 21 ; Peter v. 5, 9 =
James iv. 6, 7, 10.
   We enumerate here only the longer passages ; the number of technical
terms and isolated words which confirm these collations is still more
considerable. It will be further remarked that the parallels are supplied
by the epistles to the Romans and Ephesians alone ; this is one more
evidence that the writer had them before him, and that the coincidence
is not fortuitous. We know that criticism has made use of this fact as
an argument against the authenticity of the book itself. We have no
interest in pursuing this question here. Be the author whohe may, our
observations hold good.

flection and labour, and the relation is altogether different from that between the supposed Second Epistle of Peter and that of Jude, in which there is actual plagiarism. But it is only the more evident that the quotations are made deliberately and purposely,—that is, in the conviction that the two shades of opinion are not contradictory.

The tone of the Epistle of Peter is, as we have already said, essentially Pauline. We can easily draw from it a series of expressions which recall the teaching of the great apostle of the Gentiles. It is of course very difficult to reduce to a system the scattered statements accidentally inserted in a sort of homiletic discourse. The attempt has indeed been made, but at the expense of objective certainty. We shall confine ourselves to bringing out the numerous points of contact between the two theologians, and the differences which divide them.

The psychological basis of the Pauline theology, though merely touched upon, is yet sufficiently indicated in this epistle. Man, before his conversion to Christ, is plunged in an ignorance which makes him the victim of vice,* and his natural inclinations are opposed to the will of God. These inclinations are at war with the soul, or in conflict with its true interests. It is by the grace of God we are raised into a better condition.† This grace is the subject of the good news that has been declared to us, at the time by God appointed,‡ by men endowed for the work with the gift of the Holy Spirit, until which time·the prophets and the angels themselves had but an imperfect knowledge of it, though it was foreordained from before the creation of the world.§ The Gospel‖ reveals to us the decrees of God, the ministry of Christ, judgment and eternal life. The salvation of the individual is the effect of the particular application of grace, for

* Αἰ ἐν ἀγνοίᾳ ἐπιθυμίαι, Peter i. 14; comp. iv. 2 ; ii. 11.
† Χάρις, Peter i. 10 ; v. 10 ; ἔλεος, i. 3 ; ii. 10.
‡ Καιρός, Peter i. 11 ; comp. v. 12 ; i. 12.
§ Peter i. 20.
‖ Εὐαγγέλιον, Peter i. 25 ; iv. 6, 17.

it is a matter of God's foreknowledge ;* and those whom grace
touches are called the elect.† God has called them,‡ and they
have listened to His voice of truth,§ while other men have
remained in disobedience. ‖ The sins of the elect are taken
away by Christ,¶ the spotless Lamb, whose blood also redeems
us,** that is to say, delivers us from the habits of sin which
are our natural heritage, and brings us to God.†† Thus we
are henceforth sanctified by the Spirit of God,‡‡ which rests
upon us, having already wrought with us in our conversion.
The elect are called to be holy,§§ as God Himself is holy, and
because He is holy ; they are called a holy people, a royal and
sacred priesthood,‖‖ called to offer spiritual sacrifices acceptable to God. Their life is a progress in goodness, which may
be compared to the growth of a child fed with pure milk.¶¶
This inward health,*** this purity of heart, free from all worldly
pride, forms in the sight of God, who sees all, the most precious ornament of man.††† It is the source of that sincere
and active charity which regards as brethren ‡‡‡ all whom
gratitude binds to Christ. Men animated with this spirit
will seek to render to one another mutual services, each according to the opportunity and ability §§§ God has bestowed
on him, and of which he will hold himself to be a steward‖‖‖
for the benefit of the community. That community is

* Πρόγνωσις, Peter i. 2.
† Ἐκλεκτοί, Peter i. 1; ii. 9.
‡ Ὁ καλέσας, Peter i. 15; ii. 9; v. 10.
§ Ὑπακοή, Peter i. 2, 14, 22.
‖ Ἀπείθεια, Peter ii. 7; iii. 1, 20; iv. 17.
¶ Peter ii. 24; i. 19; ii. 22.
** Λυτροῦν, Peter i. 18.
†† Προσάγει, Peter iii. 18.
‡‡ Ἁγιασμὸς πνεύματος, Peter i. 2; iv. 14; i. 22.
§§ Ἅγιοι, Peter i. 15, and foll.
‖‖ Peter ii. 5, 9.
¶¶ Αὐξάνεσθαι, Peter ii. 2.
*** Τὸ ἄφθαρτον, Peter iii. 4; comp. i. 22.
††† Peter iii. 4.
‡‡‡ Ἡ ἀδελφότης, Peter ii. 17; v. 9; comp. i. 8. 22; iv. 8.
§§§ Χαρίσματα, Peter iv. 10.
‖‖‖ Οἰκονόμος.

called the household of God,* and this figure is dwelt upon in accordance with the allegory already familiar to us. According to another image, the faithful form a flock; their spiritual heads and overseers are shepherds; over all is Christ, the chief shepherd, the supreme guardian of the souls of His people.† The Gospel proclaims a happy existence, but in reality we are still far from enjoying it. All that is promised is ours as yet only in hope;‡ grace itself will only be perfected in the future.§ Until then, painful trials await us;‖ by these we are brought into fellowship with Christ,¶ who also suffered for us and with us, to be afterwards exalted to the right hand of God, and to reign over all principalities and powers.** Happy are we if we suffer not for our faults or crimes, but only as belonging to Christ, as Christians,†† and if we can endure temptation.‡‡ This time of trial is, moreover, of short duration; the end is at hand.§§ The Lord will come again in His glory,‖‖ and His coming will usher in our final salvation,¶¶ that state of glory and felicity*** which is to be our portion, and which is, like the victor's crown after the contest, the final recompense of our faith in God.†††

This brief summary will suffice to bring out the numerous relations between the theology of this epistle and that of Paul. It would have been easy to multiply the points of contact, by comprehending a series of other terms common to both, but

* Οἶκος θεοῦ, Peter iv. 17; comp. ii. 5, and foll.

† Ἀρχιποιμήν, ἐπίσκοπος ψυχῶν, Peter ii. 25; v. 4.

‡ Ἐλπίς, Peter i. 3, 21; iii. 15.

§ Peter i. 7.

‖ Πειρασμοί, λύπαι, παθήματα, Peter i. 6; ii. 19, and foll; iii. 14; iv. 12; v. 9, etc.

¶ Κοινωνεῖν, Peter iv. 13.

** Peter i. 11; iv. 1; v. 1; iii. 22; comp. i. 21.

†† Χριστιανοί, Peter iv. 16.

‡‡ Δοκίμιον, Peter i. 7.

§§ Peter iv. 7; v. 10.

‖‖ Ἀποκάλυψις, Peter i. 7, 13; iv. 13; v. 1.

¶¶ Σωτηρία, Peter i. 5.

*** Δόξα, Peter i. 7; v. 1.

††† Peter i. 9; v. 4.

of less importance.* The two systems, however, or to speak more correctly the two trains of thought—for Peter attempts nothing systematic—are far from being identical. That which we are at present considering, lacks the most essential and fundamental element, justification by faith, and consequently all that mysticism which is the vital principle of the theology of Paul. In fact, with Peter, the object of faith is identical with that in the Epistle to the Hebrews, namely, things to come; it is trust in the promises of God, a trust which shall be rewarded by the fulfilment of its hope if it remains steadfast and immovable.† It is thus fixed upon God, and is almost a synonym for hope. Even when Christ is its object, it does not refer to the mystic union of the believer with Him, but to the hope of one day seeing Him manifested in His glory, and of being made partakers of the same.‡ The word righteousness has in a still less degree th esense attached to it by Paul. It is simply righteousness in the Hebrew meaning of the word, —virtue, good deeds.§ The righteous man is the man who does not do evil.‖ Grace is left entirely out of the question. This fact, which is very notable in itself, is still more so as confirmed by other remarks which the epistle may suggest, and which will introduce us to a mode of presenting the truth very nearly approaching that of James. Judgment is to be passed according to every man's works.¶ Works are therefore insisted on with peculiar emphasis, and there is no word of more frequent occurrence in the epistle than *well-doing.*** Good works are the immediate end of the calling,†† and are to gain the favour of God. Similar phrases are, we know, to be found in Paul's writings, but they are there uniformly held in

---

* Χαρις καὶ εἰρήνη, Peter i. 2 ; θεὸς καὶ πατὴρ Ἰησοῦ Χριστοῦ, i. 3 ; κληρονομία, etc., Peter i. 4 ; iii. 9 ; τηρεῖσθαι, ibid. ; κομίζεσθαι, Peter i. 9, etc.

† Πίστις, Peter i. 5, 7, 9, 21 ; v. 9.

‡ Peter i. 8.

§ Δικαιοσύνη, Peter ii. 24 ; iii. 14.

‖ Peter iii. 12 ; iv. 18.

¶ Peter i. 17.

** Ἀγαθοποιεῖν, Peter ii. 14, 15, 20 ; iii. 6, 11, 13, 16, 17 ; iv. 19.

†† Peter ii. 20, and foll. ; iii. 9.

subordination to regeneration by faith; here, on the contrary, there is nothing wanting but the express declaration of justification by works; the thing itself is here.*

It is true that regeneration† is also here spoken of, and is ascribed as a fact, to the operation of God. Christians are compared to new-born babes,‡ and their life is divided into two distinct periods, before and after conversion, the former of which is likened to a kind of death.§ Here, again, the words remind us of Paul, but the spirit is not Paul's. Regeneration is not the result of a direct and inward contact of the Spirit of God with the spirit of man, and does not consist in an identification of our personality with that of Christ; it is the word, the Gospel, outward teaching,‖ in short, which, works this change, and we are not taught why the new law is more effectual than the old; it is the example¶ of Jesus which is to incite us to virtue; virtue is therefore the result of our own reflection; having beheld Christ's sufferings for us, we are to arm ourselves with an earnest resolve,** that the whole remainder of our lives may be consecrated to God. This

* Throughout this contrast between St. Paul and St. Peter, Reuss is unduly controlled by the mere form in which St. Peter expresses his thought, and fails to apprehend its underlying substance. That the doctrine of justification by faith was developed by St. Paul as it was developed by no other apostle is obvious; but all St. Peter's representations of the work of Christ contradict what Reuss has said in this paragraph about good works gaining God's grace, and about the doctrine of justification by works; see especially ii. 24, iii. 18. Such a conception of the work of Christ underlies the very conception of faith on which St. Paul insists. It is true, no doubt, that St. Peter insists much more on the faith which, according to St. Paul, is one of the fruits of the Spirit, than on the faith which is the condition of pardon and regeneration; but this is accounted for by the object of St. Peter's epistle. Nor should it be forgotten that St. Paul dwells with far greater emphasis than St. Peter upon "judgment by works."—ED.

† 'Αναγεννήν, Peter i. 3, 23.
‡ Peter ii. 2.
§ Παθὼν ἐν σαρκί, Peter iv. 1, and foll.
‖ Peter i. 23; comp. James i. 18.
¶ 'Υπογραμμός, Peter ii. 21.
** Peter iv. 1.

morality obviously has as its basis Judæo-Christian rationalism, and not Pauline mysticism. The end is the same; holiness and righteousness are in both cases the objects aimed at; but the two theories differ widely as to the path to be pursued.

The Pauline idea of faith being thus absent from the writings of Peter, the doctrine of redemption is also of necessity differently expressed. First, the thesis that Christ died for* sinners cannot be explained by the idea of mystical substitution, especially since, as we have just seen, regeneration, which ought to be its inseparable complement, is established on an entirely different basis. The atoning death of Christ† appears as a finished act, wrought, it is true, in our behalf and for our salvation, but in which our own nature has no part, —that is to say, it is not essentially changed by it; we are not told that we also have something to do in it, nor how we may appropriate its benefits. Christ has borne our sins on the cross; by His wounds we are healed;‡ but this fact is connected with our own moral life only by an external bond, which is more akin to a generous invitation, a pious desire, than to a natural necessity in the very nature of things.§ It would be perhaps more exact to say‖ that obedience to the preaching of the Gospel takes place first, and that the sprinkling with the blood of Christ,¶ that is, the remission of sins, is the recompense of a happy resolve.**

If all these remarks prove that the theology of the Epistle of Peter does not simply reproduce that of Paul, but looks at many essential matters from an entirely different point of view, this first result of our investigation will be amply corroborated by a fact of quite another kind. This is the absolute silence of the author on the subject of the law. The name *law* is not

---

* 'Υπὲρ, Peter ii. 21; iii. 8; iv. 1.
† Πάθημα, αἷμα, etc., *loc. cit.*
‡ Peter ii. 24.
§ But see Peter ii. 24, and iv. 1.—Ed.
‖ Peter i. 2.
¶ 'Ραντισμός.
** St. Paul describes faith as being obedience to the Gospel. 2 Thess. 18; Rom. i. 5.; xv. 18; xvi. 26.—Ed.

even uttered. Nothing is said of its relation to the Gospel. As the writer has read the Epistle to the Romans and to the Ephesians; as, again, his own epistle is addressed to the Churches of Galatia, this silence cannot be accidental; it must be intentional. The writer had his reasons for being silent. We may be allowed to imagine that he desired to do his part towards allaying the polemical ardour and excitement of men's minds, in the Churches of Asia Minor; he would show that the Gospel, even the Gospel of Paul, of that apostle who was repudiated as the enemy of the law, makes for the soul such abundant provision, that the questions in dispute might well be left in the background. The intention was praiseworthy, but the mediation offered was based less upon doctrinal principles than upon practical considerations. For this very reason, it was in part successful, and accomplished some good in the Church, but it could never really satisfy theology. For theology could not accept a rendering of Paul's system, incomplete in many of its fundamental portions; still less could it sanction the occasional use of Pauline formulas, detached, so to speak, from their basis, and thus deprived of their true force and value. Such a use of them has, unhappily, been in all times too prevalent.

In showing that under modes of expression generally analogous or even identical with those of Paul, we may trace in Peter's writings a really Judæo-Christian line of thought, it has not been our intention to convey any blame, which indeed would be a deviation from our duty as impartial historians. We state facts, and pronounce upon them only so far as is necessary for purposes of comparison, never with a view to determine their positive value. This we shall show further by finally examining some ideas peculiar to this writer, and derived from the same scource, which seem to us worthy ornaments of his epistle.

In the inscription, the apostle calls the Christians to whom he writes the *strangers scattered abroad* throughout the provinces of Asia.* This designation first brings to mind the

* Παρεπίδημοι διασπορᾶς.

name commonly applied to the Jews settled beyond the land of Palestine; but as the writer numbers some who were once Gentiles among his readers,* it is more natural to understand him as alluding to those who are thus regarded as strangers or proselytes—that is, members of the Israelitish nation by religious faith, but not by birth and ascetic rites. We thus recognize, in the very inscription, the point of view taken by the authors of the compromise at Jerusalem, who would neither pronounce the abolition of the law, nor exclude the uncircumcised from their communion. The latter thus became children of Abraham and of Sarah,† having through conversion and sanctification a part in the promises made to the patriarchs, without fulfilling any legal conditions for their naturalization. Thus the Epistle of Peter reads from the beginning like a paraphrase of his sermon, of which we haʌe an epitome in the fifteenth chapter of the Acts.

Believers are called the property, the heritage of God.‡ This is an expression repeatedly used in the Old Testament in speaking of Israel; and shows that, while leaving the law untouched, the apostle had no repugnance to incorporating believers of foreign nations with the people of God.

The tribulations of the present life are the beginning of the last judgment,§ a precursive sign of the approaching end of time. The more severe the trial, the more will it inspire the mind with a wholesome awe, since the end of the wicked will be yet far more terrible.

The Gospel is a principle and a promise of emancipation and liberty. Hence it is so impatiently awaited by the people of Israel. Political liberty was their very legitimate desire, and this Messiah was to give. But the Christian remembers, first of all, that he is ever the subject of God, and that God has appointed kings and magistrates. To fear God and to honour the emperor are in his eyes inseparable duties. This maxim, which suggests a new and happy application of a well-known axiom of Paul's,‖

* Peter ii. 10 ; iv. 3.
† Peter iii. 6.
‡ Κλῆροι, Peter v. 3.
§ Peter iv. 17.
‖ Ἐλευθερία, Gal. v. 13.

shows to what an extent the religious principle of the Gospel had already neutralized and corrected the political element in the old creeds.

Baptism* is not simply an ablution designed to remove outward impurities, but the appeal to God of a good conscience based upon the resurrection of Christ. That is to say, a man, in receiving baptism, forms the firm and sincere resolve to live according to the commandments of God,† and expresses the hope that God will be pleased, for the sake of this resolve, to grant him the pardon of his sins. His conscience is called good, in view of the sincerity of his intention, and his hope is not chimerical, because the resurrection of Jesus Christ proves that He had the right and the commission to offer to sinners the pardon of His Father. This is the most natural meaning of this passage, which is so variously explained ; it is in perfect agreement with what we have elsewhere found stated as the principle of conversion, and thus justifies in the most emphatic manner that which we have said of the absence of the mystical element in the theology of Peter.

We have reserved to the last the most celebrated passage in this epistle,‡ a passage which the exegesis of every age has enveloped in an impenetrable cloud of obscurity, and the real import of which ecclesiastical theology has never discerned. Setting aside all the scholastic interpretations,§ we simply

---

* Βάπτισμα, Peter iii. 21. It is evident from this passage also that baptism was by immersion ; for it is typified by the waters of the flood, fallen from heaven, and *through* which—not *by* which—Noah was saved.

† Comp. Peter iv. 1.

‡ Peter iii. 18, and foll. ; iv. 6.

§ We shall pause only over two difficulties of detail. It is not certain if the author means to say that the physical death of Christ did not interrupt the life of the spirit, or if the ζωοποιηθεὶς πνεύματι is to be understood in a general manner of the life after the resurrection. The first version is the more commonly accepted ; according to it, the descent into hell took place before the resurrection. Be this as it may, we can with difficulty per-suade ourselves that the apostles had carried dialectic subtlety so far as to distinguish various phases of existence (we mean, of course, in the physical point of view) in the posthumous life of Jesus. Peter, in the first part of the sentence, simply affirms that Christ died as to His human and earthly

show that Peter here expresses the idea that Jesus, after His death, still carried on a saving work among men, who having died in unbelief and wickedness before His coming to earth, were kept in the prison of Sheol. The thesis that God will judge the quick and the dead, has here a different meaning from that conveyed by Paul. The Gospel has been preached to those who were already dead as to the living of to-day; and the text making use, for this statement, of the familiar term, and saying nothing as to the effect of this preaching, we are perhaps authorized in supposing that this effect may not have been the same in all cases, as we know that it is not on earth. This point, however, is not raised. The apostle only insists upon the fact that the dead of all times have had the opportunity of knowing Christ no less than their successors, his contemporaries, in order that, after having undergone as men corporeal death, which is a punishment for our whole race, they might arrive at spiritual life, according to the decrees of God, which equally embrace the whole race. Thus Peter, who represents in such gloomy colours the future of the unbelieving, proclaims in substance this consoling idea, that there is no final condemnation, except where the Gospel has been knowingly rejected; and the descent into hell of which he speaks was neither a visit made to the pious patriarchs who were awaiting their deliverance, nor a spectacle for devils who were to tremble before their lord, nor

nature, without touching at all on the philosophical problem, which inquires what became of the spirit when separated from the body, which naturally went down into the grave ; in the latter part of the sentence, he simply affirms that Christ lived and lives, as to the spiritual and heavenly nature ; and he does not concern himself at all with the theological problem which inquires what became of the spirit of Christ before it was manifested to His disciples clothed in the immortal body. The second difficulty is that Peter seems to restrict the preaching to the contemporaries of Noah. This difficulty is insoluble, unless we are prepared to say that the author, in commencing the phrase in verse 20, was so preoccupied with the typological comparison he meant to institute between the flood and baptism, that he thus forgot to insert some word which would have shown that the antecedent phrase had a universal application to the unbelievers of former days, and that the victims of the deluge were introduced only as a particular example.

a further anguish endured in the stead of redeemed sinners, (interpretations which all do equal violence to the text in various arbitrary ways); but was, for the living, a new manifestation of the unfathomable grace of God; and to the dead, one crowning opportunity of casting themselves into the arms of His mercy. To Christian theologians, finally, who are so ingenious in wresting the letter and so dull in discerning the spirit, it might have become the fruitful germ of a sublime conception if, instead of narrowing more and more the circle of life and light by their anathemas and rigid formulas, they had profited by the hint here given by the apostle, that that circle of light is illimitable, and that the life-giving rays which spring from its centre can reach to the most distant spheres of the world of spirits.

CHAPTER III.

THE EPISTLE OF BARNABAS.

WE do not propose to enter here on the discussion of the arguments for or against the authenticity of the epistle which Clement of Alexandria and many other of the Fathers ascribe to Barnabas, the friend and colleague of Paul. We have refrained altogether from questions of this sort in relation to the other writings which we have analyzed, although critical science has not yet pronounced its final judgment on several of them. There would be the less occasion to change our method with regard to the document now before us, because there does not attach to it the same ecclesiastical interest as to the others. It is further anonymous, and does not contain the slightest indication which could authorize us in making a conjecture as to its writer. The testimony of several Fathers is never, in itself, a decisive argument. We know only too well how often they have been mistaken on far more important historical points. It is enough, for the moment, to show that even those among modern scholars who have not been able to recognize Barnabas as the author of the epistle attributed to him, have no hesitation in regarding it as a monument of the theology of the primitive age of the Church, and in assigning to it a date certainly not later than the early years of the second century. We shall have elsewhere occasion to confirm this chronological supposition, and perhaps even to modify it, so as to support a still further presumption of antiquity, by arguments which have partially escaped those who have preceded us. For the present, we confine ourselves to saying that, in our opinion, there are reasons more than sufficient for supposing that this epistle is far from being the most modern writing among those which form the subject of the present work. We have therefore no right to pass it over in silence, and it only remains for us to justify, by the analysis of its contents, the place we here assign to it.

That place it may claim, in our opinion, on the ground of the two most prominent characteristics which every attentive reader will at once discover in it, and which are of a nature to confound criticism by their apparent contradiction. On the one hand, we discern what might be called very decided anti-Judaism ; on the other, Paulinism reduced to the most attenuated proportions. We are so accustomed, generally, to identify the two tendencies of Paulinism and anti-Judaism, that it is difficult for us at once to enter into the spirit of a book which seems completely to belie this relation; and it is very possible that by too much stress being laid on one or other of these constituent elements, the author has come to be classed alternately with each opposing school.

But we have already seen, in the Epistle to the Hebrews, how the evangelical theory of Paul may lose much of its vigour, and especially of its mystical character. We shall soon note the same phenomenon, in growing proportions, in several other writings supposed to issue from the same school. If we find, in this respect, still greater weakness in the reputed Epistle of Barnabas, or, to speak more truly, an entire want of power to grasp the fundamental idea of Paul, with all its consequences and in all its dialectic force, we shall not be therefore justified in denying all relation of origin or tendency between the two systems. We would the less venture to pronounce a positive judgment to that effect, because the scattered fragments of the theology of Paul which are found in this epistle, and the few formulas borrowed from it, are not formed into any system, do not convey any creative or independent thought, and cannot therefore serve to establish a comparison, which would require as its basis and premise equal originality on both sides.

As to the second characteristic to which we have alluded, the anti-Judaic tendency, it is undoubtedly far more strongly marked here than in the writings of Paul, and based apparently upon a different principle, a principle which compromises even the relative authority of the Old Testament, so studiously guarded by the apostle of the Gentiles; but this will certainly not lead us to seek the starting-point of the theology of Barnabas in a less advanced stage than that of Paul, namely, in Judæo-Christianity. If it were really necessary to assign to it a separate origin, we should seek it rather beyond that of Paul, nearer to the sphere of Gnostic Antinomianism. But, on closer examination, the expressions of Paul and Barnabas are not separated by a wide gulf. In practical application they lead to the same result, the spiritualization of the law, and by the same method, that of typology. In this respect, the Epistle of Barnabas is a continuation of those of Paul, and especially of that to the Hebrews, both by the variety of examples which it gives, and by the degree of art with which it chooses and explains them. But the more it multiplies the number, the more it impoverishes the spirit of its types; such, however, is the history of typology in all ages. Its principle is beautiful and true so long as it adheres to the general facts of the providential direction of mankind. The laws which govern the spiritual world being as immutable as those which control the physical, and acting always under the high sanction of their Author, their various manifestations in the course of time must offer numerous analogies, and positive revelations especially cannot fail to present such. We may study them, examine them; we may even arrive thus at more or less spiritual resemblances, according to the measure of discretion used, and the intelligence brought to bear on the subject; but so soon as curiosity begins to take the lead, and the comparisons are carried into details and accessory facts, the danger arises of falling into puerilities and violations of good taste.

We have been led to make these remarks in order to justify the place which we assign to the Epistle of Barnabas in the great theological movement of the primitive age. But we must not forget that we are here speaking of a book which many of our readers may never have seen, and that we must therefore treat it in a different manner from the writings of the New Testament. We may say then, in a few words, that the Epistle of Barnabas is a discourse which has still less of the real epistolary character even than the Epistle to the Hebrews, and that it is of about the same length. It has come down to us in two texts—the Greek and the Latin; and the number of copies is very small. It is divided into two parts: chapters i.—xvii. doctrinal, and chapters xviii.—xxi. moral. The first part, which will especially claim our attention, proclaims the decadence of the law, and is evidently designed to liberate the Gospel and believers from any close connection with the old covenant, and the duties imposed by it. The author demonstrates his thesis in three separate ways, which we shall consider one by one, in order the more readily to discover in what it is he differs from preceding writers.

The Gospel covenant, the new dispensation for the salvation of man, brought in or fulfilled by Christ, and based upon His atoning death, was directly foretold by the prophets of the Old Testament. Among the texts which the author quotes in support of his thesis, there are some which the apostles employed for the same purpose; but there are a greater number which he seems to have been the first to discover. Generally in such cases, his quotations depend for their effect upon the more or less forced allegorical interpretation which he gives to them. In the first category, we place, for example, the prophetic passages in which Jehovah declares that He has no pleasure in the sacrifices and offerings, the fasts and feasts of the people, but seeks rather purity of heart and the moral consecration of individuals (chapters ii., iii.) In the same category we shall simply cite the explanation given (chapter vi.) of the promise made to the Israelites, that they should enter into a good land, flowing with milk and honey. As Adam was made out of the earth, so the land in this passage signifies the incarnation of Christ; the milk and honey, as the common food of children of tender age, represent the new birth of the man. Thus the two fundamental facts, the theology and morality of the new economy, are found directly foretold in the old. The author blesses God, on this occasion, for the wisdom and understanding given him to comprehend the mysteries of prophecy; he exalts this secret and profound apprehension of the word of God (γνῶσις) which is the privilege of the true believer, and to which he desires to raise his readers. The numerous quotations borrowed from the Mosaic code to establish the principal circumstances of the passion of Christ,—and hence, implicitly, the historical basis of the new economy,—belong in part to the same category of proofs.

The second series of proofs brought forward by the writer in support of his main thesis, occupies a still larger place in this epistle; these are the typical analogies, by means of which he proposes to reduce the institutions of Moses to nothing more than prophetic figures. It is here especially we see how this description of exegetical studies is always characterized by the individuality of those who pursue them. While it is the special aim of the writer of the Epistle to the Hebrews to make all his types converge to a common centre, to group them around one parent idea, that of sacrifice, this author endeavours to convince his readers by an interminable series of disconnected images, collected at hazard, succeeding each other without order, and in the explanation of which we recognize deep convictions and sometimes surprising subtlety, but little taste and still less thought. Thus, of these two unknown writers, the first has had the good fortune to win at length the general assent of the Church, by the simplicity and elevation of his parallel; while the second, who allows himself to be carried along by the current of imagination, has found numberless imitators, who have even surpassed him, and yet have not left any distinct trace in Gospel science. It might be further said that the Epistle to the Hebrews seeks in the Old Testament, the types of the great idea of the New—the priesthood of Christ offering up Himself for the sins of men; the Epistle of Barnabas, on the contrary, simply recapitulates the principal distinctive rites of Mosaism, and endeavours to explain them, almost arbitrarily, by their supposed antitypes in the New. Thus he takes up successively, the goat sent away into the wilderness, the red heifer, circumcision, forbidden meats, the Sabbath, and the Temple (chapters vi.—xvi.), and the hidden meaning of these various institutions is found sometimes in the sphere of our Lord's history, sometimes in that of the most ordinary moral precepts. Objection has often been raised against the popular superstitions which the author adopts in relation to certain animals, and against some special observances which he seems to add to the Jewish worship, and which do not appear justified by the text or by tradition: it has been hastily concluded that a Levite, an apostle, could not have written such things. This conclusion, of which we do not dispute the logical fairness, is not that which most impresses us here. We would draw attention rather to another fact, equally palpable as it seems to us, namely, that the doctrine of the desuetude of the law and the principle of typological interpretation, were fixed axioms with the author before he wrote this treatise. He evidently writes to establish them according to the means at his command, and the measure of his knowledge and capacity. Now these axioms are, in our opinion, incompatible with what is called an idealizing Judæo-Christianity. Their basis lies beyond the sphere of Judæo-Christianity altogether. They are expressed, as we shall presently see, in too absolute and trenchant a manner to be identified with Paulinism. We do not intend in saying this, to prejudge the question whether the writer was an immediate disciple of Paul or not; we merely affirm that he is of the same school as Paul, and, as is often the case, exaggerates the theory of his master. In Paul's writings we have been able to trace the path which led him from his early to his later point of view. The writer of the Epistle to Barnabas gives us no such indication of his progressive career; at the time when he began to write his treatise he had long severed all connection with the past.

The third fact which claims our attention as marking the progressive decadence of the law, is far more characteristic than the two already noticed, and may well sustain the opinion just expressed. Hitherto we have seen our present writer treading, though with less of genius and success, in the track of Paul and of the unknown author of the Epistle to the Hebrews; we shall now find him striking out for himself a new and separate path. This will give us the opportunity of ascertaining what are his peculiar theological ideas. Commencing with what is most striking and at the same time most paradoxical in the writer's theory, we shall first note what he says as to the positive value of the law, independently of its relations with the Gospel. From the very beginning of his epistle, he repudiates altogether adherence to the letter of the law; he is not satisfied with characterizing as error the Judaizing tendency,—that is, the attachment of certain Christians to the Mosaic rites (chapter iv.); he does not simply call those who manifest such a tendency *proselytes* (chapter iii.) —or deserters, changing their standard and passing over to the camp of the alien; he goes further still. He declares unreservedly that the Mosaic law, as it is written, and taken literally, never had any authority or legal existence. Moses when he came down from the mountain (chapter xiv.), and so to speak before the promulgation of the code, broke the tables of stone,—that is to say, broke the covenant made with the Jews, who henceforth were no more the people of God. And in order that we may not suppose that this fact is here taken only in its typical sense, as a prophecy of the yet distant day of another revelation, he elsewhere tells us (chapter ix.) that the circumcision of the flesh is an inspiration of the devil. All the laws of Moses had immediately and directly a spiritual meaning according to the will of the Lord; (chapter x.); but the Jews, not comprehending this, adhered to the ˙ letter. We are here, then, carried far beyond the Pauline point of view. Paul acknowledged that the law had at least a temporary value; its rites had been legitimately observed up to the day when they were replaced by the new order of things inaugurated at the cross of Christ. Here this partial validity of the letter is denied altogether; for the Jews themselves, there might and should have been an allegorical interpretation and application of these various commandments; and, in truth, the prophets, inspired by Christ Himself, had given such an interpretation, but they had been unheeded. It is naturally difficult for us to familiarize ourselves with such principles as these, accustomed as we are to speak of the Old Testament according to the ideas and expressions of Paul. But texts so clear and positive cannot be explained away. We repeat it, in this epistle Paulinism is left behind; the historical point of view is abandoned in favour of the purely spiritualistic. But one step further will lead to the declaration not only of the decadence of the letter, but of the diabolical origin of the Old Testament itself. In this aspect, the Epistle of Barnabas forms a link between Paulinism and Gnosticism. We can now understand how it was that Alexandrine spiritualism was so edified with this epistle, and so delighted to exalt its apostolic spirit; but we can understand also why the Church, which has always lingered behind Paul in doctrine, and has borrowed largely from the Mosaic institutions, has not received it into its canon. We must not suppose that the name of Barnabas, which has for us also only a conventional value here, has had any influence on these various judgments.*

A circumstance of some interest, and which will serve at the

* Reuss has, I think, greatly exaggerated the anti-Judaic character of the Epistle of Barnabas. Nothing, as it seems to me, can be much farther from the truth than to say that "one step further will lead to the declaration not only of the decadence of the letter, but of the diabolical origin of the Old Testament itself." What Barnabas contends for is that the external rites and institutions of Judaism represented spiritual ideas and truths, and that through missing these, and dwelling only on the external and transient forms in which they were embodied, the Jews had drifted into a religious condition not much better than that of the heathen. Barnabas is hostile to Judaism very much in the same sense that Isaiah is hostile to it. The statement about the "diabolical origin" of the Old Testament appears to have been suggested by a phrase of which there is a various reading in the Cod. Sin., referring to circumcision. The phrase is certainly remarkable, whichever reading is adopted, but it is as obscure and difficult as it is startling. Barnabas, however, goes on to speak of Abraham as having enjoined and practised circumcision, and he finds in the number of persons that Abraham circumcised a mystical reference to our Lord Jesus Christ.—ED.

same time as a stepping-stone to other observations, lends confirmation to that which we here assert as to the place which
the Epistle of Barnabas occupies in the development of Christian
theology.   We refer to the fact that the author, apart from the
direct and typical prophecies to which we have alluded, and
which are illustrations rather than arguments, nowhere appeals
to theological evidence in support of his assertions.   Paul, in
whose time the principle of the abrogation of the law was new,
was compelled to corroborate it by a series of arguments derived
from the nature of man, from the character of the law, and from
the work of Christ and its effects.   Here this principle is, in
the mind of the writer at least, an accepted axiom, and he feels
no necessity to render a reason for it; the truth of his thesis
has become to him a matter of direct consciousness, and he has
no remembrance of the way by which it was reached.   In his
writing, therefore, we find no attempt at a convincing demonstration of its truth or justice.   If the writer was originally a
Judæo-Christian, and had reached his present position without
passing through the school of Paul, we fail to comprehend how
he could have crossed the gulf which in such a case must lie
between his past and his present position.   The exegetical
arguments he advances in support of his thesis may have appeared sufficient to any one already convinced; but they could
never by themselves have sufficed to bring a Jew to the same
point.   An exegetical and typical demonstration of the inva-
lidity of the law is conceivable in a disciple of Paul, but not
in a Judæo-Christian.

This leads us directly to say that it is utterly impossible to
derive from this epistle a system of evangelical theology; that
is to say, a series of propositions on the causes and conditions
of the salvation of men.   Everywhere we find scattered reminiscences of the Pauline theology, but they are incoherent, and
blended with popular phrases which negative their principle.
A few examples may suffice to establish the fact, from which
we hasten to draw its legitimate conclusions.   The incarnation,
it is said (chapter v.), took place because the Saviour purposed,
by the shedding of His blood, to sanctify men by the remission

of sins. By adding, in the same connection, that Christ took part in the creation of the world, and that it was He who inspired the prophets, the writer appears to reproduce the Christology and soteriology of his great predecessor. But immediately after it is said, that the Son of God became incarnate because men could not otherwise endure His presence; again, because He would fill up the measure of the sins of His enemies; finally, because He would prove that there is a resurrection. All this is unconnected: these are incoherent propositions, one of which even borders on docetism, and none of which has any place in the theory of Paul. It would be needless to add an enumeration of the passages in which it is said that Christians are the temple of God, that they are redeemed from darkness, that they are the heirs of the new covenant, and many others of the same sort. Scattered expressions like these do not constitute a theology. In vain do we search for the idea of faith, of calling, of justification, of grace, and their corollaries, without which the Gospel preached by Paul has no unity or coherence. Instead of seeking or establishing the basis of this Gospel in the soul of the believer, in the principle of his spiritual existence, this writer speaks only of the illumination of the mind to understand the Scriptures, and of the impulse given to the will to do works which may merit the recompense of heaven.

All this, we repeat, has led many historians of Christian doctrine to think that, in spite of the anti-Judaic tendency which they were obliged to recognize in this epistle, the theology of the writer was in reality a product of Judæo-Christianity. We could not endorse this opinion without sacrificing the very definition of Judæo-Christianity, according to which it consists in the tendency to ally Jewish asceticism with the Messianic hopes attached to the person of Jesus, and more or less spiritualized. The presence of Chiliast ideas, and the absence of the mystical, do not in themselves constitute Judæo-Christianity. We have already shown how, in our opinion, the anti-Judaism of this epistle is a sign of a more advanced development than that of Paul. We may now add that we assign to it a similar position in reference to positive evangelical doctrines.

The few expressions or ideas borrowed from Pauline soteriology, do not appear to us to proceed from a Judæo-Christian who had imperfectly understood them, and who could not yet rise to the true apprehension of the system to which they belonged. On the contrary, they strike us rather as the fragments of a theory which a follower of Paul had already left behind, not because he had found anything better elsewhere, but because his mind, not being able to grasp the Pauline mysticism, and yielding to the growing desire to impart some teaching which should be entirely popular, practical, and generally acceptable to all shades of opinion, began to fall back upon the old tracks. The Epistle of Barnabas, thus regarded, is found upon the highroad which the Church has followed in reducing Paulinism to a certain number of doctrines more or less abstract, and combined promiscuously with a morality which has its basis elsewhere.*

* The first pages of the original Greek of the so-called Epistle to Barnabas have only recently been discovered in the Sinaitic manuscript. This has shown that the Latin translation which we possessed is by no means faithful. There is, however, nothing in the new text to require a modification of the exposition here given.

CHAPTER IV.

THE EPISTLE OF CLEMENT.

In the preceding chapters we have had occasion to study writers in whose works the tendency to conciliation is more or less clearly manifested, but always with a marked intention and a distinct consciousness of the end in view. The standpoint of these writers, who probably all belonged to what we might still call the first generation of Christians, although they were not all immediate disciples of Jesus, was taken amid the controversies and agitations attendant upon the progressive extension of universalist ideas, and the widening separation of the Church from the Synagogue. Thus their writings bear traces of this movement, which could not fail to make its impress upon them, even when it did not directly dictate them. But gradually there arose a younger generation, which belongs to a period when the entire separation of the two communities was an accomplished fact, beyond the scope of discussion, and when the fusion of former parties had at the same time made marked progress. The tenacity of the Judæo-Christians had been modified, more perhaps by the moral effect of the destruction of the temple, than by the intrinsic power of Gospel principles. Paulinism, on the other hand, had lost much of its force and consistency, after the eloquent voice which first preached it had become silent, and disciples who perpetuated the technicalities rather than the spirit of their master, succeeded him in the oral and written diffusion of his doctrine.

Thus it was that in the later years of the first century, evangelical theology began to enter upon that phase of vague neutrality which prepared the way for the new phase of the scientific development of the Gospel, of which history shows the predominance from the middle of the following century. As the first indications of the latter fact may be noted before the actual close of the apostolic era, it is incumbent on us to say a word on the subject here. We shall turn our attention therefore, in the present chapter, to a literary document which, if we have rightly estimated it, represents this intermediate phase, and forms, by the very absence of any luminous and vivifying idea, the natural transition between the decline of the first and the dawn of the second era of Christian theology. This document is the letter written by Clement, bishop of the Church of Rome, to that of Corinth, and which, anciently inserted in the canon of several Churches, has been preserved to us, by a happy accident, in one sole copy, and as an integral part of one of the oldest Bibles that has come down to our day.*

This epistle, composed on the occasion of certain troubles which had agitated the Church of Corinth, but the nature of which is not clearly defined, is essentially hortatory in its character. It is designed to contribute by the wisdom of its counsels and by the power of its motives, to the re-establishment of a good understanding among the Christians of the capital of Achaia, and still more to strengthen the bonds of subordination which appear to have been relaxed through these internal dissensions. It is not then properly a theological treatise; but the writer, in the course of his exhortations, which are of considerable length, is frequently led to give expression to principles which make us thoroughly acquainted with his point of view. We note an involuntary and unconscious blending of ideas and expressions of various origin, which seem to fall naturally into juxtaposition. We must not form our opinion here on the first impression which a superficial reading might produce. There are a considerable number of Pauline phrases, sometimes directly copied from the epistles, and the apostle Paul is expressly commended to the Corinthians (chapter xlvii.) as the great

* The Epistle of Clement was discovered in 1628, appended to the Codex Alexandrinus.—ED.

authority to whom they are to bow. The first lines of Clement's epistle repeat word for word the formulas of salutation so familiar to us in the writings of Paul. Again (chapter ii.) mention is made of the universal outpouring of the Spirit; Christ is frequently spoken of as Mediator (chapter xx.), and His blood as shed for us (chapter xxi.); that blood is said to be precious in the sight of God Himself, and to provide for the whole world the grace of conversion (chapter vii.) By the will of God it is said we are called in Jesus Christ, and justified, not by ourselves, by our own wisdom, piety, or works, but by faith (chapter xxxii.) It would be easy to multiply these quotations; we shall presently have occasion to bring forward others, to compare them with the explanations given of them by the writer, and which are for our purpose of the greatest importance.

In reading the Epistle of Clement more attentively, one is struck with a curious fact. The writer, belonging as he does to the second century of the Church, and drawing largely from tradition, and even from apostolic literature (although he does not usually quote the names of the authors from whom he cites), nowhere has recourse explicitly to the Epistle to the Romans, which contains that which Paul himself called his Gospel, and which Clement in his capacity as bishop of Rome must have known better than any other, while he frequently and very directly copies passages from the Epistle to the Hebrews. Thus chapter xxxvi. is composed almost entirely of extracts from that epistle. This predilection must proceed from an affinity of sentiments, such as we soon find really exists, though it does not amount to absolute identity of view or method. In every instance, however, where we can trace a divergence between the Epistle to the Hebrews and the Epistle of Clement, the latter is that which differs the more widely from Paul, and in which the evangelical idea dwindles and pales. Mysticism disappears; imputation is no longer associated with regenerating faith; salvation is effected by the operation of external causes, influencing the will of the man; works again take a high if not the first rank;

God Himself and the angels (chapters xxxiii., xxxiv.,) set the pattern of good deeds; the fear of judgment is again the motive of human virtue (chapters xxi., xxviii., xxxiv.), as under the old law, which is reinstated in high honour, as though for the benefit of the hierarchy (chapter xl., and foll.), whom we here see, for the first time, taking advantage of the Mosaic institution to exalt themselves in the Church, and claiming prerogatives incompatible with the Pauline theory of the Gospel dispensation. It is needless to say that the argument against Judaism is nowhere resumed in this book; it is dead and buried.

But it is not by such generalities as these we would characterize the theology of Clement, which was unquestionably also the theology of his Church and of a large number of his contemporaries. It contains specialities too full of interest to be passed by without briefly calling to them the attention of our readers. As we are not attempting here either to construct a system or to define a method, we may take our examples just as they present themselves, and without any more regular order than that of the interest attaching to them.

We know that Paul, James, and the writer of the Epistle to the Hebrews, all alike appeal to the history of Abraham, in confirmation of their various theories of faith and works.[*] Clement quotes it also on several occasions (chapters x. and xxxi.) According to him, Abraham gained the title of the *friend of God*, and gave the decisive evidence of his faith, by his obedience to the command to leave his native land; he believed God, when God promised him a numerous seed, and this faith was imputed to him for righteousness. Isaac was given to him on account of his faith and hospitality, and it was in obedience that he offered him up to God upon the mountain. He was blessed for having practised righteousness and truth by faith, as Isaac was for having willingly surrendered himself as a victim, and as Jacob became the father of the twelve patriarchs as the reward of having served Laban. It is impossible not to recognize in these various phrases, reminiscences of the

---

[*] Rom. iv.; James ii. 21, and foll.; Heb. xi. 8, and foll.

three passages from the apostolic writings, just quoted in the note. The term *friend* is borrowed from James; *imputation* and *faith* are taken from Paul; and the historical facts are reproduced verbatim from the Epistle to the Hebrews. Nothing but the last statement is original, and that is certainly not of a kind to exalt our estimate of his theology, the uniform tendency of which is to co-ordinate, or marry, faith and works.

Here is an example, if possible, still more instructive. James had spoken of Rahab as saved on account of the service rendered to the spies of Joshua; the Epistle to the Hebrews had extolled the faith of the woman as manifested by the same act;* Clement devotes an entire chapter (xii.) to show that she was saved on the ground of her faith and hospitality. In conclusion, he brings forward the circumstance that she owed her salvation to a red thread suspended from her house, and which was to be the signal for her recognition by the Israelite leaders. This sign indicated at the same time that by the blood of the Lord there would be redemption for all those who hoped and believed in Him. You see, adds the author, that in this woman there was not only faith, but also the gift of prophecy. Without dwelling, however, on this typological comparison, which stands alone in this epistle, we would observe that the writer, while speaking of redemption by the blood of Christ, does not preserve a vestige of the idea attached to that term in the theology of Paul. Redemption is promised to those who believe and hope in God; here then faith and hope become synonyms, as we have already noted elsewhere. Then faith is fixed upon God, and not on Christ; there is no mention of a direct and close relation between Christ and the believer; lastly, redemption is a fact accomplished outside the man who is to be benefited by it, and it becomes his in consequence of another act having no connection with the first. This fundamental point of the Gospel has then become, in the course of a few decades, a hackneyed formula, an article of a catechism which may be learned by heart without any true understanding of it, or any personal consciousness of its high import.

* James ii. 25; Heb. xi. 31.

19 *

Let it not be supposed that we are basing so severe a judgment on an isolated passage. There is a whole series of such passages all leading to the same result. Thus even while exalting the virtue of the blood of Christ (chapter vii.), Clement puts it upon the same level with all the other means of conversion spoken of in the Old Testament. For it must be understood, the sacrifice of Christ is effectual to salvation because and in so far as it leads to repentance; but the author himself is careful to remind us that the prophets also, before Christ, sought the same end by their preachings, and succeeded in securing the most happy and salutary results. It is then our repentance which is the direct cause of our salvation. Faith in Christ, it is elsewhere said (chapter xxii.), confirms the many moral precepts we have received. How does it then confirm them? Is it because faith is the character, the life of the regenerate man? Such is not the writer's meaning. His idea is still of an external teaching, of a letter, a law. It is Christ who inspired the prophets; it is Christ then who speaks to us in the Old Testament; he who believes in Christ—that is to say, he who allows himself to be taught by Christ (chapter xxi.)—is then bound to observe the commandments of Scripture. It is clear that the work of Christ, in its most direct application to the individual, consists in a teaching very nearly resembling that which was given before Christ came in the flesh. If it is said in a passage already cited (xxxii.) that justification is by faith, the numerous examples cited, both after and before the theoretic statement, and derived from the history of the people of God, point us, on the one hand, to works, on the other to a faith which is simply trust in God, as it is also defined in the Epistle to the Hebrews, from which these examples are in part taken. Future blessings, it is added, will be obtained by faith in God (xxxv.), but this faith is immediately explained by the practice of virtue and the avoidance of vice. The gate of the Lord, the entrance into life (lxvii.), is the gate of righteousness: he who has sinned must cast himself weeping at the feet of God, who will then be reconciled to him. It is as we walk in this way (xxxvi.)

that we shall find Christ, the high-priest to present our sacrifices, the Advocate in our infirmity. Christ will thus be the *patron* of those who are already in the good way, and His priestly functions will be exercised with God in behalf of those who claim His intercession (lviii.) The resurrection of men is not connected with that of Christ; it is proved by the analogy of different natural phenomena (xxiv.), and by passages from the Old Testament (xxvi.), and most of all by the history of the phœnix bird (xxv.), which is regarded as the most striking illustration of it. It is upon these arguments faith is based; faith which is therefore here simply hope, the trustful expectation of something to come.

After reading and considering all these passages, the question must necessarily arise, Why did the Son of God become man? The writer has no reply to make to this question. Christ became incarnate, we are told, in love (xlix.), but no connection is shown between this act of His and the lot of the individual. In the Epistle to the Hebrews we had at least the idea still of a priestly purification; here this is wanting; there remains only the vague assertion that Christ died for men, and side by side with it a moral theory which annexes salvation to repentance and virtue. God forbid that we should cast the slightest blame on the practical and earnest tendency of this epistle; as moral teaching it may be excellent. We wish simply to show that there is no way of constructing a specifically evangelical theology out of the few fragments of Pauline phraseology found in it, and which really impede rather than aid our understanding of its real purport.

This will be abundantly evident if we compare the various passages which set forth the Christology of this epistle. On the one hand, we have the theory of the Divine Word, without the name (xxxvi., comp. xvi.), expressed in terms copied verbatim from the Epistle to the Hebrews, and carried, it has been thought, to the length of patripassianism * (ii.) On the

* We will not take up this reproach. It is true that the syntax forces us to construe, *the sufferings of God*, but in the Greek there is αὐτοῦ, and the author might have forgotten that this word had reference to God,

other hand, the theory of the subordination of the Son is most
emphatically expressed; Christ is placed in the same relation
to God as the disciples occupy to Christ (xlii.) Precisely the
same order, the same will of God, directs all. The divine
nature appears somewhat compromised by such a phrase as
this; Jacob had the signal honour of being the father of the
Levites, of Jesus, and of the kings of Israel (xxxii.) It is true
that to the name of Jesus is added the qualification *according
to the flesh*, but His intermediate place between the Levites and
the kings is not the less singular. Lastly, God is called (lviii.)
the Ruler of spirits, and the Lord of all flesh, who has chosen
Jesus Christ, and us by Him. There is here a parallelism which
can scarcely be misunderstood. As Lord of all flesh, God might
grant His grace to whom He would. He has chosen us. Ruler
in the same way of spirits—that is, of superhuman existences—
He was free to choose among these His interpreter and Mediator
with men, and He has chosen Jesus. The latter, then, holds
His privileged position, not by virtue of His unique nature, but
by the choice of God. We do not here mention these various
theses with any idea of combining them into a system; we
believe, on the contrary, that this is impossible, and that this
epistle proves, as we have already said, that at the end of the
century, and in circles where it might have been least expected,
dogmatic theology had vastly retrograded. Its eclectic tendency
had enfeebled the great principles and broken the unity of the
system, and the progressive reaction from the impetuous ardour
of primitive days, had substituted for direct feeling, and instinctive piety, a moral teaching very necessary and in itself
very laudable, but which leant for support upon the Gospel
of redemption, rather from the force of habit than from any
theological necessity.*

named a few lines above, and not to Christ, of whom he was at this
moment thinking.

    * The immense inferiority of the Epistle of Clement to the writings of
St. Paul and the rest of the apostles is very striking and significant.
There is a thinness and poverty in the thought and an absence of intensity
and depth in the emotion which remind us on every page that we have
passed out of the creative age of the Church. But Reuss seems to me

indiscriminating in his criticism. The true account of the alleged inco-
herence of the epistle seems to be that the fulness of apostolic intuition
had ceased, and that the scientific organization of the contents of the
Christian revelation had not begun. The vital force of the apostolic
convictions gave to apostolic thought a certain organic and consistent
form, even in the absence of what we are accustomed to call scientific
theology. Clement had not the same living apprehension of the great
principles and facts of the Christian faith, and, as yet, scientific thought
had hardly any place in the Church. But a dispassionate examination
of the epistle will, I think, lead to the conclusion that Reuss is unjust in
alleging that to Clement the fundamental fact of the Gospel had become
a mere "hackneyed formula,"—this is, not true in relation to the great
fact of Redemption, nor can it be fairly maintained in relation to other
great truths on which the apostles insisted.—ED.

CHAPTER V.

THE ACTS OF THE APOSTLES.

HAVING concluded the analysis of the more directly didactic
writings which, by the basis or the scope of their teaching,
claimed a place in this particular part of our work, we propose
now to devote some pages to the study of the historical books
of the New Testament. It is needless to say that our attention
will not be directed mainly to the facts which they record; the
theological ideas presented will chiefly concern us, in so far as
the authors, in the compilation of their narratives, have either
been led casually to give expression to them, or have found it
necessary to bring them into prominence. In this respect, they
are not all equally rich in elements which will be of use to us
in our history, but from all we can derive some contribution to
its completeness.

Of all the literary monuments of the primitive age of Christianity, none bears more evident traces of the conciliatory tendency to which we have referred, than the book commonly called
the Acts of the Apostles. Although the history of apostolic
literature should never separate this book from the third gospel,
which is by the same author, and with which it has more than
one close relation, we may here consider it separately, because
the subject treated in it is of a nature to bring specially before
us the theological standpoint of the historian, while in his
earlier work he was entirely dependent upon a tradition which
it was of the first importance to transmit faithfully. Here, on
the contrary, he is himself the witness of the events, or in any
case of their immediate effects; he is in part an actor in the
scenes which he describes. He therefore pronounces judgment

upon them as he proceeds, and it is with these judgments we have to deal, for they constitute the spirit and the theology of the work.

It has been always remarked that this book, regarded simply as a history, leaves much to be desired, and does not justify the title which posterity, not the writer himself, has attached to it. If we compare it with the other authentic sources of apostolic history, especially with the epistles of Paul, we find in it very considerable omissions; and a number of facts which were well established in the time of the second generation, and which in their origin belong to the first, are passed over in silence. The early Church, both in sanctioning traditions which are sometimes doubtful, and in accepting some even apocryphal narratives, has implicitly avowed that its first historian did not satisfy it in this respect. It appears to have particularly regretted his silence in regard to the greater number of the early disciples, whose names, commended, so to speak, to the Church, by the choice of the Saviour, are allowed to fall into profound obscurity.

But instead of making this a subject of reproach against the writer of the book of the Acts, we will inquire first if his object in writing it was really to edit a volume of historical memoirs, and to preserve the traditions of the primitive age from the speedy oblivion in which they were only too likely to be involved in an age of such violent agitations. An attentive study of his narrative will show us that the object he had in view was really something different, and that he chose this history as the best method of attaining it. His intention is precisely the same as that which is readily recognized in the writings of the four evangelists, namely, not to satisfy a doubtless legitimate curiosity, but to produce or confirm religious convictions; and both he and they might, therefore, without at all impairing the value of their recitals, confine themselves to certain selected facts, among the great number of those placed at their disposal by the traditions of the Church.

However little may be known by us of the state of men's minds, and of parties in the Church, in the last quarter of the

century, an attentive reading of the account given by Luke
will show a very marked parallelism between the series of facts
which form the substance of his narrative, and those which
were occupying the thoughts of his contemporaries at the time
he wrote. What is it, in fact, of which he chiefly speaks?
Around what fact, what main idea, does his narrative revolve?
What are the proper names which, in his view, eclipse all
others? There can be no hesitation about the answer. The
names of Peter and Paul are those around which rally the two
parties, both contending over an issue which they often fail
fully to comprehend. The other historical personages are either
completely lost sight of, like the Twelve, who are only mentioned incidentally, or are subordinate to the two principal
heroes, as is the case with Stephen and James. If the writer
claimed to be a historian simply, such a predilection could
be the result only of ignorance or partiality. But the former
supposition is inconceivable in the case of Luke, and we have
no ground for holding him guilty of the latter fault. The
events recorded and the questions discussed will suggest the
same reflections. It is always the principle of universalism,
supported on the one hand, and repudiated on the other, which
occupies the foremost place. It is the admissibility or non-
admissibility of Gentiles into the Church; it is the doctrine of
the calling of strangers, or men uncircumcized, to the orthodox
synagogue, which overrides all other questions, and finally
absorbs them wholly. Undoubtedly, this was a main point, as
we well know; but not only did it not, from a doctrinal point of
view, embrace the whole preaching of the apostles, but neither
did it, historically regarded, comprise in itself alone the life of
the Church. Once more, if Luke had designed to be the
historian of the Church's life, in the modern acceptation of that
term, his book would be strangely incomplete. But we hold
it to be, on the contrary, very complete, and most carefully
arranged with a view to the special purpose we have supposed.
It collects all the facts necessary to be adduced, and shows
both the harmony of the Church's leaders on the question
which was dividing the Christian world, and the errors of

those who in their impetuous partizanship made use of the two great apostles' names, to justify the deplorable schism they sought to create. While preserving all the calmness proper to history, the book of the Acts is then, really, a theological work, didactic in it essence, apologetic and polemical in its form. He sets forth facts, but for the purpose of bringing into prominence the theories which had given rise to them, and which were apt to be forgotten or repudiated.*

Let us not be misunderstood in the use of the expressions. If we here employ the word *theory*, we do not mean by it a summary of ideas or formulas,—a system, in short, which should claim to present the entire Gospel. The theory here intended by us is simply the resolution taken at Jerusalem at the time of the conferences, a resolution of an essentially practical nature, and designed to meet the early developed wants of the Church. It may be boldly affirmed that the history of these conferences forms the centre of the entire work, and that the compromise there adopted gives the summary of its spirit. All the earlier facts lead up to it and tend to it by their natural development ; all the subsequent facts revert to it as to a standard by which its application may be understood and tested. The attentive reader will not allow himself to be diverted from this central point by accessory details, which the narrative could not suppress without being untrue to itself. Through all the various scenes which it describes, and the dramatic truthfulness of which captivates him more and more, he will discover always the guiding thread of the writer's inner thought.

We now purpose to support these assertions by an analysis of the book itself. Our task, in order to this end, will be to search out the didactic elements contained in it, holding as we do that the writer is not simply recording statements of doctrine from the lips of the recognized heads of the Church, to which he himself could not subscribe. Before entering on

* The simplest and most accurate account of St. Luke's object is that he wrote the Acts of the Apostles to show how the Gospel which was first preached to the Jews came to be spread among the Gentiles.—ED.

this investigation, however, we shall call the attention of
our readers briefly to the material facts, which represent what
may be called the body of the history, of which we desire
to ascertain the spirit. We shall at once see that the inner
is manifested in this outer life. We have said that all the
facts group themselves around the persons of Peter and Paul,
who thus stand prominently before the reader, and, as it
were, confronted with one another. The comparison between
the words, deeds, and destinies of each, is thus rendered easy,
and its tendency is altogether to the establishment of principles of unity and concord. The apostolic authority of Paul is
placed beyond question by the fact of his direct calling by the
Lord in person, and the history of this calling, which places
him on a level with Peter, is three times repeated. His special
mission, as the apostle of the Gentiles, is also directly and on
several occasions communicated to him by revelation;* the
mode of communication chosen by Providence for this end is the
same as that employed in the case of Peter† also, for a similar
purpose, and the similarity extends even to the secondary personages who in the two parallel cases carried out the designs
of God.‡ As to other forms of legitimation which might be
deemed necessary in the eyes of men, the two apostles are again
favoured in equal measure. Both work miracles, heal men
paralyzed from their birth;§ both raise the dead; ‖ their power
is exercised not only in such beneficent works, but also for the
punishment of their adversaries;¶ this supernatural influence is
so strong that it seems to dwell even in their shadow or in their
clothes,** and excites the adoration of some who witness it.††
The same miraculous protection of heaven is extended to both;‡‡

* Acts xvi. 9; xviii. 9; xxii. 17; xxiii. 11.
† Acts x. 10.
‡ Acts ix. 10; x. 3.
§ Acts iii. 2; xiv. 8, and foll.
‖ Acts ix. 36, and foll.; xx. 9.
¶ Acts v. 1, and foll.; xiii. 9.
** Acts v. 15; xix. 12.
†† Acts x. 26; xiv. 11.
‡‡ Acts xii. 7, and foll.; xvi. 26.

and, lastly, the apostolic privilege of imparting the Holy Spirit to the new converts, is possessed by both in the same measure,[*] which is evidence that they were themselves both equally inspired.

It is impossible that the reader should not be struck with this parallelism, and should not receive from it the impression of the perfect equality of the two apostles, as to their ecclesiastical authority; it is natural, therefore, that we should suppose it was the intention of the author to convey this impression. His design is yet more apparent in another series of facts which he chooses from the general history, in which it is evident that he is writing mainly for a public prejudiced against one of the two heads of the Church, and that his aim is to correct those prejudices. Now it was not so much the disciples of Paul who repudiated Peter, as the Judæo-Christians who repudiated the apostle of the Gentiles. The narrative of Luke aims, therefore, to bring into prominence the traits in the public life of Paul, which prove his personal attachment to the religious duties of his nation, and thus to vindicate him from the charge of apostasy, bitterly pronounced against him. Such traits would present themselves in abundance to the historian, Paul himself having boldly proclaimed it as his principle to be all things to all men,[†] to live with the Jews as a Jew, that he might gain the Jews, and with those who had no law, as being himself without law also. Thus Luke could point to him as the faithful observer of the law,[‡] fasting, making pilgrimages with ardent zeal, binding himself by the rites of an ascetic vow, and causing Timothy to be circumcised to bring him as his disciple into closer fellowship with himself. It was again under the patronage of the Levite Barnabas, a man highly esteemed in Jerusalem, that Paul had first entered into relations with the apostles, and had been, so to speak, installed in his ministry.[§] He has to encounter the same adversaries as his colleagues the Sadducees, the

* Acts x. 44 ; xix. 6.
† 1 Cor. ix. 19, and foll.
‡ Acts xiii. 3 ; xiv. 23 ; xviii. 18, 21 ; xx. 16 ; xxi. 24 ; xvi. 3.
§ Acts ix. 27 ; xi. 22, and foll.

opponents of tradition, and indifferent to the cherished hopes
of Israel; while the Pharisees, the warm supporters of those
traditions and hopes, espoused on occasion the cause of Paul, as
of the other apostles.* In his apostolic work, he always began
at the synagogue, and only turned to carry the Gospel message
to the Gentiles, when the Jews rejected it; this course was
marked out for him by the prophets themselves,† and it is
perhaps not without a retrospective thought of the same nature
that the history concludes with the solemn reiteration of this
fact and of this principle.‡ Lastly, we note how carefully the
apostle points out, from their very first interview,§ the harmony
which existed between the old apostles and their new colleague.
But this is especially brought into prominence by the account
of the conferences at Jerusalem, an account so much the more
significant from the solemnity with which it is given. As we
have already had occasion to study these facts in another connection, we shall not dwell here upon the reflections that
might be suggested by a comparison of Luke's text with the
narrative of Paul. We will simply remind the reader that we
have elsewhere shown that the author of the Acts does not
deserve the reproach of having modified those facts to support
his own point of view; but that, in passing lightly over the
opposition encountered by Paul at Jerusalem, he designed to
lay the more stress upon the result obtained; while Paul, whose
mind was absorbed in the necessity of raising the question to
the height of the principles involved, was led to dwell with
emphasis upon the efforts that had been required to vindicate
those principles against all opposition.

We have only spoken of these facts, because they may serve
to define the theological position of the writer. We now
hasten on to the didactic portion of his book,—that is, to the
discourses which he puts into the mouth of the principal
personages,—from which we may gather more direct and
positive statements, marking the tendency of his own mind.

* Acts v. 17, and foll.; xxiii. 6, and foll.
† Acts xiii. 46.
‡ Acts xxviii. 25, and foll.
§ Acts ix. 28.

There, again, we shall have occasion to observe that the two
parts of this work, that which brings Peter before us, and that
which is appropriated to Paul, are throughout in the móst
complete harmony, and represent the two apostles, whose
names at the time of the writer were made the rallying-points
of two hostile schools, as united in the preaching of one and the
same Gospel.

If we read over in succession the numerous epitomes of
sermons given in the book of the Acts, we shall readily
perceive that the theology taught in them is based upon this
simple exhortation: Repent, and believe in Jesus, the Christ,
that you may obtain the pardon of your sins and life.* The
wording is not the same in all the passages where it occurs,
nor is the exhortation always equally complete, but the
various shades of expression constitute no real difference. It
is still more essential to observe that this is a very general
and primitive form of expressing the Christian faith, one therefore which might the better serve as a rallying-point for all
parties, since, before their divisions arose, all had accepted
and used it in common. A few words will suffice further to
explain its import. The term repentance occurs far more
frequently than any of the rest, a fact which· marks the
character of the preaching as eminently practical. In some
places it is replaced or accompanied by the word conversion,
which is synonymous with it.† As the meaning of these words
is sufficiently familiar to us, we shall not dwell upon it now.
In reference to faith, we observe that the special idea attached
to that term in the writings of Paul and John, is nowhere
explicitly reproduced in this book. The phrase *faith in Jesus
Christ*,‡ does not, at least, necessarily contain it, especially if
we examine the other phrases in which the same word occurs.§

* Μετανοεῖτε καὶ πιστεύετε εἰς Ἰησοῦν Χριστὸν εἰς ἄφεσιν ἁμαρτιῶν καὶ ζωήν,
Acts ii. 38 ; iii. 19 ; v. 31 ; viii. 22 ; x. 43 ; xi. 18 ; xiii. 38 ; xvii. 30 ;
xx. 21 ; xxii. 16 ; xxvi. 18, and foll., etc.

† Ἐπιστρέφειν.

‡ Πίστις εἰς Χριστόν.

§ Thus πιστεύειν signifies simply to become a Christian, Acts xiii. 48 ;
xix. 2 ; ὑπακούειν τῇ πίστει, to be converted (vi. 7) ; a man full of faith and
of the Holy Spirit (vi. 5, xi. 24), is a zealous member of the Church ; to

As, however, faith is placed in direct relation with the forgiveness of sins, it is right that we should inquire what is the nature of that relation. Pardon is described as an ablution,* and baptism in the name of Jesus Christ is mentioned in the very passages where faith is not separately named.† We conclude from this, that the two formulas must be synonymous, and represent, in connection with conversion, a profession at once verbal and symbolical of belief in the Messianic dignity of Jesus, a belief which naturally expresses itself in moral reformation, and consequently brings with it the pardon of sins. This constitutes the difference between Christian baptism and the baptism of John, which presented only one of these elements.‡ We obtain the same result from the word to *blot out,*§ which is also used to express this pardon. It is well understood that salvation can be by Christ alone,‖ that He is the only leader into life;¶ and it would be erroneous to suppose that the writer, in proclaiming the principle that whosoever worketh righteousness is accepted of God,** seeks to place the Church on a basis foreign to the Gospel revelation, while in truth he says only that God is willing to receive men, without distinction of race, to the benefits of His grace. It is further said that Christ has purchased the Church with His own blood,†† that His death was a providential fact, predicted in Scripture,‡‡ and fulfilling the decree of God; §§ but we are not told what was the necessity for the death of Christ; at least in most of these passages His death is only spoken of from the

believe or to hope, or be persuaded (xv. 11), to have confidence in the possibility of receiving a benefit (xiv. 9).

* Ἀπολούω, Acts xxii. 16.
† Βάπτισμα ἐπὶ τῷ ὀνόματι Ἰησοῦ Χριστοῦ, that is, calling upon His name, *ibid.* ; comp. ii. 38.
‡ Acts xiii. 24 ; xix. 4.
§ Ἐξαλείφειν, Acts iii. 19.
‖ Acts iv. 12.
¶ Ἀρχηγός, Acts iii. 15 ; v. 31.
** Acts x. 35.
†† Acts xx. 28.
‡‡ Acts iii. 18 ; xvii. 3.
§§ Acts ii. 23 ; comp. iv. 28 ; xx. 27.

apologetic point of view, to vindicate His dignity in opposition to the exegesis of the Jews.* We might make the same remark in reference to the resurrection.† It is said again by the mouth of Peter, as by that of Paul, that purification is by faith and grace, not by the law, which hath no power to cleanse.‡ But these expressions, which moreover occur but very rarely, fail to conduct us beyond the point we have already reached in the analysis of other writings, given in the earlier chapters of this book. The law loses its absolute but not its relative value by the Gospel; it would be tempting God to seek to impose it upon the Gentiles, but it would be no less apostasy to dispense with it in the case of the Jews.§ If we were called upon distinctively to characterize the theology of the Acts, we should say that it bases salvation, not upon the mystical fact of regeneration, as does Paul, but upon the eschatological fact of the fulfilment of the prophecies, as does Judæo-Christianity.‖ In truth, the world is called to the duty of conversion, because the promised Messiah has come once, and will not delay to come a second time and finally. Conversion itself consists theoretically, in the belief of these two facts; practically, it consists in turning to account this last solemn warning from God.¶ For when it is said that God gives repentance to the world,** it means that He calls, or rather leads to repentance, all whom He has chosen. The idea of predestination comes out clearly in many passages.†† But this idea does not belong exclusively to any of the particular forms of Christian thought which we have distinguished; that of mystical substitution, on the contrary, which would form the most direct link between Luke and Paul, is not touched upon even in the one passage where we might have expected to find it introduced.‡‡

---

* Acts xxvi. 23.
† Acts ii. 14, and foll. ; xiii. 34, etc.
‡ Acts xiii. 39 ; xv. 9, and foll.
§ Acts xv. 10, 21 ; xxi. 21.
‖ Acts iii. 18, and foll. ; xiii. 32, foll., etc.
¶ Acts ii. 21.
** Acts v. 31 ; xi. 18 ; comp. ii. 39.
†† Acts ii. 47 ; xiii. 48.   ‡‡ Acts viii. 32.

It is right that we should here say a word about the Holy
Spirit, whose influence upon men is an important element in
the work of salvation, according to the Pauline theory. It is
notable that the book of the Acts is, of all the writings of the
New Testament, that in which the name of the Holy Spirit most
frequently occurs, so that the idea attached to it by the writer
cannot remain doubtful. That idea is, beyond question, a
thoroughly Christian one, but yet it is different from that which
we have traced in the book preceding this.* It does not here
represent an inward regeneration, but an impulse given by God
to the individual, leading him to speak or act for the benefit of
the Gospel cause. Setting aside the few passages in which the
reference is to special predictions,† all the rest will confirm the
definition we have just given. Thus, it is the Spirit which leads
Philip on to the road to Gaza, which tells Peter to welcome
the messengers of the centurion Cornelius, which prompts the
mission of Paul and Barnabas to the Gentiles, which guides the
missionaries in the choice of their route, which brings Paul up
to Jerusalem, chooses the pastors of the Churches,‡ and so on.
Stephen is called a man full of the Holy Ghost and of wisdom,§
because he manifested, on the one hand, the qualities necessary
for the diaconate, and on the other those required for successful controversy with the opponents of the Gospel. Such
was the case also with Barnabas, the preacher of Antioch, with
Paul, and others.|| The entire Church is animated by the Holy
Spirit in this sense, that it is disposed to do and suffer all for
the faith which it has embraced.¶ It must be especially observed that our definition is supported by the circumstance that
the communication of the Holy Spirit is not a fact unique in
the history of each individual receiving it, as in the evangelical

* It is still less the idea of traditional exegesis, which persists in regarding it as an official and exclusive inspiration of the Twelve, by which
they were endowed from day to day with absolute infallibility.

† Acts i. 16 ; vii. 51 ; xxviii. 25 ; xi. 28 ; xxi. 4, 11.

‡ Acts viii. 29 ; x. 19 ; xi. 12 ; xiii. 2, 4 ; xvi. 6, and foll.; xx. 22, 28.

§ Acts vi. 3, 5, 10.

|| Acts xi. 24 ; xiii. 9.

¶ Acts ix. 31 ; xv. 32.

theory of Paul, but that it repeats itself whenever it is required for a special purpose. The same men receive the Holy Spirit on repeated occasions, a fact which could not be understood on the other theory. Thus, the apostles, who had been already endowed with the Spirit before the ascension of Christ,* receive it again with a large number of other disciples at Pentecost.† Peter is endowed afresh with it on other occasions; so also are all the other apostles, and Paul among the rest.‡ These examples might easily be multiplied. They prove clearly that every impulse leading to a manifestation of Christian activity on behalf of the Gospel, is ascribed to a special impartation of the Spirit of God. The Pentecostal effusion is no exceptional event. It is explained beforehand by those words, "Ye shall receive power after that the Holy Ghost is come upon you, and ye shall be my witnesses."§ The power thus promised is power to act, an impulse given to the will, and not an illumination of the understanding. It is further explained subsequently in Peter's sermon.‖ It is impossible that the reference here should be to any exclusive privilege of the Twelve, for the text asserts the very contrary. All, to the number of more than a hundred, receive the Holy Spirit, and with it the gift of prophecy, that is to say, the gift of preaching the great things of God.¶ Peter even receives it, in a less degree than others, since he is more self-possessed, and not excited to the point of speaking with tongues;** he promises the same Holy Spirit to all who shall turn to the Lord,†† and the history distinctly says that this promise was fulfilled.‡‡ Lastly, it must be borne in mind that in the Acts the reference is always to a visible manifestation of the Holy Spirit,—that is, to an effect produced on the outer life,

* Acts i. 2.
† Acts ii. 4.
‡ Acts iv. 8, 31; ix. 17; xiii. 9.
§ Acts i. 5, 8.
‖ Acts ii. 17, and foll.
¶ Acts ii. 11, 33.
** Acts ii. 15.
†† Acts ii. 38.
‡‡ Acts x. 45, and foll.; xi. 15, and foll.; xv. 8.

20 *

which those who witnessed it could verify, which would not be the case if the reference were simply to an inner and purely psychological fact, or to a subjective illumination.* Even the rapture of Stephen† is not an exception, for it was not only the vision which he saw, but the words which he spoke, that attested the presence of the Holy Spirit with him.

The Christology of the Acts is thus very slightly developed, and scarcely rises above the level of the popular ideas of Judaism. We simply refer our readers to the remarks we have already made in speaking of Judæo-Christian theology. We will add only that the name Son of God occurs but three times in the Acts,‡ and always in the sense of the promised Messiah; we have therefore no means of determining its theological import.§

The eschatology of the book is no less confined to a few general ideas. •In addition to life,‖ which is spoken of as the end and final fruit of repentance and faith, mention is made also of the inheritance¶ in which the believer will share with all who are sanctified. We know that this latter term is but a figurative repetition of the former. The various expressions used to set forth the idea of salvation** are so familiar that we need do no more than allude to them. Elsewhere, the times of Messiah, the relative proximity of which is represented as dependent on the readiness of men to be converted, are called times of refreshing, or the time of the restitution of all things.†† The first expression, borrowed from the poetical language of the

* Acts ii. 4, 13; viii. 15, and foll.; x. 44, and foll.. ; xix. 2, and foll.
† Acts vii. 55.
‡ Υἱὸς τοῦ θεοῦ, Acts viii. 37, which is an interpolated passage; ix. 20; xiii. 33.
§ There are two other passages in the Acts which speak of the person of Jesus. In chapter viii. 56, υἱὸς τοῦ ἀνθρώπου is a reminiscence of a term frequently employed by Jesus Himself. In chapter xx. 28, on the contrary, the inadvertence of a copyist or a doctrinal prejudice has substituted θεὸς for κύριος.
‖ Ζωή, Acts v. 20; xi. 18.
¶ Κλῆρος, κληρονομία, Acts xx. 32; xxvi. 18.
** Σώζω, σωτηρία, Acts ii. 21; xi. 14; xiii. 26; xv. 1, 11; xvi. 30, etc.
†† Καιροὶ ἀναψύξεως, χρόνοι ἀποκαταστάσεως πάντων, Acts iii. 19—21.

Old Testament, simply denotes a state of happiness and exemption from suffering; the second, which clearly has reference to the predictions of the prophets, comprehends the three elements of the old eschatology, a religious and moral renovation, no less than a change in the outward condition of the people. As to the latter, the popular hopes, which were at first purely political, became spiritualized by degrees, but not all at once,* in the young community, and in the end the two former elements asserted their predominance over the third. It must be still further remarked, that in some places the apostolic preaching is so abridged in the narrative of our historian, as to retain simply that which is essential, so that repentance and the last judgment, the beginning and the end,† are alone mentioned, while all the evangelical ideas, properly so called, are omitted.

After all that has been said, it will be unnecessary for us to revert to the position taken by the book of the Acts in the great contest between the universalists and the particularists. It adheres expressly to the formula adopted at Jerusalem. It shows how, from the beginning, the apostles must have understood their mission as designed to comprehend the whole world. This the last words of Jesus ‡ expressly state. The nomenclature of the various nations represented in the Pentecostal gathering,§ although historical exegesis can discover in it only Jews, nevertheless appears in the intention of the writer to extend beyond the limit of this narrow circle; at least, the idea that he seems to entertain of the gift of tongues‖ leads us to such a conclusion. In his early discourses, Peter affirms that the evangelical promises are addressed to others beside the Jews, to men more remote, to all the families of the earth;¶

---

* Acts i. 6.

† Acts xvii. 30; xxiv. 25.

‡ Acts i. 8.

§ Acts ii. 9.

‖ See my article on the gifts of tongues in the *Revue de Théologie*, 1851, III., p. 89.

¶ Εἰς μακράν, Acts ii. 39; πατριαί, iii. 25.

that God makes no distinction of persons in this respect,* except on purely moral grounds. As it was not till long after this
that Peter was brought to understand the possibility of the
baptism of the uncircumcised, it is evident that the passages
above quoted must be understood of conversion in the sense
that the Gentiles on becoming Christians became by that very
fact incorporated with the Israelitish nation.   The Jerusalem
compromise is the limit of concession in the opposite direction.
In the discourses of Paul himself, there is not a word which
goes beyond this, and the Pauline theory in its logical completeness is spoken of to his very face as apostasy, and he
does not attempt to defend it.†   Add to this the stress laid in
these same discourses on the Pharisaism of Paul,‡ even after
his conversion, and it must be admitted that the theology of
the apostle of the Gentiles is singularly impoverished by his
biographer,§ and that there may be considerable reason to
question if the writer was really a disciple of Paul. If he
was so, it is at least clear that the disposition to compromise
was with him paramount to every other.

* Acts x. 15, 34.
† Acts xxi. 21.
‡ Acts xxiii. 6, and foll. ; xxiv. 14, and foll. ; xxv. 8 ; xxvi. 4, and foll.;
xxviii. 20.
§ We find but one faint reminiscence of it in chapter xiii. 39, and
foll.

CHAPTER VI.

MATTHEW AND LUKE.

IN concluding this section of our work, it remains for us to examine from a theological point of view, three books, by far the most popular in the whole New Testament, and which our readers will doubtless be surprised to see re-introduced in this later portion of our book, after having been already treated at length in the earlier. These are the gospels which tradition ascribes to Matthew, Mark, and Luke. They have served as the historical sources from which our knowledge of the Master's teaching is derived, and their authors certainly make no other claim than to be faithful historians. We should have formed, however, but an incomplete estimate of their works, if we did not attempt to study them also from a theological point of view. Let none be surprised that we should endeavour to discover in the artless words of a simple narrator, the particular shade of his own thought. The life and teaching of Jesus, as we have already shown, were so inexhaustible in their fulness, and so elevated in their scope, His person especially, if we may be pardoned the expression, was of so lofty a stature, that none of His disciples could rise to the full measure of it, and the greater part failed to apprehend even that phase of His revelation of Himself which was most accessible to the popular mind. His biographers, placed at a distance from Him, were not better qualified in this respect than their friends. The longer the distance to be traversed by the ray issuing from that great centre of light, the more would it be refracted and coloured by the medium through which it passed. We may well suppose that the evangelists, while recording most conscientiously the words of Jesus according to their own memories, and the sources at their disposal, may also have intermingled some words of their own, or at least have reproduced the impressions made upon those whose testimony they received.

We are the more naturally led to compare them in this respect, that we are accustomed and obliged to do so in other aspects of their work. The external similarity of their narratives, the numerous analogies which their method presents, even the appearances so often pointed out, and so vainly contested, of their interdependence, all provoke such a comparison. Why then should it not be extended to their religious ideas, to that which is more essential in their writings, if only to prove whether the historical elements in which they differ by additions, omissions, and variations, are derived simply from the variable nature of a tradition more or less complete and full, or whether they are traceable to a premeditated choice of the compiler, and to his own theological bias? It is not we, indeed, who propose this question. We are bound to reply to it, because it has been so long agitated. The old Fathers of the Church were alive to it, and solved it in their manner by saying, for example, that Matthew wrote for the Jews, and Luke for the Gentiles, or that Paul dictated the third gospel, Peter the second. But it is especially in modern times that science has entered into the thorough discussion of this subject. Some writers have gone so far as to see in these gospels actual manifestoes of opposing parties; almost all, without arriving at a conclusion so exaggerated, have admitted the premises on which it is based.

We are thus brought to consider the opinion, widely diffused in our day, that Matthew, by the choice of the facts which he records and the discourses which he inserts, represents, of deliberate purpose, the Judæo-Christian type of thought; that Luke, on the contrary, wrote his book to vindicate the principles of the apostle Paul; and, lastly, that Mark, following the other two, sought to serve the conciliatory school, omitting designedly that which was most characteristic of the spirit and theory of either party, and thus, by modifying the narratives of his predecessors, unfurled the flag of neutrality. It will be our duty to examine these opinions by the light of an impartial and conscientious criticism.

We shall devote the present chapter to the most tangible and least difficult part of the problem—that is, to the comparison of the gospels of Matthew and Luke. Here the facts on which a solid and positive judgment may be based, are so numerous and so well defined, that we may hope to impart to our readers the same convictions at which we ourselves have arrived. It is easy to collate the passages most favourable to the opinion we have just mentioned; they are quoted everywhere; and though we have no wish to diminish their significance, we may content ourselves with reproducing only the most prominent.

It has been observed that Matthew commences the genealogy of Jesus with Abraham the patriarch of Israel, while Luke traces it back to Adam, the common father of mankind. From the historical point of view, this is of no moment, for the ascending line from Abraham to Adam was familiar to all. The enumeration therefore of these names by Luke, while in itself superfluous, indicates that he designed to suggest the relationship of Jesus to humanity at large, rather than to the Jewish nation in particular. The number of the disciples stands related, unquestionably, to the number of the tribes of Israel. This number twelve is the symbol of the Jewish nation in its totality;* it denotes therefore a mission circumscribed within the limits of Judaism. Luke, and he only, mentions that Jesus chose other disciples to the number of seventy, and the longer and more emphatic directions which both evangelists record as addressed by Jesus to those whom He sent forth to preach the Gospel, appear according to Matthew to have been given to the Twelve (chapter x.), while Luke connects them with the mission of the Seventy (chapter x.), the charge to the Twelve being in his narrative very brief (chapter ix.) Now it must be remembered that the number seventy had also a

* Matt. xix. 28; James i. 1; Acts xxvi. 7.

symbolic value; it represented all the nations supposed to exist upon the earth, in their entirety. Here, then, we have universalism opposed to exclusiveness. But it is not by induction only we are led to this result. More direct and positive facts seem in the same way to point to it. Thus Matthew alone* makes Jesus say that His appearing will take place before the Gospel shall have overpassed the boundaries of Palestine, so that no place is left for the evangelization of the Gentiles. The same evangelist only once mentions the name of the Samaritans,† and then to affirm that Jesus had forbidden His disciples to go and preach the Gospel to them. Luke, in the corresponding passage, omits this injunction, while he speaks in three places of the, Samaritans in quite another spirit, twice to place them above the Jews in the judgment of the Saviour Himself, and the third time‡ to put into the lips of Christ, in opposition to a hostile sentiment, the declaration that He was come, not to destroy men's lives, but to save them. It is in Matthew only we read the story of the Canaanitish woman, to whom Jesus says that He is not sent but to the lost sheep of the house of Israel,§ and cannot take the children's bread to give to the dogs. On a par with this saying may be placed another, likewise recorded by Matthew only:‖ "Give not that which is holy unto the dogs, neither cast ye your pearls before swine." Luke, on the other hand, pronounces the Gentile Zaccheus to be a son of Abraham.¶

The Judæo-Christianity of Matthew and the Paulinism of Luke manifest themselves also in the position which they take, or which they represent Jesus as taking, in relation to the law. Thus, the first solemn discourse of the Saviour, as rendered in the first gospel, distinctly declares the permanent obligation of the law,** not one jot or tittle of which is ever to pass away. The first

---

* Matt. x. 23.
† Matt. x. 5.
‡ Luke x. 33 ; xvii. 16 ; ix. 52, and foll.
§ Matt. xv. 24.
‖ Matt. vii. 6.
¶ Luke xix. 9.
** Matt. v. 17, and foll.

sermon recorded in the third gospel* tends distinctly to transfer
to the Gentiles the benefit of the promises made of old to Israel.
The law and the prophets, it is said in Luke,† were until John
the Baptist. The significance of the same words is, in Matthew,‡
neutralized by the substitution of another verb. The parable of
the prodigal son, that of the Pharisee and the publican,§ and
many others, are designed to give emphasis to the idea of salvation by divine mercy, in opposition to salvation by the merit
of works; and these parables are found only in the third gospel.
In that of the royal feast,‖ the evident purport of which is to
sanction the principle of the calling of the Gentiles, Matthew
inserts a particular circumstance, which seems to impose on
these a special condition of which Luke makes no suggestion.
The absolute uselessness of works, and the absence of any claim
or merit on the part of men, is nowhere so explicitly taught
as in Luke.¶ The reverence for the Sabbath, carried to the
extreme by Jewish asceticism, is commended by Matthew,**
but not in the parallel passage of Luke. Matthew alone tells
us that on the occasion of His baptism Jesus used the words,
"Thus it becometh me to fulfil *all righteousness*,"††—that is,
all consecrated rites. It is Matthew again who emphatically
names Peter as the first of the apostles,‡‡ which must not be
restricted to a chronological priority, since we find Peter afterwards §§ (and again by this evangelist only) designated as the
Rock on which the Church is to be built. Lastly, Luke does
not mention the charge brought against Jesus before the
Sanhedrim of having sought to destroy the temple. We know
that this was not a pure invention, but the misconstruction of

* Luke iv. 16, and foll.
† Luke xvi. 16.
‡ Matt. xi. 13.
§ Luke xv. 11, and foll. ; xviii. 9, and foll.
‖ Matt. xxii. ; Luke xiv.
¶ Luke xvii. 10.
** Matt. xxiv. 20.
†† Matt. iii. 15, πᾶσαν δικαιοσύνην.
‡‡ Πρῶτος, Matt. x. 2.
§§ Matt. xvi. 17, and foll.

a word really spoken.* Matthew declares it to be simply false.†

The hopes of the consummation of all things have a much more strongly Jewish colouring in Matthew than in Luke. We have only to compare parallel passages of the two writers‡ to perceive that Luke had a marked tendency to spiritualize predictions taken literally by the other evangelist. The twenty-fourth chapter of Matthew compared with the twenty-first of Luke shows throughout the same relation.§ The famous adverb which in Matthew connects the visible coming of Christ with the destruction of Jerusalem, and which has confounded the exegesis of every age and of every school, is wanting in Luke, who, on the contrary, widens almost illimitably the horizon of prophecy. The reply made to the Pharisees,‖ who sought to know when the kingdom of God should come,—a reply which we look for in vain in Matthew,—places us upon altogether different ground from Judæo-Christianity.

These are a few of the principal texts that have been supposed to establish the diversity of tendency we have indicated between the gospels of Matthew and Luke. We cannot admit that these arguments, specious as they are, have any real force. We are well aware that ecclesiastical tradition seems in its turn to confirm them, by attributing the third gospel to a friend and fellow-worker of Paul, who wrote it especially for the instruction of the Greeks ; and the first gospel, on the other hand, to an apostle exclusively devoted to the evangelization of the Jews, in whose sacred tongue it is supposed to have been originally written.

The passages cited do not appear to us, however, to exhaust the question.¶ A more thorough examination will show that the suggested classification of the two books is not altogether

---

* Mark xiv. 58.

† Matt. xxvi. 61.

‡ For example, compare Matt. xvi. 28, with Luke ix. 27.

§ Matt. xxiv. 29 ; εὐθέως, comp. Luke xxi. 24.

‖ Luke xvii. 20, 21.

¶ Nor is the sense imposed upon many of them, under polemical pressure, capable of defence.—Ed.

supported by facts. The place we assign to them in this history shows, by anticipation, that our opinion of the tone of their theology differs essentially from that of our predecessors.

In fact, we cannot believe that the two books now before us express definitely and exclusively either one or the other of the tendencies described. We do not see that their writers were preoccupied with any system, or at least that it was their aim to assert certain dogmatic theories in opposition to others equally current among the Christians of their day. We find, on the contrary, that historical facts are the sole object of their research and labour. To collect these, and to repeat them, as they were supplied by the tradition of the Churches, to make use of them, finally, for the edification of the readers, this was their exclusive aim; and if we can succeed in showing that they had no thought of colouring the facts they related according to particular dogmatic theories, or of choosing them from a predetermined point of view, we shall have shown at the same time that their record is the faithful mirror of apostolic memories, as these were diffused and transmitted by word of mouth, till the time of their final incorporation in a written form.

We shall now begin by adducing proof of our assertion, and shall then draw some conclusions from it. The exegetical statements which we might bring forward are so many, that we shall confine ourselves to a few examples taken at hazard.

In the Gospel according to Matthew, there is a series of passages directly opposed to the Judaizing tendency, the Pharisaical spirit, which demanded the circumcision of the Gentiles, and which regarded the kingdom of God as inalienable from the Jewish nation. There are others which implicitly reverse the idea of the obligatory character of the Mosaic law, and which go beyond or even run counter to the commonly cherished hopes of Judæo-Christianity. Thus the universal preaching of the Gospel is predicted and enjoined in two passages familiar to all,* one of which formally excludes any idea of legal conditions to be imposed upon the Gentiles. Still further: this same

* Matt. xxiv. 14; and xxviii. 19.

Gospel repeatedly predicts the decadence of the Jews, to whom
Jesus declares that others to whom the Gospel had not been
at first promised, should take their place and enter the kingdom before them. This prediction is embodied both in the
history and in parable.* It is even put into the lips of John
the Baptist.† It is worthy of note that these texts, so fully
in harmony with what is supposed to be the tendency of Luke,
are not even all found in his gospel. The familiar saying of
the Saviour, that "new wine cannot be put into old bottles,"
occurs in both gospels,‡ and assuredly these words, naturally
explained, are in themselves a sufficient condemnation of
narrow Judæo-Christianity. The value of the law is in both
shown to consist in its religious and moral principle, to the
exclusion of the purely ritual portion, but this is even more
emphatically marked in Matthew than in Luke.§ So, on
another occasion, it is Matthew who points out expressly the
relative inferiority of the Levitical precepts.‖ If Jesus places
His own authority above that of the Sabbath, Matthew
gives the record as unhesitatingly as Luke.¶ The parables
of the grain of mustard-seed and of the leaven, both so at
variance with the spirit of Jewish eschatology, are also found
in the first gospel.**

On the other hand, if we were anxious to establish a thesis
in opposition to that hitherto accepted, proofs would not be
wanting, for the perpetuity of the law is proclaimed by Luke
also ;†† the hopes expressed by means of images familiar to Judaism are common to both writers.‡‡ According to both, Jesus
calls the temple of Jerusalem His house ;§§ the Son promised
to the Virgin is according to Luke's narrative far more strictly

---

* Matt. viii. 12 ; xx. 1, and foll. ; xxi. 28, and foll. ; 33, and foll.
† Matt. iii. 9.
‡ Matt. ix. 16, 17 ; Luke v. 36, and foll.
§ Luke x. 26 ; Matt. xxii. 40.
‖ Matt. xxiii. 23 ; comp. Luke xi. 42.
¶ Matt. xii. 8 ; Luke vi. 5.
** Matt. xiii. 31, and foll.
†† Luke xvi. 17.
‡‡ Luke xxii. 30; Matt. xix. 28.
§§ Luke xix. 46 ; Matt. xxi. 13.

the Jewish Messiah, the heir of the throne of David and king of the house of Jacob, than He is in Matthew's version;* and the third gospel is specially careful to show† how all the rites of the law were fulfilled in relation to Him. In the Sermon on the Mount, the rendering of Luke as compared with that of Matthew,‡ and taken literally, is suggestive of pure Ebionitism; for it is distinctly said that the kingdom of God is reserved for the poor, the sorrowful, the persecuted. It is only Matthew who marks the moral meaning of the Saviour's words. The rich man in the parable § goes to hell because he is rich; the beggar Lazarus is carried into Paradise because he is poor; at least the text does not contain, in its historical setting, a single word which characterizes the two from a moral point of view. So far from this, it is said, in so many words, that the recompense received by each is the reversal of his outward lot in this life. Lastly, in the parable of the Prodigal Son, which is intended to open the door to the Gentiles, the rights of the Jews are expressly reserved, and even with a kind of emphasis.‖ In the history of the childhood of Jesus, it is the supposed Judæo-Christian gospel which alone records the adoration of the Magi, a fact which signifies that the pagan world was the first to recognize the new King of the Jews; and it is the reputedly Pauline gospel which alone gives the narrative in which Jesus declares the temple at Jerusalem to be His true home.¶

We do not cite these passages to incline the balance in an opposite direction, or with any intention of denying *in toto* that it is possible to discover in the two evangelists, indications of the particular tendencies before described. Our object is simply to show that side by side with the facts which have been thus noted by our predecessors, there are others of an opposite tendency, equally deserving of attention. The two works appear

* Luke i. 32 ; Matt. i. 21.
† Luke ii. 22, and foll.
‡ Luke vi. 20—25 ; Matt. v. 3, and foll.
§ Luke xvi. 19, and foll.
‖ Luke xv. 31.
¶ Matt. ii. 1, and foll. ; Luke ii. 49.

to us to include, though possibly in different proportions, the same elements variously coloured. The question therefore is not exhausted, nor is the duty of the historian of doctrine fulfilled, when it is said that the first gospel is the pure and simple expression of Judæo-Christianity, and that the third reproduces, broadly and clearly, the theology of Paul.

The truth is we think this. The teaching of Jesus, as our exposition has shown, contained no contradictions; He had throughout one starting-point and one goal. In analyzing His method, theological exegesis will always find means of readily reconciling words apparently contradictory, such as those we have brought into comparison; and our attention, in endeavouring to systematize the teaching of the Saviour, has been directed especially to this very task. If there remains dubiousness anywhere, it will not exert any marked influence upon the whole, and we have the satisfaction of perfect assurance and clearness on all capital points. It is easy to conceive, moreover, that His words, caught by hearers variously predisposed towards Him, may have been also variously understood. Figures, expressions borrowed from the outer life, may have retained for some their ordinary meaning, while others may have been able to translate them into their inner and spiritual sense. Counsel wisely given in view of a present necessity, may have been transformed into a permanent rule independent of circumstances. Hence would arise, not only misapprehensions on the part of some, but even apparent contradictions between precepts uttered by the same teacher. The simultaneous presence in the same gospel of certain words of the Lord, which seem to belong to different regions of religious thought, subsequently distinguished in the Church, will not prove therefore either that Jesus contradicted Himself, or that His biographer altered the facts of the history; it will only add another proof that these books are the product of tradition which their writers made it their diligent study to collect and reproduce with all fidelity,—to give it, in short, as they had received it; not to colour it according to a preconceived idea, or to make it subservient to any previously fixed theological system, wresting and overriding the familiar facts.

The origin of these gospels is not therefore to be sought in the midst of parties, each of which had its own fixed formula, nor can it be assigned to the age of most animated discussion between the two leading schools of the first era of the Church. They belong to a phase of theological development in which the controversies which had previously agitated men's minds began to be modified, and tended towards reconciliation; and if we are not strangely mistaken in our estimate of the progress of ideas and parties in the apostolic Church, the synoptical gospels in their existing form have their true chronological place on the boundary line between the first and second age.

Hitherto we have taken our examples only from the discourses of the Saviour, inserted in the two gospels. But beside these discourses, there are facts which speak no less plainly, and to the same effect. We need not recall these to our readers, in order abundantly to prove that neither of the two evangelists now before us proceeds, in the choice of his materials, by way of exclusion, and so as to pass by in silence all that might not harmonize with a certain school of dogmatic thought. If, for example, it were true that Matthew wrote under the inspiration of a narrow Judæo-Christianity, he would unquestionably have omitted those scenes in the history in which Jesus is brought into contact with the Gentiles, grants them the blessings they seek, and extols their faith;* he might also have cast a veil of charitable forgetfulness over the denial of Peter. Luke, on the contrary, who is supposed to have written in the interests of the opposite party, must have erred in omitting other scenes, which would have entered naturally and necessarily into a complete outline of a Pauline gospel, and yet which are absent from his narrative, and present in that of Matthew.† We repeat, it is not party or polemical interests which dictate their writings; it is the history for its own sake, and in view of its high religious

* Matt. xv. 28 ; viii. 10, etc.
† Matt. xvi. 23 ; xx. 28 ; xxvi. 61.

significance, which absorbs their attention. The different shades of doctrine which may be traced in various points of their narrative, especially by a careful comparison between them, proceed not from any peculiar bias of their own, but from the fact that the sources to which they had recourse supplied the materials as they are thus presented to us. We hold that these sources of their information cannot have been any writings or testimonies arranged and conceived from a subjective point of view, and belonging to any one party, determined to colour the history so as to support its views. In this respect, Luke is faithful to the promise he makes to his readers in his preface; and Matthew, the reputed Judaizer, must be a very unskilful author, if his book is to be accepted as the manifesto of the party of exclusion.

One word more in conclusion. We find in the very commencement of the two gospels, the most unquestionable evidence that the writers sought to give facts, not theories. For we there observe this remarkable circumstance, that they both record in their books, in order the more faithfully to transmit the tradition they had received, an opinion which they themselves say cannot be accepted. We refer to the natural birth of Jesus. Many Christians, beyond a doubt, regarded Him as the son of Joseph; to these the genealogy of Joseph would be a matter of great interest. The narrative of the evangelists is as positive and explicit as possible in relation to the miraculous birth of the Saviour. Nevertheless Luke, in order not to neglect any elements of the tradition he had received, inserts this genealogy, saying expressly* that in his view it has no historical value in connection with Jesus, between whom and the husband of His mother there was no natural relation. Matthew is of the same opinion, though he expresses himself with less exactness. He begins by giving the genealogy of Joseph, as he had received it (and the first verse shows that it had been given him as that of Jesus Himself); but he affirms afterwards† that it does not go beyond Joseph; in other words, that it cannot have

---

* Ὡς ἐνομίζετο, Luke iii. 23.
† Matt. i. 16.

the value which one section of Christians attached to it. To
his mind, the genealogy of Joseph might doubtless be taken
as representing the *legal* bond which connected Jesus with
David, but beyond this there was the evangelical bond which
attached Him directly to God. Unless this view be accepted,
it must be supposed that Matthew carried syncretism so far as
to accept two contradictory theories, the one which regarded
Jesus as the son born of a virgin, and the other which supposed
Him to be the true son of Joseph; for all the other explanations which have been suggested in the apologetic literature
of fifteen centuries, do violence to the texts.

CHAPTER VII.

MARK.

THE last book which here claims our attention as contributing to the history of Christian theology in the first century, is the gospel which tradition ascribes to a disciple of the apostles named John, more commonly known by his surname of Mark, and probably a native of Jerusalem. It is not on chronological grounds, which are generally foreign to our work, that we have reserved this to the last place, but simply from the more marked absence of theological elements, which is the special characteristic of the book we have now to examine. It will supply us with fewer materials for our narrative than those we have just been considering, so that if we had not to remove some prejudices of criticism with regard to it, we might dismiss it with very few words. In other respects, this gospel is, on the contrary, of the highest importance. We have shown elsewhere that it is the oldest we possess, and was one of the sources chiefly consulted by the compilers of the other two.

The opinion most widely received in our own day in relation to the theological tenor of this gospel is as follows. It has been always remarked that the gospel of Mark is the shortest of all; not because he relates with more brevity the history of the Saviour, for he often gives details which we find nowhere else, and most graphic touches of representation; but because he omits almost entirely the discourses of Jesus, which occupy so large a space in, and form to us so valuable a portion of, the narratives of his colleagues. Nor is it only the longer discourses

(in which Luke sometimes, and Matthew still more often, gives
an arbitrary agglomeration of elements originally separate)
that are almost wholly wanting in Mark; it often happens
that at the close of the historical scenes which he describes, he
abridges the lessons elsewhere connected with them, or omits
very important words spoken by the Saviour. This cannot be
the result of chance, nor can it be supposed that the source
from which Mark derived his information, failed to supply so
important a part of the Gospel tradition. The omissions must
have been made intentionally. In order to discover the cause
of this singular fact, we may inquire first into the testimony
history gives as to the person of the evangelist himself. Mark
was cousin to the Levite Barnabas, that same Barnabas who
repeatedly acted as mediator between Paul and the apostles
at Jerusalem.* We see Mark first associated with Paul, then
parted from him, and in company with Peter,† with whom
tradition more particularly connects him. He had thus been
successively in relations with the two principal apostles, whose
names at the time when he wrote—that is, after their death—
still served as the watchwords of contending parties. If we
accept the tradition that this disciple is really the author of the
second gospel, we may fairly conclude from all these facts that
he did not belong to either faction, and that, possibly through
that timidity which Paul had felt it necessary somewhat
sharply to reprove,‡ he was anxious to remain neutral in these
party quarrels, and to be as cautious as a writer in expressing
his opinion as he had perhaps been as a missionary. It is to
this excess of caution that we must (on the hypothesis we are
for the moment accepting) ascribe the very remarkable fact
that Mark is the only evangelist who does not once use the term
law. But even should these historical data prove incorrect,—
that is to say, should we find reason to question whether Mark
was the writer of the second gospel,—that gospel would still
contain internal evidence of another kind as to its origin, which

* Acts ix. 27 ; x. 22 ; xv. 2 ; Gal. ii. 9, 13.
† Acts xv. 38 ; 1 Peter v. 13.
‡ Παροξυσμός, Acts xv. 38.

would explain to us in some measure its characteristic tone.
In all probability it was written at Rome. On this point
we have not only the weight of intrinsic arguments, but the
almost unanimous opinion of the early Church, who were so
fully convinced of it, that they in the end came to maintain—
erroneously, no doubt,—that the book had been first written
in Latin. Now we know that the Church of Rome was in its
commencement a Judaizing Church. Paul, on a closer acquaintance with it, tells us in no ambiguous terms that the spirit by
which it was animated, in relation to doctrinal tendencies, was
not that of the Gospel preached in his Epistle to the Romans.*
This he tells us shortly before his death; his presence could
not then have exercised a very powerful influence over that
community, which was destined soon to play so important a
part in the Church; and this is all the more conceivable from
the fact that he was not at that time in the enjoyment of full
liberty. Subsequently, however, ideas underwent a change in
this city as elsewhere. Judaism insensibly succumbed to the
opposite principle, not without at the same time modifying and
enfeebling that principle, as we have seen from some of the
documents already analyzed. We can understand, then, that
in this transition period, doctrinal theories should lose their
importance both to individuals and in the direction of the
Church; and a more prominent place would naturally be
assigned, both in the life and the teaching of the Church,
on the one hand to practical exhortation, and the establishment of its social institutions, and on the other to the purely
historical side of the Gospel. The latter fact especially receives
ample confirmation from that which we know of subsequent
times. Gradually the Church and the people came to attach
paramount interest to the miracle itself, to the greater or less
neglect of the teaching connected with it; the words of Jesus
were, so to speak, eclipsed by the strong light thrown upon
His marvellous works. This tendency further explains to us,
in part, how the Church became subsequently inundated with
so large a number of apocryphal writings, the design of which

* 2 Tim. iv. 16; Phil. i. 15, and foll.; ii. 20, and foll.; iii. 2.

was to satisfy an idle curiosity, and of which the often absurd legends have taken root side by side with the authentic records, in the memory of succeeding generations.

Such is the process of argument urged in support of the conciliatory neutrality said to be the prevailing characteristic of the second gospel, if indeed it be not regarded as altogether without colour or character of its own. The whole reasoning seems to us very feeble and unsound. As it is in our view a fact placed beyond dispute, that Mark wrote before his two colleagues, we must dismiss altogether the idea that he pursued with regard to their writings, a course of selection by which he betrayed party preoccupation, or a desire to avoid subjects of discord. But looking at his gospel in itself, we fail to discover the characteristics, and consequently the design, which some have thought they traced in it. His book is the first attempt to fix the evangelical tradition in writing; it is less rich than those which supplemented it by means of further information. This is all that can with truth be said of the omissions we have noted. But it is not true that the writer limited himself to material facts, that the didactic elements are wanting, or that those which he includes in his narrative are such as to suggest that he has carefully avoided touching on already controverted points.

The absence of any history of the childhood of the Saviour, and the phrase with which the second gospel opens, are fully explained and justified by the point of view of the apostolic preaching,* and we have no need to seek the cause elsewhere. The assertion that Mark has generally omitted all quotations from the Old Testament, because the practice of using them was of Judæo-Christian origin, rests upon a twofold exaggeration. Paul himself has frequent recourse to the Old Testament, and the Church never ceased to proclaim the close connection between the two phases of revelation. Again, there are enough quotations in Mark's gospel to show that he does not pass them by on principle.† The Judæo-Christian tone, moreover, is not

* Acts i. 22.
† Mark i. 2, 3 ; vii. 6 ; ix. 12, 13 ; xi. 17 ; xiv. 21, 27, 49.

completely lost, as is evident especially in the eschatological passages.* Still more often do we meet with others which contain the elements of the anti-Judaizing theory, and this should be especially observed, because, according to the received opinion which we are combating, the writer designedly eliminated these from his gospel. Among these passages there are some which Mark is not the only one to record, in which he is in unison with the two other synoptics. Thus we read repeatedly in his narrative, the account of scenes and discourses which reveal the deep antagonism between the spirit of the Gospel and that of Pharisaic legalism,† or which assign to ritual forms a value inferior to that of spiritual worship and heart morality,‡ or which characterize the nature and progress of the kingdom§ of God in a manner altogether different from the opinion current as yet, even in the Church; or, lastly, which hold out the promise of the calling of the Gentiles even to the exclusion of the Jews. ‖ But there are other elements of far greater interest which we gather from him alone, and which prove all the more positively that the object he had in view could not have required the constant and arbitrary omission of doctrinal elements. Thus, Mark is the only evangelist who gives us the saying of Jesus that "man was not made for the Sabbath, but the Sabbath for man."¶ While omitting a large portion of the invectives pronounced by the Saviour against the Pharisaic spirit, he epitomizes them in one severe phrase,** not found in any of the parallel passages. Repeatedly he records the utterance of universalist principles on remarkable occasions. On the expulsion of the buyers and sellers from the temple, Mark puts into the lips of Jesus words which seem to open the temple at Jerusalem to all nations,— a thought of which there is no trace in either of the other

* Mark ix. 1 ; xiii., *passim.*
† Mark i. 22 ; ii. 10, 22 ; x. 5 ; viii. 15.
‡ Mark ii. 18, 23, and foll. ; iii. 1, and foll. ; vii. 5, and foll.
§ Mark iv. 26, 31.
‖ Mark xii. 9.
¶ Mark ii. 27.
** Mark iii. 5.

gospels; and since it is found in the text of the prophet whose words are quoted,[*] Matthew and Luke might be accused of having, in this instance at least, taken away from the full significance of the Saviour's teaching. In another passage,[†] having reference also to the evangelization of the Gentiles, Mark is again more positive and more explicit than Matthew, while Luke furnishes us with no parallel at all. Lastly, Mark is also the only evangelist who makes a scribe[‡] give utterance to the fundamental axiom, that for a man to love God and his neighbour is better than all sacrifices. Again, on the other hand, in the gospel of Mark alone do we find the avowal made by Jesus,[§] that the Son of God Himself knows not the day nor the hour of the end, an avowal which has often appeared to the doctors of the Church incompatible with a Christology rising above the level of Judaism.

All these examples prove at least that omissions are not the only distinctive trait of Mark's gospel, that it contains also details not found elsewhere, and which must be borne in mind in forming a judgment upon it. In any case, if stress is still to be laid upon theological principles and colouring, it must be admitted that the second gospel presents precisely the same features which we have noticed in the other two.

We cannot leave this subject without drawing attention to two passages in the gospel of Mark, interesting from another point of view. In the history of the Canaanitish woman Matthew makes Jesus say, in so many words,[||] "I am not sent but to the lost sheep of the house of Israel." "It is not meet to take the children's bread and to cast it to dogs." Mark, on[¶] the contrary, thus renders the same words: "Let the children first be filled, for it is not meet," etc. All three evangelists give as from the lips of Jesus the saying, that it is hard for rich men

[*] Mark xi. 17 ; Isaiah lvi. 7.
[†] Mark xiii. 10 ; Matt. xxiv. 14.
[‡] Mark xii. 33.
[§] Mark xiii. 32.
[||] Mark xv. 24.
[¶] Mark vii. 27.

to enter into the kingdom of heaven; but Mark` alone adds,* that those intended are the men who put their trust in riches, whose wealth therefore is their sole treasure. We cite these two passages to show once more, by striking examples, how what has been called the Judæo-Christian, or Ebionite, or Pauline shade of doctrine, has come to be assigned to one gospel or another, or, to speak more correctly, how it has been suggested by one or other particular narration. The briefest and most paradoxical form of the discourse may be the most authentic. The additions found in Mark may be less historically accurate; but as interpretations, all will acknowledge their justness. Judæo-Christianity may have often adhered to the original form so tenaciously as even to narrow the religious horizon of Jesus, but tradition has not been necessarily modified on that account, and the exegesis of riper years is always at liberty to correct that of childhood.

We may say then, in conclusion, that these three gospels, so far from appearing to us as the instruments of party theological strife, or the representatives of opposite tendencies, in the service of which they were composed, are in our judgment independent of the one and alien to the other; that their object is not to formulate theories, but to collect facts, to which, undoubtedly, an interested exegesis may have given a dogmatic meaning they did not originally possess, but which, if that exegesis were in all cases equally exact, would serve rather to emphasize the contradictions between them than to uphold any one system.

* Mark x. 24.

BOOK SEVENTH.

THE THEOLOGY OF JOHN.

CHAPTER I.

INTRODUCTION.

THE theology of John has been hitherto treated less fully
and less felicitously than that of Paul. Such is at least the
impression left on our minds from the reading of some recent
works which have made it their special subject. If our impression is correct, the fact itself is easily explained by the
many difficulties which, so to speak, surround all the approaches to the subject, and by the nature of the subject itself,
especially as compared with that which we have treated in our
fifth book.

In truth, in studying the theology of Paul, we are brought
at once into contact with a strongly marked and perfectly
distinct individuality; we have before us a great historical
personage, a man of action no less than of thought, whose practice forms as it were a running commentary on his theories.
Here, on the contrary, the person whose convictions and principles we seek to ascertain, passes before us as a hazy figure
without any sharpness of outline, almost lost in the dim
distance, our impressions of whom are such that we can hardly
tell whether they are derived from the real facts of history, or
are the creations of a dreamy and poetic tradition. Paul's
career was so full of facts, that fable need lend nothing to
enrich his laborious life. With John, the reverse is the case;
of him, almost all that we know has come down to us through

the doubtful or fabricated accounts of an age full of credulity and greedy of miracles.

When we wish to reconstruct the system of the apostle of the Gentiles, every one knows where to seek the materials for the edifice. The sources of information, if not all equally abundant, are at least equally pure and transparent. The danger of intermixing any foreign element, of adulterating with any false alloy, the true thought of the theologian, exists only for those who carry distrust beyond its natural limits, or who, in the exercise of criticism, only see distinctly the slighter differences of form, and close their eyes to the more palpable analogies of the underlying current of ideas. The most determined doubt can hardly, in this sphere, impede the sure progress of history, or prevent a sound literary judgment. The system of the apostle remains intact, and no change is necessitated in his doctrinal theory, whether a few epistles more or less be supposed or denied to be his. With John the whole case is different. In the selection of the sources of information, very important preparatory work is required; the claims of some must be established, the pretensions of others examined; and whatever be the final decision, it will be found impossible to satisfy at once criticism and tradition, and we shall always be exposed either to the reproach of syncretism, or to that of a neology dangerous alike to science and the Church. The various works with which the name of John is currently associated, are of a nature so heterogeneous and incongruous, that it must be very difficult in any case to include the substance of all in any one outline.

More than this. If it is true that in history a peculiar value attaches to proper names, the advantage here again is on the side of the system we have treated in one of the preceding books. The name of Paul as a writer and theologian is a historical name, one which re-echoes through the Church, which gives unity to his ideas, and sets upon them the same seal of authority which formerly secured their power and ascendancy over an astonished world. Here, on the contrary, if we will attach a proper name to the system before us, we must first prove, or at least defend, the reality of the connection. Perhaps criticism and historical conscience may compel us to abandon it, or to use it only as a name of convenience, and to seek for the system it should represent a place beside the others, not on the ground of this external authority, but simply by virtue of its own intrinsic worth. To the theologian, this will make no difference, but a system unsupported by a great name will always lack something in popular estimation. For, as is well known, the books we are about to study are anonymous works, and though we may be persuaded that their apostolic origin can yet be successfully defended, we are far from pouring contempt upon the doubts of those who differ from us. This is not the place to deal with the question of the authenticity of the fourth gospel, and of the epistles attributed to John. We have elsewhere explained our reasons for accepting that authenticity as a fact. But in the existing condition of science, it is not by an anathema, or by superficial scorn, that we can hope to put to silence a criticism which would lead to opposite results. We repeat again, that for us this is not the main question. It concerns us far less to know the name of a writer, than the purpose and scope of his words.

Again: in the subject before treated, the writer and his works form one and the same individuality. The teacher, the preacher, the theologian, all are revealed in the pages we read: in writing, Paul drew his own portrait; all that he said was original; it was a part of himself which fitted in exactly with every other part, completing the mosaic of his inner life. Shall we find it the same here? We may hope so; but all are not of this opinion; many commence their study of the subject now before us by carefully distinguishing the historian from the theologian. They ask that we should first inquire if we have here a really apostolic conception of Christian thought, one which can be placed on a par with the other analogous conceptions, or if that which we call the theology of John does not claim, in part at least, a yet higher name and dignity. In a word, is not this the teaching of a disciple who claims to

have received it directly from the lips of his Master? Have we
then a right to speak of it here separately? Would it not be
proper for us first to inquire whether we cannot distinguish
in it elements of various origin, and assign each to its peculiar
sphere? All these are questions which embarrass the historian
at the very outset of his work, and tend to complicate the
problem to be solved. The following chapters will be specially
devoted to the discussion of the facts which may determine
our final judgment upon these questions. The first and the
most important will treat of the special nature of the chief
work to which our attention will here be directed; the second
will guide us to the solution of the subsidiary but also very
essential question, what is the part to be assigned to the theologian or compiler of the system under analysis?

Lastly: our comprehension of the theology of Paul is greatly
facilitated by a series of circumstances which are wanting in
this new inquiry. That theology, as we have seen, has a
purely psychological basis; it appeals to the inner experiences,
which are or may be common to all; it deals with a number
of facts which come within the range of reason and reflection,
with dispositions of heart, convictions of conscience, desires,
necessities, tendencies, with all those faculties of the soul which
may come into direct contact with religion. Nor must we lose
sight of the very important circumstance, that the language
peculiar to this system has long been that of Protestant theology in general, and that all are familiar with its phraseology,
which has become, so to speak, an integral part of the
scientific life of our Church. The theology of John is, on the
other hand, far less familiar to the literary world or in daily
usage, and the points of contact it presents with the teaching
and language of the schools, are by no means so numerous.
The religious idea by which it is mainly characterized does not
attract us by the same eloquent presentation of it; it hides
itself, as it were, in an inner sanctuary; it must be sought in
order to be found; it communicates itself only to sympathetic
souls; it is less attractive to the speculative mind eager for
new discoveries, and rejoicing to see its horizon widening, than

to the heart which, full of holy desire, and gratefully accepting what it thus receives, is satisfied even in its restricted sphere. This theology has not, happily for itself, been found adaptable to the framework and formulas of ecclesiastical dogmatism; it has retained its virgin purity untouched by the scholasticism of the schools, and has thus to avoid the unhappy *mésalliance* which has done such deep injury to the theology of Paul; but, at the same time, it has almost eluded the grasp of historic science.

These remarks will help our readers to understand how many difficulties beset the very first steps of those who endeavour to explain the theological systems to which the name of the apostle John is commonly attached. We have not alluded to them here under any false impression of our own powers, or to lead any to suppose that we hold ourselves more competent than those who have gone before us, to treat adequately so complex a subject. On the contrary, we would claim the indulgence of an intelligent public on the score of these very perplexities, and ask a lenient judgment from those who think that we also fail to avoid the rocks on which others have made shipwreck. We shall be satisfied that some progress has been made in this study, if we can succeed in shedding new light on any obscure facts, in demonstrating the justice of some new points of view, in discovering, lastly, some yet hidden treasures of religious speculation and devout thought.

It is needless to say that the theology of John can be studied only in the writings comprised in the New Testament canon; we have no other sources. This is even more strictly the case here than in the system of Paul, of which we can at least find some reflected rays in later writers. The system of John only begins to exercise a direct influence upon ecclesiastical theology at the end of the second century. In the New Testament itself also, if we can sometimes trace traits of resemblance between terms familiar to John, and the formulas employed by other writers, it is impossible to make any use of them in the study of the theology now before us, because it is quite certain that this theology is the latest phase through which the teaching of the apostle passed. It is not the tradition of the Church alone (always doubtful authority) which affirms that the fourth gospel was not written till the close of the first century; that tradition is fully confirmed by the historical study of doctrine.

But, finally, which among the books of the New Testament are we here to follow as guides, and refer to as true sources ? Usually, in order to decide this question, scholars enter into a critical investigation of the genuineness of the writings commonly ascribed to John, and by this means they are led to prove the thesis either affirmative or negative, which by taste or by instinct they had adopted before taking up the inquiry. We have had occasion already to state that we adopt another course, and by the very arrangement of this book, our readers know the result to which this method has led us. In our view, the purely literary interest of the question is merged in the theological. It is the thoughts conveyed which we seek to ascertain, to arrange, and to study; we are not for the present concerned with chronological facts or proper names; the conviction, which modern science has not been yet able to shake, and which is still less influenced by the sympathies or antipathies of the Fathers of the Church,—the conviction, namely, that all the writings of the New Testament now ascribed to the apostle John, do really belong to the apostolic age, and to the sphere of the first disciples, is based in our mind essentially upon the nature and contents of these books, upon their spirit and method, upon the memories they reproduce, and the allusions they contain, and not upon any collection of fragmentary assertions as to their origin, made a hundred years later by some Christian logician.

The study of these ideas, however, leads us to a result which is not new to any, except to those who have never entered on the consideration of this subject for themselves, or who are wholly ignorant of the actual state of theological science. In truth, of all the authors who have spoken of a theology of John, or who have attempted to present any outline of it, there is not one who ventures to connect that name or that system with the substance both of the fourth gospel and of the Revelation. All, without exception, have been struck with the diversity of these two books, not so much as regards their form and subject (which would not be conclusive), but in the theological conceptions apparent in them. We, likewise, are constrained to recognize the impossibility of uniting in one outline and of assigning to the same sphere the two series of ideas, the two religious horizons,—the purely material, eschatological asceticism of the Revelation, and the contemplative and spiritual mysticism of the fourth gospel. One and the same man might have successively occupied both standpoints, but it must have been at two widely separated periods of his life, or by a sudden and radical revulsion of thought. Never in any case could the two conceptions have existed simultaneously in the same individual; never in any case may history confound what psychology divides. Thus in philosophy, or in any other science, it might happen that a thinker, a scholar, might pass from one system to another essentially different, that he might become himself the author of an entirely new system, after having been the disciple of one of earlier date; but the historian who on that account should amalgamate the two theories, would simply prove that he had comprehended neither.

We have therefore placed the Revelation among the documents produced by Judæo-Christianity in its most marked and unmodified form. We shall not further advert to it here; but we shall devote a special chapter to drawing a parallel between it and the gospel which is at present our principal study. This parallel will serve better than any quotations from the Fathers to sustain a critical judgment, and will fully demonstrate, if not the diversity of the authorship, at least that of the systems. As the latter alone belongs to the scope of this work, we shall be satisfied with this result.

Beside the gospel of John, we have an epistle, also anonymous, but which the same critical process will soon show to proceed, not only from the same school, but from the same author as the gospel. It is ordinarily regarded as a supplement to it, as containing its practical application. This is true in the sense that the epistle presupposes a certain familiarity of its readers with the ideas contained in the doctrinal work; but it does not follow that that work must have been the first written. The apostle, before embodying his teaching in writing, may have widely diffused it by oral preaching, and the general course of Christian literature leads us to conclude that this was actually the case. The epistle then takes for granted this previous knowledge, and there are reasons, which we shall have occasion to specify presently, which incline us to the opinion that the gospel is the expression of the apostle's thought in its most advanced stage of development and perfection. We shall give in our next chapter an outline of what appears to us the deeply thought-out plan of the gospel of John. We have not been able to discover any such premeditated order in his epistle. Its utterances are dictated on the one hand by personal relations, on the other by strongly marked religious feelings; but reflection and method are not called into play. We might almost say that the ideas conveyed are still in a state of formation, in an elementary condition, and have not yet found their final place or their scientific expression. We shall take the same opportunity to reply to some critical doubts relative to the identity of the authorship, based upon the very nature of the ideas presented in the two writings. The real difference between them results simply from the fact that in the gospel the writer always adheres to the theoretical point of view, while in the epistle he is dealing partially with experimental facts; our quotations, all taken from these two books, will show that this constitutes no difference in the doctrinal aspect. On the other hand, the epistle exhibits in portions a polemical character foreign to the gospel, but expressed rather by way of allusion than of direct attack. We shall not dwell on this here; we have already spoken of it in another section of our work, in connection with the conflict of religious opinions in the apostolic age.

To the other two anonymous epistles ascribed to John, we

shall not further advert. Their doctrinal value is comparatively insignificant. They are writings dictated by circumstances without any theological design. They contain some of the expressions peculiar to John, but no new ideas, nothing that could throw light upon his system. We shall therefore have no occasion to make use of them, and for this reason we may abridge the formula of our frequent quotations from the first epistle by omitting its distinguishing number.

CHAPTER II.

GENERAL AND PRELIMINARY STUDY OF THE GOSPEL ACCORDING TO JOHN.

THE word *gospel* given to the work with which we shall be chiefly occupied in this book, though fully justified according to its true sense, is not of a nature to give to a superficial reader of the New Testament a very just idea of what he will find to be the nature and contents of the writing thus described. In truth, in the common acceptation of it, the word *gospel* represents a book containing the life of the Saviour; and as we, for very natural reasons, learn in our childhood to know this history in the form in which it is given by the three synoptic evangelists, it is with this more popular form that the idea of the gospel is identified in the mind of most Christians. In this way, the current use of a term which has lost, as we know, its primitive meaning, generally determines the judgment passed upon John's writings; and this is the case to such an extent, that from the most ancient ecclesiastical writers to our own day,[1] the majority of theologians have not been able to comprehend and appreciate the true relation which exists between this scripture and the three others bearing the same name. And yet this book, to which none will refuse the name of *a* gospel, or rather of *the* gospel according to John, is essentially different from the books bearing the same title, to which tradition attaches the names of Matthew, Mark, and Luke. As in this work we intend to make a different use of this gospel from that which we have made of the three others, and to derive from it, not so much reminiscences of the teaching of the Master, as the elements of the system of the disciple, it is important first of all, both for ourselves and our readers, that we should clearly establish the grounds and the proofs of this difference. We do not intend to convey the idea that the difference is absolute, so as to exclude all points of contact. The narrative follows on both sides the same historical clue: it accompanies Jesus through His whole career, from the Jordan to Golgotha, and to His resurrection. Nevertheless, it is obvious that the relation of the first three gospels to each other is altogether different from that sustained to them by the fourth.

Let us first compare the opening page of each of three writings. We find Matthew and Mark entering immediately upon their subject, and commencing their narrative abruptly, without preamble, with the simple difference that Matthew carries the series of facts back to an earlier date than Mark. Luke begins with a preface, in which he alludes to his preliminary historical researches, and reassures the reader as to the authenticity of his sources of information. All three—the first two by their very silence, the third by his explicit introduction—show that biographical narration was their immediate purpose; and if they had also the further design of confirming or establishing a religious conviction, we may suppose that the attentive reader was to derive that conviction from the simple objective statement of the facts. With John it is otherwise. He also has his prologue; but that prologue is not written to give any account of preparatory studies undertaken by its author, with a view to the discharge of his duties as a historian. It is intended to introduce the reader directly to the history itself, by placing him at the highest standpoint of theological speculation, and thus preparing him at once for a doctrinal treatise, rather than for the recital of a narrator, of whom we lose sight in the events he records. This introductory remark will be amply confirmed when we come to examine the relation of the prologue to the book itself.

Let us pass on at once to a comparison of the historical records on either hand. In the synoptics, these are all wholly objective. The outward facts, the miracles and vicissitudes of the Saviour's life, form their basis and principal subject-matter. We note in them a certain desire after completeness, so that the standard of comparison between them has always been mainly the measure of their relative fulness in anecdotic detail. The very connecting links, the brief indications, the closing summaries, sometimes appended to more circumstantial narratives, are not of a nature to suggest that the writers had only chosen a few scattered facts, by way of illustration, from among a much larger number at their disposal. On the contrary, they seem uniformly to give all that they possess, this entire and complete communication of the facts being their direct end. Beside the record of events, properly so called, they give also discourses more or less numerous and extended. These are associated with the other facts, and are recorded on the same grounds; they are sometimes given at length, sometimes in an abridged form; they are introduced not always in the same order or connection; they may even be wholly omitted, without the general scope of the book being in any way affected. It is altogether different with the gospel of John. He narrates very few facts, and it is evident that these are never with him the principal thing. They form only the framework for more important pictures, for something more spiritual within,—for the religious ideas, in a word, of which they serve as the basis, the mirrors, the interpreters, and which they combine together into one whole. These ideas are contained in the discourses, which occupy the largest place in this gospel, and form its most essential part. It is evidently with a view to these discourses that the book is written. We cannot doubt that the author might have recorded in far greater number, particular scenes in the life of Jesus; this he did not need to tell us, but it is obvious that such a multiplication of facts did not seem to him necessary to the full attainment of his end.

We find discourses of the Saviour both in the synoptics and in John; these will supply our third point of comparison, the third capital difference to be indicated. Unquestionably, this difference is not such as to exclude all analogy, affinity, or even partial coincidence; but it is always very marked and very characteristic, both as to the subjects of which it treats, and the impression it produces. In the synoptics, the discourses turn generally on rules and principles of morality, conveyed in sentences without much connection, succeeding each other almost as by accident, and without any fixed order, but of a nature to fasten themselves readily in the memory, and to be retained without much effort. In John's gospel, the discourses have generally a doctrinal bearing; their expression is far from popular; in form there is more connection between the various elements, but they are not therefore either systematic or argumentative. For rhetorical ornament, the discourses in the synoptics use the form of parable, which so commends itself to the simplicity of the uncultivated mind, and is so powerful in convincing it; in John, we find the allegory, a form adapted to more mature reflection, and supplying it with a subject for instructive meditation. In the former they are practical, in the latter speculative; there they address themselves immediately to life and its daily relations; here they soar away, so to speak, into higher regions, and find their theme, not in experiences of common occurrence, but in inward contemplation, in the hidden treasures of the spirit. In the synoptics, the discourses form and fortify the conscience; in John, they enlighten the reason and enrich the soul. Those concern chiefly the relations of man with God, with himself, and with his fellows; these, the relations of Jesus with God and with humanity. In both cases, Jesus is the Teacher; but with John, He is at the same time, and almost exclusively, the subject of the teaching.* In a word, in the synoptical gospels, Jesus is the principal figure in a historical picture in which we see many secondary personages moving in the background; in the gospel of John, we have a portrait of Him alone, with no other addition than that of the garb He has Himself chosen.

* The discourses in John contain the development by our Lord Himself of that which underlies His teaching and claims in the synoptical gospels.—ED.

In general, the synoptics appear, on close examination, only repertories of details which combine into one whole, because they have all a common centre, though they are not all equally indispensable. We feel at once, as we read these books, that the impression they are calculated to produce would remain the same, should some of the details be removed, or a new series of similar details be added. Mark is not less complete than Matthew, Luke is not more complete than Mark, as to the doctrinal results which their respective books are designed to establish, or are simply adapted to confirm; and yet the number of scenes which they cause to pass before us is not the same. The fourth gospel, on the contrary, is one whole, all the parts of which are closely connected. Each has its proper and predetermined place; none could be indifferently removed from the completed picture. Each miracle, whether the total number of those recorded be small or great, is inserted at the exact place where it is needed; each discourse contributes its own quota, and in a fixed order, to the exposition of a totality of ideas which could neither be disconnected nor transposed. If, in the synoptics, memory alone has been called into exercise, to supply a mass of isolated details, brought together by a more or less fortuitous process of agglomeration, here it is the productive faculties of the mind which have been engaged in the construction of a work of admirable and perfect unity. The close relations which subsist between all the parts of the book of John are especially important in its exegesis. They point to a number of parallel passages which may be all the more advantageously compared together, that they were written by the evangelist for this very purpose. Thus the words recorded as those of John the Baptist,* contain all the elements of the explanation of the text concerning the birth of water and of the Spirit.† Thus, again, the idea of union with Christ is introduced first by a series of images, and thus held forth to the yearning, secret

---

* John i. 30, 33.
† John iii. 5, 6.

desire of the heart, to be afterwards more clearly propounded and presented without a veil to the soul prepared to receive it.* There is especially a remarkable connection between the prologue (which we find in the first five verses) and the body of the gospel. This prologue states by anticipation, and very briefly, by means of abstract and metaphysical formulas, that which is afterwards reproduced at length· in its concrete and historical development. The Word spoken of in the prologue appears in the gospel as the Son of God; His pre-existence, expressed in popular language, is His coming down from heaven; His divine nature is explained as oneness with the Father. The Word had been the life of the universe; the Saviour would be in a more special sense the life of the spiritual world; He had been the light shining in darkness, and was about to descend in human form to shed His brightness over all that darkened the horizon of humanity. Finally, the thesis with which the prologue concludes, that the darkness would not accept the light, prefigures the death to which the divine element would temporarily succumb in its conflict with the world, and the end of the history is thus anticipated, a clear proof that it was not an accident, but a necessity.

We have said above that the facts recorded by John are fewer in number than in the other gospels, and occupy a position secondary to that of the doctrinal discourses. This remark, however, is far from exhausting our thought, and does not adequately characterize the fourth gospel from a literary point of view. We must further observe the directly spiritual and ideal significance of the scenes described by the theological compiler. We shall perceive at once that with him the *idea* is the one essential thing, to which the history serves only as the frame or vesture. We shall confine ourselves here to a few examples, since the analysis of the plan of the book will give us presently another opportunity of dwelling on this important fact. The two representations, the one of the unbelief of the Jews demanding a sign, the other of the faith of the simple Samaritan woman, produce by their

* John iv. 14; vi. 27, and foll.; 51, and foll.; vii. 37; viii. 12; xii. 44.

very juxtaposition an effect with which we cannot fail to be struck. The very same sentence pronounced by the Saviour upon Judaism, awakens in her an emotion which leads her to life, while in them it provokes the clamour for the death of Christ, which will end in their own condemnation. It is by the side of Jacob's well, where Judah and Ephraim once peacefully watered their flocks, that Jesus proclaims the reconciliation of the two divided Churches, which henceforth were to draw new spiritual life from a common source. The story of the multiplication of the loaves is here only the transparent medium to convey the idea of the spiritual sustenance offered by Christ; and the author is so much in haste to come to the development of this idea, that he falls behind the other evangelists in the exactness of his narrative in detail. The healing of the man born blind is immediately translated into a fact of much wider significance and more general application. Lazarus coming forth from the tomb is a living hieroglyph in which we read the words of Christ, "I am the Resurrection and the Life." We do not make these observations with any view to call in question the objective reality of the facts, and we are far from holding that John himself, like another Philo, sacrifices the real to the ideal. But it is an indubitable truth that, in the context of his gospel, miracles appear rather as the symbolical acts of the old prophets, or brilliant images of the perpetual miracle of the manifestation of Christ. There are, however, other examples in which the facts of history are altogether effaced by the doctrinal idea. Thus the narrative of the other gospels concerning the miracle of the Saviour's conception in the womb of the Virgin, is substituted here by the prologue which bears witness to the eternal existence of the Word. The historical enigma of the annunciation becomes the theological problem of the incarnation. History is transmuted into doctrine.

It will be doubtless objected that the fourth gospel resumes, at least in its latter portion, the character of a simple narrative, and that the importance of this part should modify our judgment of the whole. We do not think so. It is true that superficial readers will discern in it nothing more than the scenes of the passion and the resurrection, described almost as in the other gospels; but a little deeper attention will discover here the same relation between the historical and the ideal which we have already noted as the characteristic of this record. In the synoptics, the closing events of the Lord's life, as materials of history, are facts just like the rest, though of deeper importance to the Church and to the world's future. The reader is only prepared for them by the casual mention of the hatred of the Pharisees, and by some predictions of the Saviour's, to which the disciples do not listen, or which they fail to comprehend, and which we ourselves as we read them are scarcely more able to credit. The final catastrophe does not then appear in the synoptics as the inevitable result of the antecedents recorded. It takes us by surprise, even as it came upon the disciples with all the terrors of a climax as cruel as it was unexpected. In John's gospel it is otherwise. Even supposing the reader to know nothing of the history, he would anticipate the issue; he reads it in the prologue. The whole series of theological ideas, contained in the book from beginning to end, foreshadow the consummation even more distinctly than the narrative itself, which also is uniformly characterized by this one marked design—to show the moral necessity of the death of Christ, and the antipathy of the world towards Him. At the close of these discourses, the death and resurrection of Jesus have virtually already become facts to readers who have understood what they read. He has already returned, no more to leave them; and the three closing chapters are a sort of appendix (we might almost say a pleonasm) translating the ideal into the real. But to this point we shall have occasion to advert again.

If the remarks just made are well founded, (and it would be easy to corroborate them by others of a similar nature,) they may furnish us with a basis and starting-point for a very clear and unique judgment upon the nature and tendency of the fourth gospel, namely, that that gospel is essentially a doctrinal treatise. It is so in a higher degree than any other book of the New Testament, not excepting the epistles of Paul, which have not generally this character, and the theology of which is only dictated by accidental occasions. It cannot be justly placed in the category of historical writings, with the first three gospels; for it does not contain an account of the life of Jesus, but an exposition of the Christian faith, of which the person of Jesus is the central point. It is not a narrative, but a sermon in the highest sense of the word. It is not a biography, but a theological treatise; it is not, as has been said, a methodical history of the resistance offered by the Jews to their despised and rejected Saviour, but a picture of the opposition of the world to the light which comes from God, full of grace and truth. In a word, that which is most essential in this book is not the facts which memory might preserve and reproduce, but the ideas engendered by speculation, conceived by the soul and born of faith. In form, the exposition of doctrine is associated with certain facts and discourses of the Saviour; from these discourses mainly, the elements of the system have been derived; the system itself is given in an epitomized form in a prologue, which again is not the preface of a historian or of a mere writer, but the programme of a thinker and theologian.

We repeat, then, that it is not history, but theology, which the author designs to give us. In thus expressing our opinion, we do not intend to question the authenticity of the facts recorded, still less to forget that this theology itself rests upon a historical basis. Our book is, on the contrary, a striking proof of the fact that all truly Christian theology is built upon such a foundation, and that this is the special point of distinction between it and a theology merely natural or philosophical.

We might perhaps content ourselves with what has just been said, as establishing our right to treat thus separately the theological contents of the fourth gospel. At the risk, however, of taxing the patience of our readers, we are anxious to establish this right by yet other considerations, which, if they have no other merit, may claim at least that of originality. We shall occupy with these the remainder of this chapter and the chapter following.

We shall not dwell further on the object the author proposed to himself in writing this book. We have already by impli-cation replied to this question, which has greatly embarrassed our predecessors, because they started from a purely historical point of view, and endeavoured in this way to explain the special features of a work which, thus regarded, could not but remain inexplicable. Nothing can be more unworthy of the subject, and indeed more false, than all that has been said by the Fathers of the Church and their successors, down to the most modern times, with reference to the supposed design of John to supplement the three synoptical gospels. The history of the canon, and doctrinal exegesis, are equally opposed to such opinions, which would long ago have passed into oblivion, had they not been supported by the influence of tradition, which often holds the greatest ascendant over those who affect to despise it. Nothing can be more untrue than the hypothesis, or rather than the numerous hypotheses, built upon the imagined polemical design of the evangelist, whose writings are supposed to be directed against various sects, some real, some imaginary, with whom on the same theory he had come in contact. Doubtless in theology, as in all the sciences, when a principle is laid down there is the implicit or explicit contradition of an opposite principle; but there is a wide difference between this and a direct attack upon an adver-sary ; and the few isolated theses taken from this book, to prove an opposition, which has been traced in the history of the doctrine, or discovered by the imagination of the learned, cannot be sufficient evidence that such a theologian as John owes his immortal work to so low an inspiration.

He himself plainly states his purpose in his concluding words : "These things are written, that ye might believe that Jesus is the Christ, the Son of God; and that believing ye might have life through His name."* Let it not be said that this is the aim of all the evangelists, and that we must perforce seek some-thing special in the work of the beloved disciple. First, we may rejoin that in presence of so categorical an assertion, all necessity for this inquiry must be done away; but in reality

* John xx. 31.

the words just quoted are no mere commonplace. It must be remembered that this whole book is devoted to the exposition, definition, and inculcation of the three fundamental ideas of the Son of God, of faith, and of life; and it will then be at once obvious that it well deserved to be written, that these might be transfused into the inner life of the Church and of its members. This is, beyond question, a design different from that of Matthew, who aims to prove by facts of detail the fulfilment of the prophecies, or from the critical and chronological scope of Luke's gospel, who was mainly concerned to set before his friend Theophilus an exact account of the things that had come to pass. We return then to our principal thesis: the primary aim of the author of the fourth gospel was theological.

If this is so, we are authorized in inquiring what is the plan of his work. We shall not look for a logical method, proceeding by progressive reasonings, and rearing a scaffolding of ideas more or less artificial. We shall bear in mind that John seeks to present a theology which shall appeal rather to the heart than to the head; we shall still more carefully remember that he bases his theology upon a history, the outline of which is given him, and which it is not in his option to change. Nevertheless we shall look for a plan in his work, but a plan formed upon a theological not a historical principle. It will not be the chronological plan which the most highly esteemed of modern exegetes have thought they could trace in it. Applying the measure of a dwarf to a giant, they have allowed themselves to be guided by the few chronological indications of the book, by the mention of certain feast days, in the proper division of the text. We have elsewhere condemned this mode of treatment; and now that our opinion is beginning to gain ground, we need not enlarge upon it further. The evidence of the plan we are about to indicate will remove any necessity for argument on the point.

The work which we are analyzing is composed of two elements of different nature, but closely connected in the mind of the author, namely, the history of Jesus, and the religious conception sustained by it. The plan which we seek has its origin in the relation of the latter with the former. The writer would communicate to the world the result of his reflections upon the person of the Saviour, and upon His relations with the community of believers; he would at the same time bear witness to the new life manifested in himself, which was his joy, and in which he desired that those to whom he wrote should share. All this was based upon the memories of several years of close communion with Jesus, whom he regarded as the witness in His own cause most worthy of credit.[*] The history of Jesus, and especially the teaching which formed its most important part, was thus the substance of his work. That work must be cast in a historic mould. The subjectivity of the author appears in it sometimes directly, more often indirectly.

The combination of this twofold point of view, the historical and the theological, leads him to divide his book into three parts, preceded by a prologue.

The first part treats of the relations of the Incarnate Word with the world (chapters i.—xii.) We there see Him first introduced or proclaimed by John the Baptist, and attesting His mission by miracle and by His knowledge of the secrets of the heart, by His prophetic zeal and by predictions of the future (chapters i., ii.) He is next represented in His contact with the different classes of men who seek Him, and in this aspect even schismatics and Gentiles, in their simplicity, prove better disposed towards the Saviour than the theological erudite or the nationally prejudiced of the orthodox people (chapters iii., iv.) Then follows the picture of the opposition Christ encounters in the Jewish world; and here, the principal facts which form the essence of the Gospel—the mission of the Saviour, the ideas of faith, of the Spirit, of life, liberty, and light—are developed in a series of discourses, which succeed each other in the order determined by the theological point of view (chapters v., vi.) Lastly, we have opened before us the prospect of the calling of the Gentiles (chapter xii.) The speakers in these various scenes are by no means personages brought together by chance, but the representatives of certain classes of men with whom Jesus and

---

* John viii. 14.

His doctrine stood in relations more or less friendly or hostile. There is the Pharisee, who ignores the very'elements of true religion; the Samaritan woman, sunk in ignorance, whose heart opens to the faith; there are the Jews, who are won over as individuals to the side of Christ by evidence, or who are moved in tumultuous masses by the sway of evil passions and prejudices; there are the few intimate friends whom Jesus attaches to Himself, but whom He fails to raise effectually out of their former sphere; there are, lastly, the Gentile strangers, by whom the hope of salvation is embraced at the very moment of its rejection by Israel. We shall speak in the next chapter of the historical importance of all these personages. The first part of the book concludes with a few lines in which the writer gives at once a summary of the historical result, and a recapitulation of the principal ideas of his teaching (chapter xii. 37—50).

The second part (xiii.—xvii.) shows us the Saviour in the closest relations with His disciples. This might be described as the practical part of the gospel, the realization of the religious ideas in the life of the individual. Previously, Jesus had appeared engaged in conflict with the world; here He is seen in the inner circle of those who love Him; there He had shown the power of His presence over unbelief; here He shows its significance to faith; there judgment threatened those who turned away from Him; here life beams and brightens around those who seek Him. On the one hand there is doctrine, on the other morality; but these hackneyed words are far from doing justice to the thought of the writer, or to our own; we are not dealing here either with a body of articles of faith or of moral precepts. Unhappily, the schools have failed to invent a term aptly conveying the comparison between this theory and this application. In the earlier portion, the whole country is the scene of the life of Jesus; in the later, it is but one room. At first we see gathered crowds around the Teacher, hearing often without listening, still less comprehending; now it is the little band of disciples who receive the Master's words, if not with full apprehension of their meaning, at least with all readiness of heart. Doubtless, this sublime symbolism will be recognized only by those who are willing to admit that, in the intention of the writer, the Twelve are not the sole hearers of these last discourses, but that they represent all those who in any age and in any place are truly united to the Lord. Others of course may, if they please, read here a simple narrative.

The last portion (chapters xviii.—xx.) shows us the climax of the two relations previously established, the twofold crisis of the divine tragedy. The Son of God had come to draw a line of separation among men. This is effected in that He Himself succumbs outwardly in His contest with the world, and remains dead to all the unbelieving, while He rises victorious for those who believe in Him, so that the former become themselves the heirs of the death they had prepared for Him, while the latter inherit the life which is His by right, and which He was willing to give to all. Thus is this history, from the opening to the close, the mirror of religious truths.*

* F. Godet, in his admirable Commentary on St. John's Gospel, gives a different, and, as it seems to me, a more satisfactory, arrangement of its contents. He premises that preceding attempts at arrangement had shown that there are three principal factors in the history of our Lord as presented by St. John : the manifestation of Jesus as the Messiah and the Son of God ; the birth, growth, and completion of faith in Him among His disciples ; and the parallel development of unbelief among the mass of the Jewish people. These three elements, he thinks, appear side by side in the Gospel, which he divides into five parts.

Chapter I. 19—IV. The manifestation of our Lord as the Messiah; the origin and early growth of faith ; the first faint symptoms of unbelief.

V.—XII. The energetic and rapid development of unbelief; the conspicuous revelation of Jesus as the Son of God in the presence of antagonism ; the gradual growth of the disciples' faith.

XIII.—XVII. The energetic and decisive development of faith ; the supreme revelation of Jesus to His disciples by which this development was produced ; the expulsion of the disciple in whom unbelief had found access into the inner circle of Christ's friends.

XVIII., XIX. The triumph of unbelief in the crucifixion of our Lord; the calm revelation of His glory in the very depth of the darkness ; the silent growth of faith among those few disciples who were capable of recognizing His glory in the supreme crises of His history.

XX., XXI. The appearances of the risen Lord complete the revelation of His glory, and the victory of faith over the last remains of doubt among the apostles.—Ed.

CHAPTER III.

OF THE DISCOURSES OF JESUS IN THE FOURTH GOSPEL.

IT has just been remarked that the fourth gospel is composed essentially of sermons, or, to speak more exactly, of conversations in which Jesus is the chief speaker, teaching, prophesying, correcting, rebuking as the need arises, and thus everywhere presenting Himself as the revealer and interpreter of truth. All this being perfectly natural, and at first sight perfectly analogous with that which we read in the other evangelists, it was easy to draw the conclusion that the substance of these discourses had simply to be combined with those of the other narratives, to form the basis of a complete exposition of the Lord's teaching.

This has not been the opinion, however, of all critics, and the method which we ourselves adopt in the present work, and with which our readers are already familiar, shows that we are not prepared to fuse together the elements derived from the two sources.   We are about to speak of a theology of John as we have spoken of a Pauline and a Judæo-Christian theology; but we should never be able to give anything like a systematic view of it, if it could be shown that the essentially doctrinal contents of the fourth gospel are not available in the building up of such a system, on the ground that they had been used elsewhere, and could not therefore be here reproduced under a new name.   Our first inquiry must be whether we have a right to say that the apostle John, like his colleague Paul, has expressed the fundamental ideas of Scripture with more or less of individuality; and the reply to this question depends on the judgment we may form of the direct part to be assigned to him in the presentation of the discourses now before us. If the author of the fourth gospel has only literally written down the words supplied to him by his own memory or that of his friends, this literary labour will not entitle him to the name of a theologian, which the Church has always given him in preference to all his colleagues; and the few lines which would then remain to us as his own, are not sufficiently full to give the data for any complete system. His claim to a place in such a history as that we are now writing, and to a conspicuous place as a star of the first magnitude, must rest upon the freedom with which we suppose him to have handled the materials of which his gospel is composed.

The question is not a new one; it has often been debated in the course of this century, and variously resolved. Very excellent things have been said on either hypothesis. Nevertheless the subject does not seem to us to be exhausted. Neither the doubts of one party, nor the explanations of another, have as yet fully satisfied us, and we ask permission to state the reasons which have decided us to endeavour ourselves to explain the facts, and to establish some definite conclusions from them.

Many writers have said that it is scarcely probable, if not impossible, that discourses like those we have before us now, could have been preserved in their integrity, and without modification, during the long interval that elapsed between the death of Jesus and the composition of the gospel. Human memory, it is said, can well retain, for example, parables, isolated sentences, which impress themselves on the memory as much by their sharply cut and sometimes paradoxical form, as by the simplicity and self-evidence of the truths they proclaim; but not lengthened discourses, in which the sentences succeed each other sometimes without apparent connection, and without the links of serried argument which might aid the recollection. To this it is replied that John may possibly have taken notes on the spot of the words that fell from the lips of Jesus; that

23 *

this supposition would explain the particular character of the discourses we possess, which resemble rather simple outlines than a literal and complete rendering. The objection and the reply are equally wide of the mark. The reply in no way explains how it is that the fourth gospel contains no discourses of the kind found in the synoptics. It rests, moreover, upon a purely gratuitous supposition, and one alien to the whole spirit of the age of Jesus Christ. In fact, there is not a trace either in the history nor in the habits of the disciples and their contemporaries, of such an immediate, we might almost say stenographic, preservation of discourses and conversations, which were not delivered in set and solemn form, but arose spontaneously out of the necessities of the moment. The nature of the relations of the disciples with their Master, their Messianic hopes, the total absence of any fear of separation from Him, render this supposition finally untenable. But the objection itself rests upon two other hypotheses no less inadmissible. The one supposes that the apostle wrote his gospel when he was nearly a hundred years old. This is one of those absurdities which the mental indolence of Protestant orthodoxy has accepted with so much more of idle tradition, in relation to apostolic history, and which is not worthy of serious discussion. The other theory, still more arbitrary, and if possible less psychological, supposes that the author made no attempt to reproduce the discourses of the Saviour till the time of the final composition of this work,—that is to say, that he allowed a lapse of time which could not fail to obliterate them from his memory. Whether these discourses are literally authentic or not, they unquestionably contain the elements of the theology of the writer, his own convictions, whether derived from other teaching or freely formed in his own mind. Now it is evident that in his capacity as an apostle, evangelist, Christian preacher, he must have had occasion a hundred times to unfold, enforce, and explain his views, both briefly and in detail, before the time, more or less remote, when he judged it expedient to embody them in writing. The supposed length of the interval, which is urged as making it impossible that he should have retained such full and exact memories, thus proves to be an objection of little weight.

There is another critical argument which we will endeavour to weigh with equal impartiality. The style of the discourses of Jesus Christ in the fourth gospel is said, on the one hand, to be essentially different from that of the discourses transmitted by the synoptical gospels, and on the other to be absolutely identical with the style of John himself, as we are acquainted with it in the chapters in which he is himself the speaker, and especially in his epistles. We can trace the same pen throughout, and the same spirit directs it from the beginning to the end. To this it is replied that John had so thoroughly imbibed the spirit of his Master, that he had caught His very style, and the resemblance therefore only shows the profound impression made upon him by the teachings of the Saviour. This reply is specious, but it goes far beyond the mark, and yet is insufficient; for, on the one hand, it does not explain why John the Baptist, in the fourth gospel, speaks absolutely the same language as Jesus Christ and His disciples—language at once metaphysical and Christian, and singularly different from that attributed to him by Luke and Matthew.* Again, if the evangelist formed his style on that of his Master, it must be at once admitted that the teaching of the Saviour had a uniform and strongly marked character, such as we find here; but what then becomes of the authenticity of the discourses in the other gospels, the style of which is entirely different? Lastly, we would observe that this second apologetic reply is in contradiction with the first, which supposed notes taken on the spot, and subsequently reproduced

---

* This objection rests on the testimony of the Baptist contained in the closing verses of chapter iii. A very large number of authorities, however, can be alleged in support of the opinion that the testimony of the Baptist does not extend beyond verse 30, and that the "language at once metaphysical and Christian" in verses 31—36 ought not to be regarded as though it were intended to be a report of the testimony of the Baptist, but as the Evangelist's own development of the Baptist's words. On the other hand, Godet contends with considerable force that there is no reasonable objection to accepting verses 31—36 as the final statement of the Baptist's own faith concerning our Lord.—ED.

in their full and final form. In such a case the compiler is
guided, not by the style of his model, but by the more or less
ample notes he has preserved of his teaching. The objection
itself is by no means without foundation, but it goes too far.
The tone of the two books from which we chiefly derive our
summary of the theology of John is indeed generally the same
throughout, and in all the discourses designed to impart
evangelical truth, whether it be Jesus, or John the Baptist, or
the apostle himself who speaks. But in connection with this
fact there are others which it is important not to pass by.
It can be shown that the learned language of the schools, and
the more popular language of practical life, are kept more
or less distinct: the former is used only by the theorist, the
writer of the prologue. This we have already observed, in
the preceding chapter, in characterizing the relation between
the prologue and the historical narrative. We may here
remind the reader more particularly that the name of the
Word, which raises the Christian idea into the region of
speculative science, does not occur in any of the discourses
uttered by the Saviour; we are even prepared to venture the
opinion that in these discourses the abstract notion of the Word
is replaced by the more concrete idea of the Spirit. In the same
way, the designation the *only Son*, in which we cannot but
recognize a metaphysical idea (though rationalism assigns to it
a merely ethical significance), is only employed by the author
when he himself speaks in the name of his system. Thus, again,
the familiar formula, "*In the beginning was the Word*," with
which the prologue commences, and which is the distinct affirmation of the pre-existence of the Son, only occurs in the discourses of Jesus in the form of popular circumlocutions in which
it loses its exactness and full significance.* Lastly, we shall
find more than once that expressions ascribed to the Saviour
in the discourses addressed by Him to the people, do not exhaust
all that is contained in the premises of the prologue, nor deduce
from them all their logical consequences. Thus the Father is
said to be greater than the Son;† the glory of the pre-existent

* John iii. 13 ; viii. 58 ; xvii. 5, 24.   † John xiv. 28.

Word is represented as having been bestowed on Him by the love of the Father;[*] and there are constantly recurring examples of the same kind. Theological interpretation may perhaps find means to reconcile such passages with the system; but it is none the less true that the discourses which contain them appear independent of the system. We may perhaps conclude (with some exceptions) that the compiler has not actually changed the original colour of these discourses, while bringing them into closer contact with his own systematic forms.

A third objection raised against the authenticity of these discourses consists in the declaration that the difference between them and those of the synoptical gospels is absolute and radical, and that criticism in inquiring into the original character of the teaching of Jesus, which was of a nature to produce such a marvellous effect upon His hearers, must choose between those majestic popular sayings, at once so simple and sublime, which are still the inexhaustible spring of the religious instruction of the masses, and those discourses, more profound perhaps, but also more mysterious, which constantly gave rise to the grossest misconceptions, and which are to this day the problems of Christian science. To this it has been replied that John's design was to complete the narrative of his predecessors, and that his own individuality led him to treat mainly of the more elevated portion of the teaching of the Master, on which his colleagues had too slightly touched. This reply seems to us in no degree satisfactory. We have already, in the previous chapters, reduced to its true value this theory of the design of the writer of the fourth gospel; only the slaves of the most trite patristic tradition will now sustain so groundless an assertion. As to the individuality of the writer, and his personal preferences, it is at once evident that there is a logical fallacy in the argument; for we know the characteristics of the writer from the book, the particular nature of which is the problem to be solved, and it is not by moving in a circle that we arrive at any solid evidence. But we have a better rejoinder to this third objection. While we do not deny the difference alleged, we do

[*] John xvii. 24.

hold it to be less absolute than is supposed. In our second book, in giving our exposition of the teaching of Jesus, while guarding ourselves against casting into the same mould the principles of a religion preached to the common people, and the abstract ideas of a theology presented to thinking men, we have more than once found occasion to bring the words of John into comparison with those of the synoptics, and to discover analogies and relations between them, which place beyond a doubt the identity of the starting-point of all these theologian-narrators. We need not here reproduce the examples already quoted. We may simply remark that we do not attach undue importance to a few isolated sentences, common to all the gospels, and which may have been derived from the common stock of tradition.* Neither shall we insist more strongly on passages or fragments of discourses contained in the narratives of the first three evangelists, and recalling more or less the mystical colouring which is the special characteristic of the discourses given in the fourth gospel,—the characteristic in view of which the asserted difference has been most strongly maintained. The presence of these thoughts, in a fragmentary form, in the other gospels, is an evidence that the elements in question were not foreign to the discourses of the Saviour, but that they were beyond the apprehension of a certain proportion of His hearers, and that tradition has found less facility in transmitting them. It is interesting to observe here, that in many cases, when the parallelism is more evident, the mystical depth of the thought as expressed by John, is partially lost in the rendering of the other biographers.† The fact is that the

* Compare, for example, John ii. 19, with Matt. xxvi. 61; John iv. 22, with Mark xiv. 58; John iv. 35, with Matt. ix. 37; John iv. 44, with Matt. xiii. 57; John v. 17, with Mark ii. 27; John x. 16, with Matt. xxii. 1, and foll.; John xii. 8, with Matt. xxvi. 11; John xii. 36, with Luke xvi. 8; John xiii. 16, xv. 20, with Matt. x. 24; John xiii. 34, with Matt. xxii. 37; John xvi. 2, with Matt. xxiv. 9; John xx. 23, with Matt. xvi. 19.

† Compare, for example, John xiii. 20, with Matt. x. 40; Matt. x. 39, and John xii. 25; Matt. v. 6 (Luke vi. 21), and John vii. 37; vi. 57, and foll.; Matt. xxvi. 64, and John xvii. 2, 4; Matt. xii. 8, etc., and John v. 16, and foll.; Matt. xvi. 6—12, and John vi. 27.

Saviour's words contained a really inexhaustible treasure of truth, of which each hearer apprehended a portion greater or less in the measure of his moral or intellectual capacity. If illustrations of this from Scripture were wanting, we should still have abundant evidence of the fact in the numberless homiletic explanations which, in spite of their variety and often utter inadequacy to the real scope of the text treated, yet serve to the edification of the community. Lastly, to return to our subject, it will be superfluous to seek in the gospel of John for parallels to compare with certain passages, no doubt sufficiently isolated in the synoptical gospels,* which, might seem to be borrowed from the fourth. It might be said that this gospel, as a whole, is only a commentary on the last two passages cited in the note, and that the depths which we discover in it, while they were not fully appreciated, were at the same time not wholly hidden from the others.

As we are here writing, not an apologetic discourse, but a literary criticism, we shall not pursue further the train of ideas which crowd upon the mind in this connection. Were it otherwise, we might stay to compare the great variety of subjects treated in the synoptical discourses, with the marked uniformity of those recorded by John; we might show how all the thoughts presented by him converge to one centre, while in the other gospels they diffuse themselves radially over a wide area; we might combine these facts with the respective purposes of the writers; we might show once more that John did not propose to make his work a biographical memoir, but a book of theology, and that it was therefore natural he should bring into prominence only that aspect of the teaching of the Saviour which bore most directly on his own speculative idea. We might observe, further, the close relations often existing between the most elevated and mystical discourses, and the very simple historical facts, natural or supernatural, attested by the other records; we should find it easy to show how it was the habit of Jesus to use every occasion to raise the minds of His disciples to considerations of a higher order, and how under

* Matt. xxviii. 18, 20; xi. 25, and foll.; Luke x. 20, and foll.

His handling the simplest objects became the basis for spiritual
teaching appreciable by the least instructed minds. The very
elevation of the ideas presented ought to be an additional
guarantee of their authenticity. The history bears uniform
witness to the distance which divided the disciples from the
Master, to their slowness to apprehend His teaching or to enter
into His representations of the future. It would be difficult to
attribute to any one of them conceptions so pure as those by
which the fourth gospel is distinguished. Assuredly, were the
writer Hellenist philosopher or Galilean fisherman, if this eschatology so completely free from Judaism, this spiritual conception
of miracles, this depth of religious feeling, were his own creation, and did not come to him from the lips of Jesus, then the
disciple is greater than the Master. But he is not so; far from
it. We shall find that when he speaks his own thoughts only,
he is swayed by popular prejudice, misapprehends the sense
and scope of some of the Saviour's words, takes a lower range
of theologic thought, and thus by the very contrast with himself, gives us the measure of the greatness of his ideal.*

* See, for example, John v. 4, a passage the genuineness of which has
been vainly contested; ii. 21; vii. 39; xi. 51; many quotations from
the Old Testament, compared with the Hebrew text, and with the parallel
passages, xii. 15, 40; xix. 36, 37, etc., and chapter xiv. of this book, to
follow. [John v. 4 is rejected as a gloss by a very large number of critics
who were certainly not led to reject it by dogmatic reasons. John ii. 21
contains a very profound truth, which the apostle may have learnt from
the very lips of his Master after the Resurrection; all that the Temple
had been in type and symbol the body of Christ was in reality; moreover, in putting Christ to death, the Jews really destroyed their Temple
—it was no longer the home of God; the risen Christ, with whom all
that believe are spiritually united, henceforth became the true Temple of
the Most High. John vii. 39 is a comment—not on verse 37, but on verse
38—in harmony with all our Lord's teaching concerning the transcendent
blessing which was to come upon His disciples after His resurrection.
The justification of xi. 51 would exceed the limits of a note; but the
principle on which the words of St. John rest is simply this—that the
high-priest, according to the idea of his office, stood between the Jewish
race and God; in this supreme moment of the history of the Jewish
race he was led—notwithstanding his own unfaithfulness—to affirm the
real value of the act to which he wickedly consented. The discussion of
the quotations from the O. T. would require many pages instead of a few
lines.—ED.]

For the rest, the objections commonly made against the discourses of the fourth gospel, have not the logical force with which they have been credited, and err especially by the inadequate appreciation of facts. The question, however, is not exhausted by the remarks just made; and as far as our reasoning has yet brought us, the method of this history of apostolic theology would not be justified. It remains for us to show, by other considerations, that we may justly regard the discourses of John as having been cast into their present mould by the author of the gospel himself, and consequently as admirably adapted to further the object of this work, as that has been already defined; it is in these discourses mainly that we shall find the most systematic presentation of Christian theology according to John's conception of it. That which we have already established as to the plan of the fourth gospel, might, indeed, fully suffice to the demonstration of our thesis, since no one can by possibility suppose that Jesus in His teaching, which was always dependent on circumstances, could have followed a plan so carefully predetermined. But we shall not dwell further upon this point, which is no longer a matter of question in exegetical science. We shall proceed to show that it is not the only fact on which our opinion is based.

We need not detain our readers over discourses or conversations during which the writer was not present, and which could, therefore, have come to his knowledge only through the more or less detailed reports of others. It is evident that the version we possess of these cannot be supposed to be a literal record. Such is the interview with Nicodemus, and the discourse of John the Baptist, given in the same chapter; such also the conversation with the Samaritan woman. The importance of this remark is, however, small in comparison with that of some others yet to be made. These discourses and conversations, as well as a number of others, bear generally the character of a brief summary, taking up a few main points which are not even connected together. In many cases, the interpreter seeks with difficulty, and not without danger of mistake, the connecting links which are indispensable to the logical understanding of the teaching as it is here given. Doubtless, these connecting links were present to the mind of the compiler; that he leaves it to other theologians to discover them, is only one proof the more that it was not his object to give a simple historical narration suited to the many; and if he does not always succeed in making his meaning clear, even to the initiated, this further proves that Jesus, who never had an auditory fully capable of apprehending Him, cannot have used in His teaching the very phrases here given.

Again: in some of the discourses, passages occur in relation to which exegetes have been divided in opinion as to who is the speaker intended by the evangelist. It is exceedingly difficult, if not impossible, to decide, with regard to some of these, whether the writer is himself making reflections on the subject just treated, or whether the previous speaker is continuing to speak.* Some have insisted strongly on the necessity of distinguishing in these passages the various elements of the discourse; others have passed over this diversity very lightly. We agree with neither. It is very far from our intention to accuse the author of negligence in the presentation, or of want of skill in the appreciation of historical facts. We simply affirm positively, as a solution of the whole difficulty, that he does not intend in these passages to narrate a history, but to present a doctrinal idea. That Jesus did once hold a conversation by night with one Nicodemus, and that the subject of this conversation was such and such, is not the main point with him—not that which he is anxious to communicate to us. His purpose is that we should know that Jesus taught the necessity of the soul's regeneration, and of His own death for the salvation of men. This is with him the essential

* We have here principally in view the close of the discourse of Jesus with Nicodemus (John iii. 16—21), and the close of John the Baptist's discourse (iii. 31—36). Verses 16—18 of the first chapter are also often cited, but erroneously. In relation to these, the evangelist is not responsible for the misconceptions or embarrassments of the exegetes. By recurring in verse 19 to the testimony of the precursor, given in verse 15, he shows clearly that the three preceding verses, which are the subject in dispute, do not belong to that testimony.

thing; these are the truths he often after reiterates; they have become integral parts of his spiritual life. Whether it is Jesus who Himself speaks directly, or John who reproduces the thoughts of his Master, the result is the same as far as his purpose as a writer of theology is concerned. He thus insensibly drops the thread of the history; he breaks through the bounds of the narrative form he has adopted, as he finds it too strait for his object; he returns unconsciously to his true element, which is that of doctrinal exposition. Thus we observe that Nicodemus soon passes out of view; we see him come, we see nothing of his going. We are told nothing of the result of the interview. Nicodemus is forgotten; having introduced the doctrinal teaching, he has served the purpose, not of the historian who would have traced out the story to the close, but of the theologian who no longer requires him. Thus Nicodemus is not brought before us for his own sake, or as a personage of any historical importance; this Nicodemus might be any one of us, or rather it is the theology of the school which requires that Jesus should expound the first elements of the truth. The close of the interview we learn not from anything in the narrative, but from the teaching of our own consciousness. After this, who will attempt to maintain that this identification of the person of the evangelist with that of his Master, only commences with the sixteenth verse of the chapter? Is not this community of thought and conviction, this analogy of relation, clearly expressed in the plural of the eleventh verse? Will it be said that Jesus speaks of Himself in the plural? or does He here associate with Himself John the Baptist, or the prophets of the Old Testament, as has been averred by some exegetes? Surely not. It is the apostle, who in the lively consciousness of his union with the Saviour involuntarily communicates to the world his own similar and not less sorrowful experience.* That which has just been said on the subject of Nicodemus applies in like manner to all analogous scenes. Everywhere we see the writer identifying himself as a teacher with those who come in succession to bear witness to the truth,

* Comp. 1 John i. 1—3.

and primarily with Jesus Himself; and we can often trace in the discourses of the Saviour forms of expression which evidently bear the impress of the writer's own mind.*

Let us now take a glance over the longest of the discourses contained in this gospel (chapters xiv.—xvii.), always bearing in mind the historical circumstances which form, so to speak, its framework. It may be boldly affirmed that belief in the genuineness of the ideas here set forth, and above all of the prayer with which they close, rests primarily on the solemnity of that final hour, awful forebodings of which oppress our hearts as we read. If, in bidding farewell to His own, Jesus had not thus spoken and thus prayed, no disciple would have dared to imagine such a scene—a scene too touching and too sublime to be by possibility a dramatic invention. The words spoken on this occasion could not but make a profound impression on the soul of every sensitive hearer. But immediately after it, and still conversing, they go forth to Gethsemane. Other impressions succeed those just made. Another conversation on an entirely different subject engages the minds of the disciples, and points their gaze to a distant future. Then come the terrible scenes of the passion; the unlooked-for catastrophe in the garden; a night of terror and anguish in the court of the high-priest; the sanguinary tumult of the morning; the fatal indecision of the prefect, keeping the heart of every friend of Jesus in cruel alternation between fear and hope; then all the culminating agonies rending the troubled soul of the beloved disciple, from the despair of parting which seemed to be final, to the rapture of unexpected reunion. What a

* Is it more difficult to believe that our Lord said to Nicodemus all that is contained in John iii. 16—21, than to believe that He said to the woman of Samaria what is contained in chapter iv. 14, 23, 24 ? If it be said that in both cases John puts into the mouth of our Lord teaching which our Lord did not actually communicate to the persons named in the narrative, I think it is fair to reply that John would hardly have represented our Lord as communicating the great truths in chapter iv., to such a person as the Samaritan woman, if our Lord had not actually said these things to her. According to ordinary notions, a much more suitable frame for such teaching might have been found.—ED.

storm must have swept across the heart of John before rest returned to it! before his mind could gather up all these impressions, and recapitulate them! Unless we are prepared to deny to the apostles every trace of a humanity like our own, we may not demand of them here a literally exact and stereotyped reproduction of all the crises and of all the words of this long and soul-stirring drama.* Or shall we suppose that even during that parting prayer the beloved disciple stood with note-book and pencil in hand ? Nay, assuredly, his whole soul was hanging on the lips of his Master; he was drinking in, with all the deep devotion of his spirit, that life about to be taken away, and it became within him a well of living water. It is the spirit of Jesus, the mouth of John, that speaks and prays here; and if the Master alone could say, "I have glorified Thee on the earth; I have finished the work which Thou gavest me to do;" assuredly it is the disciple who makes that grand confession of the Christian faith, "And this is life eternal, that they might know Thee, and Jesus Christ whom Thou hast sent."†

There is one passage which may specially help us in forming a just idea of the nature of these discourses; it occurs in the last seven verses of the twelfth chapter, or according, to our division of the whole book, at the close of the first part of the work. The writer had just before‡ recapitulated his history by a brief statement of the general facts of the manifestation of the Son of God, and the reception given Him by the world.

---

* We may observe, again, that it is only on this principle of regarding the history and the conditions of the Gospel literature, that we can explain the numerous variations—even contradictions—in the four parallel records of the last days of the Saviour. On any other more orthodox theory, the truth of the history is irreparably compromised.

† John xvii. 3, 4. It will be observed that in the narrative the fourth gospel uniformly employs the simple name Jesus. The Saviour, in speaking of Himself, uses, according to the evangelist, the pronoun or a circumlocution. The form ὁ Χριστός belongs to Jewish theology. The full name Jesus Christ, without any article, is the doctrinal formula of the apostles (John i. 17 ; xxi. 31). [*Godet* has an excellent reply to this objection. See his *Commentaire sur L'Evangile de Saint Jean*, II. 543, *also* 566, 567.—Ed.]

‡ John xii. 37—43.

Here he is about to recapitulate, in the same manner, the elements of evangelical theology. How will he do it? Will he give us some fresh discourse of the Saviour, inserted here in true chronological order? No, for the closing words of the preceding paragraph* positively exclude this idea. Or is John himself here the speaker? The opening words of verse forty-four assert the contrary.† Rather, it is the apostle who here inserts this discourse, for the purpose indicated, using freely in its compilation a series of texts taken from various discourses of the Saviour, and forming together a summary of the teaching contained in all the preceding chapters.‡

This freedom in the form of the composition, combined with strict adherence to the substance of the discourses, is further proved by several passages in which the evangelist indulges in reflections on some of the words of Jesus, which go beyond the intention of the words themselves. We may illustrate our meaning first by reminding the reader of the famous saying of Christ's which served as the text for the charges brought against Him before the Sanhedrim,§ and the true interpretation‖ of which is in no way excluded by that which John gives to it,¶ nor by the context in which it occurs in his gospel. It is fully admitted that the allegorical interpretation put upon it by John, while doubtless in full harmony with the feeling of the disciples after the resurrection of the Lord, was foreign to the actual circumstances in which it was uttered. The same may be said of another passage relating to the communication of the Spirit promised to believers, supposed to present considerable obscurity, in which the interpretation put upon it by the evangelist, as it

* John xii. 36.
† John xii. 44.
‡ Verse 44 occurs also in chapter v. 36 ; vii. 29 ; viii. 42 ; x. 38 ; for verse 45, see (i. 18) ; viii. 19 ; for verse 46, comp. (i. 5) ; viii. 12 ; xii. 35 ; for verses 47, 48, see (iii. 17, and foll.) ; v. 24, and foll. ; viii. 15, and foll. ; for verse 49, comp. vii. 16, 17 ; viii. 21, 38 ; lastly, for verse 50, comp. vi. 63.
§ Matt. xxvi. 61 ; Mark xiv. 58.
‖ Acts vi. 14.
¶ John ii. 19.

tends to restrict and narrow the signification of the form of
the verb employed,* ignores the explanation, which would be
in harmony with the theology of the gospel, and which is
unmistakably given in other places by Jesus Himself.† In
truth, it was not at some period fixed in the future that Jesus
had promised to give to those who should come to Him the
water of eternal life. Faith was to produce this result at once.
Again, we may call attention to that which the author says
as to the meaning of the word *to be lifted up*,‡ in which he
discovers an allusion to the particular mode of the Lord's
death, while it is perfectly clear, from the discourses of Jesus
Himself,§ that this expression is designed to exhibit His death
as the commencement of His exaltation and glory. Lastly, it
may be said that the grand utterances of the sacerdotal prayer
of Jesus, in which He declares that He had taken into His
holy keeping those whom the Father had given Him, are
greatly shorn of their true glory by the application made of
them to the occurrences in the garden of Gethsemane.|| These
examples show that the writer did not invent the words he
puts into the lips of the Saviour, but that he had them before
him as materials upon which to work. These same examples
show us, further, the influence which the mental bias of the
exegete may have exercised in the compilation of his work.
Thus, in several passages,¶ it is very natural to trace in this
same word, *to lift up*, the idea of the crucifixion, which a too
literal exegesis had at first gratuitously attached to it.

We now come to a fact of great importance, which has
hitherto escaped the notice of the learned. On closer examination, we find that the so-called discourses in this gospel
are not discourses in the proper sense of the word; they are
conversations. In all there are interlocutors—that is, the
persons to whom Jesus first addresses Himself interrupt

* John vii. 38, ῥεύσουσιν, in the future.
† John iv. 14.
‡ Ὑψοῦσθαι, John xii. 32, and foll.
§ For example, John xiii. 31, and foll.
|| John xvii. 12; comp. xviii. 9.
¶ John iii. 14; viii. 28.

Him by different questions or objections, and these supply the opportunity for the further development of the thought, or for the progressive stages of doctrinal exposition. And all these questions or objections, without a single exception, arise out of misunderstandings, misconceptions, caused by the fact that the spiritual and figurative words of Jesus are invariably taken in their primary and material sense.* These misconceptions sometimes appear natural, and readily explained by the want of education and adequate information in the persons addressed. The Samaritan woman, for example, could not be expected to rise at once to the comprehension of the sublime mysticism of the Gospel. But in most cases such an explanation is not admissible; the objections are generally so palpably absurd that we may fairly ask how it was Jesus did not observe in His dealings with such hearers, the rule He had Himself given to His disciples.† Many attempts have been made by the exegetes to remove that which is singular and often grotesque in these objections; but they have been unsuccessful.‡

---

* See John ii. 20; iii. 4, 9; iv. 11, 15, 33; vi. 28, 31, 34, 52; vii. 27, 35; viii. 19, 22, 33, 39, 41, 52, 57; ix. 40; xi. 12; xiv. 5, 8, 22; xvi. 29. This catalogue might easily be made longer, if all the passages were enumerated in which exegetes have made the same mistake as to the significance of the words of Jesus, which rise above their low horizon. See the commentaries on chapters iv. 14; v. 21, 25, 26; xiii. 10, etc.

† Matt. vii. 6.

‡ All attempts that have been made to vindicate the common sense of Nicodemus (John iii. 4), have been baffled by the palpable absurdity of his objection. The words of the Jews (John vi. 28), have been vainly brought forward in proof of their comprehension of Christ's teaching. The question they ask is what they must do in order to have manna to eat, like their fathers in the desert. That which they say in verse 34 is explained by the parallel passage in John iv. 15. In John vii. 35, the misconception is so glaring that some have attempted to explain it away as a textual error. In chapter viii. 41, πορνεία must necessarily retain its ordinary meaning, as the Jews are vindicating for themselves the honour of legitimate birth, which Jesus, as they imagine, is disputing. So with all the other similar passages. [M. Godet calls attention to the fact that the disciples themselves supposed that when our Lord spoke of the "leaven of the Pharisees" they thought He meant to reproach them for not taking bread. It is hard to say what limits to assign to the gross materialism of the contemporaries of our Lord.—ED.]

There is, indeed, such a recurring similarity in the difficulties proposed, which we might venture to call caricatures of the true Gospel idea, that it is impossible to explain them on any other principle. This is so evident, that in some passages in which we might perhaps discover a more plausible or excusable* meaning, we are bound to prefer that which is most diametrically opposed to the intention of the Saviour. It is noticeable, moreover, that the narratives of the synoptics † do not present at all the same phenomena. What conclusion can we derive from this fact? Shall we say that Jesus was incapable of adapting His teaching to the comprehension of all sorts of persons? that He affected obscurity in doctrine? that He had to deal entirely with men void of understanding? Nothing of the kind. Our reply is, that not one of these objections belongs to the history itself; that they arise simply out of the form of its presentation; that they are merely the rhetorical or dialectic method used by a writer whose resources were limited. His object was to set the sublimely spiritual doctrines of the Gospel in contrast with the carnal conceptions of the world, which in its gross materialism utterly failed to comprehend the scope of the Lord's teaching. These objections, which are the despair of historical exegetes, of the slaves of the letter and of tradition, give the most striking characterization of the unregenerate world, traced by the master-hand of our theologian, for those who are able to rise to the height of his point of view. Nicodemus, the Samaritan woman, the Pharisees, the Jews, the Greeks, who pass in succession before us, are not so much individuals as types, the representatives of various classes of men, all alike called into communion with the Lord, all equally incapable of apprehending that call through the medium of their natural reason, but all more or less disposed to receive the light from above, and thus prefiguring the atti-

* For example, vii. 52; viii. 19.

† We except from this remark the single instance of the case mentioned in Matt. xvi. 7, which presents some analogy with those now before us. Other passages in which the disciples do not at once comprehend the meaning of some saying or parable of their Master, have nothing in common with this.

tude of the whole race of man with regard 'to that light.
Readers who are already initiated in the mysteries of this
theology, at once speculative and mystical, and are thus raised
above the sphere of these first hearers, by their blindness, may
yet find in them a salutary warning.

These discourses are further interrupted occasionally by
notices apparentlyhistorical, but evidently intended not so much
to recall the actual circumstances connected with some special
scene or event, as to describe in a general manner the dispositions of the minds of men, and the tendencies of the masses.
The discourse recorded in the fifth chapter, for example, is
broken more than once by the phrase, "Therefore did the Jews
persecute Jesus, and sought to slay Him."* Now it is evident
alike from the context and the form of the verb employed, that
the reference is not to one special and immediate act, but to a
permanent disposition, liable to manifest itself at any time in
hostile words and machinations. The formula with which the
writer resumes the interrupted discourse, *Jesus answered*, is
not therefore to be taken in the anecdotic sense, as referring to
words spoken on this particular occasion. According to the
common and purely historical interpretation, we might imagine
the Jews perpetually pursuing Jesus in the streets, and casting
stones at Him, while He still continues to speak. This is, to say
the least of it, an unnatural representation. There are, moreover, passages in which the historical interpretation creates
actual contradictions,† which, on the theory we propose, are
avoided. We hold then that in all these passages John is not
recounting the actual occurrences of any one day, but illus-
trating and amplifying his thesis, "The light shined in darkness, and the darkness comprehended it not."

The personages introduced in these narratives, not only pass
away from the scene without our knowing what has become of
them, as we have already observed; but they reappear, they
change places, they come and go we know not how, and thus
plainly show that they are used for didactic purposes simply.

* John v. 16, and foll.
† John vii. 30.

Let us examine, for example, the discourse contained in the eighth chapter of this gospel.* The analysis of this passage gives abundant proof that the writer is not narrating an actual event, the circumstances of a particular interview,—in short, that he is not giving us the transcript of anything that really took place,—but that his design is to set before us certain theological facts and religious truths, which he had at various times received from his Lord and Master, and that the men and the multitudes who serve to give life to his picture, are only lay figures, representing the passive or hostile element in this contact of revelation with the world. The writer, when he aims really to be a historian, and to narrate particular facts,† the details of which he derives from his own recollections, can do so with such clearness and precision, that every physiognomy stands before us with all the distinctness of a portrait. Must we then suppose that he loses this faculty, whenever theology is to be his theme at the same time? or shall we adopt the simpler explanation that it was not then the instrument adapted for his purpose?

We conclude with one more observation, which is not in our view the least important. We have already said that the gospel, as to its more essentially dogmatic portion, is divided into two parts, the one which places Jesus in contact with the unregenerate world, the other which shows His relations with His disciples. We maintain, then, that in the writer's mind there are but two discourses in his book,—that is to say, in

---

* Jesus begins at verse 12 a discourse addressed *to them*, αὐτοῖς (to whom?); in verse 13 the Pharisees object, and Jesus replies to them. In verse 21 we have another discourse also addressed *to them*, and at verse 22 there follows a reply of the *Jews*. After various interruptions, the speakers in which are not individually described, it is said in verse 30 that *many* believed in Him. The rest of the discourse, verse 31, is addressed to these *believers*, and *they* (who?) reply, verse 33, in such a way that Jesus accuses *them* (the believers?) of seeking to kill Him. [The only reply to this note is an illustration in detail of the movement of the controversy between our Lord and those to whom He was speaking. Godet has done this admirably.—ED.]

† See, for example, John ii. 1—11 ; v. 1—15 ; ix. ; xi. ; xiii., and the entire history of the passion.

each of these two sections the discourses form but one whole, and stand in logical connection with each other. This amounts to saying that these two series of discourses are not addressed to the persons who appear on the scenes in the supposed narrative, but to the readers of the book which contains them. Let us prove this by an example. The Jews say to Jesus, " If Thou be the Christ, tell us plainly."* He replies, " I have told you." Doubtless, He had on repeated occasions plainly affirmed the fact; but does the evangelist then mean to assert that those who were listening to Him at that moment were the same persons who had heard His other discourses ? " Yet," He continues, " ye believe not, because ye are not of my sheep, as I said unto you." † But Jesus had nowhere said this. The allegory of the sheep ‡ had been spoken to an entirely different auditory. He had, however, said repeatedly, and to various classes of people, that they were not in fellowship with Him. All these dogmatic and figurative assertions combine very naturally in the mind of the theologian who presents them to us. The discourses then here assume, in the life of Jesus, the form in which they would appear, when the entire history of the Saviour had become a doctrinal and ideal fact.

* John x. 24, and foll.

† This is the only true reading, John x. 26. The rendering which omits the words καθὼς εἶπον ὑμῖν, or refers them to the verse following, has its origin in the failure to recognize the close relation subsisting between all the discourses which we have here indicated.

‡ John x. 1, and foll.

CHAPTER IV.

GENERAL OUTLINE OF THE THEOLOGY OF JOHN.

THE question that now comes before us is what is the truest and most natural point of view from which to examine the theology of John. We have here not only to render an arduous task as easy as possible to ourselves, but to guard against error in its execution. We shall infallibly err, by blending foreign elements with the system of the apostle, if we allow ourselves to be guided either by our own particular mode of thought, or by the most currently accepted religious ideas. It is evident that this preliminary question is one beset with difficulties from the hesitation of our predecessors in choosing their ground, or in deciding upon what fundamental principle they should build up their system; they have, so to speak, only groped their way to a conclusion on the point. Some have even been found ready to declare that there is no system, no logically developed doctrine, in the fourth gospel, but only outlines, germs, fundamental ideas, which dogmatic theology is free to develop, but which the writer himself had neglected to arrange and to combine. Others have attempted to reconstruct the system by means of that which they call the personal and peculiar experience of the disciple, as we ourselves have essayed to do in the case of Paul. Doubtless such a natural relation between the inner life of a man and his writings may always be supposed; but in making this the basis of our conception of the system before us, we are clearly moving in a vicious circle, since the author is known to us only through his book. Others have said that the theology of John is summed up in the doctrine of the *Logos*, before and after His incarnation. Lastly, it has been described as the system which presents Christianity as the absolute religion. All this shows that the opinions held on this subject differ not only in accessories, but diverge from the very outset. We do not propose either to discuss or to refute the views of our predecessors. The idea we have formed of this theology has been obtained in an independent way, and here as in the preceding books we shall follow the guidance of the texts alone, not any literary exposition given of them. We venture to hope that under this guidance our readers will be prepared to accept the results to be placed before them. Our estimate of the theology of John as a whole, then, is the following.

The theology set forth in the fourth gospel is not the product of speculation, but rather of contemplation; though on a superficial view, and especially on the impressions derived from its opening sentences, we might be disposed to opine otherwise. It has its root, not in the reasoning faculties, not in the understanding, but in the feeling, in the heart. It is essentially a mystical theology; it requires only a few ideas, a very simple theory, from which to construct the life which it seeks to originate in the depths of the soul. That life can avail itself of support derived from other sources than its own; it can benefit by certain general facts, established beyond its own sphere and without its concurrence; but it will not feel the need of incessantly seeking fresh nutriment in deeper and wider intellectual speculation; on the contrary, it contains in itself an inexhaustible spring of satisfaction, the divine element on which it is sustained.

The principal characteristic of mystical theology is that of directness, of intuition, as opposed to reflection, dialectic demonstration, which is the leading feature of all non-mystical or rational theology. In order to preserve this characteristic unimpaired, we shall not yield to the desire to systematize, so natural to all scholars by profession, and which may be perfectly allowable when applied to a train of ideas brought into combination by an intellectual process. But this method is dangerous, and might tempt us to mingle ideas of foreign origin with those presented to our study, if applied to a theology which does not owe its birth to a mental necessity, nor its form to a law of logic. To multiply divisions and subdivisions in such a case, would be only to reduce a living organism, as it were, to a skeleton, and would ensure failure in that which should be our true end, namely, the recognition of that organism in all its vital power.

A sound and pure mysticism flows in a clear stream, transparent not only to the originating mind, but to all who have any affinity with it. It is only a false and unhealthy mysticism which is in itself turbid and obscure. As it is the essence of mysticism to foster feeling rather than reflection, it follows (always supposing it to be, as we have just said, pure and simple) that the exposition of it will not require a great multiplication of explanatory phrases. Any one who has truly grasped it, should be able without difficulty to make it intelligible to other minds possessing a like preparedness to comprehend it. If the true sentiment be once aroused, it will not fail to find of itself, and in a direct and practical manner, the further elucidation it may need. A verbose and protracted exposition would here fail as inevitably as a shorter treatise overweighted with erudition or transcendentalism. Our readers will divine, from what we have said, the method we propose to follow. We are perfectly aware that it will not satisfy those who " *seek after wisdom,*" [*] that is to say, the great body of our contemporary theologians, who are always on the watch for some sort of cloudy gnosticism ; but we deliberately and willingly renounce any claim to their approval.

A soul surrendered to mystical influences will always need a certain limited number of fundamental ideas, to serve as the basis or *substratum* of the inner life. These ideas are not necessarily themselves the product of mystical contemplation ; they may be theses borrowed from popular theology, or transcendental dogmas belonging to a speculative philosophy of religion. In either case, they will appear not so much as the integral parts of an artistically constructed system, as simple

* Σοφίαν ζητοῦντας, 1 Cor. i. 22.

premises upon which religious ideas are built up, and by means
of which they are combined in an order equally simple and
natural. These premises may even be absolutely foreign to
mysticism, and borrowed from the theology of an entirely
different school. These cannot of course be passed by in an
exposition of the system, since they determine its form, and
stand in an organic relation to it; but they do not belong to
the system in the sense of being in their origin a part of the
theology with which they are found in combination.

As these premises may thus be borrowed theses, and in the
present case actually are so, it often happens that the speculative theory to which they originally belonged, is not always
rigorously followed out to its logical consequences, nor is the
phraseology which is its natural expression always strictly
observed. The aim of the theologian now before us was not
to expound this earlier speculative theory, but to set forth a
doctrine more or less new; hence the speculative formulas
which he might use, as seeming to him best adapted to express his fundamental ideas, are incessantly dropped by him,
or replaced by other expressions equally apt in conveying
his meaning, but having no relation to the former speculative
theory, and even out of harmony with it.

As a general rule, every new system has necessarily its
polemical side. It stands in opposition to one or more earlier
or contemporary systems; it develops certain truths in view
of certain errors; its form and method depend more or less on
these relations. A purely mystical theology presents no such
antithesis; it ignores every outward and historical relation;
it acknowledges no necessity to define its exact position with
regard to principles or points of view heterogeneous to itself;
it offers no demonstration of its own claims; it makes no
attempt to point out the imperfections of other systems, or to
define its relations with those which have preceded it. All
these sources may have contributed to enrich and amplify the
theology of John by a series of dogmas and formulas. The
relations of the soul with God, in so far as they are natural
and free from impure alloy, are the same everywhere, are

everywhere equally direct, and cannot be modified by influences agitating the world beyond its own sphere. If mysticism is ever under the necessity of defending itself against theses which fetter and obstruct it, it will do so by a simple assertion or negation, examples of which we find in the epistle of John;. it will not make use of them to originate new ideas, or to add new members to its body of doctrine.

It is the essential character of mystical theology to combine the theoretical and the practical element in religion. As Christianity can never be without a mystical element, that which is commonly distinguished as the doctrinal and the ethical, should never be wholly disjoined in the consideration of it. The more decided is the mystical colouring, the more close will this association be. Thus, in a purely mystical theology, the mutual relation between faith and practice, the belief and the life, will be the complete fusion of the two, at least so long as the theoretic and speculative dogmas, of which we have spoken above as the premises of the system, are regarded as such. Any one who should speak of the doctrine and morality of John as separable the one from the other, would at once show that he had failed to understand either.

The mystical tendency does not necessarily lead to the isolation of the individual, but it may deal exclusively with the individual. The ideas relating to a community of several individuals, especially those which have reference to the objective design of their association, will not be readily developed in this sphere; and dogmas relating to the Church and cognate matters, will never be formulated by such a theology. The direct relation of the individual with God is so strongly predominant, and exerts such an ascendency over the rest, that the idea of any other,—that, for instance, which may subsist between man and man,—though not formally excluded, will never occupy a prominent place. The law of concentration limits the horizon of doctrine.*

* The doctrine of the Church does not occupy any conspicuous place in St. John's theology, but it is surely a misconception to represent it as individualistic. The law of love—of love binding together all who are in Christ—is one of the great ideas of the Gospel.—ED.

The same law also acts restrictively in another direction. The mysticism which we are here considering in its ideal perfection, satisfies so completely those who surrender themselves to its influence, that they can take but a faint interest in anything beyond the present moment. Each instant bringing with it the fulness of bliss after which their hearts aspire, there is nothing left for them to desire. Dogmatic assertions relating to the climax of earthly history, can hold but an inferior place in the programme of a mystical theology, or may even be wanting altogether.*

These preliminary remarks, which we will not unnecessarily multiply, explain to us at once why a mystical theology like that of John will always appear incomplete, both as to the sum of the ideas and doctrines composing it, and with regard to their logical arrangement, especially if we attempt to apply to it the standard of some other school—that, for example, of Paul, with which we are most familiar. We do wrong to the theology before us in judging it from such a standpoint; but these same remarks also explain, why it is the Church has never been able to make this theology the basis of its own system; why ecclesiastical formulas have found themselves fettered by those here employed; and why, in spite of this imperfection, keenly felt by the schools,—possibly even on account of it,—the yearning of the soul for mystical edification which has been no less strongly realized in every age of the Church, has always addressed itself to this theology of John as to the unfailing source of its deepest joys and sublimest aspirations.

Having thus established preliminarily the general character of the theology which we are about to develop, we have only one step further to take before entering finally on our subject; we have to inquire what is the fundamental idea of the system, the formula which is to serve as a key to open to us its meaning,—the text, in short, on which the apostle is about to preach. The more simple the system,—and it is so simple that we might almost hesitate to call it a system at all,—the

* But see John v. 17—31.—ED.

greater right have we to expect to find some very brief epitome of it. This hope is the more warranted, as we have succeeded in finding such an epitome of the theology of Paul, which is immeasurably more full and varied. We might pause at the prologue to the gospel, which, combined with the fourteenth verse of the first chapter, would give us a division of the subject into two principal parts, a division to which we might adhere throughout: 1st, The Word, regarded from a metaphysical point of view; 2nd, The Word, regarded historically.* We shall not, however, derive from these texts any systematic outline, as the author does not himself adhere to any, but speaks of the consequences of the incarnation before mentioning the incarnation itself.†

We prefer to turn to a passage at the close of the book, in which the evangelist explains his purpose. "These," he says, "are written, that ye might believe that Jesus is the Son of God, and that believing ye might have life through His name."‡ The two objects indicated in this sentence are evidently connected; and if we have a right to say that the Gospel history, as presented in this book, is not a narrative dictated by accidental circumstances, but rather a studied, normal, and systematic discourse, it will follow that that discourse has this twofold end in view. The passage quoted will be the practical epitome of the theology of John. That theology will then consist of two parts: a doctrinal thesis, serving as the premise or basis, *Jesus the Son of God;* and a mystical thesis representing the relation of the individual to the abstract truth, *life.* These two circles come into contact only at the idea of faith. By faith man rises into the speculative element, and appropriates it; by faith he realizes the mystical element.

This fundamental idea, however, which epitomizes the whole theology of the fourth gospel, "*Life by faith in Jesus, the Son of God,*" is elsewhere expressed in a fuller formula, which may show us, at the same time, how the most essential accessory

---

* Ὁ λόγος ἐν ἀρχῇ—ὁ λόγος σάρξ ἐγένετο.
† John i. 5, 12.
‡ John xx. 30, and foll.

ideas attach themselves to the main thesis. This will have the great advantage of saving us the trouble of seeking, by the aid of arguments all derived from reflection, to construct a theological system which is in reality almost entirely the product of feeling; in a word, it will preserve us from the danger of substituting our scholastic categories for the simple combinations of an essentially intuitive spirit.

We may point to two passages of this nature. One occurs* in the first discourse of Jesus; the substance of the gospel is there epitomized in a very distinct manner, in very few words. There is another passage in the epistle,† which differs from the former only by a change of expression; in combination, they give us the fundamental formula, which embodies the whole principle of this system:

"*Herein is manifested the love of* GOD, *that God* SENT *His only begotten* SON *into the* WORLD, *that whosoever* BELIEVETH *in Him might have eternal* LIFE."‡

We shall adhere to this statement reiterated by the apostle himself; the division which it suggests commends itself from its very simplicity. We shall have then two principal parts: the doctrinal premises, and the mystical theology itself. The latter belongs more exclusively to John. The premises are of two kinds, speculative and historical. The historical premises are the two facts of the manifestation of the Word as man, and the effect produced by it upon the world. The mystical theology of John itself comprehends, as we have already seen, the two spheres of faith and life. We shall content ourselves with so brief an epitome of our subject, without fear of losing anything essential. In the text which we take as our starting-point, the words we have emphasized give us at once the substance of this theology, and the outline we shall follow in these chapters.

* John iii. 16.
† 1 John iv. 9.
‡ Ἐν τούτῳ ἐφανερώθη ἡ ἀγάπη ΤΟΥ ΘΕΟΥ ἐν ἡμῖν ὅτι ΤΟΝ ΥΙΟΝ αὐτοῦ τὸν μονογενῆ ΑΠΕΣΤΑΛΚΕΝ εἰς ΤΟΝ ΚΟΣΜΟΝ ἵνα πᾶς ὁ ΠΙΣΤΕΥΩΝ εἰς αὐτὸν ἔχῃ ΖΩΗΝ αἰώνιον.

CHAPTER V.

OF THE ESSENTIAL NATURE OF GOD.

THE basis of mystical theology is the idea of God: it is so far more directly and necessarily than in dogmatic or philosophical theology, since its object is to lead to the recognition of God, not only as the centre of all that is, but still more as the centre to which all should converge. It is of the first importance, then, in the investigation of such a system, that we should inquire how this idea arose, and what forms it has assumed. We are not treating here of that which a general religious theory, or the Christian doctrine in its most familiar and popular form, may teach as to the person and attributes of God. We are rather inquiring whether John, in view of the practical tendency inherent in his theology and governing his whole system, has based his doctrine explicitly on one particular aspect of the conception of God; if he has brought into prominence some one attribute forgotten elsewhere, or at least raised into peculiar pre-eminence here; in a word, if, in the exposition of this capital point of his theory, he has adopted a form which at once impresses an individual character upon his whole theology. We must bear in mind, in entering upon this question, that at the time of the rise of the literature and theology of Christianity, there existed within the horizon of the apostles, two distinct forms of the conception of God, the one popular, the other philosophical. We shall inquire to which of the two, the form adopted by John is the more nearly allied, or whether it is alike independent of both. It will not be necessary to trace back the history of religious thought very far, in order to enable our readers to form a judgment upon this point. We have had occasion to speak of these and similar matters at the commencement of this work; and it here concerns us not so much to trace the genesis of these ideas, as to estimate their relative value, and to see what influence they are adapted to exert on Christian thought.

The popular theology, of which the books of the Old Testament are the great exponent, treats simply of one personal God, distinct from the world which He has created by a free act of His will, and who, in this act as in the government of His creation, constantly reveals His power, His goodness, His wisdom, and His justice.

Philosophical theology goes far beyond a conception so simple and so easily apprehended by even the least developed intelligences. It speaks of a God absolutely inaccessible to human reason, not to be apprehended by thought. It teaches that the only means by which reason may form, if not an adequate, at least an approximate conception of God, is by separating from His essence, by a speculative process, the sum of the attributes appertaining to it, and really contained, or, as it were, concealed in it and by thus arriving at a concrete conception of a Being who in Himself is an absolutely transcendent abstraction. We might have remarked that, unconsciously, we every day adopt the same course, substituting for the abstract idea of God, which our reason could never grasp, the sum of His attributes. But there is a great difference between this popular conception and the metaphysical, of which we are now speaking. The latter declares that that which we have just described as the result of a subjective, intellectual process, is a real, objective fact, independent of human thought, and anterior to it. The totality of the divine attributes is revealed as they emerge, so to speak, from the absolute in which they existed in a latent state; and this revelation is called a divine person, an hypostasis; it is in substance and in reality identical with the absolute; it differs only in form and by its manifestation. Every ulterior revelation of the Deity, all creation, all contact of God with creation, with that which exists out of Himself, takes place through the medium of this primary and personal revelation.

This particular metaphysical doctrine was not exclusively Jewish in its origin, but it found in Judaism all the elements necessary to its organic development. We shall see presently how, and how far, it found means to ally itself to Christian convictions, in the theology now claiming our attention. We shall observe it in yet closer combination with those convictions, in the doctrine of the Word. But even where we are standing at this moment,—namely, on the very threshold of the system,—we shall discover very distinct traces of it.

The idea that God in Himself, in His absolute nature, cannot be known by man, is the indispensable premise and the basis of the theory of the Word, and is clearly expressed in the words, "*No man hath seen God at any time,*"* words to which it would be absurd to give the restricted meaning that mortal eyes cannot look upon God in a corporeal form. Such a theory, taken literally, and even in the popular sense which we have repudiated, is contrary to narratives of the Old Testament in which God is said to have revealed Himself to the eye and ear. Thus the apostle, reasoning according to this theory, declares expressly that the manifestations spoken of in these narratives must be referred to the second hypostasis,† a fact which Jewish theology perfectly understood. We need not insist upon this first thesis of the metaphysics of our system; we shall find it confirmed in those that follow, which will come before us for analysis: for example, when it is said that there was no true revelation of God before that of Christ; that God can only be approached by faith; that God Himself, in His capacity as Judge, does not come into direct relations with the

---

* John i. 18 ; comp. vi. 46, θεὸν οὐδεὶς ἑώρακε πώποτε. The passage in John v. 37, placed in an entirely different context, seems to us to have no claim to be mentioned here, if it is held that the form of the discourse there given is wholly popular. Even under this form, however, which is too slight to convey fully the theological thought of the writer, we can recognize its reflection.

† John xii. 41.

world. These are very popular formulas, but still corollaries
of the speculative premise we here establish.

We cannot, however, refrain from making at once an observation which will often recur in the course of our exposition,
namely, that this first speculative premise is not kept free from
admixture, or followed out to all its consequences, in the books
we are analyzing. Were it otherwise, there could be no mention
of God as acting on or standing in any relation whatever with
that which is external to Himself, but simply of the Word, the
hypostasis through which the Godhead is revealed. But the
philosophical theorem has not wholly absorbed the religious
consciousness as expressed throughout the whole Bible, where
it is generally brought within the grasp of the ordinary intelligence. The faith in the heart of man demands a more direct
and immediate approach to God, and cannot be readily put off
by scientific abstractions. Yet more; Christian theology has its
starting-point, not in these philosophical abstractions, but in a
fact which belongs to it essentially and antecedently to all speculation,— we mean, in the historical and concrete manifestation of
Jesus Christ. It may then find the basis for its scientific edifice
in ideas and formulas derived from speculation ; but it will never
expose its historical basis to the danger of becoming absorbed
in abstractions. Such a danger might have arisen, however, had
there been neglect or forgetfulness of that which Jesus had
Himself said of the relation with the Father, a relation which
is that between two persons, both having the power to will and
to act, had these two persons been so separated as that to the
one should be ascribed abstract existence, to the other will and
action. Now such is the real meaning of the theory formulated by the Jewish schools, and it is at once seen that it comes
very close to that of Sabellianism, a system radically alien to
historic Christianity.

We shall not then be surprised to find that, in spite of the
original premise, which proclaimed the absolute transcendence
of God, John should ascribe to Him, in speaking of Him
apart from the Word, very positive and concrete attributes.
We shall not dwell on the well-known thesis, "God is a

Spirit."* This thesis, though not met with elsewhere in this brief and absolute form, is not peculiar to Christianity; Jewish theology adopted it explicitly, and it cannot be called a formula originated by John. It is moreover, in the context in which it occurs, simply a protest against materialism in religion and worship, and as such does not belong to any particular system of spiritualistic theology.

But that which deserves to be expressly mentioned here is, that the theology of John recognizes three attributes in the Godhead, which are designed not only to characterize its essence, but also to represent it, so that its very substance, so to speak, may be apprehended. We shall find these three attributes playing a very important part in the whole system, determining in great measure the writer's method, and furnishing him with the most natural principle for the division of his materials. The three attributes are as follows :—

1st. *God is light.*†—Light represents all that is true whether in the sphere of thought or of the will. As ascribed to God, the term conveys the ordinary ideas of omniscience and absolute holiness. Instead of the more simple formula just quoted, John, according to a constant usage of his theological speech, says also, *God is in the light,* as he might say *the light is in Him,* since he says elsewhere *in Him is no darkness at all.*‡ Everywhere in his phraseology, the preposition *in* expresses the close relation between two subjects, or, as in the present case, between the subject and the attribute. The meaning of these formulas would be by no means adequately rendered, if they were supposed to represent simply a dwelling in the light.§

2nd. *God is love.*‖—Love marks the relation God sustains to all that derives life from Him; that relation as sustained first to the Son¶ from before the creation of the world,** then to that

---

* John iv. 24.
† Φῶς, 1 John i. 5.
‡ 1 John i. 5, 7.
§ 1 Tim. vi. 16.
‖ 'Αγάπη, 1 John iv. 8, 16.
¶ John iii. 35 ; v. 20 ; x. 17 ; xv. 9.
** John xvii. 23, and foll.

world itself,* and in a peculiar manner to believers.† These three relations may be reduced by theology to the one idea that God can love only Himself; thus in that which is not Himself, He can love only that which comes from Him or tends to Him, that which is divine.‡

3rd. *God is life,*§ or according to the other formula, *in Him is life;* ‖ He is *the living God.*¶—The Hebrew idea of *the living God,* so named in opposition to the false gods of paganism,** is far from exhausting all that is implied in this conception. *Life* stands here, first, for existence in itself, or *being;* then for existence extending or diffusing itself—that is, for *creation;* lastly, for existence complete and satisfied in itself—that is, for *happiness.*††

In these three attributes the idea of God becomes concrete in the theology of John. But we must guard against considering these as so many special *qualities* of God, as phases or aspects of His essence. Each one represents the Divine Being in His completeness, and we may say *God is light,* as we say *God is a Spirit.* Light, love, life, are not, properly speaking, attributes, but the very essence of the divine nature.

* John iii. 16; 1 John iv. 10, 19.
† John xiv. 23; xvi. 27.
‡ John xvii. 26.
§ Ζωή, 1 John v. 20. We may possibly be wrong in quoting this passage here. Not that it should be understood rather of the Son, as is the ordinary interpretation (this does violence to the context); but *life eternal* is here, not so much that which belongs to God in His own nature, as that which believers have in and by Him. It is evident, however, that if He did not possess, He could not communicate it.
‖ John v. 26.
¶ John vi. 57.
** 1 John v. 21.
†† We shall note presently that the close relation between the ideas of being and creating is confirmed in John v. 17, inasmuch as creation is there spoken of as continuous.

CHAPTER VI.

OF THE ESSENTIAL NATURE OF THE WORD.

WE pass on to the second hypostasis, to that which in the philosophic system is, so to speak, the Godhead *in concreto*. This idea has not passed, any more than the other, in its pure and simple form into the theology of John. On the contrary, it there assumes a character so new that some have even denied that there is any connection between the Christian theory and that which preceded it. It will be easy, however, to show points of contact between the theology of John's gospel and the metaphysics of the school, or, if we choose so to put it, the elements borrowed by the apostle from the philosophers. We shall observe, presently, the differences which exist between the two systems.

Let us first make some observations on the names by which this divine hypostasis is spoken of. There are mainly two claiming our attention. It is called the *Word* and the *Son*. The Word,* that is to say the Word of God, the expression of His thought and will, the instrument by which He works, by which especially the act of creation was wrought, and considered under all these aspects as a personal Being; the Son,† or the Son of God, that is to say the essence of God reproduced, so to speak, by itself. As the latter term designates a relationship which has its analogue in the physical world, and at the same time another spiritual relationship into which men may

---

* Ὁ λόγος, John i. 1.

† Ὁ υἱός, John iii. 36 ; v. 19, and foll. ; viii. 35, and foll. ; 1 John ii. 22, foll., etc. ; x. 36 ; 1 John iii. 8, etc.

enter, the epithet *only** is added, signifying that He is the sole being of His kind, and marking in a distinct and positive manner that no man can stand in the same relation to God, no son in the same relation to his father, as Jesus Christ. These two names—the *Word* and the *Son*—differ from each other inasmuch as the second expresses rather the relation of the revealing hypostasis to the Godhead in the abstract conception of it, while the former expresses the relation of both to the world of creation.

Side by side with these names, we find also in the writings of John several theses, all indicated in the prologue of his gospel, and borrowed in the same way from this speculative theology.

1st. *The Word was towards God.*—The preposition chosen by the writer is such that the usual translation *with* is positively false and incomplete. The question is not of a supposed permanent local relation, but of a direction or tendency of life, of that which theological speculation has called the relation of immanence between the Word and God, which is changed into a relation of disjunction only for and by the fact of the creation. The same meaning is conveyed in a metaphor, when it is said that He was in the *bosom* of the Father.*

2nd. *The Word was God.*—The preceding thesis had asserted the distinctness of the persons ; this denies any difference of substance or essence. This is also the reason why the first proposition is again repeated ; for there is to be no identification of the persons ; the writer insists with equal firmness on their essential unity, and their logical or dialectic separation.

3rd. *The Word is the Creator of the World.*—This thesis properly has its origin in the well-known phrase of Genesis, which says that God spake, and the world was; an expression which is the first link of that long chain of philosophical ideas which ends in the system now before us. Between the

---

* Μονογενής, John i. 14, 18 ; iii. 16, 18 ; 1 John iv. 9.
† ῏Ην εἰς τὸν κόλπον τοῦ θεοῦ, verse 18.

Godhead, in its absolutely transcendent state, and the material world, there is a chasm. Speculation has bridged over this gulf by means of the creative hypostasis of the Word.

4th. *The Word is the Revealer of God.*[*]—He possesses the divine attributes,[†] not only as something essential to His true divine nature, but at the same time as something to be revealed.

All these propositions confirm our assertion that the theology of John has among its doctrinal premises, the speculative idea of the second person in the Deity. It is evident, without further demonstration by us, that any explanation which should attach to these theses a purely symbolical meaning, or reduce them to a merely moral significance, is inadmissible. We therefore formally repudiate the rationalistic explanation given of them at the commencement of this century.

In this chapter, however, as in the preceding, we shall have occasion to observe that the speculative system is not completely reproduced, or faithfully followed out to all its consequences. The end of Christian preaching could be accomplished without the too rigorous employment of certain formulas, and this practical purpose is always foremost in apostolic literature.

We say that the system is not completely reproduced in the texts of John. It is familiar to all that one of the fundamental theses of ecclesiastical speculation, is the idea of the eternity of the Word. Ever since the Council of Nicæa, this has been one of the corner-stones of Catholic theology, and its decision has come down as the common heritage of all the orthodox systems. This thesis, however, is not affirmed in the writings of John. These simply assert the *pre-existence* of the Word in several very positive passages,[‡] and, by implication, ascribe to Him the creation of the world. But none of these passages leads us necessarily beyond the idea of a relative pre-

* 1 John i. 18.

† Δόξα, verse 14.

‡ John iii. 13 ; vi. 62 ; viii. 58 ; xvii. 5, 24 ; comp. viii. 14 ; xii. 41 ; and i. 15, 30.

existence. Nowhere is there any assertion of an absolute pre-existence, or one from eternity, though neither is anything anywhere said to exclude such an idea. The formula, "*In the beginning was the Word*," * does not reach so far. The idea of the beginning is in itself always a relative idea, and as in the present case it can never be referred to God, but only to that which is apart from God—that is, to the world—so the formula in question contains nothing more than this simple assertion, that the Word was in existence at the time when the world was created; until then the Word could have had no relation to the world, but only to God.† The formula used in the epistle, "*He who was from the beginning*," ‡ does not convey any more, possibly less, for it fails to carry us back beyond the beginning, and the beginning is always in time. To assert eternal existence, we should read, "*without beginning*," and this formula is not found in John's writings. All theologians, again, acknowledge the striking parallelism between the first verse of Genesis and the first verse of the fourth gospel. Now it is evident that if the formula of John establishes the absolute eternity of the Word, the formula of Genesis must establish the absolute eternity of the world, and we ought to speak of an eternal creation as ecclesiastical theology speaks of an eternal generation, though the conjunction of the two latter terms seems a contradiction *in adjecto*.§ We shall seek in vain in the writings of John for any expression which could be regarded as the equivalent of this scholastic formula ; and the name *Son*, which is given to the Word, can never of itself, and in harmony with its primary meaning, lead to the idea of co-eternity with the *Father*.

It is then clear that the speculative theory of the gospel is so far left incomplete, at least if we may judge of it by the texts;

* 'Εν ἀρχῇ ἦν, John i. 1, 2.

† John i. 1, 18, πρὸς τὸν θεόν, or εἰς τὸν κόλπον τοῦ θεοῦ.

‡ John i. 1 ; ii. 13, 14, ὁ ἀπ' ἀρχῆς.

§ It is not contended that "in the beginning" is equivalent to "in eternity." If, when God began to create all things, the Word already *was*, and if by the Word all things were created, this implies the eternity of the Word.—ED.

NATURE OF THE WORD.

that it is not followed out to its full issues because its development was not the object the apostle had in view, and it has de-
volved upon the theology of the Church to give it its logical
complement, without which it could not satisfy speculative
inquiry. We repeat, it is not exegesis, but philosophy, which
lends its sanction to the doctrinal formula of Nicæa and the
Athanasian Creed. We do not call in question the right of
philosophy to do such a work ; we simply assert our own right
to regard as not of primary practical importance, matters which
it was not deemed needful to comprehend in the direct teachings of the gospel.

We remark, in the next place, that the logical consequences
of the speculative system, are not all respected in the essentially practical teaching of the apostle. The most popular
religious conceptions, the current notions of God and of His
direct action in the world, repeatedly find place in his
writings; and the two modes of expression, though essentially foreign to each other, and incompatible from a speculative point of view, are constantly blended. We subjoin some
examples. The idea of the duality of the divine persons, in
the speculative conception of it, is purely and simply ignored
in a passage which speaks not of the Word as the only acting
and revealing principle, but ascribes action and creation to
God Himself, apart from the Word, and in which a different
and exclusively spiritual sphere is assigned to the Word.*
Elsewhere God is called emphatically the *only true* God, and
the Son is at the same time distinguished from Him.† In such

---

* John v. 20. [But in verses 28, 29, the physical resurrection of the dead
is claimed by our Lord as His own work. The "speculative" idea that
in all things the Father works through the Son, is, no doubt, suppressed
in this passage, and it may be because our Lord during His earthly life
had divested Himself of His glory, and He ascribes the works which were
wrought through Him, directly to the Father.—ED.]

† Μόνος ἀληθινός, John xvii. 3 ; comp. vii 28 ; 1 John v. 20. In the last
passage quoted, the meaning of which has often been mistaken by doctrinal interpreters, the Son of God and the (θεὸς) ἀληθινός, are nevertheless
clearly distinguished, and that the more clearly, inasmuch as the latter is
there opposed to idols. In John, the word ἀληθινός generally signifies *true*
(chap. i. 9 ; iv. 23 ; vi. 32 ; xv. 1), and is employed in antithesis to that

an expression, the speculative idea of the unity of their essence is obviously disregarded or ignored. Or, again, the name God is given to the Father, so as to distinguish Him from the Word,[*] while the same expression is never employed of the Son alone, a distinction being even made between God and the Son of God.[†] But the most striking proof that popular language perpetually asserts its rights over the language of transcendental theology, is to be found in the many formulas which sustain the idea of a relation of dependence between the Son and the Father. It is indubitable that theology, to be consistent with its own premises, must exclude such a relation, and, in fact, it would be easy to show that it recognizes in principle the equality of the two divine persons. Thus the formula, " I and my Father are one,"[‡] cannot be understood as expressing simply a spiritual relation, though that relation is not excluded;[§] nor is there anything contrary to the spirit of the theology of John, when the employment of the names of Father and Son is explained as conveying a claim to equality,[||] etc. We know, indeed, that the theology of the primitive Church was not only careful to remain faithful to this principle, but also to proscribe the use of any expression that might seem to militate against it. It is none the less true that, beside the passage we have just quoted, there are others in which we find the idea of a relation of dependence and subordination, consequently of inequality, between the Father and Son. These two names indeed of themselves imply such an idea, for it is impossible for human reason (while it has freely chosen these terms as corresponding most closely with the speculative conception) to dissociate them from the accessory ideas of the priority of the one over the other in relation to time, and of authority and obedience as regards dignity. We willingly admit that these names,

which might falsely assume a certain name. [Reuss has associated three passages which require separate exegetical treatment.—ED.]

[*] John iii. 34 ; 1 John v. 11.
[†] John x. 35.
[‡] John x. 30.
[§] See John v. 38 ; comp. xvii. 21, and foll.
[||] John v. 17, and foll. ; comp. also xvi. 15, etc.

Father and Son, were not chosen with a view to express these accessory ideas; but it is evident that their necessary association with the terms did not deter the apostle from using them. We may further refer to the frequent employment of such words as *to send, mission, coming in the name of, not speaking of His own*, and the like.* These are all popular expressions, borrowed from the language of the Old Testament, which may, to a certain degree, be reconciled with the metaphysical theories we have set forth above, but which assuredly had an entirely different origin. This fact becomes still more evident when we find the Father spoken of as giving the Spirit to the Son,† and the Son declaring that He can do nothing of Himself.‡ In the latter passage we know that the reference is not to a physical but metaphysical necessity, which is perfectly in harmony with the idea of the Word, the more so that the intention with which the assertion is made, is to vindicate to the world the authority of the Son, not to detract in any way from His dignity. ·Nevertheless, the expressions, "the Son can do nothing of Himself but what He seeth the Father do;" "for what things the Father doeth, the same doeth the Son likewise," which form the substance of the assertion, imply, beyond a question, the idea of the superiority of the Father over the Son.

It is then an established fact that beside the formulas sanctioned by the system on which the theology of this gospel at first proceeded, there are others which differ from it. This is especially evident when that which the Son does is distinguished from that which is done by the Father,§ while the very conception of the hypostasis of the Word implies the absolute identity of the operations of both.

It is an ordinary expedient of exegesis to say that all this applies only to the word Incarnate, and not to the divine

---

* Πέμπειν, ἀποστέλλειν, ἐλήλυθα ἐν ὀνόματι (John v. 43), ἀπ' ἐμαυτοῦ οὐκ ἐλήλυθα, vii. 28; viii. 42.

† John i. 33; iii. 34.

‡ John v. 19, and foll.; 30.

§ John v. 20; comp. the phrases τὸ θέλημα τοῦ πέμψαντός με, vi. 38; iv. 34; ἐδίδαξέ με, viii. 28, 29; ἐντολὴν ἔδωκέ μοι, xii. 49; comp. xv. 10; xiv. 31; λόγον αὐτοῦ τηρῶ, viii. 55, etc.

hypostasis considered in itself. But it is obvious to remark
that such a distinction is contrary to the system; that John
does not regard the incarnation, with all that is involved in it,
as a humiliation or degradation of the Word (a very important
point to which we shall refer again); and, lastly, that there
are passages in which the divine attributes of the Word are
represented as being communicated, measured out, granted
to Him by love.* The notion of the Word is thus removed
from the metaphysical sphere to which it at first belonged.
Again, it is said that the Father gave life to the Son,† which,
combined with the formula of the prologue, cannot be understood as referring to the human birth of the man Jesus. The
same phrase, *He gave,* is used in relation to His glory, to
His power, to the Spirit; and all are summed up in this one
saying, "*He hath given all things into His hand.*"‡ Lastly, the
petitions addressed by the Son to the Father,§ belong to the
same series of ideas, which we shall not be startled to find
culminating in the thesis which has so perplexed the severe
scholasticism of ecclesiastical theology, "*the Father is greater
than I.*"‖

Modern writers, therefore, who have been of opinion that the
Logos of John is not the same as the *Logos* of Philo, have been
unquestionably justified, in view of the connection we have just
pointed out between the popular expressions and speculative
formulas employed in various passages, apart from many other
considerations, to which we shall have occasion to refer again.
But these writers are in error if they suppose they have thus
proved that the partial resemblance which exists between the
formulas of the apostle and those of the philosopher, does not

* I believe that the "orthodox" doctrine of the Trinity, while asserting
the "equality" of the Father and the Son, against all Arianizing theories,
affirms that the relation existing between the Incarnate Word and the
Father has its roots in the eternal relations of the Word to the Father.
—ED.
† John v. 26, ἔδωκε ζωὴν ἔχειν; comp. ζῶ διὰ τὸν πατέρα, vi. 57.
‡ John xvii. 24; iii. 34; v. 27; comp. xvii. 2; iii. 35; xiii. 3.
§ John xiv. 16; xvii. 5.
‖ Ὁ πατὴρ μείζων μοῦ ἐστίν, John xiv. 28.

imply any relation of origin between the two systems, at least as to their form and general features.*

It is then evident that the theology of John, in the development of its peculiar doctrinal premises, does borrow from contemporary speculation many and important expressions. It starts from certain convictions peculiar to itself, and which form its direct basis; it seeks to explain these in a scientific manner, by means of a phraseology which it finds elsewhere; but it does not so depart from its own point of view as to reject all ideas, definitions, and formulas which do not belong to the rigid and positive scholastic system, from which it has sought to borrow only the modes of thought. Such an alliance of two elements of different origin has in it nothing impossible, nothing which we must fail to comprehend. It is easily explained by the fact that the exposition is not given by the organ of any school; that the object of it was not to establish one metaphysical theory in preference to another; that speculation was not with the apostle an end, but a means; and that the final utterance of all his theology, which the premises were simply designed to support, is to be sought in an entirely different sphere. We shall arrive at it in due time and order; for the present, we have to offer some other observations bearing more closely on the subject immediately before us.

We have to consider the Word under a particular aspect, in

* The capital differences between the Logos of Philo and the Logos of John are very clearly stated by Godet, in his discussion of the Prologue to the Gospel (*L'Evangile de Saint Jean*, vol. i., 233). (1) Both Philo and John employ the same word Logos, but in altogether different senses. With John, according to the ordinary idiom of Scripture, it means the Word, *i.e.*, the medium of revelation; with Philo it has the philosophical sense, and means Reason. (2) The Logos of John is a Person; the Logos of Philo can hardly be called personal. (3) The function of the Logos according to Philo is the creation and preservation of the universe. With John the Logos is mentioned only in view of His appearance and incarnation as the Messiah. (4) The Logos of Philo is a metaphysical necessity, invented in order to effect a transition from God, who is conceived as the Absolute and the Infinite, to the finite universe. John's conception of God rendered no such intermediate element necessary, and his idea of the Logos is therefore of another kind.—ED.

which it will appear to us less abstract than before, and in direct
relation with the mystical ideas subsequently attaching themselves to His person. But we shall there see, also, that the
theology of the apostle, in the ideas peculiar to it, is perfectly
consistent with itself, and is always fully conscious both of its
starting-point and of the goal towards which it tends.

We have seen that God presents Himself to the religious
consciousness of John as light, love, and life; that these three
elements constitute His essence. The Word, inasmuch as He
is the revelation of God, or the revealing person in the Deity,
must necessarily present the same characteristics, and Himself
possess them, not as attributes only, but as His real and proper
essence.

The Word is light; He is *the* light, and the latter more exact
expression signifies that this light is the same as that which
constitutes the essence of God.*

The Word is love; He is *the* love, the same love which is the
essence of God. For just as God loves the Son, so does the
Son love God.† As the Father in love sent the Son, so
the Son in love accepted the mission.‡ Lastly, it is in love
that both look upon those who believe, and become one with
them.§

The Word is life; He is *the* life which dwells in God.|| He
has life in Himself, absolutely as the Father has,—essential,
inherent life,—life which He can communicate.¶ He is thus
called simply the Word-Life,** a phrase which must not be
explained away so as to signify nothing more than a thesis
of practical theology.

This threefold definition of the essence of the Word leads us
from the abstract region of thought into the mystical sphere
of faith. It will serve as a light to us in the study of this

* John i. 8 ; iii. 19 ; τὸ φῶς τὸ ἀληθινόν, i. 9 ; 1 John ii. 8.
† John xiv. 31.
‡ 1 John iii. 16.
§ John xiii. 1 ; xiv. 21 ; xv. 9, 12.
|| Ἐγὼ εἰμὶ ἡ ζωή, John xi. 24 ; John xiv. 6.
¶ John v. 26.
** Comp. John i. 4.

doctrinal system. We can discern in this threefold element, that which John calls "the *fulness*"* of the Word, that which changes our conception of it from an abstract into a concrete form.

Such is the dogmatic basis of the religious conception, developed in the writings of the apostle John; or, to speak more plainly, these are the theoretical premises upon which that conception is sustained. There are first, as has been said, certain speculative theses, taken from a theological system previously formed; secondly, there are ideas belonging to the general religious consciousness, combined with these theses in such a way as to bring them within the reach of minds little used to reflection, these more popular ideas often presenting the appearance of inconsistency with the speculative theses; lastly, there are the conceptions of the author himself, not very numerous, but all the more important in their bearing on the whole, and containing, as we shall presently see, the true germs of the mysticism of John.

* Πλήρωμα, John i. 16.

CHAPTER VII.

OF THE INCARNATION OF THE WORD.

WE pass on to a second series of facts, also forming part of the basis of the same mysticism. These, however, do not belong to the region of speculation, but to historical experience. They are outward, material events, which the reason apprehends first through observation, tradition, and memory, but which derive their theological importance, their significance and explanation, from the doctrinal premises with which they are brought into relation, and by becoming themselves the subject of theological reflection.

Hitherto we have spoken of only one kind of divine revelation, that which is given in the world itself, and which we speak of commonly under the name of the creation—that is, the communication of life to that which is not God, a communication which, however, was not effected once for all, in a long past moment of time, but which is continuous and unceasing.[*] This is what we might call the revelation of God in nature. Now we have to speak of a revelation of God in the world of spirits, an entirely new and distinct sphere of the divine operation. It will devolve upon us first to note the distinctive features of these two revelations.

In one aspect, the sphere of the new revelation appears at first sight more limited than that of the earlier, for it comprehends only one category of the numberless creations of God —the human race; and this is a prerogative vindicated in the view of the race thus honoured, by a direct act of the con-

---

[*] John v. 17 ; comp. i. 4.

sciousness.* It is true that the limit of this sphere is not as clearly defined above as below. John speaks of angels, a world of creatures superior to and less material than man; he uses in relation to them the common parlance of his contemporaries. They, in their turn, exercise an influence over physical nature,† and over the progress of events,‡ but the theological system does not assign to them any special place in its programme.

Again, this new revelation stands in a different relation to the world. The former was a revelation of God by creatures, animate or inanimate, so that the existence and the attributes of Deity are demonstrated by the existence, organization, preservation of His creatures, and by their relations among themselves. The latter is addressed to God's creatures—that is to say, to men. In both cases, God is the subject of the revelation, but in the second case there is a further very important end to be subserved. Man is to be separated from the series of creatures belonging exclusively to the world, to be raised to the height of that which is above the world, which is in God and with God,—that is, to the height of the Son,—a result possible, if not in the metaphysical, at least in the ethical sense.

Yet further: this second revelation brings to the world something different from the first. Creation was a communication of existence or life to that which had no existence before. The new revelation, addressed exclusively to man, is designed not only to raise this life to a higher degree of power, so that it should become eternal instead of temporal, spiritual instead of physical, perfect in every faculty; it is also designed to supply a new element on which this higher life may be nourished, namely, light and love.

* Perhaps we may regard 1 John iii. 9 as an attempt to demonstrate the fact in question, if it is allowable to put special emphasis upon the word μένει, which appears to contain implicitly the idea of a closer affinity between man and God, such as is explicitly asserted by Paul, Acts xvii. 28.

† John v. 4.

‡ John xx. 12.

Lastly: the two revelations are distinct also in the means used for their introduction into the world; this point, however, we reserve for future discussion.

All these ideas may be developed by the exegesis of a phrase of the prologue of which we have not yet made use, "*The life was the light of men.*" * This asserts that the life, the essence of the Word, becomes to men a light to lead them into the track of this higher life. It shows us, at the same time, what is the true significance of the speculative premises of the system we have been expounding, in relation to evangelical theology; for the fact that the Word is *God*, and the purely metaphysical theses connected with it, are not the essential element of Christianity, the gist of which is that the Word effects the salvation of men.

In the exposition of this second part of the system, the historical part, we shall have to direct our attention in succession to the revealing subject, the Word; to the sphere in which the revelation is given, the world; to the end and the means of the revelation; and, lastly, to its effects or results.

This new revelation of God was given by the Word in a manner also new. He appeared in bodily form; the Word became flesh.†

Before analyzing this thesis, let us well consider the cause of the extraordinary fact it establishes. This we shall discover in that one of the three essential attributes of the Godhead which appears to us the most exalted—namely, love. Love always seeks that which has affinity with itself; God will assimilate to Himself all that is divine, or is capable of becoming so; in this consists His joy, His highest satisfaction. This assimilation is wrought through the mediation of the Word, in a manner analogous to that by which the finite is brought into contact with the infinite; the infinite stoops to raise the finite to itself. This is the formula generally adopted by mystical theology, and which is found in Christian mysticism also.

The fact of the incarnation of the Word may be conceived

---

* John i. 4; ἡ ζωὴ ἦν τὸ φῶς τῶν ἀνθρώπων.
† Ὁ λόγος σὰρξ ἐγένετο, John i. 14.

and described either in a speculative or in a more popular manner. We shall find both in the writings of John, as the remarks already made will have led the reader to expect. The former being the more important, we shall speak of it first.

The Word was made flesh. Flesh is the term employed in the Bible to designate man as a corporeal, sensuous, mortal being. It is doubtless on account of this special signification that the term is here preferred to any other, as, for example, to the word *man*, because it is this particular aspect, this material element of human nature, which is to be brought into prominence to the exclusion of the spiritual element, the latter being of importance in relation to the work of the Word, but not to His essence. It will be further remarked that in the phrase we are analyzing, no article is used, which implies that it is intended to convey a purely generic idea. The author indeed employs two other formulas to express the same fact; he says, "He came to His own,"*—that is, to the world which He had created,—and He came in the flesh.† But these two phrases are far less expressive and exact than that before mentioned; for the one passes over in silence the essential fact of the incarnation; the other does not explicitly determine whether or not the Word was in the flesh before His coming into the world. In the phrase first quoted, the term *became* affirms positively that in thus coming He changed the form of His existence. In another aspect, however, the expression *He came in the flesh* is more exact than the former, because it shows that the Word only took flesh upon Him,—did not change His essence into flesh.

It is unnecessary to remind our readers that this thesis of the incarnation of the Word goes beyond the limits of Jewish theology, which takes no cognizance of it, so that we find ourselves here on more specifically Christian ground. We have been able to trace in many of the ideas analyzed in the preceding chapters, the influence exerted by Christian teaching on dogmas anterior to the Gospel. In this new dogma, that the Word became flesh, there is evidently an application of this

---

* John i. 11, εἰς τὰ ἴδια ἦλθεν.

† 1 John iv. 2, ἐν σαρκὶ ἦλθεν.

anterior speculation, and of its phraseology, to a fact which belongs essentially to the Christian faith, and to which the writer thus seeks to give a scientific expression. All the apostles might have a direct conviction of the superhuman dignity of Jesus, without being able to find at once a theological term adapted to convey the impression they had received of His mysterious and august presence. We here find that impression transferred by one of them into the domain of theological speculation.

The exposition of the doctrine, as it is given us in that gospel the substance of which we are now analyzing, is generally faithful to this speculative point of view. Some expressions, borrowed from the popular speech, and not in perfect harmony with it, will be mentioned presently. The earthly life of the Incarnate Word is and must be a ceaseless revelation of the Godhead. It is spoken of as a *dwelling* among men,* but that word gives but an imperfect rendering of the Greek or rather of the Hebrew term, which is used in Jewish philosophy to represent the personal presence of the Deity in the world He has created. The Word always maintains the uninterrupted and unwavering consciousness of this relation; He knows *whence He is,*† that is to say, He knows what He is, and what is His mission. The scene in Gethsemane, as narrated by Luke, and the exclamation on the cross, given by Matthew, find no place in the fourth gospel. They may have appeared to the evangelist John to be in contradiction with the theological fact in question.‡ The disciples themselves are

* 'Εσκήνωσεν ἐν ἡμῖν, John i. 14.

† Πόθεν ἐστί, John viii. 14, 23.

‡ In reference to the former, we may observe that there is a faint allusion to it in John xii. 27. But the ταράσσεσθαι of that passage (comp. chap. xiii. 21, and especially chap. xi. 33,) is an emotion in no way incompatible with the fullest assurance of the triumph of the spirit over the flesh, and with the utmost independence of will. [In neither of the synoptical gospels are there any stronger illustrations of the reality of our Lord's humanity than are found in the fourth gospel. St. John never shrinks from the narration of circumstances which might seem to imperil the great theological truths affirmed in his prologue. The agitation of our Lord described in John xii. 27, when He was surrounded by a crowd, and when the agony of Gethsemane and the desertion of the cross were

fully aware of the presence of the divine essence in the Saviour, in spite of the earthly form assumed by Him; and it must necessarily be thus, or the revelation would not be real and complete; it would have failed of its end. Thus it is said, "We *saw* His glory, the glory as of the only begotten of the Father;"* and again, "He that hath seen me, hath *seen* the Father."† All these expressions would be meaningless, if our supposition were erroneous. But neither are they intended to bring down the revelation of God into the sphere of the observation of the senses, for it is clear, especially from the passage last quoted, that this vision of God ‡ is not granted indiscriminately to all, and in other passages§ the divine dignity appertaining to the Word is insisted on as a thing not acknowledged by all.

We may be allowed to bring forward several other passages which appear to us to refer to a revelation of divine things, of which the prepared eye alone is receptive, and which is communicated to it only by and since‖ the fact of the appearing of the Word in the flesh. It is thus we interpret that which is said of the heavens being opened, and of the relation established between God and the Son of man, by the angels ascending and descending. These *angels* ¶ (an expression, like the *Word*, borrowed from the philosophical school) are the divine perfections common to both persons of the Deity, and maintaining between them the community of will and action, in spite of the difference in their position, for the time, in relation to the world. A literal explanation would here be equally meagre and absurd.** There is another similar passage, according to which the abstract life immanent in God has assumed a con-

still at some little distance, is just as inconsistent or just as consistent with the "theological fact" of which Reuss is speaking, as the sharper conflict and the deeper desolation which John has omitted.—ED.]

* John i. 14.
† John xiv. 9; comp. v. 7; viii. 19; xii. 45.
‡ Θεωρεῖν, θεάσασθαι.
§ John viii. 50, 54; v. 41.
‖ 'Απάρτι.
¶ John i. 52; ἄγγελοι.
** Our Lord was speaking to a Jew, and used a memorable fact in Jewish history. Jacob's dream was an assurance to him that even in the

crete form, and has been revealed to us by the Word.* All these propositions have at the same time a practical importance to which we shall refer again.

We thus verify the objective and positive equality of the revelation and of that which is revealed. A careful analysis of the texts will confirm this fact by a series of consequences and applications naturally resulting from it. Thus, to the Incarnate Word is attributed an adequate knowledge of all that relates to God,† and hence also a power of communicating that knowledge adequately.‡ Thus, again, divine prerogatives are ascribed to Him,—that, for example, of reading the secrets of all hearts,§ of freedom from sin,‖ a quality with which that of exemption from error is closely allied. Thus, lastly, that which is done by the Word is spoken of simply as the work of God.¶ The *works* referred to in these passages, inasmuch as they have a miraculous element, (for the term does not always designate what we call *miracles*) are signs and tokens to lead men to the recognition of the presence of the divine.** But regarded from a higher standpoint, miracles are no accidental feature in the operation of the Word; they are, on the contrary, something normal, natural, inherent in His being; they are not even the highest or most glorious feature of His manifestation.††

From all this it follows that the revealing Word could de-

exile which he was about to endure because of his sin he was not to be exiled from God. The angels—ministers of divine power and love—were still near to him : there was no impassable gulf between him and God. The ladder between heaven and earth was a symbol of the unbroken relations between the patriarch and God ; and our Lord Jesus Christ declares that Nathanael should see in Himself that these relations were still unbroken. The miracles of Christ and His whole character and history were a revelation of God's nearness to the human race.—ED.

   * 1 John i. 2.
   † John viii. 55 ; x. 15.
   ‡ John iii. 11 ; viii. 38.
   § John ii. 24.
   ‖ 1 John ii. 1 ; iii. 3, 5, 7 ; vii. 18 ; viii. 46.
   ¶ John ix. 4 ; x. 37, and foll. ; xiv. 10, ἔργα.
   ** John ii. 11.
   †† John i. 51 ; v. 20.

mand for Himself, on the part of men, the same sentiments and dispositions which they ought to entertain towards the person of the Father. These are expressed by a word which includes the notion of respect shown to a superior, the recognition of a dignity before which men bow.* In this respect, there is equality between the two divine Persons in relation to man. Those who believe in the one believe also in the other; to see the one is to see the other; to reject and hate the Son is to reject and hate the Father.† But in all this there is no reference to what in the practical language of the Church is called *worship*. Worship is due to God the Father, and will be henceforward presented to Him all the more willingly because He is better known, and there is no longer anything to separate between Him and the believing soul.‡

We here touch on another theological fact, which, in the system we are expounding, is a simple corollary of the premises; but which, by a caprice of the scholasticism of Protestant theologians especially, has been completely neglected and ignored. In the theology of John, the incarnation of the Word, and all that relates to His sojourn upon earth, is no humiliation. The Word did not descend (save in the purely local sense of the word §) to an existence which would have deprived Him of His dignity; He did not lay aside anything proper to His divinity. In a word, there is no suggestion of what the theology of the Church has called the *status inanitionis* of the Saviour. His earthly and corporeal existence does not stand in contrast with His spiritual and heavenly life; it is rather in the relation of an accessory to that life.‖ Christ holds upon earth uninterrupted

---

* Τιμᾷν, John v. 23.

† John iii. 33, 34; xii. 44; xv. 23.

‡ John iv. 20, and foll.; comp. xvii. 3.

§ John iii. 13.

‖ This passage seems to contradict violently the characteristic teaching of St. John's Gospel, which is to the effect that a Divine Person was not only revealed under a human form, but actually *became* man; the Personality of our Lord Jesus Christ, the Ego, was divine, the nature human. The co-existence of divine glory with human suffering in the same Person at the same time is not what is affirmed in this gospel, and is inconsistent with many passages in it, and especially with chapter xvii.—ED.

communion with heaven, which to Him is always open;* He
is in possession of the fulness of glory, as of grace and truth;†
in a word, all that we have just said as to the nature, the conditions, and the purpose of the incarnation, altogether exclude
the idea of an inferior condition. That the Word should have
taken flesh, that He should have become man, does not degrade
the Word, but exalts humanity. The human element cannot
fetter or deteriorate the divine, cannot encroach upon or compromise it. Doubtless, we shall presently see that the theology
of John speaks of the sufferings and death of the God-Man;
but even this is not regarded in this system as *inanition;*
for not only does the Word retain, through all these terrible
crises of His earthly life, all that He before possessed, but
John repeatedly speaks of His closing hour as that of His
highest glorification. His death is always called a lifting-up,‡
an exaltation. It is idle for popular theology to assert that these
expressions refer to a state of future glorification, after the
resurrection or ascension: the last passage quoted in the note,
alone proves very explicitly that such was not the idea of the
apostle, who would not have so constantly insisted upon the
point of view, which we are vindicating as his own, if his
mind had not been absorbed in the leading idea of his system,
that the Word is God, and that God cannot for a moment cease
to be God in all His fulness. Logic and metaphysics can recognize no other theory.

But, it may be said, the very term elevation or glorification
implies the idea of an inferior position, out of which the subject
of it is raised, and we are thus thrown back upon the formula
of the schools. By no means. We will not dwell upon the
vast difference between the scholastic formula and that of John,
the latter speaking of the death of Christ as a glorification,
the former as a humiliation, even the very lowest stage of

* John i. 52.
† John i. 14.
‡ 'Τψοῦσθαι, John iii. 14; viii. 28; xii. 32; δοξάζεσθαι, xii. 23; xiii. 31.
[John himself interprets this last passage as referring to the kind of death
He was to die.—Ed.]

abasement.* We have a remark of greater importance to make here. Neither the death nor resurrection of Christ makes any change at all in His dignity; He is no greater on the resurrection morning than on the eve of the resurrection, because He was even then the Divine Word, the *alter ego* of Deity. That which is changed is the relation of the Word to the world, and the disposition of the world with regard to Him. The *glory* which was henceforth to be His was not any blessedness, power, or divine quality whatever, which hitherto He had lacked (for in such a case He would not have been God); it is an external glory; it is a greater power of attraction to be exerted over men, a richer harvest to be gathered in from His labours; it is the ever-growing empire which His apostles will bring into subjection under Him; the yet greater works which they will do in His name; it is, lastly, the more and more perfect knowledge of His will and of His revelations.† Even the passage which might seem the least favourable to our view,‡ is really in accordance with it. So far from sustaining the idea that the incarnation is a humiliation, it proclaims that from the moment of the death of Jesus on the cross, (upon that cross which, by its very form, is the symbol of

* We may be permitted to observe, in passing, that Christian feeling loves, and rightly loves, to dwell on the contemplation of the sufferings and cruel outrages endured by Jesus Christ in the fulfilment of His saving work. The picture of His suffering is summed up in the well-known words, "*Behold the Man,*" which give, so to speak, the popular expression of the theological idea of the state of inanition. As this formula is taken from John's gospel, it might be brought forward in opposition to our view, but such an application of it is altogether at variance with the context. First, it is the language, not of John, but of Pilate; and the object of Pilate is not to excite compassion, as has been gratuitously supposed, but to defy the Jews. This is clear from verses 14 to 19. This seems therefore in no way to change the theological standpoint of John's gospel.

† John xii. 24, 32; xiv. 12, and foll.; xvi. 14.

‡ John xvii. 5. [How this can be in accordance with Reuss's view is not shown. The glory which the Word had with the Father before the creation of the world, and for the restoration of which He prays, had surely been laid aside, and at the time of His prayer was not actually in His possession.—ED.]

exaltation,)* there begins a period of glory for His name, of glory which is to become again universal and illimitable, as it was before the creation of the world, when evil and opposition had no existence. This glory of the Word dwells first in the hearts of those who know the Lord, and all who carry on His work will be made sharers in it.†

There is yet one more observation to be made on the Incarnate Word, before we come to speak of His work. He bears a special name, but it is one which He has Himself chosen, which was not invented by theology. Theology only endeavours to explain it in conformity with its principles.‡ He called Himself the Son of Man. This name, which is found also in the other gospels, but is never used by any but the Saviour Himself, assuredly indicates in the gospel of John, the Incarnate Word, the God-Man. In this formula, the emphasis is laid, so to speak, upon the human nature, because it is through it that saving relation is established between God and the world, which leads to redemption. This is especially evident from the one passage, where this term, employed without an article, stands rather as an adjective than a proper name.§ It thus designates the special characteristic of the person of Jesus, on which is based His prerogative of exercising a function belonging to God alone. For in this system, God, as God, does not come into contact with the world of which He is the Judge. For this work He becomes man, and it is in this capacity He exercises judgment.

Hitherto, we have found the theology of the gospel of John developing strictly the notion of the Word Incarnate, and the

* This idea probably suggested the parellelism between the death of Jesus and the lifting up of the serpent in the wilderness (John iii. 14), in which the emphasis is upon the word ὑψοῦν. If we find in it anything more than this, it is only one proof the more that the author plays upon words under a misconception of their significance, as is clearly the case in chap. xii. 32, 33, where certainly ὑψωθῆναι ἐκ τῆς γῆς does not mean *to be crucified*.

† John xvii. 10, 12.

‡ Ὁ υἱὸς τοῦ ἀνθρώπου, John i. 52; iii. 13, and foll.; vi. 27, 53, 62; viii. 28; xii. 23; xiii. 31.

§ John v. 27.

results naturally flowing from it. With regard to the exegesis there remains nothing to be added; before proceeding, however, we desire to show that this theology really does go as far as we have said, and no farther. Philosophical speculation, as it has been used by the theologians of the Church, whether in former days or in our own, finding these theses insufficient in many points, has raised fresh questions, and given more exact definitions, while always pretending to keep within the limits of apostolic teaching. Our task is accomplished when we have exhausted the texts themselves.

Thus we affirm that the texts say nothing explicit as to the moment or period of the incarnation of the Word. The Church has decided the question by the dogma of the supernatural generation of the man Jesus in the womb of a virgin. To this dogma it has been led less perhaps by the positive narrations of the first and third gospels, than by deference to logic, which pointed to such a solution as the only one possible, in view of the theological principle of the incarnation of God and the historical fact that Jesus was born of Mary. We find in John no texts which contradict this dogma, but neither do we find any directly sustaining it. We might almost be led to think that he combines the fact of the incarnation with that of the descent of the Spirit at the baptism of the Saviour; at least it is to be observed, that in the chronological exposition of the first chapter, we read first of John the Baptist, and only subsequently of the incarnation; and it is certain that many of the old Fathers make no distinction between the Spirit and the Word. We do not mention these arguments, however, as conclusive on the point; on the contrary, we believe that the idea of a union of the Word with a mere human individual existing previously apart from Him, has in it something repulsive which will incline the balance in favour of the orthodox theory, wherever the premises are the same. We conclude, then, that on this point, the speculation of the evangelist paused midway.

We shall arrive at the same conclusion in relation to another question much debated in the Church, and on which, after ages of controversy and numerous dogmas decided on by the old councils, the scholasticism of Protestants has made yet fresh discoveries. We allude to the union of the two natures. In the theology of John, the Word Incarnate is an indivisible person. There is as little suggestion of a human mind or a human will, side by side with the mind and will of God, as there is of a divine body in conjunction with the human. If in logic we may separate the two natures, and contemplate them apart, in theology they are blended. Many examples prove this assertion. The expression *Son of Man*, for instance, which can belong only to the Incarnate Word, is employed also,[*] and even in the present tense, when the reference is to His anterior existence. Elsewhere,[†] we find the name of Jesus, when the strict logic of the system would demand the name of the Word; while in another passage the contrary is true.[‡] There is no controversion of this view in the fact that the gospel attributes to Jesus, beside the physical infirmities inseparable from human nature, feelings and emotions similar to those of men.[§] John nowhere says that these psychical manifestations implied any derogation from the dignity of the Divine nature; else the Divine Spirit would have been bound to repress or repel them; or rather their very existence would be an anomaly in His being, a supposition perfectly incompatible with the system of John.[‖]

But it will be beyond our subject to show by other examples that the speculation of ecclesiastical schools has gone far beyond the limits observed by the apostle in his teaching. Our aim is rather to show that the latter, in the choice of his expressions, is often content to remain within the circle of popular

[*] John iii. 13 ; comp. vi. 62.
[†] John iv. 2.
[‡] John i. 18 ; comp. v. 17.
[§] John xi. 33 ; xii. 27 ; xiii. 21.
[‖] Why it should be more inconsistent with the " dignity " of a Divine *Person* to assume a moral and emotional nature rendering Him capable of psychical experiences which are impossible to God, than to assume a physical nature rendering Him capable of physical experiences impossible to God, Reuss does not explain.—ED.

phraseology and ideas, though they do not harmonize with the theory previously announced, for the simple reason, that he was not attempting to give a philosophical system, but to preach the Gospel, and that a deviation from the strict phraseology of the schools would not only be no detriment to such an end, but might even render his teaching more striking and suggestive.

Among the popular expressions used by him, which may claim notice in this chapter, we have, first, the name of *Christ*. No one can be ignorant that this is the name given by the Jews to a personage whose origin had nothing in common with the idea of the Logos, and that it indicates, etymologically, royal office and dignity. In the primitive Church this name was cherished, undoubtedly, because of the community of hopes connected with it. Jesus Christ became the historical and official designation of this personage, as He was recognized by the Christians. The historian, therefore, used the name in his gospel,* and the preacher still more frequently in his epistle. When we find this same name put into the mouth of the Saviour Himself,† it affords another evidence that His discourses have been freely reproduced by the disciple.

We place in the same category the often-repeated expressions *to send, to come from God, from above, from heaven,* in which the metaphysical premises are lost sight of, or, at least, thickly veiled.‡

Lastly, we may note the passage § in which the Father and Son are numerically distinguished, and formally separated, as two distinct authorities. There is repeated mention of a

---

* John i. 17 ; xx. 31.

† John xvii. 3. [Is not Reuss's suggestion cancelled by the remarkable fact that it is only once, and then when speaking to God, that this title is appropriated by our Lord Himself ? If St. John had reproduced our Lord's discourses with the freedom which the text affirms, the title would probably have occurred very often.—ED.]

‡ Ἀποστέλλειν, ὁ πέμψας, ἐξέρχεσθαι ἀπὸ θεοῦ, John xiii. 3 ; παρὰ θεοῦ, xvi. 27, and foll. ; xvii. 8; ἄνωθεν, ἐξ οὐρανοῦ, iii. 31. It will be remembered that the popular idea, as represented by Nicodemus, is expressed by the same term, iii. 2.

§ John viii. 17, and foll.

special witness borne by God to the Word,* of a consecration
of the Word to the ministry,† of works done by God for Him,
or by Him, to attest His dignity and mission.‡   In all these
phrases the metaphysical point of view is evidently abandoned,
and we find ourselves on the ground of a purely popular teaching, which speaks of Christ almost as the Old Testament might
speak of a prophet.

> * John v. 32, and foll.
> † Ἁγιάζειν, John x. 36.
> ‡ John x. 25, 32 ; σφραγίζειν, John vi. 27.

CHAPTER VIII.

OF THE WORLD.

THE Word came into the world. It was then for the world's behoof that His manifestation took place. Let us first inquire what, according to this system, the world is, and get a definite idea of it.

The world is, first and primarily, the totality of created things, without regard to moral qualities; so that beings endowed with ethical faculties are not necessarily comprised in it.*

But more frequently the world represents, as it does in our use of it, the totality of rational and intelligent beings; at least, these are not excluded when the visible order of things is spoken of. In this sense we understand the phrase *to come into the world*.† Here the manifestation of the Word is always spoken of with regard to His work, as elsewhere the same expression is used in speaking of men who are sent among their fellows on a special mission.‡ We shall connect with it the phrase *to send into the world*,§ the very idea of a mission implying that of humanity as its object. Lastly, we take in the same sense *to be in the world*,‖ a phrase which is used

---

* Ὁ κόσμος, John xi. 9 ; comp. xvii. 5, 24 ; i. 10 ; xxi. 25. In the first passage, φῶς τοῦ κόσμου is the sun ; ὁ βίος τοῦ κόσμου, 1 John iii. 17, are material riches.

† Εἰς τὸν κόσμον ἔρχεσθαι, John i. 9 ; iii. 19, where the author immediately after uses ἄνθρωποι, xi. 27 ; xvi. 28.

‡ John vi. 14 ; comp. xvi. 21 ; 1 John iv. 1.

§ Ἀποστέλλειν εἰς τὸν κόσμον, John iii. 17 ; x. 36 ; xvii. 18 ; 1 John iv. 9.

‖ Ἐν τῷ κόσμῳ εἶναι, John i. 10 ; ix. 5 ; xvii. 11, and foll.

in contrast with the return of the Word to the Father: it
designates, therefore, a local and temporal relation with the
present order of things. We may place in the same category
many other texts also;* but this signification is still more
positive in all the phrases which speak directly of a revelation,
and in which the world represents the totality of the persons to
whom this revelation is addressed: as when we read that God
revealed to the world, spake to the world, loved the world; or
of the light of the world, the Saviour of the world, the bread
which gives life to the world, of judging the world, of the
world's believing, of the whole world.†

But we have yet to point out an important modification of
the idea of the world, founded on a doctrinal thesis, which
naturally comes before us here. The world—that is to say,
the great body of men, taken as a whole, and regarded from
an ethical point of view—is evil; that is to say, is alienated
from God, and become strange to Him. The term in question
hence comes to be used of humanity, as exhibiting this particular characteristic, and the majority of passages to be quoted
belong to this category. The world is thus spoken of simply
as *this world*, the world as it is, as we know it by our own
experience, this evil world.‡ It thus forms an antithesis with
life;§ that which is of the world is worthless. This world
neither knows nor recognizes that which is of God; it neither
accepts nor receives it; it rather hates.‖ Sin is therefore an
attribute justly ascribed to it.¶ In a word, and that a very
emphatic one, we read that *the whole world lieth in the wicked
one.*** Hence, again, is derived the particular significance of

* John xviii. 36; comp. xiii. 1; xvi. 29; xvii. 15; 1 John iv. 3.
† John i. 4; iii. 16, and foll.; iv. 42; vi. 33, 51; vii. 4; viii. 12, 26;
ix. 5; xii. 46, and foll.; xvii. 21, and foll.; xviii. 20; 1 John ii. 2; iv. 14.
‡ Ὁ κόσμος οὗτος, John viii. 23; 1 John iv. 17; comp. John ix. 39;
xii. 31.
§ John xii. 25; xiv. 27.
‖ John i. 10; vii. 7; xiv. 17; xv. 18, and foll.; xvi. 20, 33; xvii.
14, 25; 1 John iii. 1, 13.
¶ John i. 29; xvi. 8; comp. xv. 22.
** Ὁ κόσμος ὅλος ἐν τῷ πονηρῷ κεῖται, 1 John v. 19.

the phrase *to be of the world :** it designates those who have the qualities of the world—who are in moral and spiritual affinity with it—who share its sentiments—who are, so to speak, born of the world, and inspired by it. Thus we understand the exhortation, given elsewhere, *to overcome the world.*† It is not even necessary to this understanding of it that we think of the world in its concrete form, that is to say that we have men specially in view in thus describing it. The existing order of things *in abstracto* possesses the same elements, because the sensible or material element and sin are paramount in it.‡

In this last sense—which, we say again, is the most frequent in the texts before us—the world and God are essentially opposed to each other. The will of God and the tendencies of the world are divergent and hostile. The attributes and characteristics of the world are simply the negation of the characteristics and attributes we have noted as essential to the Divine Being.

Instead of light, the world is darkness ;§ and the term darkness is in one passage used to represent it.‖ Elsewhere it is spoken of expressly as the negation of the divine light.¶ Hence the phrases *to walk, to be, to abide in darkness.*** The image is obviously borrowed from physical obscurity—that which seals the eyes of the body ;†† and it is thence transferred to the moral sphere. It is the equivalent of *not seeing,* in the spiritual and ideal sense.‡‡

In place of love, the world is characterized by hatred.§§ We may here point especially to the passages of the epistle in

* Ἐκ τοῦ κόσμου, John xv. 19; xvii. 14, and foll. ; 1 John ii. 16; iv. 5.
† 1 John v. 4, and foll. ; comp. xvi. 33.
‡ 1 John ii. 15, and foll.
§ Σκότος, σκοτία.
‖ John i. 5.
¶ John iii. 19; 1 John ii. 8.
** John viii. 12; xii. 46; 1 John i. 6; ii. 9, 11.
†† John xii. 35; 1 John ii. 11.
‡‡ John xiv. 19, 22.
§§ Μισεῖν, John vii. 7; xv. 18, and foll. ; xvii. 14; 1 John iii. 13.

which brotherly love and fratricidal hate are represented as the distinctive traits respectively of the children of God and the children of the world.*

Instead of life, the world is characterized by death.† The phrases in which this term is used—such as, *to abide in death, to pass from death unto life*—explain themselves.: we shall not dwell upon them. To die, to perish, are words which occur frequently, to denote the antithesis of participation in the divine life.‡

Such, according to the representation of the apostle, is the state of the world at large. We naturally look for an explanation from him of such a condition of things. The texts furnish a reply, entering on the question in various ways. The reader will judge if the explanations they suggest or attempt, are exhaustive or satisfactory to the inquiring mind.

In the first place, we cannot accept as a solution of the problem its mere reproduction in other words. The state of darkness is ascribed§ to an actual blindness on the part of men as its cause: and it is said that the Word came into the world to open the blind eyes. This intellectual defect, it is said, may extend to a moral insensibility, highly reprehensible.‖ But this explanation will not lead us to the desired end: it is only the substitution of one figure of speech for another of the same kind; and the fact of blindness, if it is the cause of darkness in the spiritual world, needs in its turn to be accounted for.

Again, we find that John, like Paul, notes in man the divergence of the constituent elements, which are summed up in the terms flesh and spirit. These two elements are directly op-

---

* For example, 1 John iv. 20. We may just indicate here that the theology of John employs the common term ψεῦδος, lie, to designate together the two characteristics of darkness and hatred, 1 John ii. 21, 27; in the same way he uses ἀλήθεια, truth, to represent both light and love. See Chapter XI., to follow.

† Θάνατος, John v. 24; 1 John iii. 14.

‡ Ἀποθνήσκειν, ἀπόλλυσθαι, ἀπώλεια, John iii. 15 and foll.; vi. 39, 40; x. 28; xi. 26; xvii. 12; xviii. 9.

§ John ix. 39, 41; comp. xv. 22.

‖ John xiv. 17; comp. vi. 52, 63.

posed to each other,* and it is said, in relation to them, that the spirit can only gain the ascendant over the flesh by divine aid. Apart from this, men walk after the flesh;† but it is to be observed that the theology of John nowhere dwells upon this opposition; it does not develop the consequences of so fruitful a principle; it does not describe, as Paul does, the conflict between the two principles, or rather it seems to reject the very idea of a conflict, the flesh being represented as exercising undisputed sway; but as we are not told why this is the case, this unfinished psychological explanation is not of a nature to satisfy us. Science requires more.

John reverts frequently to what may be called a moral explanation, according to which the refusal given, on the part of man, to the offers of God, is represented as proceeding from his moral insensibility, his egoism, his passions, his love of the world and of pleasures;‡ in a word, from his evil mind.§ Such a disposition must be without excuse, because no means have been neglected to turn man's feet into a better way.‖ Hence we are brought into direct contact with the idea of *sin*, the characteristics of which we shall observe. Sin is general.¶ It manifests itself in particular or individual acts, which are essentially the result of a moral disposition, to which the same name is applied in the singular.** There is, then, no difference, in reality, between the disposition and the acts. The transition from the sinful impulse to the positive and material deed, is called the commission of sin.†† This is represented sometimes as a real and objective fact;‡‡ sometimes as a principle, a power to which

---

* John iii. 6.

† Κατὰ σάρκα, John viii. 15; 1 John ii. 16.

‡ John v. 44; vii. 18; xii. 43; xii. 25; 1 John ii. 15; ἀγάπη τοῦ κόσμου, ἐπιθυμία τῆς σαρκός.

§ John iii. 19, and foll.

‖ John xv. 22, and foll.

¶ 1 John 7, and foll.

** Ἀμαρτίαι, ἁμαρτία, John viii. 21, 24.

†† Ποιεῖν τὴν ἁμαρτίαν, with the article; John viii. 34; 1 John iii. 4.

‡‡ John i. 29.

man has become subservient.* All this is not exactly a definition of sin, and, in truth, the texts give no such definition. It is expressly characterized, however, as disobedience, or rebellion against the law of God,† whether as a general tendency or as a special and actual transgression. To sin is, then, the opposite of being righteous; it is the reverse of conduct conformed to the will of God.‡

This is all that we discover in the writings of John in relation to the nature of sin.§ In returning, after this digression, to our original question, we may observe once again, (and none will fail to agree with us), that the apostle has not in all this traced this opposition of the world to God and the Word, to any ultimate cause. All that we have just cited is rather a change in the form of the question than a final reply to it. In fact, we have asked why the world is opposed to God, and we are told that this is the result of sin. Obviously, we have next to ask, Whence comes sin? Nor, let it be remembered, is it we who put this question for the mere pleasure of inquiry : it is a question with which theology and philosophy have been occupied in all ages. It is true that, for the present, we have nothing to do with the theories put forth by either; but, from our exegetical and historical point of view, we may inquire whether, after the attempts at explanation just adverted to, we may not find some further help in the texts themselves towards the solution of the problem. We shall now show that the theology of John does go further, and holds in reserve a reply which will lead us back one more step in our inquiry into the origin of evil.

Evil comes from the devil. The devil is designated sometimes by the common Hebrew appellation, or its translation ;‖ but most frequently John calls him by an essentially theological

---

* John viii. 34.

† Ἀνομία, 1 John iii. 4.

‡ Ἀδικία, 1 John i. 9 ; v. 17.

§ We may take this opportunity to remark that the opinion, so deeply rooted in the spirit of Judaism, that physical evil is always the result of sin, is especially repudiated, John ix. 3.

‖ Ὁ σατανᾶς, John xiii. 27   ὁ διάβολος, passim.

name—the evil one.* His nature is defined † as the negation of
all that is real and true in God and by God—the negation of
light, of love, of life ; or, again, he is described as a liar from
the beginning.‡ Thus his very essence and innermost nature
is said to be a lie. All the individual sins of men, from the
fratricide of Cain to the treason of Judas,§ are ascribed to his
inspiration. Men are therefore called his children, and even
devils.‖ Speaking generally, every ulterior negation of the
divine element, all opposition to the truth which is in God, is
his work.¶ As we have already seen that the world at large
is pronounced to be wicked, and now that all wickedness is
traced to the devil, it will be easy for us to discern the true
meaning of many passages in which the two subjects are
brought together. Thus the saying already quoted—*the whole
world lieth in the wicked one*—may be understood rather of a
spiritual fellowship of the world with the personal devil, than
of an immoral state *in abstracto*.** This explanation is directly
confirmed by the periphrase of the name of the devil : *he who
is in the world ; or the prince of this world*.†† The latter
designation does not of necessity contain the notion of an
absolutely invincible mastery, but of a power that is actually
victorious. Lastly, we may remark, again, that the works of
men receive the same qualification : they are evil.‡‡

The theology of John goes no further : it pauses here at the
foot of a rock, against which it does not indeed dash itself, like
ecclesiastical theology, but which, on the other hand, it does
not attempt to round ; we might almost say it is unconscious
of its existence. Whence comes the evil in the devil ? If all

---

* 'Ο πονηρός.

† John viii. 44 ; οὐκ ἔστιν ἀλήθεια ἐν αὐτῷ . . . ψεύστης ἐστί.

‡ 'Απ' ἀρχῆς, 1 John iii. 8.

§ John viii. 44 ; 1 John iii. 12 ; John xiii. 2.

‖ 1 John iii. 8, 10 ; John vi. 70.

¶ Πατὴρ τοῦ ψεύστου, John viii. 44.

** John v. 19.

†† 'Ο ἐν τῷ κόσμῳ, 1 John iv. 4 ; ὁ ἄρχων τοῦ κόσμου τούτου, John xii. 31 ;
xiv. 30 ; xvi. 11.

‡‡ John iii. 19 ; vii. 7

that is evil comes from him, it follows that evil had no existence before him—that it exists nowhere apart from him. He
is evil by nature from the very beginning of his existence.*
If the term *beginning*, applied to the Word,† involve the idea
of absolute eternity, it would follow that the same idea should
apply to the devil, and he should be regarded as an evil being
from all eternity—an Ahriman; and our gospel then gives the
Manichæan doctrine in its most absolute form.‡ But we have
shown that the meaning of this term is only relative. On the
one hand, John means to say of the Word, that it has existed
ever since there has been a contingent existence at all, and
before any other existence; on the other hand, he means to say
of the devil, that he has been evil ever since he had a being,
and *before* any other evil existed. But did God then create
him evil? This is impossible, and would be in flagrant contradiction with John's system. It is not for us here to undertake the solution of the problem; our task is done when we
have shown that no solution is given of it in this gospel—that
the problem itself seems scarcely to present itself to the
apostle. That we may leave no doubt at all as to the truth
of our assertion, we may add that John nowhere falls into the
very common inconsistency of speaking of the devil as a fallen
angel. It is indeed strange blindness not to perceive that this
hackneyed formula, so far from explaining the origin of evil,
only renders any explanation of it impossible. In fact, if the
principle of evil is not contained virtually in the primitive
constitution of human nature, because all that proceeds from
the hand of God must be perfect, it is evident that neither will
it be developed from the primitive constitution of the angelic
nature, which must have shared to at least an equal degree in
this original perfection; and we must needs suppose a tempter
to lead the angel to his fall, as a tempter was needed to bring
about the fall of man. But the fact is that John does not

* Ἀμαρτάνει ἀπ' ἀρχῆς, 1 John iii. 8.
† 1 John ii. 13; comp. John i. 1.
‡ But St. John says "the devil sinneth *from* the beginning," while he
says that the Word was "*in* the beginning."—ED.

speak of the fall of either man or angel. It is very probable that theological speculation may not be satisfied with the statements of the Gospel; indeed, it has shown that it is not so, by going far beyond it. But this is only a fresh proof that neither the aim of this gospel, nor the essence of its theology, is circumscribed within the narrow sphere of speculation.

Hitherto we have been considering the character of the world in general, in so far as all men are supposed to possess it in common. Even this, however, should be understood with a certain restriction. All men are not placed on the same level in a moral point of view, and in relation to the divine element, according to which relation, their individual status must be estimated. A word has already been said, in passing, as to this diversity, when we were discussing the intellectual causes of the opposition between the world and God. But the apostle is more explicit in other passages. Men are first divided by him into two categories, one of which—the evil—is so numerous, and embraces so large a majority, that the idea of the world, while it really contains both classes, has come to be characterized by all the qualities that really belong to this evil majority.

Thus it is said,* in relation to Cain and Abel, that the works of the one were evil, and of the other righteous. The former is therefore a child of the devil, and it is on account of the murder of Cain that the devil, who prompted it, is called a murderer from the beginning (of the history of men). In the same manner, at the time when the Word was manifested to the world, men were already divided into the evil (those who did evil), and the good (those who did truth);† and in relation to the latter, the text expressly says, and that before the saving influence of Christ had even begun, that their works were wrought *in God.* Even before this, the evangelist divides men into two classes, the one accepting, the other rejecting the light, without inquiring into or pointing out the cause of this difference of the relation established, as it would seem spontaneously,

* 1 John iii. 12.
† Φαῦλα πράσσοντες, ποιοῦντες τὴν ἀλήθειαν, John iii. 20, and foll.

between them and the Word.* It is, at least, only through
the acceptance of the Word that these last become children of
God. They were not, then, such already. Lastly, mention is
also made of children of God,† scattered throughout the whole
world before the commencement of Messiah's work: it is said
of these that they belonged to God‡ before they were received
by Christ.

We are well aware that John protests against the supposition that any man, whoever he be, is absolutely free from sin,
and against any claim based upon such a supposition.§ He
insists, however, with emphasis, upon the difference existing
between the natural and spontaneous tendencies of men, in the
degree of eagerness with which they receive that which is
offered to them. And on this point he can appeal to experience, no less than when the universality of sin is concerned.
It must be observed, however, that he does not explain this
diversity. We are naturally led to think here of the doctrine
of predestination, which will be discussed presently. But the
texts to which we have referred do not lead us to it; the
apostle makes no mention of it in this connection; and hence
we have been obliged to assign another place in our systematic
exposition, to this particular dogma.

In order to complete our observations on the world, we must
here recall one circumstance which is of a nature to modify
essentially its character and condition.

The revelation connected with the person of the Incarnate
Word is not the first dispensation of this kind granted to
humanity. Another revelation, coming equally from God, and
appointed by Him, had previously been given in Judaism.
This must necessarily present more or less analogy with that
which succeeds it; rather, it must necessarily stand in direct
relation to it. The theology of John, however, makes far less
allusion to Judaism than that of Paul. It is rarely mentioned,

* John i. 11, and foll.; ὅσοι ἔλαβον, etc.
† John xi. 52.
‡ Σοὶ ἦσαν, John xvii. 6.
§ 1 John i. 7, and foll.

and the old economy occupies no large or important place in the system itself. That which is said may be epitomized under two heads.

The revelation of the Old Testament centres here, as with the Jews themselves and the Judæo-Christians, in the idea of the *law*.

That law is regarded and understood as a constitution granted, an external ordinance,—one, that is to say, coming from without, and addressing man in the form of a commandment for the governance of his life and conduct. But in this aspect it is something essentially different from the life derived from the Word; there is no affinity between the two principles, no relation either between their respective bases, or their modes of operation. The law is *your* law, in John's record of the words addressed by Jesus to the Jews; it is *their* law,* that is, a law foreign to the sphere of true believers, who can draw directly from the source of light, and life, and love. The Gentile Pilate speaks of it in the same terms.† Yet again. In tracing this law back to its origin, the gospel of John pauses at the name of Moses,‡ as its author; and if we are not warranted in concluding from this, that John intentionally places himself in direct contradiction with the idea generally received, that the law on Mount Sinai was given by God, it is impossible to mistake the design with which, especially in the first of the two passages just quoted in the note, Jesus is contrasted with Moses. The parallel thus established between them leads evidently to a depreciation, we had almost said a degradation, of the old economy. In fact, in the mouth of a theologian, who has just declared Jesus to be God manifest in the flesh, this parallel is in itself sufficiently significant; it is the more so from the fact that the ideas of grace and truth are opposed—that is to say, are denied—to the law.

In presence of such a declaration, it is a strange error of our ordinary exegesis to regard the Jews as those of whom it is said

* 'O νόμος ὑμῶν, αὐτῶν, John vii. 19; viii. 17; x. 34; xv. 25.
† John xviii. 31.
‡ John i. 17; vii. 19.

that they belong *peculiarly* to the Saviour.* In that case, those who are contrasted with them must necessarily be the Gentiles, and we are led to an assertion which history directly contradicts, namely, that Gentiles alone embraced the Gospel; or, if it were admitted that those spoken of in verse 12 are but a scanty minority, and are also Jews, believing Jews, then in a passage broad and theoretic like this, the apostle would exclude the Gentiles, so to speak, from all participation in the kingdom of God. Neither interpretation is admissible; both are absolutely contrary to the spirit of John's gospel. The words, the meaning of which has to be determined, designate men in general, as belonging by creation to the pre-existing Word. But between the Word and the Jews, as such, there is no special bond. It was only with the prophets that the Word stood in previous relations as the Revealer to them of the future.†

We nowhere meet in the writings of John with any demonstration or dialectic deduction of the fact that *the spirit is not under the law.* No rhetorical arguments are adopted by him, such as those which we traced in the analysis of the theological system of Paul. In the sphere in which John taught and wrote, the Christian conscience was already freed from the fetters of Pharisaism, and had happily realized that emancipation which Jesus had made only the more sure, by gradually preparing the way for its proclamation. That one utterance of His, *God is a Spirit . . .* ‡ placed the rival pretensions of Jerusalem and Gerizim on the same level both in principle and in fact; when Judaism, instinctively suspicious of the religious phenomenon presenting itself to its view, begins its ill-advised attacks by preferring against Christ the charge of profaning the Sabbath, the reply which it receives§ (and which differs widely in John from the parallel passages in the other gospels)‖ does not stoop to borrow excuses from

* Οἱ ἴδιοι, John i. 11.
† John xii. 41.
‡ John iv. 23.
§ John v. 17; comp. ix. 39.
‖ Matt. xii. 1, and foll.; Mark ii. 23, and foll.; iii. 2, and foll.; Luke vi. 1, foll., etc.

the sphere of popular ideas; it takes at once higher ground, and sets the divine authority in direct contrast with that of the law, thus assigning to the latter a place of marked inferiority.

It is then an established fact that John recognizes no objective value in the law, or that which is connected with it, as it concerns those who have entered into the new economy founded by the Incarnate Word. Nevertheless, and this is the second point to which we would draw the reader's attention, the revelation of the Old Testament had a special end in view, in direct relation with that of the New, and thus imparting to it a sort of relative value which is permanent. It is here we meet with the word *testimony** used to describe the Scriptures, which, as the depository of the earlier revelation, bear witness to Christ. But this is not a privilege which belongs exclusively to them, nor does this impart to them any absolute importance. For, were this testimony lacking, there would still be that of John the Baptist,† as authentic as the other; and this, again,‡ might be superseded by yet higher testimony,§ the witness of Jesus Himself, of the Father who sent Him, that which is borne by the very works of Christ, and, finally, that of the Christian consciousness itself, which corroborates all.‖ By this comparison, the theological value of the Scriptures, as the basis or support of Christian conviction, is brought down almost to the level of what is called in logic an *argumentum ad hominem*. Again, it must be observed that the prophetic character of the Old Testament, with regard to the Messianic promises *generally*, is not touched upon in the gospel of John. We say *generally*, for in reference to detail the apostle, like his colleagues, quotes certain passages of the Old Testament, for the most part with a typological application.

This is true even of one well-known passage already quoted,¶

* Μαρτυρία, John v. 39, 46.
† John i. 6, and foll.; 33; iii. 28.
‡ John v. 36.
§ 1 John v. 9.
‖ John v. 36, 37; vii. 17; viii. 14, etc.
¶ John iv. 22.

which calls for special notice, because it seems to contradict
our assertion. Salvation, it is said, is of the Jews. Judaism
has then an advantage over the religion of the Samaritans, and
on the same grounds, over all other religions. The Jews may
claim faich in Messiah as their own inheritance; Messiah is,
indeed, Himself a member of their nation. Their religion, in
regard of both these facts, is, then, in direct and close relation
with the salvation to come, and thus acquires a significance
exclusively its own, and which will assure to it a place by
itself in history, even beyond the sphere of time and influence
specially allotted to it. This significance, nevertheless, cannot
secure to it any exceptional value, beyond the time when the
salvation hoped for shall be realized by the manifestation of
the Word. Judaism, in other words, is the religious fact to
which the religion of the future is to be attached; but, as it
would seem, the relation is external merely. For the testimony is only a form, a means; that which is essential—the
Word Himself—is not of the Jews, but comes down from
heaven. Christianity, which alone is grace and truth, cannot,
then, be regarded as the product of Mosaism. Thus the Judæo-
Christian point of view is altogether left behind.*

  * It deserves notice that in the discourses of our Lord contained in the
fourth gospel, He consecrates as symbols of Himself and of His work,
the brazen serpent, the manna, the water from the rock, the pillar of fire,
and the temple.—ED.

CHAPTER IX.

OF THE INFLUENCE OF THE WORD UPON THE WORLD.

WE now come to speak of the purpose of the incarnation of the Word, and this we shall deduce simply from the idea of the Word itself combined with that of the world. It is evident that the Word cannot have come to receive anything from the world; He can have come only to bestow something on the world—the very thing, in fact, which it lacked. In a word, He came to give Himself, to communicate His own essence to the world, to bring to it light, love, and life, and to destroy in those who receive these new elements, all that is in conflict with them—darkness, hatred, and death.

This purpose the theology of the fourth gospel expresses in various ways. Let us first look at the passage in which Christ says, "I am the way, the truth, and the life."* This passage appears to us well adapted to the development of the idea we have just suggested. In fact, the terms *truth* and *life* comprehend all that the world needs to obtain and possess. We shall show presently that in the phraseology of this system* the word *truth* corresponds to the two categories of light and love. In the writings of John, especially, it is at once knowledge conformed to the essence of God, and conduct conformed to His will. It is chiefly an objective term, while the two other terms, which we here use more habitually, and which give us the trilogical division, assume rather the subjective point of view. Christ is, then, the truth and the life, and the opening words of the sentence mark the relation between Him

---

* John xiv. 6 ; ἐγώ εἰμι ἡ ὁδὸς, ἡ ἀλήθεια καὶ ἡ ζωή.

430 CHRISTIAN THEOLOGY.

and the world. The term *the way* designates the means by
which the world may attain to truth and life;* in its relation
to the Word it indicates the design of His coming—of His
personal manifestation. By the absolute assertion, *I am the
way,* He excludes every other means, and expresses implicitly
the necessity of His manifestation; that is to say, at the same
time, the design of His coming. The same meaning is conveyed in the words,† "The Son of Man is come to destroy the
works of the devil." The works of the devil are sins, as the
effects of the opposition between the world and God, or, if we
will, *sin* itself as the source of that opposition. Sin once destroyed—uprooted, so to speak—the opposition ceases of itself: truth and life are acquired by or implanted in the world.
There are many other passages in which the object of the incarnation of the Word is but partially expressed, the author
bringing into prominence only one of the three elements which
the analysis has shown are all really present in combination.

Often the light only is spoken of; the Word is represented
as coming to give light, the great object being to dispel all
darkness from the world.‡ It will be observed that, in relation to this point, the present tense is used,§ and the word *now*
added; the light *now* shineth: ‖ expressions which are not only
designed to convey the continuity of the fact, but at the same
time to intimate that it did not previously exist, which is tantamount to saying that the presence of this light, to lighten
the world, is the direct object of the coming of the Word.

In other places, life is dwelt upon as the main object of the
manifestation of the Word. This is the case whenever the
words *to save* and *Saviour* are used to represent the operation
of the Word. Wherever there is a question of restoring health,
of healing and saving, there is implied danger to life, there is

---

* Our Lord Himself explains that by the "way" He means the way
to the Father, for He adds "no man cometh to the Father but by
Me."—ED.

† 1 John iii. 8.

‡ John xii. 46; comp. i. 9; viii. 12.

§ John i. 5.

‖ 1 John ii. 8.

the imminence of death. This is true in the figurative and spiritual, no less than in the primary and physical, sense.*

Lastly, we shall find that the third element, love, is in its turn placed foremost, or is, at least, brought into strong relief,† in other passages having reference to the incarnation. In one it is called a new commandment, which doubtless signifies at the same time that it has been the subject of a new revelation. In another, still more significant, the duty of loving is derived directly from the fact of the incarnation. It is needless to observe that all these passages, so far from changing our conviction as to the object of the Word in coming into the world, only confirm, by a sort of exegesis of details, the result we have already obtained from the general passages.

In order to omit nothing which might serve to familiarize us with the theological phraseology of John's gospel, we may further observe that the purpose of the incarnation is not to be regarded as something peculiar to the Word; it is but a part of the designs and decrees of God, from which it should not be disjoined. It is said expressly that Christ came into the world to do the work of God.‡ This thesis, which is only the corollary of the premises we have already laid down, does not need to be analyzed.

The design of the incarnation being thus established, we pass on to the means employed by the Word for its attainment. But, in truth, the incarnation itself was pre-eminently *the* means, which embraced all the rest, and which consequently comprises all that we have to speak of here; in other words, if we talk of various means, they are but various phases of the earthly life of the Word. That life, we must ever remember, cannot be a fortuitous or accidental thing, nor can it be regarded as dependent on outward circumstances, on a concurrence of incidental causes foreign to the providential will of God. On the contrary, it should be regarded as predetermined in all its stages, and only influenced by the world, in the measure

* Σώζειν, σωτήρ, John iii. 17 ; v. 34 ; xii. 47 ; 1 John iv. 14.
† John xiii. 34 ; 1 John iv. 11.
‡ Ἔργον θεοῦ, John iv. 34 ; vi. 29 ; xvii. 4.

designed and foreseen by the decrees of the Divine Mind.
Thus the Incarnate Word knows distinctly when His hour is
come,—the decisive hour;* and, yet more, the world is compelled, in its hostile relations with the Word, to bow to this
pre-established order.†

The different special manifestations here to be taken into
consideration, or the categories under which the acts of the
Incarnate Word may be ranged, form, first of all, two series or
distinct classes.   There are some which lead directly to the
end in view, and bear immediately upon it; there are others
which tend only mediately and indirectly to establish the
authority of the person of Jesus.   Among the latter, we may
note, first, the predictions and miracles of the Saviour.   We
need not dwell upon these, as Jesus was not the only person
whose mission might be, and was, attested by such proofs.
Let us only call to mind what is said in John's gospel about
them.   Jesus foretells many things to His disciples, or in their
presence, by the fulfilment of which their faith is awakened or
established;‡ or, again, he reads the secret history of a man,
and then calls forth a recognition of His superhuman power.§
The miracles are called *signs*, inasmuch as they are the visible
proofs of an extraordinary and divine mission.   They enter
into the more general category of *works*, the latter term com-
prehending not only miracles, properly so called,|| but also the
Messianic work itself in all its fulness.¶

Independently of predictions and miracles—which, after all,
are but proofs of a secondary order,**—Jesus appeals also to
other evidences of the authority of His person and of His
teaching, which we cannot pass over in silence.   We have,
first, His own testimony to Himself, which we shall better
consider, perhaps, as an integral part of His doctrine.   There

* John vii. 6, 8 ; xiii. 1 ; xvii. 1.
† John vii. 30 ; viii. 20.
‡ John ii. 19, and foll. ; xiii. 19 ; xiv. 29 ; xvi. 1, 4.
§ John i. 49, and foll.
|| Ἔργα, John xiv. 10; xv. 24 ; x. 38.
¶ John v. 17, 20, and foll.
** John i. 51, μείζω τούτων ὄψῃ ; comp. x. 38.

is next the absence of all sin in His actions;* the personal
disinterestedness of His preaching, which has the glory of God
as its sole aim ;† the power inherent in His doctrine, which,
in the experience of those who will practise it, bears its own
witness;‡ lastly, there is the voluntary sacrifice of His life.§
All these facts, tending to produce in the minds of men the
conviction that Jesus is the Christ, find their place in the
category of the mediate or indirect phases of His work upon
earth.

The direct means by which the purpose of the incarnation
is fulfilled—that is, those which are designed to procure for
the world light, love, and life—are three : The first is *teaching*.
This corresponds to the first element which is to aid in the
renovation of the world, namely *light*. Jesus describes Himself as a *Teacher* or *Master*.‖ He speaks of His doctrine as
coming from God, whose organ He is. Thus, that which is
called in one place the word of Jesus,¶ is in another place
called the word of God.** For the same reason, this teaching
is called the testimony of heavenly things, things appertaining
to God Himself.†† The expressions *message, declaration,* and
the like,‡‡ which we cite also for the sake of completeness,
present the same aspect of this first form of the action of the
Word upon the world.

As to the subject of the teaching, there can be no doubt or
difficulty. It is the very theology contained in the gospel. There
is first a revelation concerning the essence of God.§§ Next, as
a sort of transition from this primary subject to others which
are to follow, there is information as to the person of Jesus,

* John viii. 46.
† John vii. 18.
‡ John vii. 17.
§ John x. 11.
‖ Διδάσκαλοι, John xiii. 13 ; διδαχή, vii. 16.
¶ John v. 24 ; viii. 31, 37, 43, 51 ; 1 John i. 10 ; ii. 5.
** John v. 38 ; xiv. 24 ; xvii. 6, 14, 17 ; 1 John ii. 14.
†† John iii. 11, 32.
‡‡ 'Αγγελία, ἐπαγγελία, 1 John i. 5 ; ii. 25 ; λαλεῖν, John xiv. 10 ; xv. 22.
§§ John xvii. 6 ; i. 18 ; 1 John i. 5.

and His testimony concerning Himself, in which He asserts His
Messianic dignity.* This testimony has the stamp of absolute
truth,† because of the dignity of Him who bears it; while as
a general rule, and in purely human relations, the testimony
of a person in his own cause has no judicial value.‡ The
teaching of Christ further comprehends all that relates to life,§
and this all the more naturally as life is the culminating point
of the work of the Incarnate Word. Lastly, the teaching óf
Christ has love expressly as its subject.‖ It is by love, we are
told, that the disciples of Jesus will be known, and this love
is called a new commandment, inasmuch as what is here
intended, is not an intensified degree or a wider sphere of the
natural affection, but a new principle, a disinterested love,
loving for love's sake, for the love of God and of Christ, not
because love is useful, nor because it is commanded, nor because
a recompense is attached to it, but because it is natural to the
new life.

As in this text we find the word *commandment*¶ put into
the lips of Jesus, it has been concluded that John aims to
represent Him as a lawgiver. We repudiate this description,
not because it would derange the symmetry of our trilogical
division (for it would be easy for us to combine legislation
with teaching), but because it would introduce into it a totally
foreign idea, and one which would recall the abrogated legislation of the Old Testament, from which the new economy is
essentially distinct, and is explicitly and radically separated.

The word in question is employed here and elsewhere as a
popular and familiar expression, not intended to convey the

* John iv. 26; v. 17 foll., etc.
† John viii. 14.
‡ John v. 31.
§ See 1 John ii. 25, and many discourses in the gospel.
‖ John xiii. 34, and foll.; 1 John iii. 11. We cannot avoid collating
and combining these three passages in the epistle, i. 5; ii. 25; and iii. 11.
We there find light, life, and love successively designated as the object of
the ἐπαγγελία. Our mode of systematizing the ideas of the gospel finds
thus a fresh justification.
¶ Ἐντολή, comp. 2 John 5.

idea of a commandment in the sense of the old economy; perhaps it is only used to supply in some sort the gap left by the abrogation of the law; but it must necessarily represent here the idea of instruction given, or even of a mystical inspiration or initiation. This estimate of the import of the term is amply confirmed by other passages. Thus it is used to designate the mission given to Christ by His Father,* a case in which the ordinary acceptation of the word *law* is wholly inadmissible. In the first of the two texts just quoted, the commandment is identified with its own effect,† which is never the case with a law strictly so called. It may be observed, again, that the same term is used as synonymous with the *word*,‡ and applied to things which have no legal character, but are simply principles or theories. If then it is clear that we have here an idea perfectly homogeneous with the theology of John, but in a form borrowed from the Old Testament, we shall be on our guard, when we meet with the word in the plural, against understanding a series of particular commandments, which would at once carry us back into the sphere of the law—a sphere the apostle has left far behind.§

The second means employed is example or model. This corresponds to the second element which is to contribute to the renovation of the world, namely *love*. "I have given you an example," says Jesus, "that ye should do as I have done to you."‖ The whole scene of the washing the disciples' feet in its deep and ideal meaning might be cited here.¶ But we have not only a pattern in the fulfilment of duty, though this is presented first and with most prominence; the entire life of

* John xii. 50; xv. 10.

† Ἡ ἐντολὴ αὐτοῦ ζωὴ ἐστί.

‡ 1 John ii. 7, 8.

§ John xiv. 15, 21; xv. 10; 1 John ii. 3, 4; iii. 22, and foll.; iv. 21; v. 2, and foll.

‖ Ὑπόδειγμα ἔδωκα ὑμῖν ἵνα καθὼς ἐγὼ ἐποίησα ὑμῖν καὶ ὑμεῖς ποιῆτε, John xiii. 15.

¶ Comp. John xiii. 34; xv. 12; 1 John iv. 17; ii. 6, and foll.; iii. 3, 16.

28 *

Jesus, in its relations, its destinies, and its issues* is in a sense the type of the life of His true disciples.

The third and last means is the death of Christ. This, according to an express declaration of the Saviour Himself,† is the correlative of the third element, *life.* He says, "Except a grain of wheat fall into the ground and die, it abideth alone but if it die, it bringeth forth much fruit." The death of Christ in this system, as in the apostolic teach͵ing generally, is a fact of the highest importance. Unhappily, the texts of John are not, on all the questions which here arise, as complete and explicit as those of Paul. It is needful, therefore, to interpret them with great care, and with much self-imposed reserve, lest we be tempted to fill up the gaps we may discover, by means either of speculations foreign to the apostle, or of traditional notions not sustained by the texts.

The death of Christ was first an act of His own free will.‡ This idea is primarily conveyed in the phrase to *lay down His life,*§ which occurs several times. It is contained also in the words *I sanctify* (devote) *myself,*‖ whether we recognize in these the idea of a sacrifice, or simply that of a free resolve on the part of Him who thus devotes Himself.

The death of Christ is next a necessary act or event.¶ This will become obvious presently when we come to speak of its effects.

Of these two preliminary characters of the death of Christ, the first is a natural consequence of the idea of the Word, which by virtue of its own nature was not subject to death, and could not be coerced into such subjection; the second results from the idea of the world, which could be saved in no other way. This brings us directly to the main subject of our inquiry.

The death of Christ, we have said, is one of the means, and

* John xv. 20.
† John xii. 24, and foll.
‡ John x. 18.
§ Τιθέναι τὴν ψυχήν.
‖ Ἀγιάζω ἐμαυτόν, John xvii. 19.
¶ Δεῖ, John iii. 14 ; comp. xii. 34.

one altogether essential, by which the salvation of the world is wrought. It was undergone on man's behalf. This significance of the death of Christ is expressed by the same particle which we have already noticed in other parts of the New Testament, as, for example, when Jesus says, This is my flesh, (my body, my physical life,) which I give for the life (spiritual life) of the world;* that is, in order to procure it. In this phrase, the preposition expresses then the object of the death, and says at the same time that this object is to confer a benefit. In the same way it is said that Jesus died, not for the Jews only, but also that He might gather together in one all the children of God that were scattered abroad—that is, the Gentiles.† The parallelism here is evidently in favour of the interpretation which regards the preposition as marking a beneficent intent. The phrase, laying down his life for another,‡ —so frequently used by Christ Himself and by others,§ in speaking of Him—may be understood in the same way of a voluntary death endured for the sake of another, of what is commonly called self-sacrifice for some one else. It is obvious, however, that we thus approach very nearly another meaning of the word, according to which *by* should be translated *in the place of*, which implies the idea of a substitution. It will be observed that, in most languages, the preposition *for* renders the two shades of meaning. When a man exposes his life, or loses it, to save the life of another, the kind design is doubtless that which first strikes the mind, but the idea of substitution is not far removed, though in ordinary life it may not be always applicable, the end not being attainable. Now, as in the case of Christ, the end must be attained, it would be impossible that His death should not have availed for some one; it is therefore natural that here the idea of substitution should arise. This idea is even distinctly conveyed in the words of the high-priest.‖

* Ὑπὲρ τῆς τοῦ κόσμου ζωῆς, John vi. 51.
† John xi. 52.
‡ John xiii. 37, and foll.; xv. 13; 1 John iii. 16.
§ John x. 11, and foll.
‖ John xi. 50.

All this, however, does not suffice to enable us to construct out of the words of John, the doctrine of vicarious satisfaction. This dogma rests upon a basis of law, and speaks of a direct substitution in law and in fact; now this is not the case here. When we translate the words, Christ died *in our stead*, it must be borne in mind that we have here two kinds of death and two kinds of life, having only the name in common, and that the significance of this expression, with the idea of substitution which it represents, depends upon its being supported, as it is in Paul's writings, by a train of theological thought and argument, elucidating the difference of the two terms of the substitution; this, however, is entirely wanting both in the fourth gospel and in the epistle, which is its practical commentary. It must at least be admitted, that if · John designed to assert the dogma of actual or material substitution, he has used the most popular and indefinite formula which he could have found to express it, so that, after all, it must devolve not upon exegesis but upon speculation to raise it to the height of a theological thesis.

Again, an attempt has been made to find the doctrine of substitution in the phrase already quoted,* "For their sakes I sanctify myself," by translating it boldly, "I give myself as a victim in their stead." But this is impossible unless we are prepared to admit a strange play upon words in the midst of such solemn utterances; for the same word occurs again in the next line, and must there have a different signification from that immediately preceding. If such an expedient is obviously inadmissible, it is clear that there is no reference here to substitution, else the disciples could not be required to *devote* themselves, Jesus having been already made a victim in their stead.

There is yet another passage to be examined by us, in which the death of Christ is explained by this same preposition; but it lends itself still· less readily to the idea of substitution as that is received in the Church. We refer to the beautiful and familiar allegory of the shepherd and the sheep. † This is a

* John xvii. 19, ἁγιάζω.

† John x. 11, and foll.

figure, and we are far from wishing to press all the details of such a form of speech into the rigorous definition of any dogma. But as this image excludes the idea of material and legal substitution, he who adopted or chose it cannot have intended to express such an idea.   The good shepherd lays down his life *for* the sheep, in defending them against the wolf. Keeping close to the figure, we may find in it the *possibility*, even the probability, that one or more of the sheep might be destroyed by the wolf, but never the *necessary* loss of all the sheep, in the event of the shepherd's caring for his own safety, instead of devoting his life for them.   The shepherd dies in the struggle with the wolf, but this does not place the sheep out of danger. The sheep, again, do not belong to the wolf; he has no claim upon them ; the death of the shepherd is not then a ransom by which the sheep are released from liability to such a claim. Lastly, the shepherd, in struggling with the wolf, may vanquish and overthrow him without himself dying. All the sheep may then be saved without any necessity for the death of the shepherd.   In whatever way we turn the figure, it remains wholly inapt to convey the idea of substitution according to the ecclesiastical formula. And assuredly it was not conceived, either by Jesus or by John, with a view to represent that formula. It does not contain the slightest trace of a legal relation, of a judicial idea. The allegory has but one end in view—to exalt the love of the shepherd for his sheep, a love which prompts him even to sacrifice his life for them, for their welfare and salvation.

It remains for us to inquire in what sense and in what way the death of Christ effects the salvation of the world; in other words, what are the benefits, not possessed before, which are thus procured. We shall find more than one indication given us on this subject ; but we shall also find more than one point which will suggest questions to which the text offers no reply. We shall discover here once again, that an essentially mystical theology recognizes no absolute necessity to pursue a theory to its final consequences.

The death of Christ effects first of all a purification with

regard to sin; it takes it away, blots it out.* The expression
is in a manner figurative; it forms, with the idea which it
represents, a sort of comparison or metaphor, since, in a moral
sense, an effect is ascribed to blood which in physical nature
belongs to water only—that of washing, cleansing away a stain.
This purification must be understood at once of two distinct
facts; first, he upon whom it is wrought will sin no more; and
next, sin previously committed is blotted out. These two facts
are inseparable.† The term *to purify* has then a rich and
emphatic meaning, and refers not only to certain positive and
past facts, as might be supposed from the general use of the
word, but also to eventual or possible facts against which it
provides.

We may especially note the passage ‡ which joins together
the blood and the water—that is to say, the death of Christ,
and baptism—as the two coefficients or conditions of the new
life. It is clear that these two ideas or facts are here brought
together because of a secret bond which unites them, even were it
only a figurative or symbolical relationship. Blood is necessary
in order that the purification may have the specifically Christian
character, and may not be simply a baptismal ablution. The
passage indicated adds also the spirit as a third element, inasmuch as the first two are outward and material, and require,
in order to produce their effect, something spiritual, which
should be their correlative—namely, faith. We shall have to
speak presently of this third element.

Beside the term of which we have just spoken, we shall find
another, the meaning of which it is important to determine in
the theological phraseology of this system, the more as it has
been misunderstood in the traditional interpretation. In all

* Τὸ αἷμα Ἰησοῦ Χρ. καθαρίζει ἡμᾶς ἀπὸ πάσης ἁμαρτίας, 1 John i. 7, 9.
Let us observe in passing that in the latter passage we find also the term
elsewhere so frequently used, "the forgiveness of sins" (ἀφιέναι τ. ἁ.); comp.
ii. 12. The addition διὰ τὸ ὄνομα αὐτοῦ is far less explicit than the terms
we are about to analyze.
† Comp. 1 John iii. 5, and foll.
‡ 1 John v. 6; αἷμα καὶ ὕδωρ.

the passages * where it occurs (and they are very numerous), it signifies to *take away*, to remove something from its place; it nowhere signifies to *bear*. In most of the passages cited in the note, it would even be simply absurd to attempt to apply the latter word. We are, then, authorized in adhering to the first interpretation, the only one sustained by the texts, in the two passages† where the term is used in connection with the fact of sin. We shall translate it by *take away*, efface; and we shall thus show that it is less emphatic than to *purify*, inasmuch as it expresses only one of the two elements of the idea of purification, that which relates to sin already committed. It is precisely on this account, and in order to render the idea complete on all points, that the last of the passages quoted adds expressly these words, "And in Him was no sin." This is not to be taken as a mere historical assertion, applicable to Jesus of Nazareth; it is a theological thesis, concerning the Christ in whom is the life of the believer. The latter, uniting himself by faith with the crucified Saviour, will necessarily share henceforward in His impeccability, which is tantamount to the expression we lately noted, that the blood of Christ so purifies a man as to secure him from falling back into sin. There is, indeed, a shade of difference between the two passages: the one speaks of *sin*, the other of *sins*. The plural has in view the concrete facts to which experience testifies; the singular generalizes them, and regards them as constituting a habitual condition. But this difference makes no change in the positive meaning of the verb. It is, then, impossible for us to find in the verb the expression of the idea of substitution (*satisfactio vicaria*). But may not this idea, popularly rendered by the terms to *bear*, to *carry*, and other synonyms, be found, perhaps, in the comparison of Jesus to a lamb? When we read, as the utterance of John the Baptist, the words, *Behold the Lamb*, the figure or the idea could not be one wholly unfamiliar, either to the hearers of the prophet or to the readers

---

* Αἴρω, John ii. 16; v. 8, and foll.; viii. 59; x. 18, 24; xi. 39, and foll.; xv. 2; xvi. 22; xvii. 15; xix. 15, 31, 38; xx. 1, 2, 13, 15.

† John i. 29; 1 John iii. 5.

of the gospel.   Now, in the symbolic worship of the Old
Testament, there is only the paschal lamb sufficiently prominent to be supposed to have suggested it;* and our thoughts
are the more naturally directed to this, since the apostle, in
another passage, alludes to it expressly.† But the paschal
lamb was not an expiatory victim.‡   It must be acknowledged, then, that this figure is composed of two elements,
blended or confounded. We have first the historical or Judaic
element, inasmuch as it was natural to compare the Mediator
of the new covenant, crucified at the Passover feast, with the
lamb which was the symbol of the old covenant in the same
feast.§   We have, further, the doctrinal or Christian element
of the sacrifice of Christ. By this addition the Hebrew symbol
received a significance which it had not originally.

We pass on to a second formula which requires our investigation.   Christ is called *a propitiation for the sins of the
world.*‖ As the writer does not himself explain to us his
meaning in the sentence, it is necessary for us to seek out all
the elements which might supply it.   The Greek substantive
employed here may also be rendered *reconciliation;* it supposes the cessation of a hostile relation, and consequently the
obtaining of divine favour. All this is placed in connection
with the sins of man, which thus appear as the obstacle to
this reconciliation, and which needed to be set aside in order

* Paul also compares Christ to the paschal lamb, (1 Cor. v. 7); and
the design of his comparison is entirely practical; he is speaking of a
purification to be imitated, not of a substitution in the endurance of
penalties.
† John xix. 36.
‡ Isaiah liii. 7, is often cited as the source of this figure, but this is
unquestionably wrong.   There is no allusion in that passage to a lamb
bearing the burden of our sins, but to a servant of God, suffering inno-
cently, and whose patience and resignation resemble that of a lamb dumb
before its butchers or shearers. [The paschal lamb was, however, a
vicarious victim. In the houses of the Egyptians the first-born died ; in
the houses of the Israelites the paschal lamb.—ED.]
§ This is especially true if Jesus, having died on the eve of the feast,
and before the appointed time for eating the paschal lamb, (John xiii. 1;
xviii. 28 ;) no more ate it with His disciples.
‖ Ἱλασμὸς περὶ τῶν ἁμαρτιῶν, 1 John ii. 2; iv. 10.

that the separation might cease. But the preposition is far too vague to inform us in what way this reconciliation had been effected. We discover, however, from the context, that it comes from God, who provides it and prepares the way for it; that it is an act of His love; that it could be effected only by Christ, since it is said of Him that He *is* a propitiation; that its natural consequence to us is life; lastly, that Christ perpetually pleads it with God, as an advocate,* with the Judge, whenever a sinner claims the benefit of it. Hence we see, also, that reconciliation is to be regarded as a historical fact once accomplished, belonging to the past, but availing, under certain conditions, for all time to come.

We are thus afresh led to the death of Jesus as the means by which the world may obtain life; before, we saw it procuring purification from sin; now, the reconciliation of the sinner with his Judge, who, in justice, must needs have dealt with him in anger. It is evident that these two ideas are closely related. May we not venture to represent this benefit as coming to man through faith in Him who is the revealer of the divine love, and who suffered death in order to gain by it the victory over the world?† It is needless to repeat that we here intend to speak of faith in the sense in which John uses it—a sense we have already defined. Some theologians will, perhaps, find this explanation too simple and meagre; but we frankly confess that we have not been able to discover here, or anywhere in the writings of the apostle John, any trace whatever of a *vicarious satisfaction*, in the scholastic sense of the word, which supposes one person made the judicial substitute to bear the penalties incurred by another, thus suffering as the innocent victim of the wrath of God, or even as satisfying the claims of the devil. Simple exegesis, restricting itself scrupulously to its legitimate sphere, will discover nothing of the kind in the writings of John. It is possible that theological speculation may be naturally led to explanations of this sort; but it must seek its positive grounds of support elsewhere than in the texts we have just analyzed.

* 1 John ii. 1, παράκλητος; the Latin *advocatus*, intercessor.
† John xvi. 33.

There is yet another fact which seems to confirm the interpretation we have recommended as the most natural and most in accordance with the texts, and with the whole tenor of the system. It is said* that where purification and reconciliation are wrought, there is life: life, then, is something which comes to us through the death of Christ. But in the passage we have just quoted, that death and its significance are not indicated by the words *flesh* and *blood,* which cannot be taken in the physical sense, since the persons present at the moment when Jesus speaks are invited to feed on them. It is the concluding words, "*which I will give for the life of the world,*" which express this relation. It follows that the life which is in the Word, which by Him alone is revealed to the world, only becomes the heritage of man as he receives the Word and becomes one with Him. This union will be the more readily and perfectly realized when the Word shall have ceased to live as an individual—when He shall be spiritualized, or, to use His own words, when he shall be, so to speak, changed into a nutritive element for many. We see that here, again, all transpires in a spiritual region; the whole relation is a mystical one; the juridical or scholastic point of view is as remote as possible from that of the apostle. It will be remembered that elsewhere the death of Christ is represented as the preliminary condition to the outpouring of the Holy Spirit,† consequently of the abiding effect of the light, life, and love which He had come to bring to the world. The historical experience of all the apostles could attest that the propagation of the Gospel was carried on with greater success, and in a more extended sphere, after the death of their Master; and this fact is here regarded from the standpoint of a theological principle. Just as in nature‡ death is the condition of life, just as the disciples only attained to true spiritual power after the death of Jesus, so the divine principle of life which the Word came to communicate to the world, could only act with its full

* John vi. 51, and foll.
† John vii. 39; xvii. 19.
‡ John xii. 24; xvi. 7.

and perfect energy when it had dropped the vesture, the corporeal coil in which it had first been manifested. The truth both religious and exegetical, of these ideas, cannot be disputed; can their theological significance be so small that it is necessary to substitute others for them? The scholasticism of dogmatists has so judged; but we venture to hold for ourselves another opinion.

We may remark, in conclusion, that the resurrection of Jesus, recounted at length in John's gospel, is not there made the subject of theological study or argument, as is so frequently the case in the writings of Paul. This fact is easily explained by the circumstance that the death of Christ is, in John's view of it, not a humiliation, but an exaltation. The two facts of the death and the resurrection, so far from forming a contrast, are therefore, in the theological point of view, equal and homogeneous, we might say identical. The more prominence John gives to the speculative idea of the Word, the less need has he to dwell upon the resurrection as an extraordinary fact. It was, undoubtedly, an additional testimony to men; but after the prologue to John's gospel, it was already a necessity; it rested on à priori grounds, and theology had therefore nothing more to say in regard to it.

CHAPTER X.

THERE remains one further question for us to investigate in
this historical part of the system of John—the relation of the
result to the end proposed, or, in other words, the effect of the
incarnation of the Word. This effect is designated generally .
by a term,* the significance of which is often missed through
a faulty translation. This rather ambiguous word represents
two ideas analogous, but not identical, the one more popular,
.the other more peculiar to John, the latter being at the same
time the older, according to the etymology of the word.

This second idea is that of a *separation*, and refers to what
we have previously said of a difference existing between the
two categories of men. On the appearing of the Word, the
separation between these two classes is effected, inasmuch as
the one class, attracted by the Word, turn to Him, and are
joined with Him ; while the other, persisting in opposition,
reject light, love, and life, and thus have no part in them.

The other idea is that of a *judgment*. We know that this
term, in Scripture language, supported by the Christian consciousness with regard to sin, implies the idea of severity and
condemnation.

The circumstance that these two more or less differing ideas
are contained at the same time in the same word, will explain
some apparent contradictions in the use made of it. On the
one hand, it is said,† that the Son of God is not come to judge,

---

* Κρίσις.
† John iii. 17; xii. 47.

but to save; the believer is not judged at all, the unbeliever is judged already;* the Father, like the Son, judges no man. On the other hand, we read in the current translations that judgment is passed already, in that, on the appearing of the Word,† one class of men give themselves to Him, while the other remain in alienation; judgment is committed‡ to the Son, inasmuch as His appearing becomes the occasion or signal for it. It is even said to be the purpose of His coming.§ For the same reason, the judgment is declared to be just and right;‖ it is given in the name of the Father, and is therefore directly ascribed to Him.¶ It is clear that these two series of expressions are compatible when we substitute *separation* for judgment, but that the first alone is really consistent with the system, while the second borrows a familiar image from popular ideas.

As the whole of our subsequent exposition—that is to say, the second part of the system of John—will treat exclusively of one of the two categories of men thus distinguished, we shall embrace in this chapter all that refers to the other. We do this, however, only to give completeness to what has been already said, for these few accessory statements have but a very secondary importance in the theology of the apostle.

Let us say first a word as to the different names by which the men are designated who at the time of separation persist in their opposition to God and His Word. These are various and very characteristic. They are called first unbelievers,** which, as the opposite of believers, will find its natural explanation in the definition we shall have to give of faith. In the second place, they are represented as denying the Father and the Son,—that is to say, as rejecting the Son as the Christ, and the Father by the very fact of this opposition

* John iii. 18; v. 22, 24; viii. 15.
† John iii. 19, and foll.
‡ John v. 22, 27; comp. xii. 31, 48; xvi. 8, 11.
§ John ix. 39.
‖ John v. 30; viii. 16.
¶ John viii. 50.
** Ἀπειθοῦντες, John iii. 36.

to the Son.* A third name, *antichrists*,† has precisely the same signification. It is derived from the Jewish dogma concerning the personal antichrist; and John, while rejecting this dogma‡ in its vulgar form, spiritualizes it in his own manner. But the true antichrist is the devil,§ who communicates his spirit to the world, and prompts its opposition to the Word. Again, they are described as those who continue in sin, the sin consisting in this very unbelief,‖ or, again, as those who abide in darkness.¶ Lastly, they are called liars, enemies to the truth—that is, to light and love.** This negation of truth is carried to the length of charging God Himself with lying.†† It will be readily observed that there is a certain gradation in this series of qualifications, from the inertia of ill-will to the horrors of blasphemy, from the simple rejection of that which is offered, to aggressive and determined hostility; and it may fairly be supposed that the author intended to convey the idea that between the first step and the last was a steep decline on which no pausing was possible.

Persistence in opposition to light and love implies also persistent rejection of life—that is, abiding in death.‡‡ The latter condition is at the same time the punishment of the former, as in the general providential government of the world, pain is the natural and necessary fruit of sin. As the world can obtain life only from the Word, those who repudiate the Word Himself will necessarily remain destitute of it. It is impossible§§ to have life without faith. Elsewhere the apostle speaks of this same result in popular terms foreign to his

---

* Ἀρνούμενοι, 1 John ii. 22, and foll.

† Ἀντίχριστοι, 1 John ii. 22, and foll.; comp. 2 John 7.

‡ 1 John ii. 18.

§ 1 John iv. 3.

‖ Ἁμαρτάνοντες, John xvi. 9; comp. 1 John iii. 6, 8.

¶ Μένοντες ἐν τῇ σκοτίᾳ, John xii. 46; comp. 1 John ii. 9, 10.

** Ψεῦσται, 1 John ii. 4, 22; iv. 20.

†† 1 John v. 10.

‡‡ Μένειν ἐν τῷ θανάτῳ, 1 John iii. 14.

§§ Οὐ δύνανται, John vii. 34; viii. 21. It is clear that this phrase has quite another meaning in ch. xiii. 33, when it is spoken to the disciples.

peculiar theology, as, for example, when he says,* that the wrath of God rests upon those who do not believe, or that they are condemned already.† The penalty,‡ it will be observed, is, like the sin itself, only a negation. We shall therefore come to a better understanding of it when we proceed to develop the idea of life, with which it is placed in opposition.

The effect of the incarnation of the Word is then not only a separation of the elements of the world from a moral point of view, so that these, instead of being blended as heretofore, should henceforward find each its true and separate place; it is more than this; it is a victory. The combat preceding it was a personal struggle between the Word and the prince of darkness, as is evident from that which is said of the Jews and of Judas the traitor.§ But the devil has no power over the Son of God.‖ It is true that Jesus apparently succumbs, but even thus He conquers.¶ For it is through and in consequence of His death that light, love, and life are revealed, and begin truly to assert their sway, permeating the world and exercising over it their attractive power;** and wherever this action has begun, wherever the new germ has taken root, the devil is vanquished and forced to flee.†† He is then judged,‡‡ cast out of the sphere of those who belong to Christ, and the spirit by which in future they are governed, proves by the very fact of its presence that his judgment is already passed.

Before proceeding to the second part of the system, we must dwell for a moment longer on a special point, which we have already had occasion to touch upon, without being able to find a satisfactory reply to the question it suggested. We have seen that men are divided into two categories in relation to the

---

* John iii. 36; the word ὀργή occurs only this once in John's writings.
† John iii. 18.
‡ Θάνατος.
§ John viii. 40, and foll.; xiii. 2, 27.
‖ John xiv. 30.
¶ John xvi. 33, νενίκηκα.
** John xii. 32.
†† 1 John ii. 13, and foll.
‡‡ Νῦν, temporis; John xii. 31; comp. xvi. 11.

Word and the revelation brought by Him, and we have vainly sought hitherto the final cause of this division. In a previous chapter, we have shown that the system of John only states the fact without explaining it. Now that the same question presents itself again, and with special emphasis, we cannot pass on without looking thoroughly into it in this connection. Unhappily, the hope of seeing some new light arise, of discerning at length some new factor hitherto undiscovered, is a hope doomed to disappointment. The system confines itself, always and exclusively, to proclaiming, on the one hand, the satisfaction obtained by believers for all their needs and legitimate desires ; on the other, to affirming simply that all who will not assimilate themselves to the light and life, will abide in darkness and death. This contemplation of facts leaves no place for a chain of logical argument, for a well-studied and' well-demonstrated theory, concerning the connection in which the two spheres stand to each other, and to the primary cause of their separation.

We are about to examine, in succession, all the texts relating to this subject; and we shall thus see how they may be made to uphold the very contradictory theories promulgated in the various schools, which is equivalent to saying that the apostle has left the question undecided.

There are, first, a series of passages in which life, and that which must precede it, is spoken of as offered to all mortals without distinction, in which it is represented as accessible to all, as within the grasp of all.* We do not even except the passage in which Jesus says, " *I will draw all men unto me*,"† for if the success of this drawing is necessarily incomplete, this does not exclude in theory the universality of its design.‡ It may further be observed here, that when John gives the definition of judgment, or rather of separation,§ he

---

* John i. 7, 9 ; comp. v. 23.

† John xii. 32, πάντας ἑλκύσω.

‡ This universality, on the other hand, is not expressed in ch. xi. 52, nor in ch. x. 16. In these two passages the two categories of men are already separated. In the same way the phrase ἐξουσία πάσης σαρκός (xvii. 2; xiii. 3; iii. 35) is subordinate to the idea of the κρίσις.

§ John iii. 19, and foll.

says absolutely nothing which should be of a nature to restrict
the liberty of man; elsewhere,* when all who are athirst are
invited to come and drink, the figure is evidently based upon
the presumed existence of a subjective disposition; lastly, in
another passage,† it is said to the Jews that if they do not
come to a knowledge of God and of His revelations, and consequently to faith, it is solely because they will not. All these
quotations seem to leave a large part to the free action of man,
and to assign to him, at the least, a very important and efficient
share in the work of his salvation.

But beside these passages, there are in our texts a series of
others which not only speak of a direct influence exerted by
God upon the determination of man, but which, from a logical
point of view, must necessarily issue in complete and rigorous
predestinarianism.

We will not dwell upon the well-known phrases in which
it is said, for example, " *he who is of God heareth my voice,*" or
again, " *they that are of the truth,*" or again, " *ye are not of my
sheep.*" ‡ These phrases indeed assert an antecedent tendency
in the individual which may seem indicative of a higher
influence; but it would be possible to regard them as marking
only the separation of the two classes of men, so that they
might be taken simply as expressing the existence of a certain
disposition, not as assigning its cause.

But such an explanation can scarcely be applied to the term
choosing,§ which is put into the lips of Jesus. Ordinary
exegesis finds no difficulties in the saying, " *I have chosen you,*"
because it understands it to refer to the choice of the twelve
disciples; but the spirit of the entire gospel is opposed to so
restrictive an application, and leads us to apply it to the whole
body of believers. The last verse especially of those cited in
the note, should remove all hesitation on this point; for in
it those who are chosen are contrasted with the world. This

* John vii. 37.
† John v. 40.
‡ John viii. 47; xviii. 37; x. 26.
§ Ἐξελεξάμην, John xiii. 18; xv. 16, 19.

29 *

being admitted, the position of those who separate themselves
from the world would still seem to be the effect of a choice ;
though it might indeed be said that this *choice* is not necessarily
election in the Augustinian sense, but rather perhaps the act by
which the Saviour seeks His lost sheep.*

We find ourselves, however, brought very near the Augustinian sense, when we read the phrase, "No man *can* come
unto me except the Father draw him,"† or "except it be
given him of my Father." Jesus speaks also of this same
drawing power as to be exerted by Himself, especially after His
uplifting,‡ and many times He repeats the expression, " *those
whom Thou hast given me.*"§ All this seems to point to the
admission that, according to the theology of John, the determination of the tendency of each individual, depends on a direct
and indispensable operation of God.   Here, however, again we
shall find the logical consequence modified and circumscribed
within certain limits.   The individuals thus drawn are said to
be taught of God, or are described by other terms which, while
fully recognizing the divine influence, repudiate the idea of an
absolute negation of liberty on man's part ;‖ for even here it is
evident that life is made contingent on hearing and on faith.
Such is the case also with the passage ¶ in which the opening
phrase ("*all that the Father giveth me shall come to me,*")
places the divine influence in the foreground, and makes it
appear as determining the direction of the man, in a manner
perfectly independent of his will ; but in which this phrase is
immediately followed by another, ("*and him that cometh unto
me I will in nowise cast out,*") a phrase can have no plausible
meaning at all, if it is made to rest upon a basis of absolute
election.   The combination of these two theses in the same
verse, may be moreover easily explained by the supposition

* John xi. 52.
† Ἑλκύσῃ, John vi. 44, 65.
‡ John xii. 32.
§ John vi. 37 ; xvii. 2, 6.
‖ John vi. 45, θεοδίδακτοι, ἀκούσαντες καὶ μαθόντες; comp. v. 24.
¶ John vi. 37, πᾶν ὃ δίδωσί μοι ὁ πατὴρ πρὸς ἐμὲ ἥξει, καὶ τὸν ἐρχόμενον
πρὸς με οὐ μὴ ἐκβάλω ἔξω.

of the simultaneous action of the love proceeding from God and of the free-will of man.

But again we read, "*The Son quickeneth whom He will.*"* The expression is trenchant and positive; the context supplies nothing which might authorize us in restricting its import; and the meaning is the more absolute because this proposition is placed in direct antithesis with the universal resurrection of all the dead, without distinction, ascribed to the Father. The special dogma of individual predestination seems to come out clearly from such a text, or rather seems to have dictated it. It must be added, as worthy of remark, that in several passages unbelief is represented as a necessary, inevitable, almost compulsory thing.† This assertion is confirmed by the exegesis of certain texts in the prophetic scriptures, according to which this unbelief is foreknown by God.‡ The reader will see that the texts to which we refer are sufficiently numerous, and it would be obviously unfair to reduce the import of the quotations of the apostle, to certain moral analogies which he would establish between the disposition of his contemporaries, and those which the old prophets discovered among the people of their day. He is unquestionably speaking of a positive and special prediction; but if this be so, what becomes of the liberty of man? It is necessarily repudiated, or annulled, at least logically and in theory.

What conclusion shall we, then, draw from all this? To speak frankly our own opinion, we have never been able to admit that the texts of John, as we have just placed them with entire impartiality before the eyes of our readers, are of a nature to decide the great theological and philosophical problem. They are themselves too uncertain, too inconsequent, too fluctuating between two extreme points of view, and present no formula which might harmonize both. They cannot, then, be made the basis of a final solution of this question, which has so often already, to the detriment of the Church,

* John v. 21, οὓς θέλει.
† Δεῖ, οὐκ ἠδύναντο.
‡ John xii. 39; viii. 43; xiii. 18; xv. 25; xvii. 12.

called forth conflicting theories, each too daringly absolute in its own view. It always seems to us that John, like the other apostles, recognized with equal clearness the two axioms of the necessity of freedom as the basis of morals, and the necessity of divine influence to satisfy the religious consciousness and the mysticism of faith; but that he puts both side by side, without being able to reconcile them. He was not a logician: his theology was not sufficiently under the command of logic to lead him to give to one principle or the other the paramount place, by a process of close and logical deduction, as Augustine or Pelagius would have done. He does not even accidentally arrive at such a conclusion, thus clashing with some of his own assertions elsewhere developed, as we have seen to be the case with Paul. John appears hardly to have felt the antinomy before which the theology of the Church has always stood confounded, and from which it has only freed itself by some expedient born of despair.

Lastly, we may just observe, that, in their treatment of this question, neither John nor the other apostles have regard to that which preceded the Gospel revelation; that not one of them touches on the difficulty, so hotly contested in the schools, concerning the fate of those who had no opportunity of becoming acquainted with the Gospel; that they always speak of their contemporaries only. This is one proof the more that mere theory and questions of no practical bearing interested them but slightly, and argues that it would have been well if such questions had never been allowed to cross the threshold of the schools, to bring doubt and perplexity into the minds of the many.

CHAPTER XI.

OF FAITH.

HITHERTO we have been occupied with the metaphysical basis and the historical premises of the mysticism of John. We now enter on the more essential and characteristic portion of the system, in the consideration of that mysticism itself.

We have seen what was lacking to the world before the incarnation of the Word, that which the Word came to bring to satisfy the need, and how the world at large accepted this revelation. It only remains for us to examine one more phase of this great evangelical fact. We have to inquire how the individual grasps and appropriates that which the Word comes to offer; what are the, so to speak, organic changes which manifest themselves, in connection with this appropriation, in the soul of man; and what is the result at which he finally arrives. We have already hinted, in the introduction, that this part of the system is of the utmost simplicity. This will be further evident as we observe that, wherever the apostle sums up his theology in one short fundamental formula, he comprehends this second portion in these few words, "*that believing, they might have life.*"

This formula indicates directly that all we shall have to say here must be classed under the two capital and fundamental ideas of faith and life. But it teaches us, further, that the first of these two ideas must have a vast fulness and fecundity of meaning, since it corresponds to the two first categories of the trilogy of the apostle—light and love, to which life is naturally added as the third term. If there could be any doubt as

to this assertion, which seems at first to disturb the economy
of the system, that doubt would be removed by an indubitable
fact which we must point out here. This is, that the theology
of John knows and employs a term which comprises precisely
the two categories of light and love, and which, combined with
that of life, might serve to change the trilogy into a binary
division. This is *truth.** But we hasten to add that this word,
in the acceptation given to it by John, contains much more
than the word conveys to us, and we should be giving it far
too modern a colouring were we to divide it by analysis into
theoretical and practical truth.

We have already had occasion to note the presence of this
double element in the term; and we may for the present content ourselves with offering a few observations of detail in
relation to it. In several passages † *truth* is the teaching of
Christ, which is to reveal to men the nature and the will of
God; in other words, to bring light and love to the world.
Its theoretic element is the adequate knowledge of God in
these two spheres.‡ Its practical element is a life of action in
harmony with this knowledge.§

In one place,‖ Jesus prays the Father to sanctify His disciples through the truth—that is, to consecrate them for their
special career as apostles. This consecration is effected on the
part of God by the Word; on the part of Christ, by the
mission of the Spirit, which is to follow, and is conditional
on His own death. Now, as the design of this consecration
is entirely practical, as is apparent from the employment of
the term itself, instead of that of simple teaching, it follows
also that the truth, which is at once the means and the end
of the consecration, cannot consist in theoretic illumination
only.

* Ἀλήθεια.
† John viii. 31, and foll.; xvii. 17.
‡ John i. 14, 17; viii. 32.
§ Ποιεῖν τὴν ἀλήθειαν, John iii. 21; 1 John i. 6; περιπατεῖν ἐν ἀληθείᾳ,
2 John 4; 3 John 3, 4.
‖ John xvii. 17—19.

"*To be of the truth*"* is the same thing as "*to be of God.*" †
It signifies readiness to receive the Word, or, again, that disposition of mind which results from union with it.   The Spirit
Himself, whom we shall see acting in the two directions of
illumination and sanctification, is called simply the Spirit of
truth,‡ although the theoretic aspect seems to predominate in
this expression.

We have some difficulty in accustoming ourselves to this
standpoint, it being too much our wont in speech and thought
to dissociate theory from practice.   But it is the more necessary that we should recognize how far this is from being the
case in the apostolic theology, and especially in the system
now before us.   This is at once obvious from the fact, that in
one passage§ the knowledge of the truth is said to be derived
from its practice, while in another ‖ practice is spoken of as
the result of knowledge.   This is no contradiction; it is, on
the contrary, the most direct evidence that the two elements
presented themselves to the mind of the theologian as inseparable.

In harmony with the remarks just made, we shall divide
this closing portion of the theology of John into two sections,
the second of which will treat of the ultimatum of evangelical
religion—*life,* while the first will deal with the foundation of
that life—*truth;* that is, faith and love.   Love, however, is
here regarded as an inherent element of faith; so that, in the
general formula,¶ which epitomizes the whole theology, it is
not explicitly mentioned.

We commence with the definition of faith.   It causes some
surprise that this word, so frequently used by Paul, does not
occur once throughout the gospel of John,** though the idea is

---

* Εἶναι ἐκ τῆς ἀληθείας, John xviii. 37 ; 1 John iii. 19.

† John viii. 47.

‡ Πνεῦμα τῆς ἀληθείας, John xiv. 17 ; xv. 26 ; xvi. 13 ; 1 John iv. 6.

§ John vii. 17.

‖ John viii. 32.

¶ John xx. 31.

** We meet with πίστις once in 1 John v. 4.

reproduced on every page and in various forms. This fact may
remind us that paramount importance is not to be attached
to words in theological discussions. The derivatives of faith,
and especially the verb, occur very frequently.

In John, as in other writers of his age, we find various antecedent and non-theological ideas attaching themselves to this
root. There is the notion of fidelity to a word given;[*] that
of trust;[†] lastly, that of a simple conviction of fact, the adherence of the mind given to an assertion proceeding from the
lips of another.[‡]

On these it is unnecessary for us to dwell here. The essential idea of the Word—that which alone belongs to our subject
—is altogether different: it is specifically Christian, inasmuch
as it relates to the person of Christ as its proper and exclusive
object. It is in this sense we so frequently meet with formulas
already familiar to us throughout the writings of Paul.[§] Often
also we find the verb without any expressed subject, since
Christian theology recognizes only one faith of which it has to
speak.[||]

Even in this altogether special signification, however, the
meaning of the term is susceptible of various shades, according
to the degree of subjective development at which the Christian
consciousness has arrived in each individual. The reference
may be to faith in Jesus in His capacity of Messiah, working
miracles;[¶] it is then a kind of faith devoid of any mystical
element. There may be connected with this a more definite
conviction concerning the nature of Christ; as, for example,
His character as the Word Incarnate;[**] and yet this conviction

[*] Πιστός, 1 John i. 9.
[†] John ii. 24; comp. xiv. 1.
[‡] John v. 24, 38, 46, and foll.; xi. 26, 42; 1 John iv. 16; v. 1, etc.
[§] Πιστεύειν εἰς (for example, τὸν υἱόν, etc.), or εἰς τὸ ὄνομα, John i. 12;
ii. 23; iii. 18; 1 John v. 13; τῷ ὀνόματι, 1 John iii. 23.
[||] John i. 7; iii. 18; iv. 48, 53, etc.
[¶] John ii. 11, 23; iv. 41, 42.
[**] 1 John v. 4. In the passage John xx. 27, 29, we may be in doubt
as to the exact explanation of the object of the πίστις. Verse 27 may
refer simply to the fact of the resurrection. But verse 29 certainly goes
further.

may not go beyond the sphere of doctrinal theory. Lastly, this same expression, *faith*, may contain the idea of the inner life of the true Christian from its rise to its consummation. Such is especially the case wherever Jesus speaks of the faith of His true disciples, and where He describes the nature and advantages of that state. It is this last acceptation of the word on which we shall dwell most at length.

As we nowhere find a logical definition of the term *faith*, in the particular sense which claims our attention here, we shall endeavour to arrive at it by exegetical analysis. We at once discover in it three constituent elements.

First, the idea of faith implies that of knowledge, conviction, the affirmation of a fact, or, shall we say, the idea of an act of the thought, having for its object the Incarnate Word—that is, the twofold fact, that the Divine Word was really manifested in the flesh, and that Jesus of Nazareth was the Word. It has been said, with some show of reason, that the first of these two theses forms the main subject of the epistle; the second, that of the gospel. It is to this first element that several expressions belonging to the peculiar phraseology of this gospel have reference. There is, first, the word to *know*,[*] which is placed on a parallel with the knowledge of the Father, so that it is evident it does not signify a mere historical knowledge, an act of the memory relating to an external fact, but rather that purely religious and theological knowledge of which we have just spoken. The same parallelism is established in relation to the word to *know, to acknowledge*,[†] which occurs very frequently, and which has always this full and emphatic meaning, comprehending something far more than a purely historical knowledge, or experience gained by the senses. Thus this knowledge is described[‡] as adequate to its subject, as entering into its inmost essence. Again, it is associated with the mystical ideas which we shall pre-

[*] Εἰδέναι, John viii. 19; xv. 21; comp. iv. 42, etc.

[†] Γινώσκειν, John xiv. 7; xvi. 3; xvii. 3, 8; 1 John ii. 3, and foll.; 13; iii. 1, 6.

[‡] John x. 14.

sently notice, the subjective unity of the believer with the Son being represented as the source and basis of this knowledge.* For this second term is sometimes substituted its synonymous figure, *to see*.† Lastly, conviction is manifested outwardly by *confession*,‡ which is the opposite of denial or negation.§ The subject of either declaration is the very thesis already enunciated, that Jesus is the Christ, the Son of God, ‖ to which is added the indispensable complement that He is come in the flesh.¶ The abbreviated phrase, *to confess Christ*, must be explained in this complete sense. If the reader wishes to be assured of the justness of these observations made with reference to the scope and import of this first constituent element of the idea of faith, he has but to consider carefully the passages** in which the author derives from it theological consequences which could not be deduced from a mere historical acquaintance or a purely theoretic confession.

In the second place, the idea of faith implies that of obedience, of submission, or, to put it in another form, the idea of an act of the will directed to the same object. Here we shall notice, first, the term *to listen*, which is ill rendered by *to hear*,†† and which thus forms the natural transition from the previous category to this. The subject of this act, which is also represented by the word *to learn*,‡‡ is the word of Christ, or, which is the same thing, the word of God.§§ Here, again, as before, we mark the perpetual parallelism between the Incarnate Word and God,—in other words, the theological and speculative significance of all the expressions we are analyzing.

---

* 1 John iv. 6; v. 20.

† Ὁρᾶν, John xiv. 7, 9; 1 John iii. 6; 3 John 11.

‡ Ὁμολογεῖν, 1 John ii. 23.

§ Ἀρνεῖσθαι.

‖ 1 John iv. 15.

¶ 1 John iv. 2, 3; 2 John 7, ἐν σαρκὶ ἐληλυθώς.

** 1 John ii. 20, 21, 27.

†† Ἀκούειν.

‡‡ Μαθεῖν, John vi. 45.

§§ John v. 24, and foll.; x. 3, 27; vi. 45; viii. 47.

We find, further, the term *to follow** always used in reference
to the person of Jesus Himself, and originating in the outward
relations of the Master and the disciples who followed Him in
all His journeyings, applied also elsewhere to the figure of the
shepherd and his flock. It is needless to say that the meaning
of the word is here figurative. The same image is presented
in the word *to come,*†—for example, to come to the light, to
come to Christ. It is explained by the parallelism in which
it is placed with the term *to believe*, or, again, the action of
coming is represented as the immediate consequence of that of
listening.‡ Here also we find the expression *to come to the
Father* § as absolutely synonymous with the preceding.

Lastly, the idea of faith implies something which belongs
neither to the sphere of thought nor of will, but essentially to
that of *feeling*, to what is sometimes called the *soul*, in a more
special sense (Germ. *Gemüth*). It is only as we recognize this
third element that we arrive at a true idea of the Christian
faith, as it was felt and conceived by John. This last element
is represented in the phraseology of this gospel, first, by the
expression *to receive*, to accept. ‖ We might have comprehended this in the enumeration of texts under the two previous heads; for there are passages in which it does not go
beyond the sphere of what we have already spoken of as
initiation into the Gospel.¶ But we have reserved it for
separate consideration, because it is employed where the reference is to the reception or appropriation, so to speak, not
merely of an idea, but of the object of faith itself, of the person
of Christ. Thus we explain it, for example, in the two passages
of the first chapter just quoted; also in the twelfth verse,
where it alone is used as the synonym of complete and perfect faith; lastly, in another passage,** where the *reception* of

* Ἀκολουθεῖν, John viii. 12; x. 4, 27; xii. 26.
† Ἔρχεσθαι, John iii. 20, and foll.; v. 40; vi. 35.
‡ John vii. 37, 44, and foll.; vii. 37, etc.   § John xiv. 6.
‖ Λαμβάνειν (καταλαμβάνειν, John i. 5; παραλαμβάνειν, i. 11).
¶ For example, John v. 43, and wherever it is joined to the μαρτυρία,
iii. 11, 32, to the ῥήματα of Christ, xii. 48; xvii. 8.
** John xiii. 20.

Christ is identified with the reception of God Himself. The
consequence of this act is *having, possessing,*[*] which is far the
strongest and most forcible expression theology could use to
describe a close relation, surpassing anything that the will
or the reason is capable of attaining and realizing. In this
aspect, again, the Father and the Son are inseparable,[†] which
proves that here, as everywhere else, the theological element
is the essential in the mind of the writer.

Thus we are led by the successive and gradual enumeration
of all these elements of faith to the well-defined idea of a
community or *communion* of the believer with the person of
Him who is the object of his faith—that is to say, with the
Son first, and by Him with the Father.[‡] This idea is the
worthy consummation of the theology of John. Thus John
delights, we will not say to define more exactly, but to depict,
to *illustrate* by imagery, this rich and fundamental idea. He
even raises it to the idea of *oneness*, in which analysis readily
discovers the two elements of reciprocity and identification.
Christians are the brethren of Christ—His friends,[§] not servants under a master. They have an intimate knowledge of
Him, as He has of them.[||] This relation is permanent, un-
alterable, because it is perfect; it is an *abiding*. This expression is used and understood at first in a more external and
superficial manner, when treating of the word of Christ as
abiding in our hearts,[¶] or, what is the same thing, of our
spiritual life as finding in that word its vital principle.[**]
But it rises to the height of personal or mystic union in the
many passages in which it is said that the believer abides in
Christ and Christ in him,[††] as also that he dwells in the

[*] Ἔχειν, 1 John v. 12.
[†] Comp. 1 John ii. 23; 2 John 9.
[‡] Κοινωνία, 1 John i. 3, 6, 7.
[§] John xx. 17; xv. 15.
[||] John x. 14, 27.
[¶] Μένειν, John v. 38; xv. 7; 1 John ii. 14, 24.
[**] John viii. 31.
[††] John vi. 56; xv. 4, and foll.; 1 John iii. 24; iv. 13; comp. 1 John
ii. 6, 27, 28; iii. 6.

Father,* and the Father in him. The identity of these two relations is formally expressed and recognized in the text itself.†

The closeness of this purely mystical relation is, as we have just hinted, represented by various images chosen with intention by the author, and which have become to us terms so familiar, that very often they lose, in the use made of them, their proper and primary signification. These images are borrowed from the processes of eating and drinking, by which the aliments become changed into the substance of the body which receives them, and may thus give an idea of this fusion of souls, that spiritual identification of two natures, which forms the essence of faith. The reader will remember the words addressed to the Samaritan woman‡ about the life-giving *water* — an image which is elsewhere explained,§ as by a commentary. We call to mind also the discourse about the *bread* of life.‖ In both cases we must be on our guard against so translating the texts as to derive from them the sense of a sustenance enduring *until eternal life*, as though the apostle would speak of some future period when the effect would be produced. The effect intended is direct and immediate.¶ The bread and the water spoken of are to procure life at once, as material nutriment procures the satisfaction of hunger. The figure becomes so thoroughly blended in the apostle's mind with the thing it is to set forth, that he mingles together figurative and literal expressions, thus causing much embarrassment to dogmatists and exegetes. Thus, in place of the bread to be eaten,** the preceding verse puts the person of Christ Himself, and it is strange blindness not to see that the word *to eat* belongs to the figure, the

---

* 1 John ii. 24 ; iv. 12, 15, and foll.
† 1 John ii. 24, and v. 20.
‡ John iv. 10, and foll.
§ John vii. 37, and foll.
‖ Βρῶσις, ἄρτος, John vi. 32—58.
¶ Εἰς ζωήν, John iv. 14 ; vi. 27.
** John vi. 58.

word *me* to the idea. The personal pronoun is in another verse replaced by the expression flesh and blood,* a form of speech at that time commonly used to convey the idea of a man, of the human personality.† In the context, it is the person of Jesus in His historical manifestation, and under the aspect of His teaching, His example, His death. We repeat, only a materialistic exegesis, wholly unfamiliar with the style of the writer, could have seen doctrinal mysteries in all this, instead of the very simple idea of the mystical union of the Christian with the person of his Saviour.

In connection with these images, we must further remark the peculiar term which embodies them all in the briefest and most absolute form: *to be one.* This union comprehends God, His Son, and the believers; it is the culmination of the Christian life, the final end of faith.‡

Were any one of these three elements wanting, faith would be imperfect. Yet, from a theological point of view, they are not all of the same importance: there is among them a relation of gradation, corresponding with the order of our enumeration of them.

Hitherto we have been analyzing the idea of faith; we now come to inquire into its origin. All that is most essential and worthy of remark here, will follow naturally from what has been said above as to the elements of good in the world, and the influence which God exercises upon it. In other words, we may reduce this portion of the theology of John to the following formula: Faith arises out of the contact of divine revelation with a favourable predisposition in man. Faith is not, then, something absolutely new. If God draws man to

---

* Σὰρξ καὶ αἷμα, verse 53.

† Reuss's explanation of the phrase "flesh and blood" hardly seems to satisfy the exigencies of the whole passage. At the time that our Lord delivered this discourse the Passover was "nigh," and the great Jewish feast seems to have been present to His mind throughout the latter part of the discourse. He had come to *give His flesh* for the life of the world : He was to be a sacrifice, like the Paschal lamb, and the rest of the imagery is suggested by the Paschal feast.—ED.

‡ Ἐν εἶναι, John xvii. 21, 23.

Himself,* man is also drawn ; and the latter fact supposes, not indeed a power of independent and spontaneous action, but at least an organization which renders such drawing possible,— a hand to grasp, a capacity to receive. John, the theologian, expresses this by a most happily chosen figure. To believe is, according to him, to drink of the water which Christ gives, to drink His blood. But this act is preceded by thirst.† Only he who is athirst will come to drink. This thirst, then, is what we just now spoke of as the preparatory disposition ; it is a desire more or less deeply felt, a craving more or less conscious.

From the outward and historical point of view, faith may be called into exercise by the Gospel preaching which awakens or incites it,‡ or by a miracle which commands it.§ Theology, however, attaches no importance or value to these means and to their effect.‖ Faith has a more exalted, more direct and secret origin ; it is born when Christ is received, so to speak, directly, because of the testimony which He bears to Himself,— when there is no treating with Him, no demand for preliminary evidence, authorization, guarantee,—when the soul yields itself to Him frankly and entirely, without condition and without reserve. We must admit that the gospel of John starts from the principle that such a direct and immediate surrender is not a thing impossible in the natural condition of the individual, since it is said to the Jews, If you cannot or will not believe me, believe at least for the work's sake ; that is to say, arrive at conviction, on lower grounds, by indirect proof.

Notwithstanding the mystical character of John's theology, there is about it this speciality, that he never sets himself to give a detailed description of all the phases or stages of faith, in which vulgar mysticism delights. He does not go even so

* John vi. 44.
† John vii. 37.
‡ John i. 7 ; xvii. 20.
§ John ii. 23.
‖ John x. 38.

far as Paul, who, in the analysis of a fact, considered especially as a sudden transformation, places himself at different
points of view in succession, that he may embrace it in all its
fulness.   John dwells on the main point, and this presents
itself to him under the idea of a *birth.* He places it, as it
were, at the head of his theology, making it the subject of the
first theological discourse* which he puts into the lips of the
Master.   It is with regard to this elementary position, so to
speak, that the idea of the birth is called an "earthly thing,"
in opposition to "heavenly things;" that is, to the more exalted truths of the Gospel—truths less accessible to a mind
not yet enlightened by it.† That which is popularly called
conversion, a change wrought *on* or *in* the man, is from the
mystical point of view a birth,—that is, a change *of* the
man.

This birth is likened to the wind,‡ a comparison in which it
is impossible not to trace the influence of the twofold sense of
the Greek word, which signifies at once the wind and the
spirit.   Both are felt; no doubt can be entertained of their
existence, and yet it is impossible to analyze the mode of the
influence exerted, to tell where it begins, to regulate its
course, or to lay any constraint upon it.   In order to distinguish this spiritual and mystical birth from every sort of
physical and material birth, it is called "being born from
above," or, more definitely, "being born of God or of the
Spirit."§ We pass by for the moment this last expression, as
we shall have to revert to it presently.   The other formula,
"*being born of God,*" occurs most frequently in the epistle.||
The image is there developed into a complete allegory, by the
use of accessory formulas associated with it;¶ among which
we may especially note that of "*children of God,*"** which here

---

* John iii. 3, and foll.
† 'Επίγεια, ἐπουράνια, John iii. 12; comp. Heb. vi. 1.
‡ John iii. 8.
§ Γεννηθῆναι ἄνωθεν, ἐκ θεοῦ, John i. 13; ἐκ τοῦ πνεύματος, John iii. 6.
|| 1 John iii. 9; iv. 7; v. 1, 4, 18.
¶ Σπέρμα.
** Τέκνα θεοῦ, 1 John iii. 1, 2, 10; v. 2.

finds its natural place. We read, again, of being "*born of the Son*," and of being "*children of the light.*" * All these expressions convey essentially the same idea. Whether the birth be ascribed to the Father or to the Son, as its originator, the relation of the two persons, as already established by theology, presents an easy explanation of it: the light, in this case, also designates the Son in His active essence.

By the very elements of the idea of faith which we have already recognized, as well as by the consideration of the powerful ascendant which the person of the Word must exert over a mere mortal, we are led to conclude that faith will be passive rather than active. The image of birth may yet further convince us of the justness of this point of view. In fact, in the physical world from which the image is borrowed, that which is born is simply passive, without power or concurrence of its own will in any form. We should not venture, however, to affirm that it is necessary to adhere rigorously to all the consequences of an image, chosen perhaps for other analogies rather than for this. There is also another reason which leads us to think that a too close chain of logic would lead us beyond the real scope of the apostles' ideas. Quite as legitimate a consequence of the use of this image would, indeed, be the idea of a complete renovation, a change total and absolute, leaving no vestige of that which had previously been. This is, in fact, the use made of it and the sense attached to it by Paul. But John does not give definite expression to this result. Even in the interview with Nicodemus, the theology goes no further† than a sort of analogy between a right predisposition and subsequent faith, and does not reach the idea of a radical opposition between antecedent corruption and the new creation. This is a fact which escapes most readers of the gospel, whose minds are generally preoccupied with the meaning elsewhere attached to the figure. It is certain that John, in this figure of a birth, does not bring out the idea of *new*ness; he does not speak of a *second* birth, of

---

* Γεννηθῆναι ἐκ τοῦ υἱοῦ, 1 John ii. 29 ; υἱοὶ φωτός, John xii. 36.
† John iii. 21.

regeneration;* he does not place it in contrast with the past, but uses it uniformly and exclusively in relation to that which is to be developed in the future. When he employs this term, he is not speaking so much of a new creation based essentially upon the death of the old man, as of a new communication of power and of the Spirit which is to lead the man to life. The thoughts and expressions of Paul have become so thoroughly popularized, that this slight shade, not constituting a difference of much importance, has passed unnoticed. But every man has a right to speak and think in his own manner. And even if the difference should be reduced to a simple expression, Paul speaking of dying in order to being born, and John of being born in order to live, even so slight a distinction may be characteristic of the individuality of the two men, and hence may be suggestive and interesting to us.

Be this as it may, the influence of the divine operation is not lessened by this image of a birth under which the dawn of faith is presented to us. We shall be led to the same result in examining, lastly, the action or participation of the Divine Spirit in the same fact. For, as we have already said, this birth is represented not only as originating with God or the Son, but as being also derived from the Spirit.

* There have been many exegetes who have endeavoured to trace this idea of a second birth (*wiedergeburt*) in the word ἄνωθεν, which they translate by *denuo*. We cannot endorse their view.

CHAPTER XII.

OF THE SPIRIT.*

THE Spirit is mentioned in the theology of John—if we except the account of the baptism of Jesus—only in connection with the faith of man and the relation established by the fact of this faith. He is generally named without any qualifying adjunct; occasionally He is spoken of as the Holy Spirit, with or without the article, or as the Spirit of God. We have already adverted to the characteristic expression *Spirit of truth;* we shall presently meet with yet another term, which for the moment we pass by.

Here, as on a previous occasion, a preliminary question presents itself, the solution of which must exert a great influence on the manner in which we may regard the other questions bearing upon it. What is the Spirit? What is His essence? According to the theological system we are now examining, is He a personal being? or rather a thing, a power, a manifestation, a quality? This is not easy to decide, and very various replies have been given to the question.

First, it will not be difficult to find a series of arguments adverse to the idea of the distinct personality of the Spirit. 1st. God Himself is called a Spirit.† This is a qualification which characterizes His very essence. It must be ever impossible, both in fact and in logic, to place side by side with Him, without confounding the two, a second being, a second person, also a Spirit, unless we may suppose in the one some

---

* Τὸ πνεῦμα, τν. ἅγιον, τν. τοῦ θεοῦ, 1 John iv. 13.
† John iv. 23.

attributes not to be ascribed to the other. But in such a case, the idea of the Godhead—that is, of absolute perfection—would be compromised; and moreover in such a case, the Spirit would be less a separate person, than an attribute common to both.

2nd. We read of spirits in the plural.* Doubtless they are not all alike of divine origin, but the fact still remains that such an origin may be attributed to several at once. Evidently, here the reference is not to one person, unique in his nature, but to a principle, a tendency personified.

3rd. In the same place the author substitutes, without changing the meaning of the phrase, the expression, the Spirit that comes from God,† for the other more simple term, *the Spirit of God.* Now it is easy to see that the very possibility of this substitution and the synonymy of such expressions, does not in any way favour the idea of a personality.

4th. In a remarkable passage‡ we read, according to the true rendering, "*there was not yet any Holy Spirit.*" Assuredly this cannot mean that the Holy Spirit did not exist at this period, for this would be to deny God Himself. The sense necessarily is that at that time the manifestations of the Spirit of God in men had not yet commenced, as they are witnessed after the ascension of the Saviour. Nevertheless it may be said that the writer would never have employed a phrase so singular, so shocking to the sensitive orthodoxy of the ancients, who, as we see from the manuscripts, have made violent efforts to change it, if he had himself entertained a clearly defined opinion of the personality of the Spirit.

5th. We read in another place,§ that Jesus breathed upon His disciples, saying, "Receive ye the Holy Ghost." We do not deduce from this the materiality of the Spirit; we regard it as a natural symbolical act, supported by the very etymology of the word. We cannot, however, but think that that which is here communicated to the apostles cannot be a person, but

---

* 1 John iv. 1, 2.
† Πν. ἐκ τοῦ θεοῦ.
‡ John vii. 39; οὔπω ἦν πνεῦμα ἅγιον.
§ John xx. 22.

rather a power, a quality,—something, in short, which hence-forth they were to *possess*.

6th. The same remark will apply to a number of other passages in which the Holy Spirit is said to be *given* to believers.* In none of these cases does he appear as a proper person, concrete and *sui juris*, but always as a principle, a force, a quality, an object which may be bestowed.

7th. Yet further. In one instance we find the term anoint-ing, consecration, the communication of powers, of particular characteristics, used for the very name of the Spirit.† Precisely the same qualities or effects are attributed to this anoint-ing as are elsewhere predicated of the Spirit; for example, truth, teaching, the confession of the Son,‡ so that there cannot be the slightest doubt as to the identity of the two terms. But can the idea of the personality hold its ground against a designation so essentially hostile to it?

8th. We shall not dwell upon the formula adopted by the Church which speaks of the Spirit as proceeding from the Father,§ though that formula is, to say the least, not in con-tradiction with the negative thesis we are now stating; but we must draw attention to the passage in which the Holy Spirit is spoken of quantitatively,‖ that is to say, as a force divisible in the measure of its transmission, according to the pleasure of Him who transmits it, so that one may receive more, another less of the Spirit.

In spite of all these arguments, the contrary thesis, that which maintains the personality of the Holy Spirit, may be defended with plausibility from the texts of John, and, it would seem, even more easily. We have in our mind the many passages in which the work and manifestations of the Spirit are spoken of. In these He uniformly appears as a person. He comes, He abides, He is sent, He speaks, He teaches, He

* For example, John i. 33, Βαπτίζειν ἐν πνεύματι ἁγίῳ, etc.
† 1 John ii. 20, 27, χρίσμα.
‡ John xiv. 17, 26; 1 John iv. 2.
§ Ἐκπορεύεσθαι, John xv. 26.
‖ 1 John iv. 13; comp. John iii. 34.

guides, He corrects, He bears witness, and so forth. All these acts are performed under the control of certain conditions inherent in a personal nature. It is unnecessary to quote here passages in support of this view; they will shortly present themselves to us again.

Here then are two sets of expressions which appear even contradictory. A conscientious exegesis will be careful not to impinge upon the domain of dogmatic theology, and to endeavour to efface the difference by a forced interpretation of the texts. The solution of the problem does not devolve upon exegesis. In fact, John is not the only apostle in whose writings we can trace the simultaneous presence of these different formulas. Nay, more, they are to be found in the primary source of apostolic theology, the Old Testament. The phenomenon we are now considering is not new; it recurs repeatedly within the compass of Scriptural ideas. We are only witnessing again the conception, the birth of a theological idea which thus laboriously disengages itself from its germ, taking that which had been the enclosure of its germinal principle to form its own body, its very essence. In other words, this personification of the Spirit of God, or of any other divine manifestation, which in the language of the prophets,— so vivid, so poetical, so full of figure and prosopœia,—marks the effort of the mind to grasp the abstract, tends to become under speculative treatment, a theory, a metaphysical fact, a dogma in short. If we found ourselves just now arrested for a moment, it was not because of the doctrinal result itself, which is in perfect harmony with other facts of the same kind which we have previously established; it was rather because this transformation of a popular expression into a formula of high philosophy is here less complete than elsewhere—much less so, for example, than it is in relation to the person of the Word. In the latter case, the fact of the historical personality of Jesus could not but hasten to maturity the dogmatic system, while no such support was found for the doctrine of the personality of the Holy Spirit. Thus the history of dogmas shows that the theologians of the Church took far longer in giving precision to their ideas on the third person of the Trinity, than they required to define the second.

We must not allow ourselves, then, to confound the two series of expressions used by the apostle John, or to sacrifice the one to the other at the dictation of any system whatever, to which we may ourselves incline. The first series belongs to the ancient and popular ideas, not yet recast by philosophical reflection. The second series, on the contrary, shows that this reflection, which had already given birth, to what we have called the doctrinal premises of the system, also began to appropriate this further point of doctrine, and to impose upon it its own forms. It is for our dogmatists and philosophers to determine to which side inclines the balance of truth; with this the exegetical historian has nothing to do. He will be satisfied with having verified the fact that the system he is expounding, while seeking to rise to a speculative point of view, had not as yet fully reached it. In the chapter on the Word, we saw how popular expressions sometimes clash with the theological language of the schools, but we saw also that this did not prevent theology from being complete mistress of her own ideas. Here, on the contrary, theology is still without form, and has not as yet assimilated to itself the popular conceptions.

It might be asked, Is the author conscious of this peculiar position; and if so, to what extent? In other words, did that element of his teaching which seems to us to belong to two different forms of the religious conception, appear in the same light to himself? We venture to doubt it, both on the ground of what has already been said, and for another reason presently to be advanced.

The relation of the Spirit with the Father and the Son is that of dependence, as would naturally be supposed on the first of the two theories just stated, and as is quite consistent with the second. He is sent by the Father and the Son; given by the Father and the Son.* He does not act of Himself;†

---

* John iii. 34; xiv. 16, 26; comp. with John xv. 26; xvi. 7; xx. 22.

† Ἀφ᾽ ἑαυτοῦ, John xvi. 13, and foll.; ἐκ τοῦ ἐμοῦ λήψεται.

He speaks that which He has heard, especially from the Son, as the Son also speaks not of Himself. Jesus places Himself by the side of the Father, and on the same level with Him in relation to the object of revelation. The Spirit is placed in contact with these two personalities, deriving from them as a source. The teaching of the Spirit has the Word for its subject. It brings to the mind of the believers that which Jesus had already said to them.* He will tell that which Jesus may not or cannot utter as yet.† He bears testimony to Jesus.‡ If he pronounce sentence of reproof and condemnation on the world, it is in view of the position the world has taken with regard to Jesus.§ He will glorify Jesus by working for Him and under His direction, as the lesser glorifies the greater, as Jesus glorified God∥ by doing the work of God. Lastly, it is said that God gave the Spirit first to the Son,¶ and that He gave it abundantly.

From all this it would seem to follow that the Spirit was first in God; then in Christ also, as a power inherent in His essence; and that finally, *after the death of Christ*, it was manifested in a personal manner, and as working in the believers. If it is the first duty of biblical theology to give with all simplicity the results of a sound exegesis, without any attempt to systematize where no system is as yet fairly developed, our task must now be fulfilled, since we have shown clearly that such is the case in the present instance. The Church has been of our opinion, and has sedulously sought something beyond the incomplete theses furnished by exegesis alone; and we repeat once again, it was an illusion of the theological science of the seventeenth century, to imagine that its scholastic formularies were sustained by the texts of John.

But we have not yet reached the ultimatum of our inquiry into the essence of the Holy Spirit, as represented by the

* John xiv. 26.
† John xvi. 13.
‡ John xv. 26; 1 John v. 6.
§ John xvi. 7, and foll.
∥ John xvi. 14; comp. xvii. 4.
¶ John iii. 34; comp. i. 33.

apostle ; we have yet more to say, and are on the track of a new and very interesting discovery, which will in a sense confirm the former, without, however, leading to precisely the same result. In several passages, and more especially in the solemn promise of the Spirit to the world, where the writer speaks of Him in a more theoretic manner, he gives Him a proper and special name. He calls Him the Paraclete,* or more exactly another Paraclete in the place of Jesus, who was about to leave His disciples.† The same name is elsewhere‡ given to Jesus Himself. We willingly adopt the explanation of this name, which is accepted now by the majority of interpreters. It designates, according to its etymological meaning, some one who helps and sustains by means of speech—that is, either by teaching or by the defence of a cause. It is thus the Spirit comes in aid of the believers, first and continuously as a revealer, next in espousing their cause against the world ;§ lastly, in raising them to the dignity of judges.||

This etymological explanation appears fully to satisfy the most competent exegetes. They are the more content with it, because the Church, from the earliest times, expressed on this point a theory which seems to accord so well with the letter of the text, that doubt appears superfluous and out of place. And yet there lingers in our mind a doubt of some significance, which we venture very modestly to submit to our readers.

In chapter xiv., the Master, at the moment of parting wit. His disciples, consoles them, first, by the prospect of anoth‹ life in which they shall see Him again ;¶ in the second place, by reminding them of their mission, in the accomplishment of which they will derive the moral force they will need ;** lastly, by promising them the *Paraclete*, literally another

* 'Ο παράκλητος, John xiv. 16.
† John xiv. 26 ; xv. 26 ; xvi. 7.
‡ 1 John ii. 1.
§ Διδάσκων, μαρτυρῶν, ὑπομιμνήσκων, ἐλέγχων.
|| John xx. 23.
¶ John xiv. 2—4.
** John xiv. 12—14.

Paraclete, who shall abide with them for ever, even the Spirit of truth, whom the world cannot receive because it seeth Him not, neither knoweth Him.* After this, without further transition, He adds, " I will not leave you orphans; *I will come unto you*," etc. This promise cannot be limited to the occasional appearances of Jesus after His resurrection, during the brief space before the feast of Pentecost. It must necessarily be understood of the coming—that is, of the spiritual presence of the Lord—promised in other passages also, as continuing to the very end of the world. It would be, in the first place, a very meagre interpretation to restrict the promise here to twelve individuals only, instead of extending it to all believers. Again, the word ζήσεσθε, *ye shall live* (verse 19), has no real meaning on this supposed restriction. The same remark applies to verse 20, where this ἔρχεσθαι, this *presence* promised, has as its effect a close and mystical relation (ἐγὼ ἐν ὑμῖν) between Christ and the believers; to verse 21 also, where the presence of Christ is represented as dependent on such a relation, Christ promising to manifest Himself to the soul that loves Him; and, lastly, to verse 23, where it is said that the Father will come with the Son. All these phrases are meaningless if anything else is intended than the permanent and spiritual presence of the Saviour in the souls of His disciples. But if this be the meaning, we cannot but remark the perfect analogy which exists between the coming of Christ, and that of the Paraclete. When Jesus left this earthly scene, the world saw Him no more, but He still remained visible to the believers. To their consciousness He is still present, as is said in verse 17 in regard to the Spirit. He will be in them as the Spirit is. Now as this can be no other than a spiritual presence in the believers, and as the Paraclete is the Spirit of the Son and of the Father, proceeding from and sent forth by them, it follows that these are not two distinct and different manifestations, but that what is said of the Paraclete is the theological formula by which the idea of the relation between Christ and the believer is analyzed and changed into a hypostasis, as we have already

* John xiv. 15—17.

seen elsewhere. The perfectly simple and long-established idea of the mystical union of the disciples with the glorified Master, who continues to live in them, tends to rise into the sphere of speculation. The effort of thought, which in the abstract idea of the Divinity discovered the person of the Word, separated it and presented it as a distinct and concrete Being, here finds the person of the Paraclete in the abstract idea of spiritual communion between the Word and the believing soul, and at least endeavours to render it equally concrete and definite. It is true that this attempt is not so successful as the former, because it has not at its disposal now, as in the other case, a phraseology already formed by the philosophy of the schools. There is, however, an advance upon that philosophy, and a very marked approach to the theory subsequently accepted by the Church.

When Jesus says,* "A little while and the world seeth me no more, but ye see me ;" and again,† "A little while and ye shall not see me, and again a little while and ye shall see me ;" He is not, we repeat, speaking of the few hours passed in the tomb, and of His personal appearances between the resurrection and the ascension. He is referring, on the one hand, to the unquestionable fact that the world, which knew the Saviour only according to the flesh, knows Him no more after His earthly existence ceases; and on the other hand, to the fact, foretold by Himself and attested by experience, that the death of the Crucified brought doubt and discouragement into the hearts of the disciples, that the night of His entombment for a time obscured their faith. Undoubtedly the resurrection came to restore to them light and courage, and from it will date their *seeing Him again*,‡ but that term does not denote seeing Him with the bodily eyes. The coming of the Master and the vision of the disciples—essentially correlative terms—mark§ the elements of a life in common, the principles of a complex

* John xiv. 19.
† John xvi. 16.
‡ Θεωρεῖν.
§ John xiv. 20.

existence, the factors of a mutual relation the closest and nearest possible, neither element having any reality, effect, or value apart from the other. This relation is not transitory and accidental; it is permanent,* according to the phraseology of John. It makes absolutely no difference in the fact, whether we name that which dwells within the man, the Spirit, or Christ. Literal exegesis pleads for the distinction of the persons; speculative reason admits and sanctions it; but practical logic demurs, and sees neither the necessity nor the utility of it, for whatever effort may be made by the reason, it can never succeed in distinguishing, in reality, a double operation of the same spirit, acting in the same way, for the same end, at the same time, and on the same individual. And this being the case, the explanation we have given of the theological formula before us, will not appear so paradoxical as it may have seemed at first sight.

There is, however, one passage which, literally understood, establishes the separateness of the two personalities in a manner so positive, that our system would seem to come into collision with direct evidence. This is the verse † in which Jesus refuses to give fuller explanations to His disciples, referring them to the Paraclete, who will come afterwards to teach them. As we read these words, the necessity seems obvious to adhere to the ordinary theory of the diverse functions, apparently assigned to the two revealers separately. On fuller consideration, however, we shall feel constrained by this passage to change our opinion. We must first thoroughly realize to ourselves the fact that the Spirit has nothing essentially new to teach us. His teaching consists in *bringing to remembrance* that which Jesus has Himself spoken.‡ This necessity exists because the divine revelation, as contained in its fulness in the Word, is too profound for human reason, and can be exhausted or fathomed only by means of what we may venture to call the divine exegesis—the continuous and progressive interpretation given

* Μένειν.
† John xvi. 12, and foll.
‡ John xiv. 26.

by the Spirit of God, while the words and systems of men are soon learnt and apprehended. This exegesis must always prove that it comes from God; this it will do by showing that that which it teaches has been already revealed by the Word; otherwise the revelation made by the Word would be—that which it cannot possibly be—incomplete and inadequate. It is moreover a point of view which the New Testament never abandons, and to which the Church has still more closely adhered, that revelation, objectively considered, cannot be perfectible, or in need of being supplemented, since it would thus declare what it has given to the world by the lips and in the life of the Saviour, to be insufficient.* It appertained only to the Old Testament to speak of a progressive development of revelation. If the revealing Spirit is in future to go beyond this sphere, it must be to give special instructions in reference to particular contingencies,† and to apply the truths previously revealed to questions and doubts which may arise in the advance of thought. To this must be added the important fact that the apparent antithesis between the persons which the letter expresses in the passage above cited, is expressly negatived a few lines further on,‡ where Jesus declares that He Himself will go on to teach in the times to come, and that He will teach the very same things which just before He seemed to assign to another Teacher. This last passage, showing that the distinction of the persons exists on the surface of the words only, and not in the thought itself, is to our mind conclusive.

It is not, then, as it appears to us, a matter of difficulty to prove that the apostle predicts absolutely the same thing, and in the same terms, of the Paraclete and of Christ; and that the relation of believers with both is identical. See, again, the passage § which says distinctly, "The anointing which ye have received" (that is to say, the Spirit, or the Paraclete,) "teacheth you of all things. And now abide in Him, that

---

* John xvii. 6 ; xv. 15 ; xii. 50.
† John xvi. 13 ; comp. 1 John ii. 27.
‡ John xvi. 25.
§ 1 John ii. 27, 28.

when He shall *appear*, we may have confidence, and not be ashamed before Him at His coming." Evidently here, He whose coming was expected and the Paraclete are one and the same person. If this be so, it is natural that the action of the Paraclete should be represented sometimes as personal, sometimes as impersonal; and, in the former case, sometimes as distinct from that of Christ, sometimes as one with it. Exegesis assuredly cannot deny these facts; it remains to be determined whether the manner in which we have endeavoured to apprehend this variety of formulary, apparently incompatible and paradoxical, is really the only one possible. We must be careful, however, in examining it, not to blend unadvisedly scholastic dogma with textual exegesis.

The Spirit, then, carries on the work of Christ. The Word must needs become man, but He could not always abide as man upon earth. His object had been to give to the world that which it did not possess, light, love, life,—that is to say, His own essence or substance. This substance or essence of the Word was to remain in the world, even after the form under which it had been first communicated to it had ceased to exist. Jesus died : the Christ, the Incarnate Word, quitted this earth ; but His substance did not quit it ; the *Spirit of Christ* remained in the world, at least in that portion of the world which received and accepted it. Nothing can be more true than that which is said* of this influence of the Word upon the world. The Spirit of Christ, as an active power, as the principle of the spiritual life, was only enabled to display all its vitality and force after He who had been its personal representative, its visible source, had vanished from the eyes of the world. Such is the deep meaning of that symbolic act, in which the risen Master, on parting from His disciples,† gives them His Spirit, breathing upon them, as the Creator breathed upon the first man ; but He communicates to them a life more precious than Adam received, a life the preservation of which depends, not

* John xvi. 7.
† John xx. 22.

on abstinence from the forbidden fruit of the tree of an earthly paradise, but on the participation of a new and imperishable manna, given to whomsoever asks; a life, lastly, which, far from being lost through tasting the fruits of the tree of knowledge, offers, on the contrary, the most beautiful fruits of that tree to all who may desire them.

CHAPTER XIII.

OF LOVE.

WE have seen what faith is in itself,—how it is formed, developed, and sustained in a man; how it modifies and controls the nature and the individuality of him who possesses it, or, rather, who is possessed by it. We now come to consider its outward manifestations; this is the second element, the practical side of divine truth, the Christian life in the various phases of it with which we are familiar in our experience of society. This part of the theology of John is but very slightly developed. This is in harmony with the nature of mysticism, which delights to dwell within itself, and does not readily seek channels of communication beyond its own inner sphere. If it is of a sickly, dreamy, fantastic cast, this tendency leads it into very deplorable errors. So long as it confines itself within the limits of sound religious feeling, not under the sway of the imagination, its manifestations will be simple and concentrated, rather than various and multiform. It is for this reason no other apostle has so fully as the apostle John, comprehended and described the Christian life, under the simple idea of love.

Before speaking of love, we may dwell for a moment on the negative aspect of the effects of faith. The external proof of the existence of faith is the absence of sin. This effect is a corollary, a *postulatum* inseparable from the very idea of faith. The Christian, born of God, sins not, because sin is the attribute of the children of the devil. "Whosoever abideth in Christ," it is said, sinneth not;* he that is born of God cannot sin;

* 1 John iii. 6, 9.

whosoever sinneth, knoweth not God. This is the victory
which Christ has won over the devil in the heart of the
believer,* or which the believer himself has gained,† which is
the same thing, for this victory could. not be achieved except
by union with Christ, the conqueror of both the world and the
devil. The latter has no more hold on the believer;‡ since
a victory won by Christ cannot be other than complete and
final. Our faith is then in itself a victory over the world.§
Again, it is said that the believer is *clean,*‖ which must mean
purged from sin. If we read of this purification, sometimes as
effected by the blood, sometimes by the teaching of the Lord,¶
this does not constitute any real difference in the fact. It is
always faith which serves as the bond between cause and effect.
Lastly, it is said again that the believer is free** from sin, and
this enfranchisement is derived from the fact that he continues
in Christ's word, that he knows the truth—that is to say, he is
in union with the Son. Previous sins are pardoned;†† they are
no more to be mentioned. All these various formulas, when
fairly analyzed, lend confirmation to our thesis that faith and
sin are necessarily antipathetic, and cannot co-exist.

All that we have just said is the logical consequence of the
theory. But we find this theory confronted with experience,
which can produce no such perfect believers, exempt from all
sin ; for it would be an illusion, culpable in itself,‡‡ to hold that
we are without sin. And let it be observed, this last assertion
does not relate to the period preceding faith ; it is not designed
to refute the error of those who might think they had no need
of redemption for themselves, but it is addressed to men who
have already overcome the wicked one within them, through

* 1 John iv. 4.
† 1 John ii. 13, and foll.
‡ 1 John v. 18.
§ 1 John v. 4.
‖ John xiii. 10.
¶ 1 John i. 7; John xv. 3.
** Ἐλεύθεροι, John viii. 32, and foll.
†† 1 John ii. 12.
‡‡ 1 John i. 8.

31 *

the power of Christ.* To these the apostle deems it necessary to address every form of warning and exhortation. Jesus Himself prays God to keep the believer from the power of the evil one ;† He speaks in another place ‡ of withered, fruitless branches which are to be cut off from the vine. Nay, more, even those Christians who are in no danger of being cast away, since their hope of life is steadfast, and sustained by the intercession of their brethren,§ are still spoken of as liable to sin. They are taught to seek the pardon which they perpetually need from Christ, who, in His capacity as the Paraclete, is given to be at once their helper on earth and their intercessor with the Father.‖ All unrighteousness, all that is opposed to the strict idea of right, is sin ;¶ but every sin does not lead to death—that is, not finally and irrevocably. It is impossible for sin to lead to life, since it has no life in it ; but life is not utterly lost by every sin.**

Thus theory comes into collision with experience, and is forced to abandon its logical conclusions. The spiritual birth, which, according to the analogy of physical birth,†† was represented to us as an instantaneous fact completed at once, now appears as a continuous process carried on day by day in the life of the believer. We have noted the same phenomenon in the teaching of Paul, and found it sustained in that case by still more numerous examples. It is impossible for exegetes

* 1 John ii. 13 ; comp. v. 5.
† John xvii. 15.
‡ John xv. 2 ; comp. 1 John ii. 19.
§ 1 John v. 16.
‖ 1 John i. 9 ; ii. 1.
¶ 1 John v. 17.
** The difference between mortal and venial sins has much occupied theologians, especially the casuists. As the apostle does not explain his idea, it is not in our province to divine it. We may simply say that the most probable explanation, which is moreover sustained by a passage from the Epistle to the Hebrews (vi. 4, and foll.), is that which understands by mortal sin the denial of Christ, the falling away of those who had belonged to the number of the believers. This falling away, like some physical maladies, is regarded as so dangerous that it naturally appears incurable.
†† John xvi. 21.

to deny the fact without doing violence to the most explicit texts. On the other hand, we strongly condemn any attempt to conciliate them, and to amalgamate the two views, so as to evolve from them some middle term. We repeat, it is in our opinion one of the great merits of Biblical theology, that it does not sacrifice to logic either experience on the one hand, or the ideal on the other, but presents us in the former with a mirror which may preserve us from all self-deception with regard to our supposed moral perfection (a deception so frequent and so habitual to human nature); and gives us, in the latter, the standard and pattern to which our frail and faulty virtue is ever to aspire. If the theology of the schools should venture to sacrifice the ideal, it would destroy the spring of all Christian activity. The divinity of Christianity is evidenced most strongly by the fact, that it presents to man an ideal which he could never have evolved from his own experience, whether internal or external; an ideal towards which he is ever striving, but to which he never attains, and which upon a grander scale, but with the same apparently contradictory properties, is set forth as the ultimate and final goal of the whole race of man— the kingdom of God upon earth. That which the historical Church is to this kingdom, the experimental Christian is to the theoretical; he bears his title, not as the badge of a perfection attained, but as indicating the tendency of his life, and the means which are to lead him to perfection as his final goal.

Let us now pass on to the description of the positive effect of faith; this, as we have already said, is love.* The classic passage here is the fourth chapter of the epistle.† The source of all love is God; He has first loved, and proved His love by the sending of His Son. He who is born of God loves like God, and he who loves proves by that very fact that he is born of God. Hence it is that love turns first towards its source, namely to God and Christ; and in this sphere it is identical with faith,‡ and in opposition to the love of the

* Ἀγάπη.
† Verses 7—21.
‡ 1 John iv. 19, 20; v. 1, and foll.; John viii. 42; xiv. 21.

world and its pleasures.* It is the bond which binds indissolubly the believer to God and to Christ; for he who dwelleth in love dwelleth in God,† and in the love of Christ,—that is to say, in the love which Christ has for him.

From this love flows love to man. The love of God is perfected and manifested in love to the brethren.‡ Whenever the writer speaks of this love, he uses the expression "*to love one another*,"§ and he speaks of it in such a manner as to limit the idea to the sphere of believers, so that he always mentions at the same time the fundamental opposition between them and the world. We have found no passage which speaks of what is called the universal brotherhood of all men, and this will not surprise us when we think of the absolute antagonism which the theology of John establishes between God and the world. We have seen him adopting as a sort of motto the words "He that is not with me is against me." When it is said, ‖ "He who loveth God (the author of the spiritual birth) will love Him also that is begotten of God," the love is not extended to any who lack this qualification. It may even be said that the love of the human race at large is explicitly repudiated, or at least set aside, and ignored by one utterance put into the lips of Jesus.¶ The love which believers have for one another is not the effect of a personal inclination, it is rather a natural symptom of their common regeneration, of the equality of their relation to the Father.** Thus they are called *brethren*,†† and the passages ordinarily understood as speaking of universal love,‡‡ ought really to be interpreted in a more restricted sense.

* 1 John ii. 15.
† 1 John iv. 16; xv. 9.
‡ 1 John iv. 12.
§ John xiii. 34; xv. 12, 17; 1 John iii. 11, 23; iv. 11.
‖ 1 John v. 1.
¶ John xvii. 9. [But even our Lord's prayer for His disciples had for its ultimate object that "the *world* may know that Thou hast sent me."—Ed.]
** John xvii. 21.
†† Ἀδελφοί, *passim*.
‡‡ For example, 1 John iii. 17; iv. 20, etc.

Love is in itself a feeling, a disposition of the soul, an inclination. It attains its perfection, not by word or profession, but by deed.* Herein is our love to God manifested, that we keep His commandments.† Having reached this point, and become at the same time the complete and true expression of the faith, it has power to overcome the world. It casts out fear, and can face the world with boldness on the great final day, knowing that the Lord is on its side.‡

Love to God consists in keeping His commandments. These commandments are nowhere enumerated in detail; sometimes they are mentioned, but only by way of example, and Christ is represented as the living expression and illustration of them all.§ To Christian feeling is entrusted the charge of recognizing its duties; it cannot err on this path, since the fulfilment of duty is natural to it. He who is born of God is no more flesh, but spirit,‖ and his deeds are the deeds of the spirit. In order to understand the full scope of the idea before us, we may adhere mainly to the beautiful allegory of the branch in the vine,¶ which contains all its essential elements. The true point of comparison there, is the organic oneness of the stem and the branches, and the intimate connexion between the Saviour and the believers. Both relations alike point to the idea of the natural development of an intrinsic and innate force, without any external and artificial aid.

It would then be perfectly out of place to offer an enumeration of certain terms belonging to the writings of John, by means of which a system of ethical theology might be formed, or what is called a special moral code. A complete system could never be thus derived, and the numerous omissions would render the result meagre and inadequate. We shall confine ourselves to observing that among these terms are several which belong to the popular mode of speech, and

* 1 John iii. 18.
† 1 John v. 3; ii. 5; John xiv. 21.
‡ 1 John iv. 17, 18.
§ For example, 1 John iii. 16, and foll.; John xiii. 14, etc.
‖ John iii. 6.
¶ John xv. 1, and foll.

others which recall the peculiar forms of the theology of the apostle. In the first class we may cite *to do good, to do righteousness.** This last expression is synonymous with *loving the brethren.*† In the second class we may place the phrases *to do the truth, to walk in the light.*‡ All this, as the reader will observe, is insufficient to build up a doctrine of particular duties; and we may say, generally, that a theology which makes faith the essence of obedience,§ does not need to construct a special system of ethics, or to give an enumeration of individual acts of duty. We are justified, then, in our comprehension of the theological theory of John under the two heads of faith and life.‖

In the conception of love which we have just developed, the idea of the Church, that is of the community of believers, is virtually contained. It is true that it is present only in an abstract form, and without the special qualifications by which the Church, in the historical and dogmatic sense of the word, is distinguished from every other sort of religious assembly. We may add that these qualifications are nowhere specified by John. He does not go beyond the figure of a flock, on which he delights to dwell at length, and out of which he constructs¶ one of the most popular allegories of the Bible. But this allegory, beautiful as it is, only sets forth the relations of the sheep with the shepherd. It has no application at all to the relations which may or ought to subsist among the sheep themselves, inasmuch as they have a common purpose to fulfil, a mission to the world or for it. The idea we thus obtain is at most that of an ideal Church, a community of

---

* Ἀγαθοποιεῖν, John v. 29; ποιεῖν τὴν δικαιοσύνην, 1 John ii. 29; iii. 7, 10.

† The term δίκαιος is explained by οὐχ ἁμαρτάνων (1 John iii. 7), and is not used in a more specifically theological or Christian sense.

‡ Ποιεῖν τὴν ἀλήθειαν, John iii. 21; 1 John i. 6; ἐν τῷ φωτὶ περιπατεῖν, 1 John i. 7; ii. 9.

§ John vi. 28, and foll.

‖ We may remark, in passing, that the idea of sanctification is nowhere mentioned separately in John's writings; ἁγιασμός (John xvii. 17, and foll.) is consecration to the ministry.

¶ John x. 1—16.

believers whom the affairs of social life do not touch, not of a community which is to be the active leaven of the world, and which has itself constant need of re-organization, and re-formation.

In his epistle the writer had further occasion to speak of the Church, because it was actually in existence, with its wants and its works. In fact, we here observe a number of such expressions as *we know, we believe,* etc., expressions evidently conveying the idea of a community, of a solidarity between the writer and other persons. The same idea is apparent in the exhortation to examine in common, or at least in the common interest, every doctrine* which seeks to gain authority in the Church. The spirit which teaches and directs the individuals, becomes the spirit of the entire community, so that the members composing it are guided in the same manner and to the same end. On closer examination, however, we find that we are still in the region of abstract theory. What is before us is not the historic Church, not even the Pauline Church with its simple forms and its spiritual basis. This would be out of place here; it is unneeded when the theme is the ideal Church. What is here discussed is not a question of teachers and directors; the Spirit guides and instructs all the members directly and alike. The Twelve, or, more generally, those who were with Jesus from the beginning,† have some advantage over the rest, but an advantage altogether external and accidental, in that they could teach from their own historical experience. But even this advantage is of no moment; for the Paraclete, who comes Himself to teach and to bear witness, and who is promised to all believers, is unquestionably their equal, and even their superior. Whosoever has the Spirit, has also the keys—that is, the power to pardon or to retain sin.‡ The apostle, writing to his Christians, speaks to them as to men who already know all things,§ and

---

* Δοκιμασία πνευμάτων, 1 John iv. 1, and foll.
+ John xv. 27.
‡ John xx. 23.
§ 1 John ii. 20, 21, 27.

have no further need of teaching. Thus everything is regarded from the ideal point of view; everything tends to a close and perfect union, to an identification of all in God and in Christ. This does not infer a social organization in which each should have his special place and duties; there is no mention of working for one another, of mutual edification, of the consolidation of the work within by combined efforts, and its extension without by active co-operation in the struggle against the world. Mysticism is something too self-absorbed, seeking nothing beyond its own inner sphere; social necessities do not concern it. Such a Church as is here spoken of never had other than an ideal existence, as is the case also in reference to those Christians free from all taint of sin, of whom we have already repeatedly spoken. Experience has not furnished the elements of such a picture : all that experience can do is to bring the ideal figure into a more vivid light, by the shadows which it projects, and with which it constantly surrounds it.

It devolves on us here to say a word further upon baptism. This is certainly mentioned in the writings of John, and this fact might be brought forward to prove that the Church, as an actual and visible institution, is not altogether ignored in the outline of his theology; for baptism is an ecclesiastical institution; it is the rite of initiation into a community; it is, in a word, something material and external, which argues an organization of the same nature. Nevertheless, we maintain our assertion. There are very few passages in which baptism is spoken of from a doctrinal point of view;* and in these the reference is not to the Church, but to faith only, which is equivalent to saying that baptism is regarded from the standpoint of the union of the individuals with Christ, and not from that of the union of believers among themselves, and of the formation of the ecclesiastical community. Again: in the same passages, a lower place or value is assigned to the water than to the Spirit;† or, again, the blood of Christ is set forth as the most important element; and in any case, baptism is

---

* John iii. 5 ; 1 John v. 6, 8.
† Comp. John i. 31, 33.

represented as a symbol of the spiritual birth, and not as the commemorative sign of an association. We are not then carried beyond the limits of the individualism which we have traced throughout this system.

The Lord's Supper, which Paul takes in one place as a symbol of the communion of the Church, John does not even mention. We do not say that the exegetes are wrong, who discover an allusion to this sacred institution in the celebrated passage relating to the bread from heaven, which we have already analyzed, and who regard this as a theological explanation of the rite. But if we admit this interpretation, it is only the more evident that we are right in our main assertion. In fact, in that passage again, the reference is solely to the individual communion of the believer with the Saviour, and we shall not find in it the slightest trace of a broader application or interpretation, which should introduce us to the life of the community.

CHAPTER XIV.

OF LIFE.

WE are now brought to the ultimate design of the divine economy, and consequently to the keystone of the arch of John's theology. We find both in the words, "*that ye might have life.*"* Not only does the apostle himself constantly return to this conclusion, but there is not a single discourse of Jesus which does not proclaim it as the end of His work, as the object of all the efforts of man. There can be no need to cite the texts in support of this assertion; they are found on every page; and the most remarkable passages will present themselves on special grounds as we advance.

In thus commencing our observations on *life*, we shall first establish several facts of the highest importance, and at the same time very characteristic of the system which we are expounding. The first of these facts is that *life is an immediate effect of faith.* He who believes unto life, has *already* passed from the kingdom of death into the kingdom of life.† Life, then, is not something appertaining exclusively to the future. It has its root and source in union with the Son and the Father, who alone possess essential life.‡ He who has the Son will then necessarily§ have that which is essential to the Son, namely life, as he has already received light and. love; he will have it *in himself* no less essentially.‖ It is,

* John xx. 31.
† Ἔχει, μεταβέβηκε, John v. 24; comp. vi. 40, 47, 54.
‡ John v. 26.
§ 1 John v. 11, and foll.
‖ John vi. 53.

then, indifferent whether we say that God gives life to the believers, or rather has given it, or that the Son gives it.* We may mention, in passing, the expressions *bread of life, living water*, and others,† the explanation of which has already been given in the chapter on Faith. We merely observe here that the very image which they contain, that of vivifying nourishment,‡ which is changed into the very substance of the body receiving it, is well adapted to convey the idea of this direct impartation of life.§

Besides these expressions, we meet with others, which are not derived directly from this mystical conception, and which consequently are not of a nature to prove the thesis we are here establishing. It will be remembered that this has been the case also in reference to other points. Thus, when it is said,‖ " He who followeth me shall have the light of life," this may be understood of the illumination of the reason by the Gospel, and of a progressive advance towards life eternal. The same remark will apply to the passages which speak of the "*words of eternal life*."¶ These passages, however, while less explicit, are in no way opposed to the sense which we hold to be the most essential, and cannot be used by exegesis to lessen its significance.

In all the formulas we have just cited, life is therefore represented as flowing naturally from union with Christ as its source, and this fact will govern all that relates to it, if the system be consistent with itself. Certain passages, however, have been adduced, which would seem to suggest some doubts as to this direct connection of cause and effect. Thus some have brought forward the expression which speaks of nutriment unto life,** as though it conveyed a temporary rela-

* John x. 28; xvii. 2; 1 John v. 11.

† Ἄρτος ζῶν, or ζωῆς, John vi. 35, 48, 51; ὕδωρ ζῶν, iv. 10, and foll.

‡ John vi. 33.

§ We find the latter truth again, but stated without a figure, in John xi. 25 (xiv. 6).

‖ John viii. 12.

¶ John vi. 63, 68; xii. 50.

** Εἰς ζωήν, John iv. 14, and vi. 27.

tion, and they have interpreted it as meaning *through the present life until the future*, which will be the true life—life eternal. Such an interpretation is inadmissible. In the two passages quoted in the last note, faith, under the figures of bread and water, is indicated as the food which truly gives life,* and the quality of producing a durable and permanent effect† is ascribed to it, a quality which does not belong to physical nutriment, since that does not prevent the recurrence of hunger and thirst. Thus it is erroneous, again, to understand that which is called ‡ "fruit unto life eternal," of evangelical work, as ultimately procuring that life for the apostles, as a recompense. The fruit is the new converts themselves. The labours of the disciples are compared to a harvest; they gain or reap the souls of the men who listen to them; this is the good grain, these are the sheaves which they gather into their granary, and that granary is life eternal. Evidently this solution of the allegory, so far from being opposed to the idea of the immediate bestowment of life, tends to establish it. Lastly, it may be objected that the verb *to live*, which sometimes takes the place of the formula *to have life*, is only used in the present tense in speaking of Christ, while it is always in the future when the reference is to believers. But ˙this assertion is unfounded. Not only is the present employed of believers also,§ but the future argues nothing against our thesis; for sometimes‖ the employment of the future, or rather of the aorist, is simply dictated by the rules of syntax, and has no connection with the theological idea. Again,¶ it is said that the catastrophe which will bring Jesus Himself for a while into the night of the grave, will plunge His disciples also for a time into the darkness of despair and doubt; but that after this, the day of life, in the twofold sense of that word, will dawn again for Him and for

* Εἰς expressing the effect.
† Βρῶσις μένουσα.
‡ John iv. 36.
§ John xi. 26.
‖ 1 John iv. 9.
¶ John xiv. 19.

them. The future, in this phrase, is then another evidence in support of our assertion. Finally, in other passages,* the future is used simply because of the hypothetical nature of the discourse.

With this first doctrinal fact relating to life, is associated a second, inseparable from the former,—that of its *eternal* duration.† It would be a strange error to endeavour to make any distinction between that which is simply called life, and that which is elsewhere spoken of as life eternal, as if the latter idea contained anything more than the former, or referred to another period of human existence. The two expressions are absolutely equivalent, and are sometimes used interchangeably in one and the same phrase.‡ In truth, it could not be otherwise; it is impossible to conceive of a divine life as liable to or capable of interruption; nor can we suppose it to pass through a gradual development, or successive gradations; we nowhere find it said that this life, in being transmitted from Christ to the believer, is communicated at first in an enfeebled and modified form, to be afterwards invigorated and perfected. The qualification *eternal* may then be said to be a superfluous epithet, or an attribute already contained in the idea of the subject. We might be inclined to suggest that this epithet has only been added to declare more explicitly that the mystical theology ignores the distinction which may be made elsewhere between the present and the future life. Be this as it may, the writer is consistent with himself in affirming that physical death cannot interrupt or disturb that life,§ or in refusing to apply the common notion of death to the moment of man's departure from earth.||

After this, it only remains for us to ask what this life is in its essential properties. We nowhere find a definition of it. But etymology will supply us with the elements we need, and

* John vi. 51, 57, and foll.; xi. 25.

† Ζωὴ αἰώνιος.

‡ John iii. 36; v. 24, 39, and foll.; vi. 53, and foll.; 57, and foll.; 1 John i. 2; iii. 14, and foll.; v. 11, and foll.

§ John xi. 26.

|| John viii. 51, and foll.

the history of religious thought in biblical matters will help us to complete the definition.

We shall there discover, in the first place, the idea of a real existence, an existence such as is proper to God and to the Word : an imperishable existence—that is to say, not subject to the vicissitudes and imperfections of the finite world. This primary idea is repeatedly expressed, at least in a negative form ;* it leads to a doctrine of immortality, or, to speak more correctly, of life, far surpassing any that had been expressed in the formulas of the current philosophy or theology, and resting upon premises and conceptions altogether different. In fact, it can dispense both with the philosophical thesis of the immateriality or indestructibility of the human soul, and with the theological thesis of a miraculous corporeal reconstruction of our person; theses, the first of which is altogether foreign to the religion of the Bible, and the second absolutely opposed to reason.

In the second place, the idea of life, as it is conceived in this system, implies the idea of a power, an operation, a communication, since this life no longer remains, so to speak, latent or passive in God and in the Word, but through them reaches the believer. It is not a neutral, somnolent thing; it is not a plant without fruit; it is a germ which is to find fullest development.† In the passages which may be cited on this subject, we must be careful not to understand by the prayers which are sure of being heard, the selfish demands of private interest : the context clearly shows that the reference is to the efforts and results of Christian and apostolic labour, which appear as so many blossoms and fruits of the union of the disciples with the Saviour.

Lastly, we know already, from our summary of the elements of Mosaism, that the idea of life contains that of satisfaction and happiness. These are the direct results of union with Christ. The terms which designate this union, and which are

---

* John iii. 15, and foll. ; x. 28 ; xi. 26.
† John xiv. 12, and foll. ; xvi. 23, and foll.

at the same time synonymous with that of *having life*,* are transferred in the same way to the condition of blessedness. Thus the expression *ye shall see me*,† which must necessarily be taken in the spiritual sense, is intimately associated and employed alternately with the other expression, *ye shall rejoice, ye shall be happy*. This happiness of the Christian, by the very fact of its flowing directly from an indissoluble union, is in its turn indestructible; it increases, it becomes more perfect with each new success of apostolic labours; ‡ it gains strength by every new inward experience of the Christian; § it belonged first to Christ, and from Him it passes to the believers,‖ in whom, consequently, it has the same attributes as in Him. True, it can be realized only through sharp trials, a painful conflict, a stern apprenticeship of sorrow and privation; but the joy which follows is all the more pure and complete;¶ the anguish is forgotten when this life-travail is fulfilled.** The happiness of the believer is peace of heart, an imperturbable calm, that assurance of possessing the true treasure, which makes the soul indifferent to those mere worldly advantages which yield no satisfaction. This peace, the Master, in returning to His Father, left to the disciples as His parting gift.††

Such, as it seems to us, is the relation of the inner life to the outer, as it is defined in the writings of the apostle John. The triumph over death, and over the fear it can inspire, is here, as we see, full and final. Not only is the sting taken from death, death itself seems to be done away. From this point of view, we shall not expect to find in this system any lengthened eschatology. In fact, in the theory we have just unfolded, there is no place for this branch of ordinary theology. We

---

* John vi. 56 ; x. 28.
† John xvi. 16—22, ὄψεσθέ με.
‡ John xvi. 22, 24.
§ 1 John i. 4.
‖ John xv. 11 ; xvii. 13.
¶ Πεπληρωμένη, John xv. 11 ; xvi. 24 ; 1 John i. 4.
** John xvi. 20, and foll.
†† John xiv. 27.

shall not then be surprised to find that the gospel we are examining, and the teaching of Jesus as contained in it, remain true to this theory, and exclude by their very silence that which·we have elsewhere found to be the principal object of Christian expectation. Doubtless it is impossible for mortals altogether to disregard the change which awaits them at the close of their earthly career; but if our author touches on this subject, it is only in such a way as to divest it of all theological importance. For, in the development of the individual existence, the decisive moment, the culminating point, is not that in which the body dies, but rather that in which the soul begins to live its true life, the life which is alone deserving of the name; and this moment will necessarily take precedence of the other, if it is to have all the importance which the system attaches to it.

Thus the current eschatological ideas of primitive Christianity are not found in the gospel of John, or, at the most, if they are adverted to in some popular forms of expression, they are so isolated that they in no way affect the system as a whole. In order to show this, we shall enter into some details. The fourth gospel is the only New Testament scripture which says nothing of the approaching end of the world,* or of the second coming of Christ. It would be clearly erroneous to give this construction to words which are to be understood of the spiritual return of Christ,† of which the other gospels also speak as a promise of the Lord, and with which we identify the sending of the Paraclete. It is said expressly that this coming will depend on the love of the individual to Christ;‡ this excludes altogether the idea of the second coming, and it is needless to seek elsewhere subsidiary proofs in support of our explanation. Another text,§ which some might be disposed to connect with the idea of the second coming, evidently refers to the fact that the Lord will come to all His disciples in the

---

* The promise contained in John xiv. 16 even implies, though obscurely, a contrary expectation.

† John xiv. 18, 28.

‡ John xiv. 21.

§ John xiv. 3.

moment of death, to bear them at once into the abode of the blessed. We say *at once*, and we repudiate wholly the notion of any intervening period, because if that were admitted, the doctrine already sufficiently established of the nature of life would be overthrown, and the consolation promised to the disciples, who could not be satisfied with the prospect of a universal but distant resurrection,* would be nullified. The entire chapter, from which we have just taken a number of quotations, is moreover opposed to the interpretation we are disputing, inasmuch as it affirms that Christ will return only for His chosen ones.† In this way we have it established, at the same time, that there is no indication of an intermediate state between death and the resurrection. The promise of Christ's return to seek His own, necessarily implies their reception into the eternal mansions of the Father, and nowhere is there any allusion to a subsequent change of condition or of abode. For a little while, the disciples were about to be separated locally from the Master ;‡ but this separation was to be condoned or neutralized by His spiritual presence,§ and would cease altogether as one by one was called to Himself. They were to follow Him, first, in His ministry, and afterwards in His death,‖ and were thus to be reunited to Him even locally.¶

Of all the facts of eschatology, the only one of which passing mention is made, is the resurrection of the dead. In some passages,** the spiritual resurrection is compared to the physical, and explained, so to speak, by its analogy with it; but it is declared, at the same time, to be greater and more important.††

* John xi. 24.
† John xiv. 22.
‡ John xiii. 33.
§ John xiv. 18, and foll.
‖ John xiii. 36.
¶ John xii. 26.
** John v. 21, 28, 29.
†† Μείζονα ἔργα, verse 20. [The exegesis of this passage is very obviously incorrect. The "works" of which Christ is speaking are "greater" than such miracles as that which He had just performed—the healing of the impotent man. Nor is it at all certain that these "greater works" are to be regarded as consisting in the spiritual quickening of men, for

It is spoken of again in another connection,* where the fact that eternal life is already actually possessed by some, is in a manner confirmed by the promise of the resurrection ; this is only the repetition, in more popular terms, of the doctrine already asserted in a more mystical manner, that to the believer there is no true death.   In a word, the phrase " *I will raise him up*," says neither more nor less than the other phrase, "*though he were dead, yet shall he live* "† unless we maintain that the writer contradicts himself.   We should even say that this last passage very explicitly justifies our interpretation of the others which have just been quoted.   In fact, we see in it how the belief of Martha, that her brother would rise again at the general resurrection of the dead,—a belief in which she could not at this moment find adequate consolation,—was not precisely negatived by Jesus, but was deprived of all theological value, in comparison with that other belief, that life and resurrection begin even now, triumphing over death in him who receives both directly from the Saviour.   In the passage from chapter v., referred to above,‡ it is equally evident that the discourse is based upon this mystical idea, while the popular hope, founded upon Jewish eschatology, is thrown into the background.   It might remain for those who could not rise to the height of the other. I do not say that the notion of a resurrection in the end of time is repudiated by this teaching of John, but I do say that mystical theology only touches upon it to assimilate it and transform it into its own likeness. In how many instances will not a sound exegesis of the other gospels lead us to suppose that Jesus, in His teachings in relation to the future, voluntarily adopted forms of expression which savour of the materialism of the popular beliefs.   And shall we not be authorized in making the same supposition here, when the spiritual explanation is expressly given side by side ?

our Lord goes on to speak of Judgment and of the general Resurrection."
—Ed.]

* John vi. 39, 40, 44, 54, ἐγὼ ἀναστήσω αὐτόν.

† John xi. 25.

‡ John v. 21, and foll.

That we may omit nothing connected with our subject, we observe further that the gospel of John is profoundly silent on all the other eschatological ideas and questions which are elsewhere intimately associated with that of the resurrection. Thus we find no mention of Sheol or Hades, of the power of the devil over the dead, of the rest or sleep of the grave, or of the future body. How should the spirit concern itself about the body? For the present, at least, it will not occupy itself with the subject. The idea of a future and universal judgment is repudiated * as something superfluous, and deprived of any theological basis; † and if in this connection the last day is spoken of,‡ it is clear that the reference is to the manner in which the lot of each individual will be decided at the time of his death, according to the relation in which he has stood to the Saviour. Everywhere, then, the doctrine of the future life is absolutely spiritualized,§ and nowhere shall we discover anything to suggest that it is so in its bearing on believers only, while for others there will be a slumber in the tomb, an ultimate resurrection, and a final judgment, according to the current notion. We may add that the term *kingdom of God*, a name borrowed essentially from popular eschatology, occurs only twice in the text of John, on occasions when Jesus is led to make use of familiar formularies.‖ In the first of these passages, there is simply the negation of the political idea; and it is impossible to deduce anything from it which might serve to supplement the theory of John's gospel. In the second passage, where the object is to prepare Nicodemus for the new ideas about to be set before him, entrance into the kingdom of God is so immediately connected with the new birth and with faith, that it is obvious there can be no allusion here to the final issues of the world's history.¶

* John iii. 17, and foll.; xii. 47, and foll.
† This is in direct antagonism to John v. 27—29.—ED.
‡ John xii. 48.
§ John teaches the resurrection of the body quite as explicitly as Paul See John v. 26.—ED.
‖ John xviii. 36, and iii. 3, 5.
¶ We have found in the gospel of John only one passage in which the

For the rest, the theology of the fourth gospel contains with reference to these matters only this one thesis, that for believers it is gain to die. They will then be reunited to Christ even locally; the imperfections of earthly existence will no more affect them; they will exchange them for the bliss of heaven, and will rejoice in the glory of Christ.*

Let it be observed that we say the theology of the fourth gospel. We intend by this expression, that system, that particular mode of conceiving of the essence of Christianity, which we have called the mysticism of John, and of which we are now completing the outline. This system has no place for the ordinary eschatological ideas; it acknowledges no necessity to incorporate them. We do not say that these ideas in themselves were rejected as false and absurd by the theologian-apostle; this would be an assertion that we could not prove. When a system undertakes, as does this one, to set forth and explain one single aspect of the spiritual life, that, namely, which has its root in feeling, it must necessarily pass over in silence that which appertains exclusively to another sphere—to that of the understanding, for example, or of conscience, or to that which is connected directly with the bodily life. This silence proves nothing unless it be the absence of any necessity, whether on the part of the mind that conceives, or of the reason which demonstrates. Just as no philosopher is bound to bring into his theory all that he may know of physics, so would it be unreasonable to demand that a mystical theologian should reserve a place in his system for religious ideas which may have a practical value of their own, but which are altogether foreign to mysticism.

This assertion may seem bold and paradoxical; we will however prove it directly by a fact which cannot be contested. That which lies outside the sphere of the mystical theory of

present and the future life are really placed in opposition to each other. This is ch. xii. 25. But here again we have a popular mode of speech, and further, the antithesis refers not to the difference of time, but to the diverse nature of the life of the body and the soul.

* Δόξα, John xvii. 22, 24.

the gospel, we find embodied in the more practical teaching of
the epistle. This writing, widely differing in this respect from
the gospel, adopts and makes use of many theses borrowed
from ordinary eschatology. It does this, however, in such a
way that they may be made to sustain moral exhortations,
and does not bring them into direct relation with the mysticism of the system. Thus, we find the term and the
idea of hope employed in relation to a series of future
events.* This is the only time that this word, of so frequent
occurrence in the writings of Paul, is met with in those
of John. These future events comprehend, in the first place,
the certain expectation of the near end of the age.† It is
to be observed, however, that this event is prognosticated in
a manner altogether peculiar, and differing widely from that
of Judaism. In place of the personal Antichrist, ordinarily
regarded as the precursor of the second coming, we find here
the anti-Christian tendency of the belief and the life, spoken
of as diffusing itself more and more widely, and thus calling
for judgment. The prosopœia, engendered by a hatred at
once religious and political, has disappeared; there remains
only the practical predication, the idea of a growing antagonism between good and evil, between God and the world,—
an antagonism which must necessarily lead to a catastrophe.
This, again, is a symptom of the natural tendency of evangelical theology to spiritualize completely Jewish dogma;
we note it the more readily, because it is to us an additional
proof that, in substance, the epistle teaches a doctrine which
does not differ from that of the gospel. Next to this first fact
which we gather from the epistle, we shall note, in the second
place, the idea of the second coming,‡ and that of the last
judgment, necessarily associated with it. But here, again, the
theology of the gospel asserts itself over the popular form of the
Christian hope. The believer, it is said,§ has no reason to fear

* 1 John iii. 3, ἐλπίς.
† 1 John ii. 18.
‡ 1 John ii. 28.
§ 1 John iv. 17; comp. John iii. 18.

this judgment.   Lastly, we observe the prospect held out of a
development of our nature in the new relations upon which
we are to enter, a development of which we have as yet but
a vague presentiment, and not a clear and exact idea.*   This
prospect, it is true, directs the gaze to things external, more
than is consistent with a mysticism delighting to find within
itself the source of a happiness which is perfect; but it has
far less analogy still with the Jewish materialism, which was
but too familiar with the kind of enjoyments awaiting it in
another life.

Whatever significance may be attached to these closing
observations, the fact remains, that there does exist a difference between the gospel and the epistle on the subject of
the views of the future.   This difference has been already
remarked by others, and various explanations of it have been
offered.   It has been said that the theology of the disciple, as
expressed in the epistle, does not rise to the height of the
teaching of the Master, faithfully reproduced by the historian
in the gospel.   We have already stated, in the introduction,
that we do not believe in the possibility of thus distinguishing
in the doctrinal parts of these books, two perfectly separate
individualities.   It has been said, again, that between the
epistle and the gospel a space of time may have elapsed,
during which the ideas of the writer had become more
spiritual.   From a doctrinal point of view, we could make no
objection to this explanation; but regarded historically, we
find nothing in its favour.   Yet more: the doctrinal basis of
the epistle is so spiritual, and so entirely in harmony with
that of the gospel, that it is impossible to separate them as
appertaining to two different phases of religious thought.   In
late days, some have even gone so far as to suggest different
writers for the two works; but they are too manifestly twin
children of the same mind, for us to enter seriously into any
discussion on this point.   Perhaps the reader may be satisfied
with what we have said above on the natural relation which

----

* 1 John iii. 2.

may have subsisted between a perfect and positive mystical conception of the religion given by and in Jesus Christ, and the fragmentary residuum of notions previously familiar to the writer, which that mysticism had failed either wholly to absorb, or fully to repudiate.

CHAPTER XV.

THE FOURTH GOSPEL AND THE REVELATION.

AFTER the full and detailed exposition we have just given of the theology taught in the fourth gospel, it would seem super-fluous to compare this with the theology of the Revelation, in order to bring out the difference of the two points of view, and of the systems derived from them. This difference has been felt and acknowledged in all ages, and by all the writers who have examined the subject without prejudice; and if we believed that in such questions the authority of a name could take the place of argument, we might cite fathers and reformers in large numbers in support of our view. Such, however, is not our plan; we prefer to investigate for ourselve , and to arrive on all points at a judgment settled upon a sol   and well-defined basis. We ask permission, then, to collate   e results of our study of these two books, to prove once mo. e that within the same Church, probably on the soil of the . me province, perhaps even with a very brief interval of time, a. d, most of all, with a community of faith and hope fixed on tł. same Lord and Saviour, there could arise two theologica. conceptions, differing so widely in their individuality of ex-pression, that it is less easy to discover the points of contact which unite, than the diverging tendencies which separate them.

Let it be well understood that we do not propose to enter here on a literary criticism, in order to prove either the identity or the diversity of the authors to whom the works tradition-ally ascribed to the apostle John, should really be assigned.

We are concerned only with their theological ideas; and while the diversity of these, if it be duly proved, must be a most conclusive argument against the identity of the writers, we do not pretend that the question of the origin of these books could be finally decided by a simple examination of their contents. We shall, then, pass by here, not only a mass of arguments previously adduced, and dealing mainly with the form of the Revelation (a form which Luther, among others, deemed unworthy of a disciple of Jesus), since such arguments do not appear to us of the slightest value,—we shall also pass over in silence all the proofs discovered by philosophical and historical criticism, for or against either document, whether as to the style, the allusions to various external facts, or the tradition concerning them. Our point is to establish that the two types of Christian teaching presented in the fourth gospel and in the book of the Revelation could not exist simultaneously in the same mind.

In this parallel, as in the others we have drawn, we shall dwell less on details than on the general tone and tendency of the theology as a whole. Details can furnish no conclusive proof, either by the analogies or the variations they may offer, because, after all, it is unquestionably apostolic and Christian teaching which we have before us, and it is inevitable that certain evangelical facts and fundamental convictions should be occasionally reproduced, and that the particular design of each book, and other external circumstances, should modify the choice and the expression of them. It will not be, then, by the comparison of individual texts or formulas that any decisive result will be reached in a critical inquiry of this nature.

Let us take, for example, two most instructive instances, which will show that we cannot decide questions of this kind by mere superficial resemblances. Much importance is often attached to the fact that Christ, in the Revelation, is represented frequently under the image of a lamb. This fact has been at once connected with a familiar passage in the gospel in which the same figure occurs, and it has been concluded that the writer and the theology of both are identical. We protest against this inference on various grounds. First, the Greek word used is not the same in both passages,* and thus indicates two different pens; and the same remark will apply to the formula which expresses the idea of redemption by the Lamb. Lastly, that which is more important is that the combination of this idea, whether with the paschal lamb or with that of which Isaiah speaks, is in no way peculiar to John, but belongs to primitive Christian theology generally.† The other example we would instance is the employment of the term *Logos* to designate the person of Christ. This term does not, indeed, occur in any other of the sacred writings; but it is of earlier date than the gospel, and is not the mental creation of any one apostle, to whom, consequently, it would exclusively belong. More than this, the Revelation says, " the *Word of God*," which is the formula used in the Jewish theology of Palestine; the gospel says, simply, the *Logos*, the *Word*, as we find it in the philosophy of Philo, and the metaphysical idea is not precisely the same. In order to arrive at something positive, we must get nearer the source of the ideas.

Making our appeal to the consciousness of every attentive reader, we shall establish, first: that of all the books of the New Testament, the fourth gospel is that which goes furthest beyond the scope of Judaism, rising to the height of the ideal standpoint of the gospel, from which all previous forms of religion appear imperfect, and the Jews in particular occupy, both in practice and in theory, hostile ground. And this opposition is not only displayed in acts of hostility to the person of Jesus, but manifests itself in prejudices against His teaching, which nullify and render it barren. The forms of the religious life of the Jewish community, appear to the evangelist as elements absolutely foreign to the new order of things, as barriers separating it from the new economy; and he seems to cherish with a secret predilection, the anticipation of a far more favourable disposition among the Gentiles. In the

---

* Ἀμνός, ἀρνίον.

† Acts viii. 32; 1 Peter i. 19; 1 Cor. v. 7.

Revelation all this is reversed. The writer loves to reinstate the name of Jews, applying it as a title of honour to the true disciples of Christ; it is paganism which there appears as the real and cruel enemy of the Gospel, and which is the object of execration on the part of the Christians. Doubtless, the Christian community, according to this book, is to gather adherents from among the Gentiles also, but these are to be properly incorporated with Israel. Christ Himself is the child of a mother whom we at once perceive, by her crown of twelve stars, to be an image of the Old Testament; and the temple on Mount Zion, the decadence of which had been proclaimed by the Revealer who speaks in the gospel, is here glorified as the indestructible dwelling of the elect.

That we may not repeat ourselves unnecessarily, we forbear to carry the parallel further in this direction. A mere perusal of the two texts, and a recapitulation of the favourite terms which are found in each, will prove on every page the fairness of the contrast we have just drawn. The epithets given to Deity in the Revelation are taken directly from the theocratic language of the prophets, exalting the power, holiness, eternity, truth of Jehovah, and presenting no trace of the attributes which, in the Gospel of grace and redemption, join to compose the conception of God. The relation in which the elect stand to Him is described in the Revelation as that of men unjustly persecuted by the world, and meriting a glorious compensation for their sufferings, by their patience and faithfulness even unto death. The Almighty Avenger at length raises them to the full enjoyment of their lawful privileges by the destruction of their enemies, whose ruin enters largely as an element into the joy of their victims, who are represented as sighing for the hour of vengeance to strike. How different is this from the relation described in the gospel! So far from suffering sentiments of animosity to arise in the heart of the man filled with the love of the Saviour, it scarcely allows him to cast a glance upon this hostile and ruined world; the happiness of the believer is already perfect; the enemy is already overcome; life and blessedness have begun with faith.

In a word, the Christianity of the Apocalypse, inasmuch as it places itself in a hostile attitude towards all that is anti-Christian, aims specially to confound idolatry by means of the general truths of revelation; and thus it in a manner counts Israel among its allies, at least in theory. The Christianity of the gospel, on the contrary, treats mainly of that which distinguishes it from the old covenant; the essential elements, in its view, are the speculation which is to raise it above the popular monotheism of the prophets, and the mysticism of which morality and the law know nothing. It stands thus in as strong contrast with historic Judaism as with the religion of Greece, both of which are in relation to it almost on the same level.

The Revelation, in its ideal construction of the history, as it unfolds itself before the eyes of the prophet and his readers, confines itself entirely within the circle of the concrete and material hopes of the synagogue. The gospel, on the contrary, breathes so pure a spiritual atmosphere, that the very world itself in the midst of which the apostle and his Christians still live, feels the metamorphosis which it is to undergo from the elevating power of his mysticism. The proofs of this twofold assertion abound on every hand. How vast the distance between the Lion of Judah, who will rule the people with a rod of iron and break them in pieces like a potter's vessel, and the Good Shepherd who gives His life for the flock, who loves to carry home the sheep that are scattered abroad, and who will bring all into the same fold! In the Revelation, the conflict between the kingdom of God and the powers of hell is decided by physical force and the noise of arms. The faithful worshippers marked with the seal of Christ, are the spectators of the combat, and rejoice over the torments of their adversaries vanquished on an arena upon which they themselves are not called to appear. In the gospel, it is in the hearts of His disciples that Christ rules and triumphs; His victory is gained by spiritual weapons; and the enmity of the world, while it may grieve their pitying spirit, cannot break their inward peace. In the Revelation, evil is personified, it is placed upon the

throne of the empire, at the head of an army greedy of carnage ;
it is a pagan monarch, a personal antichrist, whose name a
secret terror shrouds in mystery, but to whom the finger of
exegesis plainly points in history. In the gospel, antichrist is
the abstract fact of opposition to the truth of Christ, and
this opposition there is no need to seek in a distant sphere;
it is manifest even in the Church itself, so long as the Spirit of
God has not gained the mastery over all hearts. Both writings
speak of a double resurrection, but how wide the distinction
between the two ideas! In the Revelation, there is first the
resurrection of a class of privileged individuals. Then, after a
millennium of blessedness for these, the universal resurrection
and the last judgment, the whole splendidly dramatized and
adorned with all those imposing elements in which the poetic
imagination of the Jews delighted. In the gospel, the essential
resurrection is the first, but it takes place here in the depths
of the heart, at the call of Christ, when He comes to live in us,
and to raise us thus out of the night of a grave far gloomier
than that which receives the body. Whosoever believeth hath
already this eternal life; and the second resurrection, that which
emancipates us from the tomb, is only the natural consequence
of the former. All that in the gospel is promised to believers
and to their community on earth, is in the Apocalypse distinctly
reserved for heaven—the presence of God and of Christ, the
food which gives immortal life, the water which quenches
thirst for ever. Again, these promises are to be taken on the
one hand in an ideal and figurative sense, while on the other
they are presented with all the accessories of a concrete and
positive meaning. The evangelist, in a word, declares that it
doth not yet appear what we shall be ; he is happy in the
present, and knows that he can find in it all that is needed to
satisfy the demands of the soul and its holiest aspirations. The
author of the Revelation expends all his powers in depicting
what we shall one day be, and can find consolation for the
tribulations of the present, only in the prospect of the future.

If either one of the two types of teaching was essentially
incompatible with the idea of the gospel, we could not under-

stand the presence of both in the collection of our sacred books, from which indeed many theologians have been ready to expunge the book of Revelation. But we by no means endorse this sentence of exclusion. Both writings represent particular phases of the Christian conception in the apostolic age, and their respective value may be measured by the more or less salutary effects they have been able to produce.*

* The general plan and intention of this History precluded M. Reuss from the consideration of the strength of the external evidence that the Revelation and the fourth gospel came from the same hand. If the evidence is admitted to be conclusive, a problem is raised which M. Reuss has not discussed. His exposition of the theological teaching of the Revelation enormously exaggerates the difficulty of solving it, but that it is not insoluble is suggested by the closing paragraph of this chapter.— ED.

CHAPTER XVI.

PAUL AND JOHN.

HAVING now concluded our exposition of the evangelical doctrine as it is expressed by the two most eminent theologians among the apostles, Paul and John, we may be permitted to cast one more retrospective glance over the ground we have traversed. We desire to compare these two particular forms assumed by Christian thought in the first century, which have a better claim than any other to the title of a theological system, both from the elevation of their idea and the perfection of their method. Independent of each other in their origin and in their composition, these two systems agree in all that is essential. The two fundamental ideas of the Gospel, the state of sin in which man is found and his redemption by the Son of God, form, though differently expressed, the basis of both systems, and in reference to the redemption itself, neither of the two theologians makes any attempt to put a scholastic construction on it, by demonstrating the judicial equilibrium between guilt and expiation. Both, on the contrary, take as their starting-point the fact and the idea of regeneration, and the mystical union of the believer with the Saviour. It would be as unnecessary as it would be easy to prove the identity of the two conceptions under these aspects. We trust we have already in our exposition of them brought out these fundamental ideas with clearness and precision, and established them by citations so numerous and explicit that we may safely leave to our readers the task of confirming by subsequent private study the conviction we have endeavoured to produce on their mind.

We devote this chapter rather to prove, by a fresh series of observations in detail, that these two great theologians treated with entire freedom of thought the fundamental ideas received and held by them in common; and that, without breaking through the bounds prescribed for them, they found abundant scope for their own mental efforts, and for the expression of their respective individuality. It is well for us that we can prove by these illustrious examples, that Christian thought is so rich and suggestive, that we are under no necessity to circumscribe the exercise of our faculties within too narrow limits; and that the causes, sometimes irresistibly powerful, which impress on each one of us his peculiar spiritual physiognomy, do not necessarily lead us into a lawless region of fallacies and errors. Education, temperament, social position, and a thousand other accidents, modify indefinitely the current of our ideas. We shall see here that this is no reason why we should either despair in the search after truth, or condemn each other, because our respective formularies may differ. It is true of these two great apostles, as of the members of the Church generally, that the certainty of realizing the desired end is not obtained at the expense of the natural development of the faculties. The possibility of arriving at an adequate expression of the divine thought in human words, will always depend upon psychological conditions inherent in the nature of the mind, and will never be subordinated to a mere effort of the memory.

The most superficial comparison of these two theories of the Gospel in external points, will show the perfect independence with which they have been constructed by their authors. The reader is struck at once with the fulness of the one and the simplicity of the other. How many terms, definitions, theses we have found in the writings of Paul, which are associated with particular studies of religious facts, and are the fruits of a knowledge as true as it is profound, of the heart and conscience ! There is no secret recess of the soul into which he does not throw light, discovering in it both the natural tendency and the possibilities it presents for the work of God; there is no impulse of the spirit, however feeble, to which he does not assign its sphere of operation in the new order of things; there is no relation so subordinate in the economy of grace, that he cannot bring it into relief and attach to it some importance in the movement of the whole. Every fact is regarded successively under the most various aspects, and the diversity of the forms is still more manifold than the diversity of the thoughts. How many times does the writer repeat the same thing without copying himself! We are really at a loss which most to admire, the richness of the analysis which brings to light the treasures of evangelical philosophy, or the order of the synthesis which so justly classifies and explains them, while the schoolmen often get so sadly embarrassed in their attempts to do the same work. The numerous images destined to familiarize the intellect with abstract things by captivating the imagination, bring, so to speak, all the spheres of human life into the domain of religion, and testify alike to the acuteness of the mind which could thus discern their analogical fitness, and to the intimate connection which really exists among all the interests of man.

Students of the theology of John find themselves in a difficulty of another kind. It cannot but appear poor to them in comparison with that of Paul, if they measure it by the number of the doctrinal points treated, or by the still smaller variety of terms used in their exposition. Ten or twelve definitions, at the most, will comprise the whole system, or, to speak more accurately, the very slightly systematized basis of a faith which itself dwells deep in the heart, and rises to an elevation of feeling such as definitions are not wont to reach. The fact is, that here we must not seek the treasure in the field of intellectual cultivation; or rather, in this case, the mind, voluntarily turning away its gaze from the world and men, has preferred to dive into the inexhaustible mine of its own purest and deepest feelings. The intellect here seems to have no cravings of its own, when the heart is satisfied; and the monotonous phrases, bare of all rhetorical adornment, which rehearse the secret joys of the heart, can be repeated

33 *

indefinitely without weariness. Lastly, the images through
which John conveys his thoughts on subjects which language
labours painfully to express, are generally borrowed from the
narrow circle of personal and domestic experiences.

We shall receive a similar impression if we watch the intellectual process by which the two sysetms were wrought out.
The method followed by the two interpreters of the evangelical
idea, explains in part the fact we have just mentioned, or,
rather, it is itself one of the characteristic features distinguishing the special genius of each. In taking their books,
as they present themselves, we should say, at first sight, that
the methodical mind, the man of set forms, is John, not Paul.
In truth, nothing can display more profound meditation, rigorously adhered to, than the plan of his principal work, which a
thoughtful study must pronounce to be more than a mere
historic narrative. In the first place, there is a prologue,
giving in a few lines a prophetic summary of the metaphysics
of the gospel; then the person of the Saviour is presented
successively in its two relations with the world, calling it to
Himself and preaching to it, but encountering at once powerful
adversaries who reject Him, and a little circle of believers who
receive Him. To the former (the latter do not need it) is
given an enumeration of the testimonies in His favour,—the
witness of John the Baptist, that of miracles, of His works and
prophetic discourses; then the series of the fundamental facts
of the gospel,—the regeneration required by all, the calling of
the sinner, the divinity of the Son, the food which He offers to
the soul, the promise of the Spirit, of liberty, light, life; and
parallel with all this the picture of the growing hostility of a
world antagonistic to light, devoid of love, and necessarily
therefore destitute of life. Lastly, there is opened the prospect
of the calling of the Gentiles, who are to take the place of ancient
and rebellious Israel. To those who believe, the second part
presents the vista of benefits into the immediate enjoyment of
which they enter through their fellowship with the Saviour,
and which are to be realized by them in the future, through
the assistance of the Paraclete, through the fulfilment of their

mission on earth, and in the prospect of victory over the world
and of the heavenly glory. The respective climax of these two
relations,—the ignominious death of the Saviour brought
about by the one section, sealing at the same time their own
doom of death, and the glorious resurrection, which is the
triumph of all believers, and the guarantee of their blessed
future,—brings this exposition to a close in accordance with
the laws of a moral rather than historical necessity. The
epistle, though less systematic, is in like manner not a writing
called forth by a passing necessity, but by a true theological
treatise.

With Paul the case is very different. In his numerous
writings, there is no trace of any methodical plan of composition. It is accidentally that he is led to speak of such
and such a dogma or principle. His system is to consult the
passing necessities of his churches, to yield to the inspiration
of his apostolic solicitude. We see clearly that he did not write
with a view to teaching; he taught before he wrote. His
letters were not designed to found or to construct, but to preserve, correct, adorn, perfect that which had been already built
by other means. If these epistles were to be regarded as
treatises, then must all the minor topics introduced—his
salutations, commissions, himself, in fact, and his humblest
friends,—be incorporated with the Gospel. Even the Epistle
to the Romans, which adopts more than any of the rest the
forms of theoretic teaching, is no exception to this remark.
In the theory as there given, there are many important
omissions, and the necessities under which it was written
lead into too many digressions foreign to the subject, to allow
us to attribute to it a character which it was not the design
of the apostle to impart to any of his writings.

But while we pass such a judgment upon the works of the
two theologians between whom we are here drawing a parallel,
we are led to an opinion almost exactly the reverse, with regard
to the nature of their theology itself. Paul's method is dis-
cursive; that of John is intuitive; the one proceeds by means
of argument, the other of contemplation; Paul expounds

his religious knowledge and supports it by logical proofs; John communicates his faith to us, as he holds it himself, by direct consciousness, and makes his appeal to our feeling. The former is essentially a logician; he argues, demonstrates, deduces syllogisms, has always present to his mind the complete sequence of all his ideas; their natural connection makes him pass perpetually from axioms to corollaries, from premises to conclusions; it is by means of examples, quotations, questions, that he leads his readers to accept his mode of view, to embrace his convictions. John makes no attempt at demonstration; he states his theses as simply as possible; he enforces them merely by repetition almost in the same terms. As he himself may be said rather to *feel* than to *know* the truths he propounds, so he expects his disciples to have the same intuition of soul. This will stand them in stead of knowledge. In default of this, arguments will have no force. The evangelical faith must spring from the fountain; if the heart is an arid rock, only the finger of God can touch it and make the waters flow; logic is powerless. After all, it would be more just to say that Paul alone has method, John none.

The remarks we have just made on the particular manner of each of the two writers, may be supplemented by another more special observation closely connected with the foregoing. In both it is easy to discern a mystical and a speculative element in the Christian theory. They can conceive of salvation only as the effect of a union with Jesus Christ,—a union which is not confined within the limits of the moral sphere, to the domain of the will and practical imitation, but is perfect and efficacious only when it becomes a true substitution of a divine principle for one that is purely human—a sort of identification of two individualities, or the absorption of one by the other. But this union itself could not produce the desired effect if the person of the Saviour were not raised above the human sphere, and had not thus a unique character, to which mere experience can supply no analogue. It is the combination of this twofold element, contained in the formula faith in the Son of God, on which both systems essentially depend. But this combination is formed in each in a different manner. This is seen not only in the diversity of their respective starting-points, but in the progress of their expositions.

John lays down at once, and in the first place, the speculative basis of his theology; his very opening sentences are dictated by metaphysics, and these must be well understood to enable the reader to enter into that which follows. He shows the Word pre-existent before the incarnation; the abstract precedes the historical fact; therefore it will necessarily precede the Gospel. Paul, on the contrary, starts from an axiom of the utmost simplicity—the necessity of righteousness in order to please God and to attain to happiness; and from a thesis accredited by all experience, the universality of sin. Paul commences, then, with anthropology, John with theology in the more restricted sense of the word. On this theory, we might be ready to suppose that we should find on the one hand an abstract and transcendental philosophy, and on the other a moral and psychological doctrine. But it is not so. The first of the two writers hastens to have done with speculation, to establish both by assertion and by argument its claims and its significance, and then to pass on to that which to him is most essential, the mystical element, to which he devotes himself more and more exclusively till it absorbs him wholly. The domain of the mystical element (we speak of mysticism in the form in which we find it in this system) is always, so to speak, separate from the metaphysical, and while at every step reminding us of the speculative principles inscribed at the head of his book, and which continue to exert the greatest influence over the development of his thought, the apostle teaches us nothing further with regard to them, absolutely nothing which has not been already, and more explicitly, said in the prologue. Paul, on his part, loves constantly to combine and to confound the two elements. With him, mysticism accords perfectly with dialectic forms; his reasonings, though savouring of the methods of the schools, never do injustice to the fervour of the deepest feeling, of the most submissive faith; and never lose sight of the end of all Christian theology, which is to produce this faith in

the hearts of men. Thought with him is never lost in feeling,
nor are the gentle aspirations of a loving soul ever sacrificed
to an imperious logic dominating his subject. Lastly, it must
not be forgotten that the two elements are with him alike
subordinate to the exigencies and claims of practical life. If
he reasons, it is less as the head of a school haranguing an
auditory, than as a preacher standing before a community. If
he abandons himself to the rapture of contemplation, it is not
as the anchorite who loves to enjoy his selfish bliss afar from the
world; it is as the apostle, whose first thought is ever of the
happiness of those entrusted to him. The secret of his power
lies essentially in this, that he is ever careful to translate his
counsels into deeds. John is generally satisfied with putting
into words his inmost feeling; life, the world, have no power
to draw him out of his sphere; he is happy in an isolation
so richly peopled; he preaches love, and feels it; but this
love, fervent as it is towards those who understand and share
it, sure as it is to resist the seductions and threats of the
world, is not of a temper to fling itself into the midst of the
throng to save the world.

This leads us to make one more remark with reference to the
form which the two conceptions we are considering seem to
us to have assumed. We allude to the principle of division
which governs the train of religious ideas comprised and set
forth in them, and which determines the place which each of
these occupies in the system as a whole. This division is
based upon a trinary combination in the writings of Paul, a
binary in those of John. The formula itself in which Paul
sums up, so to speak, his whole theology, is this: "the
righteousness of God without the law is manifested, even
the righteousness which is by faith of Jesus Christ unto
all and upon all that believe." This formulary contains in its
positive clause the elements of the division we have adopted in
the exposition of the system, both as a whole and in its details.
This division has been given us in a manner by the author
himself. God, Christ, and man are presented as the three
parties on whose concurrence the work of salvation depends,

a salvation decreed by the grace of the first, offered by the sacrifice of the second, realized by the regenerating power of the third. Man must recognize this salvation in its causes, and appropriate it in its effects, by faith; he must labour for its diffusion, and co-operate in the design of God, by love; lastly, he must grasp the ideal consummation of it by hope. Yet further: in the sphere of faith, the system dwells successively on the operation of God manifested in election, calling, and the communication of the Spirit; on the experience of man, which may be classed under the three heads of obedience, regeneration, and sanctification; and on the work of Christ, which consists in redemption, justification, and reconciliation. In the sphere of love, Paul considers first the work of Christ, that is to say, the Church; next, the help of God, that is, the gifts of the Spirit; and, lastly, the ministry of man, that is, edification. In the sphere of hope, he begins with the preparation of man, by means of the trial he has to undergo in the patient waiting for Christ; he passes on to the triumphal appearing of Christ, which is to establish His kingdom; and concludes with the glorification of God the Father, which results from the fulfilment of His eternal decrees, in the final blessedness of the elect.

John's division is more simple. His fundamental formula, which occurs both in the gospel and epistle: "God sent His Son into the world, that those who believe in Him might have life," divides theology into two parts, the doctrinal and the mystical. The latter is clearly epitomized in the two ideas of faith and life. The former is subdivided into a speculative portion, which treats of the two ideas of God and the Son, and a historical portion, which treats of the incarnation and of the world. The attributes of Deity (Father and Son) are truth (light and love) and life; the attributes of the world, governed by the evil one, are lying (darkness and hatred) and death. The purpose of the incarnation is to give to the world that which it has not; its effect is the separation of the world into two parties, violently opposed to each other, the one accepting, the other rejecting, that which the Revealing Word offers to them.

We should not dwell upon these divisions, which may appear to many of our readers simply arbitrary, if the manner in which an author divides and subdivides the materials with which he deals, did not reveal to a large extent the main direction of his thoughts. In the two cases now before us, the division has even a perceptible influence upon the theology itself, and this remark may introduce us to the second part of our subject. It is evident, alike from the part we have been led to assign to John, and from the impression always left on the mind from reading his gospel, that with him, Christ is, so to speak, confounded with God, because the fundamental idea of his theology is the radical opposition between God and the world, which are indeed the only two agents that come within his spiritual horizon, inasmuch as the Word is the organ of every act emanating from God, and God acts only by the Word. Paul, on the contrary, places Christ on middle ground, between God and the world; the part of Mediator is His distinctive character; the human aspect of His personality is brought into as great prominence as the divine, while with John the divine predominates in an unquestionable manner, and by the distinct purpose of the apostle. The death of Jesus itself is always represented by him as a glorification and a victory, and he will scarcely recognize even the momentary semblance of defeat. Hence also it is that Paul always rejoices in the thought of a universal brotherhood, of the reconciliation of the entire human race, or at least of a very large proportion of it, while John stands in doubt on the point, or rather takes pleasure in another view of the subject.

All that has been said hitherto to establish a parallel between the two writers and their systems, refers really only to the form of their thought, and does not touch as yet, even distantly, on the very essence of the great theological questions. The aspect under which these are presented to us by the two apostles will render this parallel still more interesting, and will bring out with greater distinctness the particular direction taken by the mind of each.

And, first, while we assert that with both faith is the central idea, the keystone of the system, the focus whence light radiates in every direction, and the bond which unites all the other evangelical ideas into one body of doctrine, we may remark that there is, in both cases, another idea equally important. This governs not only the succession of particular questions and their gradual development, but it impresses on the whole its special character, its peculiar colour, and makes it easy to mark the distinctive traits of the two physiognomies. We shall be careful not to exaggerate this diversity, the more as we know well how much more readily the mind apprehends differences than analogies; but we propose to establish it as a fact of history, and one having an important bearing on theology.

The two ideas we have in view, as setting each its peculiar impress on the system in which it predominates, are the idea of righteousness in the system of Paul, the idea of life in that of John. The reader will be readily convinced by an attentive study of the texts, that these are the fundamental ideas of the entire scientific systems of the two apostles. Do we ask of Paul what is the great want of man? He will answer it is righteousness. Ask what is gained for man by redemption? Again he answers, righteousness. What is the subject of the Gospel preaching? Jesus died and rose again, that we might be made righteous. What is the purport of the Gospel? To declare to men that henceforth there is a way by which they may attain to righteousness. What is that which redounds most to the glory of God? It is that He has revealed the possibility of His being at once just and a Justifier. We do not need to multiply these examples; as the reply to all questions, the substance of all arguments, the basis of all definitions, we shall find *righteousness*. This idea is, as it were, the mainspring of the whole machinery, the motive power of the thought, the guiding thread which maintains unity in variety, and which prevents our losing ourselves in the wide field of evangelical philosophy. In the case of John, on the other hand, the attentive student will find that the very same things may be predicated of the idea of life. It is life which is at the beginning with God; life which the world wants; life which is the light of men; life which Jesus came to sustain by giving us, in His own person, the living water and the living bread; it is life, lastly, which is the consummation and crown of our existence, as the resurrection of Christ, which is its symbol, was the culminating point of His earthly career. The ideas of righteousness and of life, in their abstract and theoretic sense, are the starting-points of the two systems; in their concrete and practical realization, they are the final conclusion of both.

Let us now see what is involved in this difference in the fundamental idea of each system. For it must not be forgotten that words are of value only for the ideas they represent; and we should never characterize what we may call the particular shade of any theology, by the perhaps fortuitous recurrence of a certain expression. Righteousness is essentially an ethical idea, life a mystical. The former belongs to the domain of thought, of reflection, of moral judgment; it acts upon the will, it receives its sanction from the conscience; it deals so largely with what is most practical and palpable in matters of religion, that men have often gone so far as to eliminate from ecclesiastical theology (which is nevertheless based to a great extent on the theology of Paul) all its mystical elements, thus reducing it to the meagre proportions of a theorem of jurisprudence. The idea of life, on the contrary, belongs to another sphere; it is the product of contemplation; reflection can never grasp it. It may be unhesitatingly said that any one who pretends to give a logical definition of life has no experimental knowledge of it. It is a concentrated bliss, which can only be described or understood by those who have felt it. Thus, in the theology of the Church, it has been wisely passed over in silence; the scholasticism of the schools could only caricature it. The two points of view alike tend to promote piety, love, and purity of heart; but the theology of righteousness is adapted for the world, for action, for stimulating effort without and within, for giving muscular force to the character; while the theology of life, rather shrinking from contact with that which is inimical to itself than seeking to assimilate it, delights to dwell within its own sphere. We should be ready to say it was designed for heaven rather than for earth, if it did not find a heaven even upon earth, scarcely permitting those whom it makes happy to distinguish the present from the future.

We may give yet another expression to these ideas, and supplement them at the same time by other considerations. John's point of view is generally more ideal than that of Paul. In theory, it is true, the latter cannot be reproached with not rising sufficiently high in his ideas and doctrines. On the contrary, he speaks of the necessity, the possibility, we might almost say the reality, of a faith absolutely antipathetic to sin ; of a regeneration so radical, that there should remain absolutely nothing of the old man ; of a sanctification which does not admit the very idea of a relapse ; and, finally, of a Church without spot or blemish. He also has thus embraced, and very warmly, that conception of the Christian life, which, basing its anticipations, not on the nature of man, but on the perfections of God, raises man above the low sphere in which he is dragged down in all directions by the faultiness of all that is around him, to lift him ever upwards by the incessant contemplation of an ideal to which he is destined to attain. This is so true, that the definition which Paul, who is here in complete agreement with John, gives of faith, of the believer, of the Church, though true and confirmed by the testimony of our own conscience, as enlightened by the Gospel, is entirely inapplicable to the facts and the persons of actual life. Never were there such Christians as these. Paul himself would not dare to say so. Never did such a Church exist. We have the epistles to prove that the apostolic age was as far from witnessing such an one as is our own. Experience seems to give a distinct denial to the theory ; but the theory itself stands out in only greater sublimity, and bears only the more surely the stamp of its divine origin.

It is not, then, in this sense that we for a moment dispute Paul's taking an ideal standpoint. But with this theory he

well knows how to associate that which the practical purpose
of his teaching presses upon him with still greater urgency.
Mystical theology easily maintains the high altitude of the
ideal, because it is its nature to look with contempt on meagre
realities, and to feed on visions and ecstasies. But a theology
which is in its essence ethical, will always take into account
that which actually exists. It knows well that heaven is not
yet in possession, but it keeps it always in view as a goal; it
tends heavenward, but enjoys it as yet only in prospect. Its
life is movement; its law, progress. Paul loves to remind
those who call themselves Christians that they are to grow up
to the full stature of Christ. His aim is always to build up
the Church, of which only the foundation is as yet laid. John
has no further desire to express for himself or his brethren,
than that they may abide in that fellowship with Christ in
which is fulness of joy. While Paul, in dark and troublous
days, yearns for deliverance, and would fain break the bonds
which, by holding him in the flesh, separate him from his
Saviour, John feels Christ living in his heart; he is satisfied
and happy, and death itself will make no change in a relation
already unalterable. Paul, indeed, can sometimes turn away
his eyes from that which grieves him, to rejoice in the possession of something which compensates all sorrow; but life,
duty, the external realities around, quickly resume their sway
over him, and these give again the tone to his teaching. Both
apostles have seen the world as it is—given over, that is, to the
power of evil; but while John turns away to lament, to condemn, to forget, Paul bears it ever on his heart, and feels it to
be his mission to reprove and to reform.

Both are striving with all the powers of their soul for the
same end—an end, however, which to the one seems distant,
to the other near. John, grasping the hand of the Saviour,
outstretched to him as to a friend, and never letting it go, has
already ceased to feel that hunger and thirst which once he
had known; Paul, now humbled by the memory of the past,
now uplifted by grace, continues to bow as the disciple before
the Master, and frankly confesses that he has not yet reached

the goal; but he proves at the same time, both by his words and his deeds, that he is pressing on to it without relaxation, with a persevering will, with energy for every conflict, and a full assurance of success.

The churches of Paul are the churches of to-day—assemblies of men bound together externally perhaps by a common creed, and always by a common promise, but not yet by a common perfection in faith and charity. They constantly need exhortations, warnings, promises, threats, assurances, reproof, discipline. Some of them are still such children that they cannot endure the strong meat of the Gospel teaching. The grief of a father, the severity of a schoolmaster, all the difficulties of a governor, are the daily portion of the apostle: for him there is little success without a drawback, and no rest. If he shuns danger, it is not that he fears death; this would reunite him to Christ; but he desires to live because his life is needful for the churches. The Church of John does not break the peace in the soul of its pastor; he has nothing further to teach it, since it knows all things, and has received that anointing of the Spirit which keeps it in the way of truth. He would not even write to it if he were not sure that this understanding and this holiness were already its portion. Such a Church may, perhaps, be the Church of the future; it is undoubtedly that which Paul would have desired to find in reality; but when he would draw for us such a picture, he is fain to take his colours from the pure source of an inspiration undefiled by any contact with the turbid waters of experience.

It is evident that these two points of view are essentially different, and must exert a powerful influence, not so much upon the grandest and noblest elements of either theory, as upon the direction which the systems derived from them will take, whenever they touch on questions of more or less directly practical import. It is useless here to multiply quotations, and the comparisons they might suggest. These things are so evident, that, once mentioned, every one can perceive them, and the attentive reader will find them confirmed at every step.

We have just characterized the theology of Paul as the more practical, that of John as the more ideal. This judgment will be true so long as it is simply these two tendencies which are contrasted or compared; but. there is also a more particularly philosophical and speculative tendency, which may be placed in contrast with the practical, and in such a case the relation would be entirely changed. In fact, it is universally admitted that both systems contain a very decided and most fruitful speculative element, to which ecclesiastical theology has by preference attached itself, sometimes to the neglect of all beside. Now, it will be easy to show that this element is not the end to which the theology of the apostles tends, or its ultimate design; that it is rather the premise of a purely practical conclusion, the prop to sustain an application at once ethical and mystical. A single example will suffice to demonstrate this fact, which cannot, moreover, be ignored by those who take the scholasticism of our confessions of faith and of their commentators to be the expression of the apostolic theology. Thus, all the metaphysical attributes of the Word stand in a relation of close analogy with the characteristics and the hopes of believers. If He is the image of God, they reflect His image; if He is the only Son, they are His brethren, and children of God, by Him; the glory of God which He possesses by inherent right they are to share; they draw even now from the fulness of the divine perfections which dwells in Him, and His union with the Father is not more important and more true than their union with both the Father and the Son. Every speculative idea is thus translated directly into a fact which belongs to the sphere of the religious conscience, the inner experience; and it will not be disputed that these facts occupy the attention of the sacred writers far more than the metaphysical formulas which underlie them. In all this we find our two theologians pursuing exactly the same path.

Let us pause however for a moment upon this philosophical part of the two systems, in order to point out several facts of considerable interest less generally recognized. As a rule, speculation in either system never pursues the questions it takes up beyond the point at which they cease to be of interest to the spiritual life of the Church and its members, and become the pabulum of the schoolmen. Thus it was a singular illusion of the Reformation in the sixteenth century that its theology was the natural and direct product of exegesis alone, while in truth it was the legitimate offspring of the speculation of the Fathers of the Church and of the decrees of the Councils. Exegesis alone, by which we mean that which is content with examining, without any attempt at remodelling, the scriptural idea, will never derive from the texts a system which can satisfy theological speculation. Upon all abstract or transcendental questions, such speculation will always require to know more than the apostles say, for the simple reason that it is pursuing an entirely different end from theirs, since they, happily for the Church, were not philosophers, as many of their most illustrious successors have been. There is not one dogma, of all those which our confessions describe as fundamental, which did not need a series of ages to bring it to its present form, and which, in this its supposed final expression, has not served as the text of a fresh train of philosophical lucubrations. This tendency—at least, as it manifests itself in the Church (for it was previously exhibited in the Synagogue)—dates from the age of the apostles, and we discover the first traces of it in the very writers with whom we are at present occupied. This will offer a new point of view for our parallel.

Speculation has already reached a far more advanced systematic form in the writings of John than in those of Paul, who does scarcely more than lay down its premises and describe its first outlines. That which gives to the teaching of Paul a more logical and scientific form, is, as we have already indicated, his profound apprehension of the ideas of the Gospel, relative to the nature, the powers, and instinctive tendencies of man, and to that which may serve to direct these. He treats far less completely the metaphysical portion of his subject. But it is curious to remark that with him also

transcendental questions, without becoming actually paramount, assert more and more their claim to be considered.
His later epistles rise often and easily to considerations of a
more abstract nature; and while the Corinthians and the
Galatians are simply pointed to Christ crucified as the end
of all that the Christian needs to know, the Ephesians, the
Colossians, and even the Philippians are instructed on points of
doctrine which the Church has since declared to be mysteries,
—that is to say, metaphysical problems.   But we observe that
John, writing certainly at a later date, goes far beyond Paul in
this respect.   Of this we have what we may call a palpable
proof in the fact that in the exposition of certain articles, John
employs, as sure to be understood by his readers, technical terms
belonging to the phraseology of a school anterior to Christianity,
while Paul avoids or ignores them.   Beside several others
of minor importance, we may refer to the name Logos, which
is used to designate Christ in the metaphysical point of view,
and which occurs only in the writings of the philosophers and
of John.   But we need not confine our remarks to the terms
employed; it would be easy to show a similar relation in the
subject-matter of the questions themselves.   We give a few
examples among many which we might adduce.

Let us take first the teaching of the apostles concerning the
nature of Christ and His relations with God.   If we consider
in a general manner the conviction so fully expressed of the
divinity of the person of the Saviour, we should place the two
apostles upon the same level.   But it must be admitted that
this conviction is expressed by the author of the fourth gospel
in a more scientific manner than by the pen of the apostle of
the Gentiles, and that it is connected in John's writings with a
series of formulas which, upholding and explaining each other,
merit, as a whole, the name of a speculative system.   In order
to be convinced of this, we have only to compare the prologue
of the gospel, of which many passages in the book itself form
the comment, with the few well-known verses of the Epistle to
the Colossians; or, rather, we need but to remind the reader,
that ecclesiastical theology, in its article on the person of

Christ, has simply taken as the basis of its ulterior speculations the formula of John, as the fullest and most complete.
It is from John, again, that the Church has derived the elements
of the Trinitarian formulary, which it has in fact finally made
the basis of the entire Christian doctrine, since these elements
are nowhere else so clearly indicated;* and yet we have had
occasion more than once to remark, that even here the logical
sequence is not unbroken, and that the theory presents several
notable breaches which the philosophers of later times have
been eager to fill. Let us further observe, more particularly,
that the idea of the divine hypostases, the root of which is in
the Old Testament, and which is extensively employed by both
Jewish and Christian philosophy, is far more fully developed
by John than by Paul, especially with reference to the Spirit.
We shall not enter here upon a detailed demonstration of all
these facts, as we have already given the proofs elsewhere.

We pass on to another example not less remarkable, though
on slightly different grounds ; we refer to the doctrine of predestination. We note first the fact that neither apostle uses
any absolute and invariable formula on the subject. In the
writings of both, on the contrary, we find various propositions,
sometimes favouring the predominance of human liberty,
sometimes that of divine determination. This remark is not
intended to imply any reproach, for the simple reason that the
question is above the scope of man's capacities of thought, and
it is impossible for revelation itself to impart to us a conception for the apprehension of which nature has given us no
faculty. We would merely point to the fact that the Church,
finding these incompatible formulas in the same writers, has
never arrived at any fixed opinion on the point, and has
always been tossed to and fro between the two extreme

---

* We may take this opportunity to observe that nowhere, in the course
of our study of the theology of John, have we made use of the well-known
passage, 1 John v. 7. We do not ourselves hold this passage to be genuine.
The Greek manuscripts do not give it. It has been finally received
into our editions and versions under the influence of the Vulgate and of
system. Luther never admitted it into any of his numerous editions.

theories, which can alone satisfy the requirements of logic, but the one of which shocks Christian feeling, and the other evangelical piety. Practical teaching will always be constrained to insist upon the fact that man's salvation is a free gift of God, and that his condemnation is only the just punishment of sin. But this mode of teaching, truly Christian as it is, is far from philosophical. Upon this question, again, John goes a few steps further than Paul. The latter is satisfied with asserting the equality of all men as to their natural starting-point, and in view of the moral law of God, consequently also in relation to righteousness and salvation. He expresses himself somewhat obscurely on the origin of this general state of sin; he leaves therefore untouched the question of the cause of the diversity in the destiny of individuals, or, rather, he gives within a few pages two different solutions of it, in a well-known passage which we have already analyzed. John attempts to remove the difficulty a step further back, first by admitting an inequality of individual disposition, prior to the manifestation of the Word, and next by dwelling upon the relation of causality between evil and the devil, which is here raised into the region of metaphysics, while in Paul's writings it only appears as an element in the moral relations to which experience testifies. But these two theses of John, though more advanced than anything which Paul says, lead us no further. For we are not told whence arises this inequality of disposition; and were the idea of the devil pursued to its logical issues, it would lead us into the most absolute dualism, or would at least prove that the difficulty is only transferred, not removed.

We have just said that John is in advance of Paul in a philosophical point of view; we do not pretend that a preference is therefore to be accorded to him, in view of the edification of the Church. But there is one more point of comparison in which we shall have again to mark a certain superiority on the side of John, a superiority which gives him a real vantage-ground, and marks out for the Church the path it should pursue. We refer to the spiritual nature of Chris-

tianity, which in the construction of dogma is destined to free
itself more and more from Jewish materialism. We know
that the whole life of Paul was devoted to stimulating and
consolidating this progress; his epistles are the most glorious
monument of that which the Church owes him in this respect.
Nothing is farther from our intention here than to derogate
from his merit; nevertheless we shall adduce several facts in
support of the assertion just made. We shall observe, first,
that the evangelical theology of Paul uniformly finds it necessary to accord a large place to anti-Jewish polemics; it lives,
so to speak, by this conflict, which contributes more than anything else to give it that vivacity of form, and directness of
application, which we have already noted. In this sense, also,
it may be said to stand in a certain relation of dependence
upon Judaism, which partly imposes upon it the choice of its
ground and mode of treatment. John is more free in his move-
ments. With him, the great question which agitated the apostolic Church was already long settled : the part of Moses and
that of Christ are characterized with one stroke of the pen,
when it is said that " the law was given by Moses, but grace and
truth came by Jesus Christ." Such a sentence cuts short all rival
pretensions; the theologian has no need to recur to the subject,
and indeed seems almost to have forgotten that this was a point
around which controversy had raged long and passionately.
What infinite pains—in our day either completely superfluous
or very inadequate—Paul takes to prove to the Jews, by every
sort of quotation, that Mosaism was something temporary and
preparatory, that the law and the prophets, as read in the light
of the New Testament, themselves reveal this change in the
divine economy. In what bondage he places himself to the
letter in order to prove its abolition ; by what long and often
involved arguments, by what syllogisms based upon allegories
which are, to say the least, arbitrary, does he reach the demonstration of a truth then disputed, but now clear as the day.
John arrives at the same goal by a shorter path. Gerizim
and Zion alike vanish from view. "God is a Spirit, and will
be worshipped in spirit and in truth." But it seems to us

that God has always been a Spirit, and that the adoration proclaimed by the evangelist ought to be found wherever this truth is acknowledged. The privilege of Judaism, over every other form of non-evangelical religion, is to have served as the cradle of the salvation which is in Christ; this is an honour put upon it, not a merit of its own. While Paul is careful to extenuate all that is terrible in the decline of God's chosen nation, now by assurances of sympathy, now by promises of consolation, and is especially careful to maintain the impresciptible titles of the old covenant, John goes so far as to speak to the Jews with a certain mannerism of *their* law, and *their* feast,—the same terms that Pilate uses, and as if they were altogether alien institutions. Evidently, the subjective enfranchisement from the bonds of the old faith has reached a higher degree in his experience than in that of Paul.

But this is also the case with the objective enfranchisement, and this is of still greater importance. We shall only mention here one fact, the most striking in this respect. We know with what tenacity the Church, which on this point was Judæo-Christian, maintained almost intact the eschatology of the Pharisaic synagogue, and lived in expectation of the triumphal return, the universal resurrection, the last judgment, a paradise of material enjoyments, and a hell of corporeal pains. And yet not only the teaching of Christ, but that of several of the apostles, had very decidedly spiritualized these hopes. In Paul's case, the metamorphosis is begun, and has even considerably advanced. In his early epistles, those to the Thessalonians, he adheres to the apocalyptic descriptions of his early teachers; he brings before his readers the approaching end of the world, the mysterious phantom of Antichrist, the angels with their trumpets, the saints caught up to meet the descending Lord in the air, and so on. The epistles to the Corinthians dwell by preference on the far more spiritual conception of the transformation of the body, and especially of the resurrection placed in close relation with faith. Subsequently, the Jewish images disappear altogether, or serve only to aid the apprehension of more abstract ideas. We no longer read of the nearness of the end of all things, but rather of the direct connection between the death of the individual and the determination of his ultimate destiny. All this is so true, that it may be said the philosophical sections of the ancient Church, the Greek Fathers especially, derived the form of their dogma on this point from the texts of Paul.

But John had already advanced much further. In the whole of his gospel, there is no trace of Jewish eschatology. Some phrases of his epistle, which seem to contradict our assertion, have been explained in a manner which seems to us satisfactory, and on many points we can even show how the apostle spiritualizes the dogmas of the old theology. Thus he speaks in his epistle of Antichrist, but it is only to substitute for the apocalyptic personage—half man, half demon—a pure abstraction, namely, the anti-Christian tendency represented in history by a large number of individuals. The resurrection, the second coming, as future events, are as nothing in comparison with the living presence of the Saviour in the hearts of His people, and with the henceforward imperishable life which He gives them by faith. Judgment, kept in store for some awful distant day, is but a meaningless term, for the unbelieving are already judged by the fact of the rejection of the Word; and for those who believe, there can be no judgment to come. The theology of our confession of faith yet lingers far behind these grand ideas, so venerable, and yet so mournfully neglected.

We do not pretend to have exhausted our theme. Not only might examples yet be multiplied in support of each of these comparisons, but doubtless other points of view might be found which would render this interesting parallel yet more complete. It may suffice, however, for the present, that we have shown by these pages, how exegetical theology, to which such a low and limited task is often assigned, has mines to work and treasures to discover, without doing violence to its own supreme law, which is to respect the facts of history.

We conclude this chapter with one last comparison, which

is in itself the epitome of most of the rest. With Paul, the Christian life consists in faith, love, and hope; with John, the manifestation of the Word is designed to bring the world to a participation in the essence of the Godhead, which is light, love, and life. Both trilogies form, in the systems to which they respectively belong, a sort of plan regulating the form of the thought, and thus naturally recurring frequently both in the regular progress of the discourse, and in the development of the ideas. But the former belongs essentially to the sphere of humanity, the latter to that of Deity. Both tell us how man may rise to his Creator; but the qualities enunciated in Paul's trilogy rather characterize the individual in his progressive state, reaching forth after a full salvation; those in the trilogy of John represent the means or agencies by which that salvation is accomplished. The former participate in the transitory nature of things below; faith and hope tend to rise above themselves, and may give place to other relations; light and life are in their nature perfect and eternal as God Himself. Love alone is found in both trilogies; it belongs equally to heaven and earth, to God and man, to time and eternity; and hence Paul proclaims it the greatest of the three.

CONCLUSION.

WE have reached the term of a long and laborious task, the toils of which have been, however, uniformly and amply compensated by the high and absorbing interest of the subject, and by the hope that this interest, as well as the freshness of some of the results obtained, may sustain to the end the kindly attention of our readers. We here lay down the pen, solely because our own powers seem to fail, not because we for a moment deem that we have reached an era of repose, a halting-place in the history. The history of the human spirit, the history of thought, knows no pause. Christian theology has continued its course, and continues it still, varying perhaps in its phases, changing its direction from time to time, but always pursuing one and the same end, that of attaining to a wider and deeper apprehension of the truths of the Gospel, and of applying them in perpetually new spheres, and according to fresh methods. In the view held by the Church, however, and especially by the Protestant Church, the first century is more easily detached from all that have succeeded, because of the wholly exceptional authority with which it invests the teaching of the apostles. This is the chief consideration which has led us to circumscribe our labours within the limits given. These limits, it is true, are not precisely the same as those traced by the tradition of the schools; but the changes which we have ventured to introduce in this respect into our plan, are of very secondary importance. The public which is interested in such studies, or which may come to feel a growing interest in them, may now embrace at a glance a series of facts which, linked together by a bond far more real than that of chronology, and brought near to our age by the growing influence they are destined to exert, will have lost nothing of their importance by being (for the first time in France) considered from a strictly historical point of view.

Let us now, in concluding, cast one retrospective glance over the general results which we have established, the historical accuracy and interdependence of which, ascertained by long and careful preliminary studies, have determined the plan of our exposition. In here reproducing them in the form of a summary, we shall assist our readers in forming, not a judgment upon our own work, for this must be tested by a study of the documents themselves, but an estimate of the difference between our mode of treatment and that of our predecessors.

We think we have shown, in the first place, the originality of the Gospel itself. This fact will, we hope, now be received as a testimony borne by history, not merely as an apologetic theorem. The Christian apology cannot but gain by having the fact established in this manner. But we have given yet more prominence to this important fact, that the originality of the Gospel consists not so much in the novelty of certain doctrines or moral precepts, as in the new basis on which it places the entire religious life. It did not present itself to the world as a system designed to replace earlier systems, but as a principle of life sufficiently powerful to change the very nature of man.

This originality, thus understood and defined, implies and leads us to anticipate another essential characteristic of the Gospel preached by Jesus Christ; namely, that it is the permanent model and supreme rule of all Christian teaching. The religious conscience cannot go beyond it. We have frequently traced, in the course of our narrative, the formation of theories, the adoption of formulas originating in the Church, and the design of which seems to be to extend the horizon of Christian intelligence, or to deepen the meaning of the Master's words. We recognize the lawfulness of these first essays of theological speculation applied to the Gospel, which have become for succeeding generations valuable guides in the path of progress; we have shown how much of individuality there is to be traced in these conceptions and explanations; but we carry from the study of them the fixed conviction, that all these developments were contained, at least in germ, in the original teaching of the Saviour, and that they are of importance because of that relation, and in proportion to it.

For beside the instruction they may have received from the Master in their daily and familiar intercourse with Him, there was yet another influence determining the spiritual development of the disciples. This was the influence of the ideas prevalent in their country and among their contemporaries, and which, during a large part of their life, had the exclusive privilege of moulding their mental habits. We have endeavoured to acquaint ourselves accurately with the nature and scope of these ideas, and we think we have succeeded in marking out, on the one hand, that which separated them from the thoughts and spirit of the Gospel, and, on the other, that which the Christian community borrowed from them, in its more or less happy efforts to clothe its faith in the forms of science. We have seen this work carried on with an ever-growing power of means at its command, and finally disengaging more and more completely the spiritualism of the new economy from the materialism of the old.

It is certain that the apostles were the first authors of Christian theology,—that is to say, they were the first to undertake a reflective study of the ideas and convictions which constituted the inner life of the infant Church. Far from regretting this tendency, because of the manifold errors which in the end may have arisen from it, and because of the evil it may have produced by often stifling life for the sake of theory, we are bound to own our obligations to those of the disciples who have most distinguished themselves in this respect, for the example they have given to their successors in all ages. For on every page of their writings we have been able to show that their object was not speculation for its own sake, dogmatic theory, the construction of formulas,—matters

interesting only to a few select minds,—but rather the edification of the Church, the satisfaction of the legitimate demands of all, the consolation, encouragement, deepening union
of all believers without distinction, with Him who was to be
the one source of their present and future life. We have repeatedly seen that in their most important theological speculations they have paused midway, at least in the judgment of
the doctors of the Church, who have deemed it needful to
supplement and to define their words, often losing sight in the
process of the great essential object which the apostles had
first in view. In a word, we have shown, not on any preconceived theory of our own, but by the eloquence of facts
and of history, the distance which divides the theology of the
Bible from that of the schoolmen.

We hope to have contributed also by our narrative to the
confirmation of the favourable opinion, entertained for many
centuries, of the antiquity and authenticity of the books which
compose our sacred canon. In France, it is true, a hard and
captious criticism has not hitherto made great ravages. But
we know what high pretensions it has elsewhere advanced,
and these may have excited the more alarm from the want of
a thorough investigation. The necessity of classing among
the productions of the second century, a large number of the
books commonly regarded as apostolic, is not yet established
by what appears to us any adequate proof. The immense
superiority of some of the theological conceptions we have
analyzed, which on account of this very superiority have
become the basis and authoritative canon of Christian science,
seems to us incapable of reasonable explanation, in the productions of an age which had retained but a feeble impulse
from the great originating movement of the Church, and
which must have been the less able to produce such conceptions, since it showed itself incapable of even apprehending
them. Our narrative must have shown, on the contrary, that
they were the early but ripe fruit of that exegesis of the spirit,
which does not depend necessarily on the gradual evolutions of
time and thought.

Progress is undoubtedly the law of humanity, but not a mechanical progress, the march of which is regulated with such uniformity, that it may serve as a clock to chronology. We have seen, in the narrow limits of our history, in connection with the teaching of revelation, before which science ever bows with humility, strange misconceptions as to the design and conditions of the Gospel dispensation. We have seen the obstructiveness of prejudice, slow to give place to a higher apprehension of divine truth; the impotence of reason, and the weakness of the will forcing the Gospel teaching into retrograde paths, enfeebling its principle, and depriving it of its essential characteristics. The tenacity of Pharisaism, which kept aloof from the progressive movement of ideas, and finally separated itself from a Church the vital element of which was foreign to it, proved less of an obstacle to the upward progress of the Church, than the concessions imposed on or wrested from Paulinism by the spirit of an age, which could not rise to the height of its duty.

Revelation, it may be most emphatically said, raised some men above the ordinary line of mortals. The entire generation could not keep pace with them. It remained behind, not without receiving and retaining a considerable portion of the treasures entrusted to its leaders, but without being able to preserve them in their native purity and integrity. This transmitted treasure, into which we still dive with ever fresh results, we find at the close of the apostolic age passing through various metamorphoses, which add nothing to it, but rather tend to lessen its original lustre and strong and healthful vitality. Ideas which had power to change the world, just because they were beyond its control, could not but lose in force when reflection, at once more frigid and less powerful, undertook to measure their scope and weigh their conditions. This assertion will not be deemed too bold, when we remember the prodigious efforts which, after fifteen centuries, the Church was constrained to make, and then without entire success, to disengage the true idea of the Gospel from all that had been superadded, veiling its beauty and tarnishing its brightness.

And it is this very Protestant theology which has fostered a false estimate of the historical facts of the primitive ages of the Church, by representing Paulinism—that is to say the Protestant tendency of that period—as triumphant and victorious over all rival influences, or even as exercising undisputed sway. Nothing can be more unjust than such a conception. It is true that Paulinism, seconded by external circumstances, and, yet more, strong in the truth of its principle, succeeded in familiarizing the minds of men with the idea of the abrogation of the law, and in finally leading to the abandonment of circumcision, and the complete severance of the Church from the Synagogue. But all this would have taken place in the natural course of things, though possibly a little more gradually. On the other hand, the Jewish element, never wholly neutralized, still maintained itself by the side of Paulinism with a certain vigour; it bequeathed to the Church the materialism of its eschatology, enjoined upon it its own ascetic practices, and endowed it with its hierarchy and worship, in so far as its form of worship could be applied to the new economy. All this would have been impossible, if the idea of salvation and the apprehension of its conditions had not undergone at the close of the first century a very notable alteration—in other words, if the mystical conception had not so soon begun to give place to the scholastic demonstration, which thenceforth held undivided sway.

But we should be wandering too far from our subject, if we allowed our gaze to roam over the succeeding period, so important because of the vast revolution of ideas which it witnessed, so attractive from the very obscurity which directs to it the attention of the scientific. It would take more than a lifetime of labour to illuminate this period with the torch of history. The period we have chosen presents difficulties of an opposite nature. So intense a light falls upon the eye of him who contemplates it, that its dazzling brilliance augments the possibilities of mistake. In another aspect, the veneration with which fifty generations have encircled its great names, forewarns the student that if he ventures upon independent criticism he will be regarded as a foe; that its results will appear the more daring the more they present of novelty, and the more nearly they approach to truth. The world loves twilight; tradition is hostile to all investigation; all that contains within itself a form of life and movement, is impelled by a lamentable fatality to petrify into rigid and inflexible forms. The life which comes from God, so soon as it passes into the hands of men, is transformed into dogmas, cast into the mould of formularies, and thus we had almost said extinguishes its own vitality; while the efforts, whether of the Christian heart or of science, to reanimate and restore it to itself, instead of being recognized as sincere homage rendered to truth, are but too generally branded as heresies. Nothing is so sensitive as official orthodoxy.

In spite of prejudice and opposition, however, the conscientious historian must find ample compensation in his work itself. A subject like that which is treated in this work, brings him constantly into contact with ideas the most sublime and suggestive, the most adapted to sustain the mind of man and to raise him above the petty dissensions of the world and the schools. The efforts he bestows on it are to him an inexhaustible spring of intellectual and moral happiness; they familiarize him with models so exalted and admirable, that the contemplation of them must constantly invigorate his own powers; and if it is painful to him to see how in all ages men have been divided on the very subjects which ought to have united them, he finds his consolation, not indeed in indifference or party spirit, but in the assiduous search after truth, which eludes only those who believe themselves to be its sole possessors.

THE END.

INDEX.

35

Watson aud Hazell, Printers, London and Aylesbury.

HISTORY OF CHRISTIAN THEOLOGY
IN THE APOSTOLIC AGE.

By EDWARD REUSS, Professor in the Theological Faculty and in the Protestant Seminary of Strasbourg.

Translated from the Third German Edition, by ANNIE HARWOOD.

With Preface and Notes, by R. W. DALE, M.A.

VOL. I., 8vo, price 12s., cloth.

CONTENTS.

BOOK I., JUDAISM.—1. Mosaism before the Exile. 2. The Restoration. 3. The Synagogue. 4. Pharisaism. 5. Sadduceeism. 6. Jewish Theology. 7. Hellenism. 8. Alexandrine Philosophy. 9. Ebionism and Essenism. 10. Messianic Hopes. 11. John the Baptist.

BOOK II., THE GOSPEL.—1. Introduction. 2. The Gospel and the Law. 3. The Kingdom of God. 4. Conversion. 5. Perfection. 6. Faith. 7. The Good News. 8. The Son of Man and the Son of God. 9. The Church. 10. The Future. 11. The Gospel and Judaism.

BOOK III., THE APOSTOLIC CHURCH.—1 The Master and the Disciples. 2. The Churches of Palestine. 3. The Churches of the Dispersion. 4. The Controversy. 5. The Conciliation. 6. The Rise of Theology. 7. The Gospel of Liberty. 8. The Judaizing Opposition. 9. Paganism and Gnosticism. 10. Christian Gnosticism. 11. Systematic Theology.

BOOK IV., JUDÆO-CHRISTIAN THEOLOGY.—1. Introduction. 2. Exegesis. 3. The Last Times. 4. The Revelation. 5. The Christ. 6. The Angels. 7. Salvation. 8. The Epistle of James.

* OPINIONS OF THE PRESS.

"His method is, first to examine the religious conditions of Judaism at our Lord's appearing : then to examine the personal teaching of Christ concerning fundamental Christian ideas, such as the kingdom of God, conversion, perfection, faith, the Son of Man and the Son of God, the Church, etc.; and then to expound the beliefs and teachings of the Apostolic Church, presenting the principal phases of primitive Church life in Palestine, the dispersion, and Gentile lands ; and then treating of the rise of Theology, the conception of liberty, Judaism, Paganism, and Gnosticism, etc. . . . This comprehensive plan is filled up in a most masterly way. Extensive and exact scholarship, a discriminating and sober judgment, a reverent feeling, and a pure historical spirit, combine to make M. Reuss one of the foremost of the few exegetes that French Protestantism possesses."—*British Quarterly Review.*

"In presenting this book to the English reader, Messrs. Hodder and Stoughton have made another valuable contribution to our theological literature. M. Reuss is earnest and reverent, thoughtful and instructive, and we can hardly imagine any one reading the book without feeling that he has learnt much from it. Miss Harwood's translation is worthy of all praise."—*Literary Churchman.*

"This is a book of unquestionable brilliancy and power ; and Miss Harwood's readable translation will increase the number of readers which it has already found among English theologians."—*British and Foreign Evangelical Review.*

"In this work he evinces the highest capability of an historian—impartiality, breadth, research, learning, and reverence. In the first volume, now before us, he treats historically, with great felicity of thought and breadth of view, of Judaism, the Gospel, the Apostolic Church, and Judæo-Christian Theology. The book is an invaluable addition to the early history of the Church, and of Christian Theology. No biblical student or teacher of Christianity should fail to possess this book ; no theological library can be complete without it."—*Preachers' Lantern.*

"Another contribution—and undoubtedly a most important one—to the Biblical theology of the New Testament. No reader, we imagine, will rise from the study of his work without feeling that it is one of the few important contributions that have been made in recent years to theological literature in this country, and one which is likely to affect not a little the future of English religious thought."—*Weekly Review.*

"The work, when completed, will form about the best treatise on the early Church which has yet appeared."—*Rock.*

"The work is an admirable *résumé* of the growth and development of Christian Theology, during the ministry of Christ and His Apostles, and would make a capital text-book for those who are studying that portion of Church history. The difficulties of the original have been overcome in the translation, which is really good."—*Christian World.*

LONDON : HODDER & STOUGHTON, 27 & 31, PATERNOSTER ROW.

THE NEW THEOLOGICAL AND PHILOSOPHICAL LIBRARY.

Now Ready. Complete in Two Vols.:

A HISTORY OF PHILOSOPHY,

FROM THALES TO THE PRESENT TIME.

By Dr. Friedrich Ueberweg, late Professor of Philosophy in the University of Königsberg. Translated by Professor George S. Morris, A.M. ; with Additions by the Translator.

By Noah Porter, D.D., LL.D., on English and American Philosophy. And

By V. Botta, Ph.D., on Italian Philosophy.

Vol. I.—ANCIENT AND MEDIÆVAL PHILOSOPHY. *Royal 8vo*, 18s.

Vol. II.—MODERN PHILOSOPHY. *Royal 8vo, cloth*, 21s.

"A clear, condensed, comprehensive outline of the different systems which have been propounded from the earliest to the latest time. We know of no compendium so satisfactory in all respects. It may be recommended to students of Philosophy with all confidence as an admirable text-book."—*Westminster Review.*

"Ueberweg's 'History of Philosophy' is exactly what English-speaking students want." - *Examiner.*

"The work is concise and clear, exact and suggestive, comprehensive and critical. It contains a complete presentation of the different philosophical schools, and describes, with sufficient minuteness, the principal doctrines which belong to each system and to subordinate branches of each system ; by which means a distinct picture is placed before the mind of the reader. It meets at once the wants of the ordinary student, and of the independent inquirer."—*British Quarterly Review.*

"The sketches of the various systems and the biographies of their authors, the very full and valuable lists of authorities, and the careful estimates of the bearings of the systems upon each other, all help to increase its value. For certain purposes—such, for instance, as preparing students for examination—it is admirably adapted—better perhaps than any other work of the kind."—*Spectator.*

"The late Dean Mansel, whose authority to speak on such a matter was that of a master-mind, we know placed the very highest value on this work, as the most perfect and impartial of its kind. It is clear and concise in its statements, systematic in its arrangement, accurate in detail, impartial in tone, never dull, and never tedious."—*Standard.*

"No happier selection could have been made than this work of Ueberweg's for the first volume of the 'Philosophical and Theological Library.' It is a model manual. . . . Its most conspicuous and praiseworthy features are its immense erudition, its marvellous and condensed fulness, and its singular impartiality. It might have been written by a judge, so dispassionate is its spirit. . . . We know no book on philosophy so well adapted to become a text-book and standard in colleges and universities."—*Nonconformist.*

"All lovers and students of speculative philosophy will welcome this English translation of Dr. Ueberweg's history of philosophy, unapproachable as it is in its merits as a masterly and exhaustive treatise on this vast and difficult subject. The method of arrangement adopted is eminently satisfactory. It supplies us, first, with a sketch of the personal life of the philosopher discussed ; next, with an account of his writings and teachings, given chiefly in his own words ; next, with a summary of his works, their editions and commentaries. The history of speculative truth is traced in these pages from the earliest time, in every school of philosophy—Christian, Jewish, Arabic, or Pagan, and in its every form, stage, and development. The momentous question of immortality, providence, the origin of evil, the final destiny of evil, the problem of human free-will and Divine direction, the functions of conscience, the foundation and obligations of virtue, and the nature and degree of human responsibility, are, with a thousand other problems, here discussed by the thinkers of all ages—the moralists and intellectual leaders of all mankind—and this with a clearness and precision of language which few can misunderstand or misinterpret."—*John Bull.*

LONDON : HODDER & STOUGHTON, 27 & 31, PATERNOSTER ROW.

NEW VOLUME OF THE THEOLOGICAL AND PHILOSOPHICAL LIBRARY.

Now ready, in one large Volume, Royal 8vo, price 21s.,
handsomely bound.

CHRISTIAN DOGMATICS:

A TEXT BOOK FOR

ACADEMICAL INSTRUCTION AND PRIVATE STUDY.

By J. J. Van Oosterzee, D.D., Professor of Theology in the University of
Utrecht, Author of "The Theology of the New Testament."

Translated by the Rev. J. Waton Watson, B.A., Vicar of Newburgh, Lancashire,
and Rev. Maurice J. Evans, B.A., Stratford-upon-Avon.

"This volume, which forms part of Hodder and Stoughton's 'Theological and Philosophical
Library,' is a most welcome addition to our literature. Dr. Oosterzee, Professor of Theology at
Utrecht, is already known to English students, through his 'Theology of the New Testament'
and his 'Apologetical Lectures on John's Gospels,' and this volume will gain for him still wider
admiration. . . . The general tone of the work is Evangelical and Calvinistic—in harmony
with the best works of the Dutch divines, a school long famous in Europe. The views are
moderate, and the treatment Biblical and scholarly. The publishers have done all that is required
to make the work worthy of the series to which it belongs, and the result is a *magnum opus*,
which is an admirable and well nigh an exhaustive treatise of the whole system of theological
truth."—*Freeman.*

"This is the third of the magnificent series of volumes entitled 'The Theological and Philosophical Library,' and a fitting companion it is for the history of Philosophy by Dr. Ueberweg.
What the latter has done with such completeness and efficiency for philosophy, Dr. Van Oosterzee
has done equally well for Christian Dogmatics. With clearness, comprehensiveness, and ripest
learning, he discusses the character, sources, history, claims, and all the great questions of dogmatics. Every subject has its due place and importance assigned to it, and is treated in the most
masterly manner."—*Preacher's Lantern.*

"This work is a noble monument of honest, industrious toil, and no one can fail to discern in it
a true sympathy with the best minds of all churches and all ages. We have not found a single
word of theological science from one end to the other. Preachers as well as students will find it
a rich mine of suggestive hints for public instruction."—*Nonconformist.*

DR. VAN OOSTERZEE'S HANDBOOK TO THE NEW TESTAMENT.

THE THEOLOGY OF THE NEW TESTAMENT.

A HANDBOOK FOR BIBLE STUDENTS.

By J. J. Van Oosterzee, D.D., Professor of Theology in the University of
Utrecht.

Second Edition, Crown 8vo, 6s., cloth.

"An excellent manual. The scientific method on which it is constructed, the lucidity of its
arrangement, the sagacity and abundance of information which is brought to bear in it on the
work of interpretation, call for the highest praise."—*Spectator.*

"Both in idea and execution his handbook is excellent. Let not this term allow the reader to
imagine a book of dry bones and divinity skeletons. Terse and pithy indeed is the style, and not
a word is wasted, but there is nevertheless life and breath in every sentence, and so we have the
conciseness of a handbook with the enjoyment of a chosen companion."—*Record.*

LONDON : HODDER & STOUGHTON, 27 & 31, PATERNOSTER ROW.

Lightning Source UK Ltd.
Milton Keynes UK
UKHW031944020219
336576UK00009BA/388/P